AF352431

Prosody Matters

Advances in Optimality Theory

Editors: Vieri Samek-Lodovici, University College London, and Armin Mester, University of California, Santa Cruz

Optimality Theory is an exciting new approach to linguistic analysis that originated in phonology but was soon taken up in syntax, morphology, and other fields of linguistics. Optimality Theory presents a clear vision of the universal properties underlying the vast surface typological variety in the world's languages. Cross-linguistic differences once relegated to idiosyncratic language-specific rules can now be understood as the result of different priority rankings among universal, but violable constraints on grammar.

Advances in Optimality Theory is designed to stimulate and promote research in this provocative new framework. It provides a central outlet for the best new work by both established and younger scholars in this rapidly moving field. The series includes studies with a broad typological focus, studies dedicated to the detailed analysis of individual languages, and studies on the nature of Optimality Theory itself. The series publishes theoretical work in the form of monographs and coherent edited collections as well as pedagogical texts and reference texts that promote the dissemination of Optimality Theory.

Consultant Board:
Judith Aissen, University of California, Santa Cruz
Daniel Büring, University of California, Los Angeles
Gisbert Fanselow, University of Potsdam
Jane Grimshaw, Rutgers University
Géraldine Legendre, Johns Hopkins University
John J. McCarthy, University of Massachusetts, Amherst
Alan Prince, Rutgers University
Paul Smolensky, Johns Hopkins University
Donca Steriade, MIT, Cambridge, MA
Moira Yip, University College London

Forthcoming:
Understanding Allomorphy: Perspectives from Optimality Theory
Edited by Bernard Tranel

Blocking and Complementarity in Phonological Theory
Eric Baković

Faithfulness in Phonological Theory
Marc van Oostendorp

Prosody Matters

Essays in Honor of Elisabeth Selkirk

Edited by Toni Borowsky, Shigeto Kawahara,
Takahito Shinya and Mariko Sugahara

Published by Equinox Publishing Ltd.

UK: Kelham House, 3 Lancaster Street, Sheffield, S3 8AF
USA: ISD, 70 Enterprise Drive, Bristol, CT 06010

www.equinoxpub.com

First published 2012

ISBN   978-1-84553-677-0 (hardback)

British Library Cataloguing-in-Publication Data

A catalogue record for this book is available from the British Library.

Library of Congress Cataloging-in-Publication Data

Prosody matters : essays in honor of Elisabeth Selkirk / edited by Toni Borowsky...[et al.].
    p. cm. -- (Advances in Optimality Theory)
 Includes bibliographical references and index.
 ISBN 978-1-84553-677-0
1. Phonetics. 2. Grammar, Comparative and general--Phonology. 3. Grammar, Comparative and general--Syntax. 4. Generative grammar. I. Borowsky, Toni. II. Selkirk, Elisabeth O., 1945- P217P76 2011
 414'.6--dc22
                                        2010034096

Printed and bound in the UK by MPG Books Group

Contents

SECTION 3: PHRASES AND ABOVE

SECTION 4: PROSODIC HIERARCHY AND SEMANTIC
INTERPRETATION (FOCUS)

Contributors

Hasan Basri, Tadulako University

Karim Bensoukas, Mohammed V-Agdal University

Abdelaziz Boudlal, Chouaib Doukkali University

Ellen Broselow, Stony Brook University

Katy Carlson, Moorehead University

Charles Clifton Jr., University of Massachusetts at Amherst

Caroline Féry, Goethe University, Frankfurt

Daniel Finer, Stony Brook University

Lyn Frazier, University of Massachusetts at Amherst

Sam Hellmuth, University of York

Masako Hirotani, Carleton University

Junko Ito, University of California Santa Cruz

Shigeto Kawahara, Rutgers University

Armin Mester, University of California Santa Cruz

John J. McCarthy, University of Massachusetts at Amherst

Scott Myers, University of Texas at Austin

Jaye Padgett, University of California Santa Cruz

Joe Pater, University of Massachusetts at Amherst

Jennifer Smith, University of North Carolina at Chapel Hill

Mariko Sugahara, Doshisha University

Hisao Tokizaki, Sapporo University

Hubert Truckenbrodt, Zentrum für Allgemeine Sprachwissenschaft, Berlin and Humboldt-Universität zu Berlin, Germany

Preface

We conceived this volume to acknowledge Lisa Selkirk's influential contributions to the field of linguistics. Lisa's retirement provided a further opportunity for us to recognize her accomplishments as a researcher and her generosity as a teacher, mentor, colleague, and administrator and to express our gratitude to her.

Lisa created the linguistic subfield that studies the relationship between phonology and syntax, and she remains the most imaginative and prolific contributor to this subject. Her dissertation, *The Phrase Phonology of English and French,* was extremely influential, laying out many important discoveries about the phrasal phonology of these two languages and defining a model of phonology-syntax interaction. She later moved beyond the boundary-based theory espoused in her dissertation to develop an alternative model called domains theory, in which the influence of syntax on phonology is indirect; syntactic structure is mapped onto a prosodic structure, and phonological processes are governed by that structure rather than the fine details of the syntactic representation. This idea, which is now almost universally accepted, has consequences for phonological theory that are rich and far-reaching. Among these is a typology of edge-alignment between morphosyntactic and prosodic constituents which she has developed in work on Japanese, Tohono O'odham, and Chi Mwi:ni, among other languages.

Lisa's work in Linguistics has not been confined to the syntax phonology interface. The book *Phonology and Syntax: The Relation between Sound and Structure* is as much a study of stress, linguistic rhythm, intonation and focus as it is an approach to sentence phonology, while her influential book *The Syntax of Words* outlines a theory of the interface between phonology and morphology. Her papers on focus, which establish a basis for the distinction between contrastive focus and presentational focus, are squarely at the intersection of phonology, syntax, discourse, and pragmatics. Lisa has also made important contributions to the areas of syllabic and segmental phonology. Her article on English syllable structure is recognized as one of the seminal articles in this area, and her work on Arabic syllable structure and vowel epenthesis stimulated a substantial body of research. Her study of labialization in Berber derives a complex pattern of asymmetries in dissimilation from an elegant model of adjacency relations among segments. Her articles on geminate inalterability turned on its head one of the most cherished results of the field, providing a far better explanation of the limits on rules that respect inalterability. She continues to venture into new areas, currently investigating the interactions of tone and syntax. Her research trajectory is marked by continued dynamism, moving from approaches based on boundary markers to one based on domains, and from approaches based on constituent edges to her recent Match theory of syntax-phonology mapping always in the forefront of development in the field.

A member of the UMass faculty throughout almost the entire history of the UMass Linguistics Department, Lisa served for many years as head of the department, and was instrumental in bringing the department to its current status as one of the leading linguistics programs in the world.

The papers in this volume show Lisa's influence across the many areas of her research, particularly in prosodic phonology. They represent current work across many areas of phonology combining theoretical work in Optimality Theory with experimental work reflecting not just the dynamism and diversity observed in Lisa's work but the rise of the laboratory phonology as a new approach to linguistics. All the contributors are Lisa's former students and/or are close colleagues of hers.

The first section includes three papers about syllables and syllabification issues: *Karim Bensoukas and Abdelaziz Boudlal* consider the remarkably similar phonological behavior of schwa in two languages: Moroccan Amazigh and Moroccan Arabic. They propose that a schwa syllable consists of a single branching mora shared by the schwa and a following consonant. *Joe Pater's* paper revisits the well-known sonority-based syllabification pattern in Imdlawn Tashlhiyt Berber using serial OT. He proposes a version of Optimality Theory that replaces OT's ranked constraints with weighted constraints, as in Harmonic Grammar and that also assumes a serial derivation, as in Harmonic Serialism. The paper discusses how a serial model of grammar leads to the elimination of some problematic predictions of HG, and also raises some problems for further research on serial OT and HG. *Jen Smith* proposes a formal definition of the ONSET constraint that makes no reference to syllable-ONSET internal structure beyond the head/nonhead distinction: ONSET simply requires that the head segment of a syllable not be initial in the syllable. Her approach accounts for the fact that Korean glides serve to resolve hiatus (satisfying ONSET), but in other respects appear to be part of the rime. The analysis is extended to develop a non-stipulative account of the ban on word-initial liquids found in South Korean dialects.

In the second section are four papers on the Foot and the Prosodic Word. The paper by *Hasan Basri, Ellen Broselow* and *Dan Finer* discusses word edge phenomena in three Makassarese languages: Makassarese (also called Lakiung), Selayarese, and Konjo. All three languages are characterized by distinct classes of affixes associated with different phonological effects with respect to stress, vowel epenthesis, alternation between velar and glottal stops, and gemination. They argue that the phonological patterns associated with the different affix classes reflect the ways in which the affixes are incorporated into prosodic structure and that the gemination found at the right edge of a prosodic word in Konjo is reminiscent of the phenomenon of intrusive [r] found in many dialects of English.

Scott Myers and *Jaye Padgett* address the issue of Final Devoicing. Myer's paper reports an experiment about the precise nature of the phonetic effect of utterance-final position, demonstrating that the partial devoicing in utterance-final position leads listeners to identify voiced obstruents in utterance-final position as voiceless. Scholars have long related the phenomenon of Final Devoicing to the fact that utterance-final voiced segments are realized with less vocal fold vibration than non-final voiced segments. This study investigates whether this coarticulatory effect could lead listeners to identify final voiced segments as voiceless, providing the basis for the generalization that voiced obstruents do not occur finally. Padgett's contribution looks at Final Devoicing from a theoretical perspective with an analysis of voicing assimilation and final devoicing in Russian paying particular attention to the role of prosody especially where it clarifies controversial matters of fact in Russian voicing regarding the behavior of sonorants. Padgett shows that prosodic structure at the level of the prosodic word is required to explain all of the facts involving Russian voicing and clitics. He argues against the role of syllable structure to explain the patterns of assimilation and devoicing, preferring the cue-based approach of Steriade (1997).

Mariko Sugahara's paper addresses the question of whether the head-Foot of a Prosodic Word (PW) is acoustically more salient than a non-head-Foot controlling for accent phenomena. She finds as a result of two experiments that in unaccented environments: (a) a stressed vowel of the head-Foot of PW (primary stress) is longer than the stressed vowel of a secondarily stressed Foot; and (b) the stressed vowels as well as the entire Foot lengthens when the Foot is the head of PW. Her second experiment shows that pitch accent, i.e., phrasal prominence, and PW-prominence additively affect the duration of primary stress vowels and the devoicing of post-primary stress unstressed vowels. These findings suggest that the head of PW is a phonological constituent with important phonetic correlates.

The phonetics and phonology of higher prosodic levels – the Major Phrase, the Intonational Phrase and the Utterance – characterize the papers in section Three.

Sam Hellmuth explores variation in tonal cues to prosodic phrasing across speakers as well as within speakers of Egyptian Arabic. Her aims are to establish the cues to Major Phonological Phrase (MaP)-level phrasing and to determine whether there is MaP-level marking of 'XP-edges' in Egyptian Arabic or whether a phase-based analysis can account for the phrasing facts of Egyptian Arabic. The results show that boundaries are observed in almost all XP-edge positions, but the cues are systematically stronger at the right edge of the subject than at the right edge of other XPs. Based on this result, she provides an account based on subordination between phonetic implementation domains of adjacent MaPs. In this view Egyptian Arabic is a well-behaved 'XP-edge-sensitive' language, in which phrasing is nonetheless subject to prosodic minimality constraints.

Junko Ito and *Armin Mester* propose a revision of the prosodic hierarchy, which is inherently recursive. In this paper, Ito and Mester review the evidence for the two central interface categories of the prosodic hierarchy that have been proposed for Japanese: major phrase and minor phrase. They argue that the evidence favors a model with a single category 'phonological phrase', with the option of adjunction and there is no need to postulate both interface categories. They go on to hypothesize that there are only three universal interface categories: intonational phrase, phonological phrase, and prosodic word. Additional structure is imposed on the string being parsed through adjunction.

Shigeto Kawahara reports an experimental study of the intonational properties of nominal parenthetical constructions in Japanese. The results of the experiment demonstrate that the left edges of parenthetical phrases show properties distinct from VP edges, which correspond to a Major Phrase: left edges of parenthetical phrases show strong pitch reset, raising of L, and a pause (and accompanying creakiness) as well as final lowering of the material preceding the parenthetical. He concludes that Comma Phrases are aligned with a prosodic edge that is located between a Major Phrase and an Utterance thus providing support for Selkirk's (2005) theory of the syntax-phonology mapping in which syntactic Comma Phrases are mapped to Intonational Phrases.

John McCarthy's paper analyzes complex phonological alternations affecting words in utterance-final position in Classical Arabic, traditionally called 'pause'. All pausal forms end in a heavy syllable, but the ways of achieving this result are diverse and subject to phonological and morphological conditioning. McCarthy argues that an adequate analysis of Arabic's pausal phonology requires a derivational version of Optimality Theory, called Harmonic Serialism, in which morpheme spell-out is interleaved with phonological processes.

In his paper *Hisao Tokizaki* attempts to derive the edge parameter from the head parameter (head-initial/final) in syntax considering the difference in phrasing between Shanghai and other Chinese dialects which have the same syntactic structure. He argues that the mapping from syntactic brackets onto prosodic boundaries correctly predicts phrasing differences in languages. He finds that the Shanghai dialect has a smaller prosodic domain than other Chinese dialects because it only has CV syllables, giving tone split in the prosodic domain. Incorporating larger domains into phrases would cause nouns with important information to lose their base tones. Thus, he suggests, phrasing differences in languages can be explained by the syntactic head parameter and the difference in syllable structure rather than the edge parameter.

The three papers in the final section consider the interplay between prosodic patterns and semantic interpretation.

Katy Carlson, Lyn Frazier and *Chuck Clifton* explore the effects of different Intonational Phrase boundaries on the processing of ambiguous VP Ellipsis sentences (e.g., *John said that Fred went to Europe, and Mary did too*) in five auditory experiments. The expectation was that a low boundary tone (L%) after *Europe* would favor an analysis where the sentence ends after *Europe*. Comparable to a two-sentence condition in written studies, this was expected to result in more matrix interpretations of the elided verb phrase (where Mary also said Fred went to Europe) than when the sentence contained a high boundary tone (H%), which might be expected to favor an analysis of the input as a single sentence. The duration of the pause at the boundary and the pitch range of the accent on *Mary* were both manipulated. But matrix interpretations rose significantly only when the input was syntactically disambiguated to two sentences by removing the conjunction (in addition to prosodic manipulations) and, not by prosodic manipulations alone. This surprising result is explained with the suggestion that the low boundary tone was interpreted as simply marking the end of a clause, which was true on either interpretation, and did not also influence decisions about the level of attachment of the final clause or whether it was taken to constitute a separate sentence.

In her contribution *Caroline Féry* considers the difference in meaning and accent behavior of the German particles *selbst* 'self', *wieder* 'again', and *auch* 'also' and presents an analysis in terms of information structure. These particles can function as focus particles, and when they do, they do not carry focus, but instead associate with the focus constituent. In this case, they are not accented. But they can also carry a free focus themselves, and in this case, like all foci, they have a focus domain and they elicit a set of alternatives. In this function, they are generally accented at the level of the intonation phrase. The change of information structural role comes with a change of meaning. This change of meaning is only indirectly related to the change of accent status, and cannot be considered as definitional of two lexemes. German does not contrast words by the presence vs. absence of stress, and the particles under consideration are no exception. Féry compares this information structural approach with alternative semantic approaches found in the literature.

Masako Hirotani reports on two production experiments which investigate the prosodic phrasing of scopally unambiguous wh-questions in Tokyo Japanese. She finds that wh-scope is not uniquely mapped to specific prosody but rather that various factors related to the syntax-phonology and semantics-phonology interface must play a role: Embedded scope wh-questions favored the appearance of a Major Phrase (MaP) boundary after the embedded Q-marker, while such a boundary was optional for matrix scope wh-questions. She points out that the frequency of MaP boundary insertion following the embedded Q-marker decreased when the matrix verb is Given information.

Hubert Truckenbrot discusses German phrasal stress. In German, a stressed direct object preceding the verb exempts the verb from carrying phrasal stress even if the verb is not given. Truckenbrot discusses sentences with a stressed indirect object, followed by a direct object (or its trace) followed by the verb (IO DO V). He argues that the complicated stress pattern of ditransitive sentences can be accounted for by assuming another layer in the VP shell. This account leads to an additional VP-internal topic phase. Truckenbrodt provides a second account in terms of Stress-XP, where the stress-facts similarly suggest separate VPs for indirect and direct object in a VP-shell structure. He points out that in both accounts raising of the verb in the VP-shell turns on the presence or absence of overt material in the lowest VP in the shell.

As all of the authors in this volume will attest, as well as the many others who sent their good wishes, Lisa's impact on our lives has been enormous. She has been our teacher, our mentor, our friend and our colleague. She is a versatile and cosmopolitan person with varied interests and deeply held principles. We know her as someone whose commitment extends not only to the linguistics community but to the wider world. At one stage Lisa contemplated a second career in geology. Luckily for the field however, although her retirement marked an end to her administrative and classroom teaching roles, her work in linguistics continues and she will continue to exert her influence on the field through her work and the effects on the many students she has taught and advised who now teach in linguistics programs around the world.

The editors would like to thank many people for their support and assistance in the preparation of this volume. Ellen Broselow and John McCarthy in particular provided all sorts of important assistance and advice. We also wish to thank our reviewers: John Alderete, Markus Bader, Michael Becker, Toni Borowsky, Aaron Braver, Ellen Broselow, Katy Carlson, Young-mee Yu Cho, Andries Coetzee, Masanori Deguchi, Nicole DeheÅL, Donna Erickson, Caroline FeÅLry, Kathryn Flack, Maria Gouskova, Matt Goldrick, Sam Hellmuth, Masako Hirotani, Shin Ishihara, Kiwako Ito, Shigeto Kawahara, Michael Kenstowicz, Jeff Mielke, Taka Shinya, Jennifer Smith, Stefan Sudhoff, Koichi Tateishi, Hisao Tokizaki, Hubert Truckenbrodt, Rachel Walker, Tessa Warren, Colin Wilson, and Matt Wolf for their assistance in the review process and Melanie Pangilinan, Michelle Ann Marron, and Sarah Korostoff, for helping us prepare the indices.

Section 1
Mora and syllable

1 The prosody of Moroccan Amazigh and Moroccan Arabic: Similarities in the phonology of schwa[1]

Karim Bensoukas[a] and Abdelaziz Boudlal[b]

1.1 Introduction

The aim of the present paper is to provide a unified account for the phonological behavior of schwa in Moroccan Amazigh and Moroccan Arabic, which reveals a number of salient affinities in the prosodic phonology of the two languages. Building on the work done so far on these languages, our approach is framed in Optimality Theory (OT) (Prince and Smolensky, 1993/2004; McCarthy and Prince, 1993a, 1995, 1999 and related works).

We will focus on three aspects of the prosodic behavior of schwa. First, schwa is largely treated as an epenthetic vowel that breaks clusters of consonants (Benhallam, 1980, 1989/1990; Chtatou, 1982, 1991 among others). Second, schwa never appears in an open syllable in either language. Further similarities are revealed by schwa's phonological behavior with respect to the weight and stress systems of the two languages: as opposed to closed syllables with full vowels, schwa syllables are light. We will claim that schwa is not associated with a mora unless it is followed by a consonant. The schwa syllable thus consists of a single, branching mora that both schwa and the following consonant share.

[a]   Karim Bensoukas, Mohammed V-Agdal University, Rabat, Morocco. Email: k.bensoukas@gmail.com

[b]   Abdelaziz Boudlal, Chouaib Doukkali University, El Jadida, Morocco. Email: aboudlal@gmail.com

The rest of the paper is articulated as follows. Section 1.2 presents the two languages investigated. In Section 1.3, we analyze syllable structure and show that schwa is epenthesized for syllabification purposes. We also deal with the variable syllable weight issue related to schwa syllables, provide support from the two languages that schwa syllables are monomoraic, and attempt to explain the provenance of the mora in schwa syllables. In Section 1.4, we provide an analysis in terms of constraint interaction for the non-occurrence of schwa in open syllables in either language. Finally, Section 1.5 presents evidence drawn from the stress systems of the two languages and gives further support for considering closed schwa syllables light.

1.2   Moroccan Amazigh and Moroccan Arabic

Moroccan Amazigh (MAm) and Moroccan Arabic (MA), belong to the Hamitic-Semitic family, also referred to in the literature as Afro-Asiatic.[2] These varieties have characteristics that set them apart from those spoken elsewhere (Algerian or Touareg Amazigh and Tunisian or Egyptian Arabic, for example). In this section, we will provide a brief description of the two dialects under study, namely Goulmima MAm and Casablanca MA, which are representative of other dialects of MAm and MA.

1.2.1 Moroccan Amazigh

The MAm dialect under study is the Goulmima Tamazight of Errachidia, Morocco. The description and basic (metrical and instrumental) analysis on which our study is based are those in Faizi (2002, 2007).[3] The phoneme inventory of Goulmima Tamazight consists of three vowels only and a larger number of consonants. In addition, almost every consonant has a geminate counterpart.[4]

(1) Goulmima Tamazight phoneme inventory (Faizi, 2002: 82–84):

    a- Vowels: a, i, u.

    b- Consonants: b, f, m, w, t, ṭ, d, ḍ, s, ṣ, z, ẓ, n, l, r, ṛ, j, ʃ, ʒ, tʃ, ʤ, ç, çʷ, ɟ, ɟʷ, x, xʷ, ɣ, ɣʷ, q, qʷ, ħ, ʕ, ɦ.

Of special interest in this paper is the vowel schwa, the status of which is far from unanimous. Within the general and structural tradition of Amazigh language studies, scholars limited the role of schwa to an auxiliary, non-phonemic vowel (Galand, 1988) that makes easier the pronunciation of consonant clusters (Basset, 1952). Basset (1952) further asserts that full vowels have a morphological value as opposed to the purely phonetic value of schwa. In generative studies, some authors claim an underlying status for schwa (Saib, 1976a, b), while others consider it epenthetic (Chtatou, 1991; Hdouch, 2004 among others). For others yet, schwa is totally absent, which is largely the case in Tashlhit (Dell and Elmedlaoui, 1985; Boukous, 1987, 2009).

1.2.2 Moroccan Arabic

The variety of MA which the present paper focuses on is that of Casablanca, Morocco. The data is drawn essentially from Nejmi (1993) and Boudlal (1993, 2001, 2006/7). Like MAm, MA has a simple, three-vowel system but a rich consonantal inventory in which almost every consonant has a geminate counterpart:

(2) The phoneme inventory of Casablanca MA:

    a- Vowels: a, i, u.

    b- Consonants: b, f, m, w, t, ṭ, d, ḍ, s, ṣ, z, ẓ, n, l, r, ṛ, j, ʃ, ʒ, k, k^w, g, g^w, x,
       x^w, ɣ, $ɣ^w$, q, q^w, ħ, ʕ, ɦ.[5]

In the phonology of MA, too, schwa has a controversial status. Some phonologists claim that it has a phonemic status (Benkaddour, 1982; Keegan, 1986 and others). Benkaddour (1982) distinguishes between the phonemic schwa and the epenthetic schwa, the former contrasting morphological categories such as verbs and nouns, and the latter serving to break up impermissible consonant clusters. However, most generative studies claim that schwa is epenthesized for syllabic purposes (Benhallam, 1980, 1989/1990; Al Ghadi, 1990, 1994; Boudlal, 1993, 2001, 2009, to cite a few).

1.3 Prosodic well-formedness and schwa epenthesis in Moroccan Amazigh and Moroccan Arabic

This section provides a description and analysis of schwa epenthesis in MAm and MA, focusing mainly on the similarities in the behavior of schwa. It also explores the moraic constituency of schwa syllables as opposed to that of full vowel syllables. Support for the light weight of schwa syllables is provided by verb prosodization in MA and prosodic-morphological vowel epenthesis in MAm. The section closes by explaining the source of the mora in schwa syllables.

1.3.1 Facts

We assume that schwa is an epenthetic vowel inserted to split and syllabify an otherwise unsyllabifiable consonant cluster. In this section, we sketch the relevant data that supports our generalization that schwa is epenthetic in MAm and MA.

In MAm, that schwa is epenthetic can be seen in the morphologically related words in (3), in which schwa is either absent or located in different places. With a few exceptions, schwa has a very predictable distribution phonologically.[6] We see in (4a) that in biconsonantal and triconsonantal roots, schwa appears between the two root consonants or the last two consonants, while in quadriconsonantal forms it splits every cluster. In (4b), schwa is epenthesized to break the consonant cluster in words that have both vowels and consonants and in which final or medial consonant clusters remain unsyllabified (the nature of the initial consonant cluster of triconsonantal verb roots will be dealt with later in Section 1.3.2):

(3) Schwa in different morphologically related forms (Faizi, 2002: 100–111):

zəḍ	iziḍ	'grind, Verb/Action noun'
çməḍ	anəçmuḍ	'burn, Verb/Agent Noun'
iflu	ifəlwan	'door, Sg. noun/pl. noun'
ifiɣər	ifaɣriwən	'snake, Sg. noun/pl. noun'

(4)   a- Schwa in MAm consonant-only words:

/sɣ/	səɣ	'to buy'
/bdr/	bdər	'to mention'
/t-rẓm/	tər.ẓəm	'she opened'

   b- Schwa in MAm words with vowels and consonants:

/azn/	a.zən	'to send'
/adfl/	ad.fəl	'snow'
/azuzzr/	a.zuz.zər	'winnowing'
/azuçnni/	a.zu.çən.ni	'thyme'
/iɣzdis/	i.ɣəz.dis	'rib'
/tamɣra/	ta.məɣ.ra	'marriage ceremony'

In MA, too, schwa is epenthetic as is shown by the morphologically related words in (5). Moreover, since schwa is epenthetic, its position is fully predictable. In triconsonantal roots, schwa appears before the final consonant as in (6a). In quadriconsonantal roots, schwa is epenthesized between each pair of consonants (6b), resulting in a CəCCəC pattern.[7] In (7), we give examples of words with both consonants and vowels. In (7a) schwa splits a cluster of two unsyllabified consonants. In (7b), schwa appears before C3 if its sonority index is greater than that of C2, and finally in (7c) schwa is epenthesized immediately before C2 if its sonority index is greater than that of C3:

(5) Schwa in different morphologically related forms:

ktəb	məktub	'write, Verb/Past participle'
ktəf	ktaf	'shoulder, Sg. noun/pl. noun'
qtəl	qtila	'kill, Verb/Action noun'
gləs	glus	'sit, Verb/Action noun'

(6)   a- Schwa in MA consonant-only words before C3:[8]

/ktb/	ktəb	'to write'
/gls/	gləs	'to sit down'
/kħl/	kħəl	'black'
/gml/	gməl	'lice'
/smn/	smən	'preserved butter'

b- Schwa between each CC sequence:

/krkb/	kərkəb	'to roll'
/brgg/	bərgəg	'to spy on'
/mslm/	məsləm	'Muslim'

(7) Schwa in MA words with vowels and consonants:

a-	/xdma/	xəd.ma	'job'
	/katb/	ka.təb	'writing'
b-	/mṭrqa/	mṭəṛ.qa	'hammer'
	/myʷrfa/	myʷəṛ.fa	'ladle'
c-	/snsla/	sən.sla	'chain, zip'
	/brdʕa/	bər.dʕa	'saddle-bag'

Now that we have presented the facts relevant to the discussion, we provide an analysis of the syllable structure of the two varieties investigated.

1.3.2 Syllable structure

In MAm, only word-initial syllables may be onsetless, and codas are permitted. No segment is deleted to satisfy syllable structure; instead, schwa is epenthesized to provide a nucleus for otherwise unsyllabified consonants. The constraints needed to account for syllable structure in MAm are given in (8):

(8)   Syllable structure constraints

(a)   Onset (Prince and Smolensky1993/2004): Syllables must have onsets.

(b)   No-Coda (Prince and Smolensky1993/2004): Coda consonants are prohibited.

(c)   Parse-Seg (Prince and Smolensky 1993/2004): Segments must belong to syllables.

(d)   Align-L (McCarthy and Prince, 1993b): The left edge of the stem must be aligned with the left edge of the prosodic word.

(e)   MAX (McCarthy and Prince, 1995): Segments in the input must have correspondents in the output.

(f)   DEP (McCarthy and Prince, 1995): Segments in the output must have correspondents in the input.

To ban segment deletion and to allow for vowel epenthesis, MAX ranks higher than DEP. The constraint ONS is dominated by Align-L so that it does not ban word-initial onsetless syllables. The constraint No-Coda is not ranked with respect to ONS.

We illustrate with the form /iflu/ 'door'. We see that candidate (9b), epenthesizing a consonant, fails at Align-L; candidate (9c), which deletes the coda, violates MAX. (9d), which deletes both the initial vowel and the consonant, not only fails at Align-L but also incurs a double violation of MAX, both high-ranking constraints:

(9)

/iflu/	Align-L	MAX	DEP	ONS	No-Coda
☞ a- if.lu				*	*
b- ʔif.lu	*!		*!		*
c- i.lu		*!		*	
d- lu	*!	*!*			

Similarly, coda consonants are licit in MA. Also, segments are not deleted to satisfy syllable structure. One major difference between MA and MAm is that even word-initial syllables must have onsets in MA. This is an indication that ONS dominates both Align-L and DEP. Align-L and DEP are not ranked with respect to each other. Finally, DEP dominates No-Coda.

The constraint tableau in (10) assesses candidates for the input /ataj/ 'tea'. [ʔataj] emerges as the optimal candidate since it does not have any onsetless syllables, nor does it delete any segment to achieve this effect, thus satisfying high-ranking MAX. In order to satisfy ONS, it minimally violates DEP and Align-L.

(10)

/ataj/	ONS	MAX	Align-L	DEP	No-Coda
☞ a- ʔa.taj			*	*	*
b- a.taj	*!				*
c- ʔa.ta		*!	*	*	
d- ta		*!*	*		

Now, we deal with syllables with schwa as a nucleus. We have seen above that in MAm and MA alike, consonants are not deleted when unsyllabifiable. Rather, schwa is epenthesized. This vowel epenthesis process reveals that both Parse-Seg and MAX dominate the faithfulness constraint DEP, which militates against schwa epenthesis.[9] Consider in (11) below the competing candidates for the MAm word [azən] 'to send':

(11)

/azn/	Parse-Seg	MAX	DEP	No-Coda
a- az		*!		
b- az.n	*!			*
c. a.zn	*!*			
☞ d- a.zən			*	*

Note that the optimal candidate violates No-Coda as schwa epenthesis forces the syllable containing schwa to have a coda. For the time being we assume that DEP should dominate No-Coda, an assumption that will become well-founded later. Note also here that *[azə.nə], a potential candidate, loses because of a double violation of DEP; it is also ill-formed because it has schwa in an open syllable which, as we will see, is disallowed. We will return to this in Section 1.4.

In both MAm and MA, triconsonantal roots are syllabified as CCəC, with schwa being placed before the third consonant, thus reflecting right-to-left syllabification. In the OT literature, directional syllabification is accounted for by positing the constraint Align-R(Stem, σ), which requires that the right edge of the stem coincide with the right edge of the syllable (McCarthy and Prince, 1993b).

Epenthesizing schwa before the third consonant results in forms that begin with consonant clusters. This way of syllabifying poses a problem relating to whether or not the cluster should be part of the onset of the schwa syllable or simply belong to two different syllables. In other words should the sequence CCC be syllabified as [.CCəC.] or [.C.CəC.]? In Tashlhit, Dell and Elmedlaoui (1985, 2002) and Ridouane (2008) claim that word-initial onsets contain only one consonant. The same thing is true of Tamazight words (Hdouch, 2004). In experimental data collected using electromagnetic articulometry, Goldstein *et al.* (2007: 244) show that word-initial clusters in Tashlhit Berber are heterosyllabic and, therefore, that onsets cannot host more than one consonant. While the data considered in Goldstein *et al.* (2007) differs substantially from that presented here, they nonetheless converge insofar as initial clusters are concerned. In the present paper, we adopt the simplex onset hypothesis in the analysis of the MAm variety considered.

Similar results showing that syllable structure is reflected in patterns of temporal stability have been presented in the work of Shaw *et al.* (2009) on MA. In Shaw *et al.*'s (2009: 213) model, 'segments were encoded as a series of articulatory landmarks coordinated in time. The relations between segments were encoded as temporal relations between these landmarks.' Ample evidence that the onset in MA consists of a simple consonant corroborates the claim made in works such as Boudlal (2001) and Dell and Elmedlaoui (2002) that triconsonantal roots are words that consist of two syllables.

With this background in mind, let us see next how we can account for CCəC words. We assume that in both MAm and MA, complex margins are not allowed, in compliance with *Complex. Following Boudlal (2001), we also need to establish a distinction between two types of syllables: (a) a major syllable (12a), whose nuclear element is one of the full vowels [i, u, a]; and (b) a minor syllable (12b), which consists exclusively of a moraic consonant. This distinction leads to the recognition of the light syllables in (12):

(12)　　　a.　σ　　　　　b.　σ
　　　　　　　　μ　　　　　　　μ
　　　　　　C　V　　　　　　　C

We also claim that schwa syllables are major syllables. After Bensoukas (2006/7), we propose that this syllable type has the representation in (13). A full discussion of this issue is provided in Section 1.3.3.

(13)　　　　　σ
　　　　　　　　μ
　　　　　C　ə　C

What interests us at the moment is the light minor syllable in (12b) which is dominated by a consonantal mora, and which leads to the violation of a constraint banning minor syllables (i.e. *Min-σ). To ensure that schwa is epenthesized before the final consonant in CCC roots, we posit an alignment constraint (Align-R-Maj-σ) requiring that the right edge of the stem be aligned with the right edge of a major syllable.[10] The constraints needed to account for epenthesis in CCC roots as well as their respective ranking are given in (14) below:

(14) MAX, Parse-seg, *Complex, Align-R-Maj-σ » DEP » *Min-σ » No-Coda.

We assume that the constraint Align-R-Maj-σ must dominate DEP to force schwa epenthesis between the last two consonants of triconsonantal words. Ranking DEP above *Min-σ ensures that a form such *Cə.CəC is ruled out (a form that could be ruled out as we will see later in Section 1.4 by virtue of its containing schwa in an open syllable); a form such as C.CəC, which attributes the minor syllable status to the initial consonant is ruled in, in spite of its violating the lower ranked constraint *Min-σ.

The result of this constraint interaction is shown in the MAm word in (15), where candidate (15b), with a minor syllable, is the winner.[11] Candidates (15c) and (15d) are ruled out because they violate *Complex. Given that the constraints MAX and Parse-seg are never violated in the languages considered in this paper, they will not figure in the constraint tableaux presented.

(15)

/bdr/	*COMPLEX	Align-R-Maj-σ	DEP	*Min-σ	No-coda
a- bəd.r$^{\mu}$		*!	*	*	*
☞ b- b$^{\mu}$.dər			*	*	*
c- bdər	*!		*		*
d- bədr	*!		*		*

The candidate *[bədər] is not considered in this tableau because we think that it could be ruled out because of the double violation of DEP it incurs. It could also be ruled out because it has schwa in an open syllable, an issue we consider in Section 1.4.

The same ranking can be used to account successfully for schwa epenthesis in MA. For example, consider [ktəb] 'write':

(16)

/ktb/	*COMPLEX	Align-R-Maj-σ	DEP	*Min-σ	No-coda
☞ a- kᵘ.təb			*	*	*
b- kət.bᵘ		*!	*	*	*
c- kətb	*!		*		*

The candidate that has an initial minor syllable is the winner.[12]

Words combining both full vowels and schwas can be accounted for much in the same way as is shown by the MA word [katəb] in tableau (17):

(17)

/katb/	*COMPLEX	Align-R-Maj-σ	DEP	*Min-σ	No-Coda
a- katb	*!				*
☞ b- ka.təb			*		*
c- kat.bᵘ		*!		*	*
d. kat.bə		*!	*		*

Notice especially the candidate *[katbə] which is ruled out for violating the constraint Align-R-Maj-σ. In this sense, the constraint Align-R-Maj-σ not only ensures proper epenthesis of schwa in CCC roots but also prevents such epenthesis from taking place after the stem final consonant. Note once again that candidate (17d) could be ruled out for violating another constraint banning schwa from open syllables.

Having dealt with syllable structure in the two languages, we turn next to considering the status of schwa syllables and full vowel syllables and their implication for syllable weight.

1.3.3 Light closed epenthetic schwa syllables vs. heavy closed full vowel syllables

In (13) above we assumed that closed syllables with a nuclear schwa are light as opposed to those with the nuclear full vowels [i, u, a], which we posit to be heavy. These two different types of syllables are represented in (18):

(18)   a- Epenthetic schwa syllable: b- Full vowel syllable:

$$[C \ni C^{\mu}]_{\sigma} \qquad\qquad [C \, V^{\mu} \, C^{\mu}]_{\sigma}$$

We will now sketch an analysis of the moraic constituency of MAm and MA syllables. In this section, an account is proposed which is an extension and refinement of that in Bensoukas (2006/7). Assuming the standard assumptions of moraic theory, we consider vowels to be underlyingly associated with a mora (Hyman, 1985; McCarthy and Prince, 1986, 1993a; Hayes, 1989; Pulleyblank, 1994). We also assume, following Morén (1999, 2003 and references therein), the distinction between distinctive and coerced weight. In the case at hand, distinctive weight is contributed by the underlying moras associated with vowels, while coerced weight is the result of the requirements of Weight-by-Position (WBP), which requires a coda consonant to be moraic (Hayes, 1989).

In our analysis, vowels remain faithful to their underlying moraicity and coda consonants are forced to be moraic by WBP, which leads to a violation of the markedness constraint on consonants being associated with moras. The relevant constraints along with their ranking are given in (19):[13]

(19) Mora structure in MAm and MA:

   a- Weight constraints:

   $*\mu/V$: Do not associate a mora with a vowel (after Morén, 2003).

   $*\mu/C$: Do not associate a mora with a consonant (after Morén, 2003).

   WeightByPosition (WBP): Coda consonants must surface as moraic (after Hayes 1989).

   MaxLink-Mora [SEG]: A particular segment affiliated with a mora underlyingly should remain affiliated with a mora on the surface.

   DepLink-Mora [SEG]: A segment that does not have a mora underlyingly should not have a mora on the surface (after Morén, 2003).

   b- Ranking:

   MaxLink-Mora [V], WBP » $*\mu/V$, DepLink-Mora [C], $*\mu/C$

This ranking is justified by the fact that an underlying vowel mora is preserved, breaching the markedness constraint $*\mu/V$. Coda consonants are associated with a mora, in violation of DepLink-Mora [C] and $*\mu/C$.

Consider the MA word [ʔataj] from (10) above (whose MAm correspondent, although pronounced [ataj], behaves the same way with respect to prosody):

(20)

/aᵘtaᵘj/	MaxLink-Mora [V]	WBP	*μ/V	DepLink-Mora [C]	*μ/C
a- ʔa.taj	*!*	*			
b- ʔaᵘ.taᵘj		*!	**		
☞ c- ʔaᵘ.taᵘjᵘ			**	*	*

In this and all similar cases, the candidate that incorporates the underlying vowel mora and simultaneously assigns a mora to the coda consonant is the winner.

In order that the bimoraicity of a closed syllable with a full vowel be ensured, we need to rank the constraint *APPEND, which bans syllabifying segments as syllable appendices, over *μ/C, as in Rosenthall and Hulst (1999: 503) (after Sherer, 1994). In (21), a two-by-two tableau shows how the two constraints interact:

(21) Weight of underlying full vowel syllables:

/...CVᵘC.../	*APPEND	*μ/C
☞ a- CVᵘCᵘ		*
b- CVᵘCᴬᵖᵖᵉⁿᵈ	*!	

In addition, what prevents a closed syllable with a full vowel from having a branching mora and sparing violation of *μ/C is the faithfulness constraint IdentLink-Mora, which demands identity between input and output association to moras:[14]

(22) IdentLink-Mora: An underlying mora link and its output correspondent must be identical.

IdentLink-Mora is violated whenever an underlying association to a mora is altered, as in the case where one mora is doubly associated to two segments, resulting in a shared mora. As a case in point, a vowel is associated underlyingly with a mora, and sharing its mora with a following consonant violates faithfulness to underlying association to moraic structure. This argues for the high rank of IdentLink-Mora with respect to *μ/C, as illustrated in (23), where VCᵘ indicates that the mora is shared by the vowel and consonant:

(23) Weight of underlying full vowel syllables: IdentLink-Mora » *μ/C

/...CV^{μ}C.../	IdentLink-Mora	*μ/C
a- CVC^μ	* !	
☞ b- CV^{μ}C^μ		*

The mora-sharing candidate (23a) loses for candidate (23b), which has coerced coda weight. With mora faithfulness properly ranked, the hierarchy accounts for the difference between the two types of syllables quite straightforwardly.

1.3.4 Support for the distinction

Independent support for considering schwa syllables monomoraic can be observed in a prosodic requirement that verbs correspond to two moras in MA and a morphologically motivated vowel epenthesis process in MAm.

1.3.4.1 Bimoraicity prosodic requirement in Moroccan Arabic verb roots
In MA verb prosodization, the fact that non-derived quadriconsonantal verb roots epenthesize schwa rather than a full vowel is a result of the requirement that a verb be exactly bimoraic. Boudlal (2001) proposes that the grammar of MA should incorporate a constraint of the type VERB ROOT= [μμ]:[15]

(24) VERB ROOT= [μμ]
   A verb root must correspond to two moras.

In (25) below, we show how a non-derived, quadriconsonantal CəCCəC verb is obtained (cf. [kərkəb] 'roll', for example). To that end, we need to distinguish two types of epenthesis: V-epenthesis (where V stands for i, u, and a) and schwa-epenthesis.

   In order to satisfy the constraint VERB ROOT= [μμ], the output must consist of a sequence of two light syllables, which is the result achieved through schwa-epenthesis but not through V-epenthesis. If a full vowel is epenthesized, the result would be at least one heavy syllable.

(25)

/krkb/	VERB ROOT= [μμ]	DEP-V
☞ a- kər^μ.kəb^μ		**
b- kV^{μ}r^μ.kV^{μ}b^μ	*!	**

Candidate (25b) fails because it incurs a fatal violation of the constraint VERB ROOT= [μμ]. When the nucleus is a full vowel, WBP is observed and that forces candidate (25b) to surface with four moras, a violation of VERB ROOT= [μμ].

To sum up, the bimoraic maximal requirement on verb roots explains why a sequence such as /CCCC/ surfaces as [CəCCəC] with only two moras.

1.3.4.2 *Prosodic-morphological vowel epenthesis in Moroccan Amazigh*

Additional support for the light weight of schwa syllables comes from a morphologically governed vowel epenthesis in MAm. Generally, the vowel [a] or a copy of the root vowel is epenthesized into the prefinal position of stems (Bensoukas, 2001a), as in the imperfective intensive verbs in (26a) (Basset, 1929; Dell and Elmedlaoui, 1991; Bensoukas, 2001a-b, 2002, 2004a).[16] In (26b), no such epenthesis applies to verbs with a final or a pre-final vowel:

(26) MAm morphologically motivated epenthesis: Imperfective intensive forms

	UR	Imperf. Intensive	
a-	/frɣ/	tt-fraɣ	'be crooked'
	/bbaqqi/	tt-baqqaj	'explode'
	/xinss/	tt-xinsis	'sob'
	/susm/	tt-susum	'be silent'
b-	/ddu/	tt-ddu	'go'
	/aẓum/	tt-aẓum	'fast'

Note that some of the forms in (26) are also subject to schwa epenthesis. The form ttfraɣ, is realized as [ttəfraɣ], exhibiting two types of epenthesis: V-epenthesis to satisfy a prosodic morphological requirement and schwa-epenthesis required by syllabification.

The core of the analysis of morphologically governed epenthesis follows Bensoukas (2001a) and references therein. The constraint in (27), claimed to drive this epenthesis, aims at making the stem end in a heavy syllable. Tableau (28) shows that a faithful candidate is ruled out in favor of one which epenthesizes a vowel to make the final syllable heavy:

(27) $\sigma_{\mu\mu}]_{Stem}$: The right edge of the stem must correspond to a heavy syllable.

(28)

/frɣ, intensive/	$\sigma_{\mu\mu}]_{Stem}$	DEP-V
☞ a- tt-fraɣ		*
b- tt-frɣ	*!	

Presumably, weight is coerced in this case to satisfy a prosodic-morphological requirement (Morén, 1999, 2003).[17]

However, the process of prefinal vowel epenthesis applies minimally, i.e. only when the result is a stem-final heavy syllable. Thus, in [ttaẓum], the root material ends in a heavy syllable, thus satisfying the morphological requirement. [ttddu], however, does not have a final heavy syllable. Yet, neither consonant epenthesis nor vowel lengthening applies as means of satisfying $\sigma_{\mu\mu}]_{Stem}$ since MAm does not permit such processes. Thus, forms like ddu surface with open light syllables (see Bensoukas 2001a).

(29)

/ddu, intensive/	DEP-C/*V:	$\sigma_{\mu\mu}]_{Stem}$	DEP-V
☞ a- tt-ddu		*	
b- tt-dduC	*!		
c- tt-ddu:	*!		

Unlike the full vowels [i, u, a], schwa is never used to satisfy $\sigma_{\mu\mu}]_{Stem}$. Accordingly, the items in (26a) never surface with a prefinal schwa, as shown by *[ttəfrəɣ]. Why is schwa, which is an epenthetic vowel, never inserted in this circumstance? The answer is simply that the full vowel provides an additional mora to the stem, which, as we have argued above, schwa cannot do. Forms such as *[ttəfrəɣ] with prefinal, epenthetic, non-moraic schwa are ill-formed since the moraic material of the final syllable does not satisfy the final heavy syllable requirement (as in the syllable rəɣ$^{\mu}$ with a shared mora in (30b)). Contrariwise, epenthetic full vowels contribute their mora to the weight of the syllable making it heavy:

(30)

/frɣ, intensive/	$\sigma_{\mu\mu}$]Stem	DEP-V
☞a- tt-fra$^{\mu}$ɣ$^{\mu}$		*
b- tt-frəɣ$^{\mu}$	*!	*

In other words, schwa epenthesis in MAm does not satisfy morphological prosodic requirements, a role assigned instead to full vowel epenthesis.

To sum up, MAm and MA provide support for the distinction between two types of closed syllables: a heavy syllable with a full vowel and a light syllable with a schwa. In MA, as the verb root may not be larger than a bimoraic mold, two light schwa syllables correspond to quadriconsonantal roots. In MAm, prosodic-morphologically motivated epenthesis requiring a stem final heavy syllable cannot insert schwa since this vowel does not contribute to the weight of the syllable hosting it.

Now that schwa syllables have been established as light, conjointly dominating a mora and a following consonant, we turn next to considering the provenance of this shared mora.

1.3.5 The source of the mora in epenthetic schwa syllables

The next issue related to variable syllable weight in MAm and MA is related to the source of the mora in closed schwa syllables. Three possibilities can be envisaged: (a) the vowel is associated with a mora at the underlying level; (b) the mora of the closed syllable is the result of WBP; and (c) the mora is a requirement imposed by prosodic licensing. Our analysis assumes the third possibility.

We have shown above that the first possibility is unlikely given that schwa is epenthetic and that its position is predictable. Also, we do not maintain the second possibility because, as we will show in Section 1.4, schwa is moraless on the basis of the fact that it is not permitted in open syllables. If paired with a coda, it behaves like a light syllable. If we assume that the mora of the closed syllable is contributed by the coda consonant through WBP, this will require a revision of WBP as proposed by Hayes (1989), in which the existence of one mora is a prerequisite for the coda consonant to contribute to syllable weight. In our case, schwa is moraless, so how can WBP apply?

The third possibility is inspired from prosodic licensing (Zec, 1988). Given the Strict Layer Hypothesis in Selkirk (1984), Zec (1988) argued that the relationship between the root node and the higher syllabic node has to be mediated by the moraic node, and suggested the version of the hierarchy in (31) below:

(31) Prosodic hierarchy (after Zec (1988: 140) and references therein)

        Phonological Phrase
        Phonological Word
        Foot
        Syllable
        Mora

Under this conception, the syllable node is an intermediary level in the prosodic hierarchy immediately dominating the mora. Our schwa syllable thus conforms to this configuration by having under the syllable node a mora whose role is to dominate the root node(s) immediately below it in the prosodic hierarchy.

Now that we have presented the analysis of schwa epenthesis in MAm and MA, we turn to the absence of schwa from open syllables in both of these languages. This fact is our second argument that schwa is not moraic. We then go on to show how such prosodic behavior is obtained from constraint interaction later in Section 1.5, where we consider stress assignment.

1.4   Schwa and open syllables

MAm and MA both disallow open syllables whose nucleus is the vowel schwa. Whatever its position in the word, a syllable headed by schwa must have a coda.

Unlike full vowels, which occur freely in all word positions, schwa in MAm is prohibited from occurring in open syllables. The constraint against the occurrence of schwa in open syllables is formulated as $*\textschwa]_\sigma$ (Saib, 1976b;

Chtatou, 1982, for example). This constraint is spelt out in the linear account of Saib (1976b) as *Cə, *əCV, *VCə, *əCə, *əGə, where G stands for a geminate consonant, while Chtatou (1982) simply bans schwa from open syllables.

Similarly, syllables with a nuclear schwa are never open in MA (Benkirane, 1982; Benhallam, 1989/1990; Al Ghadi, 1990, 1994; Boudlal, 2001, 2009 and references therein). Al Ghadi (1990) posits a negative constraint banning schwa syllables from being dominated by non-branching rimes. Benkirane (1982) formulates a positive constraint requiring that the rime dominating schwa be branching, i.e. requiring a coda consonant. Boudlal (2001) does not posit this constraint, showing rather that its effects can be obtained from ranking DEP above No-Coda.

So, although schwa is inserted to ensure proper syllabification, it is never inserted if an open syllable results. Consider again the case of [bdər] 'mention' in tableau (15) above. The candidate *[bədər], with two epenthetic schwas, which has been ruled out for violating the constraint Align-R-Maj-σ, could also be ruled out because it has schwa in an open syllable. The constraint hierarchy we have thus far makes the wrong prediction as to the optimal output form for a word like [taməɣra] 'marriage ceremony'. As it stands the hierarchy yields two optimal analyses which tie on all constraints including DEP.

(32)

/tamɣra/	*COMPLEX	Align-R-Maj-σ	DEP	*Min-σ	No-Coda
a- tamɣ.ra	*!	*			*
☞ b- ta.məɣ.ra			*		*
☞ c- tam.ɣə.ra			*		*

This calls for an additional constraint to untie the situation.

We know that a syllable like [məɣ] is ruled in while one like [ɣə] is ruled out. In explaining this incongruity, we build on the idea that schwa is not mora-bearing, suggested in Al Ghadi (1994) for MA and applied to MAm in Bensoukas (2004b). Basic to our discussion at this point are the assumptions of moraic theory, one of which is the fact that vowels are underlyingly associated with a mora (Hyman, 1985; Zec, 1988 for example). MAm and

MA open syllables with a nuclear schwa would have the representation provided in (33a), which is ill-formed (as opposed to that of open syllables with a full vowel in (33b) which are well-formed). Syllables with a schwa nucleus must have the structure provided in (13) above.

(33)   a- * [Cə$^{\mu}$]$_\sigma$ b- [Ca$^{\mu}$]$_\sigma$, [Ci$^{\mu}$]$_\sigma$, [Cu$^{\mu}$]$_\sigma$

In our analysis vowels remain faithful to their underlying moraicity, but we will argue that schwa does not have an associated mora. The basic interaction in this context is one between the markedness constraint *μ/V (a family of constraints) and MaxLink-Mora [SEG] (after Morén, 1999, 2003):

(34) Mora structure in MAm and MA:

 *μ/V: Do not associate a mora with a vowel.
 MaxLink-Mora [SEG]: A particular segment affiliated with a mora underlyingly
  should remain affiliated with a mora on the surface.

Since only schwa seems not to be allowed in open syllables, we suggest splitting the constraint *μ/V into *μ/ə, *μ/a, *μ/u, and *μ/i. The fact that all vowels except schwa can appear in open syllables calls for ranking them with respect to faithfulness in the following way:

(35)   *μ/ə » MaxLink-Mora [SEG] » *μ/a, *μ/u, *μ/i

This ranking will ensure that schwas never get moraic, a markedness effect.
 Even if, in compliance with Richness of the Base (Prince and Smolensky, 1993/2004; Smolensky, 1996), we posit an input schwa with a mora, this mora will not be an optimal output form as shown in the tableau below for the different analyses of the MA output form [katəb]:

(36)

/ka$^{\mu}$tə$^{\mu}$b/	*μ/ə	MaxLink-Mora [SEG]	*μ/a, *μ/u, *μ/i
a- ka.təb		*!*	
b- ka$^{\mu}$.tə$^{\mu}$b$^{\mu}$	*!		*
☞ c- ka$^{\mu}$.təb$^{\mu}$			*

Being high-ranking, *μ/ə militates against an output moraic schwa. In (36b) above, the second mora associates with schwa, resulting in a fatal violation of *μ/ə. Candidate (36a) violates MaxLink-Mora [SEG] since it fails to preserve the vowel-mora link existing in the input.

The optimal candidate (36c) has kept underlying associations but has the double association of the mora with schwa and the following consonant. The assumption we are trying to make here is that when a mora is associated solely with schwa, the constraint *μ/ə is violated, whereas when the mora associates with both schwa and a following consonant, the constraint *μ/ə is not violated. This understanding of the constraint *μ/ə is a determining factor in considering CəC to be a light, mono-moraic syllable.

*μ/ə established as an undominated constraint in the phonology of MAm and MA, let us see how this constraint coupled with the ranking in (35) above yields well-formed output forms. With the introduction of the high-ranking *μ/ə constraint into the hierarchy already established, the competing candidates (32b) and (32c) are untied. The one with an open syllable whose nucleus is schwa is ruled out, as is clear in tableau (37):

(37)

/tamɣra/	*μ/ə	*Complex	Dep	*Min-σ	No-Coda
☞ a- ta.məɣ.ra			*		*
b- tam.ɣə.ra	*!		*		*

Although the optimal candidate contains two other open syllables ([ta] and [ra]), these do not incur fatal violations as the vowels other than schwa incur only minimal violations when they are moraic. As this is clear enough, we are not including the constraints relevant to these violations in the tableau.

The constraint ranking in the tableau above also accounts for the non-occurrence of schwa in open syllables in MA. Consider in (38) the competing candidates for an input such as /ṣaħb-tu/ 'his friend (fem.)', where the candidate with an open schwa syllable is the loser:

(38)

/ṣaḥb-tu/	*μ/ə	*COMPLEX	DEP	*Min-σ	No-Coda
☞ a- ṣa.ḥəb.tu			*		*
b- ṣaḥ.bə.tu	*!		*		*

Variation affecting the pronunciation of [ṣaḥəbtu] provides further justification for the fact that schwa cannot occur in open syllables. In some varieties discussed in Boudlal (1998), the consonant [t] following schwa in (38b) is geminated and the output form is [ṣaḥbəttu], an output that does not violate *μ/ə. We suggest that this gemination, which cannot be explained as driven by morphological requirements (as in [kdəb] 'lie' and causative [kəddəb] 'belie'), results from the need to satisfy the requirements of the constraint *μ/ə.

To sum up, the analysis we propose uses an undominated constraint against the association of schwa with a mora. Schwa only associates with a mora when there is a following consonant which in fact shares the mora with the schwa. This, we claim, accounts for the absence of schwa from open syllables. In other words, unlike full vowels, schwa alone is not a mora-bearing vowel in output structure. Further evidence for this position comes from the behavior of schwa syllables with respect to stress; closed syllables containing schwa as a nucleus are never counted as heavy syllables, in contrast to other closed syllables.

1.5   Schwa epenthesis and word stress assignment

In this section, we will consider the behavior of schwa syllables with respect to the stress system of MAm and MA. We will show that in spite of being closed, schwa syllables are not heavy (Faizi, 2002, 2007; Hdouch, 2004, for MAm; and Benkirane, 1982; Boudlal, 2001, 2009; El Yamani, 2006, for MA). This will be confirmed by the behavior of these syllables when they co-occur with heavy syllables, on the one hand, and light syllables, on the other hand.

1.5.1 Word stress

MAm stress facts (Faizi, 2002: 203–212) reveal that, as in (39), heavy syllables (σ_H) attract stress no matter what their position within the word is. When the word contains two or more heavy syllables, the last heavy syllable is stressed, whereas when it contains two or more light syllables (σ_L), the initial syllable receives stress, as in (40a) and (40b), respectively:

(39) MAm: Heavy syllable attracts stress

áx.bu	'hole'
tíz.wi.ri	'beginning'
ti.wír.ja	'dreams'
i.síj.nu	'cloud'
a.fár	'grass'
a.zu.rár	'big'

(40)   a- Two or more heavy syllables in MAm:

ar.ráw	'children'
taw.ma.tín	'sisters'
al.jám.mu	'rein'
i.məd.duk.kál	'friends'

b- Two or more light syllables in MAm:

tá.ma	'side'
í.mu.la	'shadows'
tá.ra.za	'sort of hat'

The analysis we provide for the MAm stress facts follows Walker (1996), who assumes a foot-free account using relative prominence to locate syllable heads. Prominence is decided by factors such as syllabic weight, peripherality and non-finality. We assume that the prominence-based account is not in contradiction with a foot-based one and, indeed, we will show that they may complement each other. The crux of our analysis is that while the prominence-driven model accounts in a straightforward fashion for MAm stress facts, the analysis of MA requires the use of foot structure as well.

The constraints needed to account for stress facts in MAm are given in (41a) and their ranking is provided in (41b):

(41) Stress in MAm:

   a- Constraints:

Pk-Prom (Prince and Smolensky, 1993: 39) (after Prince, 1990): Peak (x) > Peak (y) if |x| > |y|: An element (x) makes a better peak than an element (y) if the intrinsic prominence of (x) is greater than that of (y).

Align-L(σ_μ, PrWd) (Zoll, 1995, see Walker, 1996): For all stressed light syllables, there exists some prosodic word such that the left edge of the stressed light syllable and the left edge of the PrWd are shared.

Align-R(Pk, PrWd) (McCarthy and Prince, 1993a): The right edge of the peak must coincide with the right edge of the PrWd.

Non-finality (Prince and Smolensky, 1993: 30): The prosodic head of the word does not fall on the word-final syllable.

   b- Ranking: Align-L(σ_μ, PrWd), Pk-Prom » Align-R(Pk, PrWd) » Non-finality

This ranking is justified as follows. The stress facts presented in (39), and (40) above show that PkProm is undominated, and this follows from the requirement that heavy syllables attract stress in MAm (Faizi, 2002; Hdouch, 2004). When stressed heavy syllables occur word-finally, they breach Non-finality without this affecting in the least their being optimal, which means that Non-finality is dominated by Align-R(Pk, PrWd). Align-L(σ_μ, PrWd) is undominated to account for the fact that in words consisting of light syllables alone, it is the initial syllable which receives stress.

The cases in which the heavy syllable attracts stress are accounted for by the ranking above:

(42)

/afar/	Pk-Prom	Align-L(σ_μ, PrWd)	Align-R(Pk, PrWd)	Non-finality
☞ a- a.fár				*
b- á.far	*!		*	

(43)

/tiwirja/	Pk-Prom	Align-L(σ_μ, PrWd)	Align-R(Pk, PrWd)	Non-finality
☞ a- ti.wír.ja			*	
b- tí.wir.ja	*!		*	
c- ti.wir.já	*!	*		*

When the word contains only one heavy syllable, stress falls on the heavy syllable as a result of the high rank of Pk-Prom in the constraint hierarchy.

The cases involving more than one heavy syllable, with final stress, are accounted for by the constraint Align-R(Pk, PrWd). When Pk-Prom is satisfied by all the syllables, only the rightmost, stressed, heavy syllable is optimal:

(44)

/arraw/	Pk-Prom	Align-L(σ_μ, PrWd)	Align-R(Pk, PrWd)	Non-finality
☞ a- ar.ráw				*
b- ár.raw			*!	

When the syllables are all light, the initial syllable receives stress. This is accounted for by the ranking of Align-L(σ_μ, PrWd) as in tableaux (45) and (46).

(45)

/taraza/	Pk-Prom	Align-L(σ_μ, PrWd)	Align-R(Pk, PrWd)	Non-finality
☞ a- tá.ra.za			*	
b- ta.rá.za		*!	*	
c- ta.ra.zá		*!		*

(46)

/tama/	Pk-Prom	Align-L(σ_μ, PrWd)	Align-R(Pk, PrWd)	Non-finality
☞ a- tá.ma			*	
b- ta.má		*!		*

This analysis also accounts for words with schwa syllables as we will show later in Sections 1.5.2 and 1.5.3.

We move on now to the analysis of the stress facts of MA. The data presented in this paper rely on the instrumental analyses of words in isolation carried out in Nejmi (1993) and Boudlal (2001). In MA, as in the variety of

MAm studied here, heavy syllables attract stress. In (47), the heavy syllable of disyllabic words is stressed whether it is in penultimate or ultimate position. In disyllabic and trisyllabic words with an initial and final heavy syllables as in (48), stress is assigned to the final heavy syllable. In (49), stress falls on the penultimate, light syllable of trisyllabic words consisting of an initial heavy syllable followed by two light syllables. Finally in words with two or more light syllables, stress is assigned to the penult syllable as in (50).

(47) Heavy syllable attracts stress in MA:

      náw.ja   'intending (fem.)'

      sa.rút   'key'

      li.mún   'orange'

(48) Two heavy syllables in MA:

      law.jín   'wilted (pl.)'

      ḍar.bín   'hitting (pl.)'

      man.ḍa.rín   'oranges'

(49) A heavy syllable followed by a sequence of light syllables in MA:

      ṣan.ḍá.la   'sandals'

      mim.sá.ħa   'eraser'

(50) Two or more light syllables in MA:

      dá.ba   'now'

      li.mú.na   'an orange'

      ba.ná.na   'a banana'

The generalization we can formulate about MA is that stress falls on the final syllable if it is heavy; otherwise, it falls on the penult.

The domain of stress in MA does not go beyond the final two syllables of a word, in contrast to MAm, where stress falls on the initial light syllable in trisyllabic words. The cases in (47) above show that it is always the rightmost heavy syllable which attracts stress, even if it is non-final. This means that Pk-Prom must dominate Align-R(Pk, PrWd) as (51) shows:

(51)

/nawja/	Pk-Prom	Align-L($\acute{\sigma}_\mu$, PrWd)	Align-R(Pk, PrWd)	Non-finality
☞ a- náw.ja			*	
b- naw.já	*!			*

In disyllabic and trisyllabic words involving more than one heavy syllable, it is once again the rightmost heavy syllable that is stressed to satisfy the constraint Align-R(Pk, PrWd):

(52)

/lawjin/	Pk-Prom	Align-L($\acute{\sigma}_\mu$, PrWd)	Align-R(Pk, PrWd)	Non-finality
☞ a- law.jín				*
b- láw.jin			*!	

Given that it is the rightmost heavy syllable of the final two syllables of a word which must be stressed, we need to make sure that the prominent syllable is word-final. In LL, HLL, and LLL words, it is always the penultimate, light syllable that is stressed. The constraint Align-L($\acute{\sigma}_\mu$, PrWd), which we have used for MAm to ensure appropriate stress on the initial syllable of words with light syllables, cannot account for penult stress we see here. It will always predict that the optimal candidate is the one with initial stress as (53) reveals:

(53)

/limuna/	Pk-Prom	Align-L($\acute{\sigma}_\mu$, PrWd)	Align-R(Pk, PrWd)	Non-finality
☞ a- lí.mu.na			*	
☹ b- li.mú.na		*!	*	
c- li.mu.ná		*!		*

To account for stress in MA words ending with a sequence of light syllables, we need to refer to foot structure which, as we have noted, is not incompatible with the prominence-based moodel (Prince and Smolensky, 1993/2004). The foot-free analysis we have provided for Amazigh above has shown that a word is scanned for a potential heavy syllable. Once this syllable is located, it receives stress no matter where it is ([tízwiri], [arráw], [afár]). In the absence of a heavy syllable, it is the initial light syllable that bears stress ([táraza]). In MA, not all heavy syllables are stressed- only those in the domain of the last two syllables of the word.

The decisive constraint will be Align-R(Ft, PrWd) (McCarthy and Prince 1993b), which requires that the prominent foot be right-aligned with the prosodic word. It must dominate Pk-Prom as well as Non-finality. Consider the examples below:

(54)

/ṣanḍala/	Align-R (Ft, PrWd)	Pk-Prom	Non-finality
☞ a- ṣan(ḍá.la)		*	
b- (ṣán)ḍa.la	*!		
c- ṣan(ḍa.lá)		*	*!

(55)

/limuna/	Align-R (Ft, PrWd)	Pk-Prom	Non-finality
☞ a- li(mú.na)			
b- (lí.mu)na	*!		
c- li(mu.ná)			*!

The winning candidate in both examples above is the form that satisfies both Align-R and Non-finality.

To recapitulate, we have presented an account for the similarities between the stress systems of both MAm and MA by using a small subset of constraints proposed within the prominence-based model of Walker (1996). We complemented this analysis with an additional constraint dubbed Align-R (Ft, PrWd) referring to foot structure to account for the MA facts. With this background in mind, we now move on to discuss the behavior of schwa syllables with respect to stress in the two languages.

1.5.2 Schwa syllables and stress in MAm

One of the similarities between MAm and MA is the fact that closed schwa syllables do not attract stress in either language. When closed schwa syllables co-occur with closed syllables with full vowels, it is always the syllable with full vowels that is stressed. This reveals that schwa syllables are light in spite of the fact that they have a coda consonant. We now turn to an account of this fact.

In MAm, when the word has a closed syllable with schwa as a nucleus, that syllable will not attract stress if there is a syllable with a full vowel. We see this in the examples in (56):

(56) The stress pattern of MAm schwa syllables:

      a- σ_∂ and σ_H: σ_H attracts stress

          ád.fəl   'snow'

          azúzzər   'winnowing'

    b- σ_∂ and σ_L: stress on the initial syllable

          í.nəɣ.mi.sən   'news'

          tá.məɣ.ra   'marriage'

Compare with the items in (40) above in which a final heavy syllable is stressed in case there are more than one heavy syllable and in which the initial syllable is stressed when the remaining syllables are light. As is clear in (56), CəC behaves like a light syllable not like a heavy syllable.[18]

Now, let us consider one word from each of the classes in (56) above using the system described above. First is the word [azúzzər] 'winnowing', which consists of a medial heavy syllable flanked by a light syllable on the left edge and a schwa syllable on the right edge. Candidate (57d), which has a bimoraic, heavy schwa syllable mistakenly emerges as optimal instead of the correct candidate, (57a). As it stands, the stress constraint hierarchy cannot rule this candidate out:

32   *Prosody Matters*

(57)

/azuzzr/	Pk-Prom	Align-L($\acute{\sigma}_\mu$, PrWd)	Align-R(Pk, PrWd)	Non-finality
☹ a- a.zúz.zər$^\mu$			*!	
b- á.zuz.zər$^\mu$	*!		*	
c- a.zuz.zə́r$^\mu$	*!			*
☞ d- a.zuz.zə́$^\mu$r$^\mu$				*

In words such as [táməɣra] 'marriage ceremony', the hierarchy selects the optimal candidate (58a) so long as we assume that the schwa syllable is light. If it is heavy, the winner is the candidate with stress on the schwa syllable, i.e. (58d).

(58)

/tamɣra/	Pk-Prom	Align-L($\acute{\sigma}_\mu$, PrWd)	Align-R(Pk, PrWd)	Non-finality
☞ a- tá.məɣ$^\mu$.ra			*	
b- ta.mə́ɣ$^\mu$.ra		*!	*	
c- ta.məɣ$^\mu$.rá		*!		*
☞ d- ta.mə́$^\mu$ɣ$^\mu$.ra			*	

Recall from our discussion above that schwa never occurs in an open syllable, in satisfaction of the high-ranking constraint *µ/ə, which rules out schwas that carry a mora. Let us reconsider the two cases above, with the constraint *µ/ə included in the evaluation:

(59)

/azuzzr/	*µ/ə	Pk-Prom	Align-L($\acute{\sigma}_\mu$, PrWd)	Align-R(Pk, PrWd)	Non-finality
☞ a- a.zúz.zər$^\mu$				*	
b- á.zuz.zər$^\mu$		*!		*	
c- a.zuz.zə́r$^\mu$		*!			*
d- a.zuz.zə́$^\mu$r$^\mu$	*!				*

(60)

/tamɣra/	*μ/ə	Pk-Prom	Align-L($\acute{\sigma}_\mu$, PrWd)	Align-R(Pk, PrWd)	Non-finality
☞a- tá.məɣ$^{\mu}$.ra				*	
b- ta.mə́ɣ$^{\mu}$.ra			*!	*	
c- ta.məɣ$^{\mu}$.rá			*!		*
d- ta.mə́$^{\mu}$ɣ$^{\mu}$.ra	*!			*	

The two candidates (59d) and (60d) are now ruled out because they incur a violation of the independently motivated markedness constraint *μ/ə.

1.5.3 Schwa syllables and stress in MA

Further support for the claim that schwa syllables are treated by the stress system as light syllables is provided by MA stress data. Consider the examples in (61) below for illustration:

(61) The stress pattern of MA schwa syllables

   a- $\sigma_ə$ and σ_H: σ_H is stressed

        məljún   'a million'

        wáʕdək   'he promised you'

        wəldátni   'she gave birth to me'

   b- $\sigma_ə$ /σ_L with $\sigma_ə$ /σ_L: stress on penult syllable

        májəl   'leaning'

        ṛə́mla   'sand'

        qərbálɑ   'mess'

The data in (61) shows that a schwa syllable behaves like a light syllable in MA, too. Although it may occur in different positions, a schwa syllable never attracts stress if it co-occurs with a heavy syllable ([wáʕdək]) or a light syllable with a full vowel ([májəl]). If the schwa syllable were heavy, we would expect stress to fall on the final schwa syllable and have *[waʕdə́$^{\mu}$k$^{\mu}$] and *[majə́$^{\mu}$l$^{\mu}$], instead.

Consider the competing candidates for the input /waʕd-k/ given in the tableau below:

(62)

/waʕd-k/	*µ/ə	Pk-Prom	Align-R(Pk, PrWd)	Non-finality
☞ a- wáʕ.dək^µ			*	
b- waʕ.də́k^µ		*!		*
c- waʕ.də́^{µ}k^µ	*!			*

Candidate (62b) fails because it assigns stress to the final light schwa syllable where there is a heavy penult with a full vowel. Candidate (62c) is ruled out because schwa is associated with a mora, thus incurring a fatal violation of *µ/ə. Forms such as *[waʕdə́^{µ}k^µ] and *[majə́^{µ}l^µ] might as well be ruled out on the basis of the constraint Non-finality; however, this constraint is frequently violated in the MA cases that end in heavy syllables with full vowels and that receive final stress, as in [məljún], for instance. In this sense, *µ/ə acts as a negative constraint against having heavy schwa syllables.

The analysis undertaken in this section shows that although the two languages share a lot in common, they have different prosodic systems characterized by the details of stress patterns. In MAm, it is the rightmost heavy syllable that is stressed; in MA, and since stress does not go beyond the last two syllables of the word, it is the rightmost heavy syllable of the final two syllables that receives stress. In the absence of a heavy syllable, the two languages assign stress to light syllables differently. In MAm, it is the initial light syllable that is stressed; in MA, it is rather the penult which receives stress.

To sum up, the similarities in the behavior of schwa syllables with respect to stress facts give further support to the unified analysis we provided for the prosodic behavior of schwa. We have shown that closed syllables with a nuclear schwa are considered light, and this explains why stress does not fall on such syllables in the presence of a heavy syllable. This is reminiscent of the fact that in both languages schwa does not occur in an open syllable because it cannot sustain an independent mora.

1.6   Conclusion

In this paper, we have discussed the prosodic similarities between MAm and MA with respect to the behavior of schwa. We have shown that schwa is an epenthetic vowel needed for syllabic purposes. Moreover, the prosodic behavior of schwa in the two languages reveals that both illustrate variable closed syllable weight, with the ensuing discrepancy between heavy full vowel syllables and light schwa syllables. Evidence for this distinction comes from two prosodic phenomena, namely prosodization in MA quadriconsonantal verbs which surface as bimoraic, and prosodic-morphological full vowel epenthesis in MAm imperfective intensive verbs, which requires words to end in a heavy syllable. Schwa syllables are light, and we claimed that they contain a branching mora which schwa and a following consonant share. The provenance of this mora has also been dealt with, and the explanation provided is that the mora is the result of prosodic licensing. The prosodic analysis of schwa in both languages has also shown that this vowel can never appear in an open syllable. We explained this by claiming that the vowel schwa cannot bear a mora on its own, an effect obtained from the work of an undominated markedness constraint against the association of schwa to a mora. The weight of schwa syllables advocated herein finds support in the stress systems of both languages which present additional evidence that schwa syllables are in fact light and, as such, should be considered monomoraic.

The explanation of these affinities is an issue we leave for future research. The similarities between the two languages can be explained as the result of the two languages belonging to the Hamitic-Semitic family; under this conception, schwa is a Hamitic-Semitic reality, and this similar phonological behavior is part of the prosodic system of this language family. A comparison of the quality of epenthetic vowels in Arabic dialects immediately proves this conception to be untenable. The second conception, which we adhere to, is that the prosodic affinities between MAm and MA are due to language contact. Schwa is attested in most Amazigh dialects, some of which do not apparently have any contact with Arabic. If this is the case, then we are in front of a situation in which constraint rankings are subject to borrowing.

Notes

1   We would like to thank the editors for having invited us to contribute to this collection. The authors are native speakers of Moroccan Amazigh (KB) and Moroccan Arabic (AB). The authors' and the languages' names appear in alphabetical order. For their comments on this paper, we would like to thank N. Amrous, K. Ansar, A. Benhallam, R. Faizi, S. Imouzaz, D. Laaboudi, N. Louriz and S. Rguibi. Valuable comments on form and content from two anonymous peer-reviewers and Toni Borowsky helped improve the paper tremendously. Correspondence concerning the paper should be addressed to both authors.

2   Commonly referred to as Berber, MAm is a Hamitic language roughly divided into three major dialectal groupings whose phonology diverges more than do their morphology and syntax: Tarifit (north), Tamazight (center), and Tashlhit (south). MA is a Semitic language claimed to have four major regional varieties (Boukous, 1998). These varieties share the bulk of the grammar, which has led some linguists to establish a 'common' MA (Benhallam and Dahbi, 1990). MAm and MA have been treated fairly extensively in the literature on linguistics (see Ameur and Boumalk, 2004, 2006; Bensoukas, 2008; Youssi, 1977, 1989, 1992 among others).

3   One major respect in which our analysis differs from Faizi's is that we consider schwa epenthetic, while Faizi considers it underlying. Faizi's data yields itself readily to an epenthesis analysis within OT.

4   Emphasis is transcribed by using a dot underneath a symbol and gemination by doubling the consonant. Otherwise, IPA symbols are used. Also, we adapted the transcriptions in our sources to the conventions herein.

5   In addition to the consonants in (2), MA has a prothetic glottal stop [ʔ], used to satisfy the requirement that syllables have onsets.

6   The exceptions include individual items and forms with feminine morphology (Faizi, 2002). Examples of individual words are: [fərn]/*[frən] 'sort out', and [ils]/*[iləs] 'tongue'. Also exceptional are forms with the feminine plural nominal morpheme (/srm-nt/- [sərmənt]/*[srəmnət] 'they sharpened it, fem.') and feminine nouns ([tudərt]/ *[tudrət] 'life'). In the individual words above, sonority can be invoked to explain the site of schwa epenthesis. The final [t] of the feminine morpheme is extraprosodic (See Faizi, 2002; Hdouch, 2004).

7   Not every sequence of four consonants is syllabified as CəCCəC. Exceptional cases include words such as /ktb-t/, which surfaces as [ktəbt] 'I wrote' instead of the expected *[kətbət]. For more details on the syllabification of such words, see Boudlal (2001, 2009).

8   There are two CCC classes that epenthesize schwa before the second consonant: (a) a group of words with a final geminate ([mədd] 'to hand', [məss] 'to touch' and [dəmm] 'blood'), in which schwa does not split the geminate; and (b) a group of nouns with three distinct consonants such as ([bərd] 'wind' and [bənt] 'girl'), where schwa is epenthesized before the most sonorous consonant in the sequence.

9   Here and in (11c), both the constraints MAX and PARSE-seg are needed since they perform different functions. MAX ensures that all input segments appear in the output, while PARSE-seg requires them to belong to syllables and, thus, triggers schwa epenthesis between consonants that would otherwise remain unsyllabified and, consequently, be adjoined to the foot or PrWd. In [az.n], for example, Parse-Seg is violated by the final consonant not belonging to a syllable.

10   Boudlal (2001, 2009) assumes that epenthesizing schwa before C3, and not C2, of CCC roots follows from the general requirement that the stem be iambic. Instead of the constraint Align-R-Maj-σ, the author proposes the constraint Align-R-σ́, which requires the schwa syllable to be right-aligned with the stem, and the minor syllable to be word initial as in words such as [k.təb].

11   In other dialects of MAm, the verb meaning 'work', for example, is pronounced [əxðəm] instead of [xðəm], which is expected given our data from Goulmima Tamazight. Interestingly, there is free variation with respect to some words that have the same pattern ([ffəɣ]/[əffəɣ] 'go out', for example). These details, although not dealt with here, present additional support for considering word-initial clusters hetero-syllabic.

12   Our analysis does not cover nouns on the pattern CəCC. To ensure proper schwa epenthesis in such words in which the sonority index of the second consonant is greater than that of the third, we need to posit an additional set of sonority constraints which should rank above Align-R-Maj-σ. Boudlal (2001, 2006/7, 2009) posits the following constraints on schwa-consonant sequences: *əS » *əF » *əN » *əL » *əG (S=stop, F=fricative, N=nasal, L=liquid, G=glide). According to this ranking, the more harmonious schwa syllables are those in which the difference between the sonority of the nucleus and that of the coda is not significant. For example, an output such as [bənt] 'girl' is optimal because it epenthesizes schwa before a nasal consonant, whereas another candidate, *[bnət], loses exactly because it epenthesizes schwa before a stop and violates high-ranking *əS.

13   Both MAm and MA have underlying geminates. A complete analysis of the two systems will have to account for this fact, which will call for the ranking MaxLink-Mora-[C] » *μ/C to be incorporated into the hierarchy. We do not pursue this issue here.

14   Our constraint IdentLink-Mora is inspired from Morén (1999, 2003), in which the constraints DepLink-Mora and MaxLink-Mora are proposed.

15 We think the constraint VERB ROOT= [μμ] is simply a different manifestation of FT-BIN observed at the moraic level (McCarthy and Prince, 1993a).

16 The phenomenon is more general and intricate than the facts herein indicate. As space does not permit a comprehensive account, the reader is referred to Bensoukas (2001a).

17 To deal with a wider array of facts than presented in the present paper, Bensoukas (1994) and Jebbour (1996) claim that what is at work is a constraint requiring the stem to correspond to an Iambic foot consisting preferably of a succession of a Light and a Heavy syllables.

18 In Faizi (2002), which focuses on nouns and adjectives, CəC.CV.CV. native words are not reported. In MAm, masculine nouns and adjectives start with an initial full vowel and feminine ones with an initial t+full vowel sequence. Our analysis predicts that such words would receive initial stress, like in [táraza]. Faizi (2002: 331) mentions the MA loan-words [ləçsáwi] 'dresses' and [ləç^{w}rása] 'chairs', with stress on the penult. He states that 'despite the fact that the loanwords ... have undergone some phonological changes ... their stress patterns remain unchanged'. Perhaps, loan-words stay faithful to their original stress pattern.

References

Al Ghadi, A. (1990) *Moroccan Arabic Plurals and the Organization of the Lexicon.* D.E.S. thesis, M5University, FLHS, Rabat.

Al Ghadi, A. (1994) An OT account of Moroccan Arabic prosody. Ms. University of Delaware.

Ameur, M. and Boumalk, A. (eds) (2004) *Standardisation de l'Amazighe.* Rabat: IRCAM.

Ameur, M. and Boumalk, A. (eds) (2006) *Structures Morphologiques de l'Amazighe.* Rabat: IRCAM.

Basset, A. (1929) *La Langue Berbère. Morphologie. Le verbe. Etude de thèmes.* Paris: Leroux.

Basset, A. (1952) *La Langue Berbère.* (First published for the International African Institute; reprinted in 1969) London: Dawsons of Pall Mall.

Benhallam, A. (1980) *Syllable Structure and Rule Types in Arabic.* Ph.D. dissertation, University of Florida at Gainesville.

Benhallam, A. (1989/1990) Moroccan Arabic syllable structure. *Langues et Littératures* 8: 177–191.

Benhallam, A. and Dahbi, M. (1990) Accents of Moroccan Arabic: a preliminary study. In J. Pleines (ed.) *Maghreb Linguistics* 111–125. Rabat: Okad.

Benkaddour, A. (1982) *A Nonlinear Analysis of Some Aspects of the Phonology and Nonconcatenative Morphology of Arabic.* Ph.D. dissertation, SOAS, London.

Benkirane, T. (1982) *Etude Phonétique et Fonction de la Syllabe en Arabe Marocain.* Third Cycle thesis, Université de Provence.

Bensoukas, K. (1994) *Tashlhit Agentive Nouns. An Optimality–Theoretic Approach.* D.E.S. thesis, M5University, FLHS, Rabat.

Bensoukas, K. (2001a) *Stem Forms in the Nontemplatic Morphology of Berber.* Doctorat d'État thesis, M5University, FLHS, Rabat.

Bensoukas, K. (2001b) Markedness and epenthetic quality in Tashlhit imperfective verbs: an OT approach. *Linguistic Research* 6 (1): 81–123.

Bensoukas, K. (2002) The emergence of the unmarked in Berber epenthetic vowel quality. ms. M5University, FLHS, Rabat.

Bensoukas, K. (2004a) On the unity of the morphology of Moroccan Amazighe: aspects of the imperfective form of the verb. In M. Ameur and A. Boumalk (eds) *Standardisation de l'Amazighe* 198–224. Rabat: IRCAM.

Bensoukas, K. (2004b) A note on the absence of schwa in Berber open syllables. Presented at *La Langue Amazighe: Approche Linguistique*, FLHS, Ben M'sik, 8 March 2004.

Bensoukas, K. (2006/2007) Variable syllable weight in Amazighe. *Languages and Linguistics* 18&19: 31–58.

Bensoukas, K. (2008) Research on Amazighe phonology in Morocco: how can the decline be remedied? Paper presented at the conference *Horizons de l'Enseignement de la Langue Amazighe à l'Université Marocaine.* FLSH Saïs, Fès, 15–16 May 2008.

Boudlal, A. (1993) *Moroccan Arabic Glides: A Lexical Approach.* D.E.S. thesis, M5University, FLHS, Rabat.

Boudlal, A. (1998) A diachronic analysis of labialization in Moroccan Arabic. *Langues et Littératures* 16: 45–60.

Boudlal, A. (2001) *Constraint Interaction in the Phonology and Morphology of Casablanca Moroccan Arabic.* Doctorat d'État thesis, M5University, FLHS, Rabat. Available at http://roa.rutgers.edu, ROA#650.

Boudlal, A. (2006/2007) Sonority-driven schwa epenthesis in Moroccan Arabic. *Languages and Linguistics* 18&19: 59–81.

Boudlal, A. (2009) *The Prosody and Morphology of a Moroccan Arabic Dialect: An Optimality–Theoretic Account.* Saarbrüchen, Germany: VDM Verlag Dr. Müller.

Boukous, A. (1987) *Phonotactique et Domaines Prosodiques en Berbère.* Doctorat d'État thesis, Université Paris VIII, Vincennes, Saint-Denis.

Boukous, A. (1998) La situation sociolinguistique au Maroc. *Plurilinguismes (Le Maroc)* 16: 5–30. Paris: Centre d'Etudes et de Recherches en Planification Linguistique.

Boukous, A. (2009) *Phonologie de l'Amazighe.* Rabat: IRCAM. Available at www.ircam.ma.

Chtatou, M. (1982) *Aspects of the Phonology of a Berber Dialect of the Rif.* Ph.D. dissertation, SOAS, London.

Chtatou, M. (1991) Syllable structure in Tarifit Berber. *Langues et Littératures* 9: 27–60.

Dell, F. and Elmedlaoui, M. (1985) Syllabic consonants and syllabification in Imdlawn Tashlhiyt Berber. *Journal of African Languages and Linguistics* 7: 105–130.

Dell, F. and Elmedlaoui, M. (1991) Clitic ordering, morphology and phonology in the verbal complex of Imdlawn Tashlhiyt Berber (Part II). *Langues Orientales Anciennes–Philologie et Linguistique* 3: 77–104.

Dell, F. and Elmedlaoui, M. (2002) *Syllables in Tashlhiyt Berber and in Moroccan Arabic.* Dordrecht: Kluwer.

El Yamani, S. (2006) *Stress Assignment in Rabati Moroccan Arabic Verbs: An Optimality Theoretic Approach.* Doctorat dissertation, M5University, FLHS, Rabat.

Faizi, R. (2002) *Stress and Syllabicity in Goulmima Tamazight Berber: A Metrical Approach.* Doctorat dissertation, M5University, FLHS, Rabat.

Faizi, R. (2007) An acoustic study of stress in Amazigh. Paper submitted to *Languages and Linguistics.*

Galand, L. (1988) Le Berbère. In J. Perrot (ed.) *Les Langues dans le Monde Ancien et Moderne. Troisième Partie. Les Langues Chamito–Sémitiques* 207–242. Paris: CNRS.

Goldstein, L., Chitoran, I., and Selkirk, E. (2007) Syllable structure as coupled oscillation modes: evidence from Georgian vs. Tashlhiyt Berber. *ICPhs XIV* 241–244.

Hayes, B. (1989) Compensatory lengthening in moraic phonology. *Linguistic Inquiry* 20 (2): 253–306.

Hdouch, Y. (2004) *Some Aspects of Extraprosodicity in Ayt–Wirra Tamazight Berber: An Optimality Theoretic Approach.* Doctorat thesis, M5University, FLHS, Rabat.

Hyman, L. (1985) A *Theory of Phonological Weight.* Dordrecht: Foris.

Jebbour, A. (1996) *Morphologie et Contraintes Prosodiques en Berbère (Tachelhit de Tiznit). Analyse Linguistique et Traitement Automatique.* Doctorat d'État thesis, M5University, FLHS, Rabat.

Keegan, J. (1986) *The Phonology and Morphology of Moroccan Arabic.* Unpublished doctoral dissertation, The City University of New York.

McCarthy, J. and Prince, A. (1986) *Prosodic Morphology.* Ms. University of Massachusetts, Amherst and Brandeis University.

McCarthy, J. and Prince, A. (1993a) *Prosodic Morphology I: Constraint Interaction and Satisfaction.* Ms. University of Massachusetts, Amherst and Rutgers University. Available at http://roa.rutgers.edu, ROA# 482.

McCarthy, J. and Prince, A. (1993b) Generalized alignment. In G. Booij, and J. van Marle (eds) *Yearbook of Morphology* 79–153. Dordrecht: Kluwer.

McCarthy, J. and Prince, A. (1995) Faithfulness and reduplicative identity. *University of Massachusetts Occasional Papers in Linguistics 18: Papers in Optimality Theory*. Available at http://roa.rutgers.edu, ROA#60.

McCarthy, J. and Prince, A. (1999) Faithfulness and identity in prosodic morphology. In R. Kager, H. van der Hulst, and W. Zonneveld (eds) *The Prosody–morphology Interface* 218–309. Cambridge: Cambridge University Press.

Morén, B. T. (1999) *Distinctiveness, Coercion and Sonority: A Unified Theory of Weight*. Ph.D. dissertation, University of Maryland at College Park. Available at http://roa.rutgers.edu, ROA#346.

Morén, B. T. (2003) Weight typology: an optimality theoretic approach. *The Linguistic Review* 20: 281–304.

Nejmi, H. (1993) *Contribution à une Etude des Processus Accentuels de l'Arabe Marocain de Casablanca: Approche Phonétique et Phonologique (Accent de Mot)*. Doctoral dissertation, Paris III, Université de la Sorbonne Nouvelle.

Prince, A. (1990) Quantitative consequences of rhythmic organization. In M. Ziolkowski, M. Noske and K. Deaton (eds) *Parasession on the Syllable in Phonetics and Phonology* 355–398. Chicago, IL: University of Chicago, Chicago Linguistic Society.

Prince, A. and Smolensky, P. (1993/2004) *Optimality Theory: Constraint Interaction in Generative Grammar*. Malden, MA, and Oxford, UK: Blackwell. (Revision of 1993 technical report, Rutgers University Center for Cognitive Science). Available at http://roa.rutgers.edu, ROA#537.

Pulleyblank, D. (1994) Underlying mora structure. *Linguistic Inquiry* 25 (2): 344–353.

Ridouane, R. (2008) Syllables without vowels: phonetic and phonological evidence from Tashlhiyt Berber. *Phonology* 25: 1–39.

Rosenthall, S. and van der Hulst, H. (1999) Weight-by-position by position. *Natural Language and Linguistic Theory* 17: 499–540.

Saib, J. (1976a) Schwa insertion in Berber: un problème de choix. *Afroasiatic Linguistics* 3/4: 71–83.

Saib, J. (1976b) *A Phonological Study of Tamazight Berber: Dialect of the Ayt Ndhir*. Ph.D. dissertation, University of California, Los Angeles.

Selkirk, E. (1984) *Phonology and Syntax: The Relation between Sound and Structure*. Cambridge, MA: The MIT Press.

Shaw, J., Gafos, A., Hoole, P. and Zeroual, C. (2009) Syllabification in Moroccan Arabic: evidence from patterns of temporal stability. *Phonology* 26: 187–215.

Sherer, T. D. (1994) *Prosodic Phonotactics*. Ph.D. dissertation, University of Massachusetts, Amherst. [Reproduced by GLSA, University of Massachusetts, Amherst.]

Smolensky, P. (1996) The initial state and 'richness of the base' in optimality theory. Technical Report JHU–CoSci–96–4. (The Johns Hopkins University.) Available at http://roa.rutgers.edu, ROA#154.

Walker, R. (1996) *Prominence-driven Stress*. Ms. University of California, Santa Cruz.

Youssi, A. (1977) *L'Arabe Marocain Conceptuel*. Third Cycle thesis, Université de Paris V.

Youssi, A. (1989) Parlers Arabes d'occident: présentation. In *Langue et Société au Maghreb: Bilan et Perspectives* 151–165. Rabat: Publications of M5University, FLHS.

Youssi, A. (1992) *Grammaire et Lexique de l'Arabe Marocain Moderne*. Casablanca: Wallada.

Zec, D. (1988) *Sonority Constraints on Prosodic Structure*. Ph.D. dissertation, Stanford University.

Zoll, C. (1995) *Licensing and Directionality*. Ms. University of California, Berkeley.

2　Serial Harmonic Grammar and Berber syllabification*

Joe Pater[a]

This paper introduces serial Harmonic Grammar, a version of Optimality Theory (OT; Prince and Smolensky, 1993/2004) that reverses two of Prince and Smolensky's basic architectural decisions.[1] One is their choice of constraint ranking over the numerically weighted constraints of its predecessor, Harmonic Grammar (HG; Legendre *et al.*, 1990; see Smolensky and Legendre 2006, and Pater, 2009 for overviews of subsequent work). The other is their choice of parallel evaluation over a version of OT in which the representation is changed and evaluated iteratively (Harmonic Serialism; Prince and Smolensky, 1993/2004: ch. 2; McCarthy, 2007 *et seq*.). I introduce serial HG with an analysis of syllabification in Imdlawn Tashlhiyt Berber (Dell and Elmedlaoui, 1985, 1988, 2002), the same case that Prince and Smolensky use to introduce OT. This analysis illustrates advantages of both serialism and weighted constraints. I also discuss some of the positive consequences of the adoption of serialism for the typological predictions of HG, as well as some outstanding issues for further research on serial versions of both OT and HG.

2.1　Serialism and Berber syllabification

I start by showing how a serial approach to syllabification allows for an improved constraint-based analysis of Imdlawn Tashlhiyt Berber (ITB; Dell and Elmedlaoui, 1985, 1988, 2002). With serial syllabification, the margin constraints of Prince and Smolensky (1993/2004: ch. 8) can be replaced by a

[a]　Joe Pater: University of Massachusetts, Amherst, MA. Email: pater@linguist. umass.edu

constraint that assigns penalties to nuclei according to their position on a sonority scale. This allows the preference for high sonority nuclei in ITB to be ascribed to the same constraint that generates absolute restrictions on nuclear sonority in many languages, including a ban on obstruent nuclei in phrase-final position in ITB. The elimination of margin constraints is not just a reductionist gain in elegance, since as we will see below, they are known to make unsupported typological predictions.

2.1.1 Background

In ITB, any consonant can occupy nuclear position. Dell and Elmedlaoui (1985) (henceforth DE85) provide the following examples of syllabicity alternations that occur across the third person masculine (marked with /i-/) and the third person feminine (marked with /t-/) forms of perfective verbs. Syllable edges are indicated with parentheses, and syllabic consonants are capitalized.

(1)   /i + *root*/   /t + *root*/
        (il)(di)   (tL)(di)   'pull'
        (ir)(ba)   (tR)(ba)   'carry on one's back'
        (in)(da)   (tN)(da)   'shake (milk)
        (if)(si)   (tF)(si)   'untie'
        (ix)(si)   (tX)(si)   'go out (fire)'

Despite the relative freedom of consonants to take on the role of nuclei, ITB does show preferences for nuclei of high sonority. DE85: 108 provide the now-famous example in (2). The asterisked form is composed of *legal* syllables, but the actual syllabification has *better* syllables in that they contain only vocalic nuclei.

(2)   (rat)(lult)   *vs.*   *(ra)(tL)(wLt) 'you will be born'

The DE85 syllabification algorithm builds core syllables consisting of an onset and a nucleus, where the nucleus has a designated sonority level. Syllables with nuclei of the highest level of sonority are built first, followed by syllables of the next highest level of sonority, and so on through the sonority scale. The sonority scale used by DE85 is as in (3).

(3)   low vowel > high vowel > liquid > nasal > voiced fricative > voiceless
        fricative > voiced stop > voiceless stop

Once the core syllabification subroutine is finished, codas are added, and then
other rules apply. The DE85 algorithm is illustrated in (4). We will return to
prepausal annexation shortly.

(4)   (ra)tlult   Build O-N, N = low vowel
        (ra)t(lu)lt   Build O-N, N = high vowel
        (ra)t(lu)(lT)   Build O-N, N = stop
        (rat)(lu)(lT)   Coda adjunction
        (rat)(lult)   Prepausal annexation

This analysis is an instance of an approach to preferences that can be referred
to as 'markedness-based rule ordering': the unmarked structure is built earlier
in the derivation than the marked one, thus capturing the preference for the
unmarked structure. Here, vowels are taken as nuclei before consonants, thus
yielding (rat)(lult) instead of *(ra)(tL)(wLt).

A general problem with markedness-based rule ordering is that it fails to
formally capture the relationship between 'soft' preferences and related 'hard'
restrictions. Examples of hard restrictions related to the Berber preference are
found in languages in which only a subset of segments can appear in nucleus
position. For instance, languages like French tolerate no consonantal nuclei at
all, while languages like English allow sonorants, but not obstruents, as
nuclei. In these and other cases, the permissible nuclei are of higher sonority
than the disallowed ones. The problem is illustrated by the fact that the early
syllabification of vowel nuclei in Berber that produces the preference is in no
way related to the morpheme structure constraint or filtering rule that would
be used to disallow consonantal nuclei in a rule-based analysis of French.

A striking further illustration of this problem can be found in Berber itself,
which has an absolute restriction against obstruent nuclei in phrase-final
position. DE85's rule of prepausal annexation (p. 119) is given as follows:

(5) *Prepausal annexation*

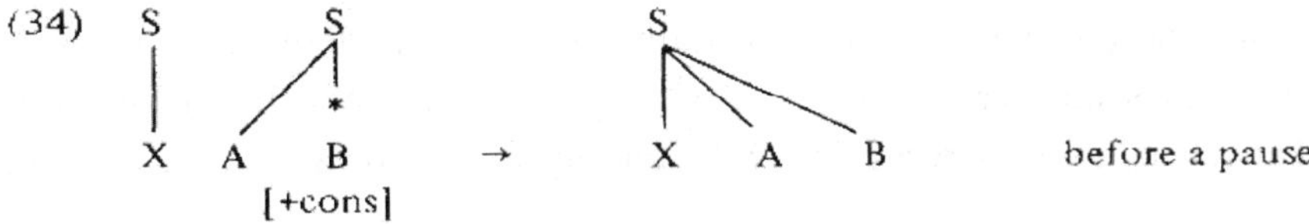

As the derivation in (4) shows, it is this rule that is responsible for the syllabification of /ratlult/ as (rat)(lult) rather than *(rat)(lu)(lT). The issue is that the rule is simply stipulated to apply obligatorily to obstruents (see Section 2.2.2 below); there is no connection drawn to the general relative ill-formedness of obstruents as nuclei in Berber and other languages.

Much of the success of OT comes from its ability to provide formal accounts of preferences that use the very same constraints that also yield hard restrictions.[2] As a simple example, we can take two effects of the constraint ONSET. Ranked above a competing faithfulness constraint like DEP, which penalizes epenthesis (McCarthy and Prince, 1999), ONSET yields a hard restriction, which is enforced by consonant insertion, as in (6). I use numbers, rather than asterisks, to indicate the violation count.

(6)

/an/	ONSET	DEP
an	1 !	
☞ [ʔan]		1

However, even when the ranking of the two constraints is reversed, producing a language that tolerates onsetless syllables, ONSET will still prefer an inter-vocalic consonant to be syllabified with the following vowel, rather than with the preceding one, as shown in (7).

(7)

/an/	DEP	ONSET
☞ [an]		1
ʔan	1 !	

/aba/	DEP	ONSET
☞ [a.ba]		
ab.a		1 !

Markedness-based rule ordering usually accounts for onset preferences of this type by ordering onset creation before coda formation, as in DE85's use of early core syllable formation (Steriade 1982; see Kenstowicz (1994) and Blevins (1995) for overviews of serial approaches to syllabification). Again, the issue is that the preference is not formally related to the hard restriction, which would be put down to a separate morpheme structure constraint or epenthesis rule.

Despite this general success in formally relating preferences to absolute restrictions, there appears to be no existing OT analysis of ITB syllabification that relates its preference for high sonority nuclei to the related absolute restrictions in Berber and elsewhere. Just as the move from inviolable to minimally violable constraints opened up the general possibility of unified analyses of hard and soft restrictions, it turns out that moving from parallel to serial evaluation allows the Berber preference to be driven by the same constraint that delivers the hard restrictions.

2.1.2 A new constraint-based serial analysis of ITB

In this section I provide a slightly modified version of Prince and Smolensky's (1993/2004; henceforth PS93) serial analysis of ITB syllabification to illustrate how the serial version of OT works, and to provide a new argument for it. The PS93 serial analysis uses the 'Nuclear Harmony Constraint'.

(8)   H-NUC
       A higher sonority nucleus is more harmonic than one of lower sonority.

This constraint is unusual in OT because it directly states a preference. Other constraints in PS93, and almost all OT constraints since, assign violation scores. McCarthy (2003) suggests the restatement of H-NUC provided in (9), which I call *C-NUC (as we will soon see, H-NUC and *C-NUC are not fully equivalent). It assigns violation marks according to the degree to which a nucleus diverges from the ideal in terms of sonority, the maximally sonorous segment [a].

(9)   *CONSONANTAL-NUCLEUS (*C-NUC)
       Assign a violation mark to a nucleus for each degree of sonority separating it
       from [a]

McCarthy (2003) rejects *C-NUC as a parallel OT constraint for reasons to be discussed in Section 2.2. For the Berber data to be discussed in this section, *C-NUC makes the desired choices between candidates, so long as evaluation is serial rather than parallel.

The statement of *C-NUC presupposes an *n*-ary sonority feature, as in Hankamer and Aissen (1974) and Selkirk (1984). For the rich set of sonority distinctions that DE85 document for ITB (as in (3)), we would need a correspondingly rich set of gradations in the sonority scale, so that *C-NUC would assign violations as illustrated in (10) for the high end of the scale.

(10)   *C-NUC(a) = 0   *C-NUC(i) = 1   *C-NUC(r) = 2,...

To deal with the examples to be discussed in this paper, we can simplify, with *C-NUC making just the distinctions in (11).

(11)   **C-NUC violations*

Vowel = 0, Sonorant Consonant = 1, Fricative = 2, Stop = 3

For their analysis, PS93 also use a constraint against hiatus to favor CV syllabification. I will use the name *HIATUS to transparently reflect how it assigns violation scores (PS93 call it ONSET):

(12)   *HIATUS

Assign a violation mark to a sequence of adjacent nuclei

The interaction between Gen (the candidate creation function) and Eval (the choice function) differs in the serial version of OT from the more familiar parallel version. PS93: 21 provide the following definition of the Gen function for their serial analysis of ITB syllabification:

(13)   Gen (input$_i$):

The set of (partial) syllabifications of input$_i$ which differ from input$_i$ in no more than one syllabic adjunction.

The adjunctions used here are provided in (14). I use the general term 'operation' to refer to these and other transformations in Gen. DE85's core syllable formation is replaced by separate steps of Nucleus Projection and Dependent Adjunction. As John McCarthy (p.c.) points out, using core syllable formation in Harmonic Serialism would amount to building an effect of the ONSET constraint into Gen (cf. PS93).

(14)   *Operations*

NUCLEUS PROJECTION
Input: Unsyllabified segment
Output: Segment syllabified as nucleus/head
    e.g.   a → (a)   m → (M)

DEPENDENT ADJUNCTION (ONSET/CODA)
Input: Unsyllabified segment adjacent to a syllable
Output: Segment incorporated into that syllable as a dependent
    e.g.   t(a) → (ta)   (M)t → (Mt)

In serial OT as in parallel OT, the candidates emitted by Gen are evaluated by the constraint hierarchy, which chooses the optimal candidate(s). The difference is that the optimum is resubmitted to the Gen function, and to subsequent evaluation by the constraint hierarchy. This loop continues until convergence, that is, until the unchanged candidate is picked as optimal.

The first step is illustrated in (15) for the verb [kšm] 'enter' (Dell and Elmedlaoui, 1988). Here we see all of the candidates formed by the projection of a nucleus (I use Americanist [š] since it can be capitalized). I assume an undominated PARSE-SEG constraint (PS93), or feature of Gen, that forces syllabification at the expense of *C-NUC. This means that when the input contains an unsyllabified segment, the fully faithful candidate is not in the candidate set (cf. fn. 8, and Section 2.2.4). The selection of the optimum is done as in standard OT; kš(M) performs best on *C-NUC.

(15) *Step 1*

/kšm/	*HIATUS	*C-NUC
(K)šm		3!
k(Š)m		2!
☞ kš(M)		1

The next tableau has as an input the optimal form from step 1. Only the new unshared violations are shown in the tableaux (in this case, the *C-NUC violations incurred by [M] are omitted). Here adding the onset to the previously established syllable violates no constraint, and so is optimal.

(16) *Step 2*

kš(M)	*HIATUS	*C-NUC
(K)š(M)		3!
k(Š)(M)	1!	2
☞ k(šM)		

In the third step, we're forced to put the stop in the nucleus. The candidate set for the next step would contain only the unchanged candidate, since there are no operations to apply, and the derivation would terminate.

(17) *Step 3*

k(šM)	*Hiatus	*C-Nuc
☞ (K)(šM)		3

This replicates the result of the DE85 algorithm. As in DE85, the least marked nucleus is created first, followed by nuclei of decreasing sonority. The difference between DE85's rule ordering analysis and the present serial constraint-based analysis is that here the ordering, and the resulting preference, is a direct consequence of the operation of the *C-Nuc constraint. The advantage of this difference is illustrated in Section 2.2, where we see that in serial HG this same constraint also yields the related hard restrictions.

These constraints produce a different result in parallel OT, shown in (18). The fricative is chosen as a nucleus because it minimizes violations of *C-Nuc.

(18) *Parallel OT*

/kšm/	*Hiatus	*C-Nuc
(K)(šM)		4!
☞ (kŠm)		2

The serial OT result is correct.[3] It differs from the parallel OT one because of the lack of derivational look-ahead in the serial model. In the first step of the derivation in (15), the best available nucleus is chosen, irrespective of the eventual result of this move, which is the formation of the worst possible nucleus in the last step in (17). The derivation is blind to the fact that the globally optimal outcome would place the fricative in nucleus, as in (18). This property of derivational 'myopia' (Wilson, 2003) is the fundamental difference between serial and parallel versions of OT, and the basis of many of the arguments in its favor (see *esp.* McCarthy, 2007a; Pruitt, 2008; see further 2.5 below).

In one parallel analysis, PS93: ch. 2 use H-Nuc, which positively rewards high sonority nuclei through comparison, as illustrated in (19).

(19)

/kšm/	*Hiatus	H-Nuc
☞ (K)(šM)		
(kŠm)		M > Š !

While this analysis succeeds for the Berber facts, it not only uses an unusual constraint type, but it also fails to deal with absolute restrictions, as discussed in PS93: ch. 8. Their revised analysis uses a set of constraints that is in a fixed ranking and that penalize margins (onsets and codas) according to their sonority. The constraints are arranged in the fixed ranking such that a higher sonority margin always violates a higher ranked constraint than a lower sonority margin. In this case, the constraint labeled *Margin-Nasal dominates *Margin-Fricative, thus picking the correct candidate.

(20)

/kšm/	*Margin- Nasal	*Margin- Fricative
☞ (K)(šM)		1
(kŠm)	1!	

PS93: 191 note that by collapsing the sonority preferences for onsets and codas, the margin constraints make undesired typological predictions. They cite Prince (1983), Zec (1988, 1995) and Clements (1990) for the observation that when a language admits only a subset of consonants as codas, these are ones of relatively high, rather than low sonority. The margin constraints predict exactly the reverse. As the tableau in (20) shows, it is crucial for the analysis of ITB that the margin constraints do penalize high sonority codas. This issue has apparently never been resolved.

The point that rising sonority sequences like [kšm] require margin constraints rather than peak constraints (≈ *C-Nuc) is due to Donca Steriade (p.c.). PS93 and Clements (1997) focus on falling sonority sequences, which pose the same problem, as shown in tableau (21) for [ršq] 'be happy' (Dell and Elmedlaoui, 1988).

(21) *Parallel OT*

/ršq/	*Hiatus	*C-Nuc
(R)(šQ)		4!
☞ (rŠq)		2

The correct form is (R)(šQ), which we again get from serial OT with these constraints, as shown in the derivation in (22). Step 2 of this derivation shows the need to have *HIATUS and NOCODA ranked above *C-NUC to get the correct result (see also PS93: fn. 49 on the need for NOCODA >> *C-NUC for a serial OT analysis).

(22) *Serial OT Derivation for a falling sonority cluster*

a. Step 1

/ršq/	*HIATUS	NOCODA	*C-NUC
rš(Q)			3!
r(Š)q			2!
☞ (R)šq			1

b. Step 2

(R)šq	*HIATUS	NOCODA	*C-NUC
(Rš)q		1!	
(R)(Š)q	1!		2
☞ (R)š(Q)			3

c. Step 3

(R)š(Q)	*HIATUS	NOCODA	*C-NUC
(Rš)(Q)		1!	
(R)(Š)(Q)	2!		2
☞ (R)(šQ)			

As well as having typological problems (see further Clements, 1997), margin constraints cannot account for the English or French restrictions on possible nuclei, since consonantal nuclei do not violate the constraint. Consider, for example, the French pronunciation of *table*, which unlike English, syllabifies the final liquid as a margin, rather than as a nucleus. I will assume that this violates a constraint against coda clusters, *COMPLEX.[4] The tableau in (23) shows that that *C-NUC correctly disfavors the English-like (tæ)(bL) *vis-à-vis* the French (tæbl). Again, I include only unshared violations of the two constraints.

(23) *French ranking*

/tæbl/	*C-NUC	*COMPLEX
(tæ)(bL)	2!	
☞ (tæbl)		1

If we try to replace *C-NUC with margin constraints, French becomes impossible to generate, since (tæbl) is harmonically bounded by (tæ)(bL).

(24) *French impossible with margin constraints only*

/tæbl/	*MARGIN-LIQUID	*COMPLEX
☞ (tæ)(bL)		
(tæbl)	1	1

PS93 do not suggest that the margin constraints could replace their peak constraints, the fixed ranking equivalents of *C-NUC. This example shows why they cannot.

2.2 Harmonic Grammar and ITB

We have just seen that a serial OT analysis of ITB allows us to use *C-NUC, a constraint that unlike H-NUC assigns violation scores, and that unlike the margin constraints is typologically well supported. This provides an argument for serial OT, alongside those developed in McCarthy's (2007a,b, 2008a,b, 2010) recent work, and in Pruitt (2008), Elfner (2009), Jesney (to appear) and Kimper (to appear). In this section we see how switching from ranked to weighted constraints also yields benefits for the analysis of Berber syllabification (see Pater, 2009 for an introduction to HG and an overview of other arguments for weighted over ranked constraints, as well as Jesney, 2009 and Potts *et al.*, 2010).

2.2.1 Cross-linguistic hard restrictions on nuclear sonority

A benefit of adopting weighted constraints is the resulting ability of *C-NUC to deal with the hard restrictions on nuclear sonority in languages like English and French, along with the Berber phrase-final one. Building on the discussion of H-NUC in PS93: ch. 8, McCarthy (2003) rejects *C-NUC as an OT constraint because it cannot handle inventory restrictions and other phenom-ena that require the constraint to impose a 'cut-off' mid-way through the sonority scale. The English nucleus inventory provides an example, because it includes sonorant consonants (in unstressed syllables), but no lower sonority nuclei. If we consider the interaction of *C-NUC with DEP, we only get two languages in OT, as shown in (25) (note that with the full version of *C-NUC needed for the DE85 sonority scale, the language in 25b. would not corre-spond to French, since it would permit only low vowels as nuclei).

(25)   a. DEP >> *C-NUC
   All segments can be nuclei (Berber)

   b. *C-NUC >> DEP
   Only vowels can be nuclei (French)

English is thus impossible with this constraint set in OT. The picture is differ-ent in HG, as illustrated in the pair of tableaux in (26). In the HG tableaux, violations are indicated with negative integers, and the weights of the con-straints are shown beneath the constraint names. The harmony of a candidate is the weighted sum of constraint scores; this number is shown at the end of each candidate's row. The candidate with the highest harmony is optimal; since the violations are negative, and the weights are positive, this will be the number closest or equal to zero. The symbol [V] stands for an epenthetic vowel. Epenthesis is worse than a sonorant consonant as a nucleus, because the weight of DEP is higher than the weight of *C-NUC. Because a fricative nucleus incurs a penalty of –2 on *C-NUC, the harmony of that candidate is lower than the epenthetic alternative.

(26) *'English' – only sonorants as consonantal nuclei*

/tn/	DEP 1.5	*C-NUC 1	
☞ (tN)		–1	–1
(tVn)	–1		–1.5

/ts/	DEP 1.5	*C-NUC 1	
(tS)		–2	–2
☞ (tVs)	–1		–1.5

The values of the weights in the tableaux in (26) are partially arbitrary, since there is an infinite number of weights that will pick the correct optima. Their non-arbitrary aspect is that they must meet the weighting conditions in (27):

(27)   /tn/ → (tN), *(tVn) $w(\text{DEP}) > w(\text{*C-NUC})$

/ts/ → (tVs), *(tS) $2w(\text{*C-NUC}) > w(\text{DEP})$

The weight of DEP must be greater than the weight of *C-NUC, so that a single violation of the markedness constraint is tolerated as in (tN), but it must be less than twice the weight of *C-NUC, so that epenthesis is preferred over two violations, as in (tVs) *vs.* *(tS). This example shows that a weighted version of *C-NUC can impose a cut-off mid-way through the scale, between fricatives and sonorants – a full analysis of English would account for the lack of nasal consonants in the nuclei of stressed syllables.

In Berber, DEP is weighted high enough to force any degree of *C-NUC violation. The weight of 4 will be sufficient if the maximum violation count on *C-NUC is the 3 we are assuming here (see (11)). The tableaux in (28) contrast with the English ones in that a nuclear fricative is now chosen over epenthesis.

(28) *Berber – all consonants as nuclei*

/tn/	DEP 4	*C-NUC 1	
☞ (tN)		−1	−1
(tVn)	−1		−4

/ts/	DEP 4	*C-NUC 1	
☞ (tS)		−2	−2
(tVs)	−1		−4

In French, *C-NUC is weighted higher than DEP. Here I am assuming that the constraint does not penalize vowels; if it penalized high vowels (see (10)), the constraint weights could be adjusted so as to permit them, but no segments of lower sonority.

(29) *French – no consonants as nuclei*

/tn/	*C-NUC 1.5	DEP 1	
(tN)	−1		−1.5
☞ (tVn)		−1	−1

/ts/	*C-NUC 1.5	DEP 1	
(tS)	−2		−3
☞ (tVs)		−1	−1

These typological results can be checked in OT-Help 2.0 (Staubs *et al.,* 2010), which uses Recursive Constraint Demotion (Tesar and Smolensky, 2000) to determine if sets of optima are consistent in OT, and uses an application of linear programming (Potts *et al.,* 2010) to make the same determination for

HG. Computational help is perhaps unnecessary to determine that HG generates just the three attested languages, while OT generates only Berber and French,[5] but this software is indispensible for comparisons between the theories in more complex cases.

The HG scalar constraint typology presented in this section, along with the serial analysis of Berber (see 2.2.2 for the HG version), add up to the goal set up in Section 2.1.1: a single constraint gets absolute restrictions on the sonority of nuclei in English and French as well as the preference for highly sonorous nuclei in Berber. As far as I know, this is the first analysis to succeed in this way. The issues for the DE85 and PS93 analyses of ITB syllabification were discussed in Section 2.1. Clements (1997) and Dell and Elmedlaoui (2002) use a SONORITY PEAK constraint for Berber that can be stated for present purposes as in (30):[6]

(30)   SONORITY PEAK

      If a segment is of greater sonority than the segments adjacent to it, it is syllabified as a nucleus.

The SONORITY PEAK constraint will not generalize to the related hard restrictions. For example, it does not penalize a syllable like (tS), which is ill-formed in English and French.

2.2.2 Phrase-final nucleus restrictions in Berber

Because of the inadequacies of scalar constraints in OT, scalar phenomena are standardly analyzed with either a set of constraints in a fixed ranking, or with a set of constraints in a specific-to-general or stringency relation (Prince, 1997; de Lacy, 2004). The last section's brief demonstration of the basic adequacy of scalar constraints in HG opens a large and important topic for further research: the comparison of OT with fixed rankings or stringency relations to HG with scalar constraints (see Flemming, 2001 on HG with phonetic scales). In this section, I provide a further demonstration of the utility of weighted constraints for a treatment of ITB syllabification, by showing that they allow *C-NUC to be recruited in the analysis of the sonority-based restrictions on phrase-final nuclei.

The first step is to add a general constraint penalizing final nuclei (cf. McCarthy and Prince's (1994) word-final-C constraint; see also Flack (2009) on parallels between word- and phrase-level constraints).

(31)   *FINAL-N
        Assign a violation mark to a phrase-final nucleus.

As shown in (32), the additive interaction of *C-NUC and *FINAL-N will produce the desired result: codas, which are generally disfavored, are created phrase finally, in order to avoid a phrase-final obstruent nucleus. To focus on the crucial interaction, I omit the candidate (rat)(lu)(Lt), which would be ruled out by *HIATUS, and once more show only violations that are not shared by the candidates.

(32) *'Prepausal annexation' as a gang effect*

/ratlult/	*CODA 4	*FINAL-N 2	*C-NUC 1	
☞ (rat)(lult)	−1			−4
(rat)(lu)(lT)		−1	−3	−5

This is a 'gang effect' in that the weighted sum of the violations of the two constraints *C-NUC and *FINAL-N is greater than the weighted violation of *CODA, but the weighted violations of the individual constraints is lower than that of *CODA. In our serial OT analysis, we have seen that a single violation of *CODA must trump the most severe violation of *C-NUC, the three incurred by a stop (see 22b; note that this tableau is for non-phrase-final position). In HG terms, this requires *CODA to have a weight greater than three times the weight of *C-NUC; the (4,1) weighting in (32) meets this condition.[7]

*FINAL-N is also not strong enough to beat *CODA on its own. For example, sonorant consonants can (optionally) surface as final nuclei (DE85).

(33)   *Sonorants as final nuclei*

(i)(gi)(dR) 'eagle'   (R)(gL) 'lock'   (du)(mN) 'they (m.) last'

This is captured in the current analysis in that a violation score of −1 on *C-NUC contributed by the sonorant is not sufficient to help *FINAL-N overcome *CODA:

(34) *Escape from prepausal annexation*

	*Coda 4	*Final-N 2	*C-Nuc 1	
/igidr/				
☞ (i)(gi)(dR)		−1	−1	−3
(i)(gidr)	−1			−4

DE85 note that most words with final sonorant consonants as nuclei in fact optionally undergo prepausal annexation, yielding the variation illustrated in (35).

(35)   *Optional prepausal annexation*

(i)(gi)(dR) / (i)(gidr)   (R)(gL) / (Rgl)   (du)(mN) / (dumn)

By increasing the weight of *Final-Nuc by 1, we get a tie in these cases.

(36) *Optional prepausal annexation as a tie*

	*Coda 4	*Final-N 3	*C-Nuc 1	
/igidr/				
☞ (i)(gidr)	−1			−4
☞ (i)(gi)(dR)		−1	−1	−4

This is an approximation of an account of this instance of variation. Actual theories of variation in HG directly generate a probability distribution over candidates ('Max-Ent-OT'; Johnson, 2002; Goldwater and Johnson, 2003; Wilson, 2006; Jäger, 2007), or use noise on the weights to generate variable outcomes across instances of evaluation (Boersma and Pater, 2008). Both of these are in principle compatible with serial HG; the choice between them will likely depend on the success of associated learning algorithms, which are being developed in ongoing research.

In the current approximate account, we get the correct obligatory coda syllabification of a final obstruent, as shown in (37).

(37) *Obligatory final obstruent coda*

/ratlult/	*CODA 4	*FINAL-N 3	*C-NUC 1	
☞ (rat)(lult)	−1			−4
(rat)(lu)(lT)		−1	−3	−6

We also get the correct obligatory nuclear syllabification of a final vocoid (i, u, a), as shown in (38).

(38) *Obligatory final vocalic nucleus*

/tldi/	*CODA 4	*FINAL-N 3	*C-NUC 1	
(tLdj)	−1			−4
☞ (tL)(di)		−1		−3

The existence of gang effects in HG creates the possibility of using a single constraint to encode both the general preference for high sonority nuclei in Berber, as well as contribution of sonority to the explanation of the related absolute restriction against phrase-final obstruent nuclei. Again, no previous analysis has succeeded in formally drawing that connection.

2.2.3 Serial HG

Section 2.1.2 discussed the role of serialism in achieving a satisfactory account of ITB syllabification, and the last two sections explained the role of constraint weighting. We can now put these together in a serial HG derivation for /ratlult/. As Smolensky and Legendre (2006) point out in their translation of the PS93 analyses into parallel HG, *HIATUS must have a value greater than the highest possible violation score on *C-NUC. Since we are assuming that this is maximum is 3, then as for *CODA, a weighting of 4 for *HIATUS will suffice.

The constraint weights are shown in (39), followed by the derivation. The optimum for each step of the derivation is shown in the left column, and the failed candidates are shown to its right. Underneath each candidate is its vector of violation scores in parentheses, followed by the weighted sum of violations. To save space, I have used positive integers for violation, and the weighted sum is also positive. The optimum hence has the lowest penalty. I have collapsed nucleus projection and onset adjunction into a single step, since this has no consequence here.[8]

(39)   *HIATUS   *CODA   *FINAL-NUC   *C-NUC
              4   4   3   1

Optima   *Failed candidates*
1. (ra)tlult   r(aT)lult   ra(tL)ult   rat(lu)lt   ratl(wL)t
(0,0,0,0)=0   (0,0,0,3)=3   (0,0,0,1)=1   (0,0,0,0)=0   (0,0,0,1)=1
                        ratlu(lT)
                        (0,0,1,3)=6
2. (ra)t(lu)lt   (rat)lult
(0,0,0,0)=0   (0,1,0,0)=4
3. (rat)(lu)lt   (ra)t(lu)(lT)   (ra)t(lu)(L)t
(0,1,0,0)=4   (0,0,1,3)=6   (1,0,0,1)=5
4. (rat)(lul)t   (rat)(lu)(lT)
(0,1,0,0)=4   (0,0,1,3)=6
5. (rat)(lult)   (rat)(lul)(T)
(0,0,0,0)=0   (0,0,0,3)=3

The first step is shown in the first row. Syllabifying either vowel as a nucleus violates none of our constraints, and is thus optimal. A full analysis of ITB would distinguish between high and low vowels, and would pick (ra)tlult over rat(lu)lt. The other failed candidates shown in step 1 include the full set of possible core syllables. All of the others have a consonantal nucleus, and thus a non-zero score as the last component of the violation vector, and a non-zero penalty. The final candidate ratlu(lT) has the worst nucleus in the worst (final) position, and thus has the highest penalty of $(3\times1) + (1\times3) = 6$.

In the second step we have an established syllable, and hence the option of adding a coda. This option is sub-optimal, however, relative to the creation of a second syllable, which again violates no constraint. In the third step, however, coda creation is optimal relative to the creation of a third new syllable, one that violates both *FINAL-NUC and has a stop nucleus. The fourth and fifth steps show the creation of the final coda. The optimum in the fourth step in fact ties with the optimum in the third, and the derivation could go in either order. In the fifth step I assume that the addition of the final consonant in the optimal candidate does not add a violation of *CODA ('every syllable ends in a vowel') and the creation of the final onsetless syllable does not violate *HIATUS ('no adjacent nuclei').

2.2.4 Serialism and HG typology

In the last few sections, the greater power of weighted than ranked constraints allowed *C-NUC to be used in the account of attested patterns that would fall out of reach of OT with the same constraint set. PS93, as well as Prince and Smolensky (1997) and Smolensky and Legendre (2006), cite this greater power as the fatal flaw of a weighted constraint version of OT, claiming that it leads inexorably to unsupported typological predictions (though cf. Jesney, 2009; Pater, 2009; Potts *et al.*, 2010).

As pointed out in Pater (2009), a switch to serialism has deep consequences for HG/OT comparisons. Here I expand on that point with a further example and more discussion. The example relates to the process of coda syllabification that we have just seen in action in Berber. Pater *et al.* (2007), drawing on Prince and Smolensky (1997), point out that a parallel version of HG can produce a system in which *CODA is satisfied at the cost of n violations of a faithfulness constraint, but not $n+1$. As Pater *et al.* (2007) point out, this example also crucially depends on a definition of *CODA that assigns a single violation for the entire coda, rather than one that assigns a violation per segment contained in the coda; the violation profiles in (40) reflect that definition.

To make the example similar to the one in the last section, we can use as our conflicting constraint PARSE-SEG, which assigns one violation per unparsed segment (PS93). A segment that violates PARSE-SEG may be unpronounced, as in PS93, or pronounced but unsyllabified; the choice is tangential to this example. As the pair of tableau in (40) shows, the result of the interaction of these constraints in parallel HG can be quite bizarre: a language that has codas with two or more consonants (e.g. ☞ [(apt)]), but not one (e.g. *[(ap)]). Further, this cut-off can be made at any point: languages with codas with no fewer consonants than three, or four, or five, or any other number can be modeled in this theory.

(40) *A problematic type of pattern in parallel HG*

ap	*CODA 1.5	PARSE-SEG 1	
☞ (a)p		−1	−1
(ap)	−1		−1.5

apt	*CODA 1.5	PARSE-SEG 1	
(a)pt		−2	−2
(ap)t	−1	−1	−2.5
☞ (apt)	−1		−1.5

This pattern is impossible in serial HG because of the limit to a single application of an operation in creating a candidate. The relevant operation here is adjunction, which adds a single consonant to an existing syllable. With our two constraints, the first application of adjunction will beat the fully faithful candidate if and only if *CODA has a greater weight than PARSE-SEG. The tableau in (41) illustrates the second step of the derivation for the UR /apt/ with the same weights as in (40). Here we already have the nucleus syllabified through the prior application of nuclear projection. Importantly, the candidate set includes only the faithful candidate and the single adjunction, and not the fully syllabified candidate (apt) that was optimal in the parallel HG tableau for /apt/ in (40). Since that candidate is missing from the candidate set, the optimum is now [(a)pt]; we no longer get the strange pattern in which a coda is formed only to syllabify some minimum number of segments.

(41) *Coda formation in serial HG*

(a)pt	*CODA 1.5	PARSE-SEG 1	
☞ (a)pt		−2	−2
(ap)t	−1	−1	−2.5

We can compare the typological predictions of serial and parallel versions of OT and HG using Staubs *et al.*'s (2010) OT-Help 2. The table in (42) provides an illustration of the ways in which the move to serialism can affect comparisons between ranked and weighted constraints. The top row displays a set of three inputs with potential codas of different lengths, and the subsequent rows show the syllabifications for four different languages. Checkmarks indicate which of the theories of constraint interaction can generate these languages with the two constraints *CODA and PARSE-SEG. Serial candidate sets are produced using the adjunction operation as illustrated here, while the parallel candidate sets include codas with all possible numbers of consonants, from zero up to the number provided in the UR. Serial OT, parallel OT and serial HG each generate only two languages: one in which all of the consonants are parsed regardless of the number available in the UR, and one in which none of the consonants are. Parallel HG can also generate the extra languages alluded to above, in which a lower bound is placed on coda size: a coda is formed to parse minimally two, or three segments.

(42)

/ap/	/apt/	/aptk/	Parallel OT	Parallel HG	Serial OT	Serial HG
(a)p	(a)pt	(a)ptk	✓	✓	✓	✓
(ap)	(apt)	(aptk)	✓	✓	✓	✓
(a)p	(ap)t	(aptk)		✓		
(a)p	(a)pt	(aptk)		✓		

This example also illustrates a more general consequence of the single change limitation on candidates: that the set of possible constraint interactions, or 'trade-offs' in the terminology of Pater (2009), is restricted relative to a parallel model. In particular, trade-offs involving multiple instances of violation of a given faithfulness constraint will never occur in a serial version of HG or OT, insofar as the operations that create candidates incur at most one violation of each faithfulness constraint (as in McCarthy, 2007b). Thus, scenarios in which a markedness constraint is satisfied at the cost of n violations of a faithfulness constraint, but not $n+1$, which can be created in a parallel version of HG, are impossible in a serial version. The typological benefit accrued by serialism in the *CODA/PARSE example is likely typical of such cases.

2.2.5 Further issues

It is important to note that under certain assumptions serialism can also lead to unwelcome typological predictions, in both OT and HG. Based on results of a typological calculation in OT-Help, Pratt (2008) identifies the following derivational path as producing an outcome in serial OT that is impossible in parallel OT, a difference that seems to weigh in parallelism's favor. The last two steps of the derivation are show in (43). Prior to this, [a] was selected as the best nucleus, and [b] was added as its onset. In the third step, shown in (43a.), the coda [t] is chosen over the nuclear [n] because the single step of nucleus projection yields an onsetless syllable (ONSET is violated by a nucleus adjacent to a left syllable boundary). In the fourth step, the [n] is syllabified as a nucleus (assuming a ranking of *COMPLEX over *C-NUC).

(43) *Partial serial OT derivation*

a. Step 3

(ba)tn	ONSET	*CODA
☞ (bat)n		1
(ba)t(N)	1	

b. Step 4

(bat)n	ONSET	*CODA
☞ (bat)(N)		

The ONSET >> *CODA ranking thus yields onsetless syllables, which is quite counterintuitive, and almost certainly empirically problematic. In the full pattern that this derivational interaction produces, only relatively marked nuclei in the second syllable have no onsets; a UR like /tnba/ in which the last segment is a relatively good nucleus would be syllabified as (tN)(ba). Syllables that are marked on one dimension (nucleus sonority) are marked on another (onset possession). Whether serial OT/HG produces other instances of such 'markedness accumulation' is a question for further research that may bear on the choice between serialism and parallelism.

One solution to this particular problem is to introduce an operation of resyllabification that changes (bat)(N) into (ba)(tN). So long as this operation is cost-free, the candidate that it produces would always triumph, since it eliminates violations of *CODA and ONSET, and adds no other violations. The resyllabification operation is defined in (44).

(44)   RESYLLABIFICATION

   Input: A segment syllabified as a dependent in syllable 1, adjacent to a segment syllabified in syllable 2
   Output: Segment adjoined to syllable 2

   e.g.   (bat)(N) → (ba)(tN)   (ba)(tN) → (bat)(N)

To check that adding Resyllabification produces the desired result, I submitted to OT-Help the two inputs /bata/ and /batn/, with constraints PARSE-SEG, *C-NUC, *CODA, and *COMPLEX. In one typology calculation, I had only the Nucleus-Projection and Dependent Adjunction operations from (15), in the second I added Resyllabification. In both, I limited Adjunction to consonants. Serial OT and HG produced the same results, and so are collapsed in the table in (45).

(45)	/bata/	/batn/	Serial OT/HG no Resyllab.	Serial OT/HG w/ Resyllab.
	bata	batn	✓	✓
	(ba)(ta)	(ba)tn	✓	✓
	(ba)(ta)	(bat)n	✓	✓
	(ba)(ta)	(batn)	✓	✓
	(ba)(ta)	(ba)(tN)	✓	✓
	(ba)(ta)	(bat)(N)	✓	

This calculation shows that the addition of Resyllabification does produce the intended result: the theory can no longer produce the final language. The languages that are produced also seem typologically sensible: one language allows sonorant nuclei, as in [(ba)(tN)], while others avoid them by having instead complex codas, as in [(batn)], or by non-parsing, as in [(bat)n] or [(ba)tn]. The remaining potentially troubling case is the first language, which parses no segments at all, which again happens because the initial step of nucleus projection creates an onset violation (and ONSET overrides PARSE-SEG). This result could be avoided if contrary to one of this paper's basic premises, nuclear syllabification and onset formation were combined into a single step (*cf.* Note 9), or if initial nucleus projection did not violate ONSET. However, a language in which the optima are unparsed is likely to be predicted by any version of OT/HG with a reasonably rich constraint set, if PARSE-SEG and other parsing constraints are ranked beneath all conflicting Markedness constraints.

Besides markedness accumulation, another potentially general problematic pattern of constraint interaction in Harmonic Serialism is one identified in Pater *et al.* (2007: 4.5), which can be termed 'multiple application blocking'. When a markedness constraint can require multiple applications of an operation to be satisfied, we can get patterns in which the operation applies only in a situation in which it in fact satisfied by a single application. An example related to syllabification is the deletion of segments from coda position. As shown in (46), if *CODA assigns a violation to every syllable that ends in a consonant (PS93), deletion of a single segment will satisfy *CODA only if there is a single consonant in coda position.

(46) *A problematic type of pattern in Harmonic Serialism*

(ap)	*CODA	MAX
☞ (a)		1
(ap)	1	

(apt)	*CODA	MAX
(ap)	1	1
☞ (apt)	1	

Just like the example of markedness accumulation above, there is a variety of ways that this particular example of multiple application blocking might be ruled out. First, it may be that the inputs to these tableaux could never occur: if *CODA is more highly valued than MAX, then each time a consonant is added to a syllable in coda position, it will be deleted, and we would never get to (apt). For this explanation to go through, it would also have to be the case that syllabification is universally absent from URs (see relatedly McCarthy and Pruitt, to appear). As Pater *et al.* note, one might also simply redefine *CODA to penalize every segment in coda position, though a more satisfactory solution would rule this sort of interaction out in principle.

Unlike some other work in Harmonic Serialism that continues to assume parallelism for prosody (see *esp.* McCarthy, 2007b), this paper assumes that both segmental and prosodic structure are constructed and revised serially (see also McCarthy, 2008b; Pruit, 2008; Elfner, 2009; Jesney, to appear; Kimper, to appear). In the analysis of ITB, the absence of derivational look-ahead was crucial to achieving the correct outcome (see the discussion following (18) above). Another important question for further research is the extent to which serial prosodification can generally be maintained. It appears that none of the arguments against 'bottom-up constructionism' in PS93 are in fact arguments against Harmonic Serialism (see e.g. McCarthy, 2008b on Tongan). It also appears that the candidate comparison that occurs at each step of the derivation gives the theory sufficient look-ahead to deal with these and many other cases that have been labeled as requiring parallelism (e.g. stress and syllabification in English; Pater 2000). There do, however, seem to be cases that are true problems for the most strictly serial account of prosodification; see McCarthy (2010) for an example and discussion (and Bakovic, 2007 for some further relevant examples). Developing a general theory of operations that yields just the right amount of look-ahead is another important topic for further research.

2.3   Conclusions

In this paper I have proposed a grammatical framework that adopts serial candidate generation and evaluation with weighted constraints, serial HG. I have provided an analysis of a subset of the data on ITB syllabification in this framework, showing that the combination of serialism and constraint weighting allows for the first time an account of the ITB preference for high sonority nuclei that extends to related hard restrictions on nuclear sonority in Berber and elsewhere. Much remains to be done in terms of the development of this framework and this analysis, but these initial results seem promising for the future of serial HG, especially since serialism also imposes restrictions on the generative power of weighted constraint interaction.

Notes

* I am happy to present to Lisa Selkirk a paper that builds on her pioneering work on the role of sonority in syllabification, that discusses data from Berber, whose phonology Lisa's own work has helped us to understand, and that even manages to sneak in a few references to French. In these small ways it pays tribute to her influence on me and on the rest of the field as a scholar. I am even happier to be able to take this occasion to pay personal tribute to Lisa in her role as a colleague, mentor and friend; *merci pour tout!* This research has also especially benefited from discussion with John McCarthy and Donca Steriade, as well as with participants in Ling 730, UMass fall 2007, Ling 751, UMass spring 2010, the 2008–2009 McCarthy-Pater NSF grant group, and colloquia at University of North Carolina, University of Chicago, SUNY Stony Brook and the University of Southern California. Thanks also to Karen Jesney, Shigeto Kawahara, Jason Riggle, Brian Smith, and two anonymous reviewers for comments on an earlier draft, and to Patrick Pratt and Robert Staubs for indispensible computational help. This research was supported by grant BCS-0813829 from the National Science Foundation to the University of Massachusetts, Amherst.

1   See also Goldsmith (1991, 1993a, 1994) and other papers collected in Goldsmith (1993b) for related precedents whose formalisms differ in various ways from the present framework. Goldsmith's Harmonic Phonology, for example, incorporates both serialism and the notion of harmonic improvement, but it does not formalize constraint interaction as in OT/HG (see Prince and Smolensky 1993/2004: 239–240, though cf. Goldsmith, 1991: Note 10 for a brief discussion of an OT-like model).

2   The success of OT in this regard has been discussed under the rubrics of 'the emergence of the unmarked', 'minimal violation' and 'nonuniformity'. See McCarthy (2002) for discussion and references.

3   This is the syllabification based on evidence from poetic meter (Dell and Elmedlaoui 1988). In phrase-initial position, the syllabification based on introspection (Elmedlaoui's judgment; DE85) would have the initial stop as starting a cluster (i.e. [(kšM)]). An approach parallel to the one proposed for phrase-final position in Section 2.2 seems possible, though I do not pursue this here.

4   Under an analysis of French in which such final clusters are syllabified with a final empty-headed syllable (e.g. Charette 1991), the operative constraint would be one against null nuclei.

5   OT-Help input files for these tableaux, as well as for other examples in this paper, can be found at http://people.umass.edu/pater/pater-othelp-files.zip.

6   Here, as elsewhere in the paper, I abstract from sonority 'plateaux'; see Dell and Elmedlaoui (2002) for discussion.

7   As Karen Jesney (p.c.) points out, a serial analysis with separate nucleus projection and onset formation will require *CODA to overcome not only *C-NUC, but also ONSET, since the first step (rat)(lu)l(T) violates both. See further Section 2.2.5.

8   It turns out that the separation of core syllable construction into separate steps is desirable not only for reason of principle (see Section 2.1.2), but may also be empirically necessary once we consider a fuller constraint set. If the constraint driving syllabification penalizes every unparsed segment (PS93's PARSE-SEG), and if core syllable construction is a single step, it will prefer the syllabification of a pair of segments over the syllabification of a single one (see relatedly Pruitt (2008) on foot parsing). In Berber, PARSE-SEG must have sufficient strength to overcome any degree of violation of *C-NUC, so as to rule out candidates that leave consonantal nuclei unparsed. As Kathryn Pruitt (p.c.) points out, this would result in (rŠ)q being chosen in step 1 of (22), leading to the ill-formed outcome of *(rŠq).

References

Bakovic, Eric. (2007) A revised typology of opaque generalizations. *Phonology* 24 (2): 217–259.

Becker, Michael, Potts, Christopher, Pratt, Patrick, Staubs, Robert, McCarthy, John and Pater, Joe. (2010) *OT-Help 2: Java tools for Optimality Theory.* Software available at http://web.linguist.umass.edu/~OTHelp/

Blevins, J. (1995) The syllable in phonological theory. In John Goldsmith (ed.) *Handbook of Phonological Theory* 206–244. London: Basil Blackwell.

Boersma, Paul and Pater, Joe. (2008) Convergence properties of a gradual learning algorithm for Harmonic Grammar. Ms, University of Amsterdam and UMass Amherst. Available at http://roa.rutgers.edu/

Charette, Monique. (1991) *Conditions on Phonological Government.* Cambridge: Cambridge University Press.

Clements, G. N. (1990) The role of the sonority cycle in core syllabification. In John Kingston and Mary Beckman (eds) *Papers in Laboratory Phonology I* 283–333. Cambridge: Cambridge University Press.

Clements, G. N. (1997) Berber syllabification: derivations or constraints? In I. M. Roca (ed.) *Derivations and Constraints in Phonology* 289–330. Oxford: Oxford University Press.

Dell, Francois and Elmedlaoui, Mohamed. (1985) Syllabic consonants and syllabification in Imdlawn Tashlhiyt Berber. *Journal of African Languages and Linguistics* 7: 105–130.

Dell, Francois and Elmedlaoui, Mohamed. (1988) Syllabic consonants in Berber: some new evidence. *Journal of African Languages and Linguistics* 10: 1–17.

Dell, Francois and Elmedlaoui, Mohamed. (2002) *Syllables in Tashlhiyt Berber and in Moroccan Arabic.* Dordrecht: Kluwer Academic Publishers.

Elfner, Emily. (2009) Syllabification and stress-epenthesis interactions in harmonic serialism. Ms, University of Massachusetts, Amherst.

Flack, Kathryn. (2009) Constraints on onsets and codas of words and phrases. *Phonology* 26: 269–302.

Flemming, Edward. (2001) Scalar and categorical phenomena in a unified model of phonetics and phonology. *Phonology* 18: 7–44.

Goldsmith, John. (1991) Phonology as an intelligent system. In Donna Jo Napoli and Judy Anne Kegl (eds) *Bridges Between Psychology and Linguistics: A Swarthmore festschrift for Lila Gleitman* 247–267. Hillsdale, NJ: Erlbaum.

Goldsmith, John. (1993a) Harmonic phonology. In John Goldsmith (ed.) *The Last Phonological Rule* 21–60. Chicago, IL: University of Chicago Press.

Goldsmith, John. (1993b) *The Last Phonological Rule: Reflections on Constraints and Derivations.* Chicago, IL: University of Chicago Press.

Goldsmith, John. (1994) A dynamic computational theory of accent systems. In

Jennifer Cole and Charles Kisseberth (eds) *Perspectives in Phonology* 1–28. Stanford, CA: CSLI.

Goldwater, Sharon and Mark, Johnson. (2003) Learning OT constraint rankings using a maximum entropy model. In J. Spenader, A. Eriksson and Ö. Dahl (eds), *Proceedings of the Stockholm Workshop on Variation within Optimality Theory* 111–120. Stockholm: Stockholm University.

Hankamer, Jorge and Aissen, Judith. (1974) The sonority hierarchy. In A. Bruck, A. R. Fox and M. W. La Galy (eds) *Papers from the Parasession on Natural Phonology* 131–145. Chicago, IL: Chicago Linguistic Society.

Jäger, Gerhard. (2007) Maximum entropy models and stochastic optimality theory. In Annie Zaenen, Jane Simpson, Tracy Holloway King, Jane Grimshaw, Joan Maling and Chris Manning (eds), *Architectures, Rules, and Preferences. Variations on Themes by Joan W. Bresnan* 467–479. Stanford, CA: CSLI Publications.

Jesney, Karen. (2009) Licensing in multiple contexts: an argument for Harmonic Grammar. Paper presented at the 45th Meeting of the Chicago Linguistic Society (CLS 45). Available at http://people.umass.edu/kjesney/papers.html

Jesney, Karen. (To appear) Positional Faithfulness, non-locality, and the Harmonic Serialism solution. In Suzi Lima, Kevin Mullin and Brian Smith (eds) *Proceedings of the 39th Meeting of the North East Linguistics Society (NELS 39)*. Amherst, MA: GLSA. Available at http://roa.rutgers.edu/

Johnson, Mark. (2002) Optimality-theoretic lexical functional grammar. In S. Stevenson and P. Merlo (eds) *The Lexical Basis of Syntactic Processing: Formal, Computational and Experimental Issues* 59–73. Amsterdam: John Benjamins.

Kenstowicz, Michael. (1994) *Phonology in Generative Grammar*. Malden, MA: Blackwell.

Kimper, Wendell. (To appear) Locality and globality in phonological variation. In *Natural Language and Linguistic Theory*.

Lacy, Paul de. (2004) Markedness conflation in Optimality Theory. *Phonology* 21 (2): 1–55.

Legendre, Géraldine, Miyata, Yoshiro and Smolensky, Paul. (1990) Can connectionism contribute to syntax? Harmonic Grammar, with an application. In M. Ziolkowski, M. Noske, and K. Deaton (eds) *Proceedings of the 26th regional meeting of the Chicago Linguistic Society* 237–252. Chicago, IL: Chicago Linguistic Society.

Legendre, Géraldine, Antonella, Sorace and Smolensky, Paul. (2006) The Optimality Theory–Harmonic Grammar connection. In Paul Smolensky and Géraldine Legendre *The Harmonic Mind: From Neural Computation to Optimality-Theoretic Grammar* 339–402. Cambridge, MA: MIT Press.

McCarthy, John J. (2002) *A Thematic Guide to Optimality Theory*. Cambridge: Cambridge University Press.

McCarthy, John J. (2003) OT constraints are categorical. *Phonology* 20: 75–138.

McCarthy, John J. (2007a) Restraint of analysis. In Sylvia Blaho, Patrick Bye and

Martin Krämer (eds) *Freedom of Analysis* 203–231. Berlin and New York: Mouton de Gruyter.

McCarthy, John J. (2007b) *Hidden Generalizations: Phonological Opacity in Optimality Theory*. London: Equinox.

McCarthy, John J. (2008a) The gradual path to cluster simplification. *Phonology* 25: 271–319.

McCarthy, John J. (2008b) The serial interaction of stress and syncope. *Natural Language and Linguistic Theory* 26 (3): 499–546.

McCarthy, John J. (2010) Studying GEN. *Journal of the Phonetic Society of Japan* 13 (2): 3–12.

McCarthy, John J. and Prince, Alan. (1994) The emergence of the unmarked: optimality in prosodic morphology. In Mercè Gonzàlez (ed.) *Proceedings of the North East Linguistics Society 24* 333–379. Amherst, MA: GLSA. Available at http://roa.rutgers.edu/

McCarthy, John J. and Prince, Alan. (1999) Faithfulness and identity in Prosodic Morphology. In René Kager, Harry van der Hulst and Wim Zonneveld (eds), *The Prosody-morphology Interface* 218–309. Cambridge: Cambridge University Press.

McCarthy, John J. and Pruitt, Kathryn. (To appear) Sources of phonological structure. In Ralf Vogel and Hans Broekhuis (eds), *Derivation and Filtering*. London: Equinox Publishing.

Pater, Joe. (2000) Nonuniformity in English stress: the role of ranked and lexically specific constraints. *Phonology* 17 (2): 237–274.

Pater, Joe. (2009) Weighted constraints in generative linguistics. *Cognitive Science* 33 (6): 999–1035. Available at http://roa.rutgers.edu/

Pater, Joe, Bhatt, Rajesh and Potts, Christopher. (2007) Linguistic optimization. Ms, University of Massachusetts, Amherst. Available at http://roa.rutgers.edu/

Potts, Christopher, Pater, Joe, Jesney, Karen, Bhatt, Rajesh and Becker, Michael. (2010) Harmonic Grammar with Linear Programming: From linear systems to linguistic typology. *Phonology* 27 (1): 77–117.

Prince, Alan. (1983) Relating to the Grid. *Linguistic Inquiry* 14 (1): 19–100.

Prince, Alan. (1997) Stringency and anti-Paninian hierarchies. Handout from LSA Institute, Cornell University. Available at http://ling.rutgers.edu/people/faculty/prince.html

Prince, Alan and Smolensky, Paul. (1993/2004) *Optimality Theory: Constraint Interaction in Generative Grammar*. RuCCS Technical Report 2, Rutgers University, Piscateway, NJ: Rutgers University Center for Cognitive Science. Revised version published 2004 by Blackwell. Page references to the 2004 version.

Pratt, Patrick. (2008) *Calculating Typologies in Harmonic Serialism*. Honor's thesis, University of Massachusetts, Amherst.

Prince, Alan, and Smolensky, Paul. (1997) Optimality: from neural networks to universal grammar. *Science* 275 (5306): 1604–1610.

Pruitt, Kathryn. (2008) Iterative foot optimization and locality in stress systems. Ms, University of Massachusetts, Amherst. Available at http://roa.rutgers.edu/

Smolensky, Paul and Legendre, Géraldine. (2006) *The Harmonic Mind: From Neural Computation to Optimality-Theoretic Grammar.* Cambridge, MA: MIT Press.

Steriade, Donca (1982) Greek prosodies and the nature of syllabification. Ph.D. Thesis. Cambridge, MA: Massachusetts Institute of Technology.

Wilson, Colin. (2003) Analyzing unbounded spreading with constraints: marks, targets and derivations. Unpublished ms, UCLA.

Wilson, Colin. (2006). Learning phonology with substantive bias: an experimental and computational study of velar palatalization. *Cognitive Science* 30 (5): 945–982.

Zec, Draga. (1995) Coda constraints and conditions on syllable weight. *Phonology* 12: 85–129.

3 The formal definition of the ONSET constraint and implications for Korean syllable structure

Jennifer L. Smith[a]

3.1 Introduction

The crosslinguistic preference for syllables to have onsets has been modeled by various rules, principles, and constraints in a number of phonological frameworks. Early generative discussions include Kahn (1976), Selkirk (1982, 1984), Steriade (1982), Clements and Keyser (1983), and Itô (1986, 1989). In Optimality Theory (Prince and Smolensky, 2004 [1993]), this preference is formalized as the ONS(ET) constraint. ONSET finds widespread acceptance among OT practitioners, but not much attention has been paid to developing and defending a precise formal definition for this constraint.

This paper provides additional support for the formal definition of ONSET proposed in Smith (2002, 2003, 2008), a definition that makes reference to no details of syllable-internal structure other than the fundamental head/nonhead distinction. This *head-based* definition of ONSET has crosslinguistic empirical support and contributes to a view of the phonology-phonetics interface according to which constraints are only indirectly related to phonetic factors, even when functionally motivated. In the discussion that follows, the head-based definition of ONSET is shown to allow for a consistent, noncontradictory phonological analysis of the syllable position of glides in Korean. Moreover, the account of glides now available under this view of ONSET is shown to

a   Jennifer L. Smith: University of North Carolina at Chapel Hill, Chapel Hill, NC. Email: jlsmith@email.unc.edu prepare the ground for a nonstipulative account of a ban on word-initial liquids in South Korean dialects, an otherwise independent phenomenon.

Prince and Smolensky's (2004 [1993]) original definition of ONSET is given in (1). According to this definition, a syllable will satisfy ONSET only if it begins with a segment syllabified as a true structural onset. A syllable that begins with a nonpeak segment that is syllabified as part of the syllable rime, as with a rising diphthong such as [i̯a], does not satisfy this version of the constraint.

(1)   Prince and Smolensky's (2004) ONSET
       (a) ONS   A syllable must have an onset (Prince and Smolensky, 2004: 106)

       (b) 'We will say a syllable "has an onset" if … it has an Ons node …'
           (Prince and Smolensky, 2004: 110)

In contrast, the formal definition of the ONSET constraint adopted in this paper is as in (2). According to this definition, ONSET is satisfied as long as the head segment of the syllable is preceded by some other segment in that syllable.

(2)   ONSET   'Syllables have onsets'
                    For all syllables σ, $a \neq b$
                         where a is the leftmost segment dominated by σ
                                b is the head segment of σ

Discussion of this definition of ONSET, and why it is preferable to other proposed or conceivable definitions, is given in §3.2.

The implications of the head-based definition of ONSET for Korean are discussed in §3.3 and §3.4. Previous research has presented apparently contradictory evidence to support both claims that Korean glides are onsets, and claims that they are rimal. However, §3.3 demonstrates that the evidence in support of Korean glides 'as onsets' reduces to evidence that the glides resolve hiatus, that is, that they satisfy ONSET. Under the definition of ONSET developed here, this is predicted to be the case *even if the glides are syllabified in the syllable rime*. Thus, all the available evidence about glide syllabification in Korean can now be seen to be compatible with the claim that Korean glides are part of the syllable rime. Once this analysis is adopted for the glides, a sonority-based, and therefore phonetically and phonologically motivated, account becomes possible for the ban on word-initial liquids in South Korean dialects. This account, and crosslinguistic support for such an approach, are presented in §3.4.

Finally, the head-based definition of ONSET has theoretical implications, because it is relevant for ongoing debates about the nature of the phonetics-phonology interface. As shown in §3.5, ONSET has the same functional motivation as the *ONSET/X constraint family, which enforces low sonority in onset consonants. However, while ONSET is independent of syllable structure beyond head/nonhead status, the *ONSET/X constraints are crucially *dependent* on syllable structure – they evaluate only segments that are syllabified as true structural onsets. Therefore, ONSET and *ONSET/X, despite their shared functional motivation, are formally distinct constraints. This shows that it is not the case that functionally motivated constraints are projected directly from the phonetics; the relationship between phonetic information and phonological constraints is indirect.

3.2 ONSET is sensitive to head/nonhead status only

There are a number of logically possible ways to give an explicit phonological definition for a constraint whose intent is to penalize onsetless syllables. The definition adopted here is the following (repeated from (2) above), proposed in Smith (2002, 2003, 2008).

(3)   ONSET   'Syllables have onsets'
                      For all syllables σ, $a \neq b$
                            where a is the leftmost segment dominated by σ
                            b is the head segment of σ

This constraint formalization demands only that the head segment of a syllable not be leftmost in its syllable; the exact position in hierarchical syllable structure taken by the desired prehead segment is irrelevant. Formally, the head segment is the syllable peak or 'designated terminal element' (Liberman and Prince, 1977); this follows the standard assumption in prosodic theory that every prosodic constituent has a dependent that is phonologically designated as its head (see, e.g., Selkirk, 1986, 1995).

The remainder of this section now considers general implications of the head-based definition of ONSET, and argues against alternative formalizations.

Adopting the head-based definition of ONSET turns out to have important consequences for glides, because two phonologically distinct syllable positions have been identifed for prepeak glides (Kaye and Lowenstamm, 1984; Davis and Hammond, 1995; Harris and Kaisse, 1999; see also Selkirk, 1982: 343). For example, in French, some prepeak glides act 'like vowels' while others act 'like consonants,' triggering different sets of allomorphs and distinct co-occurrence restrictions (Kaye and Lowenstamm, 1984). In Spanish, prepeak glides preceded by another consonant act rimal, contributing to syllable weight, while syllable-initial prepeak glides act like onsets, undergoing fortition in many dialects (Harris and Kaisse, 1999). These different patterns in glide behavior have been used to motivate a representational distinction between what are called here *true onset glides,* glides that are syllabified as structural onsets, and *rimal onglides,* glides that are syllabified as part of the syllable rime, forming a rising diphthong with the syllable peak.

This representational distinction can be made in any theory of subsyllabic structure that recognizes some kind of structural difference between onset and rime, including a model in which the rime is a separate constituent that excludes the onset (e.g., Selkirk, 1982, 1984; Blevins, 1995); for concreteness, this paper assumes moraic theory as implemented by McCarthy and Prince (1986) and Hayes (1989). On this view of subsyllabic structure, a true structural onset is defined as a prepeak segment that is a direct dependent of the syllable node. Any prepeak segment that is not a direct dependent of the syllable node, being dominated by a mora instead, is by definition part of the rime.

(4)   Two possible syllable positions for prepeak glides

    (a) Glide as true onset   (b) Glide as rimal onglide[1]

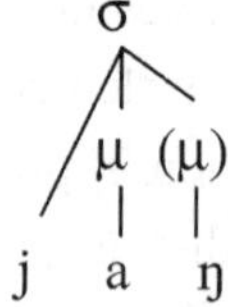
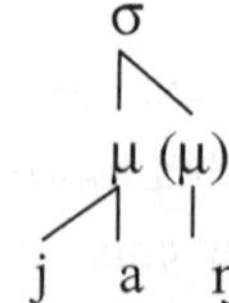

What is crucial here is that, under the head-based definition of ONSET given in (2) above, both (4a) and (4b) satisfy the constraint. Even though only (4a) is a syllable with a true structural onset (daughter of σ), both of these representations satisfy the requirement that the head segment ([a]) not be leftmost in its syllable.

In the discussion that follows, curly brackets {} are used to demarcate segments contained in the syllable rime. This notation makes it convenient to distinguish between [j{a}], a true onset glide, and [{ja}], a rimal onglide.

As outlined in §3.1, this indifference to syllable structure in the definition of ONSET is empirically motivated; justification is presented in §3.3 and §3.4 below. First, however, this section defends the proposal that ONSET must be defined on the basis of the head/nonhead distinction, rather than other conceivable distinctions, such as values for the feature [±consonantal] or relative sonority.

3.2.1 ONSET does not refer to [±consonantal] or the CV tier

Many definitions for ONSET require that syllables start with 'C' (McCarthy and Prince, 1993; Eisner, 1997; Karttunen, 1998), or that they not start with 'V' (Kager, 1999; McCarthy, 2003). Examples are given in (5).

(5)   CV-based definitions of ONSET

      (a) McCarthy and Prince (1993: 101)

          ONSET   Align (σ, L, C, L)

                               For every σ, there is some C such that the Left edge of σ and the Left edge of C are aligned

      (b) Kager (1999: 93)

          ONSET   *[σ V]

The exact conditions under which these constraints would assign violations are not clear, because this depends on how the *C/V* notation is to be interpreted. However, C and V must not simply be equivalent to the feature specifications [+consonantal] and [−consonantal] respectively, for two reasons. First, glides, which are [−consonantal] ('V'?), do satisfy ONSET; glide formation or glide spreading often occurs in order to resolve hiatus (see, e.g.,

Rosenthall, 1994 and Levi, 2004; additional evidence that glides satisfy ONSET is discussed in §3.3 below). Second, many languages allow [+consonantal] segments ('C'?) to serve as syllable peaks, so if ONSET merely demands that each syllable begin with something [+consonantal], then this constraint would inappropriately be satisfied by an onsetless syllable with a [+consonantal] peak. That this is not so is shown by Imdlawn Tashlhiyt Berber (Dell and Elmedlaoui, 1985, 1988; Prince and Smolensky, 2004; Ridouane, 2008), where onsets are obligatory (except word initially, where other constraints come into play) even when the syllable peak is a [+consonantal] segment. For example, the syllabification [tx̣.zn̩t] 'you stored', where all medial syllables have onsets, is chosen over *[tx̣z.n̩t], which does better with respect to nucleus sonority ([z̩] is better than [x̣]), but has an onsetless medial syllable (Prince and Smolensky, 2004: 24). If ONSET were satisfied by the presence of a [+consonantal] segment at the left edge of the syllable, [n̩t] would not violate this constraint.

Assuming that the CV notation used in (5) refers to slots on the CV tier does not straightforwardly rescue this definition, either. Proponents of X-slot theory (Levin [Blevins], 1985; Blevins, 1995) and moraic theory (Hayes, 1989; McCarthy and Prince, 1986) have demonstrated that the distinction between C and V slots is secondary, being derivative from the role that a segment plays in syllable structure.

Therefore, the only successful interpretation of ONSET definitions like those in (5) is to let C/V stand for 'not syllabic'/'syllabic,' which reduces to the very proposal being made here: ONSET is a constraint that requires a syllable not to begin with its peak (the 'syllabic' segment in the syllable).

3.2.2 ONSET does not refer to relative sonority

Another conceivable way to formalize the ONSET constraint is to require every syllable to begin with a rise in sonority. Such a definition would transparently reflect the functional motivation for ONSET, discussed in §5, which is to intersperse low-sonority segments between syllable peaks in order to increase the perceptual salience of the speech stream. However, another example from Imdlawn Tashlhiyt Berber shows that ONSET is satisfied even when the prepeak segment is of a *higher* sonority class than the peak. The syllabification [i.sa.wḷ] 'he talked', with a syllable [wḷ], is chosen over *[i.sa.ul], with [ul]. Again, the unattested form better satisfies constraints demanding high-sonority peaks, because [u] is better than [ḷ]. So, if [wḷ] did not satisfy high-ranking ONSET, there would be no reason to choose this syllabification over [ul] (Prince and Smolensky, 2004: 24; Ridouane, 2008: 325). And yet in this syllable, the leftmost segment, [w], is *not* lower in sonority than the nucleus, [ḷ]. Therefore, a definition of ONSET that is sensitive to differences in sonority is not empirically supported.

The examples discussed in §3.2 confirm that what the ONSET constraint requires in syllable-initial position is neither a [+consonantal] feature speci-fication nor a sequence of segments with rising sonority. The head-based definition of ONSET succeeds in avoiding these problems. Next, §3.3 and §3.4 show that the head-based definition has desirable consequences for the analy-sis of several otherwise unrelated syllable-structure phenomena in Korean. Thus, the definition of ONSET adopted here is furthermore preferable to one, like that in Prince and Smolensky (2004), that refers to the structural onset position within a syllable.

3.3   Head-based ONSET and the syllabification of Korean glides

The proposal that ONSET is insensitive to differences in the syllable position of prepeak segments sheds new light on several patterns in the phonology of Seoul Korean. For years, there has been a debate over the phonological repre-sentation of glides in Korean syllable structure. Some researchers claim that Korean glides are onsets, or 'consonants' (e.g., B. G. Lee, 1982; Y. S. Kim, 1984; Ahn, 1985; Y. Lee, 1994). Others take the position that Korean glides are rimal onglides, or 'vowels' (e.g., Martin, 1954, 1992; H. S. Sohn, 1987a,b; Han, 1990; C. W. Kim and H. Y. Kim, 1991; H. M. Sohn, 1994; I. Lee and Ramsey, 2000).

This question has been difficult to settle for a number of reasons. First, much of the evidence originally presented to support one view or the other, such as evidence from language games or place-based co-occurrence restric-tions, was later shown to be inconclusive in choosing between the two structural alternatives (for detailed discussion of this debate, see especially

Y. S. Kim, 1984; Ahn, 1985; Y. Lee, 1994; H. Y. Kim, 1998 for the pro-onset position, and H. S. Sohn, 1987a,b; C. W. Kim and H. Y. Kim, 1991; Shim, 1997 for the pro-rime position). Second, the evidence that does actually withstand scrutiny appears to be contradictory; each side of the debate has evidence that the other side has been unable to explain away.

The argument pursued here is as follows. Essentially all of the evidence in support of the claim that Korean glides are syllabified as onsets reduces to the claim that glides resolve hiatus – that is, that they satisfy the ONSET constraint. However, according to the head-based definition of ONSET, rimal onglides actually satisfy this constraint as well. Therefore, proposing that Korean glides are rimal onglides, in combination with the definition of ONSET adopted here, allows for a consistent account of glide behavior in Korean.

The remainder of this section summarizes the evidence that Korean glides resolve hiatus and presents several arguments from the literature that these glides are rimal onglides and not true structural onsets.

3.3.1 The distribution of glides in Korean

The syllable template for Korean is (C)(G)V(C) (H. M. Sohn, 1994: 445), where C is a [+consonantal] element, G is a glide, and V is a vowel (nucleus). Thus, glides may be syllable initial (6), or they may co-occur with a preceding onset consonant (7), which is the only configuration in which two segments precede the syllable peak.

(6)   Simplex glide onsets (data from H. M. Sohn, 1994)

(a) initial	[waŋ]	'king'	[jaŋ]	'sheep'
	[wən.tʃʰik]	'principle'	[jə.ɾim]	'summer'
(b) medial	[o.nju.wəl]	'May and June'	[kjoː.juk]	'education'

(7)   C+glide onsets (data from H. M. Sohn, 1994, 1999)

(a) initial	[kwaː.il]	'fruit'	[kjuːl]	'orange (n.)'
	[kwəl.ljək]	'power'	[pjəŋ]	'bottle'
			[mjoː.dʒi]	'graveyard'
(b) medial	[i.ɾwən]	'one *won*'	[hak.k'jo]	'school'
	[tʃəːn.hwa]	'telephone'	[ko.hjaŋ]	'hometown'
	[tʃi.gwən]	'staff'	[kwəl.ljək]	'power'
			[o.nju.wəl]	'May and June'

These are the only contexts in which glides are found; in particular, glides do not systematically occur to the right of the peak within a syllable.[2]

3.3.2 Evidence for Korean glides as 'onsets'

As noted above, the strongest argument in favor of the claim that Korean glides are 'consonants,' that is, that they are syllabified as onsets, is that glides resolve hiatus. Evidence that glides resolve hiatus is now presented, with data from suffix allomorphy, glide coalescence, and glide deletion in turn.

One piece of evidence showing that glides are able to resolve hiatus comes from suffix allomorphy patterns. Several suffixes in Korean have two allomorphs, one consonant initial and one vowel initial, which are combined with stems ending in the opposite segment class in order to form V+C and C+V sequences at morpheme boundaries. Examples include the suffixes that mark nominative ([-ga]~[-i]), accusative [-ɾɯl]~[-ɯl], topic ([-nɯn]~[-ɯn]), and directional or instrumental ([-ɾo]~[-ɨro] (Martin, 1992: 195–196). It is not clear for all pairs whether both allomorphs are lexically listed, or whether one is derived from the other in the synchronic phonology (H. M. Sohn, 1999: 163), but the relevant point for the current discussion is that the V-initial allomorph is not selected when a stem is V-final. The avoidance of V+V sequences in these morphological forms indicates that ONSET is being satisfied through allomorph selection. Crucially, there are suffix allomorph pairs of this type where the allomorph that occurs with V-final stems begins with a glide. This shows that glides behave like other consonants in Korean in satisfying ONSET.

The vocative is one such morpheme. This suffix alternates between [-ja] after V-final names and [-a] after C-final names.

(8)   Vocative suffix allomorphy: [ja]~[a]
        (data from Ahn, 1985: 49–50; Y. Lee, 1994: 138; Yun, 2001: 74)

	(a) Vowel-final names		(b) Consonant-final names	
	name	*vocative*	*name*	*vocative*
	[su.mi]	[su.mi.ja]	[sun]	[su.na]
	[tʃin.se]	[tʃin.se.ja]	[tʃin.suk]	[tʃin.su.ga]
	[min.su]	[min.su.ja]		

The last example in (8a) confirms that the [j] glide is not simply copied from the stem-final vowel, which would have produced *[min.su.wa].

A second example of suffix allomorphy involving a glide-initial allomorph after a V-final stem is the [-ja] allomorph of the verb infinitive suffix /-a/, as seen in (9).

(9)   Verb infinitive suffix /-a/, with idiosyncratic [-ja] alternant (Y. S. Kim, 1984: 12–13)
       /ha + A + la/ *do*-INF-IMPER   →   [ha.jə.ɾa] 'do!'   (also [ha.ɾa], [hɛ.ɾa])

The morphophonology of the infinitive suffix is complicated, so only the immediately relevant facts are presented here; see, e.g., H. S. Sohn (1987b) and Martin (1992: 465–466) for additional details. This suffix consists of a harmonizing vowel, represented as /A/, which is realized as [a] or [ə] depending on the vowel in the preceding syllable. After verb stems ending in [e], [ɛ], or [a], the infinitive suffix usually surfaces as zero, which accounts for the [ha.ɾa] form in (9). However, as discussed by Y. S. Kim (1984), certain verbs show optional consonant-initial alternants of the infinitive suffix. The consonant involved is unpredictable and depends on the individual verb; Y. S. Kim (1984: 12) gives the examples /o + a + la/ [o.nə.ɾa] 'come!' and /ka + a + la/ [ka.gə.ɾa] 'go!' in addition to the form shown in (9). What is important here, as Kim emphasizes, is that there would be no advantage to choosing the [j]-initial form of the infinitive suffix over its usual vowel-initial form if glides did not serve to avoid hiatus just as the other idiosyncratic infinitive-initial consonants [n g] do.

Another set of patterns showing that syllable-initial glides satisfy ONSET in Korean are those in which general processes of glide coalescence or glide deletion are blocked in contexts where hiatus would arise if those processes applied. For example, there is a optional pattern of glide coalescence in which [–hi, –rd] back vowels merge with [j] to become front vowels (C. W. Kim, 1968; C. W. Kim and H. Y. Kim, 1991; H. S. Sohn, 1987a,b). Specifically, [j]+[ə] becomes [e], and [j]+[a] becomes [ɛ], as exemplified in (10). However, Y. Lee (1994) notes that this coalescence process is blocked in absolute word-initial position (11a), and Yun (2001) demonstrates that it is blocked in intervocalic position as well (11b) – these are contexts where no other onset consonant is available.

(10)   Optional GV coalescence in CGV syllables

    (a) Word-initial examples
        (data from C. W. Kim, 1968: 520–521; H. S. Sohn, 1987b: 162; C. W. Kim and H. Y. Kim, 1991: 121; Martin, 1992: 39)

[pjə]	~	[pe]	'rice plant'	[pjə.ɾak]	~	[pe.ɾak]	'thunder'
[pjəl]	~	[pel]	'star'	[pjəŋ.wən]	~	[peŋ.wən]	'hospital'
[pʰjə]	~	[pʰe]	'spread'	[pʰjəŋ.jaŋ]	~	[pʰeŋ.jaŋ]	'Pyŏngyang'
[kjə]	~	[ke]	'chaff'	[hjəŋ.nim]	~	[heŋ.nim]	'elder brother'
[mjət]	~	[met]	'how much?'	[mjə.ni.ɾi]	~	[me.ni.ɾi]	'daughter-in-law'
[p'jam]	~	[p'ɛm]	'cheek'				

    (b) Medial examples (data from H. S. Sohn, 1987b: 162; Martin, 1992: 25, 38)

[pi.njə]	~	[pi.ne]	'stick hairpin'
[səl.mjəŋ]	~	[səl.meŋ]	'explanation'
[ki.ta.ɾjə.jo]	~	[ki.ta.ɾe.jo]	'waits' (/kitali + A + jo/ '*wait*-INF-POLITE')

(11)   GV coalescence blocked in .GV syllables

    (a) Word-initial examples (data from Y. Lee, 1994: 141)

[jə.dʒa]	*[e.dʒa]	'woman';	cf. [kjə.dʒa]	~	[ke.dʒa]	'mustard'
[jə.ul]	*[e.ul]	'stream';	cf. [kjə.ul]	~	[ke.ul]	'winter'

    (b) Medial example (data from Yun, 2001: 78)

[pu.jə]	*[pu.e]	(place name)

A similar argument in favor of the ability of syllable-initial glides to function as onsets is made by Yun (2001), who focuses on an optional[3] glide deletion phenomenon that, once again, affects glides in CGV syllables, but not .GV syllables. The target of the deletion process is [j] when it is followed by [e]. (Since [e] is also the output of coalescence in the case of [jə], this process of [j] 'deletion' before [e] may in fact be another case of coalescence, i.e., [je] → [e] with the value of [±back] vacuously output as [–back] as it is, nonvacuously, in the case of [ja] → [ɛ] and [jə] → [e].)

(12)   [j] deletion in C[je] sequences (data from Yun, 2001: 68)

    (a) Word-initial examples

[pʰje]	~	[pʰe]	'bother'
[nje]	~	[ne]	'yes'

    (b) Medial example

[sa.ɾje]	~	[sa.ɾe]	'reward'

(13)   Resistance to [j]-deletion in #GV (data from Yun, 2001: 68)

    (a) [je]   *[e]   'example'

       [kje]   ~   [ke]   'a traditional mutual financial association'

    (b) [je.san]   *[e.san]   'budget'

       [kje.san] ~ [ke.san] 'calculation'

For both the GV coalescence pattern and the glide-deletion pattern, there is a difference between glide-initial and C-initial syllables. Where the glide is the sole prepeak segment, it is resistant to these optional phonological processes that, in other contexts, remove glide segments from surface forms. Crucially if [je] were *not* a syllable that satisfied ONSET, the [j]-deletion form *[e] should be equally acceptable (given the general optionality of the glide-deletion rule). Thus, for [j]-deletion as for GV coalescence, the special behavior of the syllable-initial case shows that glides are relevant for the ONSET constraint.

In summary, the facts discussed above have been presented in the literature as evidence that Korean glides have the status of 'consonants,' or onsets. (Discussion of the role of glides in resolving hiatus or serving as onsets can also be found in Y. Lee (1997) and Cho (2000).) However, what these facts actually show is that glides in Korean satisfy ONSET. Under the revised definition of ONSET presented here, rimal onglides also satisfy this constraint. Therefore, these various arguments that glides are able to resolve hiatus in Korean do not contradict the claim that prepeak glides are actually syllabified as rimal onglides.

Some additional facts about Korean glides, independent of their ability to resolve hiatus, have also been presented in the literature in support of glides as onsets. However, these arguments are less compelling than those about hiatus resolution. One such argument has to do with rhyming conventions in poetry. H. Y. Kim (1998: 120) notes that '[t]he onset and the prenucleus G do not affect the rhyming pattern at all'. That is, there is no evidence from rhyming conventions that a prepeak glide functions as part of a subsyllabic constituent with the syllable peak. However, rhyme schemes have an aesthetic, conventionalized dimension in addition to their linguistically motivated dimension, and there are other known cases where the units that must match in a rhyming convention are not phonological constituents. One example is English, where rhyme involves the span from the head segment of the prosodic word to the end of the prosodic word (Clements and Keyser, 1983: 23–24); this domain includes a subpart of the head syllable plus, potentially, one or more additional syllables, and is clearly not any sort of prosodic constituent. Similarly, it may simply be the case that poetic rhyme in Korean is defined starting at the syllable peak, rather than at the left edge of the syllable rime.

Another argument has been raised by Yun (2001). This argument concerns what are sometimes described as the 'front rounded vowels' of Korean (Martin, 1992: 24; H. M. Sohn, 1999: 158). These are orthographically represented as <wi> (high) and <we>, <oj> (mid), and are transcribed sometimes as [y] and [ø] (e.g., H. M. Sohn, 1999) and sometimes as [wi] and [we] (e.g., Martin, 1992). According to Yun's intuitions, these 'vowels' are always diphthongal, consisting of a labial glide plus [i] or [e]. Moreover, Yun claims that this labial glide is realized as a front glide, [ɥ], when another onset consonant is present (C[ɥ]V), but as a back glide, [w], when the glide is syllable-initial (.[w]V).

Yun argues that because there is a difference in the phonetic realization of the glide that depends on the presence or absence of a preceding C, the syllabification of the glide is different in these two contexts. He draws a comparison with Spanish, which has rimal onglides when a consonant precedes (C{GV}), but true onset glides when the glide is syllable-initial (G{V}) (Harris and Kaisse, 1999). However, the evidence presented by Harris and Kaisse to motivate different syllable positions for glides in CGV versus .GV includes facts about syllable weight and sonority, phenomena which are known to correlate with syllable structure. It is much less clear that the backness alternation that Yun discusses is something that should depend on a difference in syllable structure. Even if the glide is undergoing some sort of assimilation or dissimilation process involving the following front vowel, it has been shown that place-of-articulation interactions are much less likely to respect syllable constituent boundaries than, for example, co-occurrence restrictions based on sonority class (Steriade, 1988b: 121). Finally, the observation that the backness of the labial glide can be determined by the following vowel is found elsewhere (e.g., Martin, 1992: 24), but the additional claim in Yun (2001), that the choice between [w] and [ɥ] is influenced by the presence of a preceding consonant, seems to be a novel claim, so it would be desirable to confirm this claim with empirical measurements.

Thus, the truly compelling evidence in favor of Korean glides as 'onsets' is, more precisely, evidence that glides satisfy the constraint ONSET. However, as ONSET is defined here, this is true even of rimal onglides. Consequently, there is in fact *no* compelling evidence that Korean glides are syllabified in true onset position.

3.3.3 Previous evidence that Korean glides are not syllabified as true onsets

The traditional view of Korean prepeak glides is that they are part of the syllable rime. This view is reflected in, and perhaps reinforced by, orthographic practice. Since its development in the fifteenth century (see H. M. Sohn, 1999: Ch 6 for an overview), *hangul* orthography has indicated a /j/ glide as a diacritic on the nuclear vowel, and a /w/ glide by linking the symbol for either /u/ or /o/ with the symbol for the nuclear vowel. Moreover, if the glide is the only prepeak element in the syllable, it is preceded by the symbol for 'zero onset' just as a syllable-initial nuclear vowel would be.

There is also evidence of a more directly phonological nature to support the view that Korean glides are not syllabified as true onsets. H. Y. Kim (1998: 120), following Duanmu (1990), observes that we expect to see consistent sonority distance effects between members of an onset cluster. In particular, if a cluster C_1C_2 with a certain sonority distance between C_1 and C_2 is allowed, then onset clusters with a greater sonority distance should be legal as well. On the assumption that CG sequences in Korean are onset clusters, the minimum required sonority distance would appear to be quite small, since even nasals or liquids can occur with glides, as seen for example in (7) above. However, the only possible 'clusters' are those that have a glide as the second member, regardless of the sonority distance; even a stop+liquid cluster is impossible, despite the fact that the sonority distance there is much larger than for a nasal+glide or liquid+glide sequence. This indicates that CGV sequences are not complex onsets; G here is not syllabified as part of a true structural onset (see Baertsch, 1998 for similar argumentation concerning Spanish).

Admittedly, some caution is necessary here, because showing that G in CGV is not an onset does not automatically prove that G in .GV is not an onset. As mentioned in §3.2 above, some languages treat glides in CGV and .GV syllables differently in precisely this way (Davis and Hammond, 1995; Rubach, 1998; Harris and Kaisse, 1999). Indeed, Yun (2001) has made this claim for Korean (see also related discussion in Shim, 1997 and K. S. Kang, 2003). Furthermore, in addition to the rimal onglide structure C{GV}, there is another possible phonological analysis for a phonetic CGV sequence in which G is not an onset: The CG sequence might be a complex consonant, C^G (H. Y. Kim, 1998).

However, the rimal onglide approach finds additional support from a phenomenon that has not yet (to my knowledge) been applied to the question of glide structure in Korean. Namely, Seoul and other South Korean dialects have a word-initial liquid onset ban, which is analyzed in the following section as a requirement for lower-sonority onsets in initial position. The fact that glides, the highest sonority 'onsets,' appear to be exempt from such restrictions receives a straightforward explanation if glides are syllabified as rimal onglides.

Thus, adopting the head-based definition of ONSET not only resolves the controversy over glide structure in Korean, but also relates two aspects of the language that were not previously seen to be connected: glide syllabification and the avoidance of word-initial liquids.

3.4   Further implications for liquid-specific sonority effects

In South Korean dialects, liquid onsets are prohibited in two structurally similar contexts: after a (nonliquid) consonant, and in word-initial position (except in recent loanwords). The two prohibitions both affect liquids that are syllable onsets, and moreover in both cases the underlying liquids surface as [n]. Because of these similarities, a number of researchers have tried to derive both patterns from a general ban on liquid onsets (Iverson and K. H. Kim, 1987; S. K. Kang, 1991; Han, 1993; H. M. Sohn, 1994: 474; McDonough, 1995; Smith, 1997). However, a different approach to the postconsonantal ban on liquids has greater explanatory success. On this view, the post-C liquid ban is part of a more general pattern of syllable-contact effects (Murray and Venneman, 1983), where no onset may be higher in sonority than a preceding coda (Iverson and H. S. Sohn, 1994; Davis and Shin, 1999; Um, 2003). Since liquids are higher in sonority than all other potential coda consonants in Korean, this syllable-contact requirement happens to resemble a prohibition against post-C liquid onsets.

Although the syllable-contact account of medial liquid-nasal alternations captures an important generalization, proposals taking this perspective on Korean liquids have left the word-initial liquid ban without a phonetically motivated phonological analysis. Several researchers have observed that a ban on word-initial liquids is consistent with the crosslinguistic tendency toward initial 'strengthening' or sonority-lowering effects (Iverson and H. S. Sohn, 1994; Um, 2003).[4] Nevertheless, formal accounts of the word-initial liquid prohibition have not incorporated this insight into the phonological analysis directly; even recent constraint-based analyses have resorted to stipulative constraints along the lines of '*$_{\text{WORD}}[l/r]$' (Um, 2003: 128).

One obstacle to pursuing a sonority-based account of this word-initial liquid ban would be the fact that glides, which are even higher in sonority than liquids, are nevertheless tolerated as word-initial onsets. However, this section demonstrates that the apparently contradictory behavior of initial liquids and glides in Korean (and in other languages with similar patterns) is resolved once we adopt the rimal onglide analysis presented in §3. If Korean prepeak glides are not true structural onsets, but instead are syllabified as part of the syllable rime, there is an explanation for why they are exempt from restrictions on sonority that apply to true structural onsets.

Section 3.4.1 first demonstrates the behavior of liquids in Korean and reviews the evidence for treating word-initial and post-C cases of liquid-nasal alternation separately. A sonority-based account of the initial liquid ban is then presented in §4.2, along with discussion of how the rimal onglide analysis from §3 makes this approach to the initial liquid-nasal alternations possible.

3.4.1 The word-initial liquid ban in Seoul Korean

Korean has a single liquid phoneme; its realization is fully predictable. The liquid surfaces as [l] in coda position, including the geminate structure V[l.l](G)V, and as [ɾ] when intervocalic or in a V.[ɾ]GV sequence; examples of these liquid realizations can be seen in (14), (15) and (16) below. Most relevant for the current discussion is the fact that in Seoul and other South Korean dialects, the liquid surfaces as a nasal [n] in word-initial position (except in recent loanwords).

(14)   Word-initial liquids surface as [n] (data from Um, 2003: 112, 113)

input[5]	output	gloss	related forms		
/lo-pjən/	[no.bjən]	'roadside'	/toː-lo/	[toː.ɾo]	'road'
/lon-tʃɨŋ/	[non.dʒɨŋ]	'proof'	/sə-lon/	[sə.ɾon]	'introduction'
/lak-wən/	[na.gwən]	'paradise'	/kʰwɛ-lak/	[kʰwɛ.ɾak]	'joy'
/lu-kak/	[nu.gak]	'pavilion'	/po-lu/	[po.ɾu]	'fort'
/lɛ-il/	[nɛ.il]	'tomorrow'	/tʃən-lɛ/	[tʃəl.lɛ]	'tradition'

As outlined above, the word-initial liquid ban in Seoul Korean is taken to be a sonority-based restriction on word-initial onsets. Before turning to the details of this analysis, however, it is necessary to clarify how the word-initial pattern relates to the other case of liquid-nasal alternation in Korean. The liquid phoneme also surfaces as [n] in word-medial onset position when another consonant (a coda) precedes (except that when the preceding consonant is coronal, /t + l/ or /n + l/, it assimilates to the liquid instead, producing a geminate [l.l]).

(15)   Noncoronal nasal + liquid → nasal + [n] (data from Davis and Shin, 1999: 288)

input	output	gloss	related forms		
/kam-li/	[kam.ni]	'supervision'	/to-li/	[to.ɾi]	'ethics'
/sam-lju/	[sam.nju]	'third rate'	/i-lju/	[i.ɾju]	'second rate'
/tʃəŋ-li/	[tʃəŋ.ni]	'arrangement'			
/jəŋ-lak/	[jəŋ.nak]	'downfall'	/tʃu-lak/	[tʃu.ɾak]	'plunge'

If the preceding consonant is an oral stop, then the stop becomes a nasal as well, so that an input stop+liquid sequence becomes a nasal+nasal sequence in the output.

(16)   Noncoronal stop + liquid → nasal + [n] (data from Davis and Shin, 1999: 288)

input	output	gloss	related forms		
/pəp-li/	[pəm.ni]	'principle of law'	/pəp + ɨl/	[pə.bɨl]	'law-ACC'
/tʃap-lok/	[tʃam.nok]	'a miscellany'	/tʃap-sə/	[tʃap.s'ə]	'sundry writings'
			/ki-lok/	[ki.rok]	'write down'
/kjək-li/	[kjəŋ.ni]	'separation'	/kan-kjək/	[kan.gjək]	'gap'
			/kə-li/	[kə.ri]	'street'
/pak-lam/	[paŋ.nam]	'exhibition'	/pak-sik/	[pak.ʃ'ik]	'knowledgeable'
			/ju-lam/	[ju.ram]	'cruise'

Davis and Shin (1999) demonstrate convincingly that the medial, post-C cases of liquid nasalization are syllable-contact effects (see also Iverson and H. S. Sohn, 1994; Um, 2003). Crucially, other segment classes also undergo alternations in onset and/or coda position that result in flat or falling sonority levels across the syllable boundary. As seen in (16), an input stop+liquid sequence is realized as nasal+nasal, rather than stop+nasal, confirming that more is at stake than a simple ban on onset liquids. The syllable-contact analysis is able to account for the change in both the coda and the onset in this circumstance – the sequence has gone from a highly marked sonority rise across the syllable boundary to a less marked, more desirable sonority plateau.

However, the *word-initial* liquid-nasal alternations in (14) cannot be attributed to a syllable-contact effect, because in initial position, syllable contact requirements are irrelevant. The word-initial pattern therefore requires a separate explanation.[6]

Indeed, there is further evidence that the two cases of liquid alternation should be treated separately. First, the post-C liquid ban is more widespread among dialects of Korean than the word-initial liquid ban; North Korean dialects have the same pattern of post-C liquid alternations as in (15) and (16) above, but allow initial liquids to surface unchanged (Cho, 1997: 91; Davis and Shin, 1999: 310). Second, Cho (1997) and Um (2003) show that (even in South Korean dialects) loanwords are exempt from the word-initial liquid ban, while still being subject to the syllable-contact requirement. Crucially, when a liquid-initial loanword appears in the post-C environment as the second element in a compound word, the liquid surfaces as [n] (Um, 2003: 116). This rules out an alternative approach in which there is just one constraint against all liquid onsets and word-initial *faithfulness* protects the initial liquids in loanwords. Instead, this pattern confirms that initial and post-C liquid alternations are separate processes, driven by distinct *markedness* constraints.

It is also worth noting that the fact that liquids surface in the same way – as nasals – in response to both syllable-contact restrictions and initial onset sonority restrictions does not prevent us from treating the two restrictions separately. This is simply a consequence of the fact that the same faithfulness constraint, IDENT[nasal], is ranked low enough to be the constraint that is violated in both cases.

Thus, the initial liquid-nasal alternations require an explanation that is distinct from the syllable-contact requirement that affects post-C liquids. This explanation is the subject of §3.4.2.

3.4.2 Liquid-onset prohibitions and *ONSET/X sonority constraints

Korean is not the only language to have a ban on word-initial liquids; similar patterns are found in a number of languages. For example, Mongolian (Poppe, 1970; Ramsey, 1987), Kuman (Trefry, 1969; Lynch, 1983; Blevins, 1994), and many Australian languages, including Guugu Yimidhirr (Haviland, 1979; Dixon, 1980), Pitta-Pitta (Blake and Breen, 1971; Blake, 1979, Dixon, 1980), and Panyjima (Dench, 1991: 133; Flack, 2006) likewise ban all initial liquids. Most of these languages have more than one liquid phoneme – Guugu Yimidhirr and Pitta-Pitta have three and four liquid phonemes respectively that would be expected to occur in word-initial position if not for the initial-liquid ban (see Smith, 2008 for more detailed discussion). Related patterns of initial-onset restriction are found as well: rhotic onsets (though not laterals) are banned from initial position in the Iglesias dialect of Campidanian Sardinian (Bolognesi, 1998) and in Mbabaram (Australian; Dixon, 1991), while the Sestu dialect of Campidanian Sardinian (Bolognesi, 1998) bans both glide and rhotic onsets in word-initial position.

A clear generalization to be made is that the segments subject to word-initial onset bans in these languages – liquids (laterals and rhotics) and glides – are the potential onset segments that have the highest sonority. Indeed, a variety of phonological phenomena demonstrate that onsets prefer to have low sonority. For example, in reduplication, an onset cluster in the base is sometimes copied as a simplex onset in the reduplicant; in some languages, the choice of which onset consonant to copy depends on which has lower sonority (Steriade, 1982, 1988a; McCarthy and Prince 1986). In child language acquisition, target onset consonants are sometimes replaced by consonants of lower sonority, and when words are truncated or clusters are reduced, it can be the lower sonority consonant that survives as the output onset (Gnanadesikan, 2004; Barlow, 1997). There are even cases of sonority-driven onset-sensitive stress (Smith, 2002; Gordon, 2003), in which stress is attracted to syllables with lower-sonority onsets. Thus, the effect observed in languages that avoid word-initial liquids and glides can be attributed to the crosslinguistically attested constraints penalizing high-sonority onsets.[7]

In order to model patterns like these, the following family of constraints can be defined (Smith, 2002, 2003).

(17)   *ONSET/X   'Onsets do not have sonority level X'
                        For every segment a that is the leftmost onset segment of some syllable σ, $|a| < X$
                            where $|y|$ is the sonority of segment y
                            X is a particular step on the sonority scale

*ONSET/X is a family of related constraints, one for each level of the sonority scale. The constraints in this family are universally ranked on the basis of the sonority scale such that the highest-sonority onsets are most strongly dispreferred. *ONSET/X is a modification of Prince and Smolensky's (2004 [1993]) original *MARGIN/X constraint family; the modification is necessary because *MARGIN/X treats onsets and codas uniformly, even though the two positions actually have different sonority preferences (Zec, 1988; Clements, 1990; see also Selkirk, 1984).

(18)   *ONSET/X constraints: sonority scale determines ranking
            *ONS/GLIDE >> *ONS/RHOTIC >> *ONS/LATERAL >> *ONS/NASAL >> ...

The fact that onset sonority restrictions sometimes occur only in word-initial position is also part of a larger pattern: Prominent positions like the word-initial syllable can be subject to positional markedness constraints (Smith, 2002). In fact, onset sonority restrictions have also been observed for another prominent position, the stressed syllable; glide onsets are avoided in stressed syllables in Niuafo'ou (de Lacy, 2001), and, as noted above, stress may be preferentially attracted to syllables whose onsets have the lowest possible sonority (Smith, 2002; Gordon, 2003).

For the initial-syllable cases under discussion here, the relevant constraint family is a positional version of *ONSET/X that is relativized to the strong position *initial syllable* (σ1) (Smith, 2002, 2003).

(19)   *ONSET/X–σ1   'Onsets in initial syllables do not have sonority level X'
For every segment *a* that is the leftmost onset segment of some syllable σ, if σ is a σ1, then $|a| <$ X
where $|y|$ is the sonority of segment *y*
X is a particular step on the sonority scale

The avoidance of high-sonority onsets in initial syllables can now be seen as a case where the *ONSET/X–σ1 constraint for the lowest prohibited sonority level outranks at least one relevant faithfulness constraint. For example, the Sestu dialect of Campidanian Sardinian (Bolognesi, 1998) avoids glide and rhotic onsets in initial syllables. Where a word-initial onset of one of those sonority classes is expected, on the basis of etymology or dialect comparison, the Sestu form has a prothetic vowel, which causes the problematic consonant to surface in a position other than onset of σ1.

(20)   Initial glide and rhotic onsets avoided in Sestu Campidanian
(a) [arːuβiu]   'red' < Lat. *rubeum*   (b) [ajaju] 'grandfather'
[arːɔða]   'wheel' < Lat. *rota*   [ajaja] 'grandmother'
[arːaðiu]   'radio' < Ital. *radio*   vs. related dialects: [jaju], [jaja]

For this language, the problematic high-sonority onsets are avoided by epenthesis, so *ONSET/GLIDE–σ1 and *ONSET/RHOTIC–σ1 must each be ranked above DEP, the constraint against epenthetic segments (McCarthy and Prince, 1995).

(21)   Ranking for Sestu Campidanian

(a) Crucial ranking for glide case: *ONSET/GLIDE–σ1 >> DEP

/jaju/ 'grandfather'	*ONS/GLI–σ1	*ONS/RHO–σ1	DEP
i. jaju	*!		
☞ ii. ajaju			*

(b) Crucial ranking for rhotic case: *ONSET/RHOTIC–σ1 >> DEP

/ruβiu/ 'red'	*ONS/GLI–σ1	*ONS/RHO–σ1	DEP
i. ruβiu		*!	
☞ ii. arːuβiu			*

The case of Sestu is straightforward, because the set of segment classes banned as onsets in word-initial syllables is a contiguous range of the sonority scale from rhotics up through the highest onset sonority class, glides. However, the pattern seen in Korean, as well as in a number of other languages as mentioned above, introduces a complication. In these languages, high-sonority onsets such as rhotics, or all liquids, are banned, but glide onsets are allowed.

This glide exemption from sonority restrictions on onsets is unexpected given the nature of the *ONSET/X constraint family.[8] Consider the Iglesias dialect of Campidanian Sardinian (Bolognesi, 1998), which differs minimally from Sestu in allowing glide onsets in initial syllables even though rhotic onsets are banned in that position. The appearance of a prothetic vowel in a putatively rhotic-initial word motivates the ranking *ONSET/RHOTIC–σ1 >> DEP, exactly as seen for Sestu in (21b). However, *ONSET/RHOTIC–σ1 >> DEP implies *ONSET/GLIDE–σ1 >> DEP, because glides are higher on the sonority scale than rhotics, and the sonority scale fixes the family-internal ranking of the *ONSET/X constraints. *ONSET/GLIDE–σ1 >> DEP is the ranking exemplified in (21a) for Sestu, but this seems to make the wrong prediction for Iglesias, where the desired winner is [jaju], not *[ajaju] as in Sestu. Moving DEP above *ONSET/GLIDE–σ1 does not solve the problem, since this ranking now incorrectly predicts that rhotic onsets are tolerated just as the higher-sonority glide onsets are.

In Korean as well, the implication is that if *ONSET/RHOTIC–σ1 and *ONSET/LATERAL–σ1 are ranked high enough to have an effect, then the even higher-ranking *ONSET/GLIDE–σ1 should have an effect as well. Contrary to this prediction, however, Korean does allow word-initial glides, as seen above in (6a).

Fortunately, the proposal defended in §3.3, that Korean prepeak glides are actually rimal onglides, provides a way to account for why glides are unexpectedly exempt from restrictions on high-sonority 'onsets'. As defined in

(17) above, *ONSET/X constraints are crucially different from the ONSET constraint in that they do refer explicitly to subsyllabic position: they assign violations for segments of a certain sonority class only when those segments are in the true structural onset position. The idea here is that *ONSET/X constraints connect an actual structural role in the syllable – the onset – with requirements pertaining to sonority level. *ONSET/X is therefore formally quite different from the (now inconveniently named) ONSET constraint, which, according to the definition in §3.2, requires the presence of some prepeak segment but does not make reference to any syllable position for that segment. (Additional implications of this difference between ONSET and *ONSET/X for our understanding of the phonology-phonetics interface are taken up in §3.5 below.)

Once we have recognized the two possible structural positions for prepeak glides, and *ONSET/X has been defined so that it enforces sonority requirements specifically on true onset segments, an explanation becomes possible for why glides are able to escape onset sonority restrictions. Namely, syllable-initial glides in languages that otherwise show the effects of bans on high-sonority onsets avoid violating *ONSET/GLIDE because they are rimal onglides.

This general approach can be applied to the specific case of Korean as follows. Liquid-related constraints of the *ONSET/X–σ1 family are responsible for the nasal realization of the liquid phoneme because they are ranked above the faithfulness constraint IDENT[nasal], which is violated when inputs and outputs differ with respect to [±nasal] (McCarthy and Prince 1995). Specifically, *ONSET/RHOTIC–σ1 dominates IDENT[nasal], prohibiting the rhotic [ɾ] in word-initial position. It may be the case that *ONSET/LATERAL–σ1 dominates IDENT[nasal] as well, but the allophonic alternation between [l] and [ɾ] already restricts [l] to coda position, so the ranking of *ONSET/LATERAL–σ1 cannot be definitively determined. Finally, the fact that word-initial nasal onsets are tolerated shows that *ONSET/NASAL–σ1 is ranked below all relevant faithfulness constraints, including IDENT[nasal]. This ranking is summarized in (22) and exemplified in (23) and (24) below.

(22)   Constraint ranking for the Korean word-initial liquid/nasal alternation

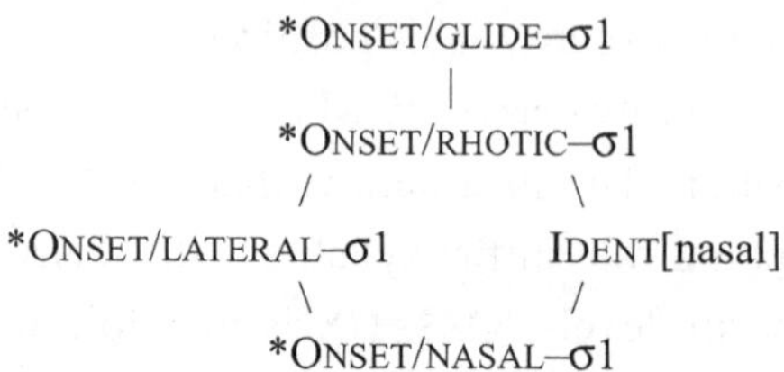

The form /lɛ-il/ [nɛ.il] 'tomorrow' demonstrates the effects of this ranking. The initial liquid is realized as a nasal because a violation of *ONSET/RHOTIC–σ1 (23-i) is worse than a violation of the faithfulness constraint IDENT[nasal] (23-ii). Other liquids do surface as liquids (except in environments where the high-ranking syllable-contact constraints, not discussed here, are relevant; see Davis and Shin for an OT analysis of the syllable-contact effects) because IDENT[nasal] is violated only if a higher-ranking constraint is at stake (23-iii).

(23)   Avoidance of word-initial liquid onsets in Korean

/lɛ-il/ 'tomorrow'	*ONS/ GLI–σ1	*ONS/ RHO–σ1	*ONS/ LAT–σ1	IDENT [nas]	*ONS/ NAS–σ1
i. ɾɛ.il		*!			
☞ ii. nɛ.il				*	*
iii. nɛ.in				**!	*

For glides, however, there is another option. Syllabifying a glide as a true onset does lead to a violation of *ONSET/GLIDE–σ1, which is a fatal violation, as expected from the sonority-based ranking of the *ONSET/X constraints. However, syllabifying a word-initial glide as a rimal onglide results in a candidate that satisfies *ONSET/GLIDE–σ1 without violating any faithfulness constraints.[9] Thus, word-initial glides are tolerated even though other sonorous onsets are prohibited.

(24)   Word-initial glides tolerated

/jaŋ/ 'sheep'	*ONS/ GLI–σ1	*ONS/ RHO–σ1	*ONS/ LAT–σ1	IDENT [nas]	*ONS/ NAS–σ1
i. j{aŋ}	*!				
☞ ii. {jaŋ}					
iii. naŋ				*!	*

For Seoul Korean, the rimal-onglide analysis is not the only possible account for the appearance of word-initial glides despite a general ban on high-sonority onsets in word-initial position. For example, a glide-nasal alternation violates IDENT[cons], while a liquid-nasal alternation does not, so ranking IDENT[cons] above *ONSET/GLIDE–σ1 would allow for the faithful realization of word-initial glides even if they were syllabified in true onset position (Smith, 1997; Flack, 2006). However, settling the controversy over the syllabification of Korean glides (§3.3) by giving them the structure of rimal onglides – a development made possible by the new definition of ONSET adopted here – automatically accounts for the ability of glides to be exempt from sonority-based restrictions on word-initial onsets.

In summary, the availability of the rimal onglide candidate, and the sensitivity of *ONSET/X constraints to subsyllabic structure, explains why glides are sometimes exempt from bans on high-sonority onsets in Seoul Korean and other languages. Treating this alternation as a sonority-based onset restriction relates it to the crosslinguistic preference for low-sonority onsets, particularly in word-initial position. As a result, for the first time, a connection is made between glide and liquid behavior in Korean.

3.5   Implications for the phonetics/phonology interface

The discussion thus far has shown that the head-based definition of ONSET resolves a controversy about how prepeak glides in Korean are syllabified. Moreover, the claim that ONSET makes no reference to syllable-internal structure, while the sonority-based constraint family *ONSET/X does make crucial reference to true onset segments only, allows for an account of the pattern seen in Seoul Korean and other, unrelated languages, in which high-sonority word-initial segments are generally prohibited, but word-initial glides are allowed – an account that relies only on constraints that have phonetically plausible motivations.

Intuitively, ONSET and *ONSET/X constraints have something in common. Crosslinguistically, syllables with onsets are preferred to syllables without onsets, and low-sonority onsets are preferred to high-sonority onsets, as noted in §3.4.2. These two preferences share a functional basis. Namely, there is a perceptual advantage when the speech stream modulates between low and high sonority (e.g., Delgutte, 1997; Ohala and Kawasaki-Fukumori, 1997; Wright, 2004). This is true because, given a constant stimulus, auditory-nerve response decays, a phenomenon known as adaptation. However, adaptation is lessened if spectrally different segments alternate. This happens when vowels are separated by onset consonants; and, the lower the sonority of those consonants the better. (On the high perceptual salience of rapid spectral changes, see also Ohala, 1992; Silverman, 1995; Warner, 1998.)

In other words, the functional motivation behind ONSET is the perceptual advantage gained by interspersing consonants between syllable peaks. It follows that the best onset is a low-sonority onset, so the same functional motivation also underlies *ONSET/X. However, as has been shown above, the two constraints are formally distinct; in particular, they refer to completely separate aspects of syllable structure.

This point turns out to be of interest, because the separation of ONSET and *ONSET/X as formally distinct constraints seems to be a problem for direct-phonetics models of the phonological constraint set. Direct-phonetics models (e.g., Boersma, 1998; Kirchner, 2000; Flemming, 2001; Zhang, 2004), which make a fundamental assumption that phonology is not distinct from phonetics, often propose families of constraints reflecting values along a continuum of some phonetic property. One example is the direct-phonetics constraint LAZY, defined as follows by Kirchner (2004).

> Formally, I assume that for each candidate provided by GEN … the effort cost (a mental estimate of the biomechanical energy required for articulatory production of the candidate) is computed; and LAZY violations are assessed for the candidate based on this effort cost. (314)

Since the complete lack of an onset consonant is even less useful, perceptually speaking, than the presence of a very high-sonority onset, the direct-phonetics approach predicts that ONSET should be formalized as the highest-ranked member of the *ONSET/X family, '*ONSET/Ø'.

However, the attempt to reformulate ONSET as '*ONSET/Ø' fails if, as argued here, ONSET and *ONSET/X evaluate different phonological structures. The head-based ONSET constraint simply cannot be viewed as part of the *ONSET/X family, which evaluates specifically true onset segments.[10] From this, we conclude that ONSET and *ONSET/X are formally distinct, and thus that the mapping from phonetics to constraints is indirect.

It is important to note that evidence against a direct-phonetics view of the universal constraint set is not automatically evidence against a model that incorporates phonetic grounding or phonetic motivation for the constraints in the constraint set. That is, it is logically possible to have a phonetically motivated grammar that is not the same as 'direct phonetics'. For example, phonetic information might be used either to rank, or to filter out from the set of actual constraints, constraints that are stated over formal phonological categories (Archangeli and Pulleyblank, 1994; Hayes, 1999; Steriade, 2001 [though Hayes and Steriade 2004 take a somewhat different perspective]; Smith, 2002). For additional evidence that the effect of phonetics on phonology is indirect or symbolically mediated, see (e.g.) Gerfen (2001); Howe and Pulleyblank (2001); Cohn (2003); Gordon (2004); Flack (2006).

3.6 Conclusions

The head-based definition of the ONSET constraint allows this constraint to be satisfied both by true structural onsets and by rimal onglides. This formal development in turn makes possible a new approach to the syllabification of Korean glides that is able to account for both their 'consonant'-like and their 'vowel'-like behavior, thereby resolving a long-standing controversy: Korean glides are rimal onglides, but this is nevertheless compatible with their ability to resolve hiatus (i.e., satisfy ONSET).

A second advantage to the rimal-onglide account of Korean glides is that an explanation for an apparently unrelated phenomenon – the prohibition on word-initial liquids in Seoul and other South Korean dialects – falls out for free. It is now straightforward to model the initial liquid ban as a sonority-based (which is to say phonetically motivated) restriction; given that glides are rimal, it is unsurprising that they are exempt from sonority-based restrictions on segments that are syllabified as true structural onsets.

In addition to the evidence from Korean that glides satisfy hiatus despite their status as rimal onglides, there is further crosslinguistic evidence that rimal onglides satisfy ONSET. Guugu Yimidhirr (Haviland, 1979; Dixon, 1980), mentioned in §3.4.2, bans initial liquids but not glides – indicating that glides are syllabified as rimal onglides, just as in Korean – while also banning vowel-initial words, due to high-ranking ONSET. If rimal onglides did not satisfy ONSET, we would expect to see glide-initial words banned just as vowel-initial words are. Pitta-Pitta is a similar example (see Smith (2008) for further discussion of both of these languages).

Finally, since ONSET is independent of syllable-internal structure beyond the head/nonhead distinction, but the *ONSET/X constraint family is sensitive to subsyllabic structure, this demonstrates that even constraints with the same fundamental phonetic motivation can be formally distinct entities, which in turn shows that the link between phonetic motivation and phonological constraint is indirect.

Acknowledgments

Many thanks to the following people for comments and discussion: Hyun Kyung Hwang, Ellen Kaisse, Eunsuk Lee, Craig Melchert, Elliott Moreton, John Whitman, and audiences at LSA 2003, CLS 41, Cornell University, and UNC Chapel Hill, as well as two anonymous reviewers. I am also indebted to John McCarthy, Lisa Selkirk and Jaye Padgett for helpful and inspiring discussion at early stages of this project. Finally, portions of §3.5 are based on some of the discussion in Smith (2008).

Notes

1   In a language where a rimal onglide contributes independently to syllable weight, as in Spanish (in cases where another onset consonant precedes; Harris and Kaisse, 1999), it would be dominated by its own mora rather than sharing the mora of the syllable peak.

2   One marginal exception may be the offglide in the diphthong [ɨj], which is described by Martin (1992: 26) and H. M. Sohn (1994: 440) as a spelling pronunciation for orthographic <ɨj> used by some younger speakers, although K. O. Kim (1978: 76–77) describes it instead as a rising diphthong with a back unrounded onglide, [ɯi]. In any case, orthographic <ɨj> in Seoul Korean is more generally pronounced [ɨ] in absolute word-initial position and [i] in other contexts, except that it is [e] in the case of the genitive marker. The other orthographic diphthongs with 'offglides' are consistently pronounced as monophthongs or *rising* diphthongs in Seoul: <əj> as [e], <aj> as [ɛ] or [æ] (a category that has merged with [e] for some speakers), and <oj> as [ø] or [we] (Martin, 1992: 11–12, 24).

3   Martin (1992: 109–110) describes this as a mandatory process: 'The phoneme string /je/ occurs only after a pause; in other positions it is automatically replaced by /e/...' [transcriptions converted to IPA]. However, Yun (2001: 68) states that for his variety of Korean, the deletion process is optional.

4   See also Kim-Renaud (1986: 41) and Iverson and K. H. Kim (1987: 379), who analyze the word-initial and post-C liquid bans as a unified onset ban rather than recognizing a role for syllable contact, but nevertheless point out the connection to sonority reduction as a plausible phonetic motivation for avoiding liquids.

5   Because this is an allophonic alternation, driven entirely by markedness constraints, the UR cannot be uniquely established as /l/ or /ɾ/ (see Prince and Smolensky 2004: §225 on richness of the base) – although it does contrast with /n/, which shows that the UR for the liquid phoneme must be distinct from /n/. For expository convenience, this discussion will follow conventional practice and represent the liquid phoneme as /l/. However, because this alternation is allophonic, it must be the case that the faithfulness constraints that enforce the [l]~[ɾ] contrast are ranked low enough to be irrelevant. Therefore, even if inputs were to contain /ɾ/ instead of /l/, the correct output candidate would still be chosen.

6   Intervocalic liquids, which are subject neither to syllable-contact effects nor to restrictions on onsets in word-initial position, simply surface as liquids. Thus, the approach adopted here does not require intervocalic liquids to be ambisyllabic – contra the proposals in, for example, S. K. Kang (1991) and Smith (1997).

7   Flack (2006) argues against an acoustically driven 'licensing-by-cue' approach to an initial (and postconsonantal) lateral ban in three Australian languages,

Ngandi, Jingulu, and Warlpiri, concluding that a sonority-based approach is better motivated.

8   An analogous point can be made if stringency constraints (Prince, 1997; de Lacy, 2004) are used in place of this universally ranked constraint scale; see Smith (2008) for discussion.

9   The rimal onglide candidate does violate constraints against diphthongs, and constraints against rising diphthongs, so a language that allows rimal onglide syllabification must rank those constraints below the relevant faithfulness constraints. In languages like Sestu Campidanian, that do not use the rimal onglide syllabification, constraints against (rising) diphthongs are ranked higher in the hierarchy. As expected from factorial typology (Prince and Smolensky, 2004: 103), languages vary with respect to this choice; languages may even use different structures for different glides (Davis and Hammond, 1995) or under different circumstances (Harris and Kaisse, 1999), according to the fine details of the constraint ranking.

10   Another argument that ONSET and *ONSET/X constraints are formally different is presented in Smith (2008). To summarize briefly, the ranking of ONSET with respect to the different members of the *ONSET/X constraint family varies from language to language; thus, ONSET cannot be a member of that constraint family.

References

Ahn, S.-C. (1985) *The Interplay of Phonology and Morphology in Korean.* Doctoral dissertation, UIUC.

Archangeli, D. and Pulleyblank, D. (1994) *Grounded Phonology.* Cambridge, MA: MIT Press.

Baertsch, K. (1998) Onset sonority distance constraints through local conjunction. In M. C. Gruber, D. Higgins, K. S. Olson and T. Wysocki (eds) *Chicago Linguistic Society 34* vol. 2, 1–15. Chicago, IL: CLS.

Barlow, J. (1997) *A Constraint-Based Account of Syllable Onsets: Evidence from Developing Systems.* Doctoral dissertation, Indiana University.

Blake, B. J. (1979) Pitta-Pitta. In R. M. W. Dixon and B. J. Blake (eds) *Handbook of Australian Languages* vol. 1, 183–242. Amsterdam: John Benjamins.

Blake, B. J. and Breen, J. G. (1971) *The Pitta-Pitta Dialects.* Melbourne: Monash University.

Blevins, J. (1994) A place for lateral in the feature geometry. *Journal of Linguistics* 30(2): 301–348.

Blevins, J. (1995) The syllable in phonological theory. In J. Goldsmith (ed.) *Handbook of Phonological Theory* 206–244. Oxford: Blackwell.

Boersma, P. (1998) *Functional Phonology.* The Hague: Holland Academic Graphics.

Bolognesi, R. (1998) *The Phonology of Campidanian Sardinian.* Amsterdam: HIL.

Cho, Y.-M. Y. (1997) Liquid specification in Korean as geminate alterability. In S. Kuno, J. Whitman, Y.-S. Kang, I.-H. Lee, Joan Maling and Y. Kim (eds) *Harvard Studies in Korean Linguistics VII* 78–92. Cambridge, MA: Harvard University and Seoul: Hanshin.

Cho, Y.-M. Y. (2000) Deriving optionality in Korean glide formation. In M. Nakayama and C. J. Quinn, Jr. (eds) *Japanese/Korean Linguistics 9* 88–99. Stanford, CA: CSLI.

Clements, G. N. (1990) The role of the sonority cycle in core syllabification. In J. C. Kingston and M. E. Beckman (eds) *Papers in Laboratory Phonology I: Between the Grammar and Physics of Speech* 283–333. Cambridge: Cambridge University Press.

Clements, G. N. and Keyser, S. J. (1983) *CV Phonology: A Generative Theory of the Syllable.* Cambridge, MA: MIT Press.

Cohn, A. C. (2003) Phonological structure and phonetic duration: the role of the mora. *Working Papers of the Cornell Phonetics Laboratory* 15: 69–100.

Davis, S. and Hammond, M. (1995) On the status of onglides in American English. *Phonology* 12: 159–182.

Davis, S. and Shin, S.-H. (1999) The syllable contact constraint in Korean: an optimality-theoretic analysis. *Journal of East Asian Linguistics* 8: 285–312.

de Lacy, P. (2001) Markedness in prominent positions. In O. Matushansky, A. Costa, J. Martín-González, L. Nathan and A. Szczegielniak (eds), *Proceedings of HUMIT 2000.* MIT Working Papers in Linguistics 40 53–66. Cambridge, MA: MITWPL.

de Lacy, P. (2004) Markedness conflation in Optimality Theory. *Phonology* 21: 145–199.

Delgutte, B. (1997) Auditory neural processing of speech. In W. J. Hardcastle and J. Laver (eds) *The Handbook of Phonetic Sciences* 507–538. Oxford: Blackwell.

Dell, F. and Elmedlaoui, M. (1985) Syllabic consonants and syllabification in Imdlawn Tashlhiyt Berber. *Journal of African Languages and Linguistics* 7(2): 105–130.

Dell, F. and Elmedlaoui, M. (1988) Syllabic consonants in Berber: some new evidence. *Journal of African Languages and Linguistics* 10(1): 1–17.

Dench, A. (1991) Panyjima. In R. M. W. Dixon and B. J. Blake (eds) *Handbook of Australian Languages* vol. 4, 125–243. Melbourne: Oxford University Press.

Dixon, R. M. W. (1980) *The Languages of Australia.* Cambridge: Cambridge University Press.

Dixon, R. M. W. (1991) Mbabaram. In R. M. W. Dixon and B. J. Blake (eds) *Handbook of Australian Languages* vol. 4, 348–402. Melbourne: Oxford University Press.

Duanmu, S. (1990) *A Formal Study of Syllable, Tone, Stress and Domain in Chinese Languages.* Doctoral dissertation, Cambridge, MA: MIT.

Eisner, J. (1997) What constraints should OT allow? Paper presented at the LSA Annual Meeting; Chicago, 4 January.

Flack, K. (2006) Lateral phonotactics in Australian languages. In L. Bateman and C. Ussery (eds) *North East Linguistic Society 35* 187–199. Amherst, MA: GLSA.

Flemming, E. (2001) Scalar and categorical phenomena in a unified model of phonetics and phonology. *Phonology* 18: 7–44.

Gerfen, C. (2001) A critical view of Licensing by Cue: the case of Andalusian Spanish. In L. Lombardi (ed.) *Segmental Phonology in Optimality Theory* 183–205. Cambridge: Cambridge University Press.

Gnanadesikan, A. (2004) Markedness and faithfulness constraints in child phonology. In R. Kager, J. Pater and W. Zonneveld (eds) *Constraints in Phonological Acquisition* 73–108. Cambridge: Cambridge University Press.

Gordon, M. (2003) The puzzle of onset-sensitive stress: a perceptually-driven approach. In G. Garding and M. Tsujimura (eds) *Proceedings of the 22nd West Coast Conference on Formal Linguistics* 217–230. Somerville, MA: Cascadilla Press.

Gordon, M. (2004) Syllable weight. In B. Hayes, R. Kirchner and D. Steriade (eds) *Phonetically Based Phonology* 277–312. Cambridge: Cambridge University Press.

Han, E. (1990) Glide formation in Korean. In H. Hoji (ed.) *Japanese/Korean Linguistics* 173–186. Stanford, CA: CSLI.

Han, E. (1993) Resolving an ordering paradox: lateralization and delateralization in Korean. In S. Kuno, J. Whitman, I.-H. Lee, J. Maling and Y. Kim (eds) *Harvard Studies in Korean Linguistics V* 159–69. Cambridge, MA: Harvard University and Seoul: Hanshin.

Harris, J. W. and Kaisse, E. M. (1999) Palatal vowels, glides and obstruents in Argentinean Spanish. *Phonology* 16: 117–190.

Haviland, J. (1979) Guugu Yimidhirr. In R.M.W. Dixon and B. J. Blake (eds) *Handbook of Australian Languages* vol. 1, 27–180. Amsterdam: John Benjamins.

Hayes, B. (1989) Compensatory lengthening in moraic phonology. *Linguistic Inquiry* 20(2): 253–306.

Hayes, B. (1999) Phonetically driven phonology: the role of Optimality Theory and inductive grounding. In M. Darnell, E. A. Moravcsik, F. Newmeyer, M. Noonan and K. M. Wheatley (eds) *Formalism and Functionalism in Linguistics* vol. I, 243–85. Amsterdam: Benjamins.

Hayes, B. and Steriade, D. (2004) Introduction: the phonetic bases of phonological markedness. In B. Hayes, R. Kirchner and D. Steriade (eds) *Phonetically Based Phonology* 1–33. Cambridge: Cambridge University Press.

Howe, D. and Pulleyblank, D. (2001) Patterns and timing of glottalisation. *Phonology* 18: 45–80.

Itô, J. (1986) *Syllable Theory in Prosodic Phonology.* Doctoral dissertation, University of Massachusetts, Amherst. [New York: Garland, 1988.]

Itô, J. (1989) A prosodic theory of epenthesis. *Natural Language and Linguistic Theory* 7: 217–259.

Iverson, G. K. and Kim, K.-H. (1987) Underspecification and hierarchical feature representation in Korean consonantal phonology. In A. Bosch, B. Need and E. Schiller (eds) *Chicago Linguistic Society 23* vol. 2, 182–198. Chicago, IL: CLS.

Iverson, G. and Sohn, H.-S. (1994) Liquid representation in Korean. In Y.-K. Kim-Renaud (ed.) *Theoretical Issues in Korean Linguistics* 77–100. Stanford, CA: CSLI.

Kager, R. (1999) *Optimality Theory.* Cambridge: Cambridge University Press.

Kahn, D. (1976) *Syllable-Based Generalizations in English Phonology.* Doctoral dissertation, MIT. [New York: Garland, 1980.]

Kang, K.-S. (2003) The status of onglides in Korean: evidence from speech errors. *Studies in Phonetics, Phonology and Morphology* 9(1): 1–15.

Kang, S. K. (1991) Moraic representation of ambisyllabicity: evidence from Korean. *Studies in the Linguistic Sciences* 21: 89–100.

Karttunen, L. (1998) The proper treatment of optimality theory in computational phonology. In L. Karttunen and K. Oflazer (eds) *Finite-State Methods in Natural Language Processing 1998* 1–12. Ankara: Meteksan A.Ş.

Kaye, J. D. and Lowenstamm, J. (1984) De la syllabicité. In F. Dell, D. Hirst and J.-R. Vergnaud (eds) *Forme sonore du langage* 123–159. Paris: Hermann.

Kim, C.-W. (1968) The vowel system of Korean. *Language* 44(3): 516–527.

Kim, C.-W and Kim, H.-Y. (1991) The *character* of Korean glides. *Studies in the Linguistic Sciences* 21(2): 113–125.

Kim, H.-Y. (1998) Prenucleus glides in Korean. *Studies in the Linguistic Sciences* 28: 113–135.

Kim, K.-O. (1978) Vowel system in Korean revisited. In C.-W. Kim (ed.) *Papers in Korean Linguistics: Proceedings of the Symposium on Korean Linguistics* 75–83. Columbia, SC: Hornbeam Press.

Kim, Y.-S. (1984) *Aspects of Korean Morphology.* Doctoral dissertation, University of Texas, Austin.

Kim-Renaud, Y.-K. (1986) The syllable in Korean phonology. In *Studies in Korean Linguistics* 31–44. Seoul: Hanshin.

Kirchner, R. (2000) Geminate inalterability and lenition. *Language* 76: 509–545.

Kirchner, R. (2004) Consonant lenition. In B. Hayes, R. Kirchner and D. Steriade (eds) *Phonetically Based Phonology* 313–345. Cambridge: Cambridge University Press.

Lee, B.-G. (1982) A well-formedness condition on syllable structure. In Linguistic Society of Korea (ed.) *Linguistics in the Morning Calm* 489–506. Seoul: Hanshin.

Lee, I. and Ramsey, S. R. (2000) *The Korean Language.* Albany, NY: State University of New York Press.

Lee, Y. (1994) Onset analysis of Korean on-glides. In Y.-K. Kim-Renaud (ed.) *Theoretical Issues in Korean Linguistics* 133–156. Stanford, CA: CSLI.

Lee, Y. (1997) Glide formation and compensatory lengthening in Korean verbal conjugation. *Studies in Phonetics, Phonology, and Morphology* 3: 223–246.

Levi, S. V. (2004) *The Representation of Underlying Glides: A Cross-Linguistic Study.* Doctoral dissertation, University of Washington.

Levin [Blevins], J. (1985) *A Metrical Theory of Syllabicity.* Doctoral dissertation, MIT.

Liberman, M. and Prince, A. (1977) On stress and linguistic rhythm. *Linguistic Inquiry* 8: 249–336.

Lynch, J. (1983) On the Kuman 'liquids'. *Languages and Linguistics in Melanesia* 14: 98–112.

Martin, S. E. (1954) *Korean Morphophonemics.* Baltimore, MD: Linguistic Society of America.

Martin, S. E. (1992) *A Reference Grammar of Korean.* Rutland, VT: Tuttle.

McCarthy, J. (2003) Comparative markedness. *Theoretical Linguistics* 29: 1–51.

McCarthy, J. and Prince, A. (1986) *Prosodic Morphology.* Ms., University of Massachusetts and Brandeis University.

McCarthy, J. and Prince, A. (1993) Generalized alignment. *Yearbook of Morphology* 1993: 79–153.

McCarthy, J. and Prince, A. (1995) Faithfulness and reduplicative identity. In J. N. Beckman, L. Walsh Dickey and S. Urbanczyk (eds) *Papers in Optimality Theory.* University of Massachusetts Occasional Papers 18 250–384. Amherst, MA: GLSA.

McDonough, J. (1995) Gemination and the prosodic enhancement strategy. In J. N. Beckman (ed.) *North East Linguistic Society 25* vol. 1, 347–359. Amherst, MA: GLSA.

Murray, R. W. and Venneman, T. (1983) Sound change and syllable structure in Germanic phonology. *Language* 59: 514–528.

Ohala, J. J. (1992) The segment: primitive or derived? In G. J. Docherty and D. R. Ladd (eds) *Papers in Laboratory Phonology II: Gesture, Segment, Prosody* 166–183. Cambridge: Cambridge University Press.

Ohala, J. and Kawasaki-Fukumori, H. (1997) Alternatives to the sonority hierarchy for explaining segmental sequential constraints. In S. Eliasson and E. Jahr (eds) *Language and Its Ecology* 343–365. Berlin: Mouton.

Poppe, N. (1970) *Mongolian Language Handbook.* Washington, DC: Center for Applied Linguistics.

Prince, A. (1997) Stringency and anti-Paninian hierarchies. Handout from LSA Linguistic Institute, Cornell University.

Prince, A. and Smolensky, P. (2004) *Optimality Theory: Constraint Interaction in Generative Grammar.* Oxford: Blackwell. [Ms., Rutgers University and University of Colorado, Boulder, 1993.]

Ramsey, S. R. (1987) *The Languages of China.* Princeton, NJ: Princeton University Press.

Ridouane, R. (2008) Syllables without vowels: phonetic and phonological evidence from Tashlhiyt Berber. *Phonology* 25: 321–359.

Rosenthall, S. (1994) *Vowel/Glide Alternation in a Theory of Constraint Interaction.* Doctoral dissertation, University of Massachusetts, Amherst.

Rubach, J. (1998) A Slovak argument for the onset/rime distinction. *Linguistic Inquiry* 29 (1): 168–179.

Selkirk, E. (1978) On prosodic structure and its relation to syntactic structure. In T. Fretheim (ed.) *Nordic Prosody II* 111–140. Trondheim: Tapir.

Selkirk, E. (1982) The syllable. In H. van der Hulst and N. Smith (eds) *The Structure of Phonological Representations* vol. 2, 337–383. Dordrecht: Foris.

Selkirk, E. (1984) On the major class features and syllable theory. In M. Aronoff and R. T. Oehrle (eds) *Language Sound Structure* 107–136. Cambridge, MA: MIT Press.

Selkirk, E. (1995) The prosodic structure of function words. In J. N. Beckman, L. Walsh Dickey and S. Urbanczyk (eds) *Papers in Optimality Theory.* University of Massachusetts Occasional Papers 18 439–469. Amherst, MA: GLSA.

Shim, M. (1997) *The Vowel Phonology of the Kyongsang Dialect of Korean.* Doctoral dissertation, Indiana University.

Silverman, D. (1995) *Phasing and Recoverability.* Doctoral dissertation, UCLA. [New York: Garland, 1997.]

Smith, J. L. (1997) Markedness and liquid alternations in Korean: Implications for the representation of ambisyllabicity. Poster presented at the Hopkins Optimality Workshop/University of Maryland Mayfest; Baltimore, 11 May.

Smith, J. L. (2002) *Phonological Augmentation in Prominent Positions.* Doctoral dissertation, University of Massachusetts, Amherst. [New York: Routledge, 2005.]

Smith, J. L. (2003) Onset sonority constraints and subsyllabic structure. Ms., University of North Carolina, Chapel Hill. [Revised version of a paper presented at Phonologica 2002, University of Vienna, 3 November 2002.]

Smith, J. L. (2008) Phonological constraints are not directly phonetic. In R. L. Edwards, P. J. Midtlyng, C. L. Sprague and K. G. Stensrud (eds) *Chicago Linguistic Society 41* vol. 1, 457–471.

Sohn, H.-M. (1994) *Korean.* London: Routledge.

Sohn, H.-M. (1999) *The Korean Language.* Cambridge: Cambridge University Press.

Sohn, H.-S. (1987a) On the representation of vowels and diphthongs and their merger in Korean. In A. Bosch, B. Need and E. Schiller (eds) *Chicago Linguistic Society 23* vol. 2, 307–23.

Sohn, H.-S. (1987b) *Underspecification in Korean Phonology.* Doctoral dissertation, UIUC.

Steriade, D. (1982) *Greek Prosodies and the Nature of Syllabification.* Doctoral dissertation, MIT.

Steriade, D. (1988a) Reduplication and syllable transfer in Sanskrit and elsewhere. *Phonology* 5: 73–155.

Steriade, D. (1988b) Review of *CV Phonology: A Generative Theory of the Syllable. Language* 64: 118–129.

Steriade, D. (2001) Directional asymmetries in place assimilation: a perceptual account. In E. Hume and K. Johnson (eds) *The Role of Speech Perception in Phonology* 219–250. New York: Academic Press.

Trefry, D. (1969) *A Comparative Study of Kuman and Pawaian.* Pacific Linguistics B-13. Canberra: ANU.

Um, Y. (2003) An ordering paradox as constraint interaction: alternation of *n* and *l* in Korean. *Studies in Phonetics, Phonology and Morphology* 9: 111–133.

Warner, N. L. (1998) *The Role of Dynamic Cues in Speech Perception, Spoken Word Recognition, and Phonological Universals.* Doctoral dissertation, University of California, Berkeley.

Wright, R. (2004) A review of perceptual cues and cue robustness. In B. Hayes, R. Kirchner and D. Steriade (eds) *Phonetically Based Phonology* 34–57. Cambridge: Cambridge University Press.

Yun, Y. (2001) Glides in Korean syllables. *University of Washington Working Papers in Linguistics* 20: 57–98.

Zec, D. (1988) *Sonority Constraints on Prosodic Structure.* Doctoral dissertation, Stanford University. [New York: Garland, 1994.]

Zhang, J. (2004) The role of contrast-specific and language-specific phonetics in contour tone distribution. In B. Hayes, R. Kirchner and D. Steriade (eds) *Phonetically Based Phonology* 157–190. Cambridge: Cambridge University Press.

Section 2
Foot and Prosodic Word

4 The end of the word in Makassar languages*

Hasan Basri,[a] Ellen Broselow,[b] and Daniel Finer[b]

4.1 Introduction

The Makassar languages, spoken in South Sulawesi (Celebes), Indonesia, include Makassarese (also called Lakiung), Selayarese, and Konjo.[1] All three languages are characterized by distinct classes of affixes which exhibit various differences in phonological patterning, some of which are illustrated by the Konjo data in (1):

(1) Konjo

	a. díŋiŋ	'cool'
	b. diŋíŋi	'make cool' (*-i* transitivizer)
	c. díŋiŋŋi	'he/she/it/they is/are cold' (*-i* absolutive)

While the two affixes in (1b) and (1c) are segmentally identical, they are associated with different phonological effects. First, both the bare stem (1a) and the form affixed with the transitivizing suffix (1b) receive (normal) penultimate stress, while the third-person absolutive affix in (1c) falls outside the stress domain. Second, the stem-final nasal is realized as a singleton before the transitivizer in (1b) but as a geminate before the absolutive marker in (1c). We will argue, following earlier proposals, that the distinct phonological patterns associated with the two affix classes reflect the different ways in which the affixes are incorporated into prosodic structure (Mithun and Basri, 1986; Aronoff *et al.*, 1987; Friberg and Friberg, 1991; McCarthy and Prince, 1994; Basri, 1999; Selkirk, 1999; Basri *et al.*, 2000). Affixes like the transi-

[a] Hasan Basri: University of Tadulako, Palu, Central Sulawesi.
[b] Ellen Broselow and Daniel Finer: Stony Brook University Department of Linguistics, Stony Book, NY. Email: ebroselow@notes.cc.sunysb.edu

tivizing *-i* are true suffixes, which adjoin to a stem and form part of the same morphosyntactic and prosodic word as their host. Affixes like the absolutive *-i* are phrasal clitics which fall outside the morphosyntactic and prosodic word.

Makassarese and Selayarese have been the focus of considerable attention (Mithun and Basri, 1986; Aronoff *et al.*,1987; McCarthy and Prince, 1994; Basri, 1999; Selkirk, 1999; Basri *et al.*, 2000), much of it directed at the interface between morphosyntactic and prosodic structure. While Konjo shares with Selayarese and Makassarese many of the patterns distinguishing suffixes and clitics, Konjo exhibits additional complex patterns involving gemination that are not attested in the other two languages. We will argue that the Konjo gemination data provide additional support for the analysis of the relationship between morphosyntactic and prosodic structure that has been proposed for the other two languages.

We begin with a review of the suffix/clitic contrasts in Makassarese and Selayarese, noting similarities and differences among the three languages. In Section 4.3 we outline the Konjo gemination facts and offer an analysis of these patterns in terms of constraints making reference to right edges of prosodic words (PWds) and right edges of stems. We argue that the gemination found at the right edge of a PWd in Konjo is reminiscent of the phenomenon of intrusive [r] found in many dialects of English (McCarthy, 1993).

4.2   Suffixes vs. clitics in Makassar languages

In this section we review evidence for the morphosyntactic and prosodic structure of suffixes and clitics in Makassarese, Selayarese and Konjo. We propose an analysis of the behavior of these affixes with respect to stress, epenthesis, and the alternation of velar and glottal stop, grounded in different structures.

4.2.1 Syntactic behavior

The differing behaviors of suffixes and clitics with respect to stress and gemination, illustrated in (1), as well as the other differences in phonological behavior that will be discussed in the following sections correlate with a difference in syntactic patterning.

The class of true suffixes includes transitivizers, comparatives and benefactives, while the class of phrasal clitics includes absolutive markers and aspectuals. While true suffixes always appear attached to a stem, phrasal clitics are mobile, generally appearing in sentential second position (Friberg, 1996; Basri, 1999; Finer, 2000, 2002). For example, the Konjo and Selayarese absolutives appear following the verb in (2a,3a) but following the fronted prepositional phrase in (2b,3b). Interlinear glosses have been regularized, using the following abbreviations: ERG (ergative), ABS (absolutive), ITR (intransitive), TR (transitive), PREP (preposition), DEF (definite) and COMP (comparative).

(2) Konjo Phrasal Clitics (Friberg, 1996; Basri field notes)

    a. am-malli-**ko**   juku? ri   pasara   sikarie?
        ITR- *buy*-2ABS *fish* PREP *market* *yesterday*
        'You bought fish at (the) market yesterday'

    b. ri pasara-**ko**   am-malli juku? sikarie?
        PREP *market*- 2ABS ITR- *buy fish*   *yesterday*
        'At (the) market, you bought fish yesterday'

(3) Makassarese (Basri field notes, 1998)

    a. am-malli-**a?**   juku? ri   pasarak-a   subaŋŋi
        ITR-*buy*-1ABS *fish*   prep *market*-DEF *yesterday*
        'I bought fish at (the) market yesterday.'

    b. ri pasarak-**a?**   am-malli juku? subaŋŋi
        PREP *market*-1ABS ITR-*buy* *fish*   *yesterday*
        'At (the) market, I bought fish yesterday'

Similarly, in Selayarese the second person absolutive in (3) may appear following a verb, a preposition, or an auxiliary verb:

(4) Selayarese (Basri, 1999; Finer, 2002)

    a la-taro-**i**   loka-ñjo   rinni
       3ERG-*put*-3ABS *banana*-DEF *here*
       'He put the bananas here'

    b. rinni-**i**   la-taro   loka-ñjo
       here-3ABS 3ERG-*put banana*-DEF
       'He put the bananas here'

    c. minaŋ-**i**   rinni la-taro   loka- ñjo
       used to-3ABS *here* 3ERG-*put* *banana*-DEF
       'He used to put the bananas here'

A representative list of suffixes and clitics, classified both according to their syntactic patterning (mobility for clitics, fixed position for suffixes) and their phonological patterning (inside the stress domain for suffixes, outside the stress domain for clitics), appears below:

(5) true suffixes (fixed position; inside stress domain)
    a. Selayarese: *-aŋ* (comparative; benefactive) *-i* (transitivizer; plural)
    b. Makassarese: *-aŋ* (comparative; benefactive), *-i* (transitivizer)
    c. Konjo: *-aŋ* (comparative; benefactive; nominalizer)
                          -i (transitivizer; prohibitivizer; perpetualizer)
                          -a (warning)

(6) phrasal clitics (mobile; outside stress domain)
    a. Selayarese: Absolutives
                          -a (first person singular)
                          -kaŋ (first person plural, exclusive)
                          -ko (second person singular)
                          -ki (second person honorific; first person plural, inclusive)
                          -i (third person singular; third person plural)
                      Aspectuals
                          -mo (used with second person, third person, first plural, excl)
                          -ma (used with first person singular, first person plural, incl)
    b. Makassarese: Absolutives
                          -aʔ (first person singular)
                          -ko (second person singular)
                          -ki (second person honorific; first person plural)
                          -i (third person singular; third person plural)
                      Aspectual: *-ma*
    c. Konjo: Absolutives
                          -a (first person singular)
                          -ko (second person singular)
                          -ki (second person honorific)
                          -i (third person)
                      Aspectual: *-ma*

4.2.2 Prosodic structure

We will assume that true suffixes attach directly to a stem to form a single morphosyntactic word, a process designated *affixation to stem* by Selkirk (1999). Phrasal clitics, in contrast, are not part of the morphosyntactic word;

they constitute functional category items (FNC) which attach directly to the phonological phrase (Selkirk's (1999) *affixation to word*). Thus, a morphosyntactic word (MWord) constitutes a prosodic word (PWord), and clitics are independent of their stems in terms of both morphosyntactic and prosodic word structure. The relationship between the morphosyntactic and prosodic structures is dictated by alignment constraints such as the following, from Selkirk (1995):

(7) Prosodic Word Alignment

   Align (PWd, L/R; Lex L/R): The left/right edge of a prosodic word must be aligned with the left/right edge of a lexical category.

Exemplary structures for the Konjo forms (1b) *diníŋi* (*diŋiŋ* 'cool/cold' plus transitivizing suffix -*i*) and (1c) *díŋiŋŋi* (*diŋiŋ* plus third person absolutive clitic -*i*) are given below:

(8) Morphosyntactic and prosodic structure

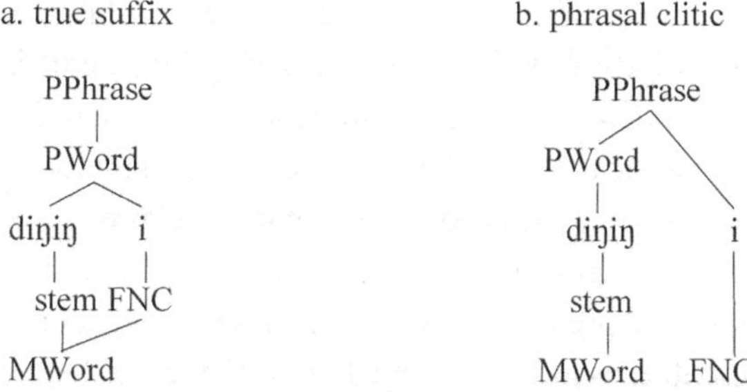

In the following sections we will examine the behavior of suffixes and clitics with respect to a number of phonological patterns: stress, vowel epenthesis, consonant place alternations, and consonant gemination, and will argue that the different patterns exhibited by suffixes and clitics are consistent with the morphosyntactic and prosodic structures posited above.

4.2.3 Stress

Stress in all three languages normally falls on the penultimate syllable, regardless of syllable makeup, as illustrated by data from Selayarese:

(9)   Selayarese
      a. sampúlo   'ten'
      b. palóla   'eggplant'
      c. balíkaʔ   'arm'
      d. barámbaŋ   'chest'
      d. kalihára   'ant'
      e. kalumánti   'big black ant'
      f. katiŋálo   'fly'

Stress may be analyzed as the realization of a bisyllabic trochaic foot aligned with the right edge of the PWd. We assume the following constraints:

(10)   a. FTBIN, FTFORM=TROCH: All feet are bisyllabic and trochaic.
      b. ALIGN (PWD, R, FT, R) : The right edge of a prosodic word must be aligned with the right edge of a foot.

The constraints requiring feet to be bisyllabic and trochaic are undominated in these languages. All lexical category words contain at least two syllables, and monosyllabic borrowed words are augmented to reach the bisyllabic minimum (Basri, 1999; Broselow, 1999; Friberg and Friberg, 1991), consistent with the requirement that a lexical word must also be a prosodic word.[2]

As mentioned above, true suffixes fall inside the stress domain while phrasal clitics fall outside it. Again, this is consistent with the claim that while the stem plus suffix combination constitutes a single prosodic word, clitics do not form a prosodic word with a preceding stem. Below, curly brackets indicate PWd edges, while parentheses indicate foot edges. Suffixes are separated from the preceding material by a dash, while clitics are preceded by =:

(11)   a. Selayarese
      (bámbaŋ)}   'hot'
      bam(báŋ-i)}   'make hot'   (*-i* TR)
      (bámbaŋŋ)}=i   'he is hot'   (=*i* 3rd person ABS)

      b. Makassarese
      (lómpo)}   'big'
      lom(pó-aŋ)}   'bigger'   (*-aŋ* COMP)
      (lómpo)}=ma=ko   'you are already big'   (=*ma* aspectual, =*ko* 2 sg. ABS)

      c. Konjo
      (hájiʔ)}[3]   'good'
      ha(jík-aŋ)}   'better'   (*-aŋ* COMP)
      (hájiʔ)}=a   'I am good'   (=*a* ABS)

The right PWd boundaries, represented by curly brackets, are aligned with the right edge of the bisyllabic trochaic foot that determines the location of stress. Phrasal clitics are therefore not part of the PWd containing the stem. These clitics cannot, however, constitute PWds on their own. Clitics are monosyllabic and therefore fall below the minimal word size. Furthermore, even a sequence of two clitics (as in the Makassarese example in (11b) *lómpo}* *=ma=ko* 'you are already big'), which could in principle support a bisyllabic foot, fails to attract stress. The absence of stress on clitic sequences is consistent with the structure posited in (8b) in which a clitic is part of the phonological phrase but not part of a prosodic word: a metrical foot must be aligned with the right edge of a prosodic word, but the clitic sequence contains no PWd edge.

4.2.4 Copy vowel epenthesis

A second difference between suffixes and clitics involves the appearance of epenthetic vowels. As has been well established (Mithun and Basri, 1986; Aronoff *et al.*, 1987; Friberg and Friberg, 1991; McCarthy, 1998; Alderete, 1999b; Broselow, 1999, 2008), the final vowel of words with antepenultimate stress is epenthetic. Stems undergoing vowel epenthesis share three characteristics: they constitute the only monomorphemic words with antepenultimate rather than penultimate stress; their final syllable begins with one of the three consonants [r,l,s]; and they end in a vowel which is identical to the vowel preceding this [r,l,s]:

(12) Selayarese r/l/s-final stems

a. sáhala	/sahal/	'profit'
b. lámbere	/lamber/	'long'
d. sússulu	/sussul/	'burn'
e. pá?risi	/pá?ris/	'painful'
f. maŋkásara	/maŋkasar/	'Makassar'

Vowel epenthesis after stem-final [r,l,s] is motivated by the fact that the only permitted word-final codas in all three languages are velar nasal and glottal stop. (Word-internally, a coda nasal is homorganic with a following consonant, and a sequence of glottal stop-voiceless consonant is realized as gemination of the second consonant.) The restrictions on possible codas prevent stems ending in [r,l,s] from surfacing faithfully, and these stems undergo copy vowel epenthesis when the stem-final consonant would otherwise surface in coda position.[4] The epenthetic status of the final copy vowel is supported by the disappearance of this vowel before a vowel-initial suffix. Lexical vowels, in contrast, remain before vowel-initial suffixes:

(13) Epenthetic vs. Lexical Vowels (Selayarese)
    a. Epenthetic vowel
        lámbere   'long'   /lamber/
        lambér-aŋ   'longer'   /lamber-aŋ/
    b. Lexical vowel
        tirére   'thirsty'   /tirere/
        tireré-aŋ   'thirstier'   /tirere-aŋ/

In Makassarese, both a copy vowel and a word-final glottal stop are inserted in [r,l,s]-final forms. We discuss the insertion of glottal stop in Section 4.2.5.2. Aside from this difference, the three languages repair [r,l,s]-final stems in the same manner:

(14)   a. Selayarese: bótolo   'bottle'   /botol/
        b. Konjo: bótolo   'bottle'   /botol/
        c. Makassarese: bótolo?   'bottle'   /botol/

Further evidence for the analysis of forms with antepenultimate stress as derived from consonant-final stems is the fact that the presence of [r,l,s] flanked by identical vowels is a necessary but not sufficient condition for antepenultimate stress (for example, alongside Selayarese *sáhala* 'profit' (12a) we find *sahála* 'sea cucumber'). We adopt the analysis of the connection between antepenultimate stress and word-final epenthesis suggested by Alderete (1999a, 1999b), which relies on the following constraint banning epenthetic vowels from the main stress foot:

(15) HEAD-DEP (Alderete, 1999a, 1999b; see also Broselow, 1999, 2008):
    Every vowel contained in the head foot in the output must have a correspondent in the input.

This constraint dominates ALIGN-R (PWD, FT), and therefore chooses the footing *(bóto)lo̠}*, in which the main foot contains only lexical vowels, over **bo(tólo)}*, with normal penultimate stress:

(16) Stress with epenthetic vowels

/botol/ 'bottle'	FtBin, Ft Troch	Head-Dep	Align(PWd,R, Ft, R)
a. bo(tólo)		*!	
☞b. (bóto)lo			*

The interesting feature of copy vowel epenthesis for the purposes of this paper involves the behavior of [r,l,s]-final stems before true suffixes and clitics. In all three languages, an epenthetic vowel is present before a clitic, even when the clitic begins with a vowel. Below we provide data from Selayarese and Konjo, postponing discussion of the parallel Makassarese data to the following section:

(17) Selayarese

  a. lámbusu} 'straight'   (/lambus/)
  b. lambús-aŋ} 'straighter'
  c. lámbusu}=a 'I am straight'

(18) Konjo

  a. jámmara} 'dirty'   (/jamar/)
  b. jammárr-i} 'make dirty'
  c. jámmara}=i 'he is dirty'

The gemination of [r] before the transitivizing suffix in Konjo is discussed in section 4.3. The question we focus on at this point is why vowel epenthesis is found in (17c) and (18c), when [r,l,s] could simply be syllabified as onsets to the following clitic-initial vowel (that is, why (17c) and (18c) are not realized as *lambus-a and *jammar-i, respectively.[5]

To account for this, we adopt the suggestion of Selkirk (1999) that a set of Output-Output constraints (Benua, 1995) demands identity between the isolation form of a morphosyntactic word and all its surface exponents (that is, forms containing the same syntactic features). The retention of the epenthetic vowel in the preclitic form is due to the following constraint:

(19) O-O(Word)Max(V): Where two strings S and S' are in an O-O$_{\text{Mword}}$ correspondence relation and S is the base and S' is the affiliate of that correspondence relation, a vocalic segment s' belonging to S' must have a vocalic segment to which it corresponds in S.

The epenthetic vowel is necessary in the base form to prevent [r,l,s] from surfacing in coda. This vowel therefore appears in the base-plus-clitic forms as well:[6]

(20) Selayarese: stem plus clitic

/lambus/ = a	*[r,l,s]CODA	O-O(WORD)MAX(V)	DEP(V)
a. lambus]$_{Wd}$ =a		*!	
☞b. lambusu]$_{Wd}$ =a			*

In contrast, no epenthetic vowel appears with true suffixes, as the output-output constraint is irrelevant in this case:

(21) Selayarese: stem plus suffix

/lambus-aŋ/ *straight*+COMP	*[r,l,s]CODA	O-O(WORD)MAX(V)	DEP(V)
☞a.lambus-aŋ]$_{Wd}$			
b. lambusu-aŋ]$_{Wd}$			*!

The identity between the isolation form and the preclitic form (as opposed to the presuffixal form) supports the claim that a stem-suffix sequence constitutes a single morphosyntactic (and therefore prosodic) word, in contrast to a stem-clitic sequence.

4.2.5 Velar stop–glottal stop alternation

4.2.5.1 *Lexical glottal stop*

A third diagnostic for suffix vs. clitic involves the alternation between velar and glottal stops. Recall that codas are limited to velar nasal and glottal stop. In all three languages, a stem-final glottal stop surfaces as [k] before a true suffix:

(22) a. Selayarese:
          bákkaʔ}   'big'
          bakkák-aŋ}   'bigger'

      b. Konjo
          hájiʔ}   'good'
          hajík-aŋ}   'better'

      c. Makassarese
          bájiʔ}   'good'
          bajík-aŋ}   'better'

This alternation reflects a distributional restriction of glottal stop to coda and velar stop to onset position.[7] We will assume that this alternation is motivated by the following constraints:[8]

(23)   a. ONSET: Syllables must have onsets.
       b. *[ʔ]ONSET: Glottal stops cannot occur in syllable onset.

The complementary distribution of glottal stop and [k] breaks down in one context, however; in Selayarese and Konjo, final glottal stop is retained before a phrasal clitic:

(24)   a. Selayarese:
           bákkaʔ}   'big'
           bakkák-aŋ}   'bigger'
           bákkaʔ}=a   'I am big'

       b. Konjo
           hájiʔ}   'good'
           hajík-aŋ}   'better'
           hájiʔ}=a   'I am good'

In contrast, Makassarese maintains the prohibition on glottal stops in all pre-vocalic contexts, before both suffixes and clitics:

(25) Makassarese
           bájiʔ}   'good'
           bajík-aŋ}   'better'
           bájik}=aʔ   'I am good'

We assume that in Makassarese, the surfacing of the stem-final consonant as glottal stop is an effect of the constraints ONSET and *[ʔ]ONSET, which together force the stem-final consonant into onset position, where it is realized as the legal onset [k]. In Selayarese and Konjo, where glottal stop surfaces before clitics, some other constraint must override either ONSET or *[ʔ]ONSET. We follow Selkirk (1999) in viewing the retention of glottal stop in preclitic forms as another reflection of the mandate for identity between all exponents of morphosyntactic words containing the same syntactic features, expressed in the following constraint:

(26)   O-O(WORD)IDENTPLACE(CONS) (Selkirk, 1999): Where two strings S and S' are in an O-O$_{Mword}$ correpondence relation and S is the base and S' is the affiliate of that correspondence relation, a consonantal segment s' belonging to S' must be identical in place feature composition to the segment s to which it corresponds in S.

In Makassarese, this constraint is ranked too low to force correspondence between the basic and derived forms:

(27) Makassarese

/baji?/ = aʔ *good* + 1st ABS clitic base: [báji?]	*[ʔ]ONSET	ONSET	O-O(WORD)IDENTPLACE(CONS)
☞a. báji .k=aʔ			*
b. báji.ʔ=aʔ	*!		
c. báji?. =aʔ		*!	

In Selayarese and Konjo, however, the output-output constraint must be ranked high enough to force glottal stop to surface even before a vowel-initial clitic. Whether the glottal stop surfaces as a coda (violating ONSET) or as an onset to the following clitic (violating *[ʔ]ONSET) depends on the relative ranking of these constraints:

(28) Konjo, with ranking *[ʔ]ONSET >> ONSET

/hajiʔ/ = a *good* + 1st ABS clitic base: [hájiʔ]	O-O(WORD)IDENTPLACE(CONS)	*[ʔ]ONSET	ONSET
a. háji.k=a	*!		
b. háji.ʔ=a		*!	
☞c. hájiʔ. =a			*

(29) Konjo, with ranking ONSET >> *[ʔ]ONSET:

/hajiʔ/ + a *good* + 1st ABS clitic base: [hájiʔ]	O-O(WORD)IDENTPLACE(CONS)	ONSET	*[ʔ]ONSET
a. háji.k-a	*!		
☞b. háji.ʔ-a			*
c. hájiʔ. -a		*!	

At this point we do not have evidence to determine the full rankings of the onset-related constraints, though we will return to this question in Section 4.3.3.3. In either case, the output-output constraint is ranked highly enough in Selayarese and Konjo to preserve a stem-final glottal stop before clitics but not before true suffixes:

(30) Rankings
    a. Makassarese: *[ʔ]ONSET, ONSET>> O-O(WORD)IDENTPLACE
    b. Selayarese, Konjo: O-O(WORD)IDENTPLACE >> *[ʔ]ONSET and/or ONSET

4.2.5.2 Epenthetic glottal stop

In Section 4.2.4 we saw that whereas a copy vowel is inserted after stems ending in [r,l,s] in all three languages, Makassarese additionally inserts a glottal stop following the copy vowel (Aronoff *et al.*, 1987; McCarthy and Prince, 1994); cf. *bótolo* 'bottle' in Selayarese and Konjo, *bótoloʔ* 'bottle' in Makassarese). In Makassarese an epenthetic glottal stop, like a lexical glottal stop, is realized as [k] before a vowel, whether that vowel is contained in a suffix or a clitic:

(31)   Makassarese

rántasaʔ}	'dirty'	(stem /rantas/)
rantás-aŋ}	'dirtier'	
rántasak}=aʔ	'I am dirty'	(*rantás}=a)

Makassarese glottal stop epenthesis was analyzed by McCarthy and Prince (1994) as an effect of a constraint which requires prosodic words to end in a consonant. Makassarese, unlike Selayarese and Konjo, ranks this constraint above DEP(C), which forbids consonant insertion:

(32) Presence vs. Absence of Epenthetic Glottal Stop
    a. Constraints
        FINAL-C: A prosodic word must end in a consonant.
        DEP(C): Any consonant in the output must have a correspondent in the input.
    b. Rankings
        Selayarese, Konjo: DEP(C) >> FINAL-C
        Makassarese: FINAL-C >> DEP(C)

The epenthetic glottal stop appears in Makassarese only after stems ending in [r,l,s] – that is, stems that undergo vowel epenthesis – while stems that end in a vowel underlyingly do not undergo glottal stop epenthesis, even though they violate FINAL-C. McCarthy and Prince ascribe the failure to epenthesize a consonant after vowel-final stems to a constraint ALIGN-STEM-RIGHT which requires the right edge of a stem to be coterminous with the right edge of a syllable. We will assume a slightly different version of this constraint, a categorical Anchor constraint rather than a gradient alignment constraint:

(33)   ANCHOR-RIGHT (STEM, SYLLABLE): The segment at the right edge of the (morphosyntactic) stem must be at the right edge of a syllable.

Glottal stop epenthesis after a vowel-final stem would violate the Anchor constraint. Stems ending in [r,l,s], however, can never satisfy this constraint, as [r,l,s] cannot surface in coda position:

(34) Makassarese epenthetic glottal stop

	ANCHOR-RIGHT (STEM, SYLLABLE)	FINAL-C	DEP(C)
vowel-final stem: /batu/ 'boat'			
☞a. batu		*	
b. batuʔ	*!		*
[l]-final stem: /botol/ 'bottle'			
a. botolo	*	*!	
☞b. botoloʔ	*		*!

Epenthetic glottal stop appears in a second context, reduplication. All three languages prefix a bisyllabic reduplicant to express notions such as diminutive or lack of intensity or seriousness (Basri, 1999). A stem of two syllables is copied in its entirety, as in Makassarese *batu-batu* 'small stones' (Aronoff *et al.*, 1987; McCarthy and Prince, 1994). However, the upper limit of two syllables on reduplicants forces incomplete copying of longer bases. In all three languages, incomplete copying is associated with the appearance of a glottal stop at the right edge of the reduplicant, as in *balaʔ-baláo* 'toy rat.' McCarthy and Prince (1994) point out that incomplete reduplication provides a second context in which the constraint demanding that the right edges of stems be coterminous with the right edges of syllables cannot be satisfied, allowing FINAL-C to be decisive.[9] We will see in the next section that FINAL-C and ANCHOR-R(STEM,SYLL) are also instrumental in accounting for Konjo gemination.

4.2.6 Summary

This section has outlined three diagnostics for true suffixes vs. phrasal clitics: stress, copy vowel epenthesis, and the velar stop-glottal stop alternation. In the following section we will consider additional diagnostics involving consonant gemination which are specific to Konjo.

4.3   Konjo gemination

Konjo exhibits two phenomena which are not attested in either Selayarese or Makassarese. The first, dubbed *ŋ-gemination* by Friberg and Friberg (1991), affects velar nasals followed by clitics. The second, Friberg and Friberg's *A-gemination*, affects consonants followed by true suffixes but not clitics. We will argue that these two gemination processes are responses to two previously motivated constraints, each dictating a relationship between morphosyntactic and phonological structure. Gemination at the right edge of the prosodic word (ŋ-gemination) is motivated by the FINAL-C constraint, while PWd-internal A-gemination is motivated by the constraint ANCHOR-RIGHT (STEM,SYLLABLE).

Our investigation of Konjo gemination is indebted to Friberg and Friberg's (1991) lucid and insightful discussion of this phenomenon. Examples in the following sections are taken from Hasan Basri's (1998) field notes or from Friberg and Friberg (1991).

4.3.1 Overview: Konjo ŋ-gemination and A-gemination

The process of ŋ-gemination is illustrated in (29), where the final nasal of the stem *diŋiŋ* 'cool' surfaces as a singleton before the transitivizing suffix in (29a) but as a geminate before the phonologically identical absolutive clitic in (29b):

(35) ŋ-gemination: stem-final C

    a. diŋíŋ-i 'cool (something)' (-*i* TR)   b. díŋiŋŋ=i 'it is cold' =-*i* ABS)

```
     σ   σ}                        σ} σ
     |   Λ                         Λ  Λ
     i   ŋ - i                     i  ŋ = i
```

Again, the curly brackets in (35) indicate the right edge of the prosodic word, as indicated by stress on the penultimate syllable within the PWd.

Velar gemination is not limited to stem-final consonants. The final nasal of the comparative/benefactive/nominalizing suffix *aŋ* also geminates in a pre-clitic environment:

(36) ŋ-gemination:

    a. diɲíŋ-aŋŋ}=i   'he is colder (than)'
       cool/cold -COMP= 3rd ABS

    b. paka-diɲíŋ-aŋŋ}=a   'cool it for me'
      imperative- *cool/cold*-benefactive=1st ABS

In contrast, A-gemination applies only to consonants followed by a true suffix: to undergo A-gemination, a consonant must be stem-final and must be followed by a vowel within its own PWd. Friberg and Friberg identify a third condition that must be met: a geminating consonant must be preceded by the vowel [a]:[10]

(37) a. A-Gemination (Friberg and Friberg, 1991)
        taráŋŋ-i}   'make (something) sharp'
        sharp-TR

    b. failure of A-Gemination after vowel other than [a] (Friberg and Friberg, 1991)
        diɲíŋ-i}   'make (something) cold'
        cool/cold-TR

Both gemination processes may apply in a single form. In (38), the true suffix (the benefactive *-aŋ*) provides the context for A-gemination of the final consonant of the stem /taraŋ/, while the clitic (absolutive = *a*) provides the context for ŋ-gemination of the PWd-final consonant.

(38) Both ŋ-gemination and A-gemination (Friberg and Friberg, 1991)
      paka-taráŋŋ-aŋŋ}=a   'sharpen it for me'
      imperative-*sharp*-benefactive=1st ABS

The [a] before the geminate surfaces as a schwa, a fact we will return to below.

While ŋ-gemination is limited to velar nasals, any stem-final consonant is subject to A-gemination in the proper context. Recall that Konjo, like Selayarese and Makassarese, exhibits a regular alternation between glottal stop in coda position and [k] in onset. With stem-final glottal stops, gemination is accompanied by change in place:

(39) a. A-gemination before true suffix

      lumpákk-i}   'jump (on something)' (stem /lumpaʔ/)
      jump-TR

  b. No A-gemination before a clitic

      lúmpaʔ}=i   'he jumps'
      jump=3rd ABS

For Friberg and Friberg's (1991) speakers, A-gemination of glottal stop, like
that of velar nasal, is limited to post-[a] context:

(40) Failure of A-gemination following vowel other than [a] (Friberg and Friberg, 1991)

      hajík-i}   'make good' (stem /hajiʔ/)
      good-TR

      tekék-aŋ}   'to carry on saddle/load carried on saddle' (stem /tekeʔ/)
      carry on saddle-Nominalizer

The remaining stem-final consonants, [r,l,s], also surface as geminate
following [a] and preceding a true suffix. Recall that stems ending in [r,l,s]
undergo epenthesis of a copy vowel. This epenthetic vowel surfaces both
when the word is final, and when it is followed by a clitic. However, no copy
vowel is inserted when the [r,l,s] is followed by a suffix vowel, and it is in
precisely this position that [r,l,s] may undergo A-gemination, as in (41b):

(41) A-gemination: Stem /ajar/ 'teach'

  a. aŋŋ-ájara}=i   'he teaches'
     TR- *teach*=3rd ABS

  b. ajárr-i}   'teach (someone)'
     teach-TR

Again, A-gemination may fail to apply if the preceding vowel is other than
[a], as in Friberg and Friberg's (1991) example *áko báňjuʔ baňjúl-i* 'don't
joke around'(root /baňjul/ plus transitivizer).[11] This restriction appears, however, to be on the road to extinction; Friberg and Friberg (1991) report a
tendency for younger speakers to generalize pre-suffixal gemination to other
vowel contexts, and the first author of this paper found that gemination was
common regardless of the quality of the preceding vowel, so long as the other
conditions were met.

It is tempting to ascribe A-gemination to the presence of a stressed vowel
preceding the geminate, since addition of a suffix places the stem-final syllable in penultimate (stressed) position. (Recall that because clitics fall outside

the stress domain, a bisyllabic stem preceding a clitic is stressed on its initial rather than its final syllable.) However, Friberg and Friberg (1991) anticipate and dismiss this argument, pointing out that A-gemination occurs even when the addition of two true suffixes moves stress to the right of the geminating consonant, as in (42b):

(42) A-gemination following unstressed vowel (Friberg and Friberg, 1991):
    a. áko} {kapáll-i}   'don't make (something) too thick' (stem /kapal/)
       neg *thick*-TR

    b. áko} {kapall-í-ʔi}   'don't make (everything) so thick'
       neg   *thick*-TR-perpetualizer

4.3.2 Interim summary: Conditions for gemination

The following chart summarizes the conditions for the two gemination processes in Konjo:

(43) Summary: Conditions for Gemination (preliminary description)

    a. ŋ-Gemination applies to a velar nasal that is
        i. before a clitic, and
        ii. followed by a vowel.

    b. A-Gemination applies to any consonant that is
        i. before a (vowel-initial) suffix, and
        ii. preceded by [a] (for some speakers).

In the following two sections we will develop an analysis of Konjo gemination, addressing the questions of the motivation for the two gemination processes, as well as for the contextual restrictions on each process.

4.3.3 ŋ-Gemination: FINAL-C effect

4.3.3.1 *English intrusive [r] as FINAL-C Effect*

As discussed in Section 4.2.5.2, the appearance of epenthetic glottal stop at the right edge of [r,l,s]-final stems in Makassarese has been analyzed (McCarthy and Prince, 1994) as an effect of the FINAL-C constraint, which requires prosodic words to end in a consonant. FINAL-C is also responsible, according to McCarthy (1993), for the appearance of intrusive [r] in a number of dialects of English. We will argue that the conditions for ŋ-gemination parallel those for intrusive [r]. We begin by briefly reviewing McCarthy's analysis of intrusive [r].

As is well known, many English dialects typically ban [r] from syllable coda (e.g., *He put the tuna down* and *He put the tuner down* will be homophonic, with no [r] in 'tuner'). Some r-dropping dialects also show an intrusive [r] following word-final [ə, a, ɔ], as in *He put the tuna[r] away,* which is pronounced in McCarthy's Eastern Massachusetts dialect as homophonic with *He put the tuner away*. McCarthy notes that this intrusive [r] appears only intervocalically, where, he argues, it is ambisyllabic (associated both with coda and with the following onset). This ambisyllabicity protects intrusive [r] from the prohibition on coda [r] that leads to the loss of [r] in, e.g., *tuner down*. However, the intervocalic context is necessary but not sufficient for the appearance of the intrusive [r], which typically appears only when the first vowel is contained in a lexical category word:

(44) Grammatical context for intrusive [r] (McCarthy, 1993)
    a. intrusive [r] after LEX
        The tuna [r] is …
    b. No intrusive [r] after FNC
        *I'm gonna [r] eat.

Appealing to Selkirk's (1984) insight that in English, lexical word edges are isomorphic with prosodic word edges, McCarthy ascribes intrusive [r] following lexical words (like *tuna*) to FINAL-C, which requires a PWd to end in a consonant. In contrast, a function word (such as *gonna*) is not subject to FINAL-C, since in English function words attach directly to the phonological phrase, much like the Makassarese, Selayarese, and Konjo phrasal clitics.[12]

(45) Intrusive [r] at PWd boundary (McCarthy, 1993)

	FINAL-C	DEP(C)
/tuna is/		
a. tuna} is	*!	
☞b. tuna r} is		*
/gonna eat/		
☞a. gonna eat}		
b. gonna r eat}		*!

The sole exceptions to the prohibition on intrusive [r] at the right edge of a functional category involve cases in which FNC appears at the right edge of a phonological phrase:

(46) Intrusive [r] after FNC
　　　　I said I was gonna [r], and I did.

This fact is consistent with the analysis of intrusive [r] as appearing at the end of PWd, since Selkirk's constraint ALIGN (PPH, R, PWD, R) ensures that the right edge of a phonological phrase will also be the right edge of a prosodic word:

(47) Intrusive [r] at PPh/PWd boundary

/gonna, and.../	CODA-COND	FINAL-C	DEP(C)
a. gonna}, and		*!	
☞b. gonna r}, and			*

4.3.3.2 ŋ-gemination

We now return to Konjo ŋ-gemination, which we will argue is quite similar to English [r] intrusion. For intrusive [r] to appear, two conditions must be met: a phonological condition (flanking vowels) and a prosodic condition (PWd edge). Konjo ŋ-gemination is subject to similar conditions.

Note first that Konjo geminates, like English intrusive [r], occur only inter-vocalically. This follows from the assumption (Hayes, 1989) that geminate consonants represent a single feature matrix linked to two prosodic positions, coda and onset. Since Konjo limits both onsets and codas to a single conso-nant, the only possible position for a geminate is between two vowels.

Second, recall that ŋ-gemination applies in preclitic contexts, but not to velar nasals followed by a true suffix. As we have seen, the preclitic context corresponds to the right edge of a prosodic word. Gemination permits the PWd to end in a consonant, while still allowing the consonant to serve as onset to the following vowel. Thus, FINAL-C accounts naturally for gemina-tion before clitics, so long as FINAL-C and ONSET outrank the constraint that forbids a lexical singleton from being realized as a geminate. FINAL-C is in turn outranked by DEP(C), making gemination the only option for satisfying both FINAL-C and ONSET. The ranking of DEP(C) over FINAL-C is necessary to prevent the Makassarese pattern, illustrated by the realization of /botol/ as [botolo?] 'bottle' discussed in Section 4.2.5.2.

Following Hayes (1989), we assume that geminates represent a single consonant linked to two prosodic positions, both coda and onset. Assuming that coda (but not onset) consonants are dominated by a mora, the realization of an underlying singleton as geminate can be prevented by MORAFAITH (Broselow *et al.*, 1997):

(48)   MORAFAITH: If the number of moras linked to S_i = n and S_i R S_o, then the number of moras linked to S_o = n. (A segment linked to n moras in the input must be linked to n moras in the output.)

A violation of MORAFAITH is incurred each time an underlyingly nonmoraic segment is assigned to coda position.[13] This constraint therefore favors the syllabification of a single intervocalic consonant as onset to the following vowel, rather than as a geminate linked to both coda and onset positions.

The phenomenon of ŋ-gemination indicates that MORAFAITH is outranked by constraint(s) favoring gemination. The following tableau illustrates the role of FINAL-C and ONSET in triggering ŋ-gemination:

(49) No ŋ-gemination before suffix; ŋ-gemination before clitic

	DEP-C	FINAL-C	ONSET	MORAFAITH
/diŋiŋ-i/ (TR) 'make cold'				
☞ a. diŋí.ŋ-i}		*		
b. diŋíŋ.ŋ -i}		*		*!
c. diŋí.ŋ-i?}	*!			
/diŋiŋ=i/ (ABS) 'he/she/it is cold'				
a. díŋi.}ŋ=i		*!		
☞ b. díŋiŋ.}ŋ=i				*
c. díŋiŋ.}=i			*!	*

If gemination is motivated by the mandate that prosodic words should end in a consonant, we would expect that all words ending in velar nasals, not only those followed by a clitic, should be subject to ŋ-gemination, so long as there is a following vowel to supply the correct phonological context. As Friberg and Friberg (1991) point out, this is indeed the case. Their example below, in which the first member of a phrase containing two lexical items exhibits ŋ-gemination, establishes that the presence of a clitic is not required for ŋ-gemination:

(50) ŋ-Gemination in V#V Context (Friberg and Friberg, 1991)
    a. bájuŋ   'ingredients'
    b. útaŋ   'vegetables'
    c. bájuŋŋ útaŋ   'vegetable makings'

We conclude, then, that Konjo ŋ-gemination, like the appearance of final glottal stop in Makassarese epenthetic words and the appearance of intrusive [r] in English, can be ascribed to a constraint requiring the right edges of PWd to be consonantal. While this constraint is ranked below DEP(C) in Konjo, thereby preventing addition of a new consonant, it is ranked above the constraint preventing gemination of a lexical single consonant. Thus gemination is a valid strategy for ensuring C-finality in PWds, so long as the phonological context supports a geminate. The next question to consider is why gemination is restricted to final velar nasals.

4.3.3.3 Restriction of ŋ-Gemination to Velar Nasals

In all three languages under consideration, words may end in a vowel, a velar nasal, or a glottal stop. In Section 4.2.5 we saw that the three languages evidence an alternation between velar and glottal stops: generally, [k] appears in onset and [ʔ] in coda, though in Selayarese and Konjo, a PWd-final glottal stop is retained even before a vowel-initial clitic:

(51) Konjo k ~ ʔ
    a. Final position
        hájiʔ}   'good'
    b. Before suffix
        hajík-i}   'make good'
    c. Before clitic
        hájiʔ}=i   'he is good'

In Section 4.2.5.1, we analyzed the retention of the glottal stop in preclitic position as an effect of an Output-Output constraint demanding identity in place between the consonants contained in the surface exponents of the same morphosyntactic word. This Output-Output constraint can account for the failure of glottal stop to geminate in preclitic position (51c), the same position where a velar nasal is realized as geminate. Recall that glottal stops may undergo A-gemination, and that the geminate realization of glottal stop is [kk]:

(52) A-gemination

    lúmpaʔ}   'jump'
    lumpákk-i}   'jump on (something)'

If ŋ-gemination of PWd-final consonants were extended to affect PWd-final glottal stops, such stops would necessarily be realized as geminate [k], violating the constraint requiring place identity between the base form and the preclitic form. The ranking of this O-O constraint above FINAL-C blocks gemination, as illustrated in the following tableau:

(53) PWd-edge gemination blocked with final [ʔ]

	O-OIDENT (CPLACE)	*[ʔ]ONSET	FINAL-C	ONSET	MORAFAITH
/hajiʔ=i/ *good*=ABS '3rd is good'	base: [hájiʔ]				
☞a. há.jiʔ.} = i				*	*
b. háji.} = ʔi		*!	*		
c. há.ji.}k =i	*!		*		
d. há.jik.}k=i	*!				*
e. ha.jiʔ.}ʔ=i		*!			*

The option of realizing glottal stop as either single or geminate [k](53c,d) is closed off by the output-output constraint. The gemination of glottal stop (e) is blocked by the constraint forbidding glottal onsets, which also rules out (b), in which single glottal stop surfaces in onset position. These facts therefore allow us to determine the relative ranking of ONSET and *[?]ONSET (discussed above). Ranking ONSET above *[?]ONSET would incorrectly choose the output with geminate glottal stop:

(54) Incorrect ranking

	O-OIDENT (CPLACE)	ONSET	FINAL-C	*[?]ONSET	MORAFAITH
/haji?=i/ '3rd is good' (ABS clitic)	base: [háji?]				
a. há.ji?.} = i		*!			*
b. háji.} = ?i			*!	*	
c. há.ji.}k =i	*!		*		
d. há.jik.}k=i	*!				*
☞e. ha.ji?.}?=i				*	*

As the tableau below shows, the earlier ranking in (53) is consistent with the presuffix context as well as the preclitic context:

No Gemination of [ʔ]

	O-OIDENT (CPLACE)	*[ʔ]ONSET	FINAL-C	ONSET	MORAFAITH
(55) /hajiʔ-i/ 'make good' (TR) suffix)					
a. ha.jí.ʔ-i}		*!	*		
☞b. ha.jí.k-i}			*		
c. ha.jíʔ.-i}			*	*!	*
d. ha.jík.k-i}			*		*!
e. hajíʔ.ʔ-i}		*!	*		*
(56) /hajiʔ=i/ '3ʳᵈ is good' (ABS clitic)	base: [hájiʔ]				
☞a. há.jiʔ.} = i				*	*
b. háji.} = ʔi		*!	*		
c. há.ji.}k =i	*!		*		
d. há.jik.}k=i	*!				*
e. há.jiʔ.}ʔ=i	*!	*!			*

Gemination is blocked in preclitic forms by the combination of the Output-Output constraint and the constraint forbidding glottal onsets. In presuffix forms, where the Output-Output constraint is irrelevant, gemination is blocked by MORAFAITH, which favors syllabifying the stem-final consonant solely as an onset.

However, we saw in Section 4.3.1 that gemination can occur in presuffixal contexts, illustrated by alternations such as *lúmpaʔ* 'jump' vs. *lumpákk-i* 'jump on'. For older speakers, this gemination is limited to contexts in which the stem-final consonant is preceded by [a]. This gemination will not be blocked by the Output-Output constraint, as the transitivizing suffix *-i* of *lumpákk-i* forms part of the morphosyntactic word, and the base form 'jump, intransitive' is not in a correspondence relation with the derived form 'jump, transitive'. But MORAFAITH, which rules out (55d) *hajíkk-i*, is not decisive in *lumpákk-i* and must therefore be outranked by some constraint which forces gemination in this context. We turn now to closer consideration of A-gemination.

4.3.4 A-gemination: Anchor effect

4.3.4.1 Motivation for A-gemination

As outlined in Section 4.3.1, A-gemination occurs in stem-final consonants which precede a suffix within the same prosodic word (and which also, for some speakers, follow [a]):

(57) A-gemination

    a. táraŋ}   'sharp'
    b. taráŋŋ-i}   'make (something) sharp'
    sharp-TR

We argue that A-gemination occurs in response to ANCHOR-R(STEM, SYLLABLE), which requires the right edge of a stem to correspond to the right edge of a syllable. Recall that McCarthy and Prince (1994) have argued that such a constraint operates in Makassarese to force insertion of a glottal stop at the right edges of stems ending in epenthetic vowels but not those ending in lexical vowels (e.g., *botolo?* 'bottle' from stem /botol/, but *lompo* 'big' (**lompo?* from stem /lompo/). We repeat the constraint below:

(58) ANCHOR-R(STEM,SYLLABLE): The right edge of a stem should coincide with the right edge of a syllable (McCarthy and Prince, 1994).

Assuming that geminate consonants are ambisyllabic, gemination permits a stem-final consonant before a vowel-initial suffix to satisfy both ONSET and ANCHOR-R. We postpone the effect of preceding vowel context to Section 4.3.4.2., considering at this point the prosodic conditioning of A-gemination. The following tableau illustrates the role of ANCHOR-R in inducing gemination of presuffixal velar nasal:

(59) A-gemination

/taraŋ - i/ 'make sharp' (TR suffix)	ONSET	ANCHOR-R(STEM,SYLL)	MORAFAITH
☞ a. σ σ ta ra ŋ - i}			*
b. σ σ ta r a ŋ - i}		*!	
c. σ σ ta ra ŋ - i}	*!		*

If untrammeled by other constraints, ANCHOR-R should cause any stem-final consonant in prevocalic position to be geminate, regardless of whether the following vowel is contained in a suffix or a clitic. However, stem-final glottal stops geminate only before true suffixes, even though the consonant is, of course, stem-final in the preclitic position as well:

(60) Stem /lumpaʔ/   'jump'

    a. gemination before true suffix
    lumpákk-i}   'jump (on something)'
    jump-TR
    b. no gemination before clitic
    lúmpaʔ}=a   'I jump'
    jump=1st ABS

We argued above that gemination of glottal stops in preclitic position is blocked by the Output-Output constraint requiring all consonants in the pre-clitic form to have the same place specification as their correspondents in the isolation form. Ranked above ANCHOR-R(STEM, SYLL), the Output-Output constraint will block gemination before clitics, but not before suffixes, because the correspondence relationship holds between the base form and the preclitic form, but not between the base and the presuffixal form, which con-stitute separate words with separate sets of morphosyntactic features.

The remaining consonants that may occur in stem-final position are [r,l,s]. Like glottal stop, these consonants geminate before true suffixes but not before clitics:

(61)   Stem /ajar/ 'teach' (Friberg and Friberg, 1991)

      a. A-gemination before suffix
          jáko} ajárr-i}=ʔi   'don't teach him'
          neg *teach*-TR=prohibitivizer
      b. No A-gemination before clitic
          aŋŋ-ájara}=i   'he teaches'
          TR- *teach*=i 3rd ABS

The failure of stem-final [r,l,s] to geminate before a following epenthetic vowel, as in (61b), is puzzling. In a form like *aŋŋ-ájara}=i* 'he teaches' the following vowel provides a context in which stem-final [r] could geminate.

We cannot appeal here to an Output-Output constraint to block gemination (as we did with final glottal stops). However, there is a difference between [r,l,s]-final stems and those ending in velar nasal or glottal stop: the anomalous stress induced by vowel epenthesis. The foot structures of the relevant forms (with foot edges marked by parentheses) are as follows:

(62)   a. a(járr-i)}   'teach (someone)'
      b. aŋŋ-(ája)ra}=i   'he teaches' (*ájar)ra}=i

Note that in (62a), the geminate [r] is contained within a foot. What is needed to rule out gemination of [r,l,s] before an epenthetic vowel, as in (62b), is a constraint that forbids syllable association lines from crossing the right edge of a foot. We appeal here to the family of constraints proposed by Itô and Mester (1994, 1999) demanding that the edges of prosodic constituents be 'crisp':

(63)   CRISPEDGE-RIGHT(FOOT): Any segment contained within a foot is linked only to syllables contained exclusively within that foot.

Ranked above ANCHOR-R(STEM, SYLLABLE), the CRISPEDGE(FOOT) constraint will prevent gemination of [r,l,s] before an epenthetic vowel.

Note that ŋ-gemination may produce violations of CRISPEDGE, as in *(díŋiŋ)ŋ}-i* 'it is cold'. This is not surprising, as we have argued that ŋ-gemination and A-gemination reflect two independent constraints: ŋ-gemination is a response to FINAL-C, which demands that prosodic words end in a consonant, while A-gemination is a response to ANCHOR-R (STEM,SYLLABLE), which demands that the final segment of a stem be syllable-final. The ranking FINAL-C, ONSET >> CRISPEDGE-R(FOOT) >> ANCHOR-R(STEM,SYLLABLE) allows ŋ-gemination, but not A-gemination, to create non-crisp edges:

(64) ŋ-gemination applies despite CRISPEDGE

/diŋiŋ = i (3rd ABS)/ 'it is cold'	FINAL-C	ONSET	CRISPEDGE-R (FOOT)	ANCHOR-R (STEM,SYLL)	MORA FAITH
a. (díŋiŋ)}= i		*!			
☞ b. (díŋiŋ)}ŋ= i			*		*
c. (díŋi)}ŋ= i	*!			*	

(65) A-gemination is blocked by CRISPEDGE

/ajar = i (3rd ABS)/ 'he teaches'	FINAL-C	ONSET	CRISPEDGE-R (FOOT)	ANCHOR-R (STEM,SYLL)	MORA FAITH
☞ a. (ája)ra}= i	*	*		*	
b. (ájar)ra}= i	*	*	*!		*

Underlying geminates (such as the [mm] in *jámmara* 'dirty') are preserved by MORAFAITH, but these geminates do not occur at the right edge of a foot. Given the overwhelming consistency of penultimate stress, the only position in which a foot may be followed by another (nonclitic) syllable is in epenthetic forms, where gemination is never found.

4.3.4.2   *Restriction of A-gemination to post-[a] context*

While Konjo speakers seem to have generalized A-gemination to other vocalic contexts, we still must explain why Friberg and Friberg's older speakers restricted presuffixal gemination to post-[a] contexts. Crucial to understanding this restriction on A-gemination is the fact that [a] is the only one of Konjo's five vowels ([i,e,a,o,u]) for which Friberg and Friberg note a distinct pregeminate allophone; they describe [a] as a schwa before nasal geminates and as a raised [a] before other geminates. We assume that the pregeminate [a] represents a reduced vowel. We further assume that for speakers who geminate only after [a], the relevant restriction is that geminates may be derived only if they are preceded by a reduced vowel. To account for this restriction, we propose that geminate consonants in Konjo share a mora with a preceding vowel, rather than occupying their own mora:

(66) Mora-sharing structure for geminates

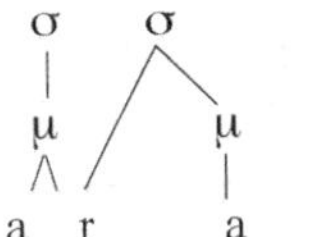

The option of geminates sharing a mora with a preceding vowel was proposed by Broselow *et al.* (1997) for Malayalam geminates, and indeed for all coda consonants that do not add weight to the syllable with which they are affiliated. Broselow *et al.* (1997) propose two constraints, NOCMORA (The head of a mora must be a vowel) and NOSHAREDMORA (Moras should be linked to single segments), which favor monomoraic VC rimes and bimoraic VC rimes, respectively. Broselow *et al.* also posit constraints restricting the types of segments that can participate in the mora sharing relation. For Konjo, high-ranking NOCMORA would force all coda consonants to share a mora with a preceding vowel (consistent with the weight equivalence of CV and CVC syllables). Additional constraints forbidding reduction of any vowel other than [a] and forbidding nonreduced vowels to share a mora with a consonant would restrict gemination to the post-[a] context:

(67)
    a. IDENTFEATUREV[-LOW]: The output correspondent of a nonlow vowel must be identical with its input correspondent.
    b. *[FULLV-C]MORA: A nonreduced vowel may not share a mora with a consonant.

The ranking for those speakers who permit presuffixal gemination only after [a] would be as illustrated in the following two tableaux:

(68) Presuffix gemination restricted to [a] (older speakers)

/diŋiŋ-i/ (TR) 'make cold'	FINAL-C	ONSET	NOC MORA	IDENTV [-LOW]	*[FULLV-C] MORA	ANCHOR-R (STEM,SYLL)
☞a. diŋi.ŋ-i}	*					*
σ σ \ | μμ μ | | / b. diŋ iŋ- i}	*		*!			
σ σ | | μ μ \ \ / c. diŋ Iŋ-i}	*			*!		
σ σ | | μ μ \ \ / d. diŋ iŋ-i}	*				*!	

(69) Presuffix gemination after [a]

/taraŋ-i/ (TR) 'make sharp'	FINAL-C	ONSET	NOC MORA	IDENTV [-LOW]	*[FULLV-C] MORA	ANCHOR-R (STEM,SYLL)
a. tara.ŋ-i}	*					*!
σ σ \ | μμ μ | | / b. tar aŋ-i}	*		*!			
σ σ | | μ μ ∧ ∧ ☞c. tar əŋ-i}	*					
σ σ | | μ μ \ \ / d. tar aŋ-i}	*				*!	

The pattern whereby presuffixal gemination is restricted to post-[a] contexts while preclitic gemination applies after any vowel is accounted for by the independent rankings of the constraints triggering ŋ-gemination and A-gemination: FINAL-C outranks the constraints that limit mora sharing to [a], while ANCHOR-R(STEM,SYLLABLE) ranks below these constraints.

(70) ŋ-gemination

/diŋiŋ=i/ (ABS) 'he/she/it is cold'	FINAL-C	ONSET	NoC MORA	IDENTV [-LOW]	*[FULL V-C] MORA	ANCHOR-R (STEM,SYLL)
a. diŋi.}ŋ=i	*!					*
σ σ |\ | μμ μ ||/| b. diŋ iŋ}=i			*!			
σ σ | | μ μ |\/| c. diŋ Iŋ}=i				*!		
σ σ | | μ μ ∧ ∧ ☞ d. diŋ iŋ}=i					*	

The diagrams below summarize the rankings of the constraints discussed above:

(80) Konjo

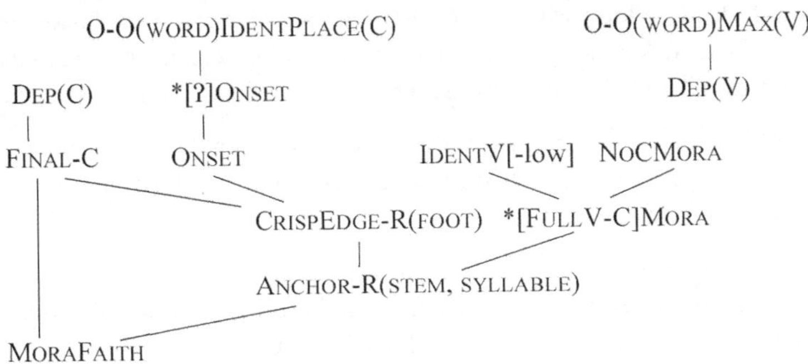

(81) Selayarese

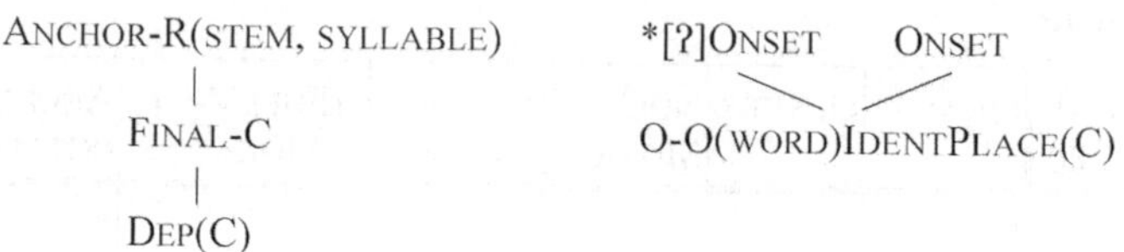

(82) Makassarese

4.5   Conclusion

We have seen how various phonological patterns in the Makassar languages – stress alternations, alternations in copy-vowel insertion, velar-glottal alternations, and the complex gemination patterns of Konjo – can be analyzed by assuming differences in prosodic structure between forms with true suffixes vs. forms with suffixal clitics, along with a set of constraints that enforce particular relationships between morphosyntactic and prosodic structure.

Notes

*   Portions of this paper were presented at AFLA VII at the Free University of Amsterdam and at the Long Island Sound meeting at Yale University, and we are grateful to audiences there for comments and discussion. This work was supported in part by NSF grant #SBR-9729108 to Ellen Broselow and Daniel Finer, co-PIs. Particular thanks are due to two reviewers and to Yunju Suh, whose perceptive comments have considerably improved this paper. Our greatest debt of gratitude goes to Lisa Selkirk, whose work inspired us to examine the phonology-syntax interface in Makassar languages and with whom we have had many discussions of this material; only her modesty prevents her from being considered a coauthor.

1   The Makassarese group (part of the Austronesian family) also includes Turatea and Bantaeng. These two languages are less well described than Makassarese, Selayarese, and Konjo.

2   Two major strategies are used to augment borrowed monosyllables, illustrated by the rendering of Bahasa Indonesia [seŋ] and [gol] as [séʔeŋ] 'pliers' and [gólo] 'ball'; see Broselow 1999 for an analysis of these facts.

3   [j] indicates a voiced palatal stop.

4   See McCarthy 1998, Broselow 1999 for competing analyses of why the lexicon does not appear to contain stems ending in any consonants other than [ŋ,ʔ,r,l,s].

5   An alternative analysis would prevent syllabification of [r,l,s] as onset to a clitic by banning syllabification which crosses a PWd boundary, although constraints banning such syllabification would need to be ranked so as to allow cases discussed below in which syllabification across PWd boundaries does take place. We will not pursue this approach here.

6   For convenience, we assume that copy vowel epenthesis involves insertion of an additional vowel slot, violating DEP(V). Under an alternative view, presented in Kitto and de Lacy 1999, copy vowel epenthesis involves copying of a base vowel, violating INTEGRITY. Nothing in our arguments hinges on this distinction.

7   In all three languages, intervocalic glottal stop is possible in some monomorphemic words when the flanking vowels are identical (e.g. Konjo *teʔeŋ* 'tea', Friberg and Friberg 1991). In the three languages in question, subminimal foreign CVC words are generally adapted as CVʔVC, with insertion of glottal stop and a copy vowel (Broselow 1999).

8   This is a special case of the constraints posited by Basri (1999), Parker (2001), and Smith (2002) requiring onset consonants to have a specified place feature.

9   While neither Selayarese nor Konjo inserts glottal stop after [r,l,s]-final stems, these languages do have epenthetic glottal stop in incomplete reduplicants. We can account for this difference by assuming that in Selayarese and Konjo, the constraint FINAL-C outranks DEP(C)B-R, which demands that any segment contained in the reduplicant also be contained in the base.

10   As discussed below, Basri found that his informants are no longer bound by this condition.

11   Friberg and Friberg (1991; 92) also note additional constraints on A-gemination: 'a preceding nasal-stop sequence and a glottal-voiced stop sequence (those perceived as /bb dd jj gg/ by native speakers) override any doubling effect, though there are counterexamples'.

12   The requirement that the lefthand context of r-intrusion must contain one of the vowels [ə,a,ɔ] stems from the fact that other English vowels are diphthongal ([ij, ej, uw, ow]) and therefore contain their own consonantal elements. In McCarthy's analysis, [r] is inserted; however, Gick (1999) argues that schwa actually contains an underlying consonantal gesture which is normally attenuated in final position; see Broselow (2005) for further discussion.

13 For reasons discussed in section 3.4.2, we assume that geminate consonants share a mora with the preceding vowel, rather than projecting a new mora. Therefore, MORAFAITH, rather than DEP(MORA), is required to block gemination.

References

Alderete, John. (1999a) Faithfulness to prosodic heads. In Ben Hermans and Marc van Oostendorp (eds) *The Derivational Residue in Phonology*. Amsterdam: John Benjamins.

Alderete, John. (1999b) Head dependence in stress-epenthesis interaction. In Ben Hermans and Marc van Oostendorp (eds) *The Derivational Residue in Phonology* 29–50. Amsterdam: John Benjamins.

Aronoff, Mark, Arsyad, Azhar, Basri, Hasan and Broselow, Ellen. (1987) Tier configuration in Makassarese reduplication. *CLS 23, Part Two*, 1–15.

Basri, Hasan. (1998) Field Notes: Buginese, Konjo, Makassarese.

Basri, Hasan. (1999) *Phonological and Syntactic Reflections of the Morphological Structure of Selayarese*. Unpublished doctoral dissertation, State University of New York at Stony Brook.

Basri, Hasan, Broselow, Ellen and Finer, Daniel. (2000) Clitics and crisp edges in Makassarese. In Catherine Kitto and Carolyn Smallwood (eds) *AFLA VI: Proceedings of the Sixth Austronesian Formal Linguistics Association* 25–36. University of Toronto (Paper presented at AFLA IV).

Benua, Laura. (1995) Identity effects in morphological truncation. *University of Massachusetts Occasional Papers* 18: 77–136.

Broselow, Ellen. (1999) Stress, epenthesis, and segment transformation in Selayarese loans. In Steve Chang, Lily Liaw and Josef Ruppenhofer (eds) *Proceedings of the 25th Annual Conference of the Berkeley Linguistics Society*, UC Berkeley: 311–325.

Broselow, Ellen. (2005) The end of the word in Makassar languages. Talk presented at Long Island Sounds Meeting, Yale University.

Broselow, Ellen. (2008) Stress-epenthesis interactions. In Bert Vaux and Andrew Nevins (eds) *Rules, Constraints, and Phonological Phenomena* 121–148. Oxford: Oxford University Press.

Broselow, Ellen, Chen Su-I and Huffman, Marie. (1997) Syllable weight: convergence of phonology and phonetics. *Phonology* 14: 47–82.

Finer, Daniel. (2000) Cyclic clitics in Selayarese. In Catherine Kitto and Carolyn Smallwood (eds) *AFLA VI: Proceedings of the Sixth Austronesian Formal Linguistics Association* 137–160. Toronto: University of Toronto.

Finer, Daniel. (2002) Phases and Selayarese movement. In Norvin Richards and Andrea Rackowski (eds) *AFLA VIII: Proceedings of the Eighth Annual Meeting of the*

Austronesian Formal Linguistics Association,155–172. MIT Working Papers in Linguistics.

Friberg, Barbara. (1996) Konjo's peripatetic person markers. In Hein Steinhauer (ed.) *Papers in Austronesian Linguisics No. 3*, 137–171. Pacific Linguistics Series A-84 (see also 6ICAL, Honolulu, 1991).

Friberg, Timothy and Friberg, Barbara. (1991) Notes on Konjo phonology. In J. J. Sneddon (ed.) *Studies in Sulawesi Linguistics, Part II* 71–115. NUSA: Linguistic Studies of Indonesian and Other Languages in Indonesia 33.

Gick, Bryan. (1999) A gesture-based account of intrusive consonants in English. *Phonology* 16: 29–54.

Hayes, Bruce. (1989) Compensatory lengthening in moraic phonology. *Linguistic Inquiry* 20 (2): 253–306.

Itô, Junko and Mester, Armin. (1994) Reflections on CodaCond and alignment. In Jason Merchant, Jaye Padgett and Rachel Walker (eds) *Phonology at Santa Cruz* Vol. 3, 27–46. Santa Cruz, CA: Linguistics Research Center, UCSC.

Itô, Junko and Mester, Armin. (1999) Realignment. In Rene Kager, Harry van der Hulst and Wim Zonneveld (eds), *The Prosody-morphology Interface* 188–217. Cambridge: Cambridge University Press.

Kitto, Catherine and de Lacy, Paul. (1999) Correspondence theory and epenthetic quality. In Catherine Kitto and Carolyn Smallwood (eds) *Proceedings of AFLA (Austronesian Formal Linguistics Association) VI* 181–200. Toronto: Toronto Working Papers in Linguistics.

McCarthy, John. (1993) A case of surface constraint violation. *Canadian Journal of Linguistics* 38: 169–195.

McCarthy, John J. (1998) Morpheme structure constraints and paradigm occultation. In M. Catherine Gruber, Derrick Higgins, Kenneth Olson and Tamra Wysocki (eds) *CLS 32, Part 2: The Panels* 123–150. Chicago, IL: Chicago Linguistic Society.

McCarthy, John and Prince, Alan. (1994) The emergence of the unmarked. *Proceedings of the North East Linguistics Society* 24: 333–379.

Mithun, Marianne and Basri, Hasan. (1986) The phonology of Selayarese. *Oceanic Linguistics* 25: 210–254.

Parker, Steve. (2001) Non-optimal onsets in Chamicuro: an inventory maximized in coda position. *Phonology* 18: 361–386.

Selkirk, Elisabeth. (1995) The prosodic structure of function words. *University of Massachusetts Occasional Papers* 18: 439–470.

Selkirk, Elisabeth. (1999) Morphologically governed Output-Output constraints in a noncyclic Optimality Theoretic grammar: evidence from the Makassar languages. Talk presented at Sophia University, Tokyo.

Smith, Jennifer. (2002) *Phonological Augmentation in Prominent Positions*. Doctoral dissertation, University of Massachusetts at Amherst.

5 Final devoicing: Production and perception studies

Scott Myers[a]

5.1 Introduction

Final devoicing is a pattern of phonological distribution in which both voiced and voiceless obstruents occur in a language, but at the end of a particular prosodic domain (Selkirk, 1978, 1986) only voiceless obstruents occur. [1,2,3] There are examples from all over the world, involving both phonological word and syllable domains (cf. Passy, 1891: 160; Grammont, 1933: 365; Locke, 1983: 118; Lombardi, 1995, 1999; Blevins, 2006; Harris, 2009):

(1) (a) All word-final obstruents are voiceless.
- Slavic: Russian (Padgett, this volume), Czech (Heim, 1976: 14), Slovak (Rubach, 1993: 283), Bulgarian (Scatton, 1984: 20), Polish (Rubach, 1984: 206)
- Romance: Walloon (Francard and Morin, 1986: 457), Friulian (Baroni and Vanelli, 2000: 27), Old French (Ewert, 1933: 75, 97), Ferrarese Italian (stops only – Dinnsen and Eckman, 1978: 5)
- Germanic: Dutch (Booij, 1995: 22), German (Jessen and Ringen, 2002), Gothic (fricatives only – Wright, 1899: 62-67; Hock, 1991: 43), Old English (fricatives only – Hock, 1991: 43)
- Saranda Ekklisies Greek (stops only – Newton, 1972: 103)
- Sanskrit (Whitney, 1879: 46)
- Daragözu Arabic and Maltese Arabic (Abu Mansour, 1996: 213, 215)
- Uyghur (Hahn, 1991: 84)
- Fur (Jakobi, 1990: 35)

[a] Scott Myers: University of Texas at Austin, Austin TX, USA. Email: s.myers@mail.utexas.edu

- Luo (Tucker, 1994: 35)
- Afar (Bliese, 1981: 242)
- Basque (Hualde, 1991: 13)

(b) All syllable-final obstruents are voiceless.
- Takelma (Sapir, 1990: 35)
- Wintu (Pitkin, 1984: 26)
- West Tarangan (Nivens, 1992: 147)
- Romansch (Montreuil, 1999: 531)
- Catalan (Hualde, 1992: 393)
- Breton (Krämer, 2000: 641)
- Haisla (Bach, 1996: 5)
- Ron (Jungraithmayr, 1970: 21)
- Malay (Ahmad, 2005: 55)
- Turkish (stops only – Clements and Keyser, 1983: 59–60)
- Buriat (Poppe, 1960: 10)
- Efik (Cook, 1969: 36)
- Manipuri (Singh, 2000: 13-16)
- Thai (Iwasaki and Ingkaphirom, 2005: 4)
- Vietnamese (Thompson, 1965: 23)
- Various Sino-Tibetan languages (Thurgood and LaPolla, 2003)

An optional pattern of word-final obstruent devoicing has been reported as a distinguishing characteristic of a number of English dialects: in some African American communities (Wolfram, 1969: 51; Luelsdorf, 1975: 42), the Appalachian region (Wolfram and Christian, 1976: 63), Wisconsin (Purnell *et al.*, 2005), and among Maori people in New Zealand (Holmes, 1996).

The pattern is also reflected in language acquisition. Already in prelinguistic babbling voiceless consonants greatly outnumber voiced consonants in utterance-final position (Oller *et al.*, 1976). When children begin to produce words, they often have a stage where they produce both voiced and voiceless obstruents, but in word-final position only voiceless ones (Velten, 1943: 283; Smith, 1973: 37; Smith, 1979: 22; Flege, 1982). Persistence of this error type later into the acquisition process is recognized as a speech disorder (Hodson and Paden, 1981: 371; Cutts and Jensen, 1983; Ingram, 1989: 115). Systematic devoicing of final voiced target consonants is also a prevalent error type in second language acquisition, even in cases where final devoicing is not a characteristic of either the target language or the learner's native language

(Eckman, 1981; Flege and Davidian, 1984; Flege *et al.*, 1992; Major and Audree, 1996; Broselow *et al.*, 1998).

Scholars have long related the phonological pattern of final devoicing to the phonetics of prepausal position (e.g. Sievers, 1901: 289–290; Jespersen, 1926: 101; Bloomfield, 1933: 373; Lindblom, 1983: 237). There is no vocal fold vibration during pause, so devoicing in prepausal position can be seen as assimilation to this voiceless state (Lightner, 1972: 332–333; Ingram, 1989: 35). Non-speech breathing is characterized by a wide glottal aperture to facilitate air passage, and speakers begin spreading the vocal folds in anticipation of this posture before they are done producing speech (Sweet, 1877: 65; Lisker *et al.*, 1969: 1545; Klatt and Klatt, 1990; Shadle, 1997: 42; Jessen, 1998; Slifka, 2006). In addition to this coarticulatory effect of the transition from speech to nonspeech, voicing in utterance-final position is also hampered by a decline in subglottal pressure over the course of the utterance (Westbury and Keating, 1986: 156). The result is a gradual breakdown in voicing as one approaches pause, often passing through nonmodal voicing before a final voiceless interval. Such utterance-final devoicing has been found in instrumental acoustic studies in English (Haggard, 1978; Docherty, 1992; Smith, 1997), French (Smith, 1999, 2003), Finnish (Lehtonen, 1970: 45; Myers and Hansen, 2007), and Kinyarwanda (Myers, 2005), and noted as well in many transcription-based studies (e.g. Michelsen's 1988 study of the Lake Iroquoian languages). Oller and Smith (1977) found utterance-final vowel devoicing to be a regular feature of prelinguistic babbling.

I would propose that this coarticulatory utterance-final devoicing is the initial impetus for a sound change that results in phonological word-final devoicing. The first step of this transformation would be that utterance-final devoicing affects the perception of voicing contrasts in utterance-final position, inducing a tendency among listeners to identify utterance-final obstruents as voiceless. This would be expected since utterance-final devoicing diminishes voicing during the constriction period, a demonstrated perceptual cue for voicing (Raphael, 1971; Wolf, 1978; Smith, 1979; Hogan and Roszypal, 1980; Kingston and Diehl, 1994). As Blevins (2006) points out, lengthening of the utterance-final consonant (Lindblom, 1968) could also contribute to this perceptual tendency, since listeners are sensitive to the fact that voiceless obstruents are longer than corresponding voiced ones (Denes, 1955). Listeners are generally adept at compensating in perception for coarticulatory effects (Lindblom and Studdert-Kennedy, 1967; Mann and Repp, 1980), but they can fail to do so, leading to hypocorrection (Ohala, 1981, 1993). In this case, the result of failing to completely compensate for the devoicing effect of utterance-final position would be a tendency to identify utterance-final obstruents as voiceless.

The second step of the sound change would be that the listener generalizes over the voicing categories he or she has identified in this way, and concludes that obstruents in this position are voiceless. This generalization is a phonological restriction on category distribution. Pierrehumbert (2001: 152) has shown how in an exemplar-based model even a small bias in identification of this sort can over time lead to such a neutralization in contrast between two speech sound categories. The extension of the pattern from utterance-final to word- and syllable-final positions would be an analogical extension based on the fact that every utterance-final consonant is also word- and syllable-final (Ewert, 1933: 75; Westbury and Keating, 1986: 161; Hock, 1991: 239).

The third step of the sound change is the spread of the pattern from the individual innovators to a broader speech community (Labov, 2001). This step depends heavily on the innovators' relations to other speakers and the dynamics of group identity (Wedel and Van Volkinburg, 2009).

In this account, phonological final devoicing is the end result of a diachronic process of phonologization (Hyman, 1976), building on phonetic utterance-final devoicing. It is a hypocorrective sound change (Ohala, 1981, 1993), beginning with a listener's failure to compensate perceptually for an effect of context on production.

Such a diachronic account would explain a number of the properties of phonological final devoicing. The phonological pattern is common and has emerged independently in numerous language groups because it results from a straightforward change based on a pervasive pattern of laryngeal coarticulation. Voiced obstruents are subject to change in final position because anticipation of the open glottis of nonspeech breathing diminishes the voicing that contributes to distinguishing those sounds. Voiced obstruents change to voiceless obstruents, because that is what a partially devoiced obstruent tends to be mistaken for. The pattern is restricted to obstruents, because partially devoiced sonorants are so low in intensity that they are mistaken for silence rather than for a voiceless segment (Myers and Hansen, 2007). The sound change is recapitulated in first- and second-language acquisition because the identification errors that are the basis for the sound change are more frequent in inexperienced learners of the sound system.

The basic phonetic prerequisites for the phonological final devoicing pattern are widespread, perhaps universal. But not every language that has the phonetic pattern ends up with the corresponding phonological pattern. This is because the phonetic pattern of utterance-final devoicing is only the first step of the change, and the emergence of phonological final devoicing depends on all the subsequent steps as well. A listener has to make an identification error due to the phonetic pattern often enough that it serves as the basis of a generalization about voicing categories, and then this innovated phonological pattern has to spread beyond that individual to a speech community. A sound change will only occur when these events happen to line up in the right way, but the point is that this series of events is more likely than one with a less frequent starting point (Yu, 2004).

The articulatory and acoustic bases of this diachronic account are well-supported – the studies cited above demonstrate the effect of utterance-final position on the actions of the vocal folds and on the resulting acoustic reflexes of voicing. But no evidence has been provided to date for the claim that these acoustic effects of utterance-final coarticulation affect identification of voicing categories and lead to a tendency to identify utterance-final obstruents as voiceless. The aim of the present study is to test this claim.

English was chosen as the language of the study, since it has a robust contrast in voicing in word-final position (e.g. *pat/pad*), and English speakers are therefore experienced in producing and perceiving contrasting voice categories in this position.

The first experiment is a production study, which is meant both to explore the conditions for the utterance-final devoicing effect and to generate stimuli for the perception experiments. The second and third experiments are perception experiments, in which English-speaking listeners identify words belonging to minimal pairs differing in final voicing (e.g. *proof/prove*), excised from utterance-final or nonfinal position.

5.2   Experiment #1: Production

5.2.1 Methods

The test items, listed in (2), all belonged to minimal pairs differing just in the voicing of a word-final obstruent: final voiceless vs. final voiced fricative (e.g. *proof/prove*), or final voiced vs. voiceless stops (e.g. *greet/greed*). There were ten test words for each class of word-final segment, for a total of 40 items.

(2) Test words

<table>
<tr><td>(a) Fricative-final (voiceless – voiced)</td><td>(b) Stop-final (voiceless – voiced)</td></tr>
<tr><td>loose – lose</td><td>greet – greed</td></tr>
<tr><td>proof – prove</td><td>feet – feed</td></tr>
<tr><td>cease – seize</td><td>beat – bead</td></tr>
<tr><td>leaf – leave</td><td>seat – seed</td></tr>
<tr><td>Bruce – bruise</td><td>loop – lube</td></tr>
<tr><td>noose – news</td><td>neat – need</td></tr>
<tr><td>belief – believe</td><td>moot – mood</td></tr>
<tr><td>grief – grieve</td><td>leak – league</td></tr>
<tr><td>relief – relieve</td><td>heat – heed</td></tr>
<tr><td>use (noun) – use (verb)</td><td>sweet – Swede</td></tr>
</table>

To control for the effects of stress (Lehiste, 1970: 36) and vowel height (Lindblom, 1968) on the duration of the vowel, the final syllable in all test words bore main word stress and had a high tense vowel.

Each test word occurred in two carrier sentences. To control for the effect of utterance length on vowel duration (Lindblom, 1968), each carrier sentence consisted of 15 syllables. In one sentence, the test word was sentence-final (e.g. *The garage can tighten any of the bolts that are too **loose***), while in the other it was non-final and preceding a word beginning with a nasal stop (e.g. *There is a **loose** nylon cover over the whole area*). Each of the 40 test words occurred in two sentence positions, so there were 80 test sentences for each speaker.

Six adult native speakers of American English produced the materials.[4] The test sentences were presented in random order at five-second intervals in a timed Powerpoint presentation on a laptop, interspersed with 60 distractor sentences (stimuli for another experiment). The speaker read them aloud seated in a sound recording booth and was recorded on a solid-state digital recorder. Six speakers produced 480 test sentences, but of those one item was excluded because the speaker produced the wrong word, and two were excluded due to background noise that made the measurements impossible. That left 477 items for analysis.

There are many acoustic correlates for voicing (Lisker, 1986), but since this study concerns the interaction of such correlates with utterance position, we focus on measures which are defined for both stops and fricatives, and which are known to be sensitive to both voicing and utterance position.

The duration of the following intervals was measured, using Praat (http://www.fon.hum.uva.nl/praat/): (a) the vowel; (b) the constriction for the postvocalic consonant (if any); (c) the release (if any); and (d) the voiced and voiceless subintervals within the VC sequence (a)–(c).

The onset of the vowel was defined as the onset of an increase in amplitude and wave complexity after the prevocalic consonant. The offset of the vowel was defined as the end of F2 and F3 of the vowel. The constriction interval was a period of minimum amplitude beginning with the vowel offset. In the case of stops this corresponded to the closure interval, while in fricatives it was the noise interval. The release was the interval of increased amplitude after the constriction and before the onset of a following sound, if any. In a released stop, this was the noise burst and aspiration. In fricatives, this was a period characterized by a shift to lower frequency and lower intensity noise. In these recordings, all utterance-final stops were released, suggesting a relatively careful pronunciation.

The voiced interval was from the onset of the vowel to the offset of quasiperiodic pulses in the waveform. The voiceless interval consisted either of noise without such pulsing, or silence (in a stop closure). In these recordings, the voiced interval was always continuous, i.e. all the VC sequences measured had an initial voiced interval, which was followed in some cases by a voiceless interval that stretched to the end of the VC sequence. The transition from voiced to voiceless always occurred either in the constriction interval or in the release.

The constriction interval was expected to be longer in voiceless obstruents than in voiced obstruents (Denes, 1955; Lisker, 1957; Stevens *et al.*, 1992), and longer in utterance-final than in nonfinal position (Byrd *et al.*, 2005).

The duration of the voiceless interval within the consonant (constriction + release) was expected to be longer in a voiceless than in a voiced consonant (Raphael, 1971; Kingston and Diehl, 1994), and longer in utterance-final than in nonfinal position (Haggard, 1978; Docherty, 1992; Smith, 1997). The absolute duration of the voiceless interval was chosen in this study as a measure rather than the proportion of the voiced interval to the whole consonant interval because the latter measure had a bimodal distribution, complicating statistical analysis (cf. Kuzla *et al.*, 2007). The duration of the voiceless interval was chosen over that of the voiced interval since it is a devoicing effect that we are aiming to measure.

The duration of the vowel was expected to be longer before voiced than before voiceless consonants (Chen, 1970), and longer in utterance-final position than in nonfinal position (Lindblom, 1968; Oller, 1973). The ratio of the vowel duration to the duration of the whole vowel + consonant sequence has been argued to be a more robust acoustic correlate of voicing than the absolute duration of the vowel alone (Kohler, 1979; Barry, 1979; Pind, 1986). This V/VC ratio is greater when C is voiced than when it is voiceless, because the vowel before a voiced coda is longer and the coda itself is shorter. The ratio is also lower in utterance-final syllables than in nonfinal syllables (Barry, 1979), because final lengthening is gradient and has more of an effect on the utterance-final coda than on the preceding vowel, proportionally (Turk, 1999).

In the statistical analysis a mixed model was used in which speaker and test word were treated as random effects, and fixed effects were voicing (voiced/voiceless), manner (stop/fricative), and (utterance) position (final/nonfinal). The alpha level was 0.05. A given acoustic measure was considered to show utterance-final devoicing when a significant effect of utterance-final position coincided with (i.e. went in the same direction as) the effect of having a voiceless obstruent in coda position.

5.2.2 Results

5.2.2.1 Constriction duration

Figure 5.1 presents the percentile distribution of constriction duration by manner, voicing and position.

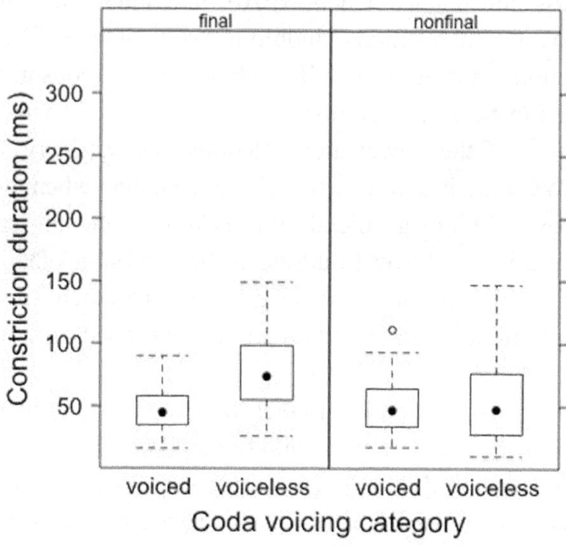

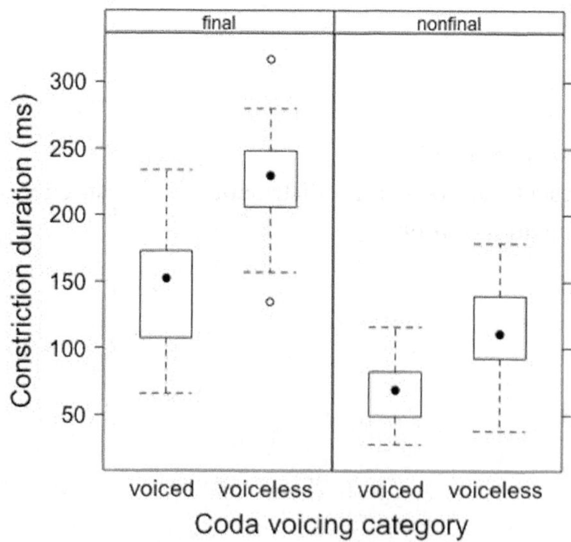

Figure 5.1: Constriction duration (ms) by manner, voicing and position

Mean constriction duration was greater in voiceless obstruents (118 ms) than in voiced obstruents (77 ms), greater in fricatives (138 ms) than in stops (57 ms), and greater in utterance-final syllables (124 ms) than in nonfinal ones (71 ms). All three main effects were significant (d.f. = 1, 469): voicing ($F = 109.0$, $p < 0.001$), manner ($F = 444.5$, $p < 0.001$), and position ($F = 433.4$, $p < 0.001$). The two-way interactions were also significant (d.f. = 1, 469): voicing*position ($F = 30.7$, $p < 0.001$), voicing*manner ($F = 36.1$, $p < 0.001$), and manner*position ($F = 274.7$, $p < 0.001$). The three-way interaction was not significant.

In order to explore the interactions, the data was split into subsets according to manner and position. Considering the manner classes, both the voicing and position main effects were significant in both stops and fricatives: voicing in stops (F (1, 234) = 17.0, $p < 0.001$), voicing in fricatives (F (1, 235) = 96.8, $p < 0.001$), position in stops (F (1, 234) = 13.1, $p < 0.001$), and position in fricatives (F (1, 235) = 612.1, $p < 0.001$). The interaction between the two factors was significant in both stops (F (1, 234) = 17.5, $p < 0.001$) and fricatives (F (1, 235) = 17.4, $p < 0.001$).

Splitting the data according to position class, voicing was a significant main effect in both final and nonfinal positions (final, F (1, 233) = 190.9, $p < 0.001$; nonfinal, F (1, 236) = 35.2, $p < 0.001$). The main effect of manner was also significant in both position classes (final, F (1, 233) = 983.4, $p < 0.001$; nonfinal, F (1, 236) = 78.7, $p < 0.001$), as was the interaction of voicing and manner (final, F (1, 233) = 41.6, $p < 0.001$; nonfinal, F (1, 236) = 23.1, $p < 0.001$).

In both stops and fricatives, and in both final and nonfinal position, constriction duration was significantly longer in voiceless than in voiced obstruents, as previously found by Denes (1955). As in Byrd *et al.* (2005), the constriction duration was longer in utterance-final than in non-final position. The two factors interacted so that the difference between the voiced and voiceless group means was greater in final position (55 ms) than in nonfinal position (27 ms). The lengthening of constriction duration associated with utterance-final position coincided with and reinforced the lengthening effect of belonging to the voiceless category, so with respect to this measure utterance-final position had a devoicing effect. The same result is obtained if the whole consonant duration (constriction + release) is used as a measure, instead of just the constriction interval.

5.2.2.2 *Duration of the voiceless interval*

Figure 5.2 presents the percentile distribution of the duration of the voiceless interval by manner, voicing, and position class.

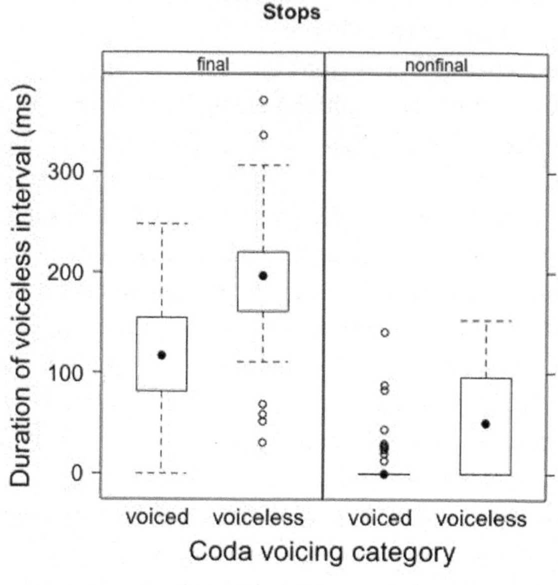

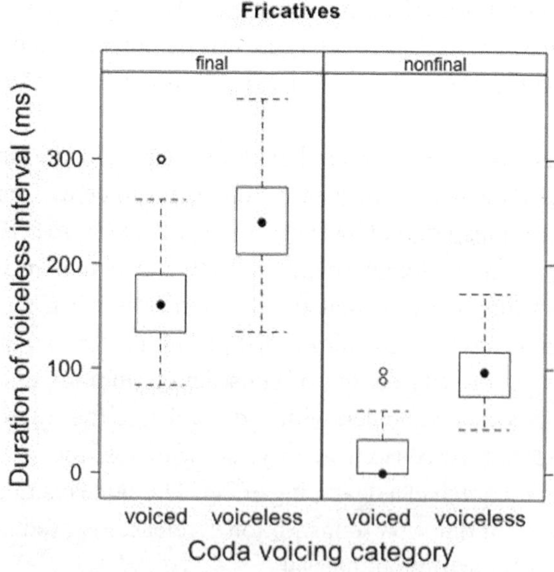

Figure 5.2: Duration of the voiceless interval by manner, voicing and position

The mean duration of the voiceless interval was greater in voiceless obstruents (146 ms) than in voiced ones (78 ms), greater in fricatives (130 ms) than in stops (93 ms), and greater in final position (181 ms) than in nonfinal position (43 ms). All three main effects are significant (d.f. = 1, 469): voicing (F = 194.8, p < 0.001), manner (F = 56.9, p < 0.001) and position (F = 1213.4, p < 0.001). All of the interactions except that of voicing and position were significant (d.f. = 1, 469): voicing and manner (F = 5.0, p = 0.03), manner and position (F = 7.8, p = 0.01), and voicing*manner*position (F = 4.4, p = 0.04).

In the manner subsets, the main effect of voicing was significant (stops, F (1, 234) = 45.5, p < 0.001; fricatives, F (1, 235) = 272.4, p < 0.001), as was the main effect of position (stops, F (1, 234) = 406.8, p < 0.001; fricatives, F (1, 235) = 970.3, p < 0.001). The interaction of voicing and position was significant in stops (F (1, 234) = 5.0, p = 0.03), but not fricatives.

In the position subsets, the main effect of voicing was significant (final, F (1, 233) = 108.0, p < 0.001; nonfinal, F (1, 236) = 104.5, p < 0.001), and so was the main effect of manner (final, F (1, 233) = 44.8, p < 0.001; nonfinal, F (1, 236) = 17.4, p < 0.001). The interaction of voicing and manner was significant in the nonfinal subset (F (1, 236) = 9.7, p = 0.002), but not in the final subset.

Thus the voiceless interval in the consonant was significantly longer in voiceless obstruents than in voiced ones in both stops and fricatives, and both final and nonfinal position. The voiceless interval was longer in utterance-final position than in nonfinal position. The voicing and position factors interacted in such a way that the difference between the voiced and voiceless group means was greater in final position (74 ms) than in nonfinal position (63 ms). For this measure, the lengthening effect of final position coincided with the lengthening effect of a voiceless obstruent, so utterance-final position had a devoicing effect. The same general pattern holds if the proportion of voicing to consonant duration is used as a measure.

5.2.2.3 Vowel duration

Figure 5.3 presents the percentile distribution of vowel duration (ms) by coda voicing and utterance position.

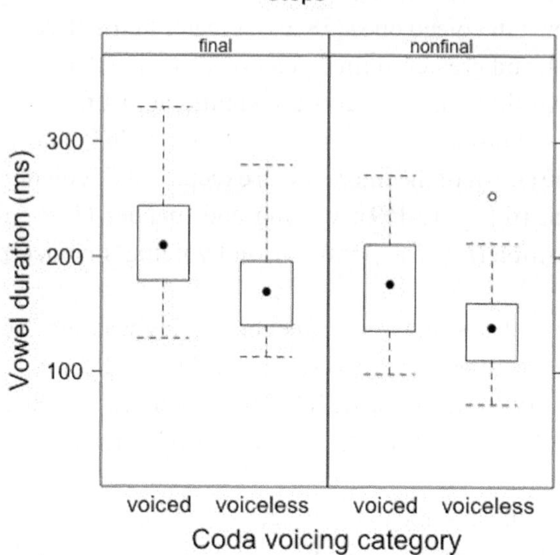

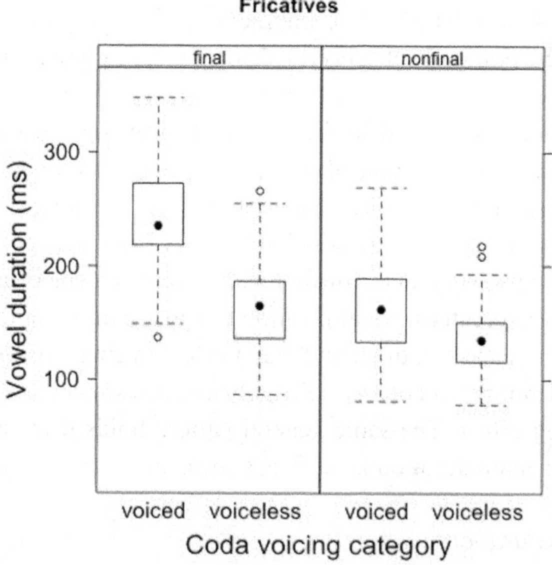

Figure 5.3: Vowel duration (ms) by manner, voicing and utterance position

Mean vowel duration was greater before a voiced obstruent (199 ms) than before voiceless ones (mean = 152 ms), slightly greater before a fricative (177 ms) than before a stop (175 ms), and greater in an utterance-final syllable (198 ms) than in a nonfinal syllable (154 ms). The main effects of voicing and position were significant (d.f. = 1, 469): voicing, $F = 57.8$, $p < 0.001$; position, $F = 255.0$, $p < 0.001$, but not the main effect of manner ($F < 1$). The significant interactions (d.f. = 1, 469) were those of voicing and position ($F = 21.0$, $p < 0.001$), voicing and manner ($F = 13.3$, $p < 0.001$), and voicing, manner and position ($F = 18.8$, $p < 0.001$). The interaction of manner with voicing was not significant ($F < 1$).

The main effect of voicing was significant in both manner subsets (stops, $F (1, 234) = 22.7$, $p < 0.001$; fricatives, $F (1, 235) = 35.6$, $p < 0.001$), as was the main effect of position (stops, $F (1, 234) = 65.5$, $p < 0.001$; fricatives, $F (1, 235) = 226.3$, $p < 0.001$). The interaction between voicing and position was significant in fricatives ($F (1, 235) = 46.7$, $p < 0.001$), but not in stops ($F < 1$).

Examining the final and nonfinal subsets separately, the main effect of voicing was significant in both the final and nonfinal subsets (final, $F (1, 233) = 79.7$, $p < 0.001$; nonfinal, $F (1, 236) = 19.2$, $p < 0.001$), while the main effect of manner was not significant in either subset. The interaction of voicing and manner was significant in the final subset (manner, $F (1, 233) = 6.9$, $p = 0.009$), but not in the nonfinal subset.

Thus, as in previous studies (e.g. Chen, 1970), vowel duration in this sample was significantly greater before a voiced consonant than before a voiceless one in stops and fricatives, and in final and nonfinal position. As in previous studies (e.g. Oller, 1973), vowel duration was significantly greater in an utterance-final syllable than in a nonfinal one. The two factors interacted in that the difference between the voiced and voiceless group means was greater in final position (60 ms) than in nonfinal position (33 ms). Umeda (1975) found a similar interaction in a study of connected speech in English, but in her study the significant effects of voicing were limited to final position. For our purposes, what matters most is that with regard to this voicing cue, the lengthening effects of utterance-final position coincide with and reinforce the effect of a voiced coda, rather than the voiceless category as with the previous two measures. Thus with respect to this measure, utterance-final position has a voicing effect, not the expected devoicing effect.

However, it should be noted that some scholars have argued that the appropriate cue for voicing in a postvocalic consonant is not the absolute duration of the preceding vowel, but the ratio of the vowel duration to the duration of the whole VC sequence (Kohler, 1979; Barry, 1979; Pind, 1986). The percentile distribution of this measure, V/VC, is presented in Figure 5.4.

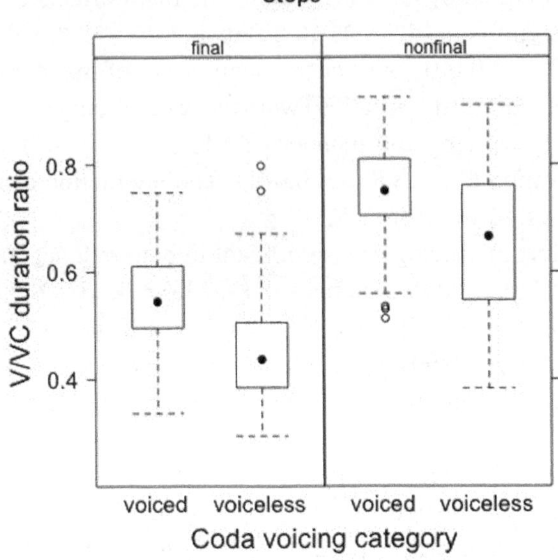

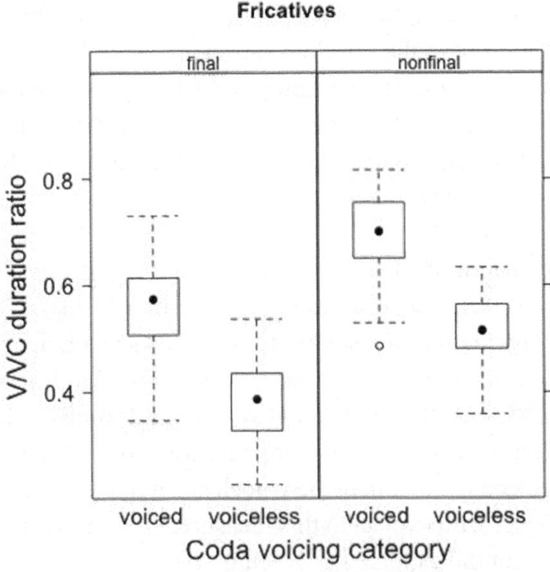

Figure 5.4: The ratio of vowel duration to VC duration, by manner, voicing and position class

The mean V/VC ratio was greater for voiced codas (0.64) than for voiceless ones (0.51), greater with stops (0.61) than with fricatives (0.54), and greater in nonfinal position (0.66) than in utterance-final position (0.49). All the main effects were significant for this measure (d.f. = 1, 469): voicing ($F = 129.2$, $p < 0.001$), manner ($F = 36.9$, $p < 0.001$), and position ($F = 568.8$, $p < 0.001$). The significant interactions (d.f. = 1, 469) were those of voicing and manner ($F = 14.6$, $p < 0.001$), and manner and position ($F = 25.8$, $p < 0.001$).

The main effect of voicing was significant in both the stop subset ($F (1, 234) = 19.6$, $p < 0.001$) and the fricative subset ($F (1, 235) = 220.3$, $p < 0.001$). The main effect of position was also significant in both manner subsets (stops, $F (1, 234) = 325.9$, $p < 0.001$; fricatives, $F (1, 235) = 269.0$, $p < 0.001$). In neither manner subset was there a significant interaction between voicing and position.

Dividing the dataset by position, the main effect of voicing was significant (final, $F (1, 233) = 133.6$, $p < 0.001$; nonfinal, $F (1, 236) = 60.4$, $p < 0.001$), as was that of manner (final, $F (1, 233) = 8.5$, $p = 0.004$; nonfinal, $F (1, 236) = 38.6$, $p < 0.001$) and the interaction of voicing and manner (final, $F (1, 233) = 14.2$, $p < 0.001$; nonfinal, $F (1, 236) = 7.1$, $p = 0.008$).

Thus the V/VC ratio was significantly greater with voiced codas than with voiceless ones in both stops and fricatives, and both final and nonfinal position. The ratio was significantly greater in final than in nonfinal position for both stops and fricatives. In this case there was no significant interaction between these two factors, so that there was no significant difference in the voicing effect depending on utterance position. The lowered ratio associated with final position coincided with the lowering effect of a voiceless coda – an utterance-final devoicing effect.

5.2.2.4 Discussion: Production study

It has been found that there are three important acoustic cues for voicing that show utterance-final devoicing in this dataset, such that the effect of final position coincides with the effect of voicelessness. Constriction duration and the duration of the voiceless interval are longer in final than nonfinal position, and longer in voiceless than in voiced consonants. The V/VC duration ratio is lower in final than in nonfinal position, and lower with voiceless than with voiced codas.

Vowel duration goes the other direction, since vowels were longer in final position and with voiced codas. There are also other cues for voicing that have not been measured in this study (Lisker, 1986), such as f0 or F1, in which the effects of final position might coincide with those of the voiced category.

The question is which class of acoustic correlates is dominant in the identification of voicing categories in utterance-final position. If, as we have hypothesized, listeners tend to identify utterance-final obstruents as voiceless, this would suggest that the cues that are most salient to listeners are those in which the effect of utterance-final position coincides with the effect of a voiceless coda. If, on the other hand, absolute vowel duration is the most salient acoustic correlate of coda voicing for listeners, then we would expect that listeners would tend to identify utterance-final obstruents as voiced. The perception experiments presented in the next session will provide evidence on this point.

5.3   Experiments #2a and #2b: Perception

We have seen in the production study that utterance-final position has significant effects on the acoustic correlates of the voicing contrast in English. The goal of the perception studies is to investigate what consequences, if any, these acoustic effects have on listeners' identification of categories contrasting in voicing.

5.3.1 Methods

The 20 obstruent-final voiced-voiceless pairs in (2) above served as the test items for the perception experiments. The test words were excised from the soundfiles produced in the first experiment, cutting at the closest zero crossing preceding the onset of the word and the closest zero crossing immediately following the end of the word (including the final consonant release, if any).

There were 477 tokens from the production study. Two of these were excluded due to speaker error, leaving 475 stimuli. The recordings were processed in Adobe Audition. They were normalized to the same peak intensity (−15 dB relative to full scale). To decrease the abruptness of the soundfile onset, a 100 ms interval of silence was added to the beginning of each soundfile, and if the initial sound wasn't a plosive, the initial portion was reset to fade in gradually.

In the stimuli for Experiment 2a, the files were presented in the clear, without any added noise. However, it was expected that the error rate would be low in this case, and perhaps too low to provide enough information about the kinds of errors listeners were prone to. Thus a new series of stimuli was created by taking the stimuli for Experiment 2a and mixing in pink noise (in which intensity is inversely proportional to frequency) at a signal-to-noise ratio of 10 dB. These stimuli were used in Experiment 2b.

Since no changes were made to f0, voice quality, or segment duration, the stimuli do not sound like isolation words, i.e. complete intonational phrases consisting of a single word, but are clearly incomplete snippets from a longer utterance. Subjects were told that the stimuli were cut out of longer sentences, and that that is why they might sound odd.

The stimuli were presented through headphones from a laptop computer using Superlab (Cedrus). The stimuli were blocked by word pair, and presented in a different random order within the block for each subject. For each block, the subject was presented with the choice of items on the laptop screen – one choice in blue on the left side of the screen, and the other in red on the right. Sound files were presented every 2 seconds, and subjects were instructed to listen to each one and press a key on a response box to indicate as quickly as possible their choice as to which word they heard. A blue key on the left of the box corresponded to the left-hand choice in blue, and a red key on the right corresponded to the right-hand choice in red. Voiced and voiceless choices were evenly distributed between left and right.

Sixteen adult native speakers of American English participated in each of the two experiments. Each subject participated in only one of the experiments, and none of the subjects for the production experiment participated as subjects in these perception experiments.

Since the experiment involves native speakers of English identifying familiar words of English, it was expected that the error rate would be quite low. But the hypothesis was that there would nevertheless be a significant tendency among listeners to identify utterance-final obstruents as voiceless, and that there would be more voiceless judgments for forms excised from utterance-final position than for forms from utterance-medial position.

The dependent variable here is a categorical response (voiced/voiceless), so the models are based on a binomial distribution. Subject (i.e. listener), talker and minimum pair were included as random effects, and the fixed effects were stimulus voicing (voiced coded as 0, and voiceless as 1) and stimulus position (final coded as 0, and nonfinal as 1). The logistic regression models expressed the likelihood of a voiceless response based on these factors.

5.3.2 Results

There were 7,600 trials in each experiment (475 stimuli * 16 subjects). In experiment 2a there were 67 nonresponses, i.e. cases in which the subject did not press either key in the 2-second interval allowed. These were excluded from the analysis, leaving a total of 7,533 responses. In Experiment 2b, 62 nonresponses were excluded, as well as two responses with suspiciously low response times below 110 ms (from stimulus onset), leaving a total of 7,536 responses.

As expected, subjects were in general quite accurate in their identification of the stimuli. 6,844 of the responses in Experiment 2a (90.9%) were correct, while in Experiment 2b, with added noise, 6,539 responses (86.8%) were correct.

The responses are broken down by stimulus category in Table 5.1 for Experiment 2a and in Table 5.2 for Experiment 2b. Correct responses are highlighted in boldface.

Table 5.1: Experiment 2a: Number (and percentage) of voicing responses by stimulus manner, position and voicing

Stimulus manner	*Stimulus position*	*Stimulus voicing*	*Number (and percentage) of voiced responses*	*Number (and percentage) of voiceless responses*
Stop	*Nonfinal*	*Voiced*	**866 (92%)**	74 (8%)
Stop	*Nonfinal*	*Voiceless*	98 (10%)	**841 (90%)**
Stop	*Final*	*Voiced*	**891 (95%)**	49 (5%)
Stop	*Final*	*Voiceless*	72 (8%)	**866 (92%)**
Fricative	*Nonfinal*	*Voiced*	**919 (97%)**	33 (3%)
Fricative	*Nonfinal*	*Voiceless*	189 (20%)	**760 (80%)**
Fricative	*Final*	*Voiced*	**820 (89%)**	106 (11%)
Fricative	*Final*	*Voiceless*	68 (7%)	**881 (93%)**

Table 5.2: Experiment 2b: Number (and percentage) of voicing responses by stimulus manner, position and voicing

Stimulus manner	Stimulus position	Stimulus voicing	Number (and percentage) of voiced responses	Number (and percentage) of voiceless responses
Stop	*Nonfinal*	*Voiced*	**802 (86%)**	136 (14%)
Stop	*Nonfinal*	*Voiceless*	114 (12%)	**825 (88%)**
Stop	*Final*	*Voiced*	**833 (88%)**	110 (12%)
Stop	*Final*	*Voiceless*	83 (9%)	**855 (91%)**
Fricative	*Nonfinal*	*Voiced*	**859 (90%)**	93 (10%)
Fricative	*Nonfinal*	*Voiceless*	184 (19%)	**766 (81%)**
Fricative	*Final*	*Voiced*	**767 (83%)**	162 (17%)
Fricative	*Final*	*Voiceless*	115 (12%)	**832 (88%)**

In both experiments, the fricatives show a higher percentage of voiceless responses for corresponding stimuli from final position than for those from nonfinal position. Thus in Experiment 2a, voiceless fricative stimuli were correctly identified as voiceless in 93% of the final cases but only 80% of the nonfinal ones. Voiced fricative stimuli in the same experiment were incorrectly identified as voiceless in 11% of the final cases, as compared to 6% of the nonfinal ones. The same generalization held for the fricative stimuli in Experiment 2b.

However, the stops did not show such a pattern. In both experiments, as with fricative stimuli, voiceless stops were correctly identified as voiceless more often in final position than in nonfinal position. For example, among stimuli with voiceless stops in Experiment 2a, 92% were identified as voiceless in final position, compared to 90% in nonfinal position. But, unlike the fricative stimuli, the incorrect identification of voiced stops as voiceless was slightly *less* frequent in final position than in nonfinal position. For example, in Experiment 2a, 8% of the final voiced stops were identified as voiceless, compared with 10% of the nonfinal voiced stops.

The results of the statistical analysis are given in Table 5.3 for Experiment 2a, and in Table 5.4 for Experiment 2b.

Table 5.3: Experiment 2a: Fixed effects

Fixed effect	Estimated coefficient	z	p
Voicing	5.2	29.0	<0.001
Position	−1.4	−6.4	<0.001
Manner	−0.9	−3.3	<0.001
Voicing * Position	0.1	0.4	0.66
Voicing * Manner	0.9	6.4	<0.001
Position* Manner	1.8	6.4	<0.001
Voicing*Manner*Position	−1.0	−2.6	0.01

Table 5.4: Experiment 2b: Fixed effects

Fixed effect	Estimated coefficient	z	p
Voicing	3.9	27.7	<0.001
Position	−0.7	−4.9	<0.001
Manner	−0.5	−2.2	0.03
Voicing * Position	0.1	0.6	0.53
Voicing * Manner	0.9	4.2	<0.001
Position* Manner	1.0	4.9	<0.001
Voicing*Manner*Position	−0.8	−2.7	0.01

In both experiments, all the main effects were significant. The positive coefficient for voicing, in conjunction with the significant z value, indicates that a voiceless stimulus (coded 1) had a significantly greater likelihood to be identified as voiceless than a voiced stimulus (coded 0) had. This just reflects the high accuracy of identification of voicing categories. The negative coefficient for position, in conjunction with the significant effect for that factor, means that a nonfinal stimulus (coded 1) had a significantly smaller likelihood to be identified as voiceless than a final stimulus (coded 0). The negative coefficient for manner meant that a stop (coded 1) was less likely than a fricative (coded 0) to be identified as voiceless. However, there were significant interactions among these factors, complicating the interpretation.

The dataset was split into stop and fricative subsets so that the effects of voicing and position could be examined in these different manner subsets. The results of these tests are presented in Tables 5.5–5.8.

Table 5.5: Experiment 2a: Fricatives

Fixed effect	*Estimated coefficient*	*z*	*p*
Voicing	5.3	28.1	< 0.001
Position	−1.4	−6.5	< 0.001
Voicing * Position	0.2	0.6	0.53

Table 5.6: Experiment 2b: Fricatives

Fixed effect	*Estimated coefficient*	*z*	*p*
Voicing	4.0	27.1	< 0.001
Position	−0.7	−4.9	< 0.001
Voicing * Position	0.1	0.6	0.53

Table 5.7: Experiment 2a: Stops

Fixed effect	*Estimated coefficient*	*z*	*p*
Voicing	6.1	27.8	< 0.001
Position	0.5	2.4	0.02
Voicing * Position	−0.8	−3.2	0

Table 5.8: Experiment 2b: Stops

Fixed effect	Estimated coefficient	z	p
Voicing	4.8	28.6	< 0.001
Position	0.3	2.0	0.05
Voicing * Position	−0.7	−3.1	0

In the fricative subset in both experiments (Tables 5.5 and 5.6), the main effect of voicing was significant, with a positive coefficient reflecting the subjects' largely accurate identification of voicing categories. The main effect of position was also significant, with a negative coefficient reflecting an association of final position with voiceless responses and nonfinal position with voiced responses. The interaction was not significant, so there was no evidence that the effect of final position on identification was different for stimuli with a voiced fricative compared to those with a voiceless fricative.

In the stop subset (Tables 5.7 and 5.8), both main effects and their interaction were significant. The coefficient for voicing was positive in both experiments, indicating that among stops, as with fricatives, voiceless stimuli were more likely to get voiceless responses than were voiced stimuli. But the coefficient for position is positive, and that for the interaction is negative. This reflects the fact, noted above, that the effect of position was different for voiced stimuli than for voiceless ones. Voiceless stops were more often correctly identified as voiceless in final than in nonfinal position, as expected and as found with fricatives, but voiced stops were unexpectedly more often identified as voiceless in nonfinal than in final position.

The nonfinal condition was expected to be a neutral control condition, and in Experiment 2b this is how it turned out, with voiced and voiceless responses evenly split. But in Experiment 2a there were more voiced responses than voiceless responses in nonfinal position (51% among the stops, and 58% among the fricatives). This tendency toward voiced responses could be due to coarticulatory voicing, since each test obstruent is between two voiced sonorants (a vowel and a nasal). But it raises the possibility that the observed effects of position are due more to nonfinal voicing than to final devoicing. To exclude this possibility, we restrict our view to utterance-final fricatives. In this set, in both experiments, the proportion of voiceless responses was significantly greater than that expected by chance: Experiment 2a, $z = 1.7$, $p = 0.04$; Experiment 2b, $z = 2.2$, $p = 0.02$.

5.3.3 Discussion: Perception studies

The hypothesis was that the acoustic effects of utterance-final devoicing observed in the production study would lead to a tendency for word-final obstruents from utterance-final position to be identified as voiceless. The two perception experiments have provided support for this hypothesis in fricative-final words, but not in stop-final words, and in particular not in words ending in voiced stops.

One explanation of this difference between stops and fricatives could lie in the effects of manner on the acoustic correlates of voicing found in the production study. Fricatives had a longer constriction duration, a longer voiceless interval, and a lower V/VC duration ratio than stops, and in all of these measures the effect of a fricative thus coincides with the effect of a voiceless sound.[5] As Ohala (1983: 201) pointed out, 'voiced fricatives have more exacting aerodynamic requirements than do voiced stops', since voicing requires supralaryngeal pressure to be lower than sublaryngeal pressure, while at the same time supralaryngeal pressure behind the oral constriction must be high enough to generate turbulent oral airflow. Ohala suggests that this aerodynamic issue is part of the reason that consonant inventories with only voiceless fricatives are twice as common in Ruhlen's (1987) survey than inventories in which all stops are voiceless. He goes on to propose that it is also the reason that 'in American English the "voiced" fricatives /v, z/ are more likely to be devoiced in word-final position than are the stops /b, d, g/'. Thus it could be that the inherently weaker voicing cues for fricatives are more susceptible to confusing interference from utterance-final devoicing than the stronger voicing cues for stops.

5.4 Conclusion

The production study reported here has replicated previous findings of a significant utterance-final devoicing effect in English. Utterance-final obstruents displayed a longer constriction duration, a longer voiceless interval, and a lower ratio of vowel duration to total VC duration in comparison to nonfinal obstruents. In all these measures, the effect of utterance-final position coincides with the effect of belonging to the voiceless category.

The two perception studies tested the hypothesis that the acoustic effects of utterance-final position lead to a tendency to identify utterance-final obstruents as voiceless. The results of the studies clearly support that hypothesis for fricatives, but not for stops. Voiceless stops in final position were more likely to be correctly identified as voiceless than those in nonfinal position, but there was no tendency in either perception study for voiced stops to be misidentified as voiceless. I have suggested that this difference might have been due to the effects of fricatives on the voicing cues coincides with the effects of voicelessness and utterance-final position.

The results provide a basis for rejecting the null hypothesis that utterance-final position has no effect on identification of voicing categories. The fact that fricatives from utterance-final position tended to be identified as voiceless further suggests that for word-final fricatives the dominant perceptual cues for voicing are those like constriction duration, voiceless interval duration, and V/VC ratio, for which the effects of final position coincide with those of the voiceless category.

The test words in the perception experiments were presented in isolation, without following context. Thus listeners were not able to use their abilities to compensate for the acoustic effects of coarticulation (Lindblom and Studdert-Kennedy, 1967; Mann and Repp, 1980), and to fill in missing information top-down from discourse context (Warren, 1970) or from knowledge of the lexicon (Ganong, 1980). These abilities are impressive, but they are not infallible, as evidenced by the fact that listeners do make identification errors in conversation even with the full phonetic and discourse context known. The perception experiments reported here provide information about a baseline pattern of errors when such contextual information is held constant by complete removal of context.

The results thus provide support, at least in the case of fricatives, for one step in the diachronic account sketched in the introduction of how utterance-final phonetic devoicing provides the basis for a sound change resulting in phonological final devoicing. In this account the phonetic basis of final devoicing is limited to utterance-final position, but the pattern is generalized from there to word-final and syllable-final position through analogical extension. The results of the perception experiments also suggest that the perceptual basis of the sound change might be limited to fricatives, and extended from that subset of obstruents to the class of all obstruents.

One might expect from this that utterance-final fricative devoicing should be the most common version of the phonological pattern of final devoicing, since it requires the fewest further steps of generalization. There are cases of devoicing limited to fricatives (e.g. Gothic: Wright, 1899: 62–67; Hock, 1991: 43) and there are cases in which the devoicing is said to be limited to utterance-final position (e.g. some Yiddish dialects: Wetzels and Mascaró, 2001: 224; Polish: Jassem and Richter, 1989; examples in Blevins, 2006: 142). But it certainly does not seem as if such cases are more common than word-final devoicing, or devoicing of all obstruents including stops.

It would appear, then, that the tendency to generalize the phonological pattern, from utterance-final words to all words and from fricatives to all obstruents is strong enough to render utterance-final phonological fricative devoicing unstable. If so, this tendency must lie not in the phonetic basis of the pattern, but in how language learners make generalizations about the distribution of speech sound categories (Hayes, 1999; Moreton, 2008).

Notes

*   I would like to thank the following people for their helpful comments on this work: Juliette Blevins, Shigeto Kawahara, two anonymous reviewers, and audiences at the University of Massachusetts at Amherst and the Acoustical Society of America meeting in Portland. Thanks also to Lisa Selkirk, who I was lucky to have as my PhD supervisor, for her mentorship, her friendship, and the example she has always provided of elegant and insightful inquiry into how language works.

1   By 'voiced' obstruents I mean obstruents that are distinguished from 'voiceless' ones by having a higher proportion of vocal fold pulsing and a lower proportion of aperiodic noise. They are generally distinguished by other phonetic properties as well (Lisker, 1986; Kingston and Diehl, 1994), and in some of these cases periodic pulsing may not be the primary cue (Jessen and Ringen, 2002).

2   Descriptions of the final devoicing pattern are often frustratingly vague. The position of neutralization is sometimes simply described as 'final', without making clear what domain it is final in (e.g. Dambriunas *et al.,* 1966: 17), and it is often not clear whether the author checked other possible domains (e.g. whether devoicing occurs at the end of a word if the word is non-final in the phrase). Most of the descriptions cited here are also based on transcriptions, so they are inherently vague as to whether the devoicing effect is gradient or categorical.

3   The neutralization of the voicing contrast in final position in some languages is incomplete, i.e. there are measurable and perceptible differences between alternat-

ing and nonalternating final voiceless consonants (Dinnsen and Charles-Luce, 1984; Port and O'Dell, 1985; Slowiaczek and Dinnsen, 1985; Charles-Luce and Dinnsen, 1987, Slowiaczek and Szymanska, 1987, Warner *et al.*, 2004; Dmitrieva, 2005). Ernestus and Baayen (2006: 47) suggest that words with alternating final voiceless obstruents are influenced in production by the activation of the corresponding voiced-final items in their paradigm.

4   The subjects were from Oklahoma, Illinois, Tennessee, Oregon, and California.

5   Manner had no significant effect on the last measure considered: absolute vowel duration.

References

Abu-Mansour, M. (1996) Voice as a privative feature: assimilation in Arabic. In M. Eid (ed.) *Perspectives on Arabic Linguistics VIII* 201–231. Amsterdam: John Benjamins.

Ahmad, Z. (2005) *The Phonology-Morphology Interface in Malay: An Optimality Theoretic Account*. Canberra: Pacific Linguistics.

Bach, E. (1996) Building words in Haisla. Unpublished manuscript, University of Massachusetts, Amherst.

Baroni, M. and Vanelli, L. (2000) The relationship between vowel length and consonantal voicing in Friulian. In L. Repetti (ed.) *Phonological Theory and the Dialects of Italy* 13–44. Amsterdam: John Benjamins.

Barry, W. (1979) Complex encoding in word-final voiced and voiceless stops. *Phonetica* 36: 361–372.

Blevins, J. (2006) A theoretical synopsis of Evolutionary Phonology. *Theoretical Linguistics* 32 (2): 117–166.

Bliese, L. (1981) *A Generative Grammar of Afar*. Arlington, TX: Summer Institute of Linguistics.

Bloomfield, L. (1933) *Language*. New York: Holt, Rinehart, and Winston.

Booij, G. (1995) *The Phonology of Dutch*. Oxford: Oxford University Press.

Broselow, E., Chen, S.-I. and Wang, C. (1998) The emergence of the unmarked in second language phonology. *Studies in Second Language Acquisition* 20: 261–280.

Byrd, D., Lee, S., Riggs, D. and Adams, J. (2005) Interacting effects of syllable and phrase position on consonant articulation. *Journal of the Acoustical Society of America* 118 (6): 3860–3873.

Charles-Luce, J. and Dinnsen, D. (1987) A reanalysis of Catalan devoicing. *Journal of Phonetics* 15: 187–190.

Chen, M. (1970) Vowel length variation as a function of the voicing of the consonant environment. *Phonetica* 22: 129–159.

Clements, G. N. and Keyser, S. J. (1983) *CV Phonology*. Cambridge, MA: MIT Press.

Cook, T. L. (1969) *The Pronunciation of Efik for Speakers of English*. Bloomington, IN: Intensive Language Training Center, Indiana University.

Cutts, H. and Jensen, P. (1983) Speech timing of phonologically disordered children: voicing contrast of initial and final stop consonants. *Journal of Speech and Hearing Science* 26: 501–510.

Dambriunas, L., Klimas, A. and Smalstieg, W. (1966) *Introduction to Modern Lithuanian*. Brooklyn, NY: Franciscan Fathers.

Denes, P. (1955) Effect of duration on the perception of voicing. *Journal of the Acoustical Society of America* 27: 761–764.

Dinnsen, D. and Charles-Luce, J. (1984) Phonological neutralization, phonetic implementation and individual differences. *Journal of Phonetics* 12: 49–60.

Dinnsen, D. and Eckman, F. (1978) Some substantive universals in atomic phonology. *Lingua* 45 (1): 1–14.

Dmitrieva, O. (2005) *Incomplete Neutralization in Russian Final Devoicing: Acoustic Evidence from Native Speakers and Second Language Learners*. Master's thesis, University of Kansas, Lawrence.

Docherty, G. (1992) *The Timing of Voicing in British English Obstruents*. Berlin: Foris.

Eckman, F. (1981) On the naturalness of interlanguage phonological rules. *Language Learning* 31 (1): 195–216.

Ernestus, M. and Baayen, R. H. (2006) The functionality of incomplete neutralization in Dutch: the case of past-tense formation. In L. Goldstein, D. Whalen, and C. T. Best (eds) *Laboratory Phonology 8* 27–49. Berlin: Mouton de Gruyter.

Ewert, A. (1933) *The French Language*. London: Faber and Faber.

Flege, J. E. (1982) English speakers learn to suppress final devoicing. In K. Tuite, R. Schneider and R. Chametsky (eds) *Papers from the 18th Regional Meeting* 111–122. Chicago, IL: Chicago Linguistics Society.

Flege, J. and Davidian, R. (1984) Transfer and developmental processes in adult foreign language speech production. *Applied Psycholinguistics* 5 (4): 323–347.

Flege, J., Munro, M. and Skelton, L. (1992) Production of the word-final English /t/ - /d/ contrast by native speakers of English, Mandarin, and Spanish. *Journal of the Acoustical Society of America* 92: 128–143.

Francard, M. and Morin, Y.-C. (1986) Sandhi in Walloon. In H. Andersen (ed.) *Sandhi Phenomena in the Languages of Europe* 453–474. Berlin: Mouton de Gruyter.

Ganong, W. (1980) Phonetic categorization in auditory word perception. *Journal of Experimental Psychology: Human Perception and Performance* 6: 110–125.

Grammont, M. (1933) *Traité de phonétique*. Paris: Librairie Delagrave.

Haggard, M. (1978) The devoicing of voiced fricatives. *Journal of Phonetics* 6: 95–102.

Hahn, R. (1991) *Spoken Uyghur*. Seattle, WA: University of Washington Press.

Harris, J. (2009) Why final devoicing is weakening. In K. Nasukawa and P. Backley (eds) *Strength Relations in Phonology* 9–46. Berlin: Mouton de Gruyter.

Hayes, B. (1999) Phonetically-driven phonology: The role of Optimality Theory and inductive grounding. In M. Darnell, E. Moravscik, M. Noonan, F. Newmeyer and K. Wheatly (eds) *Functionalism and Formalism in Linguistics, Volume I: General Papers* 243–285. Amsterdam: John Benjamins.

Heim, M. (1976) *Contemporary Czech*. Columbus, OH: Slavica Publishers.

Hock, H. H. (1991) *Principles of Historical Linguistics (2nd edition)*. Berlin: Mouton de Gruyter.

Hodson, B. and Paden, E. P. (1981) Phonological processes which characterize unintelligible and intelligible speech in early childhood. *Journal of Speech and Hearing Disorders* 46: 369–373.

Hogan, J. and Roszypal, A. (1980) Evaluation of vowel duration as a cue for the voicing distinction in the following word-final consonant. *Journal of the Acoustical Society of America* 67 (5): 1764–1771.

Holmes, J. (1996) Losing voice: is final devoicing a feature of Maori English? *World Englishes* 15 (2): 193–205.

Hualde, J. (1991) *Basque Phonology*. London: Routledge.

Hualde, J. (1992) *Catalan*. London: Routledge.

Hyman, L. (1976) Phonologization. In A. Juillard (ed.) *Linguistic Studies Offered to Joseph Greenberg, Volume 2* 407–418. Saratoga, CA: Anma Libri.

Ingram, D. (1989) *Phonological Disability in Children*. London: Whurr.

Iwasaki, S. and Ingkaphirom, B. P. (2005) *Thai*. Cambridge: Cambridge University Press.

Jakobi, A. (1990) *A Fur Grammar*. Hamburg: Helmut Buske.

Jassem, W. and Richter, L. (1989) Neutralization of voicing in Polish obstruents. *Journal of Phonetics* 17: 317–325.

Jespersen, O. (1926) *Lehrbuch der Phonetik*. Leipzig: B. G. Truebner.

Jessen, M. (1998) *Phonetics and Phonology of Tense and Lax Obstruents in German*. Amsterdam: John Benjamins.

Jessen, M. and Ringen, C. (2002) Laryngeal features in German. *Phonology* 19: 189–218.

Jungraithmayr, H. (1970) *Die Ron-Sprachen*. Glückstadt: Verlag J. J. Augustin.

Kingston, J. and Diehl, R. (1994) Phonetic knowledge. *Language* 70: 419–454.

Klatt, D. and Klatt, L. (1990) Analysis, synthesis, and perception of voice quality variations among female and male talkers. *Journal of the Acoustical Society of America* 87: 820–857.

Kohler, K. (1979) Dimensions in the perception of fortis and lenis plosives. *Phonetica* 36 (4–5): 332–343.

Krämer, M. (2000) Voicing alternations and underlying representations: the case of Breton. *Lingua* 110 (9): 639–663.

Kuzla, C., Cho, T. and Ernestus, M. (2007) Prosodic strengthening of German fricatives in duration and assimilatory devoicing. *Journal of Phonetics* 35: 301–320.

Labov, W. (2001) *Principles of Linguistic Change: Social Factors*. Malden, MA: Blackwell.

Lehiste, I. (1970) *Suprasegmentals*. Cambridge, MA: MIT Press.

Lehtonen, J. (1970) *Aspects of Quantity in Standard Finnish*. Jyväskylä: Jyväskylä University Press.

Lightner, T. (1972) *Problems in the Theory of Phonology. Vol. 1: Russian Phonology and Turkish Phonology*. Edmonton: Linguistic Research, Inc.

Lindblom, B. (1968) Temporal organization of syllable production. *Speech Transmission Laboratory Quarterly Progess and Status Report* (Royal Institute of Technology, Stockholm) 2–3: 1–6.

Lindblom, B. (1983) Economy of speech gestures. In P. MacNeilage (ed.) *The Production of Speech* 217–245. New York: Springer.

Lindblom, B. and Studdert-Kennedy, M. (1967) On the role of formant transitions in vowel recognition. *Journal of the Acoustical Society of America* 42 (4): 830–843.

Lisker, L. (1957) Closure duration and the intervocalic voiced-voiceless distinction in English. *Language* 33: 42–49.

Lisker, L. (1986) 'Voicing' in English: a catalogue of acoustic features signaling /b/ vs. /p/ in trochees. *Language and Speech* 29: 3–11.

Lisker, L., Abramson, A., Cooper, F. and Schvey, M. (1969) Transillumination of the larynx in running speech. *Journal of the Acoustical Society of America* 45: 1544–1546.

Locke, J. (1983) *Phonological Acquisition and Change*. New York: Academic Press.

Lombardi, L. (1995) Laryngeal neutralization and syllable well-formedness. *Natural Language and Linguistic Theory* 13 (1): 39–74.

Lombardi, L. (1999) Positional faithfulness and voicing assimilation in Optimality Theory. *Natural Language and Linguistic Theory* 17 (2): 267–302.

Luelsdorf, P. (1975) *A Segmental Phonology of Black English*. The Hague: Mouton.

Major, R. and Faudree, M. (1996) Markedness universals and the acquisition of voicing contrasts by Korean speakers of English. *Studies in Second Language Acquisition* 18 (1): 69–90.

Mann, V. and Repp, B. (1980) Influence of vocalic context on perception of the [S]-[s] distinction. *Perception and Psychophysics* 28 (3): 213–228.

Michelson, K. (1988) *A Comparative Study of Lake-Iroquoian Accent*. Dordrecht: Kluwer.

Montreuil, J.-P. (1999) The Romansch syllable. In H. van der Hulst and N. Ritter (eds) *The Syllable: Views and Facts* 527–550. Berlin: Mouton de Gruyter.

Moreton, E. (2008) Analytic bias and phonological typology. *Phonology* 25: 83–127.

Myers, S. (2005) Vowel duration and neutralization of vowel length contrasts in Kinyarwanda. *Journal of Phonetics* 33 (4): 427–446.

Myers, S. and Hansen, B. (2007) The origin of vowel length neutralization in final position: evidence from Finnish speakers. *Natural Language and Linguistic Theory* 25 (1): 157–193.

Newton, B. (1972) *The Generative Interpretation of Dialect: A Study of Modern Greek Phonology*. Cambridge: Cambridge University Press.

Nivens, R. (1992) A lexical phonology of West Tarangan. In D. Burquest and W. Laidis (eds) *Phonological Studies in Four Languages of Maluku* 127–227. Arlington, TX: Summer Institute of Linguistics.

Ohala, J. (1981) The listener as a source of sound change. In C. Masek, R. Hendrick and M. Miller (eds) *Papers from the Parasession on Language and Behavior* 178–203. Chicago, IL: Chicago Linguistics Society.

Ohala, J. (1983) The origin of sound patterns in vocal tract constraints. In P. Mac. Neilage (ed.) *The Production of Speech* 189–216. New York: Springer.

Ohala, J. (1993) The phonetics of sound change. In C. Jones (ed.) *Historical Linguistics: Problems and Perspectives* 237–278. London: Longman.

Oller, D. (1973) The effect of position in utterance on speech segment duration in English. *Journal of the Acoustical Society of America* 54: 1235–1247.

Oller, D. and Smith, B. (1977) Effect of final syllable position on vowel duration in infant babbling. *Journal of the Acoustical Society of America* 62: 994–997.

Oller, D., Wieman, L., Doyle, W. and Ross, C. (1976) Infant babbling and speech. *Journal of Child Language* 3 (1): 1–11.

Padgett, J. (this volume) The role of prosody in Russian voicing.

Passy, P. (1891) *Étude sur les changements phonétiques et leurs caractères généraux*. Paris: Librairie Firmin-Didot.

Pierrehumbert, J. (2001) Exemplar dynamics: word frequency, lenition and contrast. In J. Bybee and P. Hopper (eds) *Frequency and the Emergence of Linguistic Structure* 137–157. Amsterdam: John Benjamins.

Pind, J. (1986) The perception of quantity in Icelandic. *Phonetica* 43: 116–139.

Pitkin, H. (1984) *Wintu Grammar*. Berkeley, CA: University of California Press.

Poppe, N. (1960) *Buriat Grammar*. The Hague: Mouton.

Port, R. and O'Dell, M. (1985) Neutralization of syllable-final devoicing in German. *Journal of Phonetics* 13: 455–471.

Purnell, T., Salmons, J. and Tepeli, D. (2005) German substrate effects in Wisconsin English: evidence for final fortition. *American Speech* 80 (2): 135–164.

Raphael, L. (1971) Preceding vowel duration as a cue to the perception of the voicing characteristics of word-final consonants in American English. *Journal of the Acoustical Society of America* 51: 1296–1303.

Rubach, J. (1984) *Cyclic and Lexical Phonology: The Structure of Polish*. Dordrecht: Foris.

Rubach, J. (1993) *The Lexical Phonology of Slovak*. Oxford: Oxford University Press.

Ruhlen, M. (1987) *A Guide to the Languages of the World*. Stanford, CA: Stanford University Press.

Sapir, E. (1990) *Takelma Texts and Grammar (Collected Works of Edward Sapir VIII)*. Berlin: Mouton de Gruyter.

Scatton, E. (1984) *A Reference Grammar of Modern Bulgarian*. Columbus, OH: Slavica Publishers.

Selkirk, E. (1978) On prosodic structure and its relation to syntactic structure. In T. Fretheim (ed.) *Nordic Prosody II* 111–140. Trondheim: TAPIR.

Selkirk, E. (1986) On derived domains in sentence phonology. *Phonology Yearbook* 3: 371–405.

Shadle, C. (1997) The aerodynamics of speech. In W. Hardcastle and J. Laver (eds) *The Handbook of Phonetic Sciences* 33–64. Oxford: Blackwell.

Sievers, E. (1901) *Grundzüge der Phonetik, 5th Edition*. Leipzig: Breitkopf und Härtel.

Singh, C. Y. (2000) *Manipuri Grammar*. New Delhi: Rajesh Publications.

Slifka, J. (2006) Some physiological correlates to regular and irregular phonation at the end of an utterance. *Journal of Voice* 20 (2): 171–186.

Slowiaczek, L. and Dinnsen, D. (1985) On the neutralizing status of Polish word-final devoicing. *Journal of Phonetics* 13 (3): 325–341.

Slowiaczek, L. and Szymanska, H. (1989) Perception of word-final devoicing in Polish. *Journal of Phonetics* 17: 205–212.

Smith, B. (1979) A phonetic analysis of consonantal devoicing in children's speech. *Journal of Child Language* 6 (1): 19–28.

Smith, C. (1997) The devoicing of /z/ in American English: effects of local and prosodic context. *Journal of Phonetics* 25 (4): 471–500.

Smith, C. (1999) Marking the boundary: utterance-final prosody in French questions and statements. In J. Ohala, Y. Hasegawa, M. Ohala, D. Granville and A. Bailey (eds), *Proceedings of the XIVth International Congress of Phonetic Sciences* 1181–1184. Berkeley, CA: Linguistics Department, University of California.

Smith, C. (2003) Vowel devoicing in contemporary French. *French Language Studies* 13: 177–194.

Smith, N. (1973) *The Acquisition of Phonology*. Cambridge: Cambridge University Press.

Stevens, K., Blumstein, S., Glicksman, L., Burton, M. and Kurowski, K. (1992) Acoustic and perceptual characteristics of voicing in fricatives and fricative clusters. *Journal of the Acoustical Society of America* 91 (5): 2979–3000.

Sweet, H. (1877) *Handbook of Phonetics*. Oxford: Oxford University Press.

Thompson, L. (1965) *A Vietnamese Grammar*. Seattle, WA: University of Washington Press.

Thurgood, G. and LaPolla, R. (eds) (2003) *The Sino-Tibetan Languages*. London: Routledge.

Tucker, A. (1994) *A Grammar of Kenya Luo (Dholuo)*. Cologne: Rüddiger Koppe Verlag.

Turk, A. (1999) Structural influences on boundary-related lengthening in English. In J. Ohala, Y. Hasegawa, M. Ohala, D. Granville and A. Bailey (eds), *Proceedings of the XIVth International Congress of Phonetic Sciences* 237–240. Berkeley, CA: Linguistics Department, University of California.

Umeda, N. (1975) Vowel duration in American English. *Journal of the Acoustical Society of America* 58 (2): 434–445.

Velten, H. (1943) The growth of phonemic and lexical patterns in infant speech. *Language* 19: 281–292.

Warner, N., Jongman, A., Sereno, J. and Kemps, R. (2004) Incomplete neutralization and other sub-phonemic durational differences in production and perception: Evidence from Dutch. *Journal of Phonetics* 32: 251–276.

Warren, R. (1970) Perceptual restoration of missing speech sounds. *Science* 167 (917): 392–393.

Wedel, A. and Van Volkinburg, H. (2009) Modeling simultaneous convergence and divergence of linguistic features between differently-identifying groups in contact. Unpublished paper retrieved on 16 June 2009 from http://dingo.sbs.arizona.edu/~wedel/publications/

Westbury, J. and Keating, P. (1986) On the naturalness of stop consonant voicing. *Journal of Linguistics* 22: 145–166.

Wetzels, W. and Mascaró, J. (2001) The typology of voicing and devoicing. *Language* 77 (2): 207–244.

Whitney, W. D. (1879) *A Sanskrit Grammar*. Leipzig: Breitkopf and Härtel.

Wolf, C. (1978) Voicing cues in English final stops. *Journal of Phonetics* 6: 299–309.

Wolfram, W. (1969) *A Sociolinguistic Description of Detroit Negro Speech*. Washington, DC: Center for Applied Linguistics.

Wolfram, W., and Christian, D. (1976) *Appalachian Speech*. Arlington, VA: Center for Applied Linguistics.

Wright, J. (1899) *A Primer of the Gothic Language*. Oxford: Oxford University Press.

Yu, A. (2004) Explaining final obstruent voicing in Lezgian: phonetics and history. *Language* 80 (1): 73–97.

6 The role of prosody in Russian voicing

Jaye Padgett[a]

6.1 Introduction

Though Russian voicing assimilation and final devoicing have received a great deal of attention in the literature on generative phonology, there are still basic aspects of the data that are not widely understood or agreed upon. They can be unified under the question, What role does prosody play in the Russian voicing facts? The answer given here will in some ways affirm the role of prosody in the Russian facts and in others exclude it. On the affirmative side, Russian voicing assimilation cannot be understood without reference to higher prosodic units such as the prosodic word. I will present an analysis of the word-level prosody of Russian inspired by Ito and Mester (2007; 2009; see also this volume) (an approach also pursued by Selkirk to appear), one which eschews the 'Clitic Group' and other categories apart from the Phonological Word and the Phonological Phrase. On the negative side, I argue that characterizing the triggers and targets of the voicing processes by means of syllable position cannot work for Russian; the account instead requires a cue-based approach, of the sort advocated by Steriade (1997).

This paper provides an analysis of Russian voicing assimilation and final devoicing couched within Optimality Theory (Prince and Smolensky, 1993 [2004]), one that is cue-based but sensitive to questions of higher prosodic structure. An important goal will be to elucidate areas where the facts have been unclear in the past. Apart from prosody-related matters, this includes for example the controversial status of sonorants in the voicing processes. As we

[a] Jaye Padgett: University of California, Santa Cruz, CA. Email: jayepadgett@gmail.com

will see, there is an important distinction to be made between processes that apply exceptionlessly and categorically and those that do not.[1]

6.2   Basic facts

The basic facts of Russian voicing assimilation have been well described (Avanesov, 1956; Jakobson, 1956; Halle, 1959; Hayes, 1984; Kiparsky, 1985, among many others). Obstruents devoice word-finally; compare the (a) and (b) forms below.[2]

(1)

a.	/slʲeˈd-a/	slʲiˈd-a	'track (gen.sg.)'	slʲet (nom.sg.)
	/ˈraz-a/	ˈraz-ə	'occasion (gen.sg.)'	ras (nom.sg.)
	/ˈplʲaz̻-a/	ˈplʲaz̻-ə	'beach (gen.sg.)'	plʲaş (nom.sg.)
	/ˈknʲig-a/	ˈknʲig-ə	'book (nom.sg.)'	knʲik (gen.pl.)
	/guˈb-a/	guˈb-a	'lip (nom.sg.)'	gup (gen.pl.)

In addition, obstruent clusters within a word invariably agree in voicing; the cluster's voicing is predictable from the cluster-final consonant's voicing, as shown in (2). The examples in (2a–b) show prefixes ending in underlyingly voiceless obstruents, while (2c–d) show prefixes with underlyingly voiced obstruents. The underlying status of the consonants is clear from their behavior before sonorants (the (i) examples).

(2)

a.	i.	/ot-ˈjexatʲ/	ɐt-ˈjexətʲ	'to ride off'
	ii.	/ot-stuˈpʲitʲ/	ɐt-stuˈpʲitʲ	'to step back'
	iii.	/ot-ˈbrosʲitʲ/	ɐd-ˈbrosʲitʲ	'to throw aside'
b.	i.	/ˈs-jexatʲ/	ˈs-jexətʲ	'to ride down'
	ii.	/s-proˈsʲitʲ/	s-prɐˈsʲitʲ	'to ask'
	iii.	/ˈs-dʲelatʲ/	ˈz-dʲelətʲ	'to do'
c.	i.	/pod-nʲeˈstʲi/	pəd-nʲiˈstʲi	'to bring (to)'
	ii.	/pod-pʲiˈsatʲ/	pət-pʲiˈsatʲ	'to sign'
	iii.	/pod-ˈzet͡ʃ/	pɐd-ˈzet͡ʃ	'to burn'
d.	i.	/iz-laˈgatʲ/	iz-lɐˈgatʲ	'to state; set forth'
	ii.	/iz-klʲuˈt͡ʃatʲ/	is-klʲuˈt͡ʃatʲ	'to exclude; dismiss'
	iii.	/iz-ˈgnatʲ/	iz-ˈgnatʲ	'to drive out'

Final-devoicing 'feeds' voicing assimilation; that is, all of the obstruents of a word-final cluster are devoiced:

(3)

a.	/'pojezd-a/	'pojizd-ə	'train (gen.sg.)'	b.	'pojist	(nom.sg.)
	/'vʲizg-a/	'vʲizg-ə	'squeal (gen.sg.)'		vʲisk	(nom.sg.)
	/i'zb-a/	i'zb-a	'hut (nom.sg.)'		isp	(gen.pl.)

Apart from these basic facts, accounts of Russian voicing differ significantly. The areas of disagreement or unclarity fall mostly into two categories: the behavior of voicing assimilation across word boundaries, and the behavior of sonorants. It turns out that one can plausibly distinguish facts that are categorical and obligatory from others that are gradient and therefore optional.[3] My goal will be to elucidate these distinct sets of facts and provide a formal account for only the former set, since the latter are better handled by models of phonetic implementation. In taking this position on gradient effects I follow Keating (1988), Liberman and Pierrehumbert (1984), Zsiga (1993), and many others.

6.3   Sonorants

Sonorants in Russian do not participate in the truly categorical voicing processes at all. First, they never trigger voicing assimilation. The examples below show this word-initially, word-medially, and word-finally, (4)a-c respectively.

(4)	a.	knʲasʲ	'prince'	vs.	gnutʲ	'to bend'
		'tratʲitʲ	'to spend'		'drat:sə	'to fight'
	b.	'pʲisʲmə	'letters'		bəlʲşivʲi'zmə	'bolshevism (gen.)'
	c.	tʲi'atr	'theater'		kadr	'film sequence'

Nor do sonorants devoice, except for low-level gradient effects. Word-final sonorants as in (5)a are pronounced as voiced in careful speech. This is true even of sonorants preceded by a voiced ((5)b) or voiceless ((5)c) obstruent.

(5)	a.	mil	'dear'	b.	z̞iznʲ	'life'	c.	lʲitr	'liter'
		vonʲ	'stench'		bobr	'beaver'		voplʲ	'cry'

Finally, sonorants do not acquire voicelessness from a following obstruent, 6(a-b).

(6) a. bort   'side (of a boat)'   *bor̥t
         volk   'wolf'   *vol̥k
     b. rta   'mouth (gen.)'   *r̥ta
         mstʲitʲ   'to avenge'   *m̥stʲitʲ

Final devoicing and assimilation by sonorants in examples like (5) and (6) are sometimes described (Coats and Harshenin, 1971; Daniels, 1972; Hayes, 1984; Kiparsky, 1985), but once again there is a distinction to be made here between obligatory, categorical rules, and optional, gradient ones. (The references cited in fact make this distinction, especially Kiparsky, 1985.) Let us consider (5)-(6) in more detail.

First, few descriptions of Russian suggest that word-final sonorants as in (5)a devoice. Sources that do make clear that this is sporadic and partial (Bondarko, 1998:121; Kniazev, 2006:74; the latter explicitly classifies sonorant devoicing as phonetic, as opposed to phonological obstruent devoicing).[4] It is more common to suggest devoicing in words such as (5)b-c, especially for liquids, such that /bobr/ can be [bobr̥] or even [bopr̥]. Again, however, this occurs only optionally and gradiently (Isacenko, 1947; Avanesov, 1956; Baranovskaia, 1968; Reformatskii, 1975; Bondarko, 1998), being more likely in fast or casual speech and if the preceding obstruent is voiceless. According to Reformatskii (1975) and Avanesov (1956), for example, pronunciations such as [bobr̥] are merely possible, more likely in fast speech, and any devoicing of the preceding obstruent is partial. Indeed, (near)-minimal pairs such as [kadr] 'film sequence' and [tʲiatr] 'theater' are routine. These conclusions regarding (5) are supported by the phonetic investigation of Barry (1989). Turning finally to (6), assimilation in cases such as (6)a do not occur at all, as Barkaï and Horvath (1978) point out. Devoicing in (6)b is again more likely when the following obstruent is voiceless, and it is optional (Isacenko, 1947; Avanesov, 1956; Baranovskaia, 1968). Figure 6.1a–b show example spectrograms of /l/ in just this environment, before a voiced and voiceless obstruent (respectively); as can be seen at least for this speaker, the /l/ is far from voiceless in Figure 6.1b. These spectrograms are entirely representative of this speaker. (On the source of this data see below.)

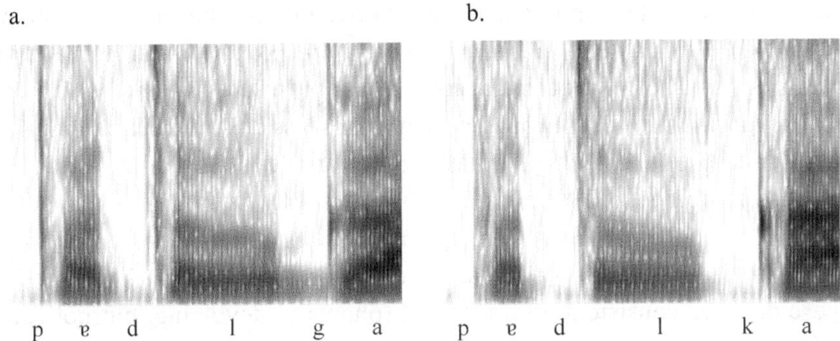

Figure 6.1: Spectrograms of word-initial [l] before a voiced (a) and voiceless (b) velar.

Sonorants have been said famously not only to devoice, but to be transparent to voicing assimilation in constructions as in (7), giving e.g., [ɐd mzdᵛi] and [is 'm̥ts͡ᵛenskə] instead of (7a–b) respectively (Jakobson, 1956; Hayes, 1984; Kiparsky, 1985). This has always been a controversial claim; some sources, such as Shapiro (1993), deny it altogether. Given the facts above, it would be very surprising if this were indeed a phonological rule of Russian. At best we expect it to occur, once again, only gradiently and optionally. Indeed, a phonetic study by Robblee and Burton (1997) examines cases involving liquids, e.g., *s lʲdʲinᵛi* 'from (the) ice floe', and finds no evidence of assimilation, though the authors do not rule out the possibility of gradient assimilation.[5]

(7)

a.	i.	/ot mzdi/	[ɐt mzdᵛi]	'from the bribe'
	ii.	/ot lʲda/	[ɐt lʲda]	'from the ice'
b.	i.	/iz 'mt͡senska/	[iʐ 'm̥ts͡ᵛenskə]	'from/out of Mcensk'
	ii.	/iz rta/	[iz rta]	'out of the mouth'

The graph in Figure 6.2 shows the duration of voicing within Russian [l,r,m] in a context similar to that shown in (7). The data are from recordings of a 20-year-old female student from St Petersburg, recorded at St Petersburg University.[6] The nonce words *lkara, rkara, mkara* were recorded in the carrier phrases [on pəlu'tʃʲil ɐt ____ 'dʲesʲitʲ ru'blʲej] 'He received 10 rubles from ____'; and the nonce words *lkarom, rkarom, mkarom* in the carrier phrase [on nɐ'ʂol pɐd ____ 'dʲesʲitʲ ru'blʲej] 'He found 10 rubles under ____'.

These carrier phrases put the nonce words in just the environment of preposition + noun seen in (7), half with a preceding [t] and half with a preceding [d]. The boxplots in Figure 6.2 each represent five tokens. If these data are representative, they suggest that [r] has less closure voicing duration than [l] and [m], and perhaps that there is more devoicing of [m] when [t] precedes compared to [l] and [r].[7] (Both of these effects are significant at $p <$ 0.001 for this speaker.) However, for our purposes what is more important is that all of these tokens have closure voicing, ranging from 13 to 143 ms. These data are consistent with gradient (phonetic) devoicing, but not categorical (phonological) devoicing.

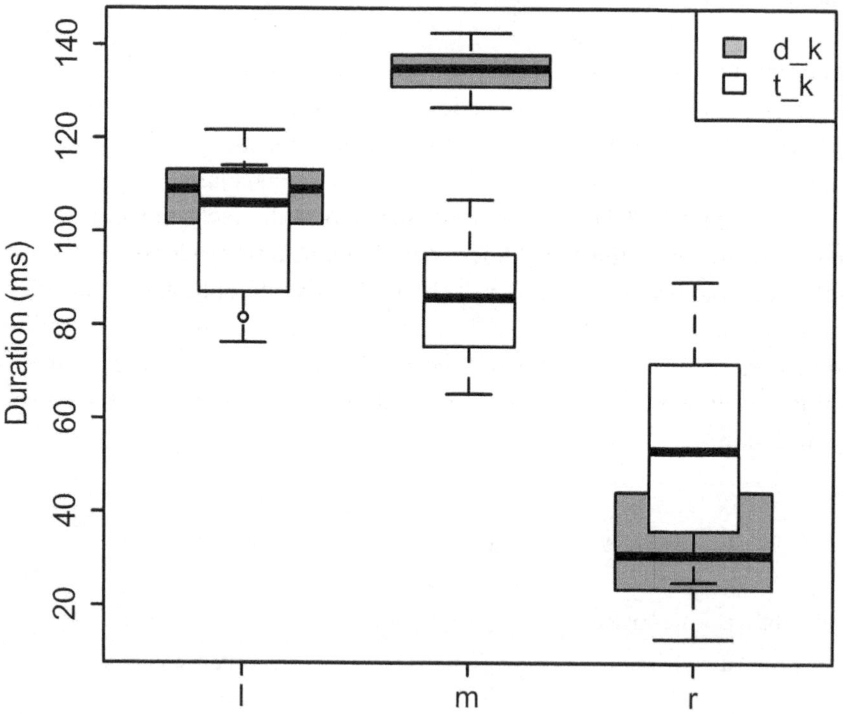

Figure 6.2: Duration of voicing within Russian [l,r,m] after [t] (white) or [d] (shaded) and before [k], in a context similar to that shown in (7).

If there is no phonological voicing assimilation in *ot mzdʲi*, etc., then why do some sources, most notably Jakobson, claim there is? We cannot rule out different dialects or idiolects, of course, but putting this aside, the claim here still allows for optional, gradient assimilation in fast or casual speech. Further, Robblee and Burton (1997) speculate that perhaps listeners perceive assimilation for other reasons: they found that the closure duration of stops in such clusters, one cue to voicing, was neutralized (though not in the way predicted by assimilation!). Perhaps listeners perceive partially neutralized stops as somehow lacking in their own voicing and so 'assimilated'. This explanation cannot extend to fricatives.

It seems likely that voicing effects involving sonorants should be handled by the phonetic component.

6.4   Voicing across words

The Russian voicing effects provide evidence of significant higher prosodic structure, in particular structure around the level of the prosodic word. First, Gvozdev (1949), Jakobson (1956), Halle (1959), Vinogradov (1960), and many others assume that one or more prepositions plus the following major category item constitutes something like a phonological word.[8] This assumption accounts for the lack of final devoicing in prepositions. Compare (8)a and (8)b: word-final voiced obstruents devoice before a following sonorant, unless the word is a preposition. Bracketing now indicates hypothesized prosodic word boundaries.

(8)	a.	/ot'kaz 'lʲeni/	[ɐt'kas]['lʲenʲi]	'Lena's refusal'
		/sad mʲi'xaila/	[sat][mʲi'xailə]	'Mikhail's garden'
		/grob 'rozi/	[grop]['rozʲi]	'Rosa's grave'
	b.	/iz lʲenʲin'grada/	[iz lʲinʲin'gradə]	'from Leningrad'
		/pod mo'skvoj/	[pəd mɐs'kvoj]	'near Moscow'
		/nad 'rozoj/	[nɐd 'rozəj]	'above the rosebush'

Voicing assimilation occurs within this same domain, as shown below. The (i) forms in (9) show the preposition-final consonant before sonorants, making clear its underlying voicing.

(9)

a.	i.	/ot 'mami/	[ɐt 'mamʲi]	'from mama'
	ii.	/ot 'papi/	[ɐt 'papʲi]	'from papa'
	iii.	/ot 'babuşkʲi/	[ɐd 'babuşkʲi]	'from grandma'
b.	i.	/'s mamoj/	['s maməj]	'with mama'
	ii.	/'s papoj/	['s papəj]	'with papa'
	iii.	/'s babuşkoj/	['z babuşkəj]	'with grandma'
c.	i.	/pod 'mamoj/	[pɐd 'maməj]	'under mama'
	ii.	/pod 'papoj/	[pɐt 'papəj]	'under papa'
	iii.	/pod 'babuşkoj/	[pɐd 'babuşkəj]	'under grandma'
d.	i.	/iz 'mami/	[iz 'mamʲi]	'out of mama'
	ii.	/iz 'papi/	[is 'papʲi]	'out of papa'
	iii.	/iz 'babuşkʲi/	[iz 'babuşkʲi]	'out of grandma'

Things are somewhat different when it comes to enclitics as in (10). Notice, first, that final devoicing applies before these enclitics: /sad/ in (10)a surfaces as [sat] before the interrogative particle [lʲi]. As the bracketing suggests, I assume therefore that clitics are not included in the prosodic word-like domain being entertained. (See Halle, 1959 for a similar proposal in terms of boundary symbols.) On the other hand, voicing assimilation applies across enclitic boundaries, as shown in (10)b-c.

(10)

	/sok/		/sad/	
a.	[sok] lʲi	'juice (interr.)'	[sat] lʲi	'garden (interr.)'
b.	[sog] zi	'juice (emph.)'	[sad] zi	'garden (emph.)'
c.	[sok] tə	'juice (topic.)'	[sat] tə	'garden (topic.)'
cf.	[sok-ə]	'juice (gen. sg.)'	[sad-ə]	'garden (gen. sg.)'

All sources agree on the final devoicing facts described above, and on the existence of voicing assimilation within the 'prosodic word' (that is, involving prepositions). A phonetic study by Burton and Robblee (1997) supports the latter. Nearly all sources describe voicing assimilation across the enclitic boundary as well, as shown in (10)b-c.[9]

Things are less clear regarding voicing assimilation across major category words.[10] Here many sources either explicitly deny it ever occurs (Isacenko,

1947), though this is incorrect, or state that it occurs optionally and/or gradiently (Isacenko, 1955; Halle, 1959; Baranovskaia, 1968; Shapiro, 1993).[11] Avanesov (1972), a work notable for its degree of phonetic detail (though also for its normative intentions), does not mention assimilation across major category word boundaries at all. In text he transcribes, assimilation is never indicated in this context, e.g. [stʲi'kajit] [doʃʲ:] 'rain flows down', [pʲi'sok] [gɐ'rʲuʧʲij] 'inflammable sand', while assimilation is always transcribed within a prosodic word, e.g., [ɐd 'znoju] 'from (the) intense heat', from /ot 'znoju/, [pɐt 'svodəm] 'under (the) arch', from /pod svodom/. (All examples p. 363.) On the other hand, phonetic studies by Paufoshima and Agaronov (1971) and Wells (1987) find assimilation across such boundaries in most instances. Even here, though, the results are not uniform, with failure to assimilate, and partial assimilation, occasionally occurring.

A conservative position, therefore, would be *phonological* voicing assimilation applies within prosodic words but not across them. Though further phonetic study is warranted, the evidence suggests that when assimilation happens across words, it happens gradiently.

This section and the last have argued that Russian voicing effects that occur across major category word boundaries, and those involving sonorants, should not be handled by the phonology, because they do not apply categorically. A shadow may be cast over this attempt to distinguish the categorical vs. the gradient by the observation that Russian final obstruent devoicing – treated as categorical here – is phonetically incomplete (Dmitrieva, 2005). Dmitrieva's careful phonetic study finds that underlyingly voiced obstruents in (largely) monosyllables like /zub/ 'tooth' show vestiges of their voicing in their surface pronunciations. This finding mirrors results for other languages having final obstruent devoicing, including Polish, German, and Catalan. (See Dmitrieva for an overview of the literature.) Given this fact, can even final obstruent devoicing be called categorical?

In fact, the gradient effects discussed above and incomplete obstruent devoicing are fundamentally different. Sonorant devoicing, for example, ranges from full to nonexistent, depending on rate/style of speech, phonetic context, etc. Crucially, it can fail to occur at all. On the other hand, obstruent devoicing cannot fail (putting aside deliberate spelling pronunciations). In fact, incomplete obstruent devoicing is subtle enough that it has become widely acknowledged over the last decades only due to instrumental phonetic techniques. For her Russian subjects that had no exposure to English (an important control, since English obviously lacks final devoicing), Dmitrieva found differences between pairs like /zub/ and /sup/ based on two measurements of the final consonant: duration of the closure, and duration of the release.

As some have argued, the existence of incomplete neutralization may require an approach in which phonology is not seen as derivationally prior to phonetics, or as different from phonetics as is widely assumed (see recent discussion and references in Gafos, 2006; Yu, 2007). However, even in Gafos's (2006) dynamical systems approach to phonology, obstruent devoicing patterns as in Russian are handled by means of 'macroscopic parameters' controlling 'qualitatively distinct modes of the voicing system' (p. 58), while incomplete neutralization results from the (parallel) interaction of these stable parameters with a scalar variable denoting 'intentional strength' (representing an intention of producing the underlying voicing). At the end of the day, any approach to phonology must represent the difference between 'stable', categorical patterns and those that are more 'scalar' or gradient.

6.5   The prosody of Russian voicing assimilation

6.5.1   Higher prosodic structure

In order to capture the special behavior of enclitics, Padgett (2002) called on a clitic group domain, assuming it encompassed a prosodic word (as described above) and additional enclitics, e.g., |[sat]$_{Pwd}$ lʲi|$_{CG}$ 'garden (interr.)', from /sad lʲi/, |[is kard]$_{Pwd}$zʲi|$_{CG}$ 'from the maps (emph.)', from /iz kart ze/. (See Hayes (1989); Nespor and Vogel (1986) on a distinction between prosodic word and clitic group.) The domain of voicing assimilation was argued to be the clitic group, while devoicing occurred at the end of a prosodic word. There is independent evidence for excluding enclitics from prosodic words in Russian: prepositions form part of the word stress domain, sometimes receiving the stress themselves (Gvozdev, 1949; Jakobson, 1956), e.g., ['pod ruku] 'by the arm' (compare [pəd ru'koj] 'at hand'). Enclitics are never stressed, and have no effect on stress.

Though the prosodic distinctions outlined above are well motivated, recent work on the prosodic hierarchy questions making a distinction between categories like prosodic word and clitic group. In a very general study of higher prosodic categories and relations, Ito and Mester (2007, 2009) argue that such distinctions are both too rich and too poor. (See also Selkirk, to appear.) They are too rich in that they imply a seemingly limitless and inconsistent inventory of prosodic categories; they are too poor in nevertheless providing too little structure to account for facts. To handle prosodic word-like facts, Ito and Mester argue for only one prosodic word-like category; following Ito and Mester I will label this category 'ω'. However, they also argue that prosodic categories like ω can form recursive structures having maximal and minimal projections, ω_{Max} and ω_{Min}. Crucially, phonological processes can make reference to ω_{Max} or ω_{Min}. They may also refer to ω, encompassing ω_{Max}, ω_{Min}, and any intermediate projections of ω. Importantly, there is no way to refer to intermediate projections exclusively. Let us consider the Russian facts within this framework.

The diagram in (11) recapitulates the facts to be explained. Prepositions together with a following open class word form a domain of final devoicing; that is, devoicing occurs at the end of this domain. This domain and a following clitic form a larger voicing assimilation domain. Voicing assimilation (at least as a categorical rule) does not apply across the boundary of this larger domain.

(11) Prosodic domains of Russian voicing

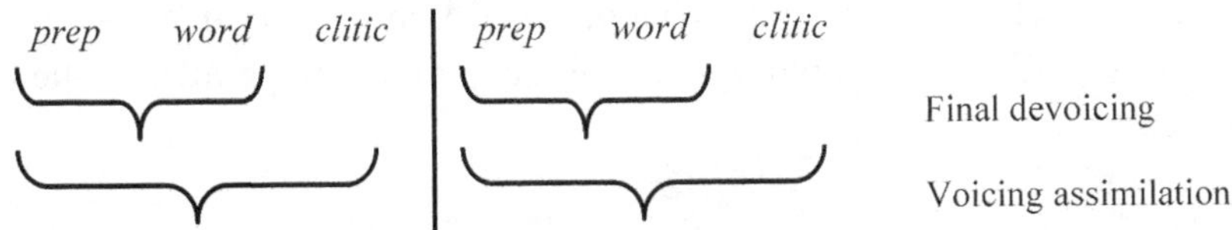

Further evidence for the smaller ω domain, as noted above, is its status as the domain of word stress. Prepositions cannot be ω themselves, because they do not bear stress independent of a following open-class item and because they do not devoice finally. However, these facts still leave the two possibilities shown in (12) for incorporating a preposition into ω: simple incorporation (as in (a)), or adjunction (as in (b)).

(12)

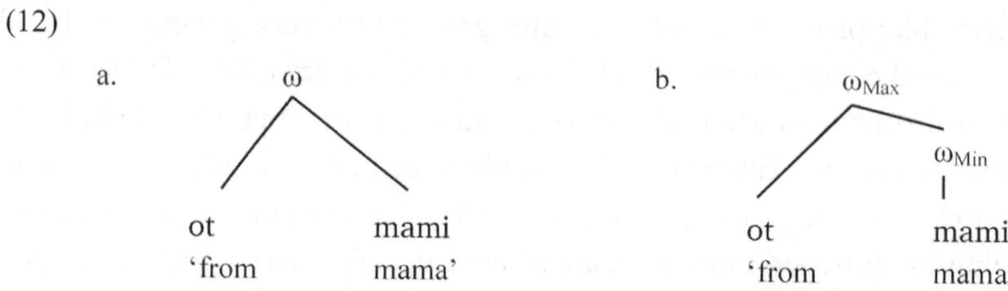

There is reason to favor (12)b for Russian. Though prepositions group with following words for the purposes of stress and voicing assimilation, they are arguably 'aloof' in other respects. First, some researchers claim that prepositions are separated from what follows by a syllable boundary, even when the sequence in question would form a fine onset. (This fact is relevant to the analysis of voicing assimilation in the next section.) Second, though adjacent consonants assimilate in secondary palatalization within words, they can fail to do so across the preposition-word boundary (see Avanesov, 1972; Darden, 1971, on both points). For just these reasons Zubritskaya (1995) treats prepositions as adjoined to the prosodic word as in (12)b. Gribanova (in progress) presents further arguments for this structure for Russian prefix-verb stem complexes, which behave identically to preposition-word complexes in many respects.[12]

Turning to enclitics, the structure for *sat lʲi* 'garden (interrogative)' cannot be (13)a. The reason, recall, is that final devoicing applies to *sat* (underlying /sad/) in such cases. For this to happen the /d/ must be ω-final. A structure such as (13)b would capture this difference in a way parallel to the clitic group idea.

(13)

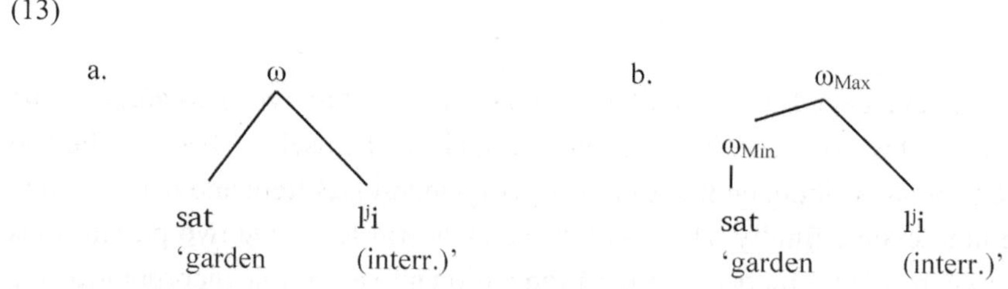

There is a problem with (13)b as well, however. Consider sequences containing both a preposition and an enclitic particle, assuming the enclitics are indeed part of ω as in (13)b. Since both kinds of clitic must adjoin, we might entertain either of (14)a-b for a phrase like /iz knʲig lʲi/ 'out of the books (interr.)'. We can immediately rule out (14)a: it does not capture the prosodic unity of the preposition-plus-following-word, e.g., the fact that this grouping constitutes the domain of stress.

(14)

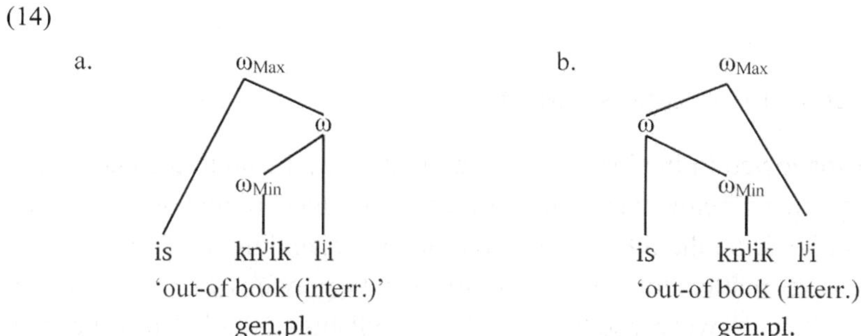

The problem is that (14)b also fails to capture this grouping adequately. Though [is knʲik]$_ω$ is indeed a prosodic word in (14)b, there is no way within Ito and Mester's theory to single out this intermediate ω domain *uniquely*. If ω is a stress domain, then $ω_{Max}$ must be a stress domain; but this is not the desired prediction.

   I therefore follow Gouskova (2009), who argues that enclitics are incorporated directly into the phonological *phrase* (notated as 'φ'):

(15)

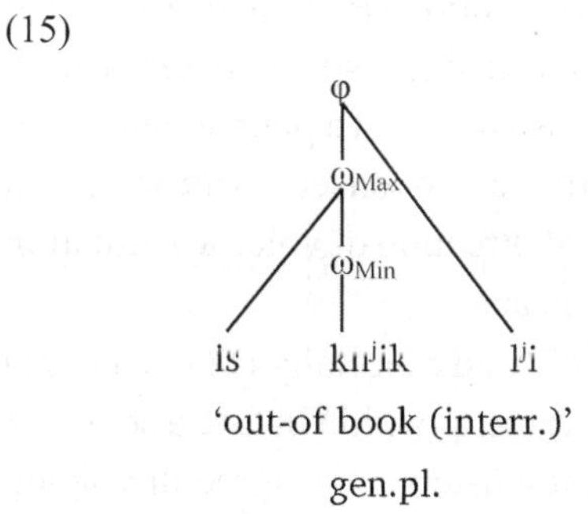

We can now generate the Russian voicing facts by assuming that devoicing is final in the prosodic word, and, following Gouskova, that voicing assimilation is blocked only by the *left* edge of a prosodic word ω. In our terms here it is specifically the onset of the *maximal* prosodic word $ω_{Max}$ that blocks assimilation. (Compare Ito and Mester's to-appear-a appeal to the onset of $ω_{Max}$ to explain the intricate facts of *r*-sandhi in English dialects.)

The larger conclusion, following up on Sections 6.3 and 6.4, is the following: voicing assimilation, as a rule of the phonology proper, affects only strings of strictly contiguous obstruents, so long as they are not separated by the left edge of ω_{Max}; devoicing affects only obstruents that are final in the prosodic word.[13]

6.5.2 Lower prosodic structure

As foreshadowed in the introduction, an important theme in the analysis of Russian voicing below has to do with the importance, on the one hand, and the limitations, on the other, of prosody in understanding the facts. Higher-level prosody matters for reasons discussed in the previous section. However, the role of lower-level prosody – namely, the syllable – is called into question. In particular, an analysis of the triggers and targets of Russian voicing processes can only be understood within a cue-based approach of the sort argued for by Steriade (1997). The account below will call on constraints that are grounded in both perception and articulation, but it is the role of perception that will be of greater interest.

The approach to perceptual distinctiveness pursued here relies on the notion of positional faithfulness (Beckman, 1997, 1998; Selkirk, 1994). According to positional faithfulness theory, one of the positions that is privileged for the purposes of faithfulness is the syllable onset position (Beckman, 1998; and see related earlier work on onset versus coda licensing, especially Goldsmith 1990; Ito, 1989). We might therefore distinguish between a plain Ident(voice) constraint and a higher-ranking one relativized to onset position (as in Lombardi, 1999), and account for the leftward direction of voice assimilation in, e.g., /ot 'brosʲitʲ/ → [ɐd 'brosʲitʲ], by this means.

There is a problem, however. As Pilch (1967) and especially Darden (1991) show, in Russian it is not onset position, but rather position before a sonorant that retains underlying voice. First, obstruent clusters must agree in voicing even when all obstruents are in the syllable onset, as shown in (16)a. When onset clusters are derived due to cliticization of monosegmental prepositions like /k/ and /v/, as in (16)b, regressive assimilation occurs. Yet according to the view that onset position licenses distinctive voicing, words like *[kdʲe] should be fine.

(16) a.   gdʲe   'where'   cf.   *kdʲe, gtʲe
            kto   'who'   *kdo, gto

      b.   kᵛ i'vanu   'to Ivan'   vᵛ i'vanʲi   'in Ivan'
            k t͡ʃilɐ'vʲeku 'to the man'   f t͡ʃilɐ'vʲekʲi 'in the man'
            'g dʲimʲi   'to Dima'   'v dʲimʲi   'in Dima'

Second, obstruent voicing in fact contrasts in coda position, so long as a sonorant follows. This can be seen in two ways. First, though onsets are usually argued to maximize within morphemes, this is not true across the prefix-stem boundary, which instead coincides with a syllable boundary, as we saw earlier. The forms in (17a–b), involving the prefixes /ot-/ and /pod-/, are therefore syllabified at the morpheme boundary. Second, words having final obstruent-sonorant sequences, as in (17c–d), preserve the underlying voicing of the obstruent. These words are monosyllabic in the literary language (Zalizniak, 1975), and the obstruents are therefore codas.[14]

(17)

    a.   i.   /pod-'jexatʲ/   [pɐd-'jexətʲ]   'to approach by vehicle'
         ii. /pod-nʲe'stʲi/   [pəd-nʲi'stʲi]   'to bring (up to)'
    b.   i.   /ot-'jexatʲ/   [ɐt-'jexətʲ]   'to ride off'
         ii. /ot-nʲe'stʲi/   [ət-nʲi'stʲi]   'to carry away'
    c.   i.   /z̩iznʲ/   [z̩iznʲ]   'life'
         ii. /pʲesnʲ/   [pʲesnʲ]   'song'
    d.   i.   /te'atr/   [tᵛi'atr]   'theater'
         ii. /kadr/   [kadr]   'film sequence'

Padgett (1995) argues that the feature [release], and not onset position, is the relevant notion of salience, for assimilation of place, as well as assimilation of voicing as in Russian. 'Release' is understood in that work to include both a burst, for consonants having one, and the following moments of consonantal offset which contain formant transitions, information on voice onset time, and other phonetic cues. The use of [release] in phonology is motivated by Selkirk (1982), Kingston (1990), and especially Steriade (1993, 1994). It is motivated also, though less directly, by Lombardi (1991, 1999), Cho (1990), and Rubach (1996); the latter two single out 'pre-obstruent' as a weak position for voice. Padgett (1995) assumes, first, that obstruents are universally [+release] before tautosyllabic sonorants (adapting the view of Lombardi), and second, that they are [+release] word-finally in some languages (in order to capture the common resistance to neutralization in specifically word-final codas).

Steriade (1997) reviews the evidence from Pilch (1967) and Darden (1991) on Russian, noting the problems with referring to syllable position. She further shows that syllable structure fails to predict patterns of voicing neutralization in a range of other languages. Other work, including Rubach (1996), Kenstowicz *et al.* (to appear), Petrova *et al.* (2001), and Wetzels and Mascaró (2001), extends this conclusion to still more languages. Steriade argues for a more articulated hierarchy of positions based on direct reference to the number and quality of phonetic cues to the obstruent voicing contrast. In this hierarchy, it is position before a sonorant, whether tautosyllabic or not, that is most perceptually privileged. On the other hand, neutralization is most likely before an obstruent. Word-final neutralization takes an intermediate position. Thus the three-way positional distinction suggested in Padgett (1995), minus the reference to syllable position, follows from a direct appeal to the relevant cues: burst properties and voice onset time are best perceived during the modal voicing of a following sonorant; pre-obstruent obstruents lack voice onset time cues, and are the most likely to lose burst cues as well, due to a following potentially overlapping obstruent. Steriade presents her account in terms of a hierarchy of markedness constraints penalizing voicing in the relevant contexts. I recast this idea in terms of positional faithfulness, assuming the constraint schema shown in (18), and the universal ranking in (19). ('PS' and 'PO' mean 'pre-sonorant' and 'pre-obstruent'.) In Russian it is only the distinction between IDENT$_{PS}$ and IDENT in other contexts that is relevant, so I collapse IDENT$_{WF}$ and IDENT$_{PO}$ into IDENT in what follows. Note the stipulation that 'pre-sonorant' must involve a sonorant in the same maximal prosodic word.[15]

(18)   IDENT$_{CUE}$(VOICE)   An output obstruent of cue strength X or higher, and its input correspondent, have identical values for the feature [voice].

       Cue strengths   PS (before a sonorant in the same ω_{Max}) >
       WF (ω-final) >
       PO (pre-obstruent)

(19)   IDENT$_{PS}$(VOICE)>>IDENT$_{WF}$(VOICE)>>IDENT$_{PO}$(VOICE)

6.6   The account

Our perceptually motivated constraints need to be supplemented with one rooted in articulatory difficulty. The basic facts involving articulatory difficulty and voicing are well known. Voiced obstruents are disfavored in comparison to their voiceless counterparts for aerodynamic reasons: it is difficult to maintain voicing given the build-up in supraglottal pressure that obstruents entail (Jaeger, 1978; Ohala, 1983; Westbury and Keating, 1986). The constraint *D below captures this aspect of the voicing facts.

The account then proceeds as follows. First, final devoicing results from the interaction of positional privilege and the general prohibition on voiced obstruents *D, following Steriade (1997) and Lombardi (1999). This is shown below for the word /god/ 'year'. A comparison of (20a–b) shows that *D dominates IDENT(voice). In pre-sonorant positions, on the other hand, the voicing contrast is maintained. Hence IDENT$_{PS}$(voice) must dominate *D, as the comparison between (20b–c) makes clear.

(20)

Input: /god/	IDENT$_{PS}$	*D	IDENT
a. god		**!	
b. ☞ got		*	*
c. kot	*!		**

Voicing assimilation requires the addition of a constraint favoring assimilation. The constraint proposed below says nothing about directionality of assimilation, since this follows precisely from the positional faithfulness constraints. The formulation of the constraint follows Bakovic (2000) and references therein. Like the Spread constraints of Padgett (1995) and Walker (1998) (and unlike alignment constraints), it does not build in directionality of assimilation.[16]

(21)   AGREE(VOICE)   Adjacent obstruents agree in [voice] specification.

As Lombardi (1999) and Steriade (1997) do, I assume that the constraint targets obstruents in particular. It would be better to derive the difference between sonorants and obstruents from independent considerations (compare the use of underspecification in Kiparsky, 1995), but this would require more discussion than is feasible here.

AGREE(voice) must dominate *D, because assimilation of voicing creates voiced obstruents; it must also dominate IDENT, since assimilation overrides underlying [voice] specifications. The two tableaux below derive [kto] 'who' and [gdʲe] 'where'. As shown, even if we specify the initial consonant for the wrong value underlyingly (as richness of the base implies must be possible), it will surface as required. The result of undominated IDENT$_{PS}$ and AGREE is clear: the underlying voicing specification of a pre-sonorant obstruent must be preserved, and any preceding obstruent must agree with this specification.

(22) (a)

Input: /gto/	IDENT$_{PS}$	AGREE	*D	IDENT
a.　　gto		*!	*	
b. ☞ kto				*
c.　　gdo	*!		**	*

(b)

Input: /kdʲe/	IDENT$_{PS}$	AGREE	*D	IDENT
a.　　kdʲe		*!	*	
b. ☞ gdʲe			**	*
c.　　ktʲe	*!			*

Given all of the above, we have the overall ranking shown below.

(23)   IDENT$_{PS}$, AGREE>> *D >>IDENT

Tableau 24 shows why devoicing of entire clusters occurs in forms like /ˈpojezd/ 'train'.

(24)

Input: /ˈpojezd/	IDENT$_{PS}$	AGREE	*D	IDENT
a.　　ˈpojizd			*!*	
b. ☞ ˈpojist				**
c.　　ˈpojizt		*!	*	*

The final element in the account involves the larger prosodic domains of final devoicing and voice assimilation. Tableaux (25)a-c compare what happens to an underlying voiced obstruent when it surfaces before a sonorant within a prosodic word (a) versus across a prosodic word boundary (b–c). (Recall that (25)c involves an enclitic that is outside of the prosodic word.) Because Ident$_{PS}$ applies only when the following sonorant is contained within the same ω$_{Max}$ as the target obstruent, it is in force for the final [z] of the preposition [iz] (and the final [d] of [lʲinʲinʲˈgradə]) in (25)a but not for the final obstruents of [ɐtˈkas] or [sat] in (25)b-c. Therefore final obstruents in prepositions do not devoice, while those ending major class words do, even when they precede an enclitic as in (25)c.

(25) (a)

Input: /iz lʲenʲinˈgrada/	IDENT$_{PS}$	AGREE	*D	IDENT
i. ☞ [iz lʲinʲinˈgradə]$_\omega$			***	
ii. [is lʲinʲinˈgradə]$_\omega$	*!		**	*

(b)

Input: /otˈkaz ˈlʲeni/	IDENT$_{PS}$	AGREE	*D	IDENT
i. [ɐtˈkaz]$_\omega$ [ˈlʲenʲi]$_\omega$			*!	
ii. ☞ [ɐtˈkas]$_\omega$ [ˈlʲenʲi]$_\omega$				*

(c)

Input: /sad lʲi/	IDENT$_{PS}$	AGREE	*D	IDENT
i. [sad]$_\omega$lʲi			*!	
ii. ☞ [sat]$_\omega$lʲi				*

However, more must be said in order to capture voicing assimilation to enclitics while blocking it across prosodic words. As (27)a shows, the account so far does correctly predict assimilation to enclitics. We need a means of ruling out assimilation in (27)b. As indicated above, I follow Gouskova (2009) in assuming that assimilation is blocked specifically by the left edge of a maximal prosodic word. (In order to allow assimilation between a word and a preposition, this must be specifically a *maximal* prosodic word.) I adapt Gouskova's NOSTRADDLING constraint for this purpose, shown below. The constraint, which depends on an understanding of assimilation as feature linking (as opposed to copying) is given rather informally here. See Gouskova for more formal treatment.

(26)   NoStraddling   A [voice] specification cannot be linked to segments separated by a ω_{Max}[boundary.

Crucially, NoStraddling is vacuously satisfied in (27)a. This is because, recall, enclitics are argued to be incorporated directly into the phonological phrase. They are neither prosodic words themselves nor incorporated into prosodic words. On the other hand, NoStraddling prevents assimilation in (27)b.

(27) (a)

Input: /sok ʐe/	NoStraddling	IDENT$_{PS}$	Agree	*D	IDENT
i. [sok]$_\omega$ʑi			*!	*	
ii. ☞ [sog]$_\omega$ʑi				**	*

(b)

Input: /sok ʑinʲi/	NoStraddling	IDENT$_{PS}$	Agree	*D	IDENT
i. ☞ [sok]$_\omega$ [ʑinʲi]$_\omega$			*	*	
ii. [sog]$_\omega$ [ʑinʲi]$_\omega$	*!			**	*

6.7   Conclusion

One goal of this paper has been to clarify, as much as possible, the facts of Russian voicing, especially with regard to prosodic structure and the behavior of sonorants. Attention to the difference between obligatory, categorical rules versus variable, gradient ones reveals, first, that sonorants do not participate in Russian voicing processes as obstruents do. It also reveals an important divide between assimilation between prosodic words and assimilation among more prosodically 'close' elements; only the latter apply regularly and categorically. I have argued, building on previous work, that lower-level prosody, in particular syllable-based prosody, cannot help us explain the conditions under which voicing assimilation and devoicing apply; rather, we must call on a cue-based analysis for this, one that is oblivious to syllabic constituency. On the other hand, the voicing facts provide strong arguments for higher-level prosodic structure. Working within Ito and Mester's (2007, 2009) framework, I have argued that devoicing affects prosodic word-final consonants. Voicing assimilation applies within prosodic words and even across right ω boundaries (in the case of clitics). However, it is blocked by the left boundary of a maximal prosodic word. The special status of the left boundary of ω_Max echoes the findings of Ito and Mester for independent facts.

Notes

* I am very grateful to Shigeto Kawahara, Rachel Walker, and an anonymous reviewer for comments that improved this paper.

1 Some of the ideas in this paper first appeared in Padgett (2002). Another goal of that paper was to analyze the controversial and interesting behavior of Russian [v] in the voicing facts. That large issue is left aside here.

2 Surface forms reflect rules of vowel reduction. Palatalization is treated as underlying in all cases, though nothing hinges on this.

3 Gradient processes by definition might apply fully, partially, or not at all, depending on matters like phonetic context and rate of speech. Such processes are 'optional' in the sense of having failure to apply as an endpoint in their gradient range of behavior. It is only in this sense that I refer to optionality in what follows.

4 Final devoicing is suggested for [r] most often (Isacenko, 1947; Boyanus, 1955), but it is still by no means necessary.

5 Hayes (1984) and Kiparsky (1985) report that whether assimilation occurs in clusters like these depends on whether the intervening sonorant is rendered syllabic. If so, then assimilation is blocked; otherwise it occurs. However, it seems the sources cited have been misunderstood on this point. Jakobson (1978) mentions a 'stylistic option' by which these sonorants can be pronounced as syllabic, but says nothing about whether assimilation then occurs. He cites Reformatskii (1971) on the existence of syllabic sonorants in Russian. Though Reformatskii argues that syllabic sonorants occur under certain conditions, the conditions stated do not include sonorants in phrases like *ot mzdʲi*, nor does Reformatskii even mention such phrases. There seems to be no clear evidence, therefore, that sonorant syllabicity is an important factor here. It is worth mentioning that Robblee and Burton threw out data in which the sonorant seemed to be syllabic (1997, footnote 7). Therefore the sonorants they analyzed were deemed to be non-syllabic, and yet these are just the sonorants that should allow assimilation to propagate through them, according to the claim entertained in this note.

6 I am very grateful to Evgenia Altukhova for carrying out the recordings for me.

7   Duration of voicing was measured, not duration relative to closure, due to the difficulty of establishing segment boundaries. Since [r] may be shorter than [l] or [m], the lower voicing values for [r] do not imply devoicing.

8   Certain prepositions count as prosodic words themselves, e.g., *skvozʲ* 'through', similar to English prepositions like 'between'. Note that Kiparsky (1985) treats prepositions as generated within the lexical phonology, since for the purposes of voicing they pattern as part of the word. As an alternative to a prosodic word-based approach, however, this cannot be correct, since they are in every way syntactic prepositions: the word to which they attach can be anything noun-phrase initial, whether a noun, adjective, adverb, or something else, e.g., *[ot otʃʲenʲ]*ₚwₐ *bolʲšovo slona* '[from (the) very] large elephant', where the word 'very' hosts the preposition. Hence the need for the prosodic word. A similar conclusion seems likely in the case of at least some enclitics, which Kiparsky also generates within the lexical phonology.

9   One exception is Baranovskaia (1968), who claims that whether assimilation occurs here depends on the position of stress in the major category word, with diminishing likelihood the farther it is away, e.g., /oˈtʲets bi/ 'father (subjunctive)' (assimilation most likely), /ˈbratʲets bi/, 'brother (dim.) (subj.)', and /ˈlʲenʲinʲets bi/ 'Leninist (subj.)' (assimilation least likely). She also states that longer clusters, as in /tʲekst ẓe/, do not assimilate fully.

10   It should be borne in mind that, given final devoicing, examples involving a voiceless consonant before another voiceless one are not evidence for assimilation across prosodic word boundaries. Final devoicing would predict, for example, [ˈgorət] [tɐˈkoj] 'such a town', from /ˈgorod taˈkoj/, whether assimilation occurs or not. This point is sometimes overlooked.

11   See note 15, p.64 of Halle (1959). Jakobson (1956) cites many examples exemplifying assimilation across words, but also notes (p. 507) that assimilation can fail, giving the example [mʲiˈdvʲetʲ] [ˈgo, ...] [ˈgolədʲin] '(the) bear (is) hungry'.

12   On the other hand, Gribanova argues that prepositions (unlike prefixes) are (at least often) adjoined not to a following ω but to a following phonological phrase. This claim is based on some differences in the behavior of jer realization in prepositions compared to prefixes. I leave the resolution of this issue to future research.

13   There are apparent cross-word assimilation facts that appear to threaten the generalization that assimilation is delimited by the ω_Max[boundary. For example, Wells (1987), who conducted a phonetic study of verbal collocations, suggests that assimilation is more likely as the verb becomes more semantically 'empty', e.g. [ˈbudʲid ˈdoktərəm] 'will be (a) doctor', from /ˈbudʲet/ 'will be', contrast [prʲivrɐˈʃʲ:ajit ˈdoktər] '(the) doctor converts'. Wells and other works suggest that the likelihood of assimilation also depends on the syntactic boundary involved, and on the close-

ness of 'contact' between the relevant words, e.g., [knʲazʲ bɐ'rʲis] 'Prince Boris', where assimilation is more likely (Halle, 1959). However, these observations about semantic 'emptiness' and 'closeness' might be interpreted to mean that such phrases in fact have the status of single maximal prosodic words, i.e., ['budʲid 'dokətrəm]ω_Max, [knʲazʲ bɐ'rʲis]ω_Max.

14 Pilch (1967) assumes that word-medial obstruent-sonorant clusters are heterosyllabic even when no prefix-stem boundary is involved, e.g., ['skorb.nij] 'sorrowful', [ɐd.'no] 'one (neut.)'. Steriade (1997) follows him in this, citing this as further evidence against the syllabic approach to voice neutralization, since here the voicing contrast is maintained also. However, most Russian sources claim that onsets are maximized in such cases, i.e., ['skor.bnij], [ɐ.'dno]. (Bondarko, 1998 provides an overview of positions on this question.) In general there is little evidence bearing on the syllabification of stem-internal clusters in Russian.

15 The phrase 'or higher' and reference to 'cue strength' are intended to make the hierarchy in (19) an 'inclusion hierarchy'. Thus, violation of one IDENT constraint entails violation of the lower ranking ones. I assume (as Steriade, 1997 does) that it is ultimately cue strength, rather than environment per se, that matters. The latter can appear formally very arbitrary.

16 It is simpler to evaluate violations of AGREE than of SPREAD: the former assesses a violation for every pair of segments that disagree in (or do not share) the relevant feature, while the autosegmentally-oriented latter assesses one for every feature(F)-segment(S) pair such that F is not linked to (S); the constraints seem to have equivalent effects for the cases discussed here.

References

Avanesov, R. I. (1956) *Fonetika sovremennogo russkogo literaturnogo iazyka*. Moscow: Izdatel'stvo moskovskogo universiteta.

Avanesov, R. I. (1972) *Russkoe literaturnoe proiznoshenie*. Moscow: Prosveshchenie.

Bakovic, E. (2000) *Harmony, Dominance, and Control*. New Brunswick, NJ: Ph.D. dissertation, Rutgers University.

Baranovskaia, S. A. (1968) Pozitsionnoe vliianie na var'irovanie soglasnykh po zvonkosti - glukhosti v sovremennom russkom literaturnom iazyke. *Trudy Universiteta Druzhby Narodov imeni Patrisa Lumumby* 29.

Barkaï, M. and Horvath, J. (1978) Voicing assimilation and the sonority hierarchy: Evidence from Russian, Hebrew, and Hungarian. *Linguistics* 212: 77–88.

Barry, S. (1989) Aspects of sonorant devoicing in Russian. *Speech, Hearing, and Language* 3: 47–59.

Beckman, J. (1997) Positional faithfulness, positional neutralization, and Shona vowel harmony. *Phonology* 14 (1): 1–46.

Beckman, J. (1998) *Positional Faithfulness*. Ph.D. dissertation, University of Massachusetts, Amherst.

Bondarko, L. V. e. (1998) *Fonetika sovremennogo russkogo iazyka*. St Petersburg.

Boyanus, S. C. (1955) *Russian Pronunciation*. Cambridge, MA: Harvard University Press.

Burton, M. W. and Robblee, K. E. (1997) A phonetic analysis of voicing assimilation in Russian. *Journal of Phonetics* 25 (2): 97–114.

Cho, Y.-m. Y. (1990) A typology of voicing assimilation *Proceedings of WCCFL 9* 141–155.

Coats, H. S. and Harshenin, A. P. (1971) On the phonological properties of Russian v. *Slavic and East European Journal* 15 (4): 466–478.

Daniels, W. J. (1972) Assimilation in Russian consonant clusters: I. *Papers in Linguistics* 5 (3): 366–380.

Darden, B. (1971) A note on Sommer's claim that there exist languages without CV syllables. *International Journal of American Linguistics* 37 (2): 126–128.

Darden, B. J. (1991) Linear assimilation in clusters *Proceedings of CLS* 27: 100–106.

Dmitrieva, O. (2005). *Incomplete Neutralization in Russian Final Devoicing: Acoustic Evidence from Native Speakers and Second Language Learners*. MA thesis, University of Kansas.

Gafos, A. (2006) Dynamics in grammar: Comment on Ladd and Ernestus and Baayen. In L. Goldstein, D. H. Whalen and C. T. Best (eds) *Laboratory Phonology 8* 51–79. Berlin: Mouton de Gruyter.

Goldsmith, J. (1990) *Autosegmental and Metrical Phonology*. Oxford and Cambridge, MA: Blackwell.

Gouskova, M. (2009). *The Prosodic Structure of Russian Compounds*: Ms., New York University.

Gribanova, V. (in progress) *Composition and Locality: The Morphosyntax and Phonology of the Russian Verbal Complex*: Ph.D. dissertation, UC Santa Cruz.

Gvozdev, A. N. (1949) *O fonologicheskikh sredstvakh russkogo iazyka: Sbornik statei*. Moscow: Izdatel'stvo akademii pedagogicheskikh nauk RSFSR.

Halle, M. (1959) *The Sound Pattern of Russian*. The Hague: Mouton.

Hayes, B. (1984) The phonetics and phonology of Russian voicing assimilation. In M. Aronoff and R. T. Oehrle (eds) *Language Sound Structure* 318–328. Cambridge, MA: MIT Press.

Hayes, B. (1989) The prosodic hierarchy in meter. In P. Kiparsky and G. Youmans (eds) *Rhythm and Meter* 201–260. Orlando, FL: Academic Press.

Isacenko, A. V. (1947) *Fonetika spisovnej rustiny*. Bratislava: Slovenska akademia vied a umeni.

Isacenko, A. V. (1955) [review of] Wolfgang Steinitz: Russische lautlehre. *Zeitschrift für phonetik* 8: 411–416.

Itô, J. (1989) A prosodic theory of epenthesis. *Natural Language and Linguistic Theory* 7: 217–259.

Ito, J. and Mester, A. (2007) Prosodic adjunction in Japanese compounds *Proceedings of the 4th Formal Approaches to Japanese Linguistics Conference* 97–112: MIT Working Papers in Linguistics.

Ito, J. and Mester, A. (2009) The onset of the prosodic word. In S. Parker (ed.), *Phonological Argumentation: Essays on Evidence and Motivation* 227–260. London: Equinox.

Jaeger, J. (1978) Speech aerodynamics and phonological universals *Proceedings of Chicago Linguistic Society* 14: 311–329.

Jakobson, R. (1956) Die verteilung der stimmhaften und stimmlosen geräuschlaute im russischen. In M. Woltner and H. Bräuer (eds) *Festschrift für max vasmer.* Wiesbaden: Harassowitz.

Keating, P. (1988) Underspecification in phonetics. *Phonology* 5: 275–292.

Kenstowicz, M., Abu-Mansour, M. and Törkenczy, M. (to appear) Two notes on laryngeal licensing. In S. Ploch and G. Williams (eds) *Living on the Edge: Phonological Essays Commemorating the Radical Career of Jonathan Kaye.*

Kingston, J. (1990) Articulatory binding. In J. Kingston and M. E. Beckman (eds) *Papers in Laboratory Phonology I* 406–434. Cambridge: Cambridge University Press.

Kiparsky, P. (1985) Some consequences of lexical phonology. *Phonology* 2: 85–138.

Kniazev, S. V. (2006) *Struktura foneticheskogo slova v russkom iazyke: Sinkhroniia i diakhroniia.* Moscow: Maks-Press.

Liberman, M., & Pierrehumbert, J. (1984) Intonational invariance under changes in pitch range and length. In M. Aronoff and R. T. Oehrle (eds) *Language Sound Structure* 157–233. Cambridge, MA: MIT Press.

Lombardi, L. (1991) *Laryngeal features and laryngeal neutralization*: Ph.D. dissertation, University of Massachusetts, Amherst [published 1994, Garland: New York].

Lombardi, L. (1999) Positional faithfulness and voicing assimilation in optimality theory. *Natural Language and Linguistic Theory* 17 (2): 267–302.

Nespor, M. and Vogel, I. (1986) *Prosodic Phonology.* Dordrecht: Foris.

Ohala, J. J. (1983) The origin of sound patterns in vocal tract constraints. In P. MacNeilage (ed.), *The Production of Speech* 189–216. New York: Springer-Verlag.

Padgett, J. (1995) Partial class behavior and nasal place assimilation *Proceedings of the South Western Optimality Theory Workshop 1995* 145–183. Tucson, AZ: The University of Arizona Coyote Papers.

Padgett, J. (2002). *Russian Voicing Assimilation, Final Devoicing, and the Problem of [v]*: Ms., UC Santa Cruz.

Paufoshima, R. F. and Agaronov, D. A. (1971) Ob usloviiakh assimiliativnogo ozvoncheniia soglasnykh na styke foneticheskikh slov v russkom iazyke. In S. S. Vysotskii, M. V. Panov, A. A. Reformatskii and V. N. Sidorov (eds) *Razvitie fonetiki sovremennogo russkogo iazyka* 189–199. Moscow: Nauka.

Petrova, O., Plapp, R., Ringen, C. and Szentgyörgyi, S. (2001). *Constraints on Voice: An OT Typology*: Ms., University of Iowa and University of Veszprém, Hungary.

Pilch, H. (1967) Russische konsonantengruppen im silbenan- und auslaut. *To Honor Roman Jakobson, volume 2* 1555–1584. The Hague: Mouton.

Prince, A. and Smolensky, P. (1993 [2004]) *Optimality Theory: Constraint Interaction in Generative Grammar*: Ms., Rutgers University, New Brunswick, NJ, and University of Colorado, Boulder [Published by Blackwell, 2004].

Reformatskii, A. A. (1971) Slogovye soglasnye v russkom iazyke. In S. S. Vysotskii, M. V. Panov, A. A. Reformatskii and V. N. Sidorov (eds) *Razvitie fonetiki sovremennogo russkogo iazyka* 200–208. Moscow: Nauka.

Reformatskii, A. A. (1975) *Fonologicheskie etiudy*. Moscow.

Robblee, K. E. and Burton, M. W. (1997) Sonorant voicing transparency in Russian. In W. Browne and D. Zec (eds) *Proceedings of Formal Approaches to Slavic Linguistics 4* 407–434. Ann Arbor, MI: Michigan Slavic Publications.

Rubach, J. (1996) Nonsyllabic analysis of voice assimilation in Polish. *Linguistic Inquiry* 27 (1): 69–110.

Selkirk, E. (1982) Syllables. In H. van der Hulst and N. Smith (eds) *The Structure of Phonological Representations* 337–383. Dordrecht: Foris.

Selkirk, E. (1994). *The Constraint Question for Feature Structure: A Review of Some Answers*: Course notes, University of Massachusetts, Amherst.

Selkirk, E. (to appear) The syntax-phonology interface. In J. Goldsmith, J. Riggle and A. Yu (eds) *The Handbook of Phonological Theory*. Oxford and Cambridge, MA: Blackwell.

Shapiro, M. (1993) Russian non-distinctive voicing: A stocktaking. *Russian Linguistics* 17 (1): 1–14.

Steriade, D. (1993) Closure, release and nasal contours. In M. Huffman and R. Krakow (eds) *Nasality*. San Diego, CA: Academic Press.

Steriade, D. (1994) Complex onsets as single segments: The Mazateco pattern. In J. Cole and C. Kisseberth (eds) *Perspectives in Phonology* 203–291. Stanford, CA: CSLI Publications.

Steriade, D. (1997). *Phonetics in Phonology: The Case of Laryngeal Neutralization*: Ms., UCLA.

Vinogradov, V. V. (ed.) (1960) *Grammatika russkogo iazyka*. Moskva: Izdatel'stvo Akademiia nauk SSSR.

Walker, R. (1998) *Nasalization, Neutral Segments, and Locality*: Ph.D. dissertation, University of California, Santa Cruz [published by Garland Press, New York, 2000].

Wells, R. (1987) Voicing assimilation across word boundaries in Russian *UCLA Working Papers in Phonetics No. 68* 170–182. Los Angeles, CA: UCLA.

Westbury, J. R. and Keating, P. A. (1986) On the naturalness of stop consonant voicing. *Journal of Linguistics* 22: 145–166.

Wetzels, W. L. and Mascaró, J. (2001) The typology of voicing and devoicing. *Language* 77 (2): 207–244.

Yu, A. (2007) Understanding near mergers: The case of morphological tone in Cantonese. *Phonology* 24: 187–214.

Zalizniak, A. A. (1975) Razmyshleniia po povodu 'iazv' a. A. Reformatskogo. *Problemnaia gruppa po eksperimental'noi i prikladnoi lingvistike Instituta russkogo iazyka AN SSSR: predvaritel'nye publikatsii* 71: 13–23.

Zsiga, E. (1993) *Features, Gestures, and the Temporal Aspects of Phonological Organization*. New Haven, CT: Ph.D. dissertation, Yale University.

Zubritskaya, E. (1995) *The Categorical and Variable Phonology of Russian*: Ph.D. dissertation, University of Pennsylvania.

7 Phonetic evidence for prosodic word prominence in American English

Mariko Sugahara[a]

7.1 Introduction

In the theory of Prosodic Phonology (Selkirk, 1978, 1980, 1986; Booij, 1983; Beckman and Pierrehumbert, 1986; Nespor and Vogel, 1986; and others), there are layered phonological constituents that are related to but not necessarily isomorphic with the morpho-syntactic constituent representation. The dominant view is that the prosodic hierarchy in English consists of at least five levels of constituents as shown in (1).

(1) Prosodic Hierarchy
    Intonational Phrase (IPh)
    Phonological Phrase (PPh)[1]
    Phonological Word (PW)
    Foot (Ft)
    Syllable (σ)

One of the important characteristics of these phonological constituents is that each level of constituents has a head, which is the most prominent constituent of one level below. The head is normally associated with a particular phonological element in English, for instance: the head of σ is associated with a vowel, the head of Ft is associated with a full vowel syllable (Selkirk, 1980; Beckman and Edwards, 1990; Ewen and Van Der Hulst, 2001), the head of

[a] Mariko Sugahara: Department of English, Doshisha University, Imadegawa-Karasuma, Kamigyo-ku, Kyoto, Japan. Email: msugahar@mail.doshisha.ac.jp

IPh is associated with a nuclear pitch accent (Beckman and Edwards, 1990, and others). Among the elements of the prosodic hierarchy in English, the head of PW, i.e., the main stress Ft, lacks a phonological associate. It is the goal of this paper to investigate whether there is any phonetic correlate of the head of PW.

Consider the following pair of words that demonstrate the relation between prosodic heads and their phonological correlates: *center* ['sɛn. tɹ] vs *centaur* ['sɛn. ˌtɔɹ].[2] They are both disyllabic and trochaic but differ in the quality of their second syllable nuclei. The second syllable nucleus of *centaur* is a full vowel with secondary stress [ɔ], while that of *center* is an unstressed syllabic sonorant [ɹ]. Selkirk (1980) and Hayes (1980) propose that the difference between the two words is captured as the difference in their Ft-level constituent structure and prominence representations. The former consists of two single-syllable feet, and therefore both syllables are the heads of separate feet as shown in (2), and the latter consists of a single trochaic foot dominating two syllables where the initial syllable is the head of the foot as shown in (3). In (2), the initial single-syllable foot is the head of PW while the second one is not. The subscripts 's' and 'w' here stand for the head and a non-head of a constituent of one level above respectively. Therefore, 'σ_S' stands for the head of Ft and 'Ft$_S$' for the head of PW.

(2)

$$
\begin{array}{ccc}
 & \text{PW} & \\
 & \diagup\diagdown & \\
\text{Ft}_S & & \text{Ft}_W \\
| & & | \\
\sigma_S & & \sigma_S \\
[\text{sɛn} & & \text{tɔɹ}]
\end{array}
$$

(3)

$$
\begin{array}{cc}
 & \text{PW} \\
 & | \\
 & \text{Ft}_S \\
 & \diagup\diagdown \\
\sigma_S & \sigma_W \\
[\text{sɛn} & \text{tɹ}]
\end{array}
$$

When a trochaic word like *centaur* that consists of two feet as in (2) is pronounced in isolation, the initial full vowel syllable (primary stress), e.g., *cen-* in *centaur*, is usually acoustically and perceptually more salient than the second full vowel syllable (secondary stress), e.g., *-taur* in *centaur*, partly because it is where a nuclear pitch accent appears (Gussenhoven, 2004: 21).

That the initial foot dominating *cen* in (2) is the head of PW does not necessarily guarantee that the syllable will automatically bear a pitch accent:
pitch accents are aligned with the designated terminal element (DTE) of IPh,
as shown in (4).[3] PW's in a post-nuclear pitch accent position that are not the
head of IPh have no pitch accent on their primary stress syllables (Pierrehumbert, 1980, among others).

(4) T* stands for a pitch accent

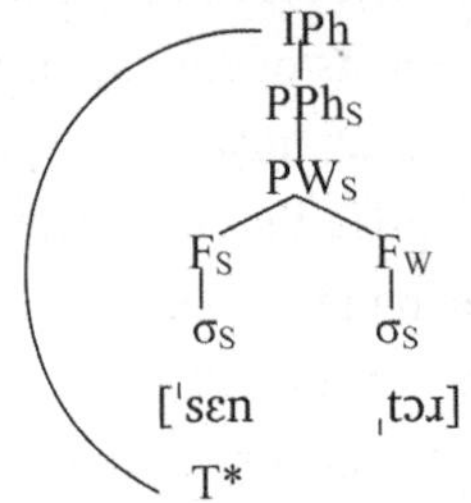

Segmental and suprasegmental elements, like full vowels and pitch accents,
are not the only correlates of prosodic representation. Other acoustic parameters such as duration also correlate with prosodic structure representation, e.g.,
pre-boundary lengthening (Beckman and Edwards, 1990; Wightman *et al.*,
1992; among many others), the lengthening of syllables bearing the phrasal
prominence (Turk and Sawush, 1997; Turk and White, 1999; Cho and Keating, 2009). Also the formant frequencies of vowels are reported to vary to the
extent they do not cross phoneme boundaries as the prominence levels of the
vowels change (Erickson, 2002, 2003).

This paper examines whether the head-Foot of PW has any phonetic correlates to distinguish it from a non-head-Foot even in an unaccented environment where the presence or absence of a pitch accent does not distinguish the
two. More specific questions are (a) whether the designated terminal element
(DTE) of the head-Foot of PW, i.e., a vowel with primary stress, is associated
with longer durations than the DTE of a non-head-Foot, i.e., a vowel with
secondary stress (Sections 7.3 and 7.4, Experiments I and II), and (b) whether
the head-Foot of PW as a whole undergoes lengthening (Section 7.4, Experiment II).

7.2 Previous studies: Primary stress and its acoustic strengthening

The phonetic correlates of English primary stress syllables in an unaccented post-nuclear focus environment have been studied by Campbell and Beckman (1997) and de Jong, (2004), Sluijter *et al.* (1995), Sluijter and van Heuven (1996), Huss (1978), and Okobi (2006). Among other things most of these studies report that primary and secondary stress vowels are acoustically distinguished by their duration and other acoustic properties such as spectral tilt.[4] Campbell and Beckman (1997), however, did not find any reliable durational and spectral tilt differences to distinguish the two levels of stress. One reason for the disagreement in these findings might be that the materials used in these studies were not well-controlled. For example, it is not clear whether primary and secondary stressed vowels were compared or whether primary and unstressed vowels were compared in Huss's (1978) and Okobi's (2006) study.[5] In addition the morphological structure and syllable count were not controlled in the studies of de Jong (2004) and Campbell and Beckman (1997). Sluijter *et al.* (1995) and Sluijter and van Heuven (1996) elicited primary and secondary stress vowels by presenting written texts with bold face letters for the primary stress syllables to their speakers. Such visual aid might have cued speakers to exaggerate acoustic differences between the syllables with and without the bold face letters.

Therefore it is worth revisiting the question whether acoustic differences between primary and secondary stressed syllables in the absence of a pitch accent adopting proper stimuli. Furthermore, none of these previous studies investigate what the domain of PW-prominence strengthening is: is it only the primary stressed syllable or the entire head-Ft of PW?

7.3 Experiment I

This experiment used two-syllable noun-verb pairs, where nouns and verbs are distinguished by the location of primary stress and secondary stress. None of the syllables in those word pairs were pronounced with reduced vowels. We compared (a) F0 values and (b) durations of full vowels with primary stress and those of full vowels with secondary stress in both a nuclear pitch accent environment (accented context) and a post-nuclear environment where no pitch accent was present (unaccented context).

The comparison of F0 values guaranteed that in the post-focus part of an utterance, not only secondary stress syllables but also primary stress syllables were unaccented. As for the duration analyses, primary stress vowels of 150 ms to 160 ms turned out to be longer than secondary stress vowels even in the unaccented environment.

7.3.1 Methods

7.3.1.1 Subjects

Eight paid speakers of American English participated in the experiment: five female and three male students at the University of Massachusetts at Amherst, aged between 18 and 30 years, without any known hearing or speaking disorders.

7.3.1.2 Materials

Three noun-verb disyllabic minimal pairs were recorded, which are shown in (5). Nouns are trochaic, i.e., primary stress followed by secondary stress, while verbs are iambic, i.e., secondary stress followed by primary stress.

(5)

    a.   *DIgest* vs. *diGEST*[6]

    b.   *MISprint* vs. *misPRINT*

    c.   *TRANSplant* vs. *transPLANT*

The target words were embedded in two different contexts: one was a neutral context where they were interpreted as presentational focus (new information), and the other was a post-focus context where they were interpreted as old information in a post-nuclear pitch accent position. We manipulated the former context so that the target words would always carry a pitch accent on a primary stress syllable, and the latter context so that the target words would be pronounced in a lower flat pitch range without any pitch accent. The contexts are provided in Appendix 7.1.

7.3.1.3 Recording

Recordings took place in a sound proof studio at the University of Massachusetts, Amherst. Scripts were presented to the speakers on a computer monitor, which the speakers read aloud. The speakers controlled the speed of text presentation by pressing the space key when they finished reading one text and move to another. The texts were ordered randomly and at least one filler text* was inserted between the texts containing the target words. Each text was recorded only once in one recording session. Speakers participated in two recording sessions conducted on different days. Therefore, 48 noun-verb pairs in total were recorded (3 pairs × 8 speakers × 2 repetitions). Their speech was directly recorded onto a hard disk (44.1 kHz, 16 bit), using an AKG C420 Cardioid Headset Condenser Microphone.

7.3.1.4   Segmentation and measurement

The vowel periods of the target words were demarcated by the beginning of voicing and the end of F2, and are henceforth called V1 (the initial syllable vowel) and V2 (the final syllable vowel). The durations and the mean F0 values were measured in Praat (Boersma and Weenick, 2009).

Some tokens of V2 in the pairs of *misprint* and *transplant* were nasalized without being followed by nasal constriction intervals, but others had a vowel region followed by separate nasal intervals. Since Repeated Measures Analyses (RMANOVA) is adopted for the comparisons of primary and secondary stress, data from nouns and those from their verbal counterparts obtained from the same speaker in the same recording session were paired with each other. The V2 data from word-pairs in which its members did not agree in the presence or absence of the following independent nasal intervals were all excluded from the analyses (eight pairs from the neutral context and two pairs from the post-focus context), just in case the presence or absence of the nasal region affects the durational outcome of V2. As a result, 40 pairs and 46 pairs were available for the analyses of V2 in the neutral and the post-focus context respectively.

In addition, the extraction of F0 values from some vowels was not possible because of their creakiness. Here, too, we only used data from cases where F0 values were available for both a noun and its verb counterpart in the same word-pair produced by the same speaker in the same recording session. The number of pairs available for the F0 analyses of V1 was 37 in the neutral context and 30 in the post-focus context, and that of V2 was 33 in the neutral context and 31 in the post-focus context.

7.3.2 Results

7.3.2.1   F0 Analyses

In order to confirm our assumption that target words in the neutral context bear an H* nuclear pitch accent (= phrasal prominence) and those in the post-focus context are unaccented, we first considered F0. If we are on the right track, the F0 of primary stress vowels should be higher than that of secondary stress vowels in the neutral context due to the H* accent. In the post-focus context, however, the F0 of primary and that of secondary stress vowels should be almost equal.

RMANOVA separately compared data for male and female speakers because their intrinsic pitch ranges are substantially different. The results are summarized in Table 7.1 for V1 and Table 7.2 for V2. Since 16 comparisons were carried out, i.e., 2 vowels × 2 contexts × 2 analyses (by-speaker and by-word analyses) × 2 genders, the alpha value was adjusted to 0.05/16 = 0.00313 (roughly 0.003).

Table 7.1 shows that the mean F0 of V1 in the primary stress (noun) condition was 27 Hz (14%) higher than that of V1 in the secondary stress (verb) condition for female speakers, which was statistically significant at the adjusted alpha level ($\alpha = 0.003$) in both by-word and by-speaker analyses. For male speakers, however, by-word measures were only 6 Hz (5%) higher than by-speaker, which turned out to be marginally significant at $\alpha = 0.05$.

In the post-focus context, primary stress V1 was unexpectedly associated with slightly lower F0 mean than secondary stress V1 for both male speakers (-4 Hz) and female speakers (-5 Hz). This result, however, does not contradict our prediction that F0 of primary stress V1 should be higher than that of secondary stress V1 in the neutral context but not in the post-focus context.

In Table 7.2, we also see that primary stress V2 was higher than secondary stress V2 in the neutral context for both male and speakers (19 Hz, 18%) and female speakers (32 Hz, 19%), and the difference was significant for both the by-word and the by-speaker analyses. In the post-focus context, however, there was no significant difference between primary stress V2 and secondary stress V2.

Table 7.1: Mean F0 values and the results of RMANOVA (by-word, by-speaker): primary stress V1 vs. secondary stress V1.

			F0 mean (StD)	Num of pairs	by-word F (df)	by-speaker F (df)
Male (3 speakers)	Neutral	Primary	134 Hz (28.7)	18	3.54* (1,15)	3.71* (1,15)
		Secondary	128 Hz (39.8)			
	Post-Focus	Primary	111 Hz (21.8)	17	−4.5 (1,14)	−5.8 (1,14)
		Secondary	116 Hz (19.8)			
Female (4 speakers)	Neutral	Primary	218 Hz (28.2)	19	14.7*** (1,16)	14.5*** (1,14)
		Secondary	191 Hz (26.1)			
	Post-Focus	Primary	157 Hz (12.6)	13	−4.9 (1,10)	−5.5 (1,9)
		Secondary	162 Hz (14)			

***$p<0.003$, **$p<0.01$, *$p<0.05$

Table 7.2: Mean F0 values and the results of RMANOVA (by-word, by-speaker): primary stress V2 vs. secondary stress V2.

			F0 mean (StD)	Num of pairs	by-word F (df)	by-speaker F (df)
Male (3 speakers)	Neutral	Primary	123 Hz (16.1)	11	22.9*** (1,8)	21.2*** (1,8)
		Secondary	104 Hz (22.9)			
	Post-Focus	Primary	105 Hz (25.6)	15	0.014 (1,12)	0.006 (1,12)
		Secondary	105 Hz (27.4)			
Female (5 speakers)	Neutral	Primary	197 Hz (38.9)	22	18.7*** (1,19)	14.6*** (1,17)
		Secondary	165 (22.4)			
	Post-Focus	Primary	165 Hz (25.9)	16	−0.26 (1,14)	−0.52 (1,11)
		Secondary	170 Hz (32.7)			

***$p<0.003$, **$p<0.01$, *$p<0.05$

For all of the comparisons above, there was neither a significant interaction between stress types and words nor an interaction between stress types and speakers.

The results confirm that neither secondary nor primary stressed vowels are accented in the post-focus context, i.e., neither carries phrasal prominence. In the following sections, the post-focus context is called the 'unaccented' environment while the neutral context the 'accented' environment.

7.3.2.2   Durational analyses

RMANOVA compared the mean durations of primary stress and those of secondary stress vowels in the accented and the unaccented environment. Since six comparisons were carried out for V1 and V2 respectively, i.e., 3 word pairs × 2 accent environments, the alpha value was adjusted to 0.05/6 = 0.0083 (roughly 0.008).

V1 durations

As shown in Table 7.3, the significant lengthening effect of primary stress on V1 was observed only in the *digest* pair regardless of the accent environments: the primary stress V1 of *digest* was more than 20 percent longer than its secondary stress V1 counterpart in both the accented and the unaccented environment.

Table 7.3: Mean durations and the results of RMANOVA (by-speaker): P (primary stress V1) vs. S (secondary stress V1).

			F0 mean (StD)	Num of pairs	by-speaker F (df)
Accented	[aɪ] in digest	P	163 ms (19.3)	16	105.4** (1,8)
		S	127 ms (13.4)		
	[ɪ] in misprint	P	71 ms (8.8)	16	1.84 (1,8)
		S	68 ms (15.8)		
	[æ] in transplant	P	119 ms (22.6)	16	1.77 (1,8)
		S	113 ms (19.9)		
Unaccented	[aɪ] in digest	P	159 ms (20.1)	16	45.6** (1,8)
		S	131 ms (13.8)		
	[ɪ] in misprint	P	70 ms (7.2)	16	1.78 (1,8)
		S	66 ms (13.9)		
	[æ] in transplant	P	104 ms (18.9)	16	−3.48 (1,8)
		S	115ms (22.9)		

**$p < 0.008$, *$p < 0.05$

There was also no significant accentual lengthening effect: the accented primary V1 was not significantly longer than its unaccented counterpart.

V2 durations

The mean duration of primary V2 of the *digest* pair [ɛ] was about 14 percent longer than that of secondary V2, and it was statistically significant at the adjusted alpha value ($\alpha = 0.008$) in both the accented and the unaccented environment.

For [æ] in *transplant*, the mean duration of primary V2 was about 17 percent longer than that of secondary V2 in the unaccented envinronment, which was statistically significant at $\alpha = 0.008$. In the accented environment, the primary stress V2 of *transplant* was 8 percent longer than secondary stress

V2, which was marginally significant at $\alpha = 0.05$. The V2 durations of the pair of *misprint*, however, showed no primary stress lengthening effect regardless of the accentual environments. Table 7.4 shows these results. We also find that there was no accentual lengthening effect: accented primary stress was not significantly longer than unaccented primary stress.

Table 7.4: Mean durations and the results of RMANOVA (by-speaker): P (primary stress V2) vs. S (secondary stress V2).

			F0 mean (StD)	Num of pairs	by-speaker F (df)
Accented	[ε] in digest	P	150 ms (24.6)	16	12.3** (1,8)
		S	132 ms (21.1)		
	[ɪ] in misprint	P	99 ms (22.7)	13	0.33 (1,6)
		S	96 ms (24.3)		
	[æ] in transplant	P	155 ms (30.2)	11	7.45* (1,4)
		S	143 ms (27.4)		
Unaccented	[ε] in digest	P	148 ms (20.3)	16	27** (1,8)
		S	130 ms (21.6)		
	[ɪ] in misprint	P	98 ms (23.5)	16	0.65 (1,8)
		S	94 ms (20.4)		
	[æ] in transplant	P	151 ms (20)	14	11** (1,6)
		S	129ms (22.3)		

**p <0 .008, *p< 0.05

7.3.2.3 Discussion

Our major finding here is that the lengthening of primary stressed syllables is not ubiquitous. For V1, only the *digest* pair showed a significant difference between the two types of stress in both accentual environments. Similarly for V2, only the *digest* and *transplant* pairs showed significant differences in both accentual environments. What these cases have in common is that the mean durations of their primary stressed vowels were 150 ms to 160 ms regardless of the accent conditions. In contrast, the mean durations of primary stress vowels that did not undergo lengthening were less than 120 ms (see in Tables 7.3 and 7.4). This suggests that longer syllables may be more likely to show stress-related durational adjustments.

Another finding is that there was no accentual lengthening effect, contra Turk and Sawusch's (1997), Turk and White's (1999) and Cho and Keating's (2009) results. They showed that the mean vowel duration was longer for the accented primary stress than for the unaccented primary stress. It may be due to the difference in the types of accent used in their studies and in the present study. In Turk and Sawusch's (1997), Turk and White's (1999) and Cho and Keating's (2009) studies, accented words were interpreted as contrastive narrow focus (a.k.a. correction focus), whereas in the present study, accented words were interpreted as presentational focus. Selkirk (2002) reports that contrastive narrow focus and presentational focus are associated with different shapes of pitch accents: the former with a bitonal accent L + H* while the latter with a monotonal accent H*. The bitonality of the accented words with narrow focus could have added extra length to the accented words in Turk and Sawusch (1997), Turk and White (1999) and Cho and Keating (2009), which might have resulted in the significant durational difference between accented and unaccented vowels with primary stress.

7.4   Experiment II

The results of Experiment I do not provide clear answers to the question of what the domain of PW-prominence lengthening is, because in these cases the head-Foot of each PW consisted only of the syllable with primary stress. Experiment II addresses this issue.

In Experiment I the members of each noun-verb pair have the same segmental sequence, so speakers had to rely on the syntactic and semantic information in carrier sentences to detect the grammatical category of each word. In Experiment II we manipulated the stimuli so that the members of each word pair did not share entirely the same segmental content. Here the target words consist of four-syllables, and the two members of each word pair partially share the same segmental sequence up to their penultimate syllables, e.g., *prosecutor* vs. *prosecution*. The position of the primary stress and that of the secondary stress is also different: the former has primary stress on its initial syllable and secondary stress on its penultimate syllable, while the latter has it the other way round. Because the final syllables help indicate the stress pattern differences, it was not necessary to manipulate the syntactic and the semantic content of the carrier sentences to indicate the location of primary and secondary stress. Therefore, the target words used in this experiment were embedded in syntactically simple carrier sentences as in Appendix 7.2 (e.g., *I said _________, you know*).

Despite the difference in the location of primary and secondary stress, each pair of words has two trochaic feet. The presence of two feet in these word-pairs makes it possible to examine whether the domain of lengthening related to PW-prominence is the primary stressed syllable only or the entire head-Ft of PW. Consider the minimal pair: ${}'PROse_{,}cutor$ and ${}_{,}prose'CUtion$ in more detail: the initial foot (${}'PRO.se$) of ${}'PROse_{,}cutor$ is the head of PW as shown in (6) while the initial foot in ${}_{,}prose'CUtion$ is not. (The head-Ft of PW is marked with a subscript 's'.)

(6)

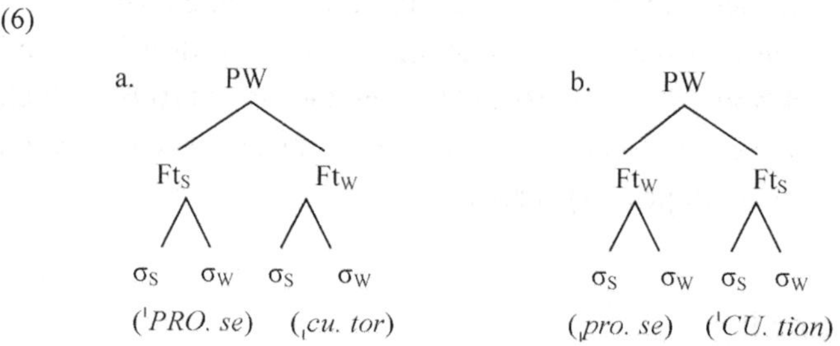

If the entire head-Ft of PW lengthens then both the initial stressed syllable and the following unstressed syllable in (6a) should be longer than the parallel constituents in (6b).

7.4.1 Methods

7.4.1.1 Speakers

Five paid native speakers of American English participated in the experiment (two female and three male). The participants were undergraduate exchange students at Doshisha University, aged between 20 and 25 years.[7] They had no known hearing or speaking disorders.

7.4.1.2 Materials

The list of word-pairs used in this experiment is shown in (7).

(7)

    (a) *'DOmi,nating* vs. *,domi'NAtion*

    (b) *'FAsci,nating* vs. *fasci'NAtion*

    (c) *'NAvi,gator* vs. *,navi'GAtion*

    (d) *'PROse,cutor* vs. *,prose'CUtion*

    (e) *'TERmi,nating* vs. *,termi'NAtion*

Each of the words in (7) was embedded in two contexts, as in Experiment I i.e. neutral accented context and post-focus unaccented context. See Appendix 7.2 for details. A pitch accent appears at the primary stress location in the accented context while no accent is present in the unaccented context.

7.4.1.3 Recording

Recordings took place in a quiet room at Doshisha University. Speakers' speech was directly recorded to a hard disk (44.1 KHz, 16 bit) using a RØDE NT2-A microphone. Speakers read each aloud four times in two sessions: two repetitions in each recording session on different days. Since there are five speakers, five word pairs, two contexts and four repetitions, the total number of utterances recorded was 400 (200 pairs).

7.4.1.4 Segmentation and measurement

We labeled the vowel period of the first stressed syllable (V1) and that of the second unstressed syllable (V2) following the same labeling procedure as for Experiment I. For the V1 interval of the pair of *terminating* and *termination*, the rhotic part that follows the vowel was also included in the V1 interval, because it was impossible to segment the vocalic and rhotic intervals; instead the whole interval was labeled as /ɚ/. Duration and mean F0 values were automatically extracted by Praat (Boersma and Weenick, 2009).

7.4.2 Results

7.4.2.1 The analyses of V1

F0 analyses

In order to make sure that vowels with primary stress in the neutral context were accented while those in the post-focus context were not, the mean F0 values of each V1 period was considered first. If V1 with primary stress is associated with a higher mean F0 value than that with secondary stress in the neutral context, then we can conclude that V1 with primary stress is accented. If V1 with primary stress and V1 with secondary stress are associated with almost equal mean F0 values in the post-focus context, then we can conclude that V1 with primary stress is unaccented. Since four comparisons (RMANOVA) were carried out (2 genders $\times$ 2 contexts), the alpha value was adjusted to $0.05/4 = 0.0125$ (roughly 0.01). Table 7.5 shows the results.

The mean F0 values of V1 with primary stress in the neutral context were significantly higher than V1 with secondary stress vowels in the same context. In the post-focus context, however, the mean F0 values were almost the same for both primary stress and secondary stress. This result supports the hypothesis that V1 with primary stress in the neutral context is accented while that in the post-focus context is not. There was no significant interaction between stress patterns and word pairs/speakers.

Table 7.5: Mean F0 values and the results of RMANOVA (by-word, by-speaker): primary stress V1 vs. secondary stress V1.

			F0 mean (StD)	Num of pairs	$F_{\text{by-word}}$ (df)	$F_{\text{by-speaker}}$ (df)
Male (2 speakers)	Neutral	P	124 Hz (18.5)	40	24.6** (1,35)	61.03** (1,37)
		S	116 Hz (25.3)			
	Post-Focus	P	97 Hz (18.5)	40	0.053 (1,35)	0.048 (1,37)
		S	97 Hz (19.1)			
Female (3 speakers)	Neutral	P	236 Hz (22.3)	60	93.6** (1,55)	234.3** (1,57)
		S	207 Hz (13.4)			
	Post-Focus	P	181 Hz (15.9)	60	0.084 (1,55)	0.083 (1,57)
		S	181 Hz (17.1)			

$**p<0.01, *p<0.05$

Durational analyses

RMANOVA (by-word and by-subject) tested whether the mean duration of V1 with primary stress was longer than that of V1 with secondary stress both in an accented environment and in an unaccented environment. Since separate comparisons were carried out for the accented and the unaccented environment, the alpha value was adjusted to $0.05/2 = 0.025$. Table 7.6 summarizes the results: V1 with primary stress is significantly longer than V1 with secondary stress regardless of the accentual environments in both the by-word and the by-speaker analyses.

Table 7.6: Mean durations and the results of RMANOVA (by-word, by-speaker): P (primary stress V1) vs. S (secondary stress V1).

			Duration mean (StD)	Num of pairs	by-word F (df)	by-speaker F (df)
5 speakers	Accented (Neutral)	P	109ms (23.6)	100	125** (1, 95)	111** (1, 95)
		S	96ms (20)			
	Unaccented (Pos-Focus)	P	103ms (22.1)	100	14.9** (1, 95)	14.5** (1, 95)
		S	98ms (22.8)			

***p*<0.01, **p*<0.05

There was, however, an interaction between stress patterns and word-pairs according to the by-word analyses: in the accented environment $F(4, 95) = 4.73$, $p = 0.002$; in the unaccented environment $F(4, 95) = 2.55$, $p = 0.02$. Given this, additional RMANOVA (by-speaker) tests were carried out separately for each word pair to examine the durational difference between primary and secondary stress in each word-pair. Since ten comparisons were carried out, i.e., 5 word pairs × 2 accent environments, the alpha value for this statistical test was adjusted to $0.05/10 = 0.005$. Results are summarized in Table 7.7.

Primary stress was consistently longer than secondary stress for all word-pairs in the accented environment: the difference was significant at $\alpha = 0.005$ for four pairs. One pair: *terminating* vs. *termination*, was marginally significant at $\alpha = 0.05$. In the unaccented environment, however, this pair: *termi-*

nating vs *termination,* was the only one that showed a significant difference at $\alpha = 0.005$. Two pairs, i.e., *fascinating* vs. *fascination* and *dominating* vs. *domination,* were marginally significant at $\alpha = 0.01$ and $\alpha = 0.05$ respectively, whereas the pair of *prosecuting* vs. *prosecution* showed no significant difference between the two stress conditions. That is, although there was a general tendency for primary stress to be longer than secondary stress regardless of the accentual environments, the tendency did not hold for all word pairs in the unaccented environment.

The mean durations of the primary stress vowels in this experiment were much shorter than 150 ms. Nonetheless, they were longer than secondary stress vowels. In contrast, primary stress vowels that underwent primary stress lengthening in Experiment I were either approximately 150 ms or more than 150 ms. We will come back to this point again in Section 7.4.3.

Table 7.7: Mean durations and the results of RMANOVA (by-speaker): P (primary stress V1) vs. S (secondary stress V1).

Word Pairs	Stress	Accented			Unaccented		
		Duration (Std)	Num of pairs	$F_{by\text{-}speaker}$ (Df)	Duration (Std)	Num of pairs	$F_{by\text{-}speaker}$ (Df)
[ɑ] in *domi-*	P	124 ms (17.6)	20	38.5*** (1,15)	114 ms (11.3)	20	6.29* (1,15)
	S	110 ms (15)			110 ms (12.2)		
[ɑ] in *prose-*	P	102 ms (16.5)	20	13.5*** (1,15)	97 ms (14.3)	20	−1.43 (1,15)
	S	94 ms (12.3)			100 ms (13.9)		
[æ] in *fasci-*	P	118 ms (12.2)	20	25.6*** (1,15)	117 ms (16.9)	20	6.77** (1,15)
	S	105 ms (14)			112 ms (18.1)		
[æ] in *navi-*	P	124 ms (14)	20	56.1*** (1,15)	114 ms (14.2)	20	3.94* (1,15)
	S	103 ms (15.8)			107 ms (13.3)		
[ɝ] in *termi-*	P	75 ms (11.9)	20	4.96* (1,15)	71 ms (12.5)	20	8.71*** (1,15)
	S	68 ms (13.3)			64 ms (14.3)		

***$p < 0.005$, **$p < 0.01$, *$p < 0.05$

An additional finding is that there was accentual lengthening of primary stress vowels: accented primary stress vowels (109 ms) was about 6 percent longer than the unaccented primary stress vowels (103 ms). This accentual lengthening effect was statistically significant according to ANOVA: $F(1, 198) = 3.38, p = 0.03$.

7.4.2.2 The analysis of unstressed V2

The mean durations of the unstressed V2 were also compared between a post-primary stress position and a post-secondary stress position. As discussed later, there were cases where V2 lacked its independent voicing period, which were treated as zero ms in the analyses here. We carried out RMANOVA (both by-word and by-subject). The alpha value was adjusted to .05/2=.025. Post-primary stress V2 was significantly longer than post-secondary stress V2 in both the accented and the unaccented environment as shown in Table 7.8. Furthermore, there was no interaction between the word-pair factor and the speaker factor, which means that the durational relationship between post-primary stress V2 and post-secondary stress V2 is consistent across all word pairs and all speakers.

Table 7.8: Mean durations and the results of RMANOVA (by-speaker): P (post-primary stress V2$_{Unstressed}$) vs. S (post-secondary stress V2$_{Unstressed}$).

5 speakers			Duration mean (StD)	Num of pairs	by-word F (df)	by-speaker F (df)
	Accented (Neutral)	P	40 ms (13.9)	100	6.75** (1, 95)	7.09** (1, 95)
		S	37 ms (14.6)			
	Unaccented (Post-focus)	P	35 ms (17.3)	100	9.59** (1, 95)	9.67** (1, 95)
		S	31 ms (17.9)			

**p<0.01, *p<0.05

An additional finding is that the unstressed V2 of *fasci-* and that of *prose-* often lacked voicing periods, and the phrasal prominence (pitch accent) and the PW-prominence (primary stress) additively affected the frequency of the V2 devoicing of *prose-*. V2 in the foot lacking PW-prominence (V2 following V1 with secondary stress) was more likely to be devoiced than that in the foot associated with PW-prominence (V2 following V1 with primary stress) though it was not statistically significant for accented nor for unaccented cases according to Fisher's exact test. V2 in PW lacking the phrasal prominence (V2 following unaccented V1) was more frequently devoiced than that of PW associated with the phrasal prominence (V2 following accented V1), which was marginally significant according Fisher's exact test (+PW-prom: $p<0.1$; -PW-prom: $p<0.1$). That is, V2 in the foot with both the PW-prominence and the phrasal prominence (V2 following V1 with accented primary stress) was the least likely to be devoiced while that in the foot with neither of the prominence (V2 following V1 with secondary stress in an unaccented environment) was the most likely to be devoiced for the *prose*-words. Such a tendency was not obtained for the V2 devoicing of *fasci-*, however. Figure 7.1 shows the frequency of devoicing in percentages, and how it varies depending on the presence or absence of PW-prominence (±PW Prom) and phrasal prominence (±IPh Prom).

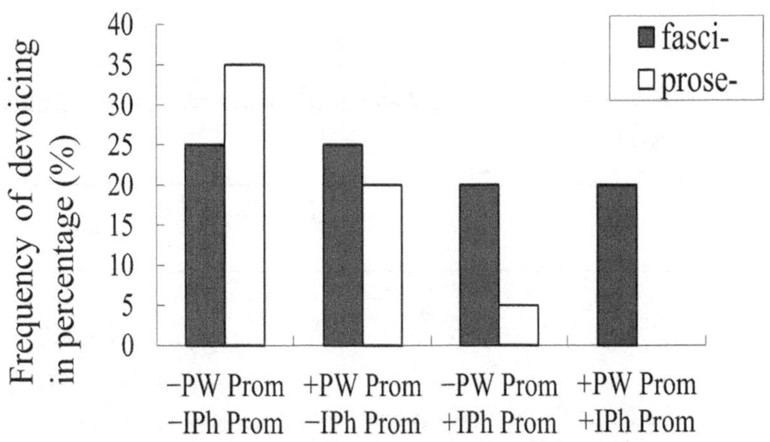

Figure 7.1: Percent V2 devoicing

7.4.3 Discussion

We observe that both the primary stress V1 and the unstressed V2 that follows the primary stress V1 undergo lengthening. The domain of lengthening triggered by the PW-prominence extends to the entire foot.

In this experiment, primary stress vowels of less than 150 ms underwent PW-prominence lengthening. This result differs from that found in Experiment I, where only those of 150 ms to 160 ms underwent PW-prominence in Experiment I. The discrepancies between the two experiments may be due to the difference in the rhythmic patterns of the target words used in these two experiments. Experiment I used disyllabic words in which two stressed syllables were next to each other while in this experiment, words with two feet were used in which an unstressed reduced syllable intervened between the two stressed syllables. Although the primary stress V1 by itself was shorter than 150 ms in this experiment, the foot as a whole undergoes lengthening. The fact that the relatively short primary stress V1 lengthened in this experiment may be a side effect of the lengthening applied to the entire foot that bears the PW-prominence.

Additionally, we found an effect of phrasal prominence (accent) on vowel duration: the accented primary stress V1 was longer than the unaccented primary stress V1. We also see in Tables 7.6 and 7.7 that the unaccented primary stress V1 was longer than not only the secondary stressed V1 in the unaccented environment but also that in the accented environment. This result indicates that both PW prominence and phrasal (IPh) prominence cumulatively contribute to the lengthening of vowels: the DTE of IPh (= accented primary stress vowels) > the DTE of PW (= unaccented primary stress vowels) > the DTE of Ft (= secondary stress vowels in both accented and unaccented environments). This outcome contradicts Cho and Keating's (2009) observation: they do not positively show that primary stress vowels in an unaccented environment were longer than secondary stress vowels. The discrepancy between Cho and Keating's results and ours may be due to the difference in the types of focus/accents involved or the kinds of target words used in the two studies. In Cho and Keating's experiment, target words were interpreted as 'contrastive narrow focus' while those in this experiment were not. They also used nonce words such as ˈNEbaˌben vs. ˌnebaˈBEN, while we used existing words. It could be that when producing nonce words, speakers can roughly distinguish the acoustic properties of the accented primary stress syllables and the rest of the syllables, but cannot make more subtle distinctions, for example, between the unaccented primary stress and the unaccented secondary stress. When producing real words, however, they can adjust more subtle durational differences with different levels of prosodic prominence. A possible hypothesis is that familiar and more frequently used words are stored in the mental lexicon together with more fine-grained prosodic and acoustic information. In contrast, no such information is stored for nonce words, and speakers cannot therefore perform as well in distinguishing the different levels of prominence when producing them.

Another finding is that the PW-prominence and the phrasal prominence additively contributed to the frequency of post-stress unstressed V2 devoicing of *prose-* (see Fig. 7.1): the devoicing tended to be the least frequent when the post-stress V2 was dominated by the head-Ft of PW and the head-PW of IPh at the same time, and the most frequent when it was dominated by neither of them though it was not necessarily statistically significant. This outcome may also indicate that the accentual (phrasal-prominence) factor and the PW-prominence factor each contribute to the acoustic property adjustment of vowels independently.

7.5   Conclusions

The present study investigated the effects of PW-prominence on the duration of vowels and the domain of the lengthening associated with PW-prominence.

The results accord well with previous studies such as Huss (1978), Sluijter and van Heuven (1996), de Jong (2004) and Okobi (2006): primary stress vowels were longer than secondary stress vowels not only in an accented context but also in an unaccented context. In the comparison of disyllabic noun-verb pairs where the location of primary stress and that of secondary stress alternated such as ʹDIˌgest vs. ˌdiʹGEST (Experiment I), only vowels that were longer than 150 ms showed a durational difference between the primary stress and the secondary stress in both the accented and the unaccented contexts. In the comparison of four-syllable words, where the location of primary stress and secondary stress alternated between the initial and the penultimate syllable (Experiment II), e.g., ʹDOmiˌnating vs. ˌdomiʹNAtion, the initial primary stress vowels were consistently longer than their secondary stress counterparts in both the accented and the unaccented contexts despite the fact that all of the target vowels were less than 150 ms. Apart from the subtle discrepancy between Experiment I and Experiment II in duration of vowels, results obtained in these two experiments are convincing enough to support the claim that PW-prominence, i.e., the prosodic prominence that is responsible for the assignment of the primary stress, contributes to the durational adjustments of vowels.

Finally, both primary stress vowels and the following unstressed vowels undergo lengthening (Experiment II). From this result, we can conclude that the domain of PW-prominence lengthening is the entire head-Foot of PW. Furthermore, in Experiment II, the PW-prominence and the IPh-prominence additively affect both duration of primary stress vowels and the frequency of devoicing of post-primary unstressed vowels. These results suggest that the PW-prominence is an independent prosodic factor contributing to the acoustic property of an entire foot.

Acknowledgments

I am grateful to Donna Erickson, Shigeto Kawahara and anonymous reviewers for their helpful comments and suggestions to the earlier version of this paper, and to Toni Borowsky and Shigeto Kawahara for editing this paper. All mistakes are mine, however. I would like to also thank Elisabeth Selkirk, Stefanie Shattuck-Hufnagel, and Anthony Okobi for having insightful discussions at an earlier stage of this study, during the summer of 2006. This study is supported by MEXT (Grant No.18720133) to the author.

Notes

1   Beckman and Pierrehumbert (1986) further distinguish the two levels of PPh in English: the Intermediate Phrase and the Accentual Phrase. The Intermediate Phrase in English, according to Beckman and Pierrehumbert, is a domain which is demarcated by a phrase-edge marking tone (a.k.a. phrase accent) and in which the downstep of H* pitch accents takes place. They define the Accentual Phrase as a domain in which one and only one pitch accent is realized, which has been already attested in Japanese. In English, however, there are neither boundary tones nor edge-marking tones to support the level of Accentual Phrase. Beckman and Pierrehumbert's Intermediate Phrase and Accentual Phrase correspond to Selkirk's Major Phrase and Minor Phrase respectively (Selkirk, 1986; Selkirk and Tateishi, 1991).

2   The example pair of *center* and *centaur* was taken from Sugahara and Turk (2009).

3   A designated terminal element of a constituent Ci is a terminal element that is exclusively dominated by strong nodes in Ci (Liberman and Prince, 1977; Selkirk, 1984). Therefore, DTE of IPh is the head (the nucleus vowel) of the head-σ that is dominated by the head-Ft of the head-PW.

4   Spectral tilt (H1-A3) is a measure of H1 (the amplitude of first harmonic) relative to A3 (the amplitude of the third formant (F3)).

5   Huss (1978), for example, used pairs of words such as *DEcrease* (noun) vs. *deCREASE* (verb). However, his noun-verb pairs do not necessarily constitute minimal pairs in terms of primary stress and secondary stress, because the initial syllable of Huss' iambic verbs may be pronounced with a reduced unstressed vowel as in [dəˈkris]. Huss, then compared the strong initial syllable in *DEcrease* (noun) and the weak and possibly unstressed syllable in *deCREASE*. In Okobi's (2006) study, he compared the acoustic properties of the initial primary stress syllables and those of the second syllables in *DIdi* [di.di], *DOdo* [doʊ.doʊ] and *DAda* [dɑ.dɑ], for example. In English, however, unstressed vowels may contrast between [i] and [oʊ] at a word-final position as discussed in Kahn (1976), Flemming (2009: 91) and Flemming and Johnson (2007: 91–93), and it is not clear whether the weaker second syllables in *DIdi* and *DOdo* really carried secondary stress.

6   According to Upton *et al.* (2003) and Wells (2007), the initial syllable of the verb form *diGEST* may be pronounced as reduced. However, in our experiment, none of our speakers produced the word with an initial reduced syllable: they always pronounced it as [daɪ. dʒɛst].

7   The students are from California, the Midwest or the Northeast.

References

Boersma, Paul and Weenink, David. (2009) Praat: doing phonetics by computer (Version 5.1.15) [Computer program]. Retrieved August 30, 2009, from http://www.praat.org/.

Booij, Geert. (1983). Principles and parameters in prosodic phonology. *Linguistics* 21: 249–280.

Beckman, Mary E. and Edwards, Jan. (1990) Lengthening and shortening and the nature of prosodic constituency. In J. Kingston and M. E. Beckman (eds) *Papers in Laboratory Phonology I: Between the Grammar and Physics of Speech* 152–214. Cambridge: Cambridge University Press.

Beckman, Mary E. and Pierrehumbert, Janet. (1986) Intonational structure in Japanese and English. *Phonology Yearbook* 3: 255–309.

Campbell, Nick and Beckman, Mary E. (1997) Stress, prominence, and spectral tilt. *Proceedings of ESCA Workshop on Intonation*, 18–21.

Cho, Taehong and Keating, Patricia. (2009) Effects of initial position versus prominence in English. *Journal of Phonetics* 37 (4): 466–485.

De Jong, Kenneth. (2004) Stress, lexical focus, and segmental focus in English: Patterns of variation in vowel duration. *Journal of Phonetics* 32 (4): 493–516.

Erickson, Donna. (2002) Articulation of extreme formant patterns for emphasized vowels. *Phonetica* 59 (2–3): 134–149.

Erickson, Donna. (2003) Some effects of prosody on articulation in American English. In T. Honma, M. Okazaki, T. Tabata and S. Tanaka (eds) *A New Century of Phonology and Phonological Theory: A Festschrift for Prof. Haraguchi* 473–491. Tokyo: Kaitakusha.

Ewen, Colin J. and Van Der Hulst, Harry. (2001) *The Phonological Structure of Words*. Cambridge: Cambridge University Press.

Flemming, Edward. (2009) The phonetics of schwa vowels. In D. Minkova (ed.) *Phonological Weakness in English* 78–95. Hampshire: Palgrave MacMillan.

Flemming, Edward and Johnson, Stephanie. (2007) Rosa's roses: reduced vowels in American English. *Journal of the International Phonetic Association* 37 (1): 83–96.

Gussenhoven, Carlos. (2004) *The Phonology of Tone and Intonation*. Cambridge: Cambridge University Press.

Hayes, Bruce. (1980) *A Metrical Theory of Stress Rules*. PhD dissertation, MIT. Published 1985, New York: Garland.

Hayes, Bruce. (1995) *Metrical Stress Theory: Principles and Case Studies*. Chicago, IL: University of Chicago Press.

Huss, Volker. (1978) English word stress in the post-nuclear position. *Phonetica* 35: 86–105.

Kahn, Daniel. (1976) *Syllable-based Generalizations in English Phonology*. PhD dissertation, MIT. Published 1980, New York: Garland.

Liberman, Mark Y. and Prince, Alan. (1977) On stress and linguistic rhythm. *Linguistic Inquiry* 8 (2): 249–336.

Nespor, Marina and Vogel, Irene. (1986) *Prosodic Phonology*. Dordrecht: Foris.

Okobi, Anthony. (2006) *Acoustic Correlates of Word Stress in American English*. PhD dissertation, MIT.

Pierrehumbert, Janet. (1980) *The Phonology and Phonetics of English Intonation*. PhD dissertation, Cambridge, MA: MIT.

Selkirk, Elisabeth O. (1978) On prosodic structure and its relation to syntactic structure. In T. Fretheim (ed.), *Nordic Prosody II* 1–31. Trondheim: TAPIR.

Selkirk, Elisabeth O. (1980) The role of prosodic categories in English word stress. *Linguistic Inquiry* 11 (3): 563–605.

Selkirk, Elisabeth O. (1984) *Phonology and Syntax: The Relation between Sound and Structure*. Cambridge, MA: MIT Press.

Selkirk, Elisabeth O. (1986) On derived domains in sentence phonology. *Phonology Yearbook* 3: 371–405.

Selkirk, Elisabeth O. (1995) Sentence prosody: intonation, stress and phrasing. In J. Goldsmith (ed.) *The Handbook of Phonological Theory* 550-569. Oxford: Blackwell.

Selkirk, Elisabeth O. (2002) Contrastive *FOCUS* vs. presentational *focus*: prosodic evidence from right node raising in English. *Proceedings of Speech Prosidy 2002*, 643–646.

Selkirk, Elisabeth O. and Tateishi Koichi. (1991) Syntax and downstep in Japanese. In C. Georgopoulos and R. Ishihara (eds), *Interdisciplinary Approaches to Language* 519–543. Dordrecht: Kluwer Academic Publishing.

Sluijter, Agaath M. C., Shattuck-Hufnagel, Stefanie, Stevens, Kenneth N. and van Heuven, Vincent J. (1995) Supralaryngeal resonance and glottal pulse shape as correlates of stress and accent in English. *Proceedings of the 13th ICPhS* vol 2, 630–633.

Sluijter, Agaath M. C. and van Heuven, Vincent J. (1996) Acoustic correlates of linguistic stress and accent in Dutch and American English. *Proceedings of ICSLP* vol 2, 630–633.

Sugahara, Mariko and Turk, Alice. (2009) Durational correlates of English sublexical constituent structure. *Phonology* 26: 477–524.

Turk, Alice and Sawusch, James R. (1997) The domain of accentual lengthening in American English. *Journal of Phonetics* 25 (1): 25–41.

Turk, Alice and White, Laurence. (1999) Structural influences on accentual lengthening in English. *Journal of Phonetics* 27 (2): 171–206.

Upton, Clive, Kretzschmar, William A. Jr and Konopka, Rafal. (2003) *Oxford Dictionary of Pronunciation for Current English*. Oxford: Oxford University Press.

Wells, J. C. (2007) *Longman Pronunciation Dictionary*. Harlow: Pearson Education Limited.

Wightman, C. W., Shattuck-Hufnagel, S., Ostendorf, M. and Price, P. J. (1992) Segmental durations in the vicinity of prosodic phrase boundaries. *Journal of the Acoustical Society of America* 91 (3): 1707–1717.

Appendix 7.1.   Test materials used in Experiment I

Target words are italicized here for clarity. They were not italicized in the scripts presented to speakers.

1.1.   Neutral (Accented) Context

Trochaic Noun Forms

    (a) What is Amy doing? Amy is reading the news and *digest*, I think.

    (b) What does the paper look like? The paper suffers from typos and *misprints*, I think.

    (c) Tell me about your heart. My heart suffers from a cut and *transplant*, I think.

Iambic Verb Forms

    (a) What is good about cookies? Cookies are easy to eat and *digest*, I think.

    (b) Tell me about these new fonts. The fonts are easy to type and *misprint*, I think.

    (c) Please tell me about hearts. Hearts are easy to move and *transplant*, I think.

1.2.   Post-Focus (Unaccented) Context

Trochaic Noun Forms

    (a) Mary is reading the news and digest. But Amy ISN'T reading the news and *digest*, I think.

    (b) Their paper suffers from typos and misprint. But our paper DOESN'T suffer from typos and *misprint*, I think.

    (c) His heart suffers from a cut and transplant. But your heart DOESN'T suffer from a cut and *transplant*, I think.

Iambic Verb Forms

    (a) Bread is easy to eat and digest. But cookies AREN'T easy to eat and *digest*, I think.

    (b) These fonts are easy to type and misprint. But those fonts AREN'T easy to type and *misprint*, I think.

    (c) Livers are easy to move and transplant. But hearts AREN'T easy to move and transplant, I think.

Appendix 7.2. Test materials used in Experiment II

Target words are italicized here for clarity. They were not italicised in the scripts presented to speakers.

2.1.   Neutral (Accented) Context:

Initial Primary stress

    a.   I said '*prosecutor*', you know.

    b.   I said '*navigator*', you know.

    c.   I said '*fascinating*', you know.

    d.   I said '*dominating*', you know.

    e.   I said '*terminating*', you know.

Initial Secondary stress

    (a) I said '*prosecution*', you know.

    (b) I said '*navigation*', you know.

    (c) I said '*fascination*' you know.

    (d) I said '*domination*', you know.

    (e) I said '*termination*', you know.

2.2.   Post-Focus (Unaccented) Context

Initial Primary stress

    (a) I didn't say 'prosecutor'. HE said '*prosecutor*', you know.

    (b) I didn't say 'navigator'. HE said '*navigator*', you know.

    (c) I didn't say 'fascinating'. HE said '*fascinating*', you know.

    (d) I didn't say 'dominating'. HE said '*dominating*', you know.

    (e) I didn't say 'terminating'. HE said '*terminating*', you know.

Initial Secondary stress

    (a) I didn't say 'prosecution'. HE said '*prosecution*', you know.

    (b) I didn't say 'navigation'. HE said '*navigation*', you know.

    (c) I didn't say 'fascination'. HE said '*fascination*', you know.

    (d) I didn't say 'domination'. HE said '*domination*', you know.

    (e) I didn't say 'termination'. HE said '*termination*', you know.

Section 3
Phrases and above

8 Variable cues to phrasing: Finding edges in Egyptian Arabic*

Sam Hellmuth[a]

8.1 Introduction

This paper explores variation in the tonal cues to prosodic phrasing observed in a corpus of read speech sentences in Egyptian Arabic (EA). There is variation between speakers in the cues employed to mark instances of the same type (or level) of prosodic juncture in the same position in the sentence, and there is also (what proves to be principled) variation in the types of cues employed at distinct instances of (what are expected to be) the same type/level of juncture occurring at different positions in syntactic structure. This paper seeks first to establish what the cues to Major Phonological Phrase (MaP)-level phrasing are in EA, amid all this variation, and, as a secondary goal, to determine whether there is MaP-level marking of 'XP-edges' in EA.

The rationale for this secondary question is to find out whether or not EA presents a challenge to edge-based mapping algorithms (Selkirk, 1986, 1995, 2000; Truckenbrodt, 1999), and their phase-based equivalents (Kratzer and Selkirk, 2007). Under edge-based mapping (Selkirk, 1986, 1995, 2000), Major Phonological Phrase (MaP) boundaries are expected at the right edge of each embedded XP, whereas, under a canonical phase-based analysis, with CP and *v*P as phase heads (Chomsky, 2001, 2005), a MaP boundary is predicted only at the right edge of the subject. Prior work on EA phrasing, in Hellmuth (2004), suggests that EA permits long MaPs which straddle XP boundaries, and these facts were there analysed in terms of interaction between prosodic

[a] Sam Hellmuth: Department of Language and Linguistic Science, University of York, UK. Email: sam.hellmuth@york.ac.uk

minimality constraints and edge-based syntax-phonology interface constraints. An alternative analysis of this lack of sensitivity to XP-edges, as yet unexplored, is that EA's long prosodic phrases may map directly to spellout domains (Adger, 2006; Ishihara, 2007). In order to determine whether a phase-based analysis of EA is plausible, the present corpus comprises SVO sentences in which both the subject and object position host complex noun phrases containing an embedded prepositional phrase adjunct, to probe EA phrasing for any signs of sensitivity to XP-edges.

In the present data we find conflicting evidence: boundaries are indeed observed in almost all XP-edge positions, but the cues are systematically stronger at the right edge of the subject than at the right edge of other XPs. One solution would be to treat the different cue sets as marking prosodic constituents of different levels, but this fails to take account of the fact that cues to MaP boundaries appear to be variable anyway, and that, even though the cues vary, for each speaker there is a consistent subset relation between the cues observed in different positions. We will argue that all of the variability can be understood in terms of subordination between phonetic implementation domains of adjacent MaPs (following Truckenbrodt, 2002, 2004, 2007). Under this view EA proves to be a well-behaved language, with MaP boundaries at XP-edges as predicted by edge-based mapping – albeit subject to prosodic minimality constraints – and we revise the analysis of Hellmuth (2004) accordingly.

8.2   Rationale for the study

8.2.1   Background

Egyptian Arabic (EA) is defined here as the dialect of Arabic spoken in Cairo, which also functions as a national standard (Haeri, 1996: Bassiouney, 2009). The segmental and metrical phonology of EA is well-described (see Watson, 2002 for a summary), and syntactically EA displays SVO basic word order (Benmamoun, 2000; Edwards, 2009). Watson (2002) describes a number of segmental sandhi processes which are sensitive to (major) phonological phrase (MaP) level prosodic boundaries. The only segmental sandhi process investigated experimentally is epenthesis (which applies to break up any illicit CCC cluster), which has been shown to apply across MaP boundaries within the intonational phrase (IP) (Hellmuth, 2004; Aquil, 2006).

A salient feature of spoken colloquial EA intonation[1] is its unusually rich distribution of pitch accents: in EA a pitch accent is observed on almost every content word (Hellmuth, 2006), and shows a very restricted range of pitch accent types (analysed as a single phonological category, L+H*, in Hellmuth, 2006). The twin properties of rich accent distribution and restricted accent inventory are shared with a number of other languages including Spanish and Greek (Jun, 2005). For EA, this accent distribution pattern can be formalized in terms of a requirement that phonological tone, in the form of an intonational pitch accent, be associated with every Prosodic Word (PWd) (Hellmuth, 2007), and this pattern sets EA apart from languages in which the distribution of pitch accents is better explained relative to a phrase level prosodic constituent (see Truckenbrodt, this volume, for an overview).

Prosodic phrasing in EA was investigated in Hellmuth (2004), on the basis of a corpus of read speech sentences in which the syntactic complexity and prosodic weight of arguments was systematically varied (replicating the design of Frota *et al.*, 2007). The key finding was that phrases at the MaP level are long in EA, in that most utterances were realized within a single MaP, straddling utterance internal XP-edges. A mid-utterance boundary was only observed when the subject NP was both syntactically complex and prosodically heavy; in particular, a phrase boundary only occurred after the subject NP when it contained at least four PWds.[2] The findings were subsequently checked in a corpus of semi-spontaneous speech (narratives re-told from memory) and the same generalization was found to hold (Hellmuth, 2007): utterances were in general realized within a single MaP in EA, and straddled XP edges.

Examples from the Hellmuth (2004) dataset are reproduced below, showing the sentence in (1) realized either within a single MaP, as in Figure 8.1, or in two MaPs, with a phrase break at the right edge of the subject (after [muhimm] 'important'), as in Figure 8.2. The cues to phrasing observed in Figure 8.2 are pre-boundary lengthening and a local pitch reset after the boundary.

(1) il-mu'handis l-maʕ'maːri l-mu'himm bij'xumm ba'lad-na

the-engineer the-architectural the-important cheats-1ms our-country

[[[[ ]AP [ ]AP]NP]DP [[[ ]DP]VP]vP]TP

'The important architect is cheating our country.'

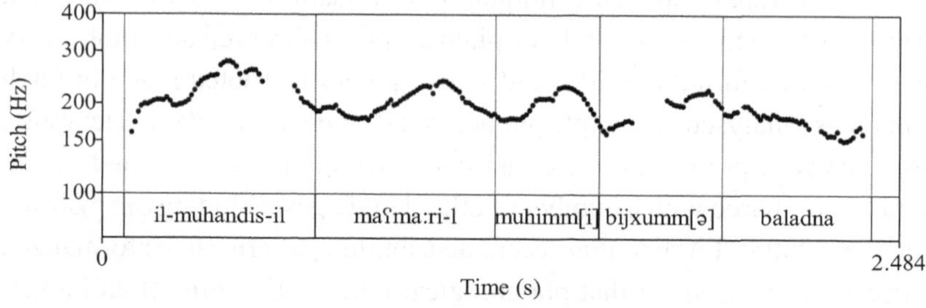

Figure 8.1: Sample SVO sentence realized in a single MaP from Hellmuth (2004: 102)

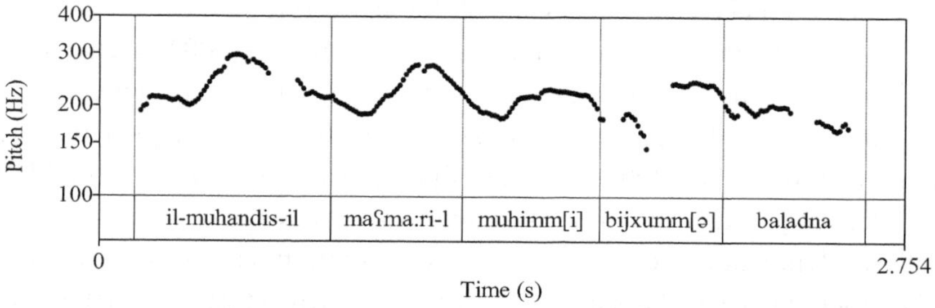

Figure 8.2: Sample SVO sentence realized in two MaPs from Hellmuth (2004: 102)

In an edge-based formalization of the syntax-phonology interface (Selkirk, 1986; Truckenbrodt, 1999) an MaP boundary is expected at XP edges, in particular at the right edge of the subject in an SVO sentence. Following Selkirk (2000), the EA facts were formalized in an OT analysis in terms of interaction between an edge-based interface constraint (ALIGNXP) and constraints on the phonological well-formedness of prosodic constituents. Specifically, Hellmuth (2004) proposed two relevant well-formedness constraints in EA: BINMAP requires each MaP to be comprised of at least two Minor Phonological Phrases (MiP), and BINMIP requires each MiP to be comprised of at least two PWds. In EA BINMAP outranks ALIGNXP so that a subject is only phrased alone if of sufficient prosodic weight, that is, when it contains four PWds. To account for the fact that some 3-PWd MaPs were observed in slower speech (e.g. in Figure 8.2), it was suggested that BINMIP is reranked or redefined in slow speech, but the analysis was not fully worked out.

The cues to phrasing observed in Hellmuth (2004) were chiefly tonal. A phrase boundary was transcribed whenever two or more of the following were observed: local pitch reset, final lowering, pre-boundary lengthening, failure of epenthesis, pause or a phrase tone (H-/L-). Very few phrase boundaries were found, just 20 in a corpus of 234, and the two speakers in the study appeared to use slightly different sets of cues. Evidence to confirm that the phrase-boundaries observed were at MaP level came from additional sentences in the dataset which contained a mid-sentence parenthetical, which are expected to be phrased as independent IPs (Nespor and Vogel, 1986; Kawahara, this volume). The phrasing cues observed at the edges of parentheticals differed somewhat from those observed at the (few) other boundaries, in that epenthesis failed to apply across boundaries at the edges of parentheticals, but did apply across other boundaries even in the presence of the other tonal and durational cues outlined above.[3]

8.2.2 Aims

This paper seeks to address issues which remain outstanding or arise from the findings of Hellmuth (2004). The first of these is to pin down the cues to phrasing in EA. In many other languages the cues to prosodic phrase edges are well-established, and indeed seem to be shared across speakers (e.g. the use of phrase tones, pre-boundary lengthening or other tonal cues). The two speakers investigated in Hellmuth (2004) varied in the cues to phrasing that they used, making it difficult to make generalizations about how phrasing is cued in EA. In this paper we examine data from six speakers in an attempt to establish more clearly what the cues to phrasing are in EA, and in particular to find out whether there are any consistent cues used by all speakers.

Given the claim advanced in Hellmuth (2004) that the long phrases observed in EA arise due to a phonological constraint on the minimum size of MaPs, and that this is what causes phrases to straddle XP edges, we investigate here read speech data using stimuli in which all arguments are prosodically heavy and syntactically complex. This should trigger a greater number of phrase boundaries, facilitating the task of establishing cues to phrasing described above, but also providing a testing ground for the formal analysis proposed in Hellmuth (2004).

An alternative explanation for the lack of boundaries at some XP-edges is that the syntax-phonology mapping does not call for a boundary in that position in the first place. In a canonical phase-based formulation of the syntax-phonology interface, only CP and *v*P act as phase heads, spelling out TP and

VP respectively as prosodic domains (Chomsky, 2001; Adger, 2006; Ishihara, 2007; Kratzer and Selkirk, 2007; cf. Truckenbrodt, this volume). If we assume that in SVO sentences in EA the subject is merged in vP (cf. Ackema and Neeleman, 2003), this predicts a prosodic boundary between the subject and verb (VP is spelled out), but not at embedded XP edges within a complex NP. The current dataset comprises SVO sentences in which the object argument has an NP complement and a following (VP-internal) PP adjunct: thus an edge-based mapping predicts a boundary between the two XPs but a phase-based analysis does not.

The influential edge-based mapping first proposed in Selkirk (1986) has provoked fruitful work in many languages over a long period (Inkelas and Zec, 1990; Truckenbrodt, 1995, 1999), and a fundamental role for XPs in the syntax-phonology mapping is maintained in Match Theory (Selkirk, 2009). This paper looks for evidence of a role for XPs in the syntax-phonology mapping, in a language which appears at first glance to have no need of them.

8.3   Methodology

The present study is designed to allow us to pick up where Hellmuth (2004) left off, eliciting read speech productions of target sentences in which all arguments are both syntactically complex and prosodically heavy. The present paper presents a fine-grained analysis of 8 SVO sentences produced three times each by six female speakers, yielding 108 tokens for input to both qualitative and quantitative analysis.[4] The materials and recording procedures are set out in §8.3.1, followed by a description of the qualitative and quanti-tative analyses in §8.3.2.

8.3.1 Materials and data collection

Eight SVO sentences were constructed in which both subject and object argu-ment positions contained a complex NP which was both syntactically complex and prosodically heavy. The verb and object NP were the same in all eight sentences, but the subject NP varied from each other in the number of sylla-bles, feet and prosodic words that they contained. The stimuli are provided in Tables 8.1 and 8.2 in transliteration. Potential XP-edge boundary positions are indicated with an arrow, at the right edge of the subject ('after S' position) and at the right edge of the complement NP within the VP ('within VP' position).

subject			verb	object		
head + complement		*adjunct PP*		*head + complement*		*adjunct PP*
il-muˈdiːr	il-giˈdiːd	min juˈnaːn	bijitˈʕallim	it-tadˈriːb	il-ħadiːs	fi kulˈlejat it-tarˈbeja
the-manager	the-new	from Greece	teaches.3ms	the-pedagogy	the-modern	[in [faculty the-education
[[[	[ ]AP]NP	[ ]PP]DP	[[	[[	[ ]AP]NP]DP	[[ ]CS]PP]VP]vP]TP
		after S ☞			*within VP* ☞	

Table 8.1: Structural template for target sentences analysed in the present study (indicating potential XP-edge boundary positions)

Table 8.2: Internal structure of the *subject* in the eight target sentences analysed in the present study (the number of PWds, feet and syllables in the subject as a whole are indicated in the leftmost columns)

target	*PWds*	*Ft*	*σ*	*subject* *head + complement*	*adjunct PP*
008	3	3	9	il-mu'diːr il-gi'diːd [[the-[manager [the-new]AP]NP	min ju'naːn [from Greece]PP]DP
010	3	4	9	il-ʔus'taːz il-gi'diːd [[the-[professor [the-new]AP]NP	min ju'naːn [from Greece]PP]DP
012	3	4	11	il-mu'diːr il-muta'dajjin [[the-[manager [the-devout]AP]NP	min ju'naːn [from Greece]PP]DP
014	3	5	11	il-ʔus'taːz il-muta'dajjin [[the-[professor [the-devout]AP]NP	min ju'naːn [from Greece]PP]DP
022	4	4	13	mu'ʕallim wi'laːdi il-mu'ʔaddab [[[teacher my-children]CS [the-polite(m.s.)]AP]NP	min ju'naːn [from Greece]PP]DP
018	4	5	14	mu'ʕallim wi'laːdi il-muta'dajjin [[[teacher my-children]CS [the-devout(m.s.)]AP]NP	min ju'naːn [from Greece]PP]DP

The VP contains five PWds in all of the sentences, and is thus of sufficient weight to allow the subject to be phrased alone. If the findings of Hellmuth (2004) generalize to other speakers, then we would expect all of the four-word subjects to be phrased alone, and at least some of the three-word subjects (depending on speech rate). Since the sentence-final adjunct PP comprises only two PWds we would not expect to observe within-VP boundaries other than at slow speech rates. Note that the four-word subject target sentences have a complex Construct State (CS) in head noun position.[5]

The eight sentences formed part of a larger set of 44 sentences with varying lexical content and structure, which were pseudo-randomized and interspersed with distractors. The sentences were presented in Arabic typescript, using EA spelling conventions in order to elicit colloquial productions (cf. Siemund *et al.*, 2002). Each speaker read all of the sentences through three times, performing another unrelated task between each repetition. The recordings were made in Cairo with six female speakers of EA. All were mother tongue speakers of EA, born and raised in Cairo, aged between 21–34 years, and none had any auditory or speech production difficulties. Speakers received a small payment as thanks for their participation. The recordings were made in a draped classroom using AKG headset condenser microphones, directly to digital .wav format in ProTools 6.0 on MBox at 44,100 Hz 16 bit, then re-sampled at 22,050 Hz 16 bit.

8.3.2 Qualitative and quantitative analysis

The full dataset of 108 tokens was submitted to both qualitative and quantitative analysis. All tokens were included in the analysis, even if they contained minor disfluencies and/or an atypical phrasing pattern. All analyses were undertaken using Praat (Boersma and Weenink, 2009).

The qualitative analysis took the form of hand-labelling of information on three tiers, carried out by the author based on auditory impression and inspection of the pitch trace and spectrogram, as illustrated in Figure 8.3 below. First, the orthography tier segments the utterance into words and provides a broad phonetic transcription for each one; enclitics were grouped with their preceding host word. The actual transcription used a standard transliteration system for Arabic, but examples for the present paper have been re-transcribed into IPA for ease of exposition.

Second, on the Break Indices tier, phrase-level junctures were transcribed using the break indices listed in Table 8.3 below. These are prototype break indices used here for the first time for EA, in order to test their usability. They assume the number of levels of phrasing proposed in Hellmuth (2004) and are modelled on the Break Indices proposed for Hebrew by Shaked (2007), which also assume an intermediate level of phrasing between the PWd and MaP. Break indices levels 0 and 1 were not transcribed for the present study, in order to speed up transcription.

Table 8.3: Prototype break indices for EA used in the present study

BI		*Labelled?*
0	Morphosyntactic word boundary	no
1	PWd boundary	no
2	MiP boundary	yes
3	MaP boundary	yes
4	IP boundary	yes

Table 8.4: Break indices proposed for Hebrew (Shaked 2007:180)

BI	Definition
0	Phonetically marked boundaries internal to the clitic group.
1	Clitic-group boundaries which are not prosodic word boundaries (e.g. internal to compounds and construct state nominals).
2	Word boundaries marked by pitch accent but no intonational phrase boundaries (minor/accentual phrase boundaries).
3	Intonational phrase boundaries marked by a single rising phrase tone (major/intermediate phrase boundaries).
4	Full intonation phrase boundaries, marked by a falling boundary tone.

Table 8.4 provides the definitions given by Shaked (2007) for Hebrew, for the boundaries of interest here. We have adopted a similar number of levels, but the definitions were not adopted a priori from Hebrew. An obvious case where the two languages appear to differ is in the distribution of pitch accents. Since in EA every PWd is expected to bear a pitch accent, the definition of BI-2 used for Hebrew by Shaked would in EA yield segmentation at every PWd boundary, rather than at MiP boundaries. Instead, we used BI-2 in EA to label MiP boundaries marked with clear phrasing cues.

Similarly, Shaked's definition of BI-1 expects a construct state (CS) nominal to be treated as a single PWd in Hebrew. CS nominals appear throughout the present dataset (e.g. utterance-final: [kullejat it-tarbeja] faculty-the-education 'the Faculty of Education') and were treated as two separate PWds by most speakers with a pitch accent on each word, as is the case in prior studies on EA (including Hellmuth, 2004). We note in §8.4 below however that one speaker in the present dataset did produce an atypical tonal pattern on these final CS constructions, which could be seen as prosodification of the whole CS into a single PWd, and such an analysis would require an additional BI for EA defined similarly to Shaked's BI-1 for Hebrew.

The final layer of qualitative transcription was a list of the cues to phrasing observed at each labelled BI juncture point, which were transcribed using the codes listed in Table 8.5. These codes were based on the set of cues observed in Hellmuth (2004). Examples of many of the cues can be seen in the sample labelled textgrid in Figure 8.3. Note, for example, the contrast between H (denoting rising pitch on and beyond the accented syllable) and U (denoting a peak at a higher level than the previous peak, following by a fall immediately after the accented syllable).

Table 8.5: Cue labels used for fine-grained description of each juncture (BI 2-4)

Label	Name	Definition
B	boundary tone	boundary shows a full boundary tone (usually a final fall)[6]
D	downstep	peak of the word at the boundary is produced at a lower level than expected[7] from effects of downstep alone, relative to pitch level of the previous peak (final lowering)
H	phrase tone	boundary shows either a H- or L- phrase tone
L	lengthening	word at the boundary is lengthened
P	pause	boundary is followed by pause (filled, e.g. with an in-breath, or unfilled)
R	reset	following peak is produced at a higher level than the peak of the word at the boundary[8]
S	suspension of downstep	peak of the word at the boundary is produced at the same level as the previous peak
U	upstep	peak of the word at the boundary is produced at a higher level than the previous peak

Figure 8.3 shows a fully labelled textgrid as created for each soundfile. The labelled tiers are as follows (from top to bottom): cues, BI, peaks, orthography, rhymes.

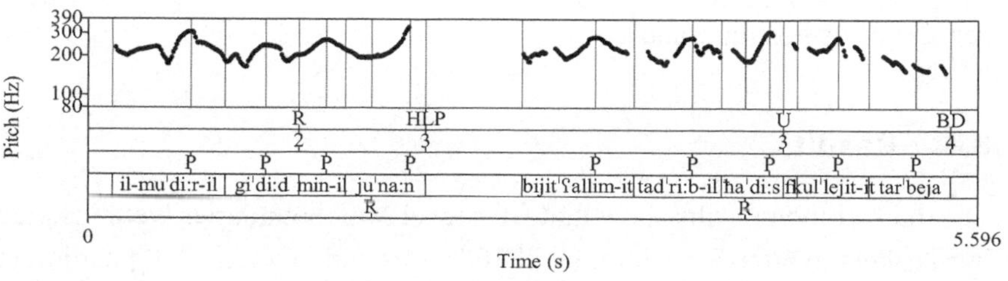

Figure 8.3: Sample textgrid showing qualitative transcription and labelling for quantitative analysis.

In order to provide independent support for the qualitative analysis, two sets of quantitative measures were extracted from each sound file: f0 and duration. To facilitate accurate f0 measurements, a Pitch object was created for each sound file in Praat (floor 75 Hz, ceiling 600 Hz) and each Pitch object hand-corrected for pitch tracking errors, such as doubling, halving or faulty pitch tracking due to voice quality variation (for example, creaky voice was very common in the last one or two syllables of each utterance). After hand-correction of the pitch trace, a Praat script was used to identify the pitch maximum within each labelled interval on the orthographic tier, and a peak label inserted at that point. During hand-labelling of BIs and phrasing cues, the position of peak labels was also hand-checked (e.g. to delete automatically inserted peak labels on any function words which were not in fact assigned a pitch accent). A further Praat script harvested the f0 value in Hertz (measured in the hand-corrected Pitch object) at each labelled peak position in the utterance. The f0 maximum identified for a PWd at a boundary could be the reflex either of a pitch accent on that word or of a phrase tone at its right edge (e.g. if the boundary is marked with a high phrase tone). This ambiguity was tolerated so that the f0 values could act as an independent source of evidence alongside the qualitative analysis.

As a source of independent evidence for pre-boundary lengthening we measured the duration of the rhyme portion of target words at the right-edge of XP constituents that might reasonably be expected to trigger a prosodic boundary (Wightman *et al.*, 1992). The rhyme of the final word in the subject ([junaːn] 'Greece') and of the final word in the complement NP of the VP ([ħadiːs] 'modern') was hand-labelled in each utterance. The duration of each labelled rhyme was extracted in milliseconds, then normalized by dividing each rhyme duration by the length of the whole sentence of which it was a part, and multiplying by 100, yielding a measure of each rhyme as a percentage of its host utterance.

8.4   Results

The transcription results show that BI-3 level MaP boundaries were inserted by speakers in after-S position in all 108 cases and in within-VP position in 91/108 cases.[9] In this section we first set out those aspects of inter-speaker behaviour which did not vary in relevant ways in §8.4.1 (looking at speech rate effects and utterance-final cues). The main body of the section then discusses the cues to phrasing used in after-S position, which do show inter-speaker variation, in §8.4.2, with comparison to the cues observed at within-VP boundaries, which are different again, in §8.4.3.

8.4.1 Lack of inter-speaker variation in speech rate effects and utterance-final cues

Since phrasing in EA has been found to vary according to speech rate (Hellmuth, 2004), a preliminary analysis of the speech rate used by each speaker was carried out to determine whether this affected phrasing choices in the present dataset. Figure 8.4 shows mean values of speech rate (syllables per second) for each speaker, presented in order from slowest speaker to fastest. An ANOVA reveals that the speakers fall into two clear subsets (F = 19.944, df = 107, $p<0.001$):[10] 'slow' speakers are fhg, fhm, fna; 'fast' speakers are fsf, faa, fhx.

Figure 8.5 shows the mean number of phrase boundaries (at BI 3 or above) observed for each speaker per utterance, again presented in order from slowest to fastest speaker.[11] At first glance it would appear that the two fastest speakers (faa and fhx) do indeed produce fewer boundaries, but an ANOVA shows that the difference between speakers is only significant between the fastest speaker (fhx) and the two speakers who produced the most boundaries (fhm and fsf), who are not the slowest speakers.[12] Speech rate is thus excluded as a factor in the remainder of this paper.

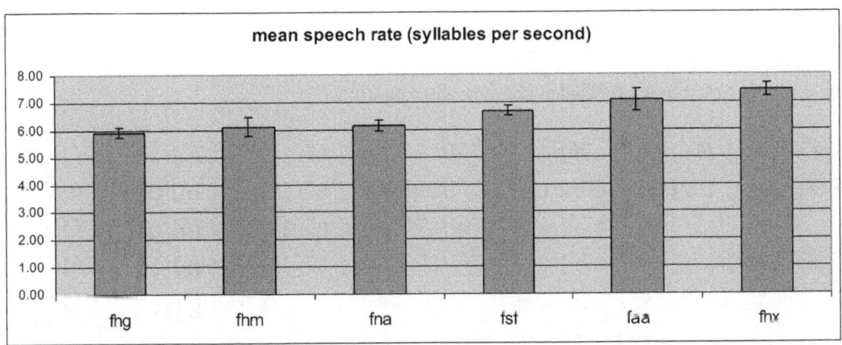

Figure 8.4: Mean speech rate by speaker (slowest on the left, fastest on the right)

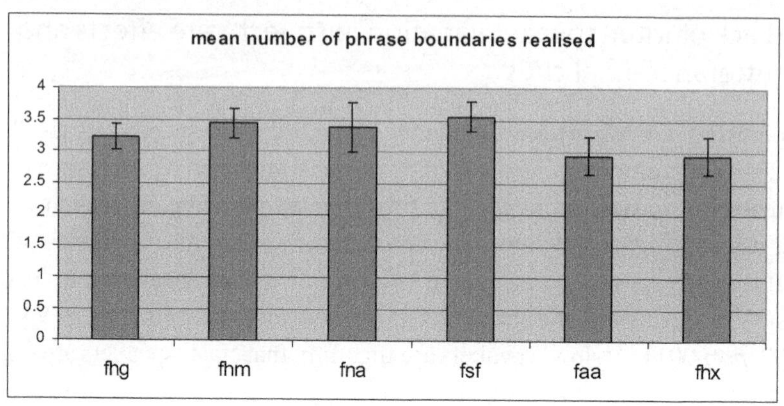

Figure 8.5: Mean number of boundaries per utterance (by speaker)

Speakers also showed little variation in their use of cues in utterance-final position, as shown in Table 8.6. All speakers used a boundary tone (B), and in most cases, the height of the final peak was realized lower than expected, showing final-lowering (Liberman and Pierrehumbert, 1984).[13] The only exception to this pattern was speaker fna (see Figure 8.10) who often realized the utterance-final word with upstep relative to the peak height of the previous word.[14]

Table 8.6: Cue clusters transcribed in utterance-final position

fhg	*fhx*	*fhm*	*fsf*	*faa*	*fna*
BD (18)	BD (18)	BD (18)	BD (18)	BD (17)	BU (12).
				B (1)	BD (3)
					BS (1)
					B (2)

8.4.2 Speaker variation in cues to phrasing

There is inter-speaker variation in the types of cues used to mark prosodic constituents of the same type in EA. To demonstrate this we will first present a summary of the auditory transcription results, to identify which speakers used which sets of cues. We support the transcription results with independent quantitative evidence of two kinds: measurements of the f0 of successive H peaks through each utterance and the duration of target words at putative XP-edge positions. Finally, although pre-boundary-lengthening is used by most speakers at most boundaries, it is not observed at all of the cases labelled as boundaries during transcription: we explore evidence from the f0 of successive peak heights to determine whether it is possible to have an MaP boundary in EA which is not cued by pre-boundary lengthening.

All of the speakers realized a boundary after the subject in all of their utterances. This means that they pattern with the slow speech phrasing generalizations observed in Hellmuth (2004), in that they allow a three-word subject to be phrased alone. The full set of cues observed in the after-S potential boundary position for each speaker are listed in Table 8.7.

All six speakers make use of pre-boundary lengthening, at most boundaries (though not all). Pauses were also used by all of the speakers but much less. With regard to their use of tonal cues, the six speakers can be divided into three groups according to their preferred cue choice in this position: speakers who tend to mark boundaries with partial reset (R), speakers who tend to mark boundaries with a phrase tone (usually H-),[15] and speakers who use a mixture of cues.

Table 8.7: Cue clusters transcribed in 'after-S' position, speakers grouped by cue preferences (for each speaker the most frequent cluster is underlined, most frequent cue(s) are in bold).

R-speakers		*H-speakers*		*Mixed-cue speakers*	
fhg	*fhx*	*fhm*	*fsf*	*faa*	*fna*
BLR (1)	DhLP (1)	<u>**HL** (11)</u>	BLP (1)	HLP (3)	**HL** (1)
BPR (1)	**DhLPR** (1)	HLP (5)	HL (2)	LP (1)	**HLP** (3)
HLPR (1)	**hLP** (5)	HLR (1)	<u>HLP (14)</u>	LPRU (1)	HLR (1)
HPR (1)	HLP (1)	U (1)	LPRS (1)	LRU (2)	L (2)
LP (1)	<u>**hLPR** (6)</u>			<u>**LS** (7)</u>	LPU (1)
<u>LPR (6)</u>	LRS (1)			LSP (1)	LRU (1)
LPRS (3)	LRU (1)			LU (1)	<u>**LS** (4)</u>
LR (3)	LS (2)			S (2)	LU (2)
LRS (1)					R (1)
					S (1)
					U (1)

Speaker fhg consistently marks the after-S boundary with partial reset (R, in 17/18 cases) and speaker fhx frequently makes use of partial reset in combination with a low phrase tone on the boundary itself; they are grouped together as *R-speakers* as a result (see Figures 8.6–8.7). Speakers fhm and fsf are *H-speakers* (see Figures 8.8–8.9): both consistently mark after-S boundaries with a high phrase tone (H). In contrast, speakers faa and fna are *mixed-cue speakers* who vary in their use of f0 cues (see Figures 8.10–8.11): for faa, the most common cue is to suspend downstep on the last item in the phrase (S), but phrase tones (H), upstep (U) or a following partial reset (R) are also observed; speaker fna varies between using a phrase tone (H), upstep (U) and suspension of downstep (S).

The cue labels and clusters listed in Table 8.7 are derived from impressionistic transcription but find independent support from quantitative analysis of the f0 properties of the utterances. The mean value of the f0 measurements for successive peaks throughout the utterance is provided in Figures 8.6–8.11, for each speaker in turn. The f0 values for each speaker are represented scaled within her own pitch range (measured across all utterances).

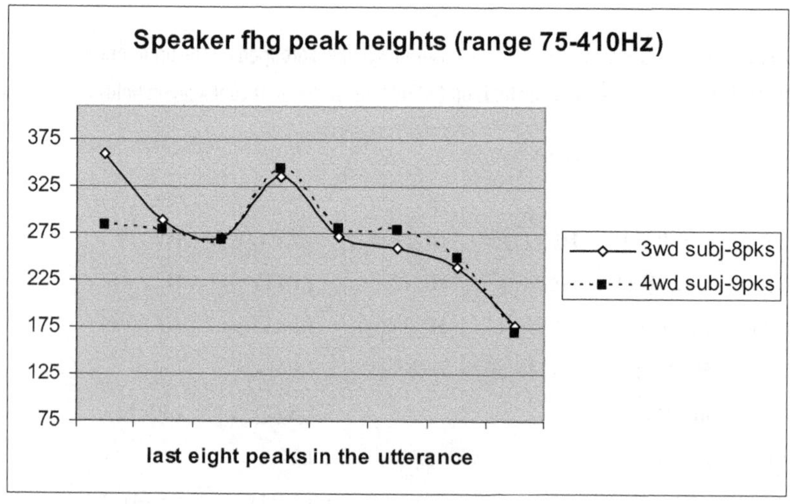

Figure 8.6: Speaker fhg peak heights

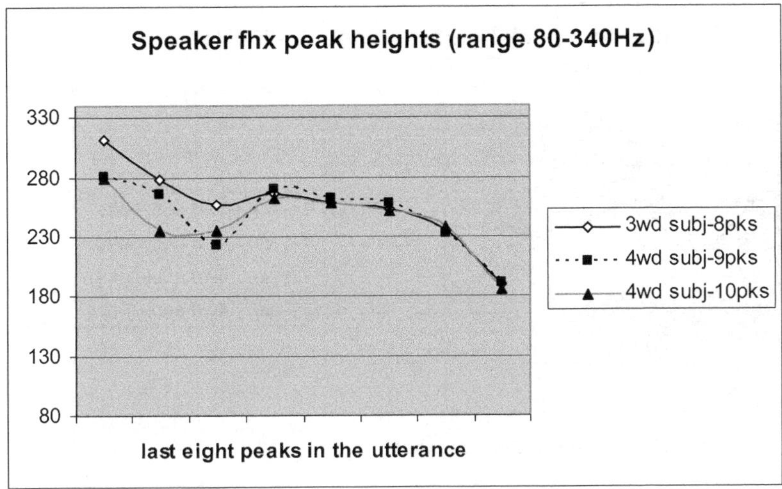

Figure 8.7: Speaker fhx peak heights

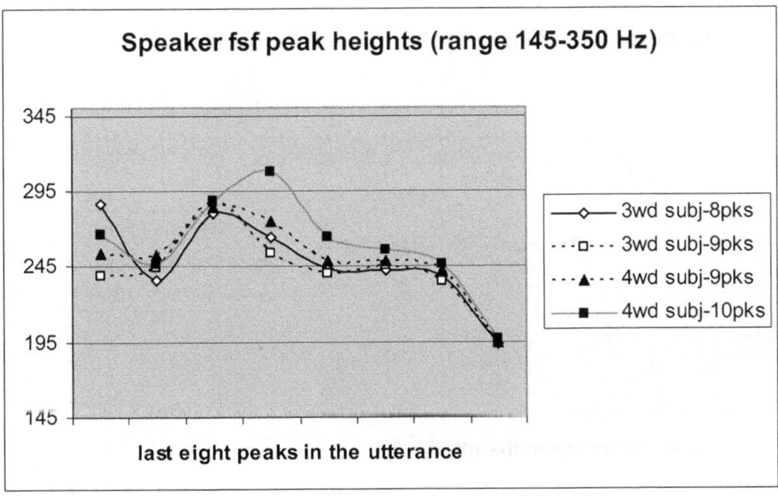

Figure 8.8: Speaker fsf peak heights

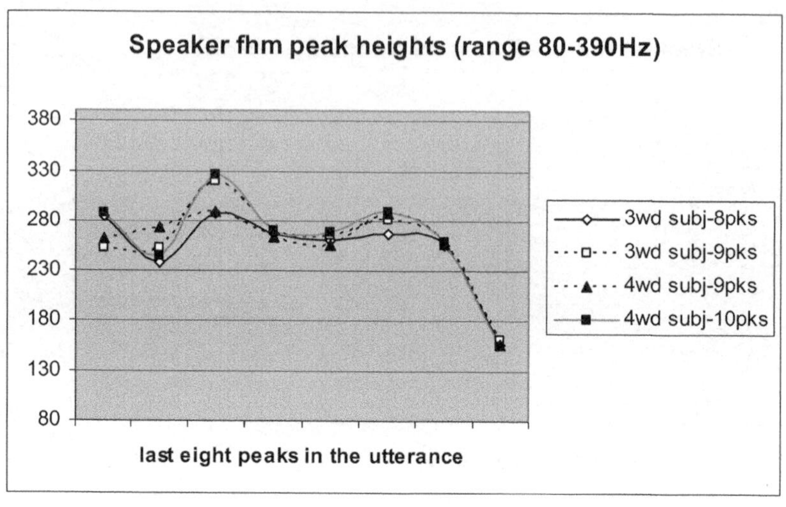

Figure 8.9: Speaker fhm peak heights

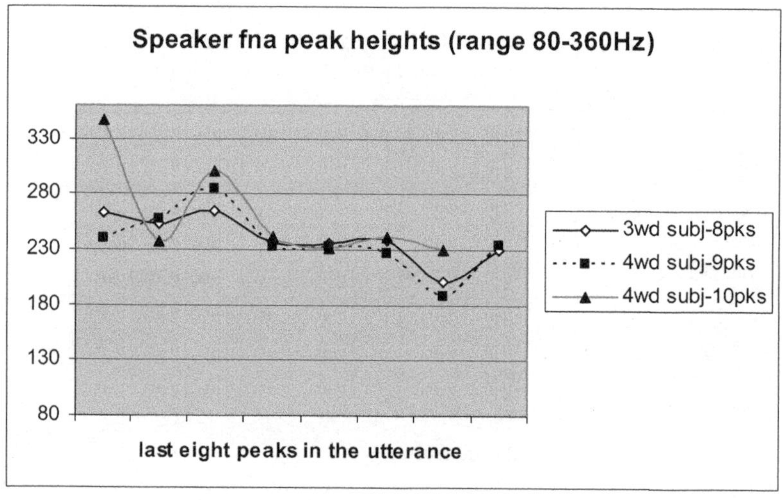

Figure 8.10: Speaker fna peak heights

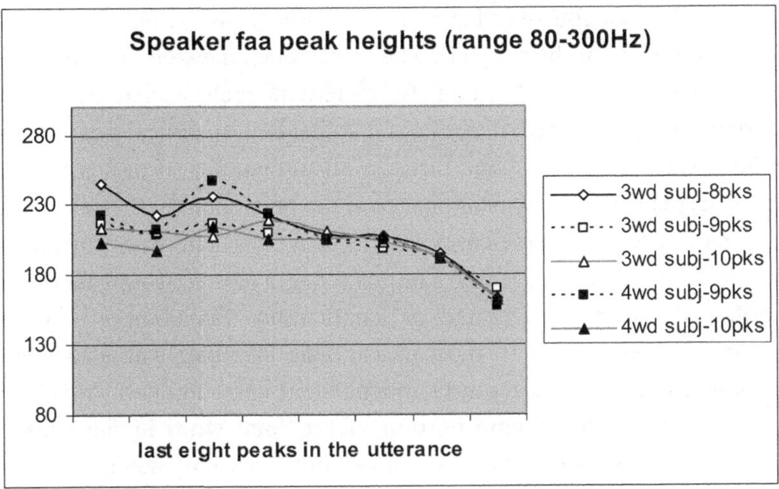

Figure 8.11: Speaker faa peak heights

When interpreting Figures 8.6–8.11 note that only the f0 values of the last eight peaks in the utterance are presented, for two reasons. The utterances vary in length, since some contain a three-word subject and some a four-word subject, but it is also possible for speakers to vary the number of pitch accents they produce when realizing an utterance, even across productions of an identical sentence.[16] Variation in the number of accents only occurred within the subject, so in the representations below we present the last eight peaks, showing the whole utterance in eight peak realizations but excluding the first one to two peaks in longer realizations. This presentation allows direct comparison across utterances with different numbers of peaks: the first three peaks in each figure represent the average f0 values in the last three peaks of the subject in every case.

In Figures 8.6–8.7, for speakers fhg and fhx respectively, we see a clear reset of pitch at the start of the VP (on the fourth peak from the left), which matches the impressionistic transcription of their frequent use of partial reset (R) as a boundary cue. For fhx, the third peak (at the right edge of the subject) appears especially low in four-word-subject sentences due to her consistent use of a low phrase tone at the after-S boundary in these sentences. Figures 8.8–8.9 show peak heights for the two H-speakers. In Figure 8.8, for speaker fsf, we can see a clear rise in pitch for the H- phrase tone, at the right edge of the subject (on the third peak). In Figure 8.9, for speaker fhm, the rise is somewhat smaller for four-word subject sentences with the phrase tone on peak 4 (i.e. at the end of the subject). The mixed cues speakers f0 values are shown in Figures 8.10–8.11. Although the pattern of labels needed to describe the pattern used here is mixed, it turns out that that both speakers' peaks show a clear downward stepping shape through all utterances, so that the combination of suspension of downstep/upstep at the boundary itself, with use of following partial reset in some cases, produces a consistent overall pattern, closely resembling that observed in Figures 8.8–8.9 (for the H-speakers).

We noted above that pre-boundary lengthening was observed for all speakers in after-S position in most cases. This labelling was also made impressionistically and thus requires independent corroboration. Measurements were taken of the rhyme portion of the final word in the subject ([juna:n] 'Greece') as a means of detecting pre-boundary lengthening (Wightman *et al.*, 1992), then normalized for speech rate variation by calculating the duration of each rhyme as a percentage of its host utterance.

The present dataset contains only utterances with prosodically heavy subjects, so we do not have any tokens without a boundary in after-S position. Nevertheless we can test the reliability of the impressionistic use of the 'L' label in after-S position in the present data by comparing these cases with those which were transcribed as having a boundary in after-S position but without the use of lengthening (L) as a cue. Comparison of mean normalized rhyme durations (nr1dur) in the final word of the subject, grouped by labelling with/without lengthening, shows that the cases transcribed impressionistically as +L ($n = 100$) are all indeed longer than those transcribed as –L ($n = 8$), as illustrated in Figure 8.12 below. A oneway ANOVA confirms that the difference in mean values between the two groups is statistically significant (F = 9.110, df = 106, $p = 0.003$).

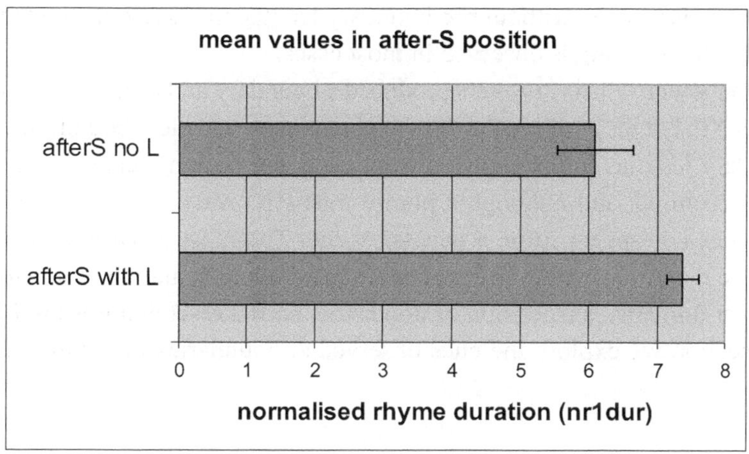

Figure 8.12: Mean normalized rhyme durations in last word of the subject, labelled with/without an L cue.

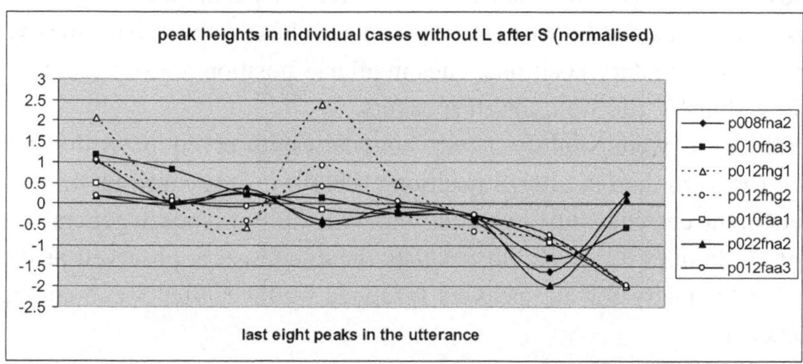

Figure 8.13: Normalized f0 values in cases labelled as a boundary without an L cue, in after-S position.

The durational evidence confirms that boundaries labelled as lengthened were indeed lengthened. What evidence is there to support the claim that boundaries marked without an L cue are indeed boundaries? Peak f0 measurements for the seven tokens labelled with exclusively tonal cues in after-S position are shown in Figure 8.13.[17] Speaker fhg shows partial reset on peak 4, and peaks 3 and 4 are similar in height for the other two speakers, who use a combination of suspension of downstep at the edge of the subject and following partial reset. This suggests that it is justified to treat these tokens as having a boundary, even without pre-boundary lengthening as a cue, though we note that lengthening is observed in most cases.

In summary then, all six speakers produced a boundary at the right edge of the subject XP, but they vary in the cues to phrasing used at these boundaries. Pre-boundary lengthening is almost always used, but does not appear to be absolutely required, and although a phrase tone (H-) was frequently used, again, it does not appear to be a necessary cue. The most consistent cues appear to be those that are the reflexes of phonetic implementation of down-step register domains: suspension of downstep, partial reset and upstep. In the next section we explore the cues observed at boundaries in within-VP position.

8.4.2 'Positional' variation in cues to phrasing

In this section we motivate the claim that there is 'positional' variation in the types of cues used to mark XP edges in EA. To do this we detail the cue clusters observed at BI-3 boundaries in the within-VP position, and argue that there is a subset relation between the types of cue clusters observed in the two key predicted boundary positions: cues in after-S position are stronger than those in within-VP position, for all speakers.

Overall there were slightly fewer boundaries observed in within-VP position (91/108) than in after-S position (108/108). This confirms that the speakers in the current study are patterning with the slow speech generalizations of Hellmuth (2004). Table 8.8 lists the cue clusters observed at the within-VP boundary for all speakers (grouped by their after-S cue choice preferences).

Table 8.8: Cue clusters transcribed in within-VP position, speakers grouped by after-S cue preferences (for each speaker the most frequent cluster is underlined, most frequent cue(s) are in bold)

After-S 'R-speakers'		*After-S 'H-speakers'*		*After-S 'mixed-cues'*	
fhg (n = 18)	*fhx (n = 11)*	*fhm (n = 18)*	*fsf (n = 18)*	*faa (n = 11)*	*fna (n = 15)*
HL (1)	LPS (1)	H (1)	HLR (1)	**L** (5)	HLP (2)
HLP (1)	LS (1)	LU (1)	**L** (2)	**LS** (3)	**LS** (2)
L (9)	LU (1)	R (2)	LPS (1)	**S** (3)	LU (1)
LR (1)	R (1)	RS (1)	LR (4)		**R** (5)
LS (5)	**S** (5)	RU (1)	LS (9)		**RS** (2)
LU (1)	U (2)	S (3)	S (1)		**S** (3)
		U (9)			

Here, again, the speakers differ from each other in their preferred cue clusters, but if we were to propose groupings among them based on within-VP cue preferences these would require different groupings: cue preferences at after-S position do not directly predict cue preferences at within-VP position. Overall there is less use of pre-boundary lengthening (L), but it is still the primary within-VP cue for speakers fhg, fsf and faa. The other three speakers mostly rely on tonal cues: fhx mostly uses suspension of downstep (S), as does fna in combination with partial reset (R); fhm mostly uses upstep (U).

In order to confirm the impressionistic labelling of 'L' at within-VP position measurements were taken of the rhyme portion of the final word in the complement NP ([ħadiːs] 'modern'), then normalized by calculating the duration of each rhyme as a percentage of its host utterance. Since there are cases both with and without a boundary in within-VP position, as well as instances of boundaries labelled with/without L, we make a three way comparison. Comparison of mean normalized rhyme durations (nr2dur) in the final word of the complement NP to the verb, grouped by presence of a boundary and labelling with/without lengthening, illustrated in Figure 8.14 below, shows first that the boundary cases transcribed impressionistically as +L ($n = 54$) are all longer than the boundary cases transcribed as –L ($n = 38$) and than the cases transcribed without a boundary ($n = 16$). Second, there is no difference in mean values of rhyme duration between non-boundary cases and those transcribed with a boundary but without lengthening. A one-way ANOVA confirms that the differences are significant (F = 34.512; df = 105; $p<0.001$).[18]

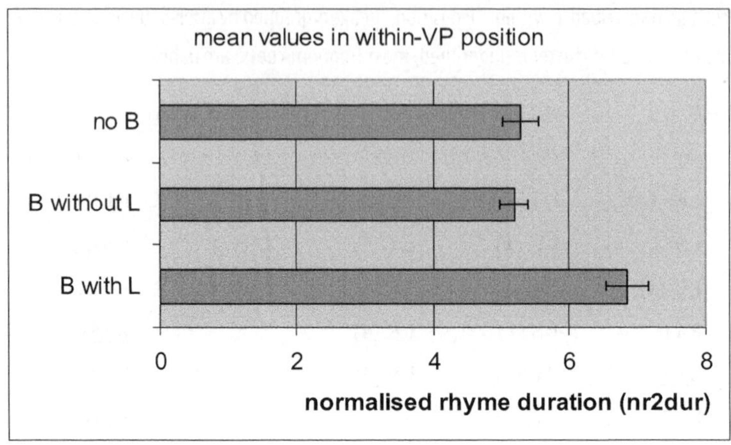

Figure 8.14: Mean values for normalized rhyme durations in the final word of the complement NP in the VP, labelled with/without a boundary and with/without an L cue.

Is there any evidence that the cases labelled as having boundaries at within-VP position, but without pre-boundary lengthening (L) as a cue, are indeed boundaries? Figure 8.15 shows f0 peak heights averaged for each speaker in the last five peaks of the utterance (that is, in the entire VP), in the 39 cases labelled as a boundary but without pre-boundary lengthening at the within-VP boundary. For comparison, Figure 8.16 shows the parallel peak measurements in 17 tokens labelled as having no boundary at all.

In interpreting Figures 8.15–8.16 recall that a within-VP boundary is expected to pick out the middle peak in the VP (at the right edge of the complement NP), which should show signs of upstep or suspension of down-step, or a following reset. The f0 trends in Figure 8.15 do all show some kind of suspension of the downstep pattern on or after the middle peak, though the effect is smaller for some speakers (e.g. fna) than others (e.g. fhm). Examination of the f0 trends in Figure 8.16 suggests that a within-VP boundary should have been transcribed in at least some of these cases for speaker fhx (non-boundary cases for fhx, $n = 7$), whose peaks (on average) show a reset before the final PP adjunct phrase. In contrast, there was indeed no boundary here for speakers faa and fna (compare level pitch between peaks 2 and 3 in the VP in Figure 8.15 with falling pitch between peaks 2 and 3 in Figure 8.16, for these speakers).

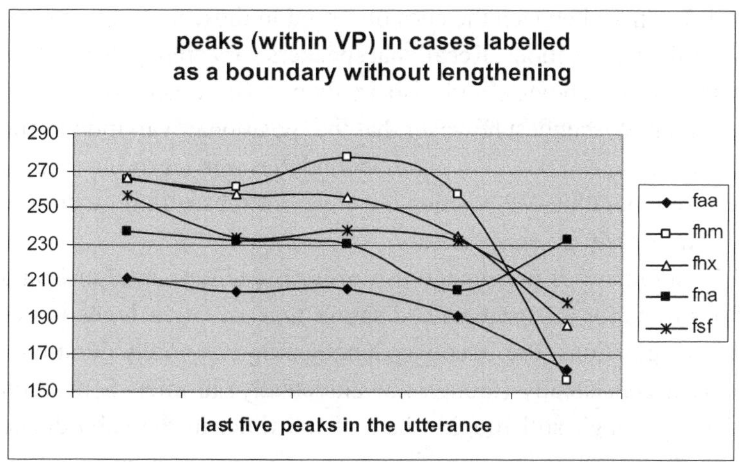

Figure 8.15: Average f0 of the last five peaks in the utterance (the VP) by speaker, for cases labelled as a boundary in within-VP position but without an L cue.

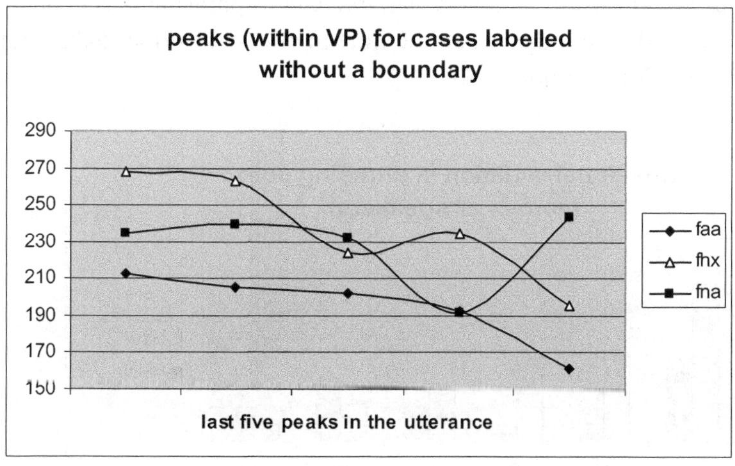

Figure 8.16: Average f0 of the last five peaks in the utterance (the VP) by speaker, for cases labelled as having no boundary in within-VP position.

The impressionistic transcription and the cue clusters that arise from it (in Tables 8.7–8.8) are thus substantially confirmed by the supporting evidence from durational and f0 measurements. Our final task in this section is to explore the differences between the cues observed in those tables, that is, in after-S and within-VP positions. Recall that speakers vary among themselves in their preferred cue choices, and also in their own choices of cues in different positions. We suggest however that the 'positional' variation in cue choices between these two potential phrase boundaries is in fact principled, in that the cues used in within-VP position are always a subset of those used in after-S position, for any given speaker.

Figure 8.17 summarizes percentage use of each cue type in after-S and within-VP positions for all speakers and shows that use of each cue varies between the two positions. Pre-boundary lengthening is a purely durational cue, and is used consistently (though not universally) in after- S position (93%), and less, though still roughly half of the time, in the subordinate within-VP position (48%). The use of a phrase tone can be seen as a pho-nological cue, which we might expect to be a required cue to a phrase edge (for example following Beckman and Pierrehumbert, 1986; Pierrehumbert and Beckman, 1988). In fact in the present corpus it is used only roughly half the time in after-S position (53%), and is somewhat rare in within-VP position (5%). Pauses are known to be a very variable cue to phrasing (Cruttenden, 1997) and are used here roughly half the time in after-S position (54%), but are rare in within-VP position (5%).

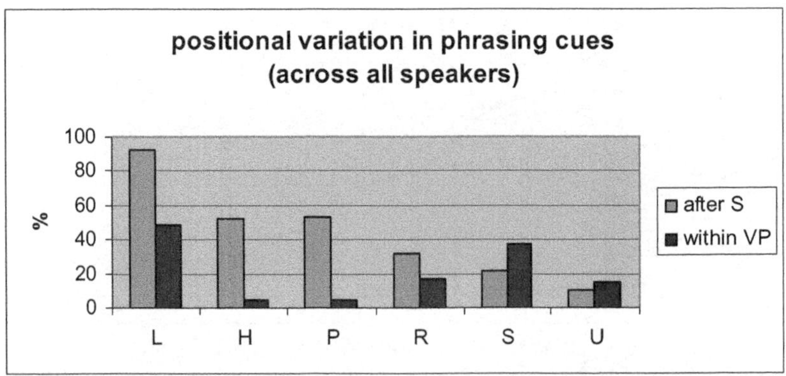

Figure 8.17: Percentage use of phrasing cues in different positions (across all speakers)

The remaining cues, partial reset (R), suspension of downstep (S) and upstep (U), are arguably all related to phonetic implementation, and can be seen as the reflexes of the register domains of successive prosodic constituents (cf. Truckenbrodt, 2002, 2004, 2007). As with the other cues, the proportion of R use is lower in within-VP position (18%) than in after-S position (34%). In contrast however, use of both S and U increases in within-VP position (37% and 15% respectively), compared to after-S position (21%, 10%). We suggest therefore that increased use of these 'phonetic' cues to register domains is in fact the norm in the subordinate within-VP boundary position, and that use of R was under-reported in the present analysis due to the definition of reset used during the labelling process. A reset was defined here relative to the immediately previous peak, so a reset would not be transcribed in cases where the preceding (phrase-final) peak bears a high phrase tone or is subject to upstep. We expect that transcription using a definition of reset relative to the level of the preceding domain (rather than the preceding peak) would yield a higher proportion of R cases in within-VP position than in after-S position.

Finally, as already mentioned above, we note that the cues used by an individual speaker in after-S position are not a clear predictor of the cues that she will use in within-VP position. The two speakers who mostly use R after-S (fhg and fhx) diverge in VP position: fhg only retains L while fhx switches to use of S (a register domain cue). Similarly, the two after-S H-speakers (fhm and fsf) both dispense with the phonological phrase tone cue: fsf only retains L while fhx switches to use of upstep (U). The after-S mixed-cue speaker faa retains only lengthening in within-VP position. The only speaker to use the same (mixed) set of cues in both positions is fna (note that this speaker is also distinct from all the others in her use of utterance-final upstep, as discussed above, and also has some instances of boundaries inserted within the subject).

In summary then, somewhat different sets of phrasing cues are used by speakers in within-VP and after-S positions, and the within-VP cues are a 'weaker' subset of those observed in after-S position. In the next section we set out arguments for and against choosing to treat these boundaries as junctures at the same level of prosodic phrasing, and explore the theoretical implications of that choice.

8.5   Discussion

In this section we seek to interpret the inter-speaker and positional variation in cues to BI-3 in EA described in §8.4 above. We first explore the possibility that some of the boundaries labelled as BI-3 should instead be treated as boundaries at some other level (that is, either IP or MiP, in §8.5.1), then explore how and why boundaries at the same level might be realized with different cue sets (in §8.5.2). Section 8.5.3 revisits the formal analysis of Hellmuth (2004) in the light of the findings of the present study.

8.5.1 Should 'different cues' imply 'different phrasing level'?

An obvious question that arises is whether the different cues that we observe here are really all cues to the same level of phrasing in the prosodic hierarchy. Perhaps some speakers are breaking the utterance up into constituents at some higher or lower level, such as IP or MiP, and consequently use different cues. We treat this question by examining the degree of reset at boundaries for each speaker (as a diagnostic for IP level boundaries) and by looking at the cues to phrasing observed at boundaries labelled BI-2 (MiP) in the present dataset for comparison with those labelled as BI-3 (MaP).

The most likely candidates for reanalysis as full IP boundaries are those in after-S position. In order to determine whether an after-S boundary is an IP or a MaP level boundary we rely on the observation made in Truckenbrodt (2002, 2004, 2007) for German, which we take to hold cross-linguistically, that boundaries between two MaP level constituents within a single IP will show partial reset only, due to global downstep between the two MaP register domains. In contrast, a full IP boundary is expected to show a full reset to the level of the initial peak in the utterance. We exclude from this investigation three tokens in the dataset which were transcribed with an IP boundary after the subject.[19] Figure 8.18 shows mean peak heights by speaker in three positions: on the first and second peaks in the utterance, and on the verb (the peak immediately following the after-S boundary). All speakers show partial reset on the verb, either to the same height as the second peak (faa, fhx, fna) or to a level intermediate between that of the first and second peaks (fhg, fhm, fsf). Crucially however, none of the speakers show reset after S to the initial level of the utterance. We conclude therefore that it is indeed appropriate to treat these boundaries as instances of MaP level boundaries,[20] even though they are cued differently by different speakers.

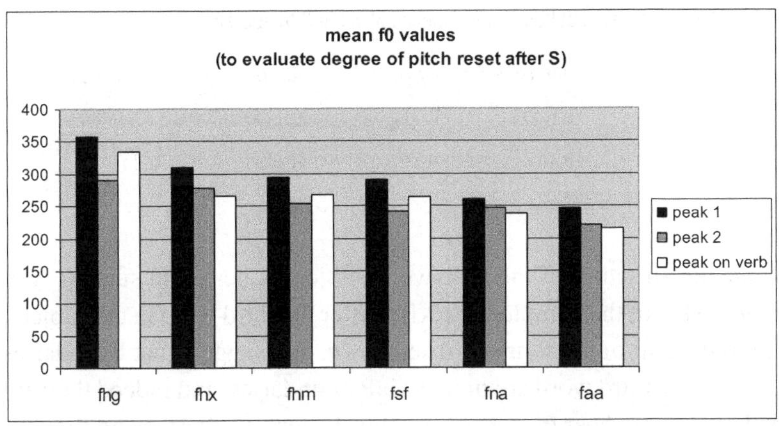

Figure 8.18: Mean f0 values on the first and second peak of the utterance and on the verb (by speaker).

A possible reanalysis of the weaker cues in within-VP position would be to suggest that some of the boundaries labelled here as BI-3 are in fact BI-2 MiP level boundaries. To explore whether this is a plausible analysis, we look at the cues observed at boundaries which were labelled BI-2 in the dataset, and where they occurred. In total, just 28 MiP level boundaries were labelled in the dataset. The cues observed at these boundaries for different speakers are detailed in Table 8.9. The most common cue used was a partial reset (relative to the previous peak), which was also the cue to MiP boundaries observed in Hellmuth (2004). There were however a number of more complex cue clusters observed, which resemble those observed at MaP boundaries for the relevant speaker (e.g. 'HL' was the most common cluster for speaker fhm in after S position, and 'LS' was the most common cluster for speaker fhg in within-VP position).

All of the 28 boundaries labelled MiP were observed within the subject, and of these 13 were observed in three-word subject sentences and 15 in four-word subject sentences. In three-word subject sentences the MiP boundary was always found between the complement NP and the adjunct PP (that is, before [min(-il) juna:n] 'from Greece'). The four-word subject sentences allow us to test whether the subject-internal boundaries labelled as BI-2 are MiP or MaP boundaries: we would expect a MaP boundary to occur at the right-edge of a syntactic XP, whereas an MiP constituent, which appears in EA to be purely rhythmic in nature, should enhance eurhythmy by forming binary MiP domains (containing two PWds each).

Table 8.9: Cue clusters observed at boundaries labelled BI-2 (MiP) by speaker

fhg (n = 4)	*fhx (n = 6)*	*fhm (n = 5)*	*fsf (n = 7)*	*faa (n = 4)*	*fna (n = 2)*
LS (1)	L (2)	HL (1)	L (1)	LS (1)	LR (1)
R (1)	R (4)	R (4)	R (6)	R (1)	R (1)
S (2)				S (2)	

The syntactic structure of the four-word subject is nested in such as way that the right edge of the complement XP is after the third word in the subject, not at the mid-point of the four-word sequence. We suggest that boundaries observed after the third word are in fact MaP boundaries, and indeed they are the ones that prove to bear the 'stronger' cue clusters: LS for faa and fhg, HL for fhm, L for fhx, LR for fna and L for fsf. All of the MiP boundaries falling at the mid-point of the four-word subject (after [wila:di-l] 'my children', $n = 8$) are marked by partial reset (R) only, suggesting that this is indeed the best diagnostic for an MiP boundary. This in turn implies that at least some of the boundaries labelled as BI-3 (MaP) in within-VP position which bear only partial reset (R) as a cue, can plausibly be reanalysed as MiP boundaries. There are however only eight such boundaries (for speakers fhx, fhm and fna; see Table 8.8). The remaining majority of boundaries labelled BI-3 at within VP position ($n = 83$) can indeed be considered MaP level boundaries, even though they bear a variety of cues.

We have set out evidence in support of treating the boundaries that are variably cued in EA as instances of the same level of prosodic phrasing. In the next section we explore why the cues are so variable.

8.5.2 How can 'different cues' imply 'same phrasing level'?

How can it be that boundaries at the same level of phrasing are marked with different cue sets by different speakers? We explore this question by comparing the degree of pitch reset observed in within-VP position and the degree of lengthening in after-S and within-VP positions.

The cues most consistently used *across all speakers* in after-S position are lengthening (L) and tonal register cues (R, S, U). These are reflexes of phonetic implementation, rather than phonological cues (such as a phrase tone), and are also the cues most likely to be retained, or made use of in within-VP position.

For the tonal register cues, we have a principled way of understanding why f0 effects are smaller at the within-VP boundary than at the after-S boundary following Truckenbrodt (2002, 2004, 2007), the degree of reset/upstep will be relatively less at the start of a more embedded domain (such as within-VP position) than at the start of a less embedded domain (such as after-S). Figure 8.19 shows mean f0 by speaker in the three phrase-initial positions (initial, on the verb and on the penultimate PWd), for 8/9 peak utterances containing a within-VP MaP boundary ($n = 72$).[21] We can see that there is a clear downstep relationship between phrases and that the degree of downstep among phrases is remarkably even (except for speaker fhg who shows reduced downstep between the first two phrases). For comparison, Figure 8.20 shows the downstep relation that holds for each speaker among the first three peaks of the utterance, within the first phrase. According to Truckenbrodt (2002, 2004, 2007) we should expect the degree of downstep among phrases to resemble that observed between individual peaks within each phrase. The third peak in the utterance is somewhat raised relative to the second for the four 'other' speakers (fhm/fsf/faa/fna), reflecting their use of a high phrase tone and/or upstep on the third peak in eight peak utterances. The degree of downstep among phrases most resembles that between the first two peaks for speakers fhx and faa, but the norm in this dataset is for the degree of downstep to be somewhat greater within phrases than between them.

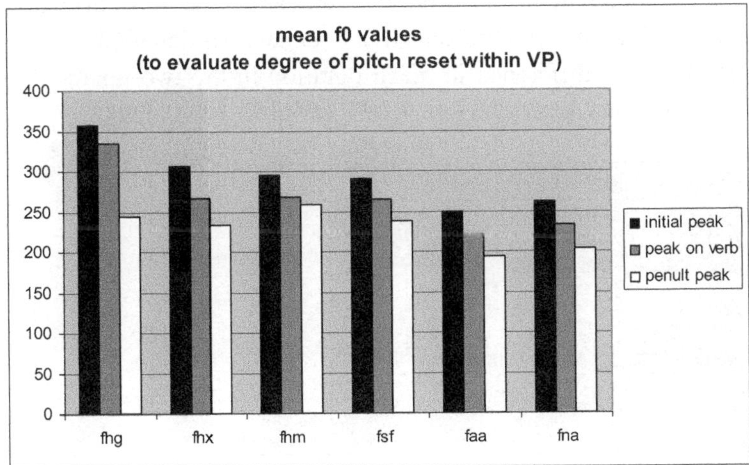

Figure 8.19: Mean f0 values on phrase-initial peaks, by speaker (for eight or nine peak utterances containing a within-VP boundary, $n = 72$).

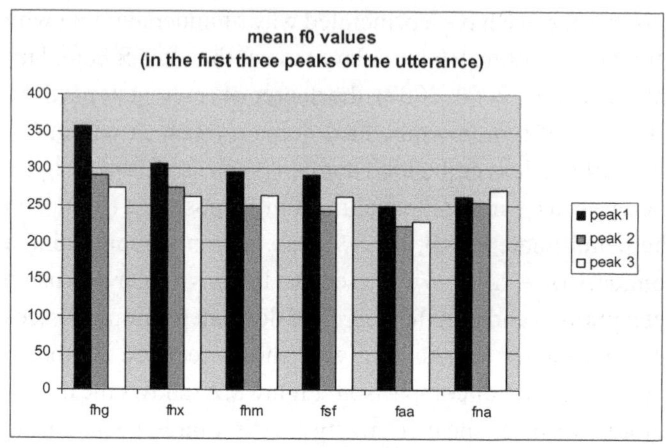

Figure 8.20: Mean f0 values on the first three peaks in the utterance, by speaker (for eight or nine peak utterances containing a within-VP boundary, $n = 72$).

The phonetic implementation theory of Truckenbrodt (2002, 2004, 2007) allows us to accommodate variant f0 cues at boundaries of the same type, due to the notion of embedding of register domains. Is there any evidence that the degree of lengthening observed at MaP boundaries in the two positions is similarly reduced? Figure 8.21 shows mean values of normalized rhyme duration for target words: (a) at the right edge of the subject (nr1dur) iff a boundary was labelled L in that position ($n = 100$); and (b) at the right edge of the complement NP of the verb (nr2dur) iff a boundary was labelled L in that position ($n = 54$). The difference in mean duration in the two positions is statistically significant (ANOVA: F = 7.097, df = 152, $p = 0.009$).

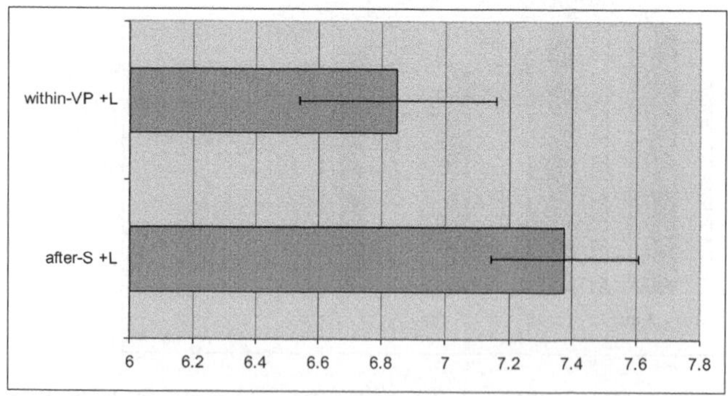

Figure 8.21: Mean values of normalized rhyme duration for target words labelled L in their respective position, after-S or within-VP, across all speakers.

It could be argued that a statistically significant difference in the degree of lengthening in the two positions is evidence for a different level of phrasing (cf. Chahal, 2001, 2003), but we suggest that to do so would require treatment of varying degrees of f0 excursion in tonal cues to phrasing as evidence of different levels also (contra Truckenbrodt, 2002, 2004, 2007). We therefore analyse this durational difference not as evidence for different levels of phrasing but as evidence that our adjacent MaP domains are embedded within a single IP. Since pre-boundary lengthening is another reflex of phonetic implementation it is to be expected that we find a degree of durational difference similar to that seen in f0 values between adjacent register domains (cf. Ladd, 2008: 299).

8.5.3 Re-analysis

The formal analysis proposed in Hellmuth (2004) was based on double-embedding of MiPs within MaP in order to arrive at a requirement that MaPs contain minimally four PWds. The empirical phrasing generalizations in the present dataset appear to be somewhat less restrictive, since a large number of MaPs containing less than four PWds are observed.

Why might the facts be different here? One reason might be that the speech dataset analysed in Hellmuth (2004) comprised two speakers who both used a somewhat fast speech rate, whereas the present dataset contains a greater mix of fast/slow speakers. Furthermore, Hellmuth (2004) employed a prosodic transcription protocol in which only boundaries bearing two or more cues to phrasing were labelled as boundaries, on the a priori assumption that fixed cues to phrasing would be identified. The results of the present study suggest that even reduced tonal cues to phrasing may still indicate the presence of a prosodic boundary and that the most reliable cues to phrasing are the relative heights of successive peaks in the utterance, which provide information about where downstep register domains begin and end.

Given these new empirical insights, the implications for the analysis proposed in Hellmuth (2004) are twofold. We reconsider the status of MiP and sketch how the analysis would be reformulated in a phase-based approach.

8.5.3.1 *Re-visiting MiP in EA*

There were two reasons for proposing an MiP level of phrasing in Hellmuth (2004): (a) as a theoretical means to generate a requirement for a 4 PWd MaP, by requiring doubly-embedded binary domains; and (b) to account for instances of apparent 'rhythmic boost' occurring in some adjacent PWd pairs (cf. the consistent 'R' cue to a MiP boundary observed here). The present study appears to eliminate the first of these two reasons, but provides further confirmation that the second reason still holds. How are we to analyse these facts?

One could maintain the analysis of Hellmuth (2004) with the caveat that BINMIP is a feature of fast speech only. Alternatively, one could dispense with BINMIP altogether and instead analyse the phrasing generalizations of EA with BINMAP only (formulated as a requirement that each MaP contain at least two PWds), but lose some of the empirical coverage, including the key fact that relatively short SVO sentences can be phrased in a single MaP, such as the three-word subject sentence reproduced from Hellmuth (2004) in Figure 8.2.

A more promising approach would be to revisit the status of MiP. We propose instead that EA has only a single level of phrasing between the IP and the PWd, namely the MaP, and that the rhythmic boost effect observed both here and in Hellmuth (2004) arises due to compounding of PWds, in violation of the Strict Layer Hypothesis (cf. Ladd, 2008: 297ff.; Itô and Mester, this volume). If we propose, plausibly, that compounding is a feature of fast and/or rhythmic speech, then faster speech will yield somewhat longer MaPs on the assumption that BINMAP pays attention to the maximal PWd (the 'non-minimal' PWd, cf. Elfner, 2010; Itô and Mester, this volume).[22]

8.5.3.2   Re-visiting the role of XP in the syntax-phonology mapping in EA?

If we accept the foregoing arguments that cues to phrasing are variable in EA, and that the boundaries observed within-VP are of the same order as those observed after-S, then EA does display sensitivity to XP constituency after all.

Could the facts of EA nonetheless be amenable to re-analysis in a multiple-spell-out approach? One option would be to adopt the Highest Phrase Condition (HPC, Kratzer and Selkirk, 2007), which predicts a within-VP boundary as well as an after-S boundary in our target sentences, as shown in (2) below: the HPC causes the highest phrase in VP, which is the spellout domain of vP, to be mapped to a MaP. The highest phrase in VP is the head + complement, shown in bold. This produces an MaP boundary at the right edge of the complement within the VP just as we observe in many cases in the present dataset.

(2)   [[[head [complement]$_{AP}$]$_{NP}$ [verb [[**head [complement**]$_{AP}$]$_{NP}$ [adjunct]$_{PP}$]]$_{VP}$]$_{vP}$]$_{CP}$

[adjunct]$_{PP}$]$_{DP}$ [*v*

spell out domain of vP phase: <--->

Highest Phrase in spellout domain: <----------------------------------->

In order to account for the variability in our dataset (the fact that not all speakers realize a within-VP boundary) however, we must however retain a role for BINMAP (in its revised form). Thus to maintain the HPC analysis, we would have to propose, contra Kratzer and Selkirk (2007), that the final adjunct PP is phrased as an MaP under an exhaustive parse. This is because, in cases where the speaker fails to realize a within-VP boundary, we infer that the adjunct PP (formed of two PWds) has formed a compound PP and that it is BINMAP that prevents the adjunct from being phrased into a separate MaP. Unfortunately however, the proposal that the parsing of syntactic material into prosodic structure is exhaustive would prevent the HPC from accounting for the original facts of German for which it was proposed (Kratzer and Selkirk, 2007). An alternative would be to adopt a prominence-driven phase-based account (such as Stress-XP, Truckenbrodt, this volume), but this is not readily adapted to analysis of a language in which accentual prominences are distributed at the PWd level, rather than the MaP level.

The only remaining option for explaining the many within-VP boundaries observed in the current dataset in a phase-based approach would be to argue for a different syntactic analysis of the target utterances. We have assumed thus far that the utterance-final adjunct PP is VP-internal as in (3); if however it were analysed as a vP-adjunct, as in (4), spellout of VP as the complement to vP would yield a prosodic break in the position that we have here termed within-VP position.

(3)   [[the- [manager [the-new]$_{AP}$]$_{NP}$ [from Greece]$_{PP}$]$_{DP}$
[[teaches$_{3ms}$ [the-[pedagogy [the-modern]$_{AP}$]$_{NP}$]$_{DP}$ [in [faculty-the-education]$_{CS}$]$_{PP}$
]$_{VP}$]$_{vP}$]$_{TP}$

(4)   [[the- [manager [the-new]$_{AP}$]$_{NP}$ [from Greece]$_{PP}$]$_{DP}$
[teaches$_{3ms}$ [[the- [pedagogy [the-modern]$_{AP}$]$_{NP}$]$_{DP}$]$_{VP}$ [in [faculty-the-education]$_{CS}$]
$_{PP}$]$_{vP}$]$_{TP}$

We note therefore that what is needed to fully rule out a role for XPs in the syntax-phonology mapping in EA is evidence that a sequence of unambiguously VP-internal XPs (e.g. in a ditransitive) also trigger within-VP boundaries of the sort observed here, and we leave this question to future research.

8.6   Conclusion

This paper has explored in detail the cues to phrasing observed in a corpus of read speech sentences, using quantitative measurements of f0 and rhyme durations to support the results of a fine-grained qualitative transcription. It appears that there is no required phonological cue to the edges of MaP boundaries in EA, though phrase tones are sometimes observed. The most common and consistent cues to MaP edges are phonetic (cf. Kawahara and Shinya, 2008): pre-boundary lengthening and peak height manipulation reflecting downstep register domains, and speakers are free to interpret these in a number of ways. This is parallel to Truckenbrodt's (2002, 2004, 2007) findings for Southern German in which speakers also varied in how phonological tones (of pitch accents or phrase tones) were associated to prosodic domains (and thus varied in their phonetic implementation). It is known that cues to phrasing also vary in e.g. English, hence the adoption of BI-2 for indeterminate cases in the MAE-ToBI labelling system (Beckman *et al.*, 2005; Brugos *et al.*, 2008).

A question that arises is what governs the distribution of phrase tones in EA, if they are not obligatory MaP edge markers. An obvious answer is that their distribution is likely to reflect pragmatic meaning and/or information structure. One hypothesis would be that low phrase tones (L-) act as a focus marker and that high phrase tones (H-) act as a marker of continuation, and thus of topics, as has been suggested by El Zarka (2008). The evidence presented here indicates that if what is inserted is indeed a phrase tone, which forces a prosodic boundary, then this would obligatorily condition boundary cues in the form of phonetic implementation of downstep register reset, and optionally also other cues such as pause or lengthening. The status of these tones is now testable in that if a boundary is indeed inserted it should condition a register domain reset of the type observed here; if no reset is found then the inserted tone might be better analysed as a free-floating tone which functions as a focus/topic marker. We leave investigation of this possibility to future research.

As for the syntax-phonology mapping in EA, we have suggested that the analysis of Hellmuth (2004) can be amended by dispensing with the MiP level and instead allowing for compounding of PWds in fast or rhythmic speech. This means that EA has only one level of phrasing between the IP and the PWd, the MaP, which is consistent with the claim that there are universal restrictions on the set of prosodic constituents (Itô and Mester, this volume; cf. Selkirk, to appear).

The edge-based analysis of Hellmuth (2004) could be re-cast in a phase-based approach by appeal to the HPC, but requires exhaustive parsing of the utterance into prosodic structure (contra Kratzer and Selkirk, 2007) if it is to account for inter-speaker variability in the occurrence of within-VP boundaries (a final MaP must be present for BINMAP to prevent its formation if composed of too few PWds). To work for EA then, the HPC requires a revision which means it no longer captures the data for which it was originally proposed (the distribution of stressless XPs in German, cf. Truckenbrodt, this volume). Since the distribution of pitch accents is PWd level in EA, rather than MaP level, phase-based approaches that govern the distribution of MaP prominences (rather than MaP domains) such as StressXP (Truckenbrodt, this volume) won't work for EA either. An alternative syntactic analysis of the target sentences, with the final PP as a vP-adjunct rather than a VP-adjunct, could be consistent with a spellout-domain approach though.

Nonetheless, assuming that our syntactic analysis is correct, it turns out that EA, which appeared to be a language which did not mark XP edges, does display sensitivity to XP constituents, *iff* sufficient prosodic material is available (that is, in long utterances such as those analysed here). So, even if a spellout-domain approach can be shown to explain the occurrence of within-VP boundaries in long and complex sentences, the fact that MaPs in EA are nonetheless subject to prosodic minimality constraints, calls for an intervening prosodic representation between the syntax and phonology, rather than a purely syntactic solution, as Selkirk has long argued.

Notes

*   The author thanks the Egyptian participants for their time, and Laura Downing, Shigeto Kawahara, Bernadette Plunkett, Hubert Truckenbrodt and the audience of the ZAS Syntax-Phonology Colloquium in Berlin for comments.

1   Most early descriptions of intonation and prosodic phrasing in EA (Rifaat, 1991; Rastegar-El Zarka, 1997) treat the Egyptian pronunciation of the formal register of

the language, Modern Standard Arabic (MSA), which exists alongside the spoken variety in the well-known diglossia of the Arab world (Ferguson 1957). The two varieties are however similar in many intonational properties (see El Zarka and Hellmuth, 2009 for discussion).

2   Some three-word subjects were phrased as separate MaPs when speakers were asked to slow their speech rate, as in the realization illustrated in Figure 8.2.

3   The stimuli were constructed so that a CCC cluster straddled all potential XP edge boundary positions. See for example the subject-final adjective [muhimm] 'important' followed by the verb [bijxumm] 'he cheats' in (1) above.

4   This subset is part of a larger database of 44 SVO and VOO (double object constructions) sentences recorded with 12 speakers of EA (six male, six female).

5   A Construct State (CS) phrase is usually analysed as a single morphosyntactic word (Borer, 1996) but functions prosodically as two PWds in EA (Hellmuth, 2006). We analyse it here as a 'CS' sequence, without further discussion of its internal syntactic structure, for ease of exposition, but assume that it does constitute a lexical XP projection.

6   A small number of mid-utterance complex boundary configurations were observed which required analysis using a phrase tone + boundary tone sequence (e.g. H-L%).

7   The relative height of peaks was judged by eye during labelling, for later corroboration with quantitative results.

8   Note that reset was defined relative to the height of the preceding peak, rather than with reference to domain register levels.

9   Cues observed at junctures labelled as BI-2 (MiP) are discussed in §8.5 below.

10   Levene's test shows that the variances among speakers are not equal ($p = 0.001$), so Tamhane's test was used to determine for each speaker pair whether the two speakers fall into the same or a different subset.

11   In this and all other figures, errors bars denote 95% Confidence Intervals.

12   Overall the ANOVA shows a significant difference among speakers ($F = 4.074$, $df = 107$, $p = 0.002$) but Tamhane's test shows that the only significant differences are between fhx and fhm ($p = 0.13$) and between fhx and fsf ($p = 0.25$); Tamhane's test was used because Levene's statistic shows that the variances are not equal ($p<0.001$).

13   This can be observed in the low f0 values seen on the final peak in Figures 8.6–8.11.

14   The final adjunct PP of the utterances is a construct state. Speaker fna produced these with a qualitatively different pitch accent on the first word than that observed

on other words; the pitch rises throughout the first word to a peak late in the stressed syllable of the second word. One analysis would be that she is treating the CS nominal as a single PWd, with a single rising pitch accent realized across the both words. Further investigation of this atypical realization is beyond the scope of this paper and is left for future research.

15   All phrase tones were labelled 'H' during transcription, whether low or high. The only speaker who used low phrase tones was fhx, and this is shown here by presenting the phrase tone in lower case.

16   This is because it is possible in EA to assign PWd status to a function word if it is bimoraic. In the current dataset the function word most often realized with an accent was [min] 'from', with encliticization of the following definite article [il] 'the', yielding bimoraic [min-il] 'from the'. The planned stimuli sought to avoid this; the printed text was [min junaa:n] 'from Greece'; but many speakers inserted the definite article yielding [min-il-junaa:n] 'from (the-) Greece'.

17   One further token was labeled with an after-S boundary but without L, but the whole utterance was phrased atypically (with a full IP boundary within the subject) and is not discussed further here.

18   By Levene's statistic the variances are not equal ($p = 0.002$), so Tamhane's test was used for post-hoc comparisons; the difference is significant for 'no B' vs. 'B with L' ($p<0.001$) and 'B no L' vs. 'B with L' vs. ($p<0.001$) only.

19   Two from speaker fhg and one from speaker fsf.

20   A check on individual tokens reveals that the differential between the peak on the verb and the first peak is positive (i.e. the verb peak is realized at a higher f0 level than the initial peak) in just three cases (p022fhg1, p022fhg3, p08fna1). These cases should probably therefore be reclassified as IP level boundaries.

21   Within-VP boundaries which were labelled with R only, and which should probably be reanalysed as MiP boundaries, are excluded.

22   This proposal would require BI-2 to be redefined for EA, either along the lines of Shaked (2007) for Hebrew, or by leaving BI-2 free for use in indeterminate cases as in MAE-ToBI (Beckman and Elam, 1993).

References

Adger, David. (2006) Stress and phasal syntax (Ms.). Queen Mary, University of London.

Ackema, P. and Neeleman, A. (2003) Context-sensitive spell-out. *Natural Language and Linguistic Theory* 21: 681–735.

Aquil, Rajaa M. (2006) *The Segmentation/parsing Unit in Cairene Arabic.* PhD, Georgetown University.

Bassiouney, Reem (2009) *Arabic Sociolinguistics.* Edinburgh: Edinburgh University Press.

Beckman, Mary and Elam, G. A. (1993) *Guidelines for TOBI Labelling (version 3.0 1997).* The Ohio State University Research Foundation.

Beckman, Mary, Hirschberg, Julia and Shattuck-Hufnagel, Stefanie (2005) The original ToBI system and the evolution of the ToBI framework. In Jun, Sun-Ah (ed.) *Prosodic Typology: The Phonology of Intonation and Phrasing* 9–54. Oxford: Oxford University Press.

Beckman, Mary and Pierrehumbert, Janet (1986) Intonational structure in Japanese and English. *Phonology Yearbook* 3: 255–309.

Benmamoun, Elabbas (2000) *The Feature Structure of Functional Categories.* Oxford: Oxford University Press.

Boersma, Paul and Weenink, David. (2009) *Praat: Doing Phonetics by Computer* (Version 5.1.19) [http://www.praat.org].

Borer, Hagit. (1996) The construct in review. In J. Lecarme, J. Lowenstamm and U. Shlonsky (eds) *Studies in Afroasiatic Grammar* 30-61. The Hague: HAG.

Brugos, Alejna, Veilleux, Nanette, Breen, Mara and Shattuck-Hufnagel, Stefanie. (2008) The alternatives (Alt) tier for ToBI: advantages of capturing prosodic ambiguity. *Speech Prosody 2008 (Campinas, Brazil),* 273–276.

Chahal, Dana. (2001) *Modeling the Intonation of Lebanese Arabic Using the Autosegmental-metrical Framework: A Comparison with English.* PhD, University of Melbourne.

Chahal, Dana. (2003) Phonetic cues to prominence in Arabic. *Proceedings of the 15th International Congress of Phonetic Sciences,* 2067–2070.

Chomsky, Noam. (2001) On derivation by phase. In M. Kenstowicz (ed.) *Ken Hale: A Life in Language* 1–52. Cambridge, MA: MIT Press.

Chomsky, Noam. (2005) *On Phases.* Cambridge, MA: MIT.

Cruttenden, Alan. (1997) *Intonation.* Cambridge: Cambridge University Press.

Edwards, Malcolm. (2009) Word order in Egyptian Arabic: form and function. In Jonathan Owens and Alaa Elgibali (eds) *Information Structure in Spoken Arabic* 93–110. Oxford: Routledge.

Elfner, Emily. (2010) Recursive phonological phrases in Conamara Irish. (Paper presented at WCCFL 28, University of Southern California. 19 February).

El Zarka, Dina. (2008) Leading, linking and closing tones and tunes in Egyptian Arabic – what a simple intonation system tells us about the nature of intonation. (Paper presented at the annual meeting of the Arabic Linguistics Society, Michigan, March 2008.)

El Zarka, Hellmuth, Dina and Hellmuth, Sam. (2009) Variation in the intonation of Egyptian Formal and Colloquial Arabic. *Langues et Linguistique* 22: 73–92.

Ferguson, C. A. (1957) Two problems in Arabic phonology. *WORD: Journal of the International Linguistic Association* 13 (3): 461–479.

Frota, Sonia, D'Imperio, Mariapaola, Elordieta, Gorka, Prieto, Pilar and Vigario, Marina. (2007) The phonetics and phonology of intonational phrasing in Romance. *Amsterdam Studies in the Theory and History of Linguistic Science IV* 282: 131–154.

Haeri, Nilofaar. (1996) *The Sociolinguistic Market of Cairo: Gender, Class and Education.* London: Keegan Paul International.

Hellmuth, Sam. (2004) Prosodic weight and phonological phrasing in Cairene Arabic. *Proceedings of Annual Meeting of Chicago Linguistic Society.* 40.

Hellmuth, Sam. (2006) *Intonational Pitch Accent Distribution in Egyptian Arabic.* PhD, SOAS.

Hellmuth, Sam. (2007) The relationship between prosodic structure and pitch accent distribution: evidence from Egyptian Arabic. *The Linguistic Review.* 24 (2): 289–314.

Inkelas, S. and Zec, D. (1990) *The Phonology-syntax Connection.* Chicago, IL: University of Chicago Press.

Ishihara, Shinichiro. (2007) Major phrase, focus intonation and multiple spellout. *The Linguistic Review.* 24 (2): 137–167.

Itô, Junko and Mester, Ralf-Armin. (2010) Trimming the prosodic hierarchy. In Toni Borowsky, Shigeto Kawahara, Tahahito Shinya and Mariko Sugahara (eds) *Prosody Matters: Essays in Honor of Elisabeth Selkirk.* London: Equinox.

Jun, Sun-Ah. (2005) Prosodic typology. In Sun-Ah Jun (ed.) *Prosodic Typology: The Phonology of Intonation and Phrasing* 430–458. Oxford: Oxford University Press.

Kawahara, Shigeto. (2010) The intonation of nominal parentheticals in Japanese. In Toni Borowsky, Shigeto Kawahara, Takahito Shinya and Mariko Sugahara (eds) *Prosody Matters: Essays in Honor of Lisa Selkirk.* London: Equinox.

Kawahara, Shigeto and Shinya, Tahahito. (2008) The intonation of gapping and coordination in Japanese: evidence for Intonational Phrase and Utterance. *Phonetica: International Journal of Speech Science* 65 (1–2): 62–105.

Kratzer, Angelika and Selkirk, Elisabeth O. (2007) Default phrase stress, prosodic phrasing and the spellout edge: The case of verbs. *The Linguistic Review* 24 (2): 93–135.

Ladd, D. R. (2008) *Intonational Phonology.* Cambridge: Cambridge University Press.

Liberman, M. and Pierrehumbert, Janet (1984) Intonational variance under changes in pitch range and length. In M. Aronoff and R. T. Oehrle (eds) *Language Sound Structure: Studies in Phonology present to Morris Hallé* 157–233. Cambridge, MA: MIT Press.

Nespor, M and Vogel, Irene (1986) *Prosodic Phonology*. Dordrecht: Foris.

Pierrehumbert, Janet and Beckman, Mary (1988) *Japanese Tone Structure*. Cambridge, MA: MIT Press.

Rastegar-El Zarka, Dina. (1997) *Prosodische Phonologie des Arabischen*. PhD, Karl-Franzens-Universität Graz.

Rifaat, Khalid. (1991) *The Intonation of Arabic: An Experimental Study*. PhD, University of Alexandria.

Selkirk, Elisabeth O. (1986) On derived domains in sentence phonology. *Phonology Yearbook* 3: 371–405.

Selkirk, Elisabeth O. (1995) Sentence prosody: intonation, stress and phrasing. In J. Goldsmith (ed.) *The Handbook of Phonological Theory* 550–569. Cambridge, MA: Blackwell.

Selkirk, Elisabeth O. (2000) The interaction of constraints on prosodic phrasing. In Merle Horne (ed.) *Prosody: Theory and Experiment* 231–262. Dordrecht: Kluwer.

Selkirk, Elisabeth O. (2009) On clause and intonational phrase in Japanese: The syntactic grounding of prosodic constituent structure. *Gengo Kenkyu: Journal of the Linguistic Society of Japan* 136: 35–73.

Selkirk, Elisabeth O. (to appear) The syntax-phonology interface. In John Goldsmith, Jason Riggle and Alan Yu (eds) *The Handbook of Phonological Theory*, 2nd edition. Cambridge, MA: Blackwell.

Shaked, Amit. (2007) Competing syntactic and prosodic constraints in Hebrew prosodic phrasing. *The Linguistic Review* 24 (2–3): 169–199.

Siemund, R., Heuft, B., Choukri, K., Emam, O., Maragoudakis, E., Tropf, H., Gedge, O., Shammass, S., Moreno, A., Nogueiras Rodriguez, A., Zitouni, I. and Iskra, D. (2002) OrienTel – Arabic speech resources for the IT market. LREC 2002 (Arabic workshop).

Truckenbrodt, Hubert. (1995) *Phonological Phrases: Their Relation to Syntax, Focus and Prominence*. PhD, MIT.

Truckenbrodt, Hubert. (1999) On the relation between syntactic phrases and phonological phrases. *Linguistic Inquiry* 30 (2): 219–255.

Truckenbrodt, Hubert. (2002) Upstep and embedded register levels. *Phonology* 19: 77–120.

Truckenbrodt, Hubert. (2004) Final lowering in non-final position. *Journal of Phonetics* 32 (3): 313–348.

Truckenbrodt, Hubert. (2007) Upstep on edge tones and on nuclear accents. In Tomas Riad and Carlos Gussenhoven (eds) *Tones and Tunes: Experimental Studies in Word and Sentence Prosody. Volume 2: Phonology and Phonetics* 349–386. Berlin: Mouton de Gruyter.

Truckenbrodt, Hubert. (2010) Stress and VP-shells in German. In Toni Borowsky, Shigeto Kawahara and Mariko Sugahara (eds) *Prosody Matters: Essays in Honor of Lisa Selkirk.* London: Equinox.

Watson, Janet C. E. (2002) *The Phonology and Morphology of Arabic.* Oxford: Oxford University Press.

Wightman, Colin W., Shattuck-Hufnagel, Stefanie, Ostendorf, Mari and Price, Patti J. (1992) Segmental durations in the vicinity of prosodic phrase boundaries. *Journal of the Acoustical Society of America* 91 (3): 1707–1717.

9 Recursive prosodic phrasing in Japanese*

Junko Ito and Armin Mester[a]

9.1 Background and identification of the problem

A key result of studies in phrasal phonology since the 1970s has been the finding that, cross-linguistically, phrase-level phonological processes do not make use of the vast set of potential domains that are in principle made available by grammatical (i.e., syntactic and morphological) structure. Rather, they are localized in a small set of domains that are phonological in nature, even though defined in reference to grammatical structure, and that turn out to play a decisive role in language after language. The model that developed in response to this central finding is *prosodic hierarchy theory* (Selkirk, 1978; Nespor and Vogel, 1983; Inkelas, 1989: 4, etc.), building on key insights in earlier work (such as Halliday, 1960 and Pike, 1967): Speech is organized into a set of prosodic domains that form a hierarchy of containment, with each non-terminal constituent made up of a sequence of constituents at the next level down (the *Strict Layer Hypothesis,* see Selkirk, 1984 and Nespor and Vogel, 1986, among others).

The hierarchy comprises two groups of categories, as shown in (1). The word-internal units (syllable, foot, and perhaps mora) are intrinsically defined in terms of sonority-related phonetic factors and speech rhythm, whereas the parsing of higher-level units (prosodic word, phonological phrase, intonational phrase, etc.) is regulated by constraints, alignment-based and other, on the correspondence between syntactic/morphological and phonological

[a]   Junko Ito and Armin Mester: University of California, Santa Cruz, CA, USA. Email: ito@ucsc.edu, mester@ucsc.edu

constituents. We will sometimes refer to the word-internal prosodic units as *rhythmic* categories, and the larger prosodic units as *interface* categories.

(1)

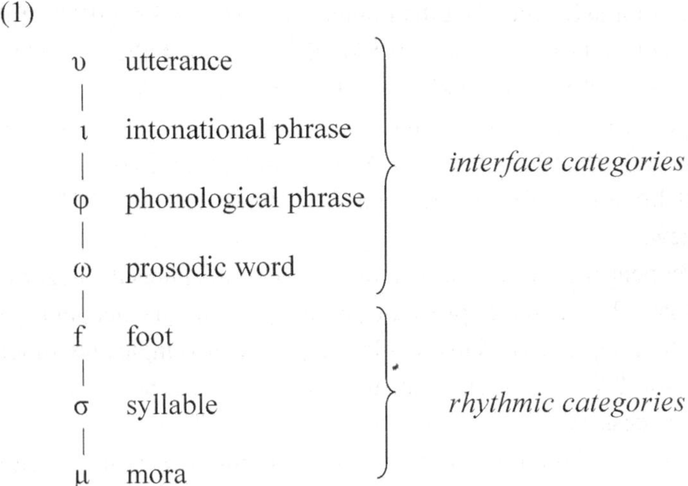

While the general form of the rhythmic categories is relatively uncontroversial, apart from specific issues (such as the status of the mora as a genuine prosodic constituent vs. a property of syllables, see Ito and Mester, 2003 [1992]), the picture is far less clear for the interface categories. The overall research program has been vastly successful in advancing our understanding of the relation between syntactic structure and phonological form, but many questions of both detail and principle have remained open, even as to the exact number and/or content of the units of the hierarchy. To make matters worse, categories are sometimes literally defined in terms of the processes associated with their instantiations in specific languages, resulting in labels like 'accentual phrase', 'tone group', etc. While this is mnemonically useful for the description of a single language, the lack of truly cross-linguistically valid and constant properties associated with these units creates additional obstacles in identifying categories between languages and grammars (see Selkirk, 2005 and Truckenbrodt, 2006 for discussion). The underlying research program has valued the postulation of new descriptive categories, designed to serve as domains for various processes in various languages, over restrictiveness.

One of the main points of dispute is, perhaps unsurprisingly, the mid-range of the prosodic hierarchy, where at least two distinct phrasal categories have been proposed, the minor phrase and the major phrase (alternatively named 'accentual phrase' and 'intermediate phrase'). The distinction seems to have grown out of research on Japanese, one of the best-studied prosodic systems. The two kinds of phrases were first distinguished in McCawley (1968), followed by Haraguchi (1977), Poser (1984), Beckman and Pierrehumbert (1986), Kubozono (1988), and Selkirk and Tateishi (1988). The distinction was then adopted for many other languages, including Basque (Elordieta, 2007), English (Selkirk, 1996), German (Kratzer and Selkirk, 2007), Italian (Petrone and D'Imperio, 2008), and Korean (Jun, 1998). See Jun (2005) for a general overview.

This paper reopens the question of whether two distinct phrasal categories are truly necessary. Is a model of prosodic parsing possible that accounts for all the facts, both in Japanese and in other languages, with a single phonological phrase category? We will argue that such a conception is not only possible, but in fact necessary: multiple categories create problems.

The starting point of the new approach is the simple observation that a single phrasal category does not mean a single layer of structure at a given level of prosody. Equating the two presupposes subscribing to the doctrine, long abandoned as part of orthodox strict layering, that only a new category can introduce a new level of structure. Even though prosodic structure shows nothing like the depth of embedding created by recursion in syntax,[1] it is a far cry from this uncontroversial observation to the strict layering conclusion that, given a prosodic hierarchy with n categories, each path (from root to terminal node) in a prosodic tree must have a length of exactly n layers. On the contrary, both level skipping and level repetition have been well motivated, resulting in paths with fewer and more levels, respectively. Level skipping occurs in weakly layered structures, as argued in Ito and Mester (2003 [1992]), and level repetition is found in recursive prosody, as was assumed in early prosodic theory (see, for example, Nespor and Vogel, 1983) and forcefully argued by Ladd in a number of publications (see Ladd 1996 for a summary). Following this growing body of work, we allow for additional layers to arise through recursion, in particular, through adjunction, as shown in (2).

(2) Prosodic recursion for interface categories:

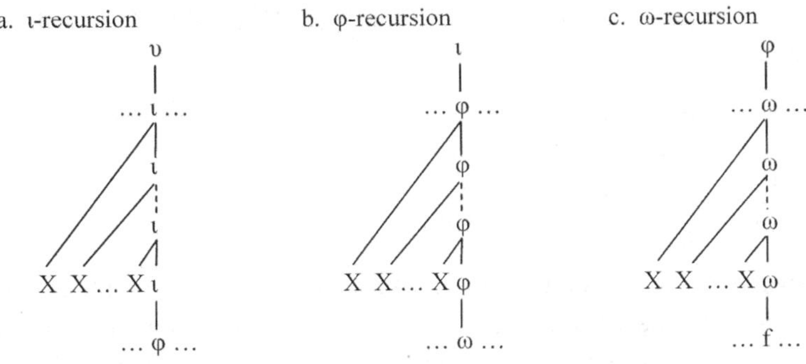

e.g., Ladd (1986, 1988) on nested coordinate structures in English

e.g., Gussenhoven (1991, 2005) on the rhythm rule in Dutch and English

e.g., Ito and Mester (2007) on Japanese compounds and Ito and Mester (2009a, 2009b) on English and German function word complexes

Constituent does not equal category once recursive structures are admitted. The crucial point is that recursion imposes further levels of structure on the string being parsed without claiming that each time a different category is involved. We are assuming an optimality-theoretic analysis (Selkirk, 1996; Truckenbrodt, 1999), where a NonRecursivity constraint prevents unlimited recursion and vacuous recursion. In fact, one layer for each category is optimal given appropriate parsing constraints, and recursive structures arise only if they serve to fulfill a higher ranking constraint (e.g., a syntax-prosody alignment constraint, a binarity restriction, etc.).

9.2   Interface categories in Japanese

Most previous work on the phrase-level prosody of Japanese (e.g., McCawley, 1968; Haraguchi, 1977; Poser, 1984; Beckman and Pierrehumbert, 1986; Kubozono, 1988; Selkirk and Tateishi, 1988) distinguishes the two phrasal interface categories in (3).

(3)

MaP   major ($\approx$ 'intermediate') phrase

MiP   minor ($\approx$ 'accentual') phrase

The rationale for this supposedly irreducible distinction is that MaP and MiP are domains for different processes. The three main generalizations are summarized in (4).

(4)

    a. MiP: Domain of accent culminativity
    b. MiP: Domain of initial rise
    c. MaP: Domain of downstep

How can a model with a single and undifferentiated category φ ('phonological phrase') make the necessary distinctions? The key lies in a better understanding of what the facts really imply about 'domains', and of the ways in which domains relate to categories.

The first generalization (4a) is more of a definition than an argument for a domain, and simply states that there can be at most one accent (H*L) in a MiP (hence the alternative name 'accentual phrase'). The generalization in (4b) is schematically illustrated in (5) (after Selkirk and Tateishi, 1991), where several unaccented prosodic words are joined into a single MiP. The central observation is that MiP, the domain of accent culminativity, is also the locus of the initial rise (a %L boundary tone followed by a phrasal H- tone).

(5) Initial rise within MiP

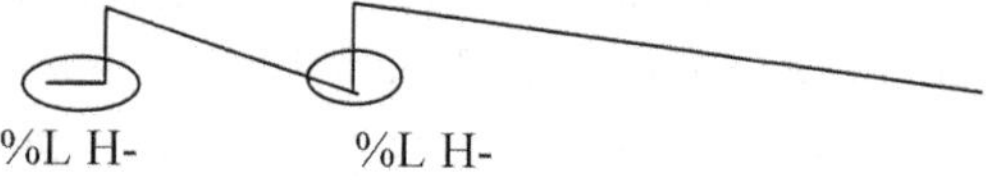

    a.   [MaP(MiP Oomiya-no) (MiP Inayama-no yuujin-ga inai)]
                                       friend isn't there
       'Mr. Inayama's friend from Oomiya isn't there.'

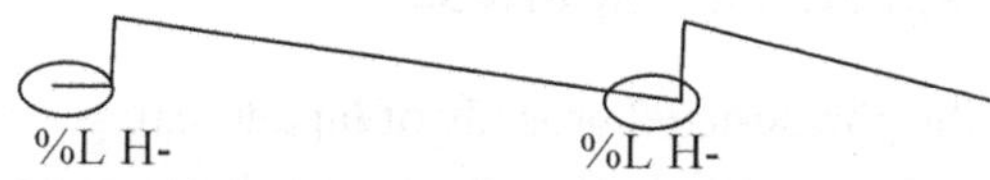

    b.   [MaP(MiP Oomiya-no Inayama-ga)(MiP yuujin-o yonda)]
                                   friend   called
       'Mr. Inayama from Oomiya called his friend.'

Downstep (or catathesis) refers to the lowering of the pitch register following an accented syllable (Poser, 1984). This is illustrated in (6) (after Selkirk and Tateishi, 1991), where each prosodic word is accented and therefore projects a MiP of its own. The domain of downstep is MaP in the sense that post-accent lowering takes place throughout MaP, and the pitch register is reset only at the beginning of the next MaP, not at the beginning of each MiP.

(6) Downstep within MaP

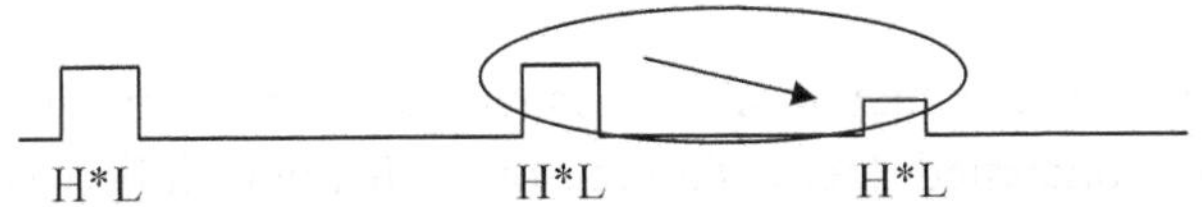

a. [$_{MaP}$($_{MiP}$ Aóyama-no)][$_{MaP}$($_{MiP}$ Yamáguchi-no)($_{MiP}$ aníyome-ga inai)]
               sister-in-law isn't there
'Mr. Yamaguchi's sister-in-law from Aoyama isn't there.'

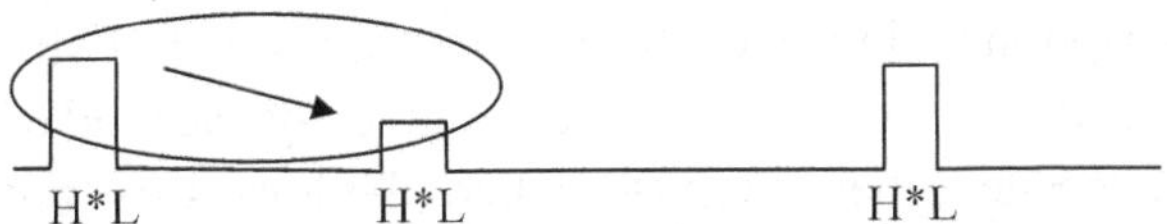

b. [$_{MaP}$($_{MiP}$ Aóyama-no) ($_{MiP}$ Yamáguchi-ga)][$_{MaP}$($_{MiP}$ aníyome-o yonda)]
               sister-in-law called
'Mr. Yamaguchi from Aoyama called his sister-in-law.'

A schematized diagram (with two MaPs, each with two MiPs) illustrating the initial rise (at the beginning of each MiP) and downstep (indicated by arrows within MaP) is given in (7).

(7)

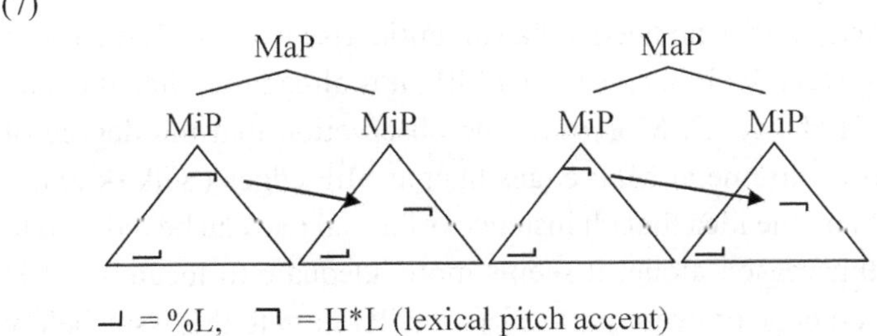

┐ = %L,   ┐ = H*L (lexical pitch accent)

How solid are these domain arguments? Are they sufficient grounds to motivate distinct categories? What goes wrong if both MaP and MiP are simply recursive undifferentiated φs, as in (8)?

(8)

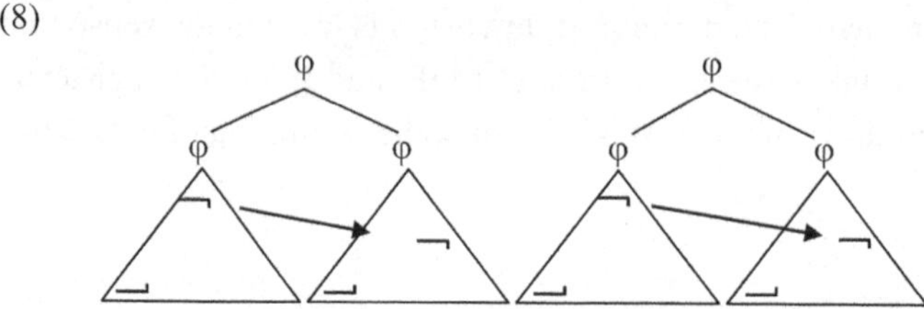

The surprising result is that nothing goes wrong: As far as the initial rise and downstep are concerned, there is no reason to distinguish between different kinds of phrases, MaP and MiP (or intermediate phrase and accentual phrase).

First, by accent culminativity a MiP contains maximally one accent; since downstep requires two accents, the first one downstepping the second, it cannot have any effect within a single MiP. Since it already follows from the structural description of downstep that it cannot apply within MiP, there is no need to specifically exclude it from this domain. Only one kind of phonological phrase φ is needed, then, as in (8), where the lowest φs (not containing other φs) are automatically excluded as 'domains of downstep'.

In structures like (8), minimal φs alone serve as domains of accent culminativity. Ito and Mester (2007: 100) argue that accent is a *head feature*: Each accent must be the head of some prosodic phrase φ. This ensures that every minimal φ has at most one accent (any additional accent would be a non-head), but non-minimal φs are free to contain more than one accent. The accent-as-head idea explains why it is the minimal φ that is the domain of accent culminativity.

In a similar way, there is no need to ban an initial rise from the left edge of MaP. As long as every MaP begins with a MiP, it is already predicted in any case: [$_{\text{MaP}}$ [$_{\text{MiP}}$ %LH …]…]. Moreover, the observation that the degree of initial rise is more extreme at MaP edges than at MiP edges (Selkirk *et al.,* 2003) casts doubt on the idea that all instances of initial rise can be reduced to MiP-rises. For this reason alone, it seems more adequate to locate a %LH sequence at the left edge of every phrase φ (we will return to this issue below in Section 9.4.3).

Downstep and initial rise, then, work without problems in the one-φ model. Our immediate conclusion is that the initial rise applies to all φ-phrases (not just to MiP), and likewise downstep applies to all φ-phrases (not just to MaP). The more interesting conclusion is that we can contemplate abolishing the entire MaP/MiP distinction: Let there be only one phonological phrase φ!

9.3   Recursion-based subcategories

What the facts and generalizations seem to demand is not enough *categories,* as the standard view of prosodic form has it, but rather enough *levels of structure.* But structure can be provided in a number of ways, the 'level = category' approach being just one of a number of possibilities, and arguably not the optimal one. In this context, it is significant that work over the last twenty years has firmly established recursivity as an indispensable attribute of prosodic form in a number of languages. The existence of recursive phrasing has been demonstrated at the level of the intonational phrase by Ladd (1986, 1988) and Ladd and Campbell (1991), and at the level of the phonological phrase by Gussenhoven (2005); prosodic word recursion has been shown to hold for compounds and function word complexes by Booij (1996) and Ito and Mester (2007, 2009a, 2009b). Further development, with additional evidence, is found in Kubozono (1988, 1993, 2005), van den Berg *et al.* (1992), Truckenbrodt (2002), and Féry and Truckenbrodt (2005), among others. Extensive study and motivation of recursive structures in prosody is provided in two recent dissertations (Wagner, 2005 (MIT); Schreuder, 2006 (Groningen); see also Wagner, 2010).

Building on this line of work, we will here outline a model that we refer to as *recursion-based subcategories.* Each prosodic category defines its own network of projections, where the usual tree-structural notions apply, such as minimal and maximal projection and head vs. non-head. Phonological and phonetic processes are part of the realization of this structure, and signal important boundaries by selecting different subconstituents as their domains. Using standard tree-structural terminology, the largest projection of a prosodic category κ is the 'maximal κ', and its smallest projection is the 'minimal κ', as defined in (9).

(9)

κ_{max} = κ not dominated by κ
κ_{min} = κ not dominating κ

The schematic structure in (10) shows how these definitions apply to the interface categories *intonational phrase* (ι), *phonological phrase* (φ), and *prosodic word* (ω). Taking up a suggestion by Shigeto Kawahara, we propose that *utterance* (υ), usually posited as the highest category in the prosodic hierarchy, is not a separate category, but rather the maximal projection of the *intonational phrase* (ɩ). The empirical prediction is that *utterance* cannot be recursive; its only role is to gather up the smaller chunks of prosodic structure.

(10) Prosodic adjunction:

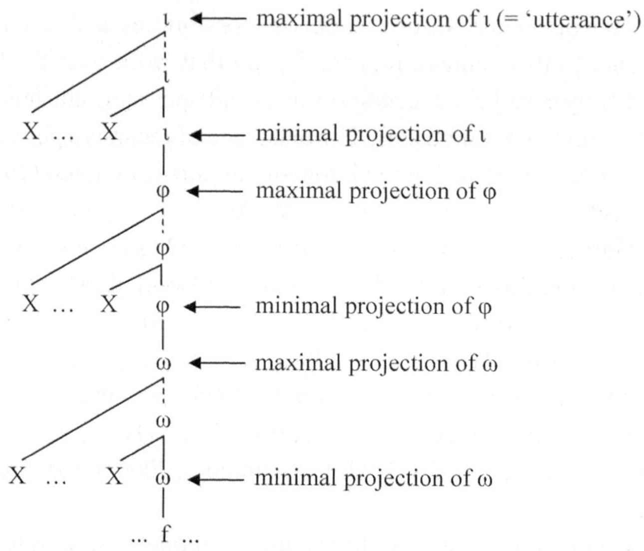

A reviewer raises the very pertinent question why the intonational phrase and the phonological phrase need to be different categories. Could the intonational phrase, as well as the utterance, simply be projections of the phonological phrase? This is obviously an empirical question that cannot be decided on a priori grounds. A relevant finding is that there seem to be substantial and 'categorical' (i.e., not merely gradient) differences such as pause and other phonetic correlates identified in Kawahara and Shinya (2008) between these levels of prosody. A similar question can be asked about the prosodic word and the phonological phrase: Might the phrase just be a higher projection of the word? Again this can only be decided on empirical grounds: For example, Kahnemuyipour's (2003) finding that stress in Persian involves opposite headedness at the word and at the phrase level argues that we are dealing with different units of prosody.

Rather than pursuing a bottom-up phonetic approach, as in Jun (2005), Venditti *et al.* (2008), and other works, where higher prosodic categories are defined solely in terms of their phonetic manifestation, we continue to assume the syntax-prosody mapping hypothesis in the tradition of prosodic theory, as inaugurated in the work of Selkirk (1978): all interface categories, i.e., prosodic categories above the rhythmically defined foot, are defined in relation to grammatical/syntactic structure and information structure. A reasonable guiding idea is to map *Lex*, the syntactic word (the lexical categories N, V, and A) to the prosodic interface unit ω, the syntactic phrase *LexP* (the maximal projection of *Lex*) to φ (roughly corresponding to the Major Phrase), and the syntactic clause (CP) to ι. This idea is one of the cornerstones of the Match Theory recently developed by Selkirk (2009, to appear).

In connection with defining minor phrasing in Japanese, Selkirk and Tateishi (1988) point out that the syntax-prosody mapping hypothesis may be too strong since it is not the case that there is a syntactic constituent type whose edge must coincide with the edge of a Minor Phrase, nor that a Minor Phrase edge must coincide with the edge of a syntactic constituent of a particular type. Selkirk and Tateishi's observation actually reveals higher ranking constraints at work, such as Accent Culminativity, which dominate the mapping constraints and result in φs that are smaller than XPs. A syntactic phrase $_{XP}[a\ a]$, where a is an accented word, would be expected to map onto a phonological φ as $_\varphi(a\ a)$. But because of Accent Culminativity, the two *a*s cannot both be heads of φ, and are optimally mapped as recursive $_\varphi(_\varphi(a)_\varphi(a))$. On the other hand, an unaccented combination $_{XP}[u\ u]$ simply maps onto a single phonological φ as $_\varphi(u\ u)$. Thus with recursive prosodic subcategories and violable constraints, there is no need to weaken the syntax-prosody mapping hypothesis – or better, the weakening involved here reveals itself simply as an intrinsically optimality-theoretic effect: The domination of an interface constraint by prosodic constraints.[2]

9.4   Recursive φ vs. MiP/MaP

How do recursion-based subcategories and MiP/MaP theory match up? In specific instantiations, MiP simply corresponds to the minimal φ, MaP to the maximal φ, as depicted in (11), leaving us wondering whether we have just recreated MiP and MaP under different names.

(11) MiP/MaP vs. minimal-φ/maximal-φ

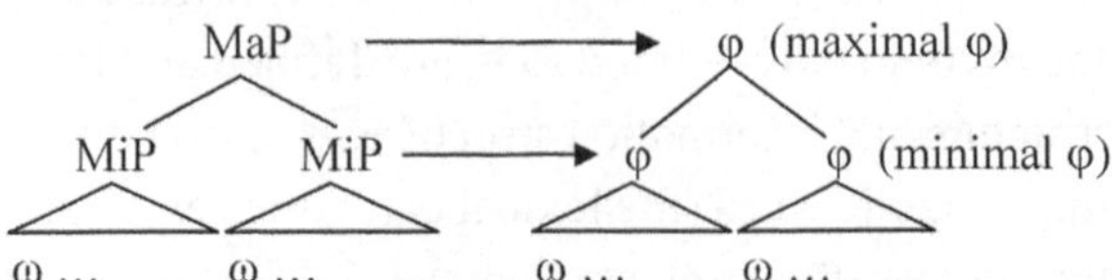

Closer inspection reveals, however, that the two theories are far from being notational variants. There are significant differences between the two, and the evidence favors the single φ-category approach. MiP/MaP theory faces a dilemma in that it gives rise to two diametrically opposed problems at the same time: It provides too much structure in some respects, and too little structure in others.

9.4.1. Too much structure in MiP/MaP

Recursivity is an established attribute of prosodic form – in OT-terms, the anti-recursivity constraint is violable (Selkirk, 1996). But whenever this constraint is low ranking in the grammar, MiP/MaP theory in principle allows both phrases to appear recursively, as in (12).

(12)

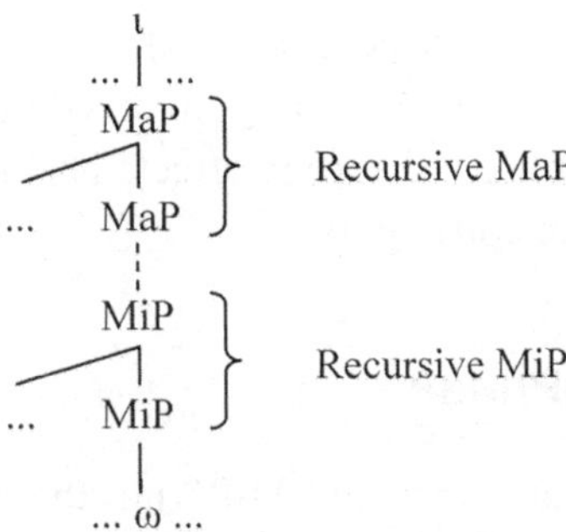

Such nested MaP/MiP structures have no equivalent in a theory with recursion-based subcategories. While MaP and MiP are actual categories and can be recursive, 'maximal φ' and 'minimal φ' are relational terms, not separate categories, and it makes no sense for something to be 'recursively maximal' or 'recursively minimal' in a single projection: Only one instance of a category is maximal, and only one is minimal (see (9)).

(13)

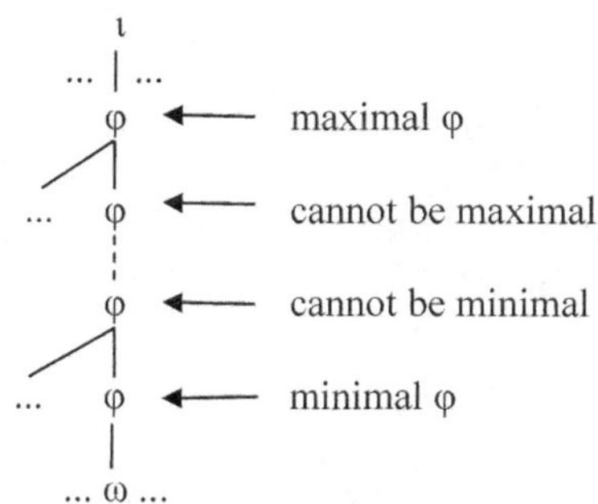

Given the independent need for recursive structures, the single-φ approach is thus inherently more restrictive than the MiP/MaP approach in (12).

Whether this difference is of consequence remains an empirical question, and will require careful investigation. Interestingly, Selkirk (2000: 25) argues explicitly that in English recursive MaP structures need to be ruled out by specifically assuming high ranking NONRECURSIVITY-MAP. If 'MaP' ≈ maximal φ, this follows automatically without invoking other constraints or ranking.[3]

9.4.2   Too little structure in MiP/MaP

Evidence that the standard MiP/MaP approach does not provide enough structure to represent the ways downstep plays out in Japanese was first pointed out by Kubozono (1993: 205–208), who found that a sequence of four accented MiPs with the grammatical structure [ÁB][ĆD], while exhibiting downstep throughout, i.e., clearly constituting a single MaP, has a systematically higher pitch on Ć than what the flat prosodic structure $_{MaP}$[MiP MiP MiP MiP] predicts. Kubozono (1989: 58–59) argues that one way of understanding this metrical boost is as a phonetic reflex of a binary, recursively restructured MiP-MiP sequence as in (14).

(14) Recursive MiPs

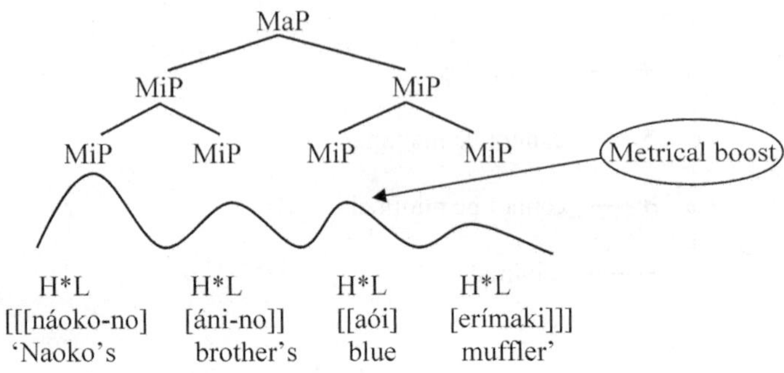

This is a subtle finding with important consequences, and the proposed recursive MiP structure clearly makes sense of the metrical boost, which remains baffling under the standard view.[4] But now a different and unexpected problem arises: Each of the higher MiPs contains two accents, inherited from the two subordinate MiPs, and therefore violates accent culminativity, the defining property of MiP.

(15)

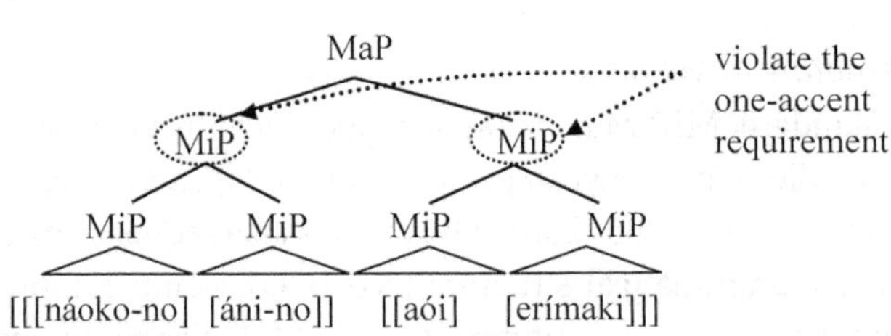

The contradictory domain desiderata – nonrecursive MiPs to observe accent culminativity vs. recursive MiPs to account for the metrical boost – did not go unnoticed (Shinya *et al.*, 2004), and the response was the standard one of introducing yet another category, 'SMiP' ('Superordinate Minor Phrase'), between MiP and MaP. SMiP, and not MiP, takes care of the metrical boost, and the one-accent requirement holds of MiP, not of SMiP.

(16)

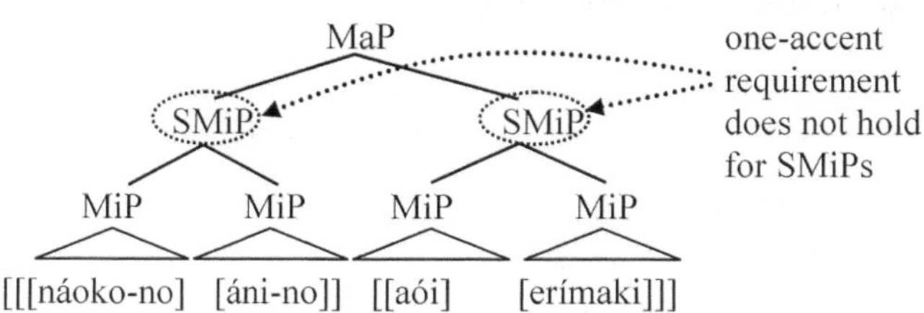

In the φ-only model, the problematic contradiction does not arise, because the one-accent requirement holds of minimal φ, and the branching φs are necessarily non-minimal. The metrical boost, on the other hand, is associated, as in Kubozono's conception, with φ in a right-branching recursive configuration, which is necessarily non-minimal.

(17)

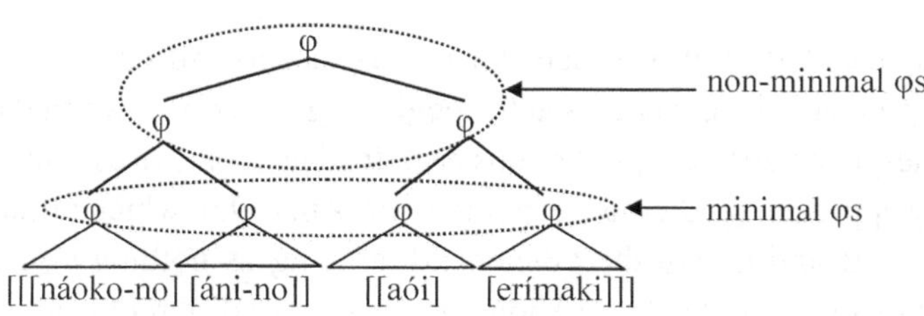

No new intermediate category (such as SMiP) is necessary in the φ-only approach. The larger lesson to be learned here is that separate labels become a liability where recursive structures are called for: They require further elaboration of the labeled hierarchy, dimming the prospects for a cross-linguistically valid hierarchy.[5]

Given the prosodic parses assigned by the φ-only approach, which are accessed by phonetics, an important question is whether phonetics can 'count' the nodes – for example, determine how many instances of φ are initiated by a given word. The answer is that such information must in principle be accessible and is of obvious relevance since it is a manifestation of what is often informally referred to as 'boundary strength'. Thus the first word *náoko* in the example below stands at the beginning of three φs, *áoi* at the beginning of two φs, and *áni* and *erímaki* are at the beginning of only one φ. Since the initial rise is computed on the basis of beginnings of φs, these distinctions are crucial (the same basic idea is expressed by the OT-mechanism of constraint conjunction in Ito and Mester 2003: 201–206).

(18)

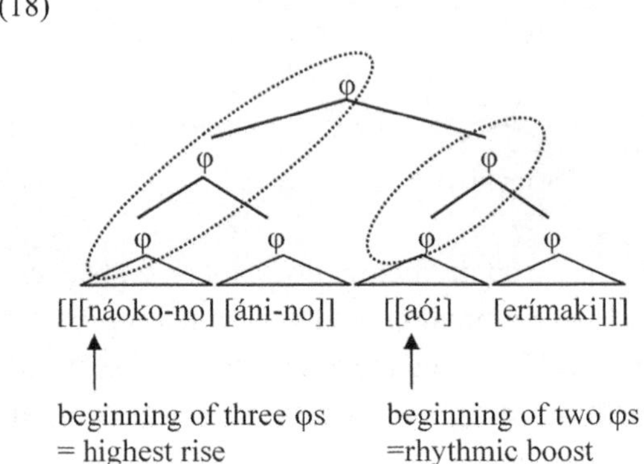

9.4.3 Cumulative rise in recursive φ

Comparing the MiP/MaP approach, where a rise occurs MiP-initially, with the φ-only approach, where it occurs at the beginning of *every* φ, we find that the two theories make different predictions for left edges. If the rise is cumulative, the φ-only approach predicts a steeper rise for A in (19a), which initiates two φs, than for B and C. On the other hand, as long as nothing else is said, MiP/MaP theory predicts that A should be in no way different from B and C in (19b).

(19)

    a. $[_\varphi\ [_\varphi\ A\ ][_\varphi\ B\ ][_\varphi\ C\ ]\ ]$

    b. $[_{MaP}[_{MiP}\ A\ ][_{MiP}\ B][_{MiP}\ C\ ]\ ]$

The facts here favor the φ-only approach: Selkirk *et al.* (2003) and Kawahara (2010, this volume) found that the degree of initial rise is more extreme at left edges – a puzzling result for the view that the initial rise is a MiP-exclusive property. Such upwards-inheritance of strengthening effects is a general feature of the prosodic hierarchy, according to Fougeron and Keating (1997) and Flack (2007). What accounts for the different degrees of initial rise? In the φ-only approach, a rise occurs at the beginning of all φs, and if it is cumulative,[6] more rise is immediately predicted at the left edge of structures like (19a) without special pleading. The MiP/MaP approach, on the other hand, needs a separate stipulation that MaP edges have a more extreme rise.[7]

9.4.4 Initial rise in weakly layered structures

We have so far considered one way in which prosodic structures are not strictly layered, namely, through level repetition (recursivity). A second way is by skipping prosodic levels, as in situations where syllables remain un-footed and are directly dominated by the prosodic word (see Ito and Mester, 2003 [1992]; Selkirk, 1996; Peperkamp, 1996; and Kabak and Schiering, 2006 for examples). In terms of Ito and Mester (2009a), these involve viola-tions of the constraint PARSE-INTO-X, where X is some level of the prosodic hierarchy.[8] It turns out that the MiP/MaP approach and the φ-only approach make different predictions in cases where level-skipping is involved, i.e., when MaP does not begin with MiP and directly dominates ω (skipping the MiP level), as in (20a), to be compared with the structurally equivalent φ-only structure (20b). The circled prosodic word is not MiP-initial in (20a), which would mean no initial rise. On the other hand, it is φ-initial in (20b), pre-dicting a rise. In order to force an initial rise MaP-initially, the MiP/MaP approach must stipulate that every MaP begins with a MiP: [MaP[MiP...]...].

(20)

    a. MiP/MaP theory:

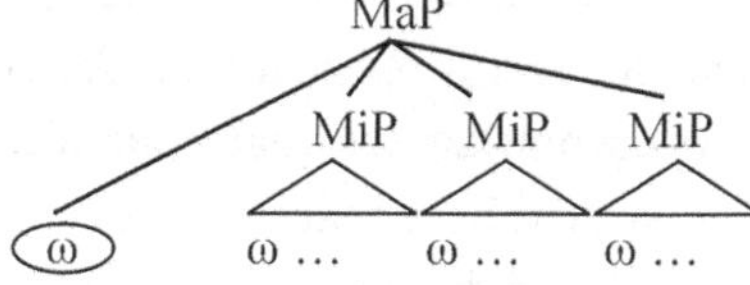

    b. φ-only theory:

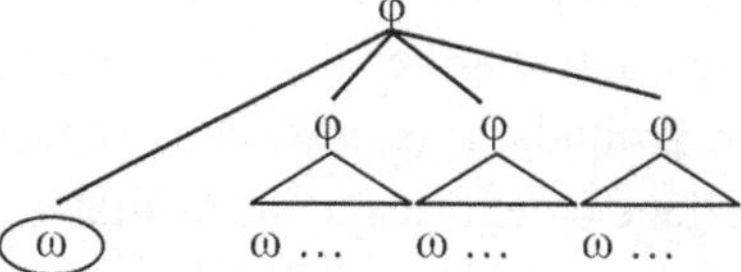

No examples are known to us that would directly bear on this issue, but plausibility is certainly on the side of the φ-only theory, especially in light of the fact that the initial rise effects in general increase with the level of phras-ing (see the previous section).

9.5 Summary and further consequences

In prosodic hierarchy theory, a large number of different interface categories have been proposed in order to provide enough separate domains for different processes, including *utterance, intonational phrase, phonological phrase, major phrase, intermediate phrase, minor phrase, accentual phrase, tone group, clitic group, prosodic word,* and *minor word.* The totality of these categories has never been instantiated in a single language, however, and their cross-linguistic identification (Does the X-Phrase of Language A really correspond to the X-Phrase of Language B?) has remained a largely unsolved problem. Even within a single language, the insistence on strictly layered representations has led to a considerable multiplication of categories. Whenever a process is found to operate in a slightly different domain than some other process, the model requires setting up two separate categories. Once repetition of levels through recursion becomes an option, however, 'domain' no longer equals 'category', raising the suspicion that perhaps some of the categories proposed in the earlier prosodic literature are in reality only larger recursive structures built on a single basic interface category. Loosening the doctrine of strict layering allows us to strengthen the theory on the category side, and limit the interface categories to a small and universally well-defined set, much like the broadly agreed-on set for rhythmic categories (foot, syllable, and mora).

In this paper, we reviewed the evidence for the distinction between the central interface categories proposed for Japanese, major phrase and minor phrase. While everyone agrees that constituents of different sizes are involved, we have argued here that there is no need to postulate two separate interface categories, and that the evidence favors a model with a single category φ 'phonological phrase', with the option of recursion. Since the φ-only theory is more restrictive, given that recursion has been shown to be necessary on independent grounds, it is up to the proponents of theories with a larger number of interface categories to show that additional categories are in fact necessary.

In a more general vein, we hypothesized that there are only three universal interface categories: *intonational phrase* (ι), *phonological phrase* (φ), and *prosodic word* (ω). Additional structure is imposed on the string through recursion.

Investigations along these lines, where relational notions such as maximal and minimal projections of categories play a natural role, have resulted in some interesting and promising results in a variety of languages. Woodbury (2002) shows in detail, using both prosodic and segmental phenomena as evidence, that Cup'ik prosody distinguishes two 'word' constituents: The grammatical word minus all enclitics, and the grammatical word plus all enclitics. In our terms, the two domains ('PW–' vs. 'PW' in Woodbury's notation) correspond exactly to the minimal and the maximal prosodic word (ω), respectively. The analysis of the word-level stress domain and the *Ezafe* construction in Persian (Kahnemuyipour, 2003) can be interpreted along similar lines, with an appeal to minimal and maximal projections of ω.

In work on the prosody of Irish, Dowd (2009) has identified the maximal ω as the domain of synthetic agreement; and Bennett and McCloskey (2008) show with several diagnostics (including pause, downstep, and lengthening) that phonological phrases (φ) are right-aligned to XP, and that the syntactically baffling distribution of weak pronouns has a prosodic rationale (see also Elfner, 2008): They appear at the right edge of the maximal φ. Henderson (2008) shows that in K'ichee' *h*-final allomorphs occur as phonological phrase markers. In conjoined phrases, they are optionally found on the first conjunct, which can be understood as recursive φ-phrasing, with *h*-final allomorphs appearing either on the minimal or the maximal φ.

In our own work, we have shown that a theory with recursion-based subcategories can be fruitfully applied to illuminate the interplay between *rendaku,* accent, downstep, and initial rise in Japanese complex compounds (Ito and Mester, 2007), the prosodic conditioning of intrusive-*r* in non-rhotic English (Ito and Mester, 2009b), and the phonology of English and German function word complexes, which involves various segmental fusion processes (Ito and Mester, 2009a).

While these preliminary results inspire some confidence in the general outlook on prosody presented here, it remains to be seen in future work whether a theory with such a minimal set of interface categories and recursion-based subcategories can be upheld cross-linguistically.

Notes

* An earlier version of this paper appeared in the conference proceedings of Japanese/Korean Linguistics 18 (CSLI, Stanford). The present version takes into consideration the comments and critiques of the reviewers and editors of the Festschrift volume. For helpful comments and suggestions on this work, we would like to thank Mary Beckman, Ryan Bennett, Kenneth de Jong, Andrew Dowd, Caroline Féry, Steven Franks, Shosuke Haraguchi, Shin Ishihara, Dan Kaufman, Shigeto Kawahara, Yoshi Kitagawa, Haruo Kubozono, Jim McCloskey, Bruce

Morén, Marina Nespor, Jeremy O'Brien, Marc van Oostendorp, Dave Odden, Jaye Padgett, Anthi Revithiadou, Tomas Riad, Curt Rice, Shin-Ichi Tanaka, and Satoshi Tomioka.

1   As shown by time-honored examples like the following (after Chomsky and Halle, 1968), where syntactic structure and ι-phrasing are radically different:

ι(This is   the cat)ι   ι(that chased   the rat)ι   ι(that ate   the malt)ι
CP[DP[CP[DP[CP[DP[   ]DP]CP]DP]CP]DP]CP

All embedding is removed in the prosodic representation, resulting in a flat sequence of three ι-phrases whose left edges coincide with those of clauses (CPs), and not of the syntactically superordinate DPs.

2   The basic idea here goes back to the earliest work on minor phrasing in McCawley (1968: 177–180), who inserts minor phrase boundaries by a strictly syntax-based rule and then adjusts the phrasing with rules sensitive to (un)accentedness. Just as minor phrases can be understood as part of recursive φs, Clitic Groups have been argued to be recursive ωs in Ito and Mester (2009a), taking up an earlier proposal by Inkelas (1989), among others.

3   Kratzer and Selkirk (2007) use recursive MaPs in explaining the accentual variation found with main clause word order in German. MaP recursivity is not essential to the proposal, however, which can be straightforwardly recast with extended word projections (ω-recursion) for MiP and φ-phrase recursion for MaP (see Ito and Mester, 2008).

4   Among other things, it involves the recognition that the notion downstep has a *paradigmatic* component, besides the obvious *syntagmatic* one: Kubozono argues that Ć in [ÁB́][ĆD́] in (14) is downstepped relative to B́, even though at roughly the same pitch as B́, because it is significantly lower in pitch than Ć in [ÁB][ĆD́], where it follows unaccented B.

5   See also Wagner (2005, 2010) for a more radical departure from the standard labeled hierarchy, with arguments for a 'label-free' purely metrical model of prosodic structure.

6   For concreteness, assume that each φ begins with %L, a lowering operator, and that stacked lowering operators are interpreted in a cumulative way.

7   A reviewer reminds us that Kawahara and Shinya (2008) found even more extreme rises at ι-edges than at φ-edges. This does not mean, however, that φ-only theory, like MiP/MaP theory, still has to have recourse to separate stipulations of the same property for separate categories. The slogan of MiP/MaP theory – and, more generally, of theories insisting on strictly layered structures – is that each level is

identified with a particular phonetic property, constituting its 'domain': MiP is the domain of the initial rise, MaP the domain of downstep, etc. In such a theory, it is odd to find more pronounced rises at the left edge of MaP, which is not a rise domain. On the other hand, since our theory does not correlate 'domain' and 'phonetic property' in this way, we do not expect a one-to-one correspondence between them. In particular, a specific phonetic property can characterize several domains. Intonational phrases and phonological phrases are both phrases, and nothing is more natural than certain properties, such as the presence of %L, being associated with all phrasal categories.

8   Or in the terminology of Selkirk (1996), violations of EXHAUSTIVITY$_Y$, which demands that the higher category Y dominate only X.

References

Beckman, Mary and Pierrehumbert, Janet. (1986) Intonational structure in English and Japanese. *Phonology* 3: 255–309.

Bennett, Ryan and McCloskey, James. (2008) Donegal Irish and the Syntax/Prosody Interface. UC Santa Cruz. Presented at PRIG (Prosody Interest Group), UC Santa Cruz.

Booij, Geert. (1996) Cliticization as prosodic integration: The case of Dutch. *The Linguistic Review* 13: 219–242.

Chomsky, Noam and Halle, Morris. (1968) *The Sound Pattern of English*. New York: Harper & Row.

Dowd, Andrew. (2009) Aspects of the Prosody of Irish Synthetic and Analytic Forms. UC Santa Cruz. Presented at PRIG (Prosody Interest Group), UC Santa Cruz.

Elfner, Emily. (2008) The Interaction of Linearization and Prosody: Evidence from Pronoun Postposing in Irish and Scottish Gaelic. Amherst, MA: University of Massachusetts.

Elordieta, Gorka. (2007) Minimum size constraints on intermediate phrases. http://www.icphs2007.de/conference/Papers/1682/1682.pdf.

Féry, Caroline and Truckenbrodt, Hubert. (2005) Sisterhood and tonal scaling. *Studia Linguistica* 59: 223–243.

Flack, Kathryn Gilbert. (2007) *The Sources of Phonological Markedness*. University of Massachusetts: Doctoral dissertation.

Fougeron, Cécile and Keating, Patricia. (1997) Articulatory strengthening at edges of prosodic domains. *Journal of the Acoustical Society of America* 101: 3728–3740.

Gussenhoven, Carlos. (1991) The English rhythm rule as an accent deletion rule. *Phonology* 8: 1–35.

Gussenhoven, Carlos. (2005) Procliticized phonological phrases in English: Evidence from rhythm. *Studia Linguistica* 59: 174–193.

Halliday, M. A. K. (1960) Categories of the theory of grammar. *Word* 17 (3): 241–292.

Haraguchi, Shosuke. (1977) *The Tone Pattern of Japanese: An Autosegmental Theory of Tonology.* Tokyo: Kaitakusha.

Henderson, Robert. (2008) Allomorphy and K'ichee' Prosodic Structure. UC Santa Cruz. Presented at PRIG (Prosody Interest Group), UC Santa Cruz.

Inkelas, Sharon. (1989) *Prosodic Constituency in the Lexicon*, Stanford University: Doctoral dissertation. Published 1990, Outstanding Dissertations in Linguistics Series. New York: Garland Press.

Ito, Junko and Mester, Armin. (2003) *Japanese Morphophonemics: Markedness and Word Structure.* Linguistic Inquiry Monographs, 41. Cambridge, MA, and London, England: MIT Press.

Ito, Junko, and Mester, Armin. (2003 [1992]) Weak layering and word binarity. In Takeru Honma, Masao Okazaki, Toshiyuki Tabata and Shin-Ichi Tanaka (eds) *A New Century of Phonology and Phonological Theory. A Festschrift for Professor Shosuke Haraguchi on the Occasion of His Sixtieth Birthday* 26–65. Slightly revised version of 1992 UC Santa Cruz Linguistics Research Center working paper.

Ito, Junko and Mester, Armin. (2007) Prosodic adjunction in Japanese compounds. In *Formal Approaches to Japanese Linguistics 4* 97–111. Cambridge, MA: MIT Department of Linguistics and Philosophy.

Ito, Junko and Mester, Armin. (2008) Rhythmic and Interface Categories in Prosody. UC Santa Cruz. Presented at PRIG (Prosody Interest Group), UC Santa Cruz.

Ito, Junko and Mester, Armin. (2009a) The extended prosodic word. In Janet Grijzenhout and Bariş Kabak (eds) *Phonological Domains: Universals and Deviations*, Berlin: Mouton de Gruyter.

Ito, Junko and Mester, Armin. (2009b) The onset of the prosodic word. In Steve Parker (ed.) *Phonological Argumentation: Essays on Evidence and Motivation* 227–260. London: Equinox.

Jun, Sun-Ah. (1998) The Accentual Phrase in the Korean prosodic hierarchy. *Phonology.* 15: 189–226.

Jun, Sun-Ah. (2005) Prosodic typology. In Sun-Ah Jun (ed.) *Prosodic Typology: The Phonology of Intonation and Phrasing* 430–458. Oxford: Oxford University Press.

Kabak, Bariş and Schiering, René. (2006) The phonology and morphology of function word contractions in German. *Journal of Comparative Germanic Linguistics* 9: 53–99.

Kahnemuyipour, Arsalan. (2003) Syntactic categories and Persian stress. *Natural Language and Linguistic Theory* 21 (2): 333–379.

Kawahara, Shigeto. (2011) The intonation of nominal parentheticals in Japanese. In Toni Borowsky, Shigeto Kawahara, Takahito Shinya and Mariko Sugahara (eds) *Prosody Matters* 320–356. London: Equinox.

Kawahara, Shigeto and Shinya, Takahito. (2008) The intonation of gapping and coordination in Japanese: Evidence for Intonational Phrase and Utterance. *Phonetica* 65: 62–105.

Kratzer, Angelika, and Selkirk, Elisabeth. (2007) Phase theory and prosodic spellout: The case of verbs. *The Linguistic Review* 24: 93–135.

Kubozono, Haruo. (1989) Syntactic and rhythmic effects on downstep in Japanese. *Phonology* 6: 39–67.

Kubozono, Haruo. (1988) *The Organization of Japanese Prosody*, University of Edinburgh: Doctoral dissertation.

Kubozono, Haruo. (1993) *The Organization of Japanese Prosody*. vol. 2: Studies in Japanese Linguistics. Tokyo: Kurosio Publishers. Revision of 1988 University of Edinburgh thesis.

Kubozono, Haruo. (2005) Focus and intonation in Japanese: Does focus trigger pitch reset?. In S. Ishihara, M. Schmitz and A. Schwarz (eds) *Interdisciplinary Studies on Information Structure (Working Papers of the Sonderforschungsbereich 632)*. Potsdam: Universitätsverlag Potsdam.

Ladd, D. Robert. (1986) Intonational phrasing: The case for recursive prosodic structure. *Phonology* 3: 311–340.

Ladd, D. Robert. (1988) Declination 'reset' and the hierarchical organization of utterances. *Journal of the Acoustical Society of America* 84 (2): 530–544.

Ladd, D. Robert. (1996) *Intonational Phonology*. Cambridge: Cambridge University Press.

Ladd, D. Robert, and Campbell, Nick. (1991) Theories of prosodic structure: Evidence from syllable duration. In *Proceedings of the 12th International Congress of the Phonetic Sciences* 290–293. Aix-En-Provence, France.

McCawley, James D. (1968) *The Phonological Component of a Grammar of Japanese*. The Hague, The Netherlands: Mouton.

Nespor, Marina and Vogel, Irene. (1983) Prosodic structure above the word. In A. Cutler and D. R. Ladd (eds) *Prosody: Models and Measurements* 123–140. Berlin, Heidelberg, New York, Tokyo: Springer.

Nespor, Marina, and Vogel, Irene. (1986) *Prosodic Phonology*. Dordrecht: Foris.

Peperkamp, Sharon. (1996) On the prosodic representation of clitics. In Ursula Kleinhenz (ed.) *Interfaces in Phonology* 102–127. Berlin: Akademie Verlag.

Petrone, Caterina, and D'Imperio, Mariapaola. (2008) Tonal structure and constituency in Neapolitan Italian: Evidence for the Accentual Phrase in statements and questions. ISCA Archive, http://www.isca-speech.org/archive.

Pike, Kenneth L. (1967) *Language in Relation to a Unified Theory of the Structure of Human Behavior*. Janua Linguarum series major 24. The Hague: Mouton.

Poser, William J. (1984) *The Phonetics and Phonology of Tone and Intonation in Japanese*. MIT: Doctoral dissertation.

Schreuder, Maartje. (2006) *Prosodic Processes in Language and Music*. Rijksuniversiteit Groningen, The Netherlands: Doctoral dissertation.

Selkirk, Elisabeth. (1978) On prosodic structure and its relation to syntactic structure. In T. Fretheim (ed.) *Nordic Prosody* 111–140. Trondheim: TAPIR.

Selkirk, Elisabeth. (1984) *Phonology and Syntax: The Relation between Sound and Structure.* Cambridge, MA: MIT Press.

Selkirk, Elisabeth. (1996) The prosodic structure of function words. In James L. Morgan and Katherine Demuth (eds) *Signal to Syntax* 187–213. Mahwah, NJ: Lawrence Erlbaum.

Selkirk, Elisabeth. (2005) Comments on intonational phrasing in English. In Sónia Frota, Marina Vigário and Maria João Freitas (eds) *Prosodies: Selected Papers from the Phonetics and Phonology in Iberia Conference, 2003 (Phonetics and Phonology Series).* Berlin and New York: Mouton de Gruyter.

Selkirk, Elisabeth. (2009) On clause and intonational phrase in Japanese: The syntactic grounding of prosodic constituent structure. *Gengo Kenkyuu* 136: 35–73.

Selkirk, Elisabeth. (to appear) The syntax-phonology interface. In John Goldsmith, Jason Riggle and Alan Yu (eds) *The Handbook of Phonological Theory. 2nd edition.* Oxford: Blackwell Publishing.

Selkirk, Elisabeth, Shinya, Takahito and Sugahara, Mariko. (2003) Degree of initial lowering in Japanese as a reflex of prosodic structure organization. In *Proc.15th ICPhS, Barcelona, Spain.* 491–494.

Selkirk, Elisabeth and Tateishi, Koichi. (1988) Constraints on minor phrase formation in Japanese. In *Papers from the 24th Annual Regional Meeting of the Chicago Linguistic Society* 316–336. Chicago, IL: Chicago Linguistic Society.

Selkirk, Elisabeth, and Tateishi, Koichi. (1991) Syntax and downstep in Japanese. In C. Georgopoulos and R. Ishihara (eds) *Interdisciplinary Approaches to Language: Essays in Honor of S.-Y. Kuroda* 519–544. Dordrecht: Kluwer.

Shinya, Takahito, Selkirk, Elisabeth and Kawahara, Shigeto. (2004) Rhythmic boost and recursive minor phrase in Japanese. In *Proceedings of the Second International Conference on Speech Prosody* 345–348.

Truckenbrodt, Hubert. (1999) On the relation between syntactic phrases and phonological phrases. *Linguistic Inquiry* 30: 219–255.

Truckenbrodt, Hubert. (2002) Upstep and embedded register levels. *Phonology* 19: 77–120.

Truckenbrodt, Hubert. (2006) The syntax-phonology interface. In Paul de Lacy (ed.) *The Cambridge Handbook of Phonology* 435–456. Cambridge: Cambridge University Press.

van den Berg, Rob, Gussenhoven, Carlos, and Rietveld, Toni. (1992) Downstep in Dutch: Implications for a model. In Gerard J. Dochtery and D. Robert Ladd (eds) *Papers in Laboratory Phonology, Vol. II: Gesture, Segment, Prosody* 335–358. Cambridge: Cambridge University Press.

Venditti, Jennifer J., Maekawa, Kikuo and Beckman, Mary E. (2008) Prominence marking in the Japanese intonational system. In Shigeru Miyagawa and Mamoru

Saito (eds) *The Oxford Handbook of Japanese Linguistics* 456–512. Oxford: Oxford University Press.

Wagner, Michael. (2005) *Prosody and Recursion*, Department of Linguistics and Philosophy, MIT: Doctoral dissertation.

Wagner, Michael. (2010) Prosody and recursion in coordinate structures and beyond. *Natural Language and Linguistic Theory* 28 (1): 183–237.

Woodbury, Anthony. (2002) The word in Cup'ik. In R. M. W. Dixon and Alexandra Y. Aikhenvald (eds) *Word: A Cross-linguistic Typology* 79–99. Cambridge: Cambridge University Press.

10 The intonation of nominal parentheticals in Japanese

Shigeto Kawahara[a]

10.1 Introduction

Syntactic structures affect prosodic patterns, but not every detail of syntactic information seems to have an effect on prosody. The theory of the prosodic hierarchy thus maps syntactic structures to phonological, prosodic structures, and only the latter are accessible to phonological and phonetic processes (Nespor and Vogel, 1986; Selkirk, 1986). Two important questions in this research program are: what the mapping principles between syntax and phonology are, and how universal these principles are.

The issue that I take up in this paper is the cross-linguistic variation in the number of prosodic levels, focusing on the case of Japanese. Some previous work on Japanese intonation, including those on J-ToBI and X-JToBI, has not posited an Intonational Phrase (IntP), a level above a Major Phrase and below an Utterance (Beckman and Pierrehumbert, 1986; Pierrehumbert and Beckman, 1988; Maekawa *et al.*, 2002; Venditti, 2005). However, it has been proposed that an IntP plays a role in many other languages – for example, in Italian, an IntP defines a domain of spirantization (Nespor and Vogel, 1986: 205–211); in English, an IntP is signaled by so-called 'comma intonation' with a distinct pause and boundary tones (Nespor and Vogel, 1986; Selkirk, 2005). Admitting some gaps in the prosodic hierarchy in particular languages is in fact not uncommon in the literature; for example, Jun states that '[l]anguages vary in the number of prosodic units above the Word, ranging from one to three' (Jun, 2006: 15). In TobI

---

[a] Shigeto Kawahara: Rutgers University, New Brunswick, NJ, USA. Email: kawahara@rci.rutgers.edu

systems, couched within a general framework for transcribing intonational patterns (see the contributions in Jun, 2005b), different numbers of prosodic levels are posited for different languages (Jun, 2005a: 434–435).

However, although the research positing language-specific categories has achieved – and will most likely continue to achieve – descriptive success, from the viewpoint of theoretical restrictiveness, admitting language-particular gaps in the prosodic hierarchy is not desirable, especially because the prosodic hierarchy serves as 'a general organizing principle for the phonology' (Hayes, 1995: 82). It is not theoretically restrictive to admit language-particular variations at this fundamental level of phonological organization. Itô and Mester (2007, 2009, to appear, this volume) raise this problem: 'A universal hierarchy cannot easily admit language-specific gaps' (2007: 97). Another research program that shares the same fundamental concern is initiated by Selkirk (2005).[1]

To address the problem of proliferation of language-particular prosodic categories, Selkirk (2005) proposed that we should seek a theory of universal prosodic categories. In particular, she suggests that we can use syntax as a guide to search for evidence for prosodic hierarchy – to the extent that we find consistent correspondences between some syntactic edges and prosodic edges cross-linguistically, those correspondences imply general, syntax-phonology mapping principles, and we can use those principles as a guide in our prosody research (see Selkirk, 2009 for a recent reiteration of this claim). (This strategy does not assume that prosodic phrasing can be predicted solely from syntactic structures; it just postulates that syntax is one factor that affects prosodic phrasing along with other factors – see subsection 10.4.2.)

This research program advanced in Selkirk (2005) builds on the framework of the Edge-based theory of the prosodic hierarchy primarily developed by Selkirk herself (1986, 2000, 2005) and a number of other scholars (Chen, 1987; Hale and Selkirk, 1987; Selkirk and Shen, 1990; Selkirk and Tateishi, 1991; Kenstowicz and Sohn, 1997; Truckenbrodt, 1999) (see Selkirk, 2009 and Kratzer and Selkirk, 2007 for related, but different, ideas). The Edge-based theory of the syntax-phonology interface posits that certain syntactic edges correspond with certain prosodic edges, and has been formalized in terms of Generalized Alignment constraints (McCarthy and Prince, 1993) in several recent works (Truckenbrodt, 1999; Selkirk, 2000; Selkirk *et al.*, 2004). Building on the Edge-based theory, Selkirk

(2005) advances a theory of 'syntactic grounding of prosodic categories' (p. 31), and in particular proposes the mapping principles in Table 10.1. In this model, a (branching) syntactic non-maximal level corresponds to a Minor Phrase (MiP), a maximal projection level corresponds to a Major Phrase (MaP), and a syntactic Comma Phrase corresponds to an Intonational Phrase (IntP) (p. 29). (Selkirk also argues that a Prosodic Word corresponds to a morphosyntactic word, but this correspondence does not concern us much in this paper.) This paper focuses on the last correspondence, formalized as ALIGN(CommaP, IntP).

Table 10.1: Selkirk's 2005 theory of syntax-phonology mapping

Syntax	X	XP	CommaP
	↓	↓	↓
Phonology	Minor Phrase	Major Phrase	Intonational Phrase

A CommaP includes an epithet, a parenthetical phrase, a non-restrictive relative clause, etc. (Potts, 2003). To simplify a bit, the [+comma] feature conveys an independent and complete speech act (Potts, 2003). In (1) for example, an embedded CommaP, *an English teacher*, conveys an independent proposition (a) with respect to the assertion made by the main clause (b).

(1) John, an English teacher, went to a Thai restaurant.

    (a) John is an English teacher.

    (b) John went to a Thai restaurant.

CommaPs have been shown to correspond to an IntP in many languages (see below), and therefore Selkirk (2005) argues that this correspondence may be universal. Then to the extent that a CommaP exists in Japanese and that ALIGN(CommaP, IntP) is universal, we should expect that Japanese also has an IntP as well.

To address this prediction, Kawahara and Shinya (2008) investigated the intonation of multiple-clause constructions in Japanese, namely, gapping and coordination. First, they found that left edges of clauses – or left edges of CommaPs – show properties distinct from left edges of maximal projections, which in turn show distinct properties from non-maximal projection edges. For example, they found that clause edges show larger initial rise and more extensive pitch reset than VP-edges. Moreover, they found that each clause is bound by a pause and is signaled by final creakiness and final tonal lowering. They thus conclude that clause edges correspond to IntP edges in Japanese phonology and that the principles in Table 10.1 govern the prosodic organization of Japanese phonology, as expected if the syntax-phonology mapping is governed by universal principles.

This paper follows up on Kawahara and Shinya (2008) and further supports the three-way distinction found in that work. In particular, this paper tests another instance of a CommaP, namely nominal parentheticals in Japanese. This paper shows that nominal parentheticals exhibit many of the properties of the Japanese IntP documented in Kawahara and Shinya (2008).

Nominal parentheticals in Japanese are side-remarks, often introduced by connective phrases like *iwa'ba* 'so-called', *iwa'yuru* 'so-called', and *tsu'mari* 'that is'. (Here and throughout I represent Japanese accents with an apostrophe.) These phrases do not need to contain tense, and I refer to those that lack tense as nominal parentheticals. Intonational patterns of parenthetical phrases in other languages have been investigated in the literature (e.g. Downing, 1970; Cooper and Sorensen, 1981; Selkirk, 1984, 2005; Nespor and Vogel, 1986; Bolinger, 1989; Taglicht, 1998; Fagyal, 2001; Frota, 2001; Wichmann, 2001; Dehé, 2009),[2] and some of these works find evidence that parenthetical phrases form an independent IntP (Selkirk, 1984; Nespor and Vogel, 1986; Fagyal, 2001; Frota, 2001; Truckenbrodt, 2005; Dehé, 2009). However, a systematic experimental investigation of Japanese nominal parentheticals has not been performed in the literature, and the current experiment aims to fill this gap. The experiment reported below supports the position that parenthetical edges show properties distinct from maximal projection edges, as predicted by ALIGN (CommaP, IntP).

This paper, as with Kawahara and Shinya (2008), concludes that it is too soon to give up the universality of the prosodic hierarchy, and that we can use syntax as a guide for our experimental research to pursue the universality of the prosodic hierarchy. All in all, this paper demonstrates that an explicit theory of the syntax-phonology interface can inform us about where to look in search of evidence for particular prosodic levels.

10.2 Method

10.2.1 Background

First, to illustrate the experimental design, some background discussion on basic Japanese accentual patterns is in order. Accents are (generally) lexically contrastive, and are realized as pitch falls (H*L). Words can be unaccented. An (accented) word and a following particle form a MiP (minor phrase) (Selkirk and Tateishi, 1988; Kubozono, 1993), which is signaled by an initial LH rise. This initial rise is realized on the first two moras of a MiP, unless the initial mora is accented, in which case the first two moras show the accentual H*L. See Pierrehumbert and Beckman (1988) for a more comprehensive description of Japanese intonational phonology.

The aim of the experiment was to test the different behaviors of the three syntactic boundaries in Table 10.1, following Kawahara and Shinya (2008). To do so, this experiment first investigated two major F0-related phonetic correlates of the left edges of prosodic levels identified by Kawahara and Shinya (2008) and earlier work. One is the degree of pitch reset across a boundary: generally, given two consecutive H-tones, the second H-tone is realized lower than the first. Across a higher boundary, the amount of this lowering is smaller i.e. pitch reset is more extensive (Ladd, 1988, 1990; Selkirk and Tateishi, 1991; Selkirk *et al.*, 2004; Truckenbrodt, 2005; Kawahara and Shinya, 2008). Another phonetic correlate of phrasal level is magnitude of initial rise: the stronger the prosodic boundary, the larger the initial rise (Truckenbrodt, 2002, 2005; Selkirk *et al.*, 2003; Selkirk, 2005; Kawahara and Shinya, 2008). In addition, Kawahara and Shinya (2008) found that sentential clauses, corresponding to distinct IntPs, are separated by a substantial pause and final tonal lowering. The following experiment sets out to use these cues to test prosodic phrasing of Japanese nominal parentheticals.

10.2.2 Stimuli

To test prosodic phrasing of nominal parentheticals in Japanese, four sets of three sentences were created. Within each set, the first and second words had the same number of moras and accent placement in all sentences. The first and the second words were separated by three types of syntactic boundaries: a noun boundary, a VP boundary or a parenthetical boundary, as schematized in (2). While the primary focus of this experiment was the distinction between the VP boundary condition and the parenthetical condition, and while the distinction between a noun boundary and a VP boundary has been investigated in several papers before (Selkirk and Tateishi, 1991; Selkirk *et al.*, 2003, 2004; Kawahara and Shinya 2008), the current experimental paradigm nevertheless included the second comparison to test the generality of the claim in Table 10.1.

(2) Schematic illustration of the three conditions

     (a) xx'xx [Noun xx'xx (Noun boundary condition)

     (b) xx'xx [VP xx'xx (VP boundary condition)

     (c) xx'xx [Par xx'xx (Parenthetical boundary condition)

Among the four sets of stimuli, in one sentence in one set, accents varied too much between the speakers in one sentence, and hence the entire set was dropped. The stimulus sentences of the remaining three sets are given in (3)–(5). Within each set, the first word and second word were separated by a noun boundary, a VP boundary, and a parenthetical boundary. The first and second words only contained light syllables to control for syllable weight. The distances between the accent in the first word and the accent in the second word were also controlled in terms of mora and syllable counts. The first two syllables of the first two words only contained sonorants so that F0 contours could be measured. All words had non-initial accents because initially-accented words do not show initial rises.

(3) Set A

  (a)   Nomi'ya-no [Noun awa'uri-no   Mori'mura-ni   deatta.
       bar-GEN   millet-seller-GEN Morimura-DAT   met
       '(I) met Morimura who is a millet seller at a bar.'

  (b)   Nomi'ya-ni [VP   ame'uri-no   Mori'shita-o   shootai-shita.
       bar-DAT   candy-seller-GEN Morishita-ACC   invited
       '(I) invited Morishita who is a candy seller to a bar.'

  (c)   Ae'mono   [Par   iwa'yuru   gomayo'goshi-o   tsukuttemita.
       mixed-salad   that is   sesame salad-ACC   made
       'I made mixed salad, that is, sesame salad.'

(4) Set B

(a) Nomi'ya-no [Noun oni'giri-to   i'ngen-ga   nusumaremashita.

     bar-GEN   rice ball-and   kidney bean-NOM   stolen

     'A rice ball and kidney beans were stolen from a bar.'

(b) Nomi'ya-ga [VP ume'ya-no   ori'jinaru-o   maneshimashita.

     bar-NOM   Umeya (place name)-GEN original   mimicked

     'The bar mimicked an original product of Umeya'

(c) Nara'matsu [Par iwa'ba   senne'nmatsu-o   sagashimashita.

     Nara pine tree   that is   thousand-year-old pine tree-ACC   looked for

     'I looked for the Nara pine tree, that is, thousand-year-old pine tree.'

(5) Set C

(a) Ame'ya-no [Noun ami'do-no   daidokoro-ga   kowaremashita.

     candy seller-GEN   screen-GEN   kitchen-NOM   broke

     'A kitchen with a screen at a candy seller broke.'

(b) Nira'ya-ga [VP ame'ya-no   zarameae-o   mochidashita.

     Leek seller-NOM   candy seller-GEN   candy mix-ACC   brought out

     'The leek seller stole the candy mix from the candy seller.'

(c) Ani'yome [Par   iwa'yuru   giri-no   ane-o   tsureteitta.

     Brother's wife   that is   in-law-GEN   sister-ACC   took

'   (I) took my brother's wife, that is, my sister in law (to somewhere).'

These stimuli were written in Japanese orthography on index cards. Parenthetical phrases were surrounded by em-dashes, following the standard practice in Japanese writing. Em-dashes, rather than commas, were used because commas can be used for other purposes, but em-dashes are used specifically for parenthetical expressions. No punctuation marks were used to indicate noun and VP boundaries.

10.2.3 Speakers and recording

Nine Japanese speakers participated in this study (HK, FG, PE, KL, PO, MJ, QS, KW, and ZZ). Five of them were female (HK, FG, PO, MJ, QS) and four of them were male (PE, KL, KW, ZZ). All speakers were from Tokyo or surrounding areas and spoke the standard dialect of Japanese. The first three speakers were recorded through a VR88 Velocity Ribbon microphone (Samson) amplified via a USB-pre ver. 1.5 using Audacity (Sound Devices, LCC). The other six speakers were recorded using a Marantz digital recorder (Sennheiser, PMD 6701F1B). The speech was automatically digitized upon recording with 44k sampling rate. The recording took place in sound-attenuated, quiet rooms. All the speakers first started with a practice run when they familiarized themselves with the sentences. During the practice run, they all confirmed the accentual patterns of the target sentences. After the practice run, they repeated the sentences 10 times in total, and the order of the items was randomized between each repetition. They were encouraged to read out the sentences at their comfortable speech level. In case they stumbled in the middle of a sentence, they were asked to start over again. Speakers took a short break between each repetition. Including pre-experimental explanation and debriefing, the overall experiment took about half an hour per participant.

10.2.4 Measurement

F0 contours were measured by Pitch Works (SciCon R & D), using autocorrelation for F0 calculation. Figures 10.1–10.3 show representative F0 contours for each condition based on Speaker HK's speech. Measurement points are shown by H and L (illustrative sound pictures in this paper were created using Praat: Boersma and Weenink (1999–2010); Boersma (2001)). Peaks and valleys for all pre-verbal elements were measured. For the noun and VP boundary conditions, the trailing L of the accentual H*L in the first word and the phrase-initial L% of the second word (or MiP) merged together, so only one point was measured (see Pierrehumbert and Beckman (1988) for the distribution of these tones in Japanese). For the parenthetical boundary condition, due to the presence of the pause (see Section 10.3.5), these two L-tones were separated and hence measured separately. Peaks on verbs were not measured because no visible peaks were available due to heavy downstep and sentence-final creakiness.

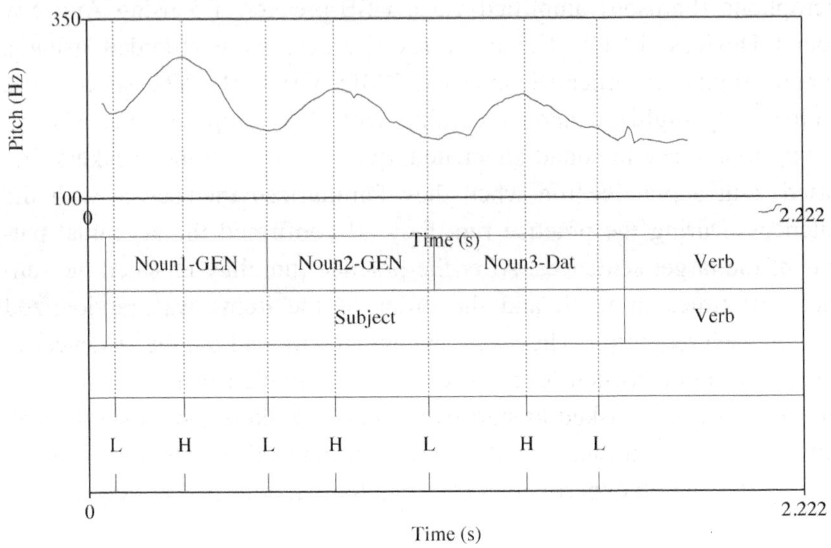

Figure 10.1: A representative contour of the noun boundary condition.

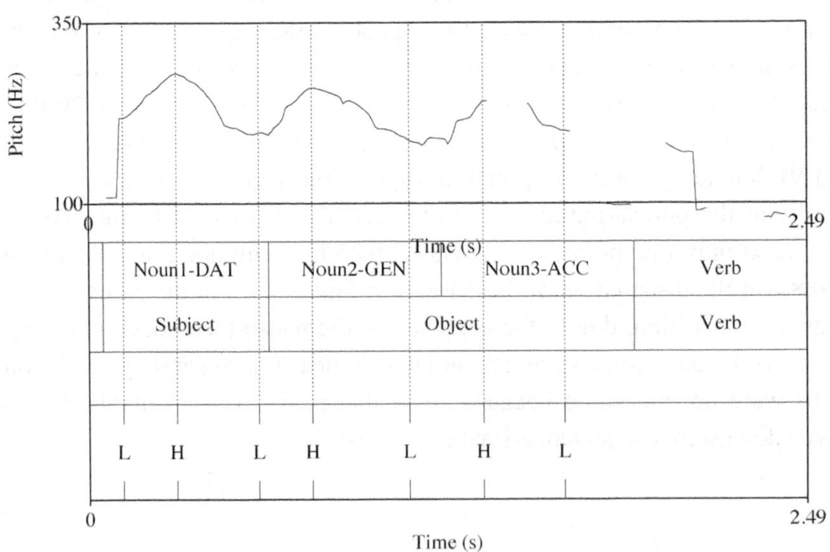

Figure 10.2: A representative contour of the VP boundary condition.

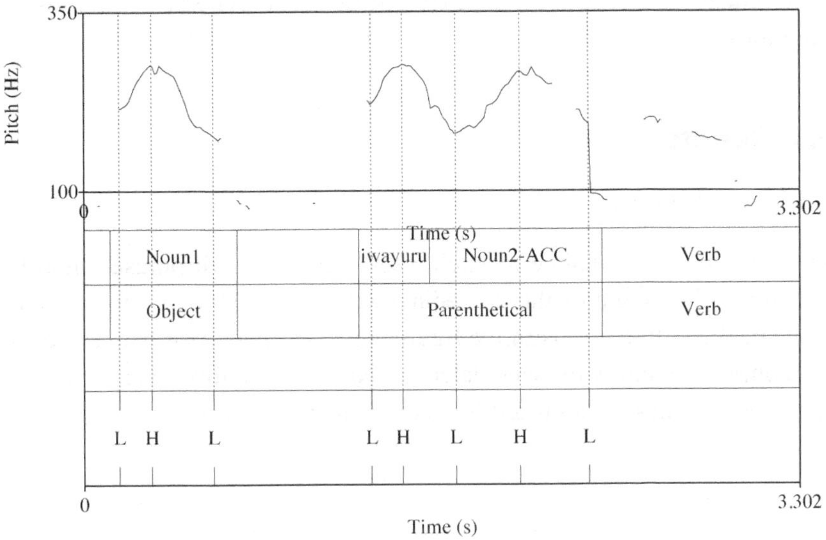

Figure 10.3: A representative contour of the parenthetical boundary condition.

From the pitch values obtained, two major phonetic correlates of prosodic levels mentioned above – pitch reset and initial rise – were calculated.

10.2.5 Statistical analyses

The effect of the three different boundaries on the calculated measures was statistically assessed via multivariate ANOVA (MANOVA). The dependent variable was a matrix in which set differences were encoded as separate column vectors and the main independent variable was the three boundary conditions. The model also included speaker as an independent variable as well as its interaction with the boundary conditions. Although we do observe inter-speaker differences, these differences are not of particular interest and will not be discussed due to space limitation. These variables were instead included in the statistical model to soak up variance in the dependent variable. The general MANOVA was followed by more specific comparisons with appropriate degrees of Bonferroni adjustments. To avoid the inflation of Type 1 errors, multiple comparisons of all conditions for all speakers were avoided. All statistical analyses were performed using R (R

Development Core Team, 1993–2010), which also generated the illustrative graphs.

10.3 Results

10.3.1 Pitch reset

Figure 10.4 plots the degree of pitch reset – the height of phrase-initial H-tones minus the height of the immediately preceding H-tone – for each set for all speakers. In the illustrative figures in this paper, error bars represent 95% confidence intervals, calculated based on variability over 10 repetitions. Y-axis scales are adjusted for each speaker.

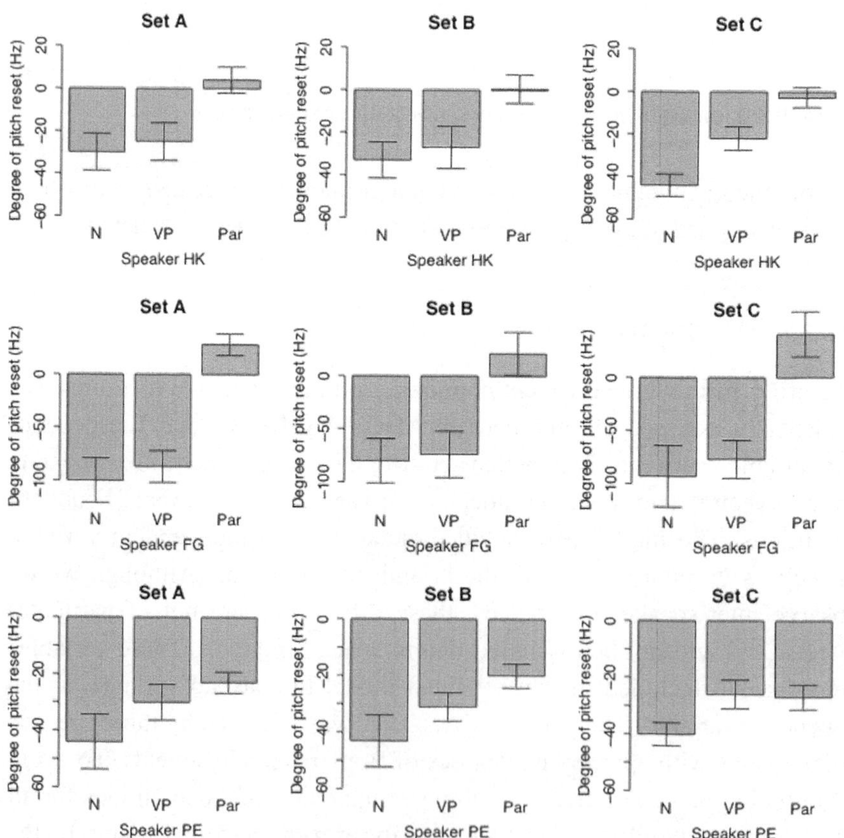

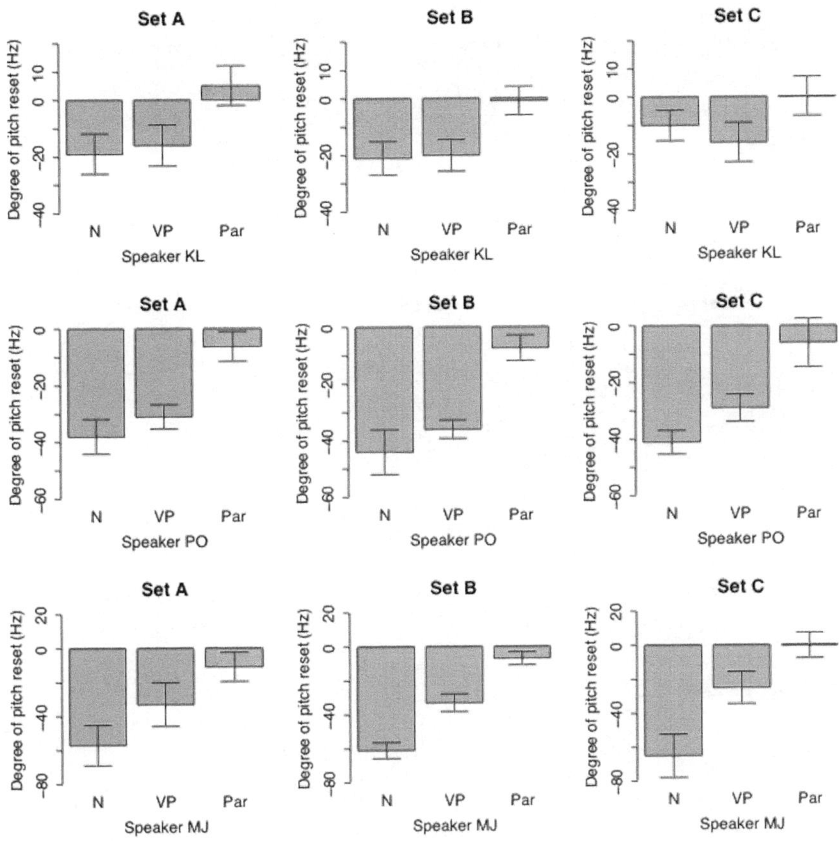

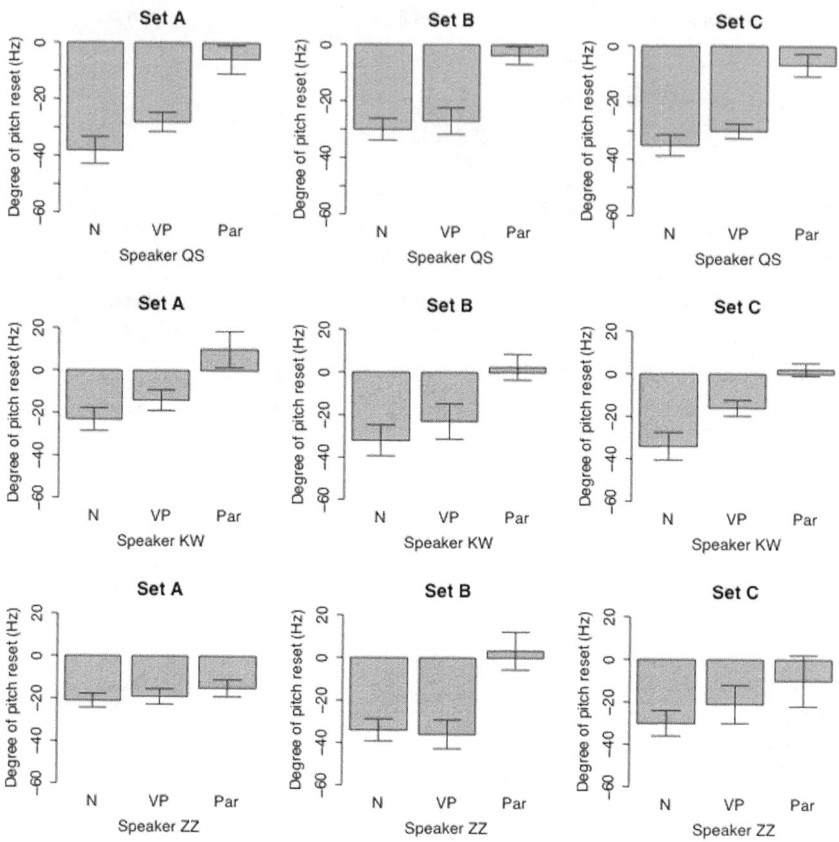

Figure 10.4: The degree of pitch reset for each speaker for each set. Error bars represent 95% confidence intervals across 10 repetitions. The y-axis scales are adjusted for each speaker.

The phrase-initial H-tones were lowest with respect to the preceding tones when only a noun boundary intervened; the degree of pitch reset was stronger when a VP boundary intervened, and it was strongest when a parenthetical boundary intervened. There were only a few exceptions; the differences between the noun boundary condition and the VP boundary condition were not observed in, for example, Set B of Speaker FG, and the direction was reversed in Set C of Speaker KL; the differences between the VP boundary condition and the parenthetical condition were not observed in Set C of Speaker PE. However, in the majority of comparisons, we observe the pitch reset hierarchy, N < VP < Par. In fact, the pitch reset across a parenthetical boundary was almost complete – that is, the parenthetical-initial H was almost as high as the preceding H – for all speakers but Speaker PE. Speaker PE nevertheless showed more extensive pitch reset across a parenthetical boundary than across a VP boundary, at least in Set A and Set B.

The general MANOVA comparing the three boundary conditions was significant ($F(2,264) = 29.4$, $p < 0.001$). The subsequent post-hoc analyses comparing the difference between the noun boundary condition and the VP boundary condition and the difference between the VP boundary condition and the parenthetical boundary condition both revealed significant differences ($F(1,176) = 3.2$, $p = 0.02$, $F(1,176) = 56.2$, $p < 0.001$, respectively).

10.3.2 Initial rise

Next we turn to the discussion of initial rise. The height of phrase-initial L-tones was subtracted from the height of phrase-initial H-tones in the three boundary conditions. Figure 10.5 presents the results.

VP-initial rises were generally higher than noun-initial rises, although we see some cases in which the difference was not substantial (e.g. Set B of Speaker FG and Set C of Speaker PE) and also a case in which the direction was reversed (Set B of Speaker ZZ). However, surprisingly, parenthetical-initial rises were generally not higher than VP-initial rises, except for Speaker FG who showed larger initial rises in the parenthetical condition than in the VP condition.

The general MANOVA turned out to be significant ($F(2,164) = 2.67$, $p < 0.05$), and the difference between the noun-initial rises and the VP-initial rises was also significant ($F(1,176) = 3.91$, $p < 0.01$). The difference between the VP-initial rises and the parenthetical-initial rises did not reach significance ($F(1,176) = 1.70$, *n.s.*). The difference between the noun-initial rises and the parenthetical-initial rises did not reach significance either after Bonferronization ($F(1,176) = 3.05$, $p = 0.03$).

This outcome was unexpected, because as we saw above, parenthetical-initial Hs undergo the strongest pitch reset – so why were parenthetical-initial rises not higher than the noun-initial rises or the VP-initial rises? To address this question, the next subsection looks at both the initial L and H for the three boundary conditions under discussion.

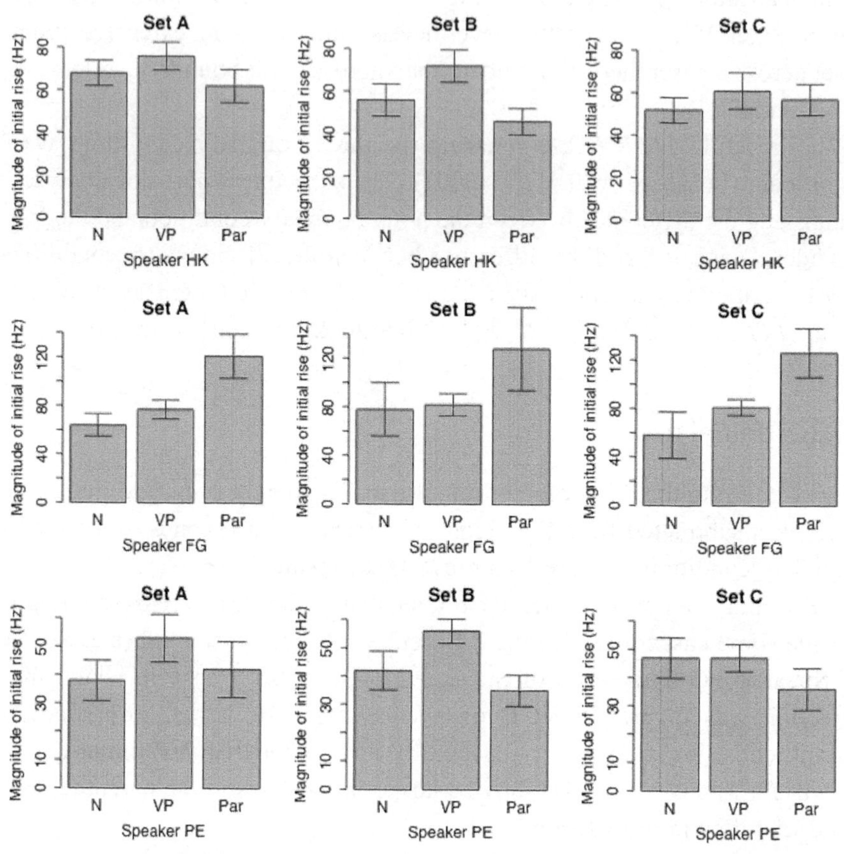

Set A
Magnitude of initial rise (Hz)
N VP Par
Speaker HK
Set B
Magnitude of initial rise (Hz)
N VP Par
Speaker HK
Set C
Magnitude of initial rise (Hz)
N VP Par
Speaker HK
Set A
Magnitude of initial rise (Hz)
N VP Par
Speaker FG
Set B
Magnitude of initial rise (Hz)
N VP Par
Speaker FG
Set C
Magnitude of initial rise (Hz)
N VP Par
Speaker FG
Set A
Magnitude of initial rise (Hz)
N VP Par
Speaker PE
Set B
Magnitude of initial rise (Hz)
N VP Par
Speaker PE
Set C
Magnitude of initial rise (Hz)
N VP Par
Speaker PE

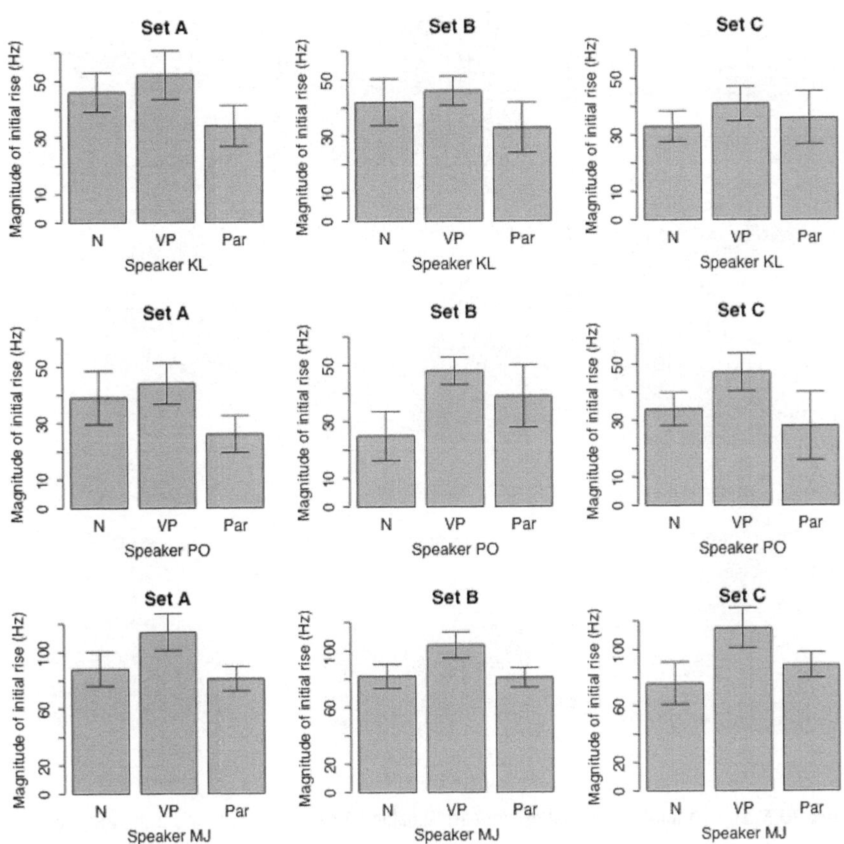

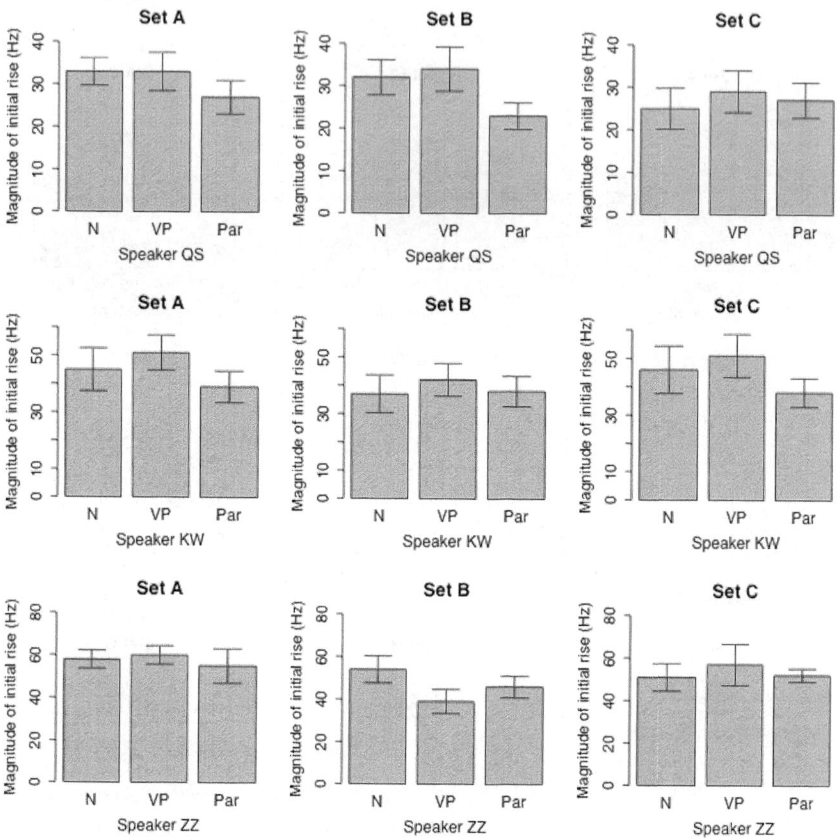

Figure 10.5: The magnitude of initial rise for each speaker for each set. The y-axis scales are adjusted for each speaker.

10.3.3 Initial L- and H-tones

Looking at L-tones first, the boundary condition affected the height of L-tones ($F(2,264) = 5.07$, $p < 0.001$) (due to space limitation, figures are not shown). More specifically, L-tones were slightly higher in the VP-initial positions than in the noun-initial positions ($F(1,176) = 3.29$, $p = 0.02$) (see also Subsection 10.3.4), and the L-tones in parenthetical-initial positions were higher than those in the VP-initial positions ($F(1,176) = 5.08$, $p < 0.01$). The height of H-tones was also affected by the boundary conditions ($F(2,264) = 6.79$, $p < 0.001$). The H-tones were higher in the VP-initial positions than in the noun-initial positions ($F(1,176) = 4.20$, $p < 0.01$) and also higher in the parenthetical-initial positions than in the VP-initial positions ($F(1,176) = 3.99$, $p < 0.01$). In other words, both L-tones and H-tones were raised in the parenthetical-initial positions.[3]

10.3.4 Final lowering

We now turn our attention to preceding materials. The three-way distinction motivated above also implies differences in the preceding materials. Assuming the EXHAUSTIVITY constraints, which require that a prosodic level *n* immediately dominates a prosodic level *n*–1 (Selkirk, 1995, 1996), material preceding a boundary is by default parsed as the same category that parses the post-boundary materials. Therefore, if parenthetical phrases are parsed as IntPs, then materials preceding the parenthetical phrases should be parsed as IntPs.

This prediction was tested using final tonal lowering. Kawahara and Shinya (2008) found that clause-final (i.e. IntP-final) tones are systematically lowered. If parenthetical phrases are separated by IntP boundaries, then it predicts that the L-tones before the parenthetical phrases are lowered. In Figures 10.1–10.3, we see that this prediction may indeed be borne out, as the pre-parenthetical L-tone looks lower than the other two corresponding L-tones. To test the prediction statistically, Figure 10.6 shows the averages of pre-boundary L-tones.

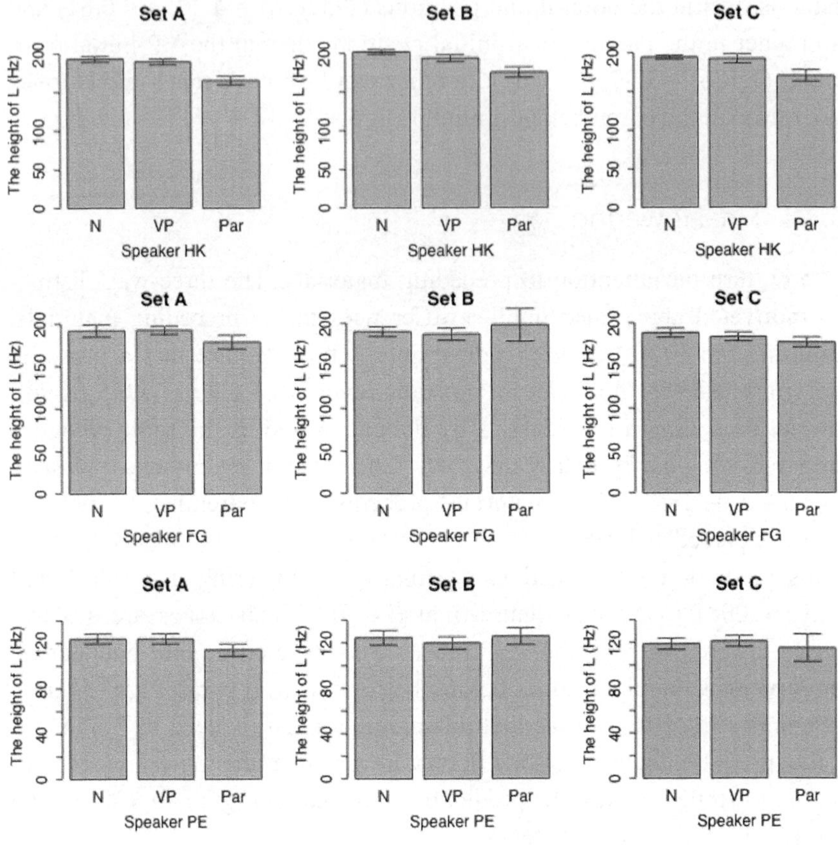

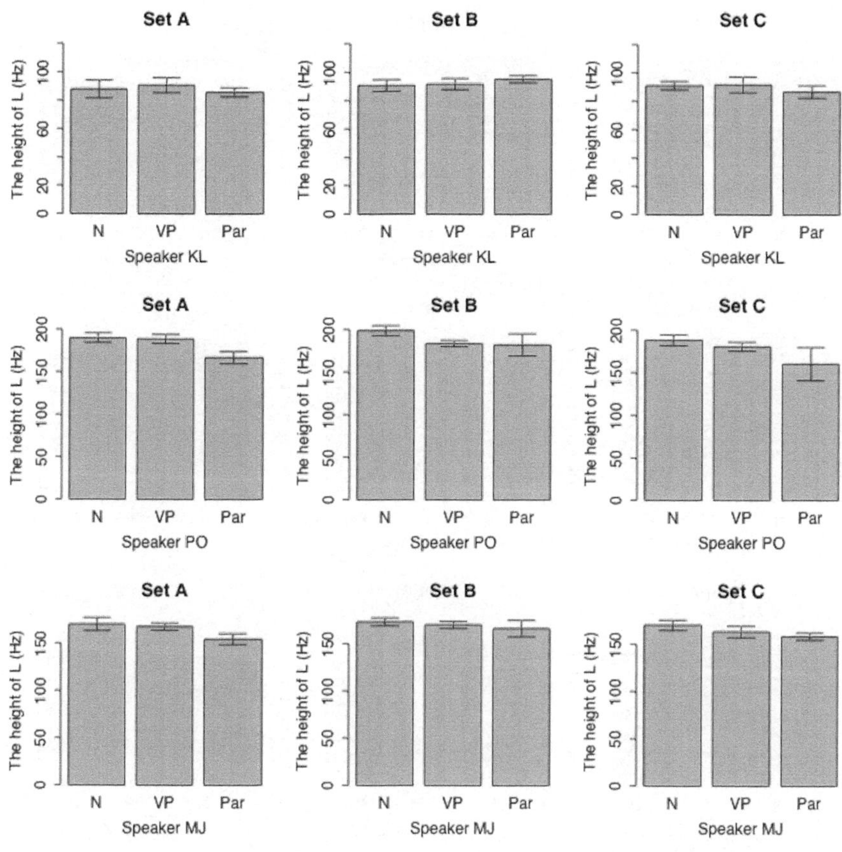

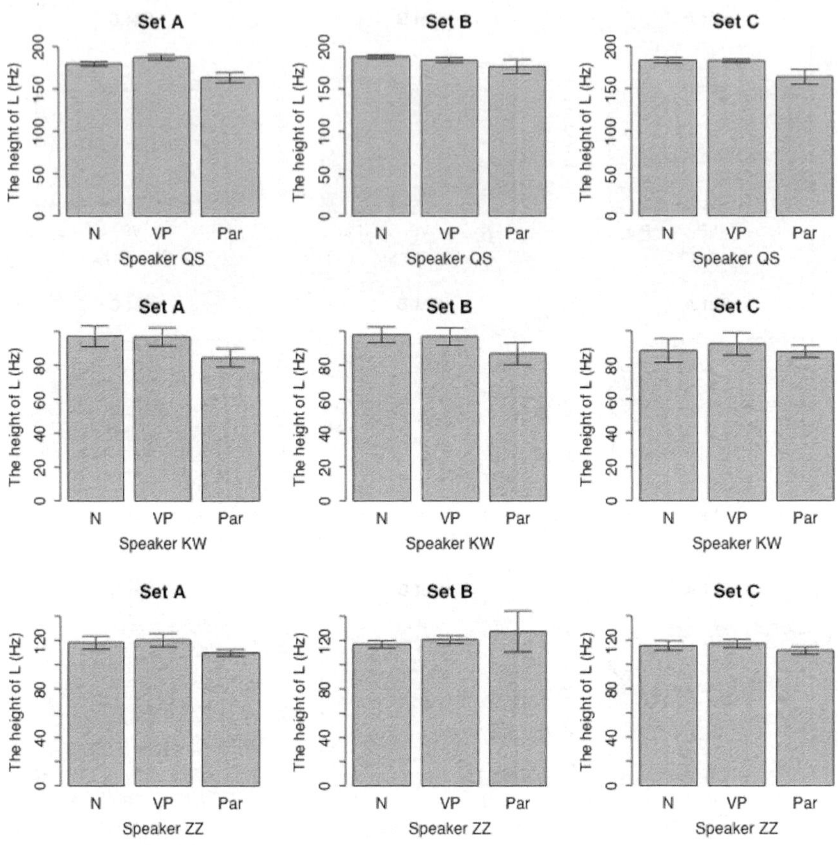

Figure 10.6: The height of L-tones in the three pre-boundary conditions. The y-axis scales are adjusted for each speaker.

The general MANOVA revealed a statistical difference among the three boundary conditions ($F(2,264) = 10.89$, $p < 0.001$). Noun-initial Ls and VP-initial Ls were comparable in height, although overall the VP-initial L-tones were slightly higher than noun-initial L-tones, as we saw in Subsection 10.3.3 ($F(1,176) = 3.29$, $p = 0.02$). More importantly, pre-parenthetical L-tones were lower than noun-initial L-tones ($F(1,175) = 10.58$, $p < 0.001$), although we observe some reversals (e.g. Set B of Speakers FG, PE and ZZ). This difference thus shows that there is final lowering right before the parenthetical phrases, which is predicted if parenthetical phrases are separated by an IntP boundary.

10.3.5 Pause and creakiness

Finally we turn to non-tonal cues. Kawahara and Shinya (2008) found that in multiple-clause constructions in which each clause corresponds to an IntP, each clause was obligatorily separated by a pause. Figures 10.7–10.9 compare spectrograms of representative tokens of the three conditions from the current experiment, based on utterances of Speaker QS. There were no substantial pauses anywhere in the noun and VP conditions, whereas in the parenthetical condition, there was a substantial pause before – but not after – the parenthetical clause. (The short silence we observe near the end of Noun2 in the noun boundary condition is the closure phase of [t] in the comitative particle [to].) The presence of a pause at the left edge of a parenthetical clause was consistently observed in all tokens for all speakers with a few exceptions (see Table 10.2). Some speakers inserted a pause both before and after a parenthetical clause, though the pause at the left edge was longer than the pause at the right edge, as illustrated in Figure 10.10 (based on Speaker MJ's speech). In such cases, interestingly, the accusative particle [o] was phrased with the following verb rather than with the preceding noun.

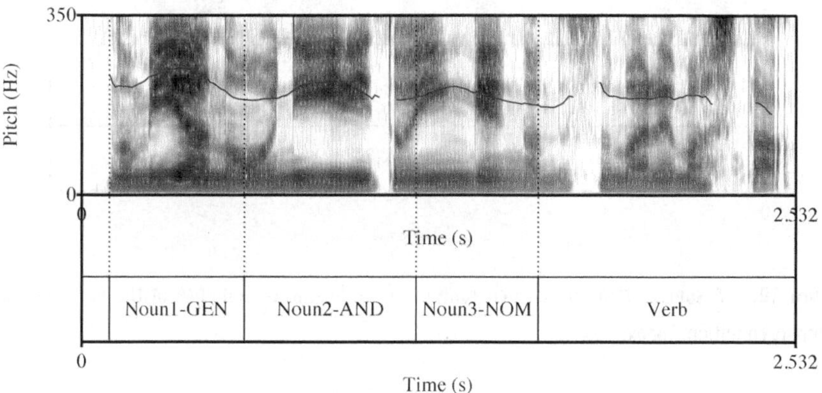

Figure 10.7: A spectrogram and a pitch contour of an illustrative sentence of the noun boundary condition. Speaker QS.

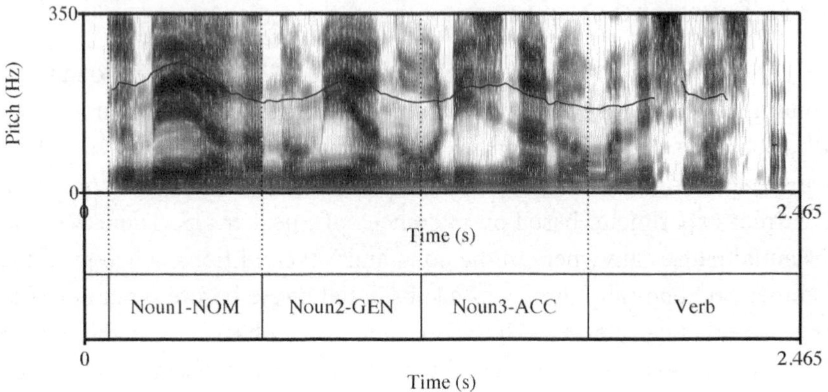

Figure 10.8: A spectrogram and a pitch contour of an illustrative sentence of the VP boundary condition. Speaker QS.

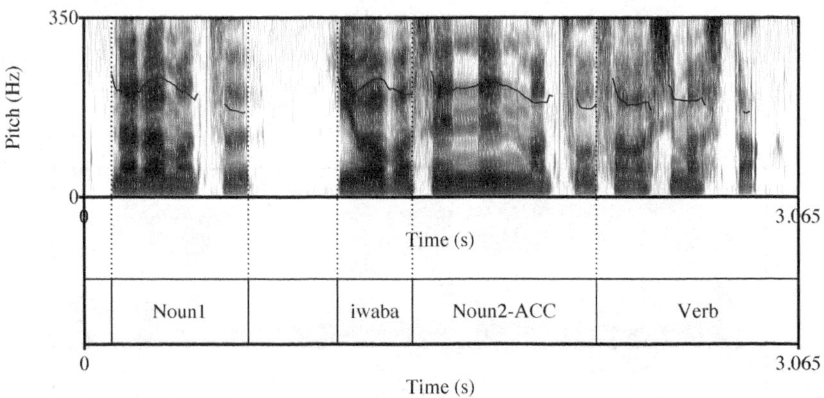

Figure 10.9: A spectrogram and a pitch contour of an illustrative sentence of the parenthetical boundary condition. Speaker QS.

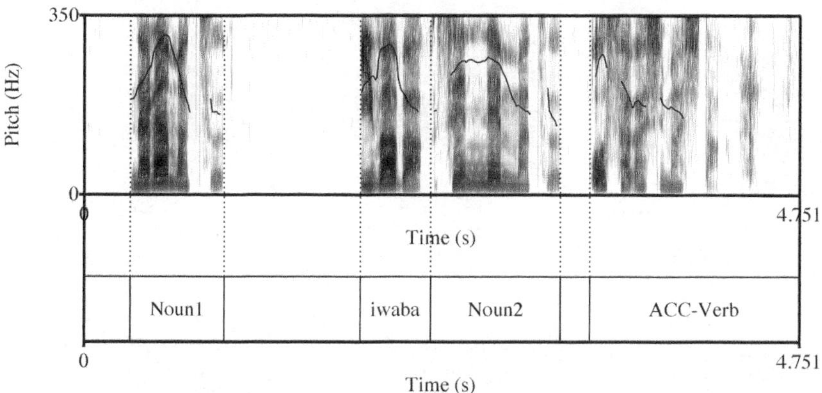

Figure 10.10: A spectrogram and a pitch contour of an illustrative sentence of the parenthetical condition. Speaker MJ.

The presence of pauses before and after the parentheticals was assessed by inspecting the spectral (dis-)continuity in spectrograms with the aid of auditory impression, and when pauses were detectable, their durations were measured using Praat (Boersma and Weenink, 1999–2010; Boersma, 2001). The result is shown in Table 10.2. All speakers always had a pause before parenthetical phrases except for Speaker ZZ who did not show detectable gaps in four out of 30 tokens.[4] Speakers FG and KW always had a pause at the right edge of parentheticals, whereas Speakers HK, KL, QS, and ZZ rarely or never did. Speakers PE, PO and MJ showed a pause at the right edge about 70-80% of the tokens.

Table 10.2: The number of utterances that show pauses (out of 30 utterances).

Speakers	before	after	Speakers	before	after
HK	30	0	MJ	30	24
FG	30	30	QS	30	0
PE	30	22	KW	30	30
KL	30	1	ZZ	26	1
PO	30	21			

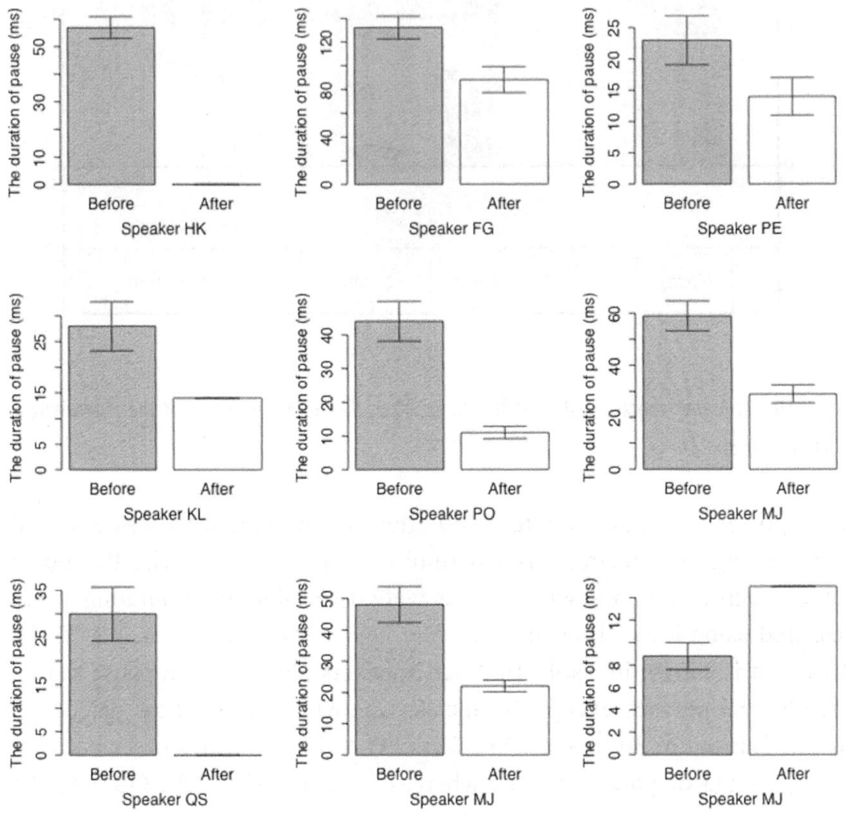

Figure 10.11: The durations of pauses before and after parentheticals. The y-axis scales are adjusted for each speaker. Error bars are not shown if there is only one relevant item.

Now turning to durations, as exemplified in the spectrogram in Figure 10.10, pauses at left edges were longer than those at right edges, and this pattern was generally true, as shown in Figure 10.11.[5] This difference is statistically significant according to ANOVA with positions and speakers as independent variables ($F(1,376) = 63.1$, $p < 0.001$). We observe one reversal in Speaker ZZ, but this reversal is not a robust counterexample, as this speaker showed only one token in which there was a detectable pause after the parenthetical phrase.

Finally, Kawahara and Shinya (2008) observe that vowels before pauses were often creaky. In the current experiment, this correlation was also observed. The distribution of creaky vowels is illustrated in Figures 10.12 and 10.13 based on an utterance by Speaker PO. As observed, the vowels before pauses – the one before the parenthetical phrase and the one at the end of the parenthetical phrase – showed some creakiness, as indicated by their irregular glottal pulses as well as excitation of high frequency energy.[6]

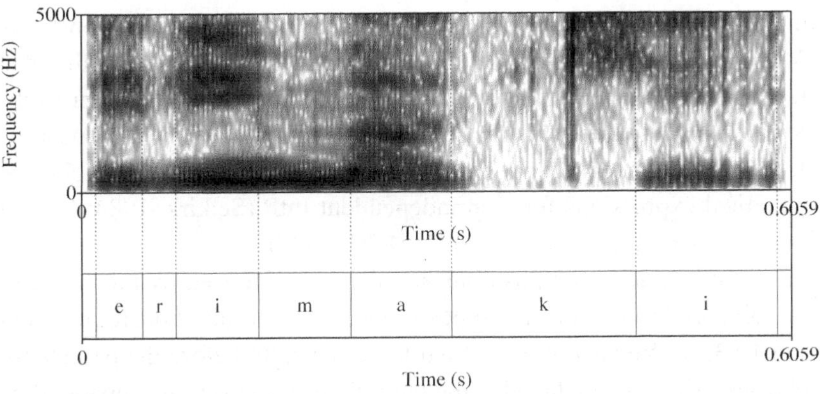

Figure 10.12: A spectrogram of a pre-parenthetical phrase. Speaker PO.

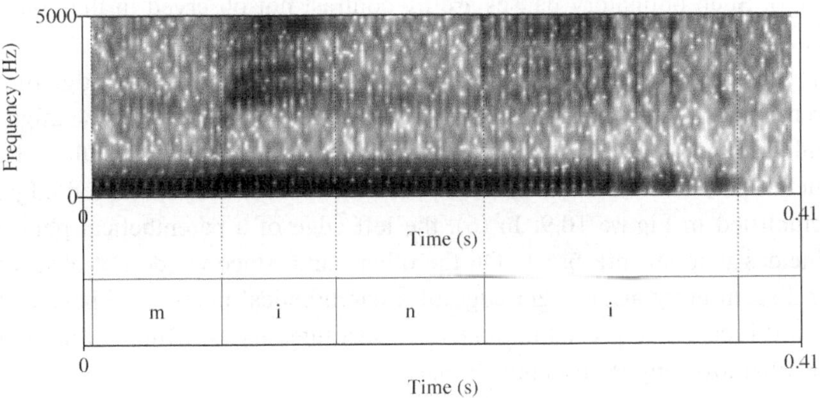

Figure 10.13: A spectrogram of a phrase at the end of a parenthetical phrase. Speaker PO.

10.4 Discussion

10.4.1 Prosodic structure

The observed hierarchy N < VP < Par in pitch reset (Subsection 10.3.1) supports the hypothesis that a noun boundary, a VP boundary and a parenthetical boundary each corresponds to a MiP boundary, a MaP boundary, and an IntP boundary, respectively. In other words, we observe a three-way distinction in terms of pitch reset between the noun boundary condition, the VP boundary condition, and the parenthetical condition, and this distinction motivates the postulation of three distinctive levels of the prosodic hierarchy. This three-way distinction in turn supports Selkirk's proposal in Table 10.1, and also accords well with observations in other languages that parenthetical expressions form an independent IntP (Selkirk, 1984; Nespor and Vogel, 1986; Truckenbrodt, 2005; Dehé, 2009).

The parenthetical-initial positions are also characterized by raising of L-tones, compared to the VP-initial positions and noun-initial positions (Subsection 10.3.3). We also observe final lowering right before the parenthetical phrases, which is predicted if the parenthetical phrases are separated by an IntP boundary (Subsection 10.3.4). Finally, substantial pauses signal the onset – and sometimes the offset – of parenthetical phrases (Subsection 10.3.5). Such obligatory pauses are by contrast not observed in the noun-initial or VP-initial positions.

These experimental results support the hypothesis that the left edge of a parenthetical phrase corresponds to an IntP edge, as predicted by the alignment constraint ALIGN-L(CommaP, IntP). We can therefore postulate the structure in (6) for cases in which a pause is observed only at the left edge, exemplified in Figure 10.9. In (6), the left edge of a parenthetical phrase coincides with an IntP break. On the other hand, since we do not observe any discontinuity at the right edge of a parenthetical phrase, we postulate no IntP break. The preceding material constitutes its own IntP, exhibiting IntP-final lowering (Subsection 10.3.4).

(6)

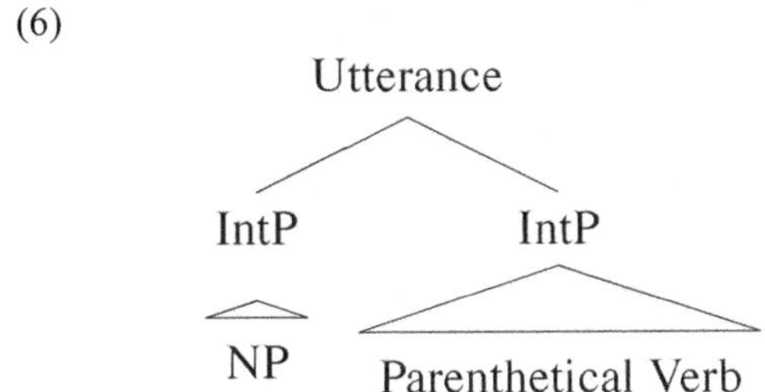

For cases in which a pause is present at both edges, I postulate the structure in (7). This structure involves recursive IntPs (Ladd, 1986; Frota, 2001). The lower IntP is aligned with both edges of a parenthetical phrase, which explains the substantial breaks before and after the parenthetical phrase.[7] The higher IntP contains both the parenthetical phrase and the following verb (I assume that the verb is parsed as MaP due to the EXHAUSTIVITY constraint). Since the left edge of a parenthetical phrase coincides with two boundaries and the right edge corresponds with one boundary, the left edge induces a longer pause (cf. Selkirk's 1984 notion of silent demibeats).[8]

(7)

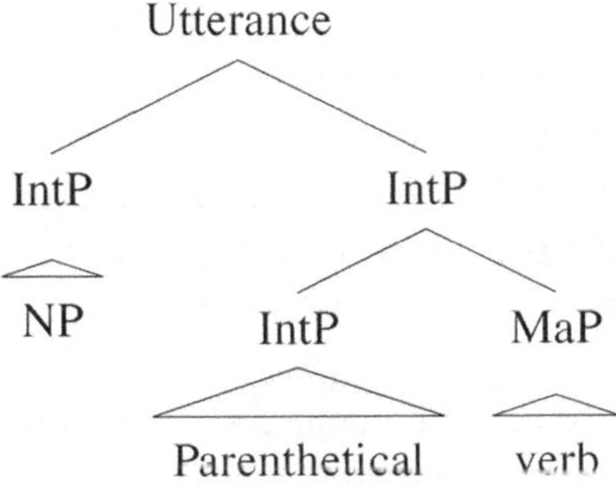

It is also conceivable to posit a structure in (8) for cases in which pauses appeared at both edges. However, this structure does not explain why pauses before the parenthetical phrases are consistently longer than pauses after the parenthetical phrases. In other words, the medial IntP in (8) is equally cohesive to the preceding material and to the following material, but in fact, the preceding material is separated by a more substantial pause from the parenthetical phrase than the following material.

(8)

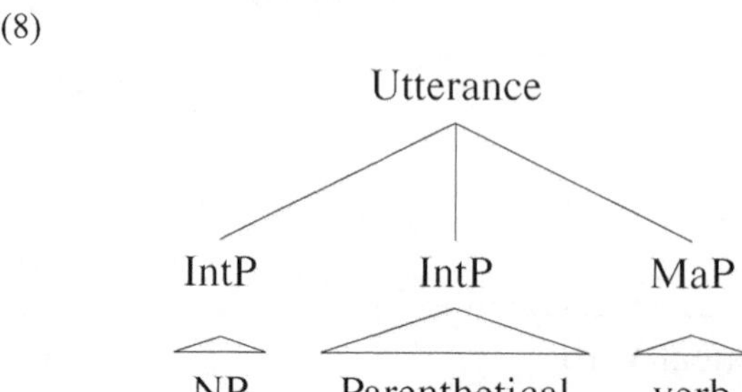

In summary, Japanese parenthetical phrases show a variable pattern of phrasing on its right edge, but the left edge is consistently aligned with an IntP edge.[9] It is interesting to observe that in both (6) and (7) it is the left edge of a parenthetical phrase in Japanese that always corresponds to an IntP edge, and the right edge is only optionally aligned with an IntP edge. In English on the other hand, the right edge of CommaPs is aligned with an IntP edge (Dehé, 2009; Taglicht, 1998, references cited therein; Selkirk, 2005).[10]

10.4.2   Directions for future research

Although the current experiment has revealed some aspects of parenthetical phrases in the Japanese intonational system, it is exploratory and leaves several questions for future research. The first question is why parenthetical-initial L-tones are raised. Kawahara and Shinya (2008) did not find raising of L-tones at the beginning of each clause, at least not to a degree such that the magnitude of initial rises is as small as that of noun-initial or VP-initial rises.

The second major issue that should be pursued in future research is the effect of orthography in intonation. The current study shows that orthography is not the only factor in that em-dashes before the parenthetical phrase always induced a pause whereas those after the parenthetical phrase did not. However, several questions arise: is the presence of pauses affected by orthography?; are the other prosodic correlates of IntP we found influenced by orthography?; what about the effect of orthography on intonation in languages other than Japanese? (see e.g. Fagyal, 2001; Frota, 2001; Watson and Gibson, 2004 for relevant discussion). These questions are beyond the scope of this paper, but one way to address these questions is to look at natural speech rather than read speech.

In fact it is an interesting question whether we observe the same three-way distinction in natural utterances. The current data are based on experimental elicitation, and so were the data in Kawahara and Shinya (2008). While it may be difficult to control for various factors in natural utterances (e.g. the phonological distances between two H-tones, the accent placement and the syllable structures of the target words, etc.), it would be interesting to investigate the properties of parenthetical phrases in natural utterances (see Dehé 2009 for a study of English parenthetical based on natural speech).

Finally, the experiment shows that a syntactic parenthetical phrase is left-aligned with an IntP. But does this mean that syntactic structures and prosodic structures are isomorphic (i.e. prosodic structures are superfluous)? Not necessarily – the IntP in (6) and the higher IntP in (7) contain both the parenthetical phrase and the verb in exclusion of its object. This grouping implies that the syntax-phonology mapping is not perfect – only the left edge, but not the right edge, of a parenthetical phrase needs to be obligatorily aligned with an IntP in Japanese phonology. Moreover, much work on the formation of intonational phrasing shows a variety of non-syntactic factors affecting the phrasing of parenthetical elements – for example, IntP phrasing has been argued to depend on rate of speech in English (Nespor and Vogel, 1986; Selkirk, 2005, and references cited therein; Dehé, 2009); information structure and constituency length are other factors that seem to affect prosodic phrasing (e.g. Selkirk and Tateishi, 1988; Selkirk *et al.*, 2004; Selkirk, 2005). This paper is limited in its scope in that it focused on the mapping between syntax and phonology. Future research should thus investigate the interaction of syntactic structures as well as phonological and other features in shaping the prosodic patterns of parentheticals in Japanese.

10.4.3 Brief remarks on a recursive, label-less model of phrasing

Before closing this paper, brief remarks on Itô and Mester's recent model of phrasing (2007, 2009, to appear, this volume) are in order. Although the current research was framed within the framework of the Selkirkian tradition of prosodic phonology, Selkirk (2005) and Itô and Mester address the same theoretical concern: the proliferation of language-particular prosodic categories. As a solution, Itô and Mester propose to reduce the difference between the MaP and the MiP to a difference in projection levels of the same phrase ϕ: MaP is simply a higher projection of ϕ than MiP. Although their model is not yet explicit about phonetic implementation such as pitch reset, the results reported in this paper offer two implications for their model.

First, in their model, the phonetic implementation module must be able to refer to the number of layers so that pitch reset at a higher level of ϕ is stronger than the pitch reset at a lower level of ϕ (the difference that I framed as a difference between the MaP and the MiP). The size of initial rise must also increase as a function of layers of projections of ϕ.

Second, the results also imply, as noted by Itô and Mester (to appear, this volume), that IntP must be qualitatively different from ϕ, and cannot be reduced to a projection of ϕ. If IntP were to be defined as the highest projection of ϕ, then the pause would need to be a property of the highest projection of ϕ. However, this postulation predicts (wrongly) that the structure in (7) exhibits only one pause, because IntP is defined as the highest projection of ϕ and the lower IntP in (7) cannot be an IntP by definition. More generally, defining an IntP as the highest projection of ϕ does not allow us to postulate recursive IntPs, which may be too restrictive (see Ladd, 1986; Frota, 2001; Selkirk to appear and references cited therein for other cases of recursive IntPs). Rather, IntP must be a level that qualitatively differs from ϕ, which can also be recursive as in (7) and is phonetically associated with a pause. Another piece of evidence for the qualitative difference between IntP and ϕ is the fact that IntP-final L-tones are lowered whereas no such lowering was observed at pre-VP positions (i.e. the highest projection of ϕ) (Subsection 10.3.4).

10.5 Conclusion

To conclude, left edges of parenthetical phrases show several distinct properties compared to VP edges: strong pitch reset, raising of L, and a pause (and accompanying creakiness). Moreover, materials preceding parenthetical phrases show final lowering. We have also observed differences between noun edges and VP edges in terms of degree of pitch reset and size of initial rise. This three way distinction supports Selkirk's (2005) theory of syntactic grounding of prosodic categories. Overall, this paper provides a hope that it may be too soon to give up the universality of the prosodic hierarchy, and that we can use syntax as a guide to what to look for in experimental intonation research.

Acknowledgments

This research is partly supported by a Research Council Grant from Rutgers University. The experiment reported in this paper has been presented at New York University, Rutgers University, the University of Calgary, the University of Delaware, and the University of Massachusetts, Amherst. I am grateful to the audiences at these occasions, especially Lyn Frazier, Jeff Heiz, Bill Idsardi, Satoshi Tomioka and Irene Vogel. I would also like to express my thanks to two anonymous reviewers, Aaron Braver, Toshikazu Ikuta, Jeremy Perkins and Taka Shinya for their extensive comments on earlier versions of this paper. Finally, a particular thanks goes to Lisa Selkirk and my former colleagues at UMass, Amherst, without whom I would not have been interested in intonational studies. Any remaining errors are my own.

Notes

1   Itô and Mester (2007, 2009, to appear, this volume) and Selkirk (2005) address the same theoretical issue (i.e. the proliferation of language-particular prosodic categories), although their implementations are different. I frame my study within the Selkirkian approach, and I will briefly come back to Itô and Mester's framework in Subsection 10.4.3.

2   For other various aspects of parentheticals including non-phonological ones, see the contributions in Dehé and Kavalova (2007).

3   By contrast, in some other languages, including English, French, German and Romanian, parenthetical phrases are signaled by a lower pitch range compared to the surrounding materials (Bolinger, 1989: 47 and Chapter 7; Fagyal, 2001; and Wichmann, 2001: 188).

4   In English, the opposite pattern holds: pauses are more consistently observed after a parenthetical phrase than before the phrase (Taglicht, 1998; Selkirk, 2005; Dehé, 2009).

5   Speaker FG had very long pauses before and after the parenthetical phrases. During recording, I asked her if she was deliberately lengthening the pauses, but she said that she was most comfortable with such long pauses in pronouncing parenthetical sentences.

6   Since creakiness was not the main concern of this experiment, the stimulus set did not control for vowel quality of phrase-final vowels. Controlling vowel quality in different phrase-final positions in a future experiment would enable us to assess the distribution of creakiness from a statistical perspective.

7   Both-edge alignment patterns are found in other languages including Kanakuru (Samek-Lodovici, 1998) and Maori (de Lacy, 2003).

8   The two proposed structures predict that pitch reset may be more extensive in (7) than in (6), because (7) involves two IntP boundaries at the left edge of the parenthetical phrase. To test this prediction, a post-hoc analysis was performed to compare two groups of speakers: those who always showed both edge pauses (Speakers FG and KW) and those who (almost) always show only left edge pauses (Speakers HK, KL, QS, ZZ). MANOVA compared the differences in pitch reset between the parenthetical boundary condition and VP boundary condition as an indication of how strong the parenthetical pitch reset is, and showed that the first group exhibited stronger pitch reset ($F(1,58) = 14.7$, $p < 0.001$). A comparison was also made for three speakers who showed variability (Speaker PE, PO, MJ) between cases with pauses at both edges and those with pauses only at left edges, but the difference was not significant ($F < 1$). Investigating the effect of recursivity of IntPs on pitch reset in Japanese requires a more controlled experiment.

9   The difference between (6) and (7) is derivable from the interaction of conflicting demands on intonational phrasing, which can be modeled in Optimality Theoretic terms (Prince and Smolensky, 1993/2004). The structure in (7) aligns the right edge of a parenthetical phrase with an IntP phrase, i.e., ALIGN-R(CommaP, IntP) is satisfied, but involves a recursive IntP, violating NONRECURSIVITY (Selkirk, 1995). The structure in (6) satisfies NONRECURSIVITY but does not achieve right-edge alignment. The structure in (8) can be ruled out by a binarity constraint on the level of the Utterance (see McCarthy and Prince, 1986; Selkirk, 2000; Selkirk *et al.*, 2004; Truckenbrodt, 2007, for binarity constraints on prosodic categories).

10   The same difference is observed at the Major Phrase level: Japanese shows left-edge alignment (Selkirk and Tateishi, 1991) whereas English shows right-edge alignment (Selkirk 2005: 18–19).

References

Beckman, M. and Pierrehumbert, J. (1986) Intonational structure in English and Japanese. *Phonology Yearbook* 3: 255–309.

Boersma, P. (2001) Praat, a system for doing phonetics by computer. *Glot International* 5 (9/10): 341–345.

Boersma, P. and Weenink, D. (1999–2010) *Praat: doing phonetics by computer.* A software.

Bolinger, D. L. (1989) *Intonation and its Uses: Melody in Grammar and Discourse.* London: Arnold.

Chen, M. (1987) The syntax of Xiamen tone sandhi. *Phonology Yearbook* 4: 109–150.

Cooper, W. E. and Sorensen, J. M. (1981). *Fundamental Frequency in Sentence Production.* New York: Springer.

de Lacy, P. (2003) Constraint universality and prosodic phrasing in Maori. In A. Carpenter, A. Coetzee and P. de Lacy (eds), *University of Massachusetts Occasional Papers in Linguistics 26: Papers in Optimality Theory II 59–79.* Amherst: GLSA.

Dehé, N. (2009) Clausal parentheticals, intonational phrasing, and prosodic theory. *Journal of Linguistics* 45: 569–615.

Dehé, N. and Kavalova, Y. (2007) *Parentheticals.* Amsterdam/Philadelphia, PA: John Benjamins.

Downing, B. (1970) *Syntactic Structure and Phonological Phrasing in English.* Doctoral dissertation, University of Texas, Austin.

Fagyal, Z. (2001). Intonation in utterance-medial parentheticals and the syntax-phonology interface in French. In M. Andronis, C. Ball, H. Elston and S. Neuvel (eds), *Proceedings of Chicago Linguistic Society 37 149–160.* Chicago, IL: CLS.

Frota, S. (2001) *Prosody and Focus in European Portugese: Phonological Phrasing and Intonation.* New York: Garland.

Hale, K. and Selkirk, E. (1987) Government and tonal phrasing in Papago. *Phonology Yearbook* 4: 151–183.

Hayes, B. (1995) *Metrical Stress Theory: Principles and Case Studies.* Chicago, IL: The University of Chicago Press.

Itô, J. and Mester, A. (2007) Prosodic adjunction in Japanese compounds. *Proceedings of Formal Approaches to Japanese Linguistics*, 4, 97–112.

Itô, J. and Mester, A. (2009) The onset of the prosodic word. In S. Parker (ed.), *Phonological Argumentation.* London: Equinox.

Itô, J. and Mester, A. (this volume) Recursive prosodic phrasing in Japanese. In T. Borowsky, S. Kawahara, T. Shinya and M. Sugahara (eds), *Prosody Matters 208–303.* London: Equinox Publishing.

Itô, J. and Mester, A. (to appear) Recursive prosodic phrasing in Japanese. In M. den Dikken and W. McClure (eds), *Japanese/Korean Linguistics 18*. Stanford, CA: CSLI.

Jun, S.-A. (2005a) Prosodic typology. In S.-A. Jun (ed.), *Prosodic Typology: The Phonology of Intonation and Phrasing*. Oxford: Oxford University Press.

Jun, S.-A. (ed.). (2005b) *Prosodic Typology: The Phonology of Intonation and Phrasing*. Oxford: Oxford University Press.

Jun, S.-A. (2006) Intonational phonology of Seoul Korean revisited. In T. Vance and K. Jones (eds), *Japanese/Korean Linguistics 14* 15–26. Stanford, CA: CSLI.

Kawahara, S. and Shinya, T. (2008) The intonation of gapping and coordination in Japanese: Evidence for Intonational Phrase and Utterance. *Phonetica* 65 (1–2): 62–105.

Kenstowicz, M. and Sohn, H.-S. (1997) Phrasing and focus in Northern Kyungsang Korean. In P. M. Bertinetto, L. Gaeta, G. Jetchev and D. Michaels (eds), *Certamen Phonologicum III* 137–156. Turin: Rosenberg and Sellier.

Kratzer, A. and Selkirk, E. (2007) Phase theory and prosodic spellout: The case of verbs. *The Linguistic Review* 24 (2–3): 93–135.

Kubozono, H. (1993) *The Organization of Japanese Prosody*. Tokyo: Kurosio Publishers.

Ladd, D. R. (1986) Intonational phrasing: The case for recursive prosodic structure. *Phonology Yearbook*, 3: 311–340.

Ladd, D. R. (1988) Declination 'reset' and the hierarchical organization of utterances. *Journal of the Acoustical Society of America*, 84: 530–544.

Ladd, D. R. (1990) Metrical representation of pitch register. In M. Beckman and J. Kingston (eds), *Papers in Laboratory Phonology I: Between the Grammar and Physics of Speech* 35–57. Cambridge: Cambridge University Press.

Maekawa, K., Kikuchi, H., Igarashi, Y. and Venditti, J. (2002) X-JToBI: An extended J-ToBI for spontaneous speech. *Proceedings of the 7th International Congress on Spoken Language Processing:* 1545–1548.

McCarthy, J. J. and Prince, A. (1986) *Prosodic Morphology*. (ms, University of Massachusetts and Rutgers University).

McCarthy, J. J. and Prince, A. (1993) Generalized alignment. In G. Booij and J. van Marle (eds), *Yearbook of Morphology* 79–153. Dordrecht: Kluwer. (Excerpts appear in John Goldsmith (ed.) *Essential Readings in Phonology* 102–136. Oxford: Blackwell. 1999.)

Nespor, M. and Vogel, I. (1986) *Prosodic Phonology*. Dordrecht: Foris.

Pierrehumbert, J. B. and Beckman, M. (1988) *Japanese Tone Structure*. Cambridge, MA: MIT Press.

Potts, C. (2003) *The Logic of Conventional Implicatures*. Doctoral dissertation, University of California at Santa Cruz.

Prince, A. and Smolensky, P. (1993/2004) *Optimality Theory: Constraint Interaction in Generative Grammar*. Malden and Oxford: Blackwell.

R Development Core Team. (1993–2010) *R: A Language and Environment for Statistical Computing.* Software, available at http://www.R-project.org. Vienna, Austria.

Samek-Lodovici, V. (1998) Opposite constraints: Left and right focus-alignment in Kanakuru. *Lingua* 104 (1–2): 111–130.

Selkirk, E. (1984) *Phonology and Syntax: The Relation Between Sound and Structure.* Cambridge, MA: MIT Press.

Selkirk, E. (1986) On derived domains in sentence phonology. *Phonology Yearbook,* 3: 371–405.

Selkirk, E. (1995) The prosodic structure of function words. In J. Beckman, L. Walsh Dickey and S. Urbanczyk (eds), *Papers in Optimality Theory* 439–470. Amherst, MA: GLSA.

Selkirk, E. (1996) The prosodic structure of function words. In J. L. Morgan and K. Demuth (eds), *Signal to Syntax: Bootstrapping from Speech to Grammar in Early Acquisition* 187–214. Mahwah, NJ: Lawrence Erlbaum Associates.

Selkirk, E. (2000) The interaction of constraints on prosodic phrasing. In M. Horn (ed.), *Prosody: Theory and Experiment* 231–271. Dordrecht: Kluwer Academic Publishers.

Selkirk, E. (2005) Comments on intonational phrasing in English. In S. Frota, M. Vigário and M. J. Freitas (eds), *Prosodies: With Special Reference to Iberian Languages* 11–58. Berlin: Mouton de Gruyter.

Selkirk, E. (2009) On clause and intonational phrase in Japanese. *Gengo Kenkyu* 136: 35–76.

Selkirk, E. (to appear) The syntax-phonology interface. In J. Goldsmith, R. Riggle and A. Yu (eds), *The Handbook of Phonological Theory, 2nd edition.* Oxford: Blackwell Publishing.

Selkirk, E. and Shen, T. (1990) Prosodic domains in Shanghai Chinese. In S. Inkelas and D. Zec (eds), *The Phonology-syntax Connection* 313–337. Chicago, IL: University of Chicago Press.

Selkirk, E., Shinya, T. and Kawahara, S. (2004) Phonological and phonetic effects of minor phrases length on f0 in Japanese. *Proceedings of the Second International Conference on Speech Prosody 2004,* 183–186.

Selkirk, E., Shinya, T. and Sugahara, M. (2003). Degree of initial lowering in Japanese as a reflex of prosodic structure organization. *Proceedings of the 15th International Congress of Phonetic Sciences,* 491–494.

Selkirk, E. and Tateishi, K. (1988) Constraints on minor phrase formation in Japanese. In L. MacLeod, G. Larson and D. K. Brentari (eds), *Proceedings of Chicago Linguistic Society 24* 316–336. Chicago, IL: Chicago Linguistic Society.

Selkirk, E. and Tateishi, K. (1991) Syntax and downstep in Japanese. In C. Georgopoulos and R. Ishihara (eds), *Interdisciplinary Approaches to Language: Essays in Honor of S.-Y. Kuroda* 519–544. Dordrecht: Kluwer.

Taglicht, J. (1998) Constraints on intonational phrasing in English. *Journal of Linguistics* 34: 181–211.

Truckenbrodt, H. (1999) On the relation between syntactic phrases and phonological phrases. *Linguistic Inquiry* 30: 219–256.

Truckenbrodt, H. (2002) Upstep and embedded register levels. *Phonology* 19: 77–120.

Truckenbrodt, H. (2005) A short report on intonational phrase boundaries in German. *Linguistische Berichte* 203: 273–296.

Truckenbrodt, H. (2007) The syntax-phonology interface. In P. de Lacy (ed.), *The Cambridge Handbook of Phonological Theory* 435–456. Cambridge: Cambridge University Press.

Venditti, J. (2005) The ToBI model of Japanese intonation. In S.-A. Jun (ed.), *Prosodic Typology: The Phonology of Intonation and Phrasing* 172–200. Oxford: Oxford University Press.

Watson, D. and Gibson, E. (2004) The relationship between intonational phrasing and syntactic structure in language production. *Language and Cognitive Processes* 19 (6): 713–755.

Wichmann, A. (2001) Spoken parentheticals. In K. Aijmer (ed.), *A Wealth of English: Studies in Honour of Gøran Kjellmer* 177–193. Gųteborg: Acta Universitatis Gothoburgensis.

11 Pausal phonology and morpheme realization*

John J. McCarthy[a]

11.1 Introduction

Among her many contributions to phonological theory, Lisa Selkirk initiated the study of prosodic domains (Selkirk, 1980), and she developed influential ideas about the phonology-morphology interface (e.g., Selkirk, 1984: chapter 3). This chapter addresses both of these topics in the context of an analysis of the pausal forms of Classical Arabic.

Words in Classical Arabic,[1] a few modern Arabic dialects (Fleisch, 1968: 29; Fischer and Jastrow, 1980: 111), and Biblical Hebrew (Prince, 1975; McCarthy, 1979; Goerwitz, 1993) undergo various morphophonemic alternations when they occur in utterance-final position. Traditionally, the utterance-final context is referred to as *pause*, and the words that appear there are described as *pausal forms* or *in pause*. These terms will be adopted here.

Among the observed alternations between non-pausal contextual forms (marked with subscripted *Cont*) and pausal forms (marked with *Pau*) are the following:

---

[a]   John J. McCarthy: University of Massachusetts Amherst, Amherst, MA, USA

(1)   Some Classical Arabic pausal alternations[2]

      a. No change

        jaqtul-u:$_{Cont}$ jaqtul-u:$_{Pau}$ 'kill (3rd m. pl. subjn.)'

      b. Absence of suffix vowel

        ʔalkita:b-u$_{Cont}$ ʔalkita:b$_{Pau}$ 'the book (nom.)'

      c. Epenthesis of [h] after stem vowel

        ʔiqtadi$_{Cont}$ ʔiqtadih$_{Pau}$ 'imitate (m. sg. imptv.)'

      d. Metathesis of suffix vowel

        ʔalbakr-u$_{Cont}$ ʔalbakur$_{Pau}$ 'the young camel (nom.)'

      e. Absence of suffixal [n]

        kita:b-u-n$_{Cont}$ kita:b$_{Pau}$ 'a book (nom.)'

        kita:b-a-n$_{Cont}$ kita:b-a:$_{Pau}$ 'a book (acc.)'

      f. [ah] for suffix [at]

        ka:tib-at-u-n$_{Cont}$ ka:tib-ah$_{Pau}$ 'a writer (f. nom.)'

There is an obvious consistency here: pausal forms must end in a heavy syllable. But the various ways of achieving this result – apocope, epenthesis, and metathesis – have to be reconciled. Furthermore, the ancillary phenomena – absence of [n] and debuccalization of [t] – do not seem to fit the pattern. And it is already apparent that any account of these phenomena will need to be sensitive to morphology, phonology, and prosodic domains.

In this chapter I will present an analysis of Classical Arabic pausal phenomena that is couched in terms of a derivational version of Optimality Theory in which morpheme realization interacts freely with the phonology. The key idea is that phonological markedness constraints on pre-pausal syllables – principally, the requirement that these syllables be heavy – affects morpheme realization. These constraints force non-realization of suffixes in (1b) and (1e), epenthesis in (1c), infixation in (1d), and allomorphy in (1f).

This chapter begins (Section 11.2) with an overview of the theoretical background necessary to support the analysis. It then continues by looking at the various aspects of Classical Arabic pause: apocope and epenthesis (Section 11.3), metathesis (Section 11.4), absence of suffixal [n] (Section 11.5), and the replacement of suffixal [at] with [ah] (Section 11.6). Section 11.7 shows how the analysis in the previous sections interacts with cliticization. Finally, Section 11.8 draws some general conclusions.

11.2 Theoretical background

It is usually assumed that the mapping from underlying to surface forms happens in a single step in Optimality Theory (Prince and Smolensky, 1993/2004). This assumption is questioned in recent work on a derivational version of OT called Harmonic Serialism (HS). HS was briefly considered by Prince and Smolensky, but then set aside. Lately, I and others have begun to reexamine HS, finding that it has a number of attractive properties (see McCarthy, 2000, 2002, 2007a, b, c, 2008b, c; Pruitt, 2008; Wolf, 2008; Kimper, to appear; Pater, to appear).

HS's differences from 'classic' OT can be described very briefly. In HS, GEN is limited to making one change at a time. Since inputs and outputs may differ in many ways, the output of each pass through GEN and EVAL is submitted as the input to another pass through GEN and EVAL, until no further changes are possible. This is the sense in which HS is a derivational version of OT.

For example, suppose a language maps underlying /pat/ to surface [patʃi] by a combination of [i]-epenthesis and [t]-palatalization. On the first pass through GEN and EVAL, shown in tableau (2a), the competing candidates include [pat], [pati], and [patʃ], among others. Because GEN can make only one change at a time, doubly-changed [patʃi] is not a candidate at this step of the derivation.[3] The grammar selects [pati], which becomes the input to another pass through GEN, shown in tableau (2b). Now the candidate set includes [patʃi], as well as [pati], [pat], and others. EVAL selects [patʃi], which is passed along to GEN. The new candidate set in tableau (2c) includes faithful [patʃi] (i.e., faithful relative to the current input) and singly-unfaithful alternatives like [pati], [patʃ], etc. EVAL finds none of the alternatives to be better than [patʃi], so [patʃi] is again the winner. At this point, the GEN-EVAL loop ends, and we say that the grammar has *converged* on its final output. The full derivation can be represented compactly as <pat, pati, patʃi>, or it can be spelled out in detail with the tableaux in (2). (On this tableau format, see Prince (2002) or McCarthy (2008a).)

(2)   <pat, pati, paʧi> in detail

a. Step 1

	pat	CODA-COND	*ti	DEP	IDENT(anterior)
i. →	pati		1	1	
ii.	pat	1 W	L	L	
iii.	paʃ	1 W	L	L	1 W

b. Step 2

	pati	CODA-COND	*ti	DEP	IDENT(anterior)
i. →	paʧi				1
ii.	pati		1 W		L
iii.	pat	1 W			L

c. Step 3 — Convergence

	paʧi	CODA-COND	*ti	DEP	IDENT(anterior)
i. →	paʧi				
ii.	pati		1 W		1 W
iii.	paʃ	1 W			

Because EVAL applies repeatedly, each step in the derivation <pat, pati, paʧi> must better satisfy the constraint hierarchy than its predecessor. This property of HS is called *harmonic improvement*. Harmonic improvement is always determined relative to a particular constraint hierarchy that is invariant across all iterations of the GEN → EVAL → GEN … loop.

HS has potential implications not only for phonology proper but also for the phonology-morphology interface. Wolf (2008) has proposed an HS-related theory of this interface called Optimal Interleaving theory (OI). OI's key idea is that morpheme realization is one of the operations that GEN performs, so derivational steps that realize morphemes are interleaved among steps that perform phonological operations. Concomitantly, constraints on morpheme realization are interleaved among phonological constraints in the ranking that EVAL applies.

Realizational theories of morphology, such as OI or Distributed Morphology (Halle and Marantz, 1993), assume that the phonological forms of morphemes are the result of processes that spell out morphosyntactic features. Thus, OI's ultimate inputs are feature structure trees – trees whose terminal nodes are abstract morphemes represented by their morphosyntactic features, such as /DOG-PLURAL/. The lexicon consists of phonological forms that may bear these features: /dɔg/$_{DOG}$, /z/$_{PLURAL}$. OI's GEN includes, in addition to familiar phonological operations like epenthesis, a spell-out operation that inserts the phonological representation of a single root or affix drawn from the lexicon.

Spell-out can occur at any location in the phonological representation, so the constraint hierarchy, rather than GEN, determine whether an affix is prefixed, infixed, or suffixed. Spell-out can also establish correspondence relations between features in the morphosyntactic representation and their counterparts in the phonological representation:

(3)   Correspondence relation in OI

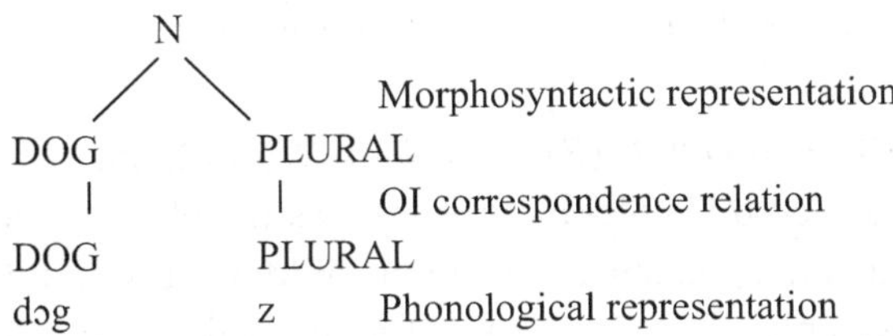

Constraints on this correspondence relation are crucial to OI's account of language typology.

In this chapter, I will often employ a compact representation for HS/OI derivations, such as <DOG-PLURAL, dɔg-PLURAL, dɔgz>. This representation, though convenient, oversimplifies in one important respect: Despite appearances, [dɔg] does not literally replace DOG, nor does [z] replace PLURAL. Rather, the morphosyntactic representation remains separate and unchanged, as in (3), while spell-out and the phonology proper occur in the phonological representation.

OI is, as its name suggests, a theory with interleaving of phonology and spell-out. So much so, that it is possible to get competition between, say, a candidate that has spelled out PLURAL and a candidate that has undergone voicing assimilation. The only limitation on the diversity of the candidate set is the one that is standard in HS: no candidate at step n can differ from the input to step n by more than the effect of a single operation in GEN.[4]

As usual in HS derivations, spell-out will not occur unless it improves harmony. It is harmonically improving by virtue of OI's constraints on the correspondence relation between features in the morphosyntactic and phonological representations. Among them are these three, all of which will be important later

(4)   MAX-M(F)

> For every token φ of the feature F, if φ is in the morphosyntactic structure and has no correspondent in the phonological structure, assign a violation mark.

(5)   DEP-M(F)

> For every token φ of the feature F, if φ is in the phonological structure and has no correspondent in the morphosyntactic structure, assign a violation mark.

(6)   UNIFORMITY-M(F_1, F_2) (abbreviated UNIF-M(F_1, F_2))

> For every token φ_1 of the feature F_1 and φ_2 of the feature F_2, with output correspondents φ_1' and φ_2' respectively, assign a violation mark if φ_1' and φ_2' are carried by the same phonological element.

MAX-M(F) and DEP-M(F) come from Wolf (2008: 26). UNIFORMITY-M(F) was suggested by Wolf (p.c.); it follows the obvious parallel with the phonological correspondence constraints in McCarthy and Prince (1995, 1999).

For example, MAX-M(PLURAL) requires the feature PLURAL in the morphosyntactic structure to be spelled out by phonological elements that are lexically marked as PLURAL, such as the suffix [-z] or the root [giːs] 'geese'. DEP-M rules out using, say, PLURAL-marked [giːs] in the singular. UNIFORMITY-M(PLURAL, GENITIVE) is violated by genitive plurals like *dogs'*, where the [-z] suffix does double duty as the exponent of both PLURAL and GENITIVE.

Atypical spell-out effects occur when OI correspondence constraints like MAX-M are dominated by phonological markedness or faithfulness constraints. The English genitive plural is an example, since UNIFORMITY-M(PLURAL, GENITIVE) is dominated by a phonological constraint that disfavors the sequence of [z]s in *[dɔgzz]. I will argue that atypical spell-out is the source of many of the pausal alternations in (1).

11.3 Non-realization and epenthesis in pause

As we already saw, Arabic words in pause have to end in a heavy syllable. This requirement is codified by the markedness constraint in (7), which prohibits monomoraic syllables utterance-finally.

(7)   HEAVYINPAUSE (HIP)

> Assign one violation mark for each configuration of the form $[\mu]_\sigma]_{Utt}$ (i.e., an utterance-final light syllable).

The configuration favored by this constraint recalls the well-known utterance-final phonetic effects of lengthening and weakening. But it is clearly not reducible to the phonetics (cf. Barnes, 2006; Myers and Hansen, 2007), since its diverse effects in Arabic are conditioned by the phonology and morphology.

Words whose contextual forms end in a heavy syllable satisfy HEAVYIN-PAUSE without further ado, and so in most cases their contextual forms are identical:

(8)   Identical contextual and pausal forms with final heavy syllable

qatal-at$_{Cont}$	qatal-at$_{Pau}$	'kill (3rd f. sg. perfv.)'
jaqtul-u:$_{Cont}$	jaqtul-u:$_{Pau}$	'kill (3rd m. pl. subjn.)'
qatal-a:$_{Cont}$	qatal-a:$_{Pau}$	'kill (3rd m. du. perfv.)'
qatal-at-a:$_{Cont}$	qatal-at-a:$_{Pau}$	'kill (3rd f. du. perfv.)'

When a word's contextual form ends in a short vowel, however, something has to change. The details of the change depend on morphological and syllabic structure. When the word-final short vowel is a suffix, then it is absent in pause:

(9)   Absence of final short suffixal vowels

ʔalkita:b-u$_{Cont}$	ʔalkita:b$_{Pau}$	'the book (nom.)'
ʔalkita:b-i$_{Cont}$	ʔalkita:b$_{Pau}$	'the book (gen.)'
ʔalkita:b-a$_{Cont}$	ʔalkita:b$_{Pau}$	'the book (acc.)'
jaqtul-u$_{Cont}$	jaqtul$_{Pau}$	'kill (3rd m. sg. impfv.)'

Although this might look like a phonological apocope process, I will argue below that it is not. OI offers an alternative to apocope: the suffix vowel is absent not because it was deleted but rather because it was never realized in the first place. If HEAVYINPAUSE dominates MAX-M instead of phonological MAX, then the suffix will remain unrealized for phonological reasons: <BOOK-NOM]$_{Utt}$, kita:b-NOM]$_{Utt}$> is the derivation. (The implicit assumption that the edges of utterances are known in advance of spell-out will be addressed shortly.) The tableaux in (10) show how this derivation is obtained.

(10)   <BOOK-NOM]$_{Utt}$, kita:b-NOM]$_{Utt}$>

    a. Step 1

BOOK-NOM]$_{Utt}$	MAX-M(ROOT)	HIP	MAX-M
i. → kita:b-NOM]$_{Utt}$			1
ii. BOOK-NOM]$_{Utt}$	1 W		2 W
iii. BOOK-u]$_{Utt}$	1 W	1 W	1

    b. Step 2: Convergence

      Ranking proven: HEAVYINPAUSE ≫ MAX-M

kita:b-NOM]$_{Utt}$	MAX-M(ROOT)	HIP	MAX-M
i. → kita:b-NOM]$_{Utt}$			1
ii. kita:b-u]$_{Utt}$		1 W	L

Top-ranked MAX-M(ROOT) is an ad hoc expedient to ensure that the root is spelled out first; see Wolf (2008: chapter 3) for the real story and Sections 11.5 and 11.7 below for related discussion.[5] The interesting action – actually inaction – occurs at step 2. A candidate that leaves NOM unrealized competes against one that realizes it but in doing so violates HEAVYINPAUSE. Since HEAVYINPAUSE is ranked higher, the candidate with incomplete realization of the morphosyntactic feature structure is the winner of this evaluation. It is also the final output of the grammar, since step 2 in (10) is convergent.

Before we continue, two issues must be dealt with. One involves the details of Arabic affixes, and the other involves the availability of information about utterance edges to the word phonology.

The first issue is this: the analysis will produce the desired effect only when an entire affix remains unrealized; partial realization is not an option permitted to GEN. The traditional morpheme segmentation in Classical Arabic looks like a problem, because it posits many CV suffixes and clitics that appear to lose just their final vowel in pause:

(11)   Traditional segmentation includes CV suffixes and clitics

      jaqtul-u:-na$_{Cont}$ jaqtul-u:-n$_{Pau}$ 'kill (3rd m. pl. ind.)'
      qatal-tu-ka$_{Cont}$ qatal-tu-k$_{Pau}$ 'I killed you (m. sg.)'
      qatal-tu-ki$_{Cont}$ qatal-tu-k$_{Pau}$ 'I killed you (f. sg.)'
      qatal-na:-hu$_{Cont}$ qatal-na:-h$_{Pau}$ 'we killed him'

This textbook morpheme segmentation is almost certainly wrong, however. The following is an exhaustive list of multisegmental suffixes and clitics ending in a short vowel:

(12)   Apparently multisegmental suffixes and clitics with a final short vowel

    a. Indicative mood

-na	'2nd, 3rd m. pl.'
-ni	'2nd, 3rd m. & f. du.'

    b. Subject agreement

-tu	'1st sg.'
-ta	'2nd sg. m.'
-ti	'2nd sg. f.'
-na	'2nd, 3rd pl. f.'

    c. Clitic

-ka	'2nd sg. m.'
-ki	'2nd sg. f.'
-hu	'3rd sg. m.' (cf. -ha: '3rd sg. f.')
-kunna	'2nd pl. f.' (cf. -kum '2nd pl. m.')
-hunna	'3rd pl. f.' (cf. -hum '3rd pl. m.')

Although these suffixes and clitics are traditionally analyzed as monomorphemic, the resemblances among them justify a finer morphological analysis (Trager and Rich, 1954; McCarthy, 1979: 295ff.). For example, [ta] and [ti] mark second person singular subjects, while [ka] and [ki] mark the corresponding objects. This suggests an analysis where [a] and [i] are separate suffixes with the meaning 'masculine' and 'feminine', respectively. If this more careful morpheme segmentation is correct, then there is no reason to prefer the apocope analysis to the realizational one.

The second issue is this: information about a word's location in the utterance must be available at the point of morpheme spell-out. In classic OT, this would come as no surprise, since all aspects of output structure are determined simultaneously. But in a derivational version of OT like HS/OI, one might expect derivations to proceed from the bottom up, as they do in Lexical Phonology (Kiparsky, 1982; Mohanan 1982 and many others). One possibility is that Lexical Phonology is simply wrong on this point, as Dresher (1983, 2008) has argued from the evidence of Tiberian Hebrew pausal alternations. Another imaginable approach is precompiled phrasal phonology, but this is clearly not appropriate when pause is the conditioning factor (Hayes, 1990: 107).[6]

A third option is to recognize the special status of the utterance constituent in the prosodic hierarchy. In an extensive body of research (e.g., Selkirk, 1986, 1995; Kratzer and Selkirk, 2007), Lisa Selkirk has shown how prosodic constituents like the phonological phrase or intonation phrase are projected from the syntax. The utterance is an exception, however. Utterances have no necessary or even regular relationship with the syntax. An utterance can consist of a single word or several sentences. An utterance can even consist of a part of word: *Q: When you aspirate a stop, do you **abduct** or **adduct** the vocal folds? A: Ab.* All that can be said about an utterance is that it is bounded by pauses and contains no internal pauses. Perhaps this is the reason why the utterance level of the prosodic hierarchy confounds the intuition that structure is built bottom-up.

Back to the main line of analysis and argument. There is a very good reason to prefer an analysis based on morphological realization over one based on phonological apocope: the realizational analysis explains why only affixal vowels disappear in pause. When an utterance-final short vowel belongs to the stem rather an affix, the obligations of HEAVYINPAUSE are met by epenthesizing [h]:

(13)   Epenthesis of [h] after final short stem vowels

    a. Verbs

ʔiqtadi$_{\text{Cont}}$	ʔiqtadih$_{\text{Pau}}$	'imitate (m. sg. imptv.)'
ʔirmi$_{\text{Cont}}$	ʔirmih$_{\text{Pau}}$	'throw (m. sg. imptv.)'
jarmi$_{\text{Cont}}$	jarmih$_{\text{Pau}}$	'throw (3rd m. sg. juss.)'

    b. Other

kajfa$_{\text{Cont}}$	kajfah$_{\text{Pau}}$	'how?'
θumma$_{\text{Cont}}$	θummah$_{\text{Pau}}$	'then'

The verbs in (13a) are derived from triconsonantal roots with final [w] or [j], and that is the source of the stem-final vowel. Since the imperative and jussive moods have no suffix, the final vowel could not be affixal. The final vowels in (13b) could not be affixal because these words do not belong to any of the inflectable lexical categories noun, verb, and adjective. Hence, these final vowels are also part of the stem.

When words like those in (13) occur in pause, non-realization of a suffix is not an option, since there is no suffix. In that case, [h]-epenthesis takes over the job of satisfying HEAVYINPAUSE. The derivation in (14) shows the ranking that produces this result.

(14) [h]-epenthesis

    a. Step 1

        Ranking proven: MAX-M(ROOT) ≫ HIP

HOW]Utt	MAX-M(ROOT)	HIP	DEP	MAX-M
i. → kajfa]Utt		1		
ii. HOW]Utt	1 W	L		1 W

    b. Step 2 (converges at step 3)

        Ranking proven: HEAVYINPAUSE ≫ DEP

kajfa]Utt	MAX-M(ROOT)	HIP	DEP	MAX-M
i. → kajfah]Utt			1	
ii. kajfa]Utt		1 W	L	

Tableau (14a) shows that MAX-M(ROOT) must dominate HEAVYINPAUSE, since spelling out the root can introduce an utterance-final light syllable. Tableau (14b) establishes that HEAVYINPAUSE dominates DEP, so it can compel epenthesis.

To ensure the internal consistency of the analysis, we need to check that the introduction of dominated DEP does not affect the account of affix non-realization in (10). It does not because there is no point in (10) where non-realization competes against a viable epenthetic alternative. That is, the intended winner [kita:b-NOM] never competes against [kita:buh], which realizes the nominative suffix as [u] and satisfies HEAVYINPAUSE by epenthesizing [h]. They do not compete because they come from different GEN 'generations'. The ultimate input is [BOOK-NOM], and [kita:b-NOM] is one step away from that. But [kita:buh] is three steps away – spell-out of BOOK, spell-out of NOM, and epenthesis.

In sum, the OI analysis presented here explains two properties of the Arabic pausal system. It explains why affix vowels are absent in pause but stem vowels are not – non-realization is an option only for the former. It also explains why affix vowels never undergo [h]-epenthesis – non-realization wins before epenthesis is a viable option. Both explanations rely on OI's eponymous ability to interleave phonological and morphological operations and constraints.

A conventional OT analysis of these data might seem to be possible with root faithfulness constraints (McCarthy and Prince, 1995, 1999). MAXroot

prevents stem vowels from deleting. If it dominates DEP, which itself dominates unadorned MAX, then the right results are obtained:

(15)   Classic OT analysis with MAX$_{root}$

a. Deletion of suffix vowel

kita:b-u	MAX$_{root}$	HIP	DEP	MAX
i. → kita:b]$_{Utt}$				1
ii. kita:bu]$_{Utt}$		1 W		L
iii. kita:buh]$_{Utt}$			1 W	L

b. Epenthesis after stem vowel

kajfa	MAX$_{root}$	HIP	DEP	MAX
i. → kajfah]$_{Utt}$			1	
ii. kajfa]$_{Utt}$		1 W	L	
iii. kajf]$_{Utt}$	1 W		L	1 W

The problem with this analysis is that it requires rankings that are con-
tradicted elsewhere in the language. Phonotactic requirements prohibit
word-initial consonant clusters. With MAX$_{root}$ dominating DEP dominating
plain MAX, we would expect clusters composed of root consonants to
undergo epenthesis, while clusters with an affixal consonant would simplify by deletion. This is false; clusters of both types have epenthesis of
prothetic [ʔi] or [ʔu]: /ktub/ → [ʔuktub] 'write!'; /sta-ktab-a/ → [ʔistaktaba],
*[taktaba] 'he asked someone to write'. Therefore, MAX must dominate
DEP, contradicting (15).

11.4 Infixation in pause

When a noun whose stem ends in a consonant cluster appears in the nominative or genitive case in pause, the suffix vowel appears to be metathesized into the cluster (16). This does not occur in the accusative case,
however.

(16)   Apparent metathesis in pause

ʔalbakr-u$_{Cont}$	ʔalbakur$_{Pau}$	'the young camel (nom.)'
ʔaddalw-u$_{Cont}$	ʔaddaluw$_{Pau}$	'the leather bucket (nom.)'
ʔalbakr-i$_{Cont}$	ʔalbakir$_{Pau}$	'the young camel (gen.)'
but		
ʔalbakr-a$_{Cont}$	ʔalbakr$_{Pau}$	'the young camel (acc.)'

OI offers an alternative to metathesis. The idea is that the nominative suffix [-u] is not *moved* into the preceding cluster; rather, the morphosyntactic feature NOM is *realized* in that position. This suffix is, in short, infixed for phonological reasons.

Consider the fate of utterance-final [CAMEL-NOM] (ignoring the definite article). At the second step of the derivation, the root has already been spelled out and the input to GEN is [bakr-NOM]. One option for spelling out NOM is [bakur], with NOM realized internally to the stem. This is a violation of the OI constraint MIRROR, which says (approximately) that the phonological exponent of NOM has to follow the phonological exponent of CAMEL, mirroring in phonological structure the relation between these morphemes in morphosyntactic structure. Wolf (2008: 81) defines MIRROR so it assesses violations gradiently by counting segments. Therefore, [bakur] receives one mark from this constraint.

Infixation of the suffix occurs with cluster-final stems like [bakr], but not with stems ending in a single consonant, such as [kitaːb], [dʒabal] 'hill', or [θaʕlab] 'fox'. In pause, these latter nouns opt for non-realization of NOM, as we have already seen. The explanation for this difference is that infixation avoids the final consonant cluster of *[bakr-NOM]. On this view, *COMPLEXCODA (*CMP) dominates MIRROR, thereby compelling infixation in cluster-final stems like the one in tableau (17). *COMPLEXCODA is irrelevant in non-cluster-final stems, as tableau (18) shows.

(17)   Step 2 of <CAMEL-NOM]$_{Utt}$, bakr-NOM]$_{Utt}$, bakur]$_{Utt}$>

Ranking proven: HEAVYINPAUSE, *COMPLEXCODA, DEP >> MIRROR

	bakr-NOM]$_{Utt}$	HIP	*CMP	DEP	MIR	MAX-M
a. →	bakur]$_{Utt}$				1	
b.	bakr-NOM]$_{Utt}$		1 W		L	1 W
c.	bakir-NOM]$_{Utt}$			1 W	L	1 W
d.	bakru]$_{Utt}$	1 W			L	

(18)   Step 2 of <FOX-NOM]$_{Utt}$, θaʕlab-NOM]$_{Utt}$> — Convergence

Ranking proven: MIRROR >> MAX-M

	θaʕlab-NOM]$_{Utt}$	HIP	*CMP	DEP	MIR	MAX-M
a. →	θaʕlab-NOM]$_{Utt}$					1
b.	θaʕlabu]$_{Utt}$	1 W				L
c.	θaʕulab]$_{Utt}$				3 W	L

These two tableaux merit close study. From previous discussion we know that HEAVYINPAUSE dominates DEP and MAX-M. These tableaux introduce two more constraints, *COMPLEXCODA and MIRROR. Tableau (17) shows that MIRROR has to be dominated by three constraints: *COMPLEXCODA, to rule out non-realization with cluster-final stems; DEP, to prevent *COMPLEXCODA from being satisfied by ordinary vowel epenthesis; and, as usual, HEAVYINPAUSE. But MIRROR must itself dominate MAX-M, as shown in (18), so that infixation does not become a more generally applicable alternative to non-realization.[7]

Interestingly, it is not possible in OI to construct an actual metathesis analysis of these data that is consistent with the results of the previous section. To get to the output by way of metathesis, the derivation would have to proceed as <CAMEL-NOM]$_{Utt}$, bakr-NOM]$_{Utt}$, bakru]$_{Utt}$, bakur]$_{Utt}$>. At step 2, NOM is realized at the expense of violating HEAVYINPAUSE — an impossibility because the previous section established that MAX-M is ranked below HEAVYINPAUSE. In OI, as in HS generally, there is no look-ahead, so the prospect of fixing [bakru]'s HEAVYINPAUSE violation by metathesis is not in sight. Derivations must steadily improve harmony, and violating undominated HEAVYINPAUSE is not the way to do that.

The analysis so far is crucially incomplete in one respect: it does not account for the contextual ~ pausal alternation in accusative nouns like [ʔalbakr-a]$_{Cont}$ ~ [ʔalbakr]$_{Pau}$. Evidently the accusative suffix resists infixation. It is by no means unusual for similar-looking affixes to differ in infixability within a language. For example, Prince and Smolensky's (1993/ 2004) analysis of the Tagalog infix [um] 'actor focus' relies on the fact that it starts with a vowel and ends in a consonant. But [ipag] 'benefactive focus' is also vowel-initial and consonant-final, yet it does not infix. Facts like this show that MIRROR, like the affixal alignment constraints it replaces, is morpheme-specific. Tagalog assigns a different ranking to MIRROR (ACTOR FOCUS) and MIRROR(BENEFACTIVE FOCUS), violating the former but not the latter. In Arabic, MIRROR(ACC) is unviolated, but MIRROR(NOM) and MIRROR(GEN) are ranked lower.

Tableau (19) illustrates this effect of MIRROR(ACC):

(19)   Step 2 of <CAMEL-ACC]$_{Utt}$, bakr-ACC]$_{Utt}$> — Convergence
       Ranking proven: HEAVYINPAUSE, MIRROR(ACC) >> *COMPLEXCODA

bakr-ACC]$_{Utt}$	HIP	MIR(ACC)	*CMP	DEP	MIR(NOM/GEN)	MAX-M
a. → bakr-ACC]$_{Utt}$			1			1
b. bakar]$_{Utt}$		1 W	L			L
c. bakra]$_{Utt}$	1 W		L			L

Splitting MIRROR in this way has no effect on previous results; for example, substituting MIRROR(NOM/GEN) for undifferentiated MIRROR does not change the outcome in tableau (17).

A final point about this analysis. When the final short vowel is not affixal, it is not 'metathesized' into the preceding cluster. This is exemplified by [ʔirmi]$_{Cont}$ ~ [ʔirmih]$_{Pau}$ and several other words in (13). The pausal form *[ʔirim]$_{Pau}$ is impossible because there is no actual metathesis – no violation of the faithfulness constraint LINEARITY. The final vowel of [ʔirmi]$_{Cont}$ is not affixal, so there is no possibility of treating it as an infix. Thus, although DEP has to dominate MIRROR(NOM/GEN) (see (17)), *[ʔirim]$_{Pau}$ is not a successful challenger to [ʔirmih]$_{Pau}$.

I will now compare this OI account with the alternative OT analyses that are available if OI is not assumed. There are two: infixation in the style of Prince and Smolensky (1993/2004) and McCarthy and Prince (1993), which I will refer to alignment-based infixation (ABI); and infixation by phonological metathesis, as proposed by Horwood (2002, 2004).

The main premise of ABI is that morphemes are unordered in the input and affix placement is determined by the ranking of affix-specific alignment constraints, such as ALIGN-L(*um*, stem) in Tagalog.[8] In Arabic, ranking ALIGN-R(u_{NOM}, stem) below *COMPLEX-CODA and HEAVYINPAUSE will favor infixation of this suffix. In contrast, ALIGN-R(a_{ACC}, stem) is ranked above these two constraints. The form *[ʔirim]$_{Pau}$ is a non-starter because it has no affix to infix.

Although ABI can supply a working analysis of these Arabic data, it has bigger problems. Horwood's (2002, 2004) critique of ABI is that independent ranking of affix-specific alignment constraints cannot capture generalizations subsumed by Baker's (1985) Mirror Principle.[9] For example, it is an accident of ranking that the case suffixes follow the feminine plural suffix [aːt]. The Mirror Principle and the cognate OI constraint MIRROR relate this observation about the phonological representation to properties of the morphosyntactic representation

Earlier, I argued that metathesis is not a viable approach to these facts in OI, but perhaps it would work in classic OT. The idea is that /bakr-u/ becomes [bakur] in pause because LINEARITY is dominated by *COMPLEX-CODA and HEAVYINPAUSE:

(20)   Fragment of metathesis analysis

	bakr-u	*CMP	HIP	LINEARITY
a. →	bakur]$_{Utt}$			1
b.	bakru]$_{Utt}$		W 1	L
c.	bakr]$_{Utt}$	W 1		L

If LINEARITY dominates MAX, then this analysis will also account for why /θaʕlab-u/ becomes [θaʕlab] and not *[θaʕulab] in pause.

This classic OT analysis also has to deal with the pausal forms where metathesis fails to occur, accusatives like [bakr]$_{Pau}$ and [h]-epenthesis cases like [ʔirmih]$_{Pau}$. The obvious move in the case of the accusative is to recruit a high-ranking morpheme-specific faithfulness constraint LINEARITY$_{ACC}$, which is violated by the mapping /bakr-a/ → *[bakar]$_{Pau}$. As for the [h]-epenthesis cases, the root faithfulness constraint LINEARITY$_{root}$ (McCarthy and Prince, 1995, 1999) could rule out the mapping /ʔirmi/ → *[ʔirim]$_{Pau}$.

Though superficially plausible, these applications of morpheme- or root-specific faithfulness do not actually work. The problem centers on identifying the *locus of exceptionality* in the sense of Pater (2006). For example, suppose MAX is indexed to a particular morpheme or class of morphemes. The scope of this indexed constraint is limited to segments that are exponents of that morpheme or morpheme class. Other segments that happen to occur in the same word as one of these morphemes are not protected by indexed MAX. Therefore, the locus of exceptionality is the segment whose deletion would violate MAX.

What is the locus of exceptionality for LINEARITY? Unlike MAX, LINEARITY refers to a pair of segments. If LINEARITY is morphologically indexed, do both segments have to meet the morphological condition, or is it enough that one of them does? Is the locus of exceptionality two segments or one? I do not know the answer to this question, but I do know that LINEARITY$_{ACC}$ and LINEARITY$_{root}$, if they are to have the desired effect in Arabic, must be inconsistent in exactly this respect. To prevent the mapping /bakr-a/ → *[bakar]$_{Pau}$, LINEARITY$_{ACC}$ has to be active when only one of the segments involved, the [a], is an exponent of ACC. But to prevent the mapping /ʔirmi/ → *[ʔirim]$_{Pau}$ while still allowing the mapping /bakr-u/ → *[bakur]$_{Pau}$, LINEARITY$_{root}$ has to be active only when both of the segments involved, the [m] and the [i], are exponents of a root. It would, of course, be possible to solve this problem by stipulating for each indexed LINEARITY constraint how its locus of exceptionality will be reckoned, but then the *reductio* would be well advanced on the road to the *absurdum*.

To sum up the analysis so far, I have argued that Wolf's (2008) Optimal Interleaving theory provides the framework for an analysis of the absence of final short vowels in pause that is superior to a more conventional OT approach. The central claim of the analysis is that the effects of the markedness constraint HEAVYINPAUSE are both morphological – blocking realization of affixes as final short vowels – and phonological – triggering epenthesis.

For convenience, I provide a list of all the ranking results and where they are established:

(21) Ranking so far

MAX-M(ROOT) ≫ HIP	(14a)
HEAVYINPAUSE ≫ MAX-M	(10b)
HEAVYINPAUSE ≫ DEP	(14b)
HEAVYINPAUSE ≫ MIRROR(NOM/GEN)	(17)
HEAVYINPAUSE ≫ *COMPLEXCODA	(19)
MIRROR(ACC) ≫ *COMPLEXCODA	(19)
*COMPLEXCODA ≫ MIRROR(NOM/GEN)	(17)
DEP ≫ MIRROR(NOM/GEN)	(17)
MIRROR(NOM/GEN) ≫ MAX-M	(18)

As evidence that the analysis is internally consistent, note that HEAVYINPAUSE dominates MIRROR(NOM/GEN) by direct argument and by two arguments from transitivity of domination, one via DEP and the other via *COMPLEX-CODA. Likewise, the ranking of HEAVYINPAUSE above MAX-M is shown by direct argument and by transitivity through MIRROR

(NOM/GEN). This is an indication that the analysis is on the right track.

In the next section, we will see how this analysis extends to other pausal phenomena.

11.5 Consequences of sequential spell-out

In HS, GEN is limited to making one change at a time. In OI, this means that spell-out can insert only one morpheme at a time. For example, in the derivation of [ROOT-F1-F2], after ROOT has been spelled-out, it is not possible to spell out both F1 and F2, unless the lexicon happens to supply a single morpheme that matches both of these features. This sequential spell-out requirement, which follows from basic HS/OI assumptions, has consequences for the phonology of pause in Classical Arabic.

Under certain circumstances, indefinite nouns are marked by a suffix [n], called 'nunation', that follows the case desinence. In pausal forms of indefinite nominatives and genitives, the desinence and the [n] are both absent (22a). In pausal forms of indefinite accusatives, the desinence and [n] are replaced by [a:] (22b).

(22)   Nunation disappears in pause

a. Nominative and genitive

kita:b-u-n$_{Cont}$	kita:b$_{Pau}$	'a book (nom.)'
bakr-u-n$_{Cont}$	bakur$_{Pau}$	'a young camel (nom.)'
kita:b-i-n$_{Cont}$	kita:b$_{Pau}$	'a book (gen.)'
bakr-i-n$_{Cont}$	bakir$_{Pau}$	'a young camel (gen.)'

b. Accusative

| kita:b-a-n$_{Cont}$ | kita:b-a:$_{Pau}$ | 'a book (acc.)' |
| bakr-a-n$_{Cont}$ | bakr-a:$_{Pau}$ | 'a young camel (acc.)' |

From the perspective of a classic OT or rule-based analysis, the forms in (22a) are puzzling. Since [kita:bun]$_{Cont}$ ends in a heavy syllable, the contextual and pausal forms should be identical (cf. (8)). Furthermore, the data in (23) show that there is no general [n]-deletion process in pause. In fact, the absence of suffix vowels in pause can actually expose [n]s to utterance-final position, where they remain intact.

(23) [n] otherwise preserved in pause

    a. Root [n]

?addi:n-i$_{Cont}$	?addi:n$_{Pau}$	'the judgment (gen.)'
ħi:n-in$_{Cont}$	ħi:n$_{Pau}$	'time (gen.)'

    b. Suffixal [n]

?alʕa:lam-i:n-a$_{Cont}$	?alʕa:lam-i:n$_{Pau}$	'the worlds (gen.)'

It is clear that the absence of nunation in pause is not the result of some conventional phonological process.

In fact, the absence of nunation in pause follows from the OI analysis already proposed, without any additional stipulations. Tableau (24) addresses the situation that obtains after root spell-out, when there is a choice between realizing the case suffix or failing to realize it. HEAVYINPAUSE and *COMPLEX-CODA dominate MAX-M, and these candidates violate no other constraints under discussion. Hence, the candidate that fails to spell out NOM or INDEF is the winner. And since this candidate is identical with the latest input to GEN, the derivation converges.

(24) Convergence at step 2 of <BOOK-NOM-INDEF]$_{Utt}$, kita:b-NOM-INDEF]$_{Utt}$>

kita:b-NOM-INDEF]$_{Utt}$	HIP	*CMP	MAX-M
a. → kita:b-NOM-INDEF]$_{Utt}$			2
b. kita:b-u-INDEF]$_{Utt}$	1 W		1 L

As I noted earlier, HS/OI has no capacity to look ahead to what might be possible at later steps of the derivation. For that reason, [kita:b-u-INDEF] enjoys no advantage, even though spell-out of INDEF as [n] at the next step would provide the sought-for heavy syllable while spelling out all of the morphosyntactic features.

Because of sequential spell-out, tableau (24) does not include the candidate [kita:b-u-n]. HS/OI's GEN cannot draw two morphemes from the lexicon in a single step, so input [kita:b-NOM-INDEF] cannot yield this candidate. This fact is crucial, because [kita:b-u-n] would otherwise win, as it satisfies both HEAVYINPAUSE and MAX-M. Furthermore, under the assumption that spell-out proceeds from the root outward (see Wolf, 2008: chapter 3) as well as Sections 11.3 above and 11.7 below), it is impossible to spell out INDEF before NOM, so [kita:b-NOM-n] is non-viable. Succinctly, nunation is absent in the pausal forms of indefinite nominative and genitive singular nouns because the case suffix is absent, and the case suffix is absent because nunation is absent. This explanation crucially relies on HS/OI's serial character.

The pausal form of the indefinite accusative also lacks nunation, but it satisfies HEAVYINPAUSE in a different way: [kita:b-a:]$_{Pau}$.[10] The [a:] suffix, I propose, is a portmanteau morpheme. That is, it realizes two morphosyntactic features that the language usually spells out with separate morphemes. In the derivation <BOOK-ACC-INDEF]$_{Utt}$, kita:b-ACC-INDEF]$_{Utt}$, kita:b-a:]$_{Utt}$>, suffixation of [a:] at the final step spells out both ACC and INDEF without running afoul of HEAVYINPAUSE:

(25)   The portmanteau suffix [a:]

kita:b-ACC-INDEF]$_{Utt}$	HIP	*CMP	MAX-M
a. → kita:b-a:]$_{Utt}$			
b. kita:b-a-INDEF]$_{Utt}$	1 W		1 W

As tableau (25) shows, no changes in the grammar are necessary to account for why [a:] appears in the pausal indefinite accusative. Because a portmanteau morpheme spells out two or more morphosyntactic features at once, it is always favored by MAX-M over spelling out the features one at a time (Wolf, 2008: 191 ff.).[11] Of course, there is no portmanteau morpheme [u:] for the nominative, so pausal [kita:b] has no such competitor in (24).

In fact, the attractiveness of the portmanteau is such that we must take care to explain why [kita:b-a-n]$_{Cont}$, rather than *[kita:b-a:]$_{Cont}$, is the contextual form of the indefinite accusative. Specifically, we need the intermediate form [kita:b-a-INDEF]$_{Cont}$ to beat [kita:b-a:]$_{Cont}$. Since MAX-M(INDEF) favors the latter, it has to be dominated by a constraint that the portmanteau violates. That constraint is UNIFORMITY-M in (6). Tableau (26) shows how this works, and tableau (27) establishes that this move does not affect the analysis of the pausal form if UNIFORMITY-M is dominated by HEAVYINPAUSE and MAX-M(ACC).

(26)   No portmanteau [a:] in contextual indefinite accusative[12]

kita:b-ACC-INDEF]$_{Cont}$	HIP	MAX-M(ACC)	UNIF-M	MAX-M(INDEF)
a. → kita:b-a-INDEF]$_{Cont}$				1
b. kita:b-a:]$_{Cont}$			1 W	L
c. kita:b-ACC-INDEF]$_{Cont}$		1 W		1

(27)   Portmanteau [aː] in pausal indefinite accusative (expanding (25))

kitaːb-ACC-INDEF]_Pau	HIP	MAX-M(ACC)	UNIF-M	MAX-M(INDEF)
a. → kitaːb-aː]_Pau			1	
b. kitaːb-a-INDEF]_Pau	1 W		L	1 W
c. kitaːb-ACC-INDEF]_Pau		1 W	L	1 W

11.6 Allomorphy

To introduce the now standard approach to allomorphy in OT, I will begin
with an example. In Korean, the nominative suffix has two alternants, [i]
and [ka]. There is no reasonable way of deriving them from a single underlying representation, but their distribution is determined phonologically: [i]
follows consonant-final stems and [ka] (voiced intervocalically to [ga]) follows vowel-final stems:

(28)   Korean nominative suffix allomorphy

     cib-i   'house (nom.)'
     cʰa-ga   'car (nom.)'

The standard approach to allomorphy in OT is based on the following
premises (e.g., Burzio, 1994; Mester, 1994; Hargus, 1995; Mascaró, 1996,
2007; Tranel, 1996a, b, 1998; Hargus and Tuttle, 1997; Perlmutter, 1998):

(a)   The allomorphs of a morpheme are listed together in the underlying
      representation: /cip-{i, ka}/, /cʰa-{i, ka}/ (Hudson, 1974).
(b)   GEN creates candidates that include all possible choices of an allo-
      morph: [cib-i], [cip-ka], [cʰa-i], [cʰa-ga].
(c)   Faithfulness constraints like MAX and DEP treat all allomorph choices
      equally.
(d)   So markedness constraints determine which allomorph is most har-
      monic. In Korean, the markedness constraints ONSET and NO-CODA
      correctly favor [cib-i] and [cʰa-ga] over [cip-ka] and [cʰa-i], respec-
      tively. Because no faithfulness violation is involved in allomorph
      selection, the markedness constraints that make the choice can be
      emergent in the sense of McCarthy and Prince (1994).

The following tableaux illustrate:

(29)   Allomorph selection in Korean

a.

	/cip-{i, ka}/	ONSET	NO-CODA
i. →	cibi		
ii.	cipka		1 W

b.

	/cʰa-{i, ka}/	ONSET	NO-CODA
i. →	cʰaga		
ii.	cʰa.i	1 W	

NO-CODA is an emergent constraint in Korean – it is unable to compel faithfulness violation, since the language permits syllables with codas.

OI's theory of allomorphy is similar, except for one not unexpected difference: allomorphs compete at the point of spell-out, not at surface structure (Wolf, 2008: chapters 2 and 3). Thus, [cʰaga] and *[cʰa.i] compete as different ways of continuing the derivation that begins with <CAR-NOM, cʰa-NOM, …>. This difference is important when we apply OI to the problem of allomorphy in the feminine singular suffix of Classical Arabic.

The feminine singular suffix is normally [at], but it takes the form [ah] when it occurs utterance-finally:

(30)   Feminine singular suffix [at] in pause

ka:tib-at-un_Cont	ka:tib-ah_Pau	'a writer (f. nom.)'
ħamz-at-a_Cont	ħamz-ah_Pau	'Hamza (masc. name) (acc.)'

When [t] comes from any other source, such as the root, the feminine plural suffix [a:t], or the homophonous third person feminine singular subject agreement suffix [at], it does not alternate with [h] (Hoberman, 1995: 168):

(31)   Other [t]s in pause

mustanbat-un_Cont	mustanbat_Pau	'cultivated (nom.)'
ka:tib-a:t-un_Cont	ka:tib-a:t_Pau	'writers (f. nom)'
katab-at_Cont	katab-at_Pau	'write (3rd f. sg. perfv.)'

As in Korean, the [t]~[h] alternation is phonologically conditioned, but no general phonological process is involved. This too is an example of allomorphy, as Hoberman (1995) argues.

It follows that the feminine singular suffix has two synonymous allo-morphs, [at] and [ah]. They compete at the point of spell-out of FEM, and phonological constraints determine which is more harmonic. These con-straints must favor, e.g., [ka:tib-*at*-NOM-INDEF]_{Cont} over *[ka:tib-*ah*-NOM-INDEF]_{Cont}, but they must also favor [ka:tib-*ah*-NOM-INDEF]_{Pau} over *[ka:tib-*at*-NOM-INDEF]_{Pau}. In short, they must favor [h] over [t] utterance-finally and [t] over [h] elsewhere. The effects of these constraints are emergent in allomorph selection but not in unfaithful mappings, since the language otherwise allows utterance-final [t] (as in (31)) and non-utterance-final [h] (as in [ʔahlaka] 'ruin (3rd m. sg. perfv.)').

I will now elucidate these constraints. One piece of the analysis comes from the observation that some languages limit codas to the laryngeals [h] and [ʔ] (Lombardi, 1995/2001; Kaneko and Kawahara, 2002; Parker 2001). This follows if laryngeals are placeless and the constraint CODACOND bans place from codas (Ito 1989; Goldsmith, 1990: 123–128;). Another key piece of the analysis comes from Flack's (2007, 2009) proposal that conditions on the onsets or codas of syllables are paralleled by conditions on the 'onsets' or 'codas' of words, phrases, or utterances. Thus, we expect to find a constraint CODACOND_{Utt} that is violated by non-laryngeal conso-nants utterance-finally. It is this constraint that favors [ka:tib-*ah*-NOM-INDEF]_{Pau} over *[ka:tib-*at*-NOM-INDEF]_{Pau}. Its effect is limited to allomorph selection because it is ranked below faithfulness, so it does not cause, say, [mustanbat]_{Pau} to become [mustanbah]_{Pau}.

There is independent support for CODACOND_{Utt} in Classic Arabic. It ex-plains why [h] and not some other consonant is epenthesized in the pausal forms in (13), since all other consonants except [ʔ] violate it. This too is an emergent effect. Furthermore, CODACOND_{Utt} is plausibly implicated in inser-tion of final [h] in phrases beginning with the so-called [wa:] of lamenta-tion (Wright, 1971: vol. i, 295): [wa: ʔami:ra lmuʔmini:na**h**] 'alas for the Prince of Believers'. CODACOND_{Utt} is also supported by Sanskrit *visarga*, a process that replaces /s/ and /r/ with [h] utterance-finally (Whitney, 1889: 58; Selkirk, 1980: 118).

Another emergent constraint disfavors the [ah] allomorph in non-pausal contexts. This constraint, HAVE-PLACE, is violated by the laryngeals [h] and [ʔ] because of their placelessness (Padgett, 1995; Parker, 2001; Smith, 2002). With CODACOND_{Utt} ranked above HAVE-PLACE, the correct allo-morph is selected in both contexts:

(32) Pausal allomorph selected

ka:tib-FEM-NOM-INDEF]Pau	CODACOND_Utt	HAVE-PLACE
a. → ka:tib-ah-NOM-INDEF]Pau		1
b. ka:tib-at-NOM-INDEF]Pau	1 W	L

(33) Non-pausal allomorph selected

ka:tib-FEM-NOM-INDEF]Cont	CODACOND_Utt	HAVE-PLACE
a. → ka:tib-at-NOM-INDEF]Cont		
b. ka:tib-ah-NOM-INDEF]Cont		1 W

After the step in (33), the derivation continues with spell-out of NOM and INDEF, in that order. The derivation in (32) converges at the next step, however, for reasons discussed previously.

11.7 Interaction with cliticization

When a noun or verb is followed by a possessive or object clitic, the pausal alternation occurs on the clitic, with the preceding noun or verb in its contextual form. Several examples of this type appeared in (11) and are repeated in (34); some additional examples have been included as well.

(34) Words with clitics

qatal-tu-ka_Cont	qatal-tu-k_Pau	'I killed you (m. sg.)'
qatal-tu-ki_Cont	qatal-tu-k_Pau	'I killed you (f. sg.)'
kita:b-a-ka_Cont	kita:b-a-k_Pau	'your (m. sg.) book (acc.)'
ka:tib-at-u-ki_Cont	ka:tib-at-u-k_Pau	'your (f. sg.) writer (f. nom.)'

A fairly standard view of Arabic clitics is that they are adjoined to their hosts (Broselow, 1976) by incorporation (Fassi Fehri, 1993).[13]

(35) Cliticization as incorporation (Fassi Fehri 1993:102)

The host of cliticization is the nearest c-commanding head (Fassi Fehri, 1993: 98ff.; Shlonsky, 1997: 178–179), which can be a noun, verb, adjective, preposition, quantifier, or complementizer. Incorporation is blocked under various conditions, such as when the pronoun is in a coordinate structure (Fassi Fehri, 1993: 103–106). In that case, the pronoun is instead cliticized to the dummy noun [ʔijjaː]: [raʔajtu ʔijjaː-ka wazajdan] 'I saw *ʔijjaː*-you (m. sg.) and Zeyd'.

It follows, then, that clitics and inflections have different morphosyntactic representations. Clitics are adjoined to the root's X°, but inflections are in it: [[WRITER-FEM-NOM]$_N$ [2ND-SG-FEM]$_D$]$_N$ (= (34d)). As we saw in (10) and (32), when [WRITER-FEM-NOM]$_N$ occurs uncliticized and in pause, phonological constraints force FEM to be spelled out as [ah] rather than [at], and they block spell-out of NOM entirely. But when [WRITER-FEM-NOM]$_N$ bears a clitic, it is not the rightmost X° in the utterance; instead, the clitic is. In words with clitics, then, the clitic's X° is the locus of the pausal alternation.

The explanation for why the pausal alternation affects only the clitic's X° has to do with how spell-out works. Spell-out within an X° goes from the bottom up, root first followed by the lowest/least peripheral affix, and so on (see Wolf (2008: chapter 3) as well as sections 11.3 and 11.5 above). But this says nothing about the order of spell-out of the adjoined X°s in cliticized forms. The most reasonable hypothesis is that they are spelled out simultaneously, in parallel with one other. This is by no means a new idea, since it is exactly how generative phonology has always dealt with cyclic rule application in X° compounds like *language requirement* (Chomsky and Halle, 1968: 21; Liberman and Prince, 1977).

On this view, the explanation for why [kaːtib-at-u-k]$_{Pau}$ has a host in its contextual form and a clitic in its pausal form can be seen in the following partial derivation:

(36)   Derivation of [kaːtib-at-u-k]$_{Pau}$

Morphosyntactic representation	[[WRITER-FEM-NOM]$_N$ [2ND-SG-FEM]$_D$]$_N$
Step 1	[[kaːtib-FEM-NOM]$_N$ [k-FEM]$_D$]$_N$
Step 2	[[kaːtib-at-NOM]$_N$ [k-FEM]$_D$]$_N$
Step 3	[[kaːtib-at-u]$_N$ [k-FEM]$_D$]$_N$

At step 1, spell-out proceeds bottom-up in both [WRITER-FEM-NOM]$_N$ and [2ND-SG-FEM]$_D$, simultaneously. At step 2, FEM in the host noun is spelled out as contextual [at] rather than pausal [ah] because the [ah]-favoring phonological constraint CODACOND$_{\text{Utt}}$ is applicable only to utterance-final consonants and the [k] of the clitic is utterance-final. In the clitic's D°, spell-out of FEM as [i] is blocked by HEAVYINPAUSE. Finally, at step 3 the nominative suffix [u] is spelled out, since it too is protected from the effects of pause by the following [k].[14]

11.8 Conclusion

This chapter has examined the phonology of utterance-final words in Classical Arabic. Although well-motivated markedness constraints determine the properties of utterance-final syllables, the satisfaction of these markedness constraints is deeply entangled with the morphology. Wolf's (2008) Optimal Interleaving theory, I have argued, offers the best account of how phonology and morphology interact in these phenomena.

OI's principal contribution to the understanding of Arabic pausal forms is that it establishes a formal connection among four seemingly disparate phenomena: missing suffixes, infixation, portmanteau morphology, and allomorphy. The connection is that all are types of (non-)realization. Suffixes remain unrealized or are infixed for phonological reasons; a portmanteau morpheme appears under phonological conditions; and phonological constraints choose between allomorphs. OI also accommodates the one purely phonological consequence of pause, epenthetic [h].

It is clear from these results that OI offers a new and valuable perspective on phonology-morphology interaction.

Personal remark

I first met Lisa Selkirk in 1976 at NELS VII. She was a dashing figure who wore an École Polytechnique cape and gave a talk in which she boldly laid out a novel theory of syntax-phonology relations. She impressed me more, however, because she took a genuine interest in my work even though I was just a second-year graduate student at another school.

I later learned that Lisa's intellectual boldness at NELS was not unusual. When she engages with a topic, she does not hesitate to set out all the premises of her approach. This might seem dangerous, but experience shows that more often than not she is on the right track.

Having Lisa as a colleague was one of the most important reasons why I came to UMass in 1985. She has been a good friend and a continuing inspiration. I am excited to see how her work develops in the future.

Notes

* This research was supported by grant BCS-0813829 from the National Science Foundation to the University of Massachusetts Amherst. I am grateful to Matt Wolf, Shigeto Kawahara, and two anonymous reviewers for extensive comments.

1 The principal Western references on Classical Arabic pausal forms are Birkeland (1940), Fleisch (1968: 28–30), Hoberman (1995), Howell (1986: 772–929), Schaade (1911: 55–63), and Wright (1971: vol. II, 368–373). For evidence that the pausal forms were productive in Classical Arabic, see Hoberman (1995: 162–164).

2 Abbreviations used in glosses in this chapter: *1st, 2nd, 3rd* first, second, third person; *acc.* accusative; *du.* dual; *f.* feminine; *gen.* genitive; *impfv.* imperfective; *imptv.* imperative; *juss.* jussive; *m.* masculine; *nom.* nominative; *perfv.* perfective; *pl.* plural; *subjn.* subjunctive.

3 Because [paʃi] is not in the candidate set at Step 1, CODA-COND and *ti are in conflict. Hence, CODA-COND must dominate *ti for the derivation to proceed any further, though these constraints would be unrankable in classic OT. To ensure that intermediate candidates win on the way to the ultimate surface form, HS often imposes additional ranking requirements like this. This difference from classic OT forms the basis of many of HS's typological predictions (e.g., McCarthy 2007b, 2008b)

4 An exception may be needed for syllabification; see McCarthy (2010).

5 Throughout this chapter, unmodified *root* refers to what is usually called the *stem* in analyses of Arabic. It does not refer to the consonantal root.

6 Precompilation theory treats sandhi forms as a kind of morphology. It is therefore limited to sandhi alternations that are conditioned by the syntax. Pause is clearly not syntactic, so the Arabic pausal alternations cannot be analyzed with precompilation.

7 In (18) I use a noun with a medial cluster, [θaʕlab], rather than [kitaːb] or [dʒabal], because *[kitaː.ub] or *[dʒabu.al] are independently ruled out by ONSET.

8 ALIGN-L(*um*, stem) is violated once for each segment intervening between the left edge of the stem and the infix [um]. It therefore favors placing this affix as close to the beginning of the stem as possible.

9   The Mirror Principle says that affix order reflects the order of syntactic opera-
    tions.

10 The [aː] indefinite accusative suffix must also bear the feature MASCULINE, since
    it is limited to nouns that are formally masculine.

11 An anonymous reviewer points out that the two anomalous properties of the
    accusative suffix – resistance to infixation and pausal indefinite [aː] – receive
    different explanations in (19) and (27), respectively. Although it might seem that
    a generalization has been missed, in reality these two anomalies have a very
    different status. The indigenous grammatical tradition describes the accusative
    suffix's resistance to infixation as variable or inconsistent, but the use of pausal
    indefinite [aː] is quite regular.

12 At the next step of this derivation, [kitaːb-a-INDEF]$_{Cont}$ becomes [kitaːb-a-n]$_{Cont}$,
    after which the derivation converges.

13 See Borer (1984) and Shlonsky (1997) for other views.

14 An anonymous reviewer has drawn my attention to Kenstowicz's (2005: 162)
    remark that the Arabic [at]~[ah] alternation is a counterexample to the claim that
    phonologically-conditioned allomorph selection never 'looks ahead' to higher/
    later morphology (Carstairs[-McCarthy] 1987, 1990; Kiparsky, 1994; Paster,
    2006, to appear), a claim that follows from the assumptions made here about
    sequential spell-out (see Section 11.5). This counterexample is only apparent,
    however; it disappears once clitics are analyzed as they are in (36).

References

Baker, Mark. (1985) The Mirror Principle and morphosyntactic explanation. *Lin-guistic Inquiry* 16 (3): 373–415.

Barnes, Jonathan. (2006) *Strength and Weakness at the Interface: Positional Neutralization in Phonetics and Phonology*. Berlin and New York: Mouton de Gruyter.

Birkeland, Harris. (1940) *Altarabische Pausalformen*. Oslo: Jacob Dybwad.

Borer, Hagit. (1984) *Parametric Syntax: Case Studies in Semitic and Romance Languages*. Dordrecht: Foris Publications.

Broselow, Ellen. (1976) *The Phonology of Egyptian Arabic*. Doctoral dissertation, University of Massachusetts Amherst, Amherst, MA.

Burzio, Luigi. (1994) Metrical consistency. In Eric Sven Ristad (ed.), *Language Computations* 93–125. Providence, RI: American Mathematical Society.

Carstairs[-McCarthy], Andrew. (1987) *Allomorphy in Inflexion*. London: Croom Helm.

Carstairs[-McCarthy], Andrew (1990) Phonologically conditioned suppletion. In Wolfgang U. Dressler, Hans C. Luschütsky, Oscar E. Pfeiffer and John R. Rennison (eds), *Contemporary Morphology* 17–23. Berlin: Mouton de Gruyter.

Chomsky, Noam and Morris Halle. (1968) *The Sound Pattern of English*. New York: Harper & Row.

Dresher, B. Elan. (1983) Postlexical phonology in Tiberian Hebrew. In M. Barlow, D. Flickinger and M. Wescoat (eds), *The Proceedings of the West Coast Conference on Formal Linguistics 2* 67–78. Stanford, CA: Stanford Linguistic Association.

Dresher, B. Elan. (2008) The word in Tiberian Hebrew. In Kristin Hanson and Sharon Inkelas (eds), *The Nature of the Word: Essays in Honor of Paul Kiparsky* 95–111. Cambridge, MA: MIT Press.

Fassi Fehri, Abdelkader. (1993) *Issues in the Structure of Arabic Clauses and Words*. Dordrecht and Boston: Kluwer Academic.

Fischer, Wolfdietrich and Otto Jastrow (eds). (1980) *Handbuch der Arabischen Dialekte*. Wiesbaden: Otto Harrassowitz.

Flack, Kathryn. (2007) *The Sources of Phonological Markedness*. Doctoral dissertation, University of Massachusetts Amherst, Amherst, MA.

Flack, Kathryn. (2009) Constraints on onsets and codas of words and phrases. *Phonology* 26: 269–302.

Fleisch, Henri. (1968) *L'Arabe Classique*. Beirut: Dar Al Machreq.

Goerwitz, Richard. (1993) *Tiberian Hebrew Pausal Forms*. Doctoral dissertation, University of Chicago, Chicago, IL.

Goldsmith, John. (1990) *Autosegmental and Metrical Phonology*. Oxford and Cambridge, MA: Blackwell.

Halle, Morris and Alec Marantz. (1993) Distributed Morphology and the pieces of inflection. In Kenneth Hale and Samuel Jay Keyser (eds), *The View from Building 20* 111–76. Cambridge, MA: MIT Press.

Hargus, Sharon. (1995) The first person plural prefix in Babine-Witsuwit'en. Unpublished paper, University of Washington, Seattle. Available on Rutgers Optimality Archive, ROA-108.

Hargus, Sharon and Siri G. Tuttle. (1997) Augmentation as affixation in Athabaskan languages. *Phonology* 14: 177–220.

Hayes, Bruce (1990) Precompiled phrasal phonology. In Sharon Inkelas and Draga Zec (eds), *The Phonology-Syntax Connection* 85–108. Chicago, IL: University of Chicago Press.

Hoberman, Robert. (1995) Subtractive morphology and morpheme identity in Arabic pausal forms. *Yearbook of Morphology 1995* 161–74.

Horwood, Graham. (2002) Precedence faithfulness governs morpheme position. In Line Mikkelsen and Christopher Potts (eds), *Proceedings of the 21st West Coast Conference on Formal Linguistics* 166–79. Cambridge, MA: Cascadilla Press.

Horwood, Graham. (2004) *Order without Chaos: Relational Faithfulness and Position of Exponence in Optimality Theory*, Doctoral dissertation, Rutgers University, New Brunswick, NJ.

Howell, Mortimer Sloper. (1986) *A Grammar of the Classical Arabic Language Translated and Compiled from the Works of the Most Approved Native or Naturalized Authors*. Delhi, India: Gian Publishing House.

Hudson, Grover. (1974) The representation of non-productive alternation. In John Anderson and Charles Jones (eds), *Historical Linguistics* 203–229. Amsterdam: North Holland.

Ito, Junko. (1989) A prosodic theory of epenthesis. *Natural Language & Linguistic Theory* 7: 217–59.

Kaneko, Ikuyo and Shigeto Kawahara. (2002) Positional faithfulness theory and the emergence of the unmarked: The case of Kagoshima Japanese. *ICU English Studies* 5: 18–36.

Kenstowicz, Michael. (2005) Paradigmatic uniformity and contrast. In Laura J. Downing, T. Alan Hall and Renate Raffelsiefen (eds), *Paradigms in Phonological Theory* 145–169. Oxford: Oxford University Press.

Kimper, Wendell. (to appear) Locality and globality in phonological variation. *Natural Language & Linguistic Theory*. Available on Rutgers Optimality Archive, ROA-988.

Kiparsky, Paul. (1982) Lexical phonology and morphology. In I. S. Yang (ed.), *Linguistics in the Morning Calm* 3–91. Seoul: Hanshin.

Kiparsky, Paul. (1994) Allomorphy or morphophonology. In Rajendra Singh and Richard Desroches (eds), *Trubetzkoy's Orphan: Proceedings of the Montréal Roundtable 'Morphonology: Contemporary Responses'* 13–31. Amsterdam: John Benjamins.

Kratzer, Angelika and Elisabeth Selkirk. (2007) Phase theory and prosodic spellout: The case of verbs. *The Linguistic Review* 24: 93–135.

Liberman, Mark and Alan Prince. (1977) On stress and linguistic rhythm. *Linguistic Inquiry* 8: 249–336.

Lombardi, Linda. (1995/2001) Why Place and Voice are different: Constraint-specific alternations in Optimality Theory. In Linda Lombardi (ed.), *Segmental Phonology in Optimality Theory: Constraints and Representations* 13–45. Cambridge: Cambridge University Press.

Mascaró, Joan. (1996) External allomorphy as emergence of the unmarked. In Jacques Durand and Bernard Laks (eds), *Current Trends in Phonology: Models and Methods* 473–483. Salford, Manchester: European Studies Research Institute, University of Salford.

Mascaró, Joan. (2007) External allomorphy and lexical representation. *Linguistic Inquiry* 38 (4): 715–735.

McCarthy, John J. (1979) *Formal Problems in Semitic Phonology and Morphology*. Doctoral dissertation, MIT, Cambridge, MA.

McCarthy, John J. (2000) Harmonic serialism and parallelism. In Masako Hirotani (ed.), *Proceedings of the North East Linguistics Society 30* 501–524. Amherst, MA: GLSA Publications.

McCarthy, John J. (2002) *A Thematic Guide to Optimality Theory*. Cambridge: Cambridge University Press.

McCarthy, John J. (2007a) *Hidden Generalizations: Phonological Opacity in Optimality Theory*. London: Equinox Publishing.

McCarthy, John J. (2007b) Restraint of analysis. In Sylvia Blaho, Patrik Bye and Martin Krämer (eds), *Freedom of Analysis* 203–231. Berlin and New York: Mouton de Gruyter.

McCarthy, John J. (2008a) *Doing Optimality Theory*. Malden, MA, and Oxford: Blackwell.

McCarthy, John J. (2008b) The gradual path to cluster simplification. *Phonology* 25: 271–319.

McCarthy, John J. (2008c) The serial interaction of stress and syncope. *Natural Language & Linguistic Theory* 26: 499–546.

McCarthy, John J. (2010) Studying Gen. *Journal of the Phonetic Society of Japan* 13: 3–12.

McCarthy, John J. and Alan Prince. (1993) Generalized alignment. In Geert Booij and Jaap van Marle (eds), *Yearbook of Morphology* 79–153. Dordrecht: Kluwer.

McCarthy, John J. and Alan Prince (1994) The emergence of the unmarked: Optimality in prosodic morphology. In Mercè Gonzàlez (ed.), *Proceedings of the North East Linguistic Society 24* 333–79. Amherst, MA: GLSA Publications.

McCarthy, John J. and Alan Prince. (1995) Faithfulness and reduplicative identity. In Jill Beckman, Laura Walsh Dickey and Suzanne Urbanczyk (eds), *University of Massachusetts Occasional Papers in Linguistics 18* 249–384. Amherst, MA: GLSA Publications.

McCarthy, John J. and Alan Prince. (1999) Faithfulness and identity in Prosodic Morphology. In René Kager, Harry van der Hulst and Wim Zonneveld (eds), *The Prosody-Morphology Interface* 218–309. Cambridge: Cambridge University Press.

Mester, Armin. (1994) The quantitative trochee in Latin. *Natural Language & Linguistic Theory* 12: 1–61.

Mohanan, K. P. (1982) *Lexical Phonology*. Doctoral dissertation, MIT, Cambridge, MA.

Myers, Scott and Benjamin B. Hansen. (2007) The origin of vowel length neutralization in final position: Evidence from Finnish speakers. *Natural Language & Linguistic Theory* 25: 157–193.

Padgett, Jaye. (1995) Partial class behavior and nasal place assimilation. In Keiichiro Suzuki and Dirk Elzinga (eds), *Proceedings of the 1995 Southwestern Workshop on Optimality Theory (SWOT)* 145–83. Tucson, AZ: Department of Linguistics, University of Arizona.

Parker, Steve. (2001) Non-optimal onsets in Chamicuro: An inventory maximized in coda position. *Phonology* 18: 361–386.

Paster, Mary. (2006) *Phonological Conditions on Affixation*. Doctoral dissertation, University of California, Berkeley, CA.

Paster, Mary. (to appear) Phonologically conditioned suppletive allomorphy: Cross-linguistic results and theoretical consequences. In Bernard Tranel (ed.), *Understanding Allomorphy: Perspectives from OT*. London: Equinox Publishing.

Pater, Joe. (2006) The locus of exceptionality: Morpheme-specific phonology as constraint indexation. In Leah Bateman, Adam Werle, Michael O'Keefe and Ehren Reilly (eds), *University of Massachusetts Occasional Papers in Linguistics 32: Papers in Optimality Theory III*. Amherst, MA: GLSA.

Pater, Joe. (to appear) Serial Harmonic Grammar and Berber syllabification. In Toni Borowsky, Shigeto Kawahara, Takahito Shinya and Mariko Sugahara (eds), *Prosody Matters: Essays in Honor of Lisa Selkirk*. London: Equinox Publishing.

Perlmutter, David (1998) Interfaces: Explanation of allomorphy and the architecture of grammars. In Steven G. Lapointe, Diane K. Brentari and Patrick M. Farrell (eds), *Morphology and its Relation to Phonology and Syntax* 307–38. Stanford, CA: CSLI Publications.

Prince, Alan. (1975) *The Phonology and Morphology of Tiberian Hebrew*. Doctoral dissertation, MIT, Cambridge, MA.

Prince, Alan (2002) Arguing optimality. In Angela Carpenter, Andries Coetzee and Paul de Lacy (eds), *University of Massachusetts Occasional Papers in Linguistics 26: Papers in Optimality Theory II* 269–304. Amherst, MA: GLSA.

Prince, Alan and Paul Smolensky. (1993/2004) *Optimality Theory: Constraint Interaction in Generative Grammar*. Malden, MA, and Oxford: Blackwell.

Pruitt, Kathryn. (2008) Iterative foot optimization and locality in stress systems. Unpublished paper, University of Massachusetts Amherst, Amherst, MA. Available on Rutgers Optimality Archive, ROA-999.

Schaade, A. (1911) *Sibawaihi's Lautlehre*. Leiden: E. J. Brill.

Selkirk, Elisabeth. (1980) Prosodic domains in phonology: Sanskrit revisited. In Mark Aronoff and Mary-Louise Kean (eds), *Juncture* 107–129. Saratoga, CA: Anma Libri.

Selkirk, Elisabeth. (1984) *Phonology and Syntax: The Relation between Sound and Structure*. Cambridge, MA: MIT Press.

Selkirk, Elisabeth. (1986) On derived domains in sentence phonology. *Phonology* 3: 371–405.

Selkirk, Elisabeth (1995) The prosodic structure of function words. In Jill Beckman, Laura Walsh Dickey and Suzanne Urbanczyk (eds), *University of Massachusetts Occasional Papers in Linguistics 18: Papers in Optimality Theory* 439–470. Amherst, MA: GLSA Publications.

Shlonsky, Ur. (1997) *Clause Structure and Word Order in Hebrew and Arabic: An Essay in Comparative Semitic Syntax*. New York: Oxford University Press.

Smith, Jennifer L. (2002) *Phonological Augmentation in Prominent Positions*. Doctoral dissertation, University of Massachusetts Amherst, Amherst, MA.

Trager, George L. and Frank A. Rich. (1954) The personal-pronoun system of Classical Arabic. *Language* 30: 224–229.

Tranel, Bernard. (1996a) Exceptionality in Optimality Theory and final consonants in French. In Karen Zagona (ed.), *Grammatical Theory and Romance Languages* 275–91. Amsterdam: John Benjamins.

Tranel, Bernard. (1996b) French liaison and elision revisited: A unified account within Optimality Theory. In Claudia Parodi, Carlos Quicoli, Mario Saltarelli and Maria Luisa Zubizarreta (eds), *Aspects of Romance Linguistics* 433–455. Washington, DC: Georgetown University Press.

Tranel, Bernard. (1998) Suppletion and OT: On the issue of the syntax/phonology interaction. In E. Curtis, J. Lyle and G. Webster (eds), *The Proceedings of the West Coast Conference on Formal Linguistics 16* 415–29. Stanford, CA: CSLI Publications.

Whitney, W. D. (1889) *Sanskrit Grammar*. Cambridge, MA: Harvard University Press.

Wolf, Matthew. (2008) *Optimal Interleaving: Serial Phonology-Morphology Interaction in a Constraint-Based Model*. Doctoral dissertation, University of Massachusetts Amherst, Amherst, MA.

Wright, W. (1971) *A Grammar of the Arabic Language*. Cambridge: Cambridge University Press.

12 Reconsidering the edge parameter

Hisao Tokizaki[a]

12.1 Introduction

The edge based theory of prosodic hierarchy (Selkirk, 1986, among others) has succeeded in explaining typological differences between languages. In this paper, I will derive the edge parameter from the head parameter in syntax and discuss the difference in phrasing between Shanghai and other Chinese dialects. In Section 12.2, I will briefly review the edge parameter theory of Selkirk (1986) and the prosodic differences between Xiamen and Shanghai. Section 12.3 illustrates the bare mapping from syntactic structure onto phonological representation (Tokizaki, 1999, 2008). Section 12.4 discusses how the differences between Chinese dialects can be explained without the edge parameter. Section 12.5 concludes the discussion.[1]

12.2 The edge based theory of prosodic hierarchy

First, let us reconsider the edge parameter proposed by Selkirk (1986) and Chen (1987). The end-based theory assumes that languages have an edge parameter in prosodic phrasing whose values are right or left. For example, Chi Mwi:ni shows that the right edge of a lexically headed XP is a phonological phrase boundary.

(1) (a) $[_{VP} [_{V'} [_{V}$ pa(:)nzize] $[_{NP}$ cho:mbo]] $[_{NP}$ mwa:mba]]
     'He ran the vessel on to the rock'
   (b)   ....$]_{Xmax}$ ....$]_{Xmax}$
   (c) $_{PPh}$(__________________________) $_{PPh}$(__________)

[a] Hisao Tokizaki: Sapporo University, Sapporo, Japan.

Selkirk argues that in (1) the left edge of the NP *cho:mbo* does not make a prosodic boundary, but its right edge does.

On the other hand, Selkirk and Tateishi (1988, 1991) argue that in Japanese the value of the phrasing parameter is left. The following example shows that verbs take their complements to their left (Selkirk and Tateishi, 1991: 524):

(2)   (a) [$_S$ [$_{NP}$ [$_{NP}$ Ao'yama-no] [$_N$ Yama'guchi-ga]] [$_{VP}$ [$_{NP}$ ani'yome-o]   [$_V$ yonda]]]
            Aoyama-from   Yamaguchi-Nom   sister-in-law-Acc called
        'Mr. Yamaguchi from Aoyama called his sister-in-law.'

    (b) $_{MaP}$(Ao'yama-no Yama'guchi-ga) $_{MaP}$(ani'yome-o yonda)

They argue that the right edge of the NP *ani'yome-o* does not make a Major Phrase boundary but its left edge does.

In this way, according to the end-based theory, languages can be grouped in terms of the edge parameter of prosodic phrasing. The following is a list of languages that have right and left as the edge parameter value:

(3) Right edge of lexically headed XPs:
    Chi Mwi:ni (Kisseberth and Abasheikh 1974, Selkirk 1986)
    Kimatuumbi (Odden 1987)
    Xiamen (Chen 1987)
    Papago (Hale and Selkirk 1987)

(4) Left edge of lexically headed XPs:
    Ewe (Clements 1978)
    Japanese (Selkirk and Tateishi 1991)
    Korean (Cho 1990)
    Northern Kyungsang Korean (Kenstowicz and Sohn 1997)
    Shanghai Chinese (Selkirk and Shen 1990)

Notice that there seems to be a parallelism between the syntactic head parameter and the prosodic edge parameter. Head-initial (i.e. complement-right) languages such as Chi Mwi:ni (cf. (1)) and Xiamen have right edge as the parameter value, and head-final (i.e. complement-left) languages such as Japanese (cf. (2)) and Korean have left as the value. It is desirable if we can dispense with the edge parameter by deriving its effect from the head parameter. In the next section, I will briefly illustrate the bare mapping theory I proposed in Tokizaki, (1999, 2008).

Note here that we cannot explain optional tone sandhi in Shanghai straightforwardly if we suppose that the phrase structure of Shanghai is the same as that of Xiamen, as Hale and Selkirk (1987: 179) argue. One possible explanation is to suppose that the prosodic domain in Shanghai is smaller than that in Xiamen. See also Selkirk and Shen (1990: 335). This issue is discussed in Section 3.1.3 in Tokizaki (2008). However, I will reconsider it in Section 12.4 below focusing on phonological properties in Shanghai.

12.3 Bare mapping from syntax onto phonology

12.3.1 Bare mapping

First, let us reconsider the example (1) from Chi Mwi:ni in terms of bare phrase structure (cf. Chomsky, 1995).

(5) [$_{VP}$ [$_{V'}$ [$_V$ pa(:)nzize] [$_N$ cho:mbo]] [$_N$ mwa:mba]]

Chi Mwi:ni is head-initial (i.e. complement-right) and has right as the edge parameter value. We can explain why this is the case with the bare mapping theory. In Tokizaki (1999, 2008), I proposed the following mapping rule as shown in (6).[2]

(6) Interpret boundaries of syntactic constituents […] as prosodic boundaries / … /.

Now let us consider the reported data in turn. First consider Chi Mwi:ni (5). As we have seen, the mapping rule places the minimum number of prosodic boundaries, that is two, between heads and non-branching complements, i.e. *pa(:)nzize* and *cho:mbo*, because they are sisters in phrase structure. It also places three boundaries between the first object and the second object if they are non-branching, as shown in (7).

(7)   /// pa(:)nzize // cho:mbo /// mwa:mba //

If we apply the boundary deletion rule (8), which I proposed in Tokizaki (1999, 2008), with $n = 2$ to (7), we have the demarcated string as in (9).

(8)   Delete *n* boundaries between words.   (*n*: a natural number)

(9)   / pa(:)nzize cho:mbo / mwa:mba   ($n = 2$)

This is the correct prosodic phrasing for the sentence. The left edge of the first object does not make a prosodic boundary because the object is the sister of the preceding verb. The right edge of the object makes a prosodic boundary because the second object is not the sister of the first object, but the sister of the category branching into the verb and the first object. Thus we do not have to specify the edge parameter of the language as right. The phrasing pattern is predicted from phrase structure.

This also holds with head-final languages like Japanese. As the examples in (2) show, verbs take their complements to their left. I will show bare phrase structure and the result of applying the mapping rule (6) together below. Consider (10) for example.

(10) (a) $[_S [_{NP} [_{NP}$ Ao'yama-no] $[_N$ Yama'guchi-ga]] $[_{VP} [_{NP}$ ani'yome-o] $[_V$ yonda]]]
               Aoyama-from   Yamaguchi-Nom   sister-in-law-Acc called
          'Mr. Yamaguchi from Aoyama called his sister-in-law.'

      (b) $_{MaP}$(Ao'yama-no Yama'guchi-ga) $_{MaP}$(ani'yome-o yonda)

In (10a), the subject NP branches. So there are four boundaries between the head of the subject NP *Yamaguchi-ga* and the object NP *ani'yome-o*, and only two boundaries between the verb *yonda* and its object *ani'yome-o*, as shown in (11a). The Boundary Deletion (8) with $n = 2$ applies to (11a) to give (11b).

(11) (a) /// Ao'yama-no // Yama'guchi-ga ///// ani'yome-o // yonda ///
      (b) / Ao'yama-no Yama'guchi-ga // ani'yome-o yonda /   ($n = 2$)

We can explain the phrasing (10b) straightforwardly, as shown in (11b), without assuming that Japanese has left as the edge parameter value.

12.3.2 Syntactic constituents and prosodic boundaries

Let us consider the relation between syntactic constituents and prosodic boundaries in general. Suppose that α and β are sisters of γ, and that A and B are as follows: A is a word dominated by and is the right edge of α: B is a word dominated by and is the left edge of β. Or α equals A and β equals B. This is shown with a tree diagram in (12).

(12)

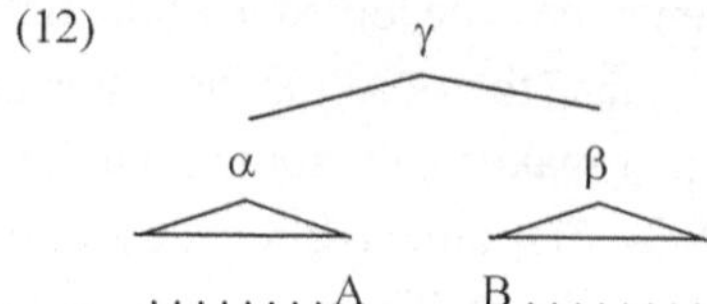

This is shown with brackets in (13) where possible brackets are italicized.

(13) [γ [α ... *[... [... A]]*] [β *[[* B ... *] ...]* ...]]

We can make the following generalization. The number of boundaries between words is at its minimum when both α and β are non-branching. The deeper A or B is embedded in α or β, the larger the number of brackets between A and B becomes.

Let us consider what phonological representations the mapping rule makes in different syntactic structures. First consider the syntactic structure of head initial languages. For example, look at the following right-branching structure where X-Z is a head word, S specifier, and C complement. SY, for example, shows the specifier of Y.

(14)

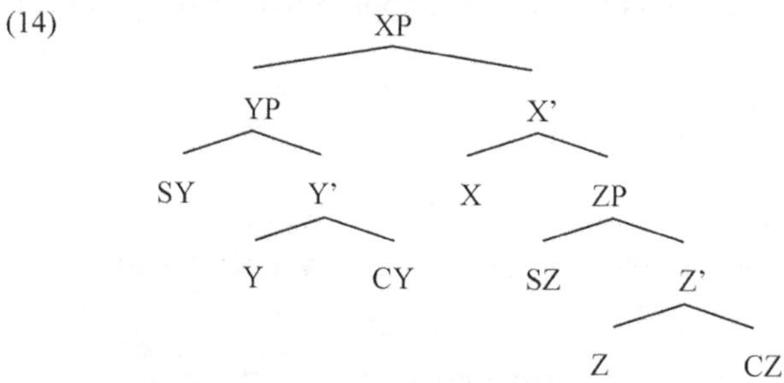

Here I show the X-bar theoretic structure for the purpose of exposition. (14) is represented as (15) with brackets.

(15) [XP [YP SY [Y' Y CY]] [X' X [ZP SZ [Z' Z CZ]]]]

Applying the bare mapping rule (6), we get the following representation:

(16) *//* SY / Y CY *///* X */* SZ / Z CZ *///*

The number of boundaries between CY and X is three. CZ also has three boundaries to its right. CY is on the right edge of YP, and CZ is in the right edge of ZP and XP. On the other hand, the number of boundaries between X and SZ is one. SY has two boundaries to its left. SZ is on the left edge of ZP, and SY is on the left edge of YP and XP. Thus, bare mapping theory predicts more boundaries at the right edge of a maximal projection in right-branching structure than at the left edge.

(17)   //   SY / Y CY /// X /   SZ / Z CZ ///
        [$_{XP}$ [$_{XP}$ SY   Y CY] X [$_{XP}$ SZ   Z CZ]]

Next, consider the syntactic structure of head final languages. For example, look at the following (partly) left-branching structure where I assume that specifiers are merged at the left of the intermediate projection of heads:

(18)

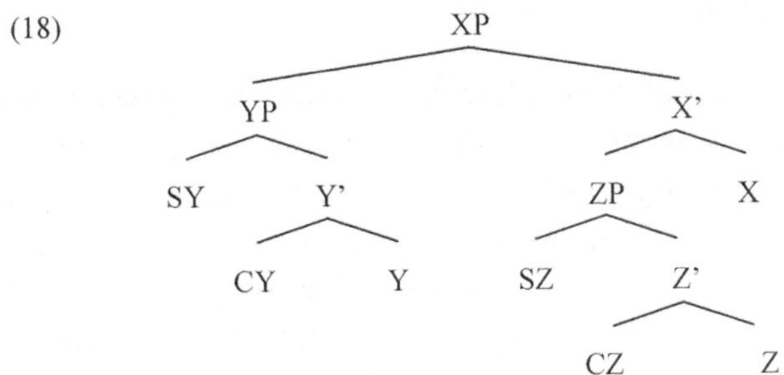

(18) is represented as (19) with brackets.

(19) [$_{XP}$ [$_{YP}$ SY [$_{Y'}$ CY Y]] [$_{X'}$ [$_{ZP}$ SZ [$_{Z'}$ CZ Z]] X]]

Applying the bare mapping rule (6), we get the following representation:

(20) // SY / CY Y ////   SZ / CZ Z // X //

The number of boundaries between Y and SZ is four. SY has two boundaries to its left. SZ is in the left edge of ZP, and SY is in the left edge of YP and XP. On the other hand, the number of boundaries between Z and X is two. X has two boundaries to its right. SZ is in the left edge of ZP, and SY is in the left edge of YP and XP.

(21)   // SY / CY Y //// SZ / CZ Z // X //
        [$_{XP}$ [$_{YP}$ SY CY Y] [$_{ZP}$ SZ CZ Z] X]

The position between Y and SZ corresponds to both the right edge of YP and the left edge of ZP in (21). Things are not as clear as in the right-branching case. However, if the position between Z and X, which corresponds to the right edge of ZP, does not block any prosodic rule, we may conclude that the left edge of a maximal projection is more relevant in prosodic phrasing than its right edge. This is what the end based theory predicts in right-branching structure. Bare mapping can make the same prediction as shown in (21).

12.4 Phonological differences between Taiwanese and Shanghai

12.4.1 Domain size difference

In this section, I will discuss how the differences between Chinese dialects can be explained without the edge parameter. First, I show that Shanghai Chinese has smaller prosodic units than other dialects of Chinese. In Section 12.4.2, I argue that the domain size difference arises from the difference of syllable structure: Shanghai has CV syllables only while other Chinese dialects have many CVG or CVC syllables (cf. Duanmu, 2008). In Section 12.4.3, I discuss the effects of rhythm, functional words and compounds on prosodic phrasing.

The most difficult problem for bare mapping theory is to explain the different parameter values among Chinese dialects. As the lists in (3) and (4) show, the value of the edge parameter is reported to be right in the Xiamen dialect and left in Shanghai Chinese (Chen, 1987; Selkirk and Shen, 1990). These languages share basic properties of grammar, especially word order and phrase structure. Both languages are syntactically head initial. If we are trying to derive the edge parameter from the syntactic head parameter, how can we make a prosodic difference in two languages that have the same parametric value of the syntactic parameter?

One solution is to suppose that the sensitivity to boundaries is different in the two languages. Let us first consider the rules and the data of these languages. Chen (1987: 131) argues that Tone Group Formation in Xiamen can be formulated as (22).

(22) Mark the right edge of every XP with #, except where XP is an adjunct c-commanding
its head.

The rule (22) correctly predicts the tone group boundary (#) in (23a) and
(23b).

(23) (a) yi   tsiong   hit   pun ts'eq #   sang   hoo   tang-oq
           he   Obj-marker   that Cl   book   give   to   schoolmate
           'He gave that book to his schoolmate.'

      (b) yi kap tang-oq   #   kai-siao   tsit e   lu-ping-yu
           he to   schoolmate   introduce   one Cl   girlfriend
           'He introduced a girlfriend to his schoolmate.'

hit pun ts'eq in (23a) and *kap tang-oq* in (23b), which are XPs, have a tone
group boundary to their right.

Selkirk and Shen (1990: 320, 332) argue that Shanghai Chinese has syntax-
phonology mapping rules with the parameter setting in (24) and (25).

(24) Shanghai Chinese Prosodic Word Rule: (p. 320)
      Prosodic Word: {Left, Lex^0}
      where Lex^0 stands for word belonging to the lexical categories N, V, A.

(25) Shanghai Chinese Major Phrase Rule: (p. 332, p. 328)
      Major Phrase: {Left, Lex^{max}}

Shanghai and Xiamen have almost the same syntax, but their edge parameter
values seem to be different. First, let us examine the data shown by Selkirk
and Shen (1990).

(26) (a) 'zaw   'mo
           toward   horse
           (LH)   (LH)
           'toward the horse'

      (b) peq   'mo   tshaw
          give   horses   grass
          (MH)   (LH)   (MH)
          'give horses grass'

(26a) is a crucial example. Prepositions and their objects make their own prosodic phrase. This is also the case with verbs and their objects as shown in (26b). Remember that in Xiamen, prepositions or verbs and their objects are grouped into the same prosodic phrase, as shown in (23a) and (23b).[3]

How can we derive prosodic phrasing in Shanghai if we eliminate the phonological edge parameter? First, note that the prosodic domain in Shanghai is smaller than that of Xiamen or Taiwanese. Consider the following examples from Yip (2002: 118):

(27) V-NP

    (a) Taiwanese: One tonal domain

       $[_V$ pang] $[_{NP}$ hong-ts'e]   'fly kite'

          fly   kite

    (b) Shanghai: Two tonal domains

       $[_V$ taN] # $[_{NP}$ 'niN]   'hit people'

         hit   people

As shown in (24), Selkirk and Shen (1990) also assume that the prosodic domain is prosodic word in Shanghai, unless there is focus effect. Then, if we assume that the variable n in the boundary deletion rule (8) is relatively small, say n = 1, in Shanghai, we can explain the data in (26).

(28) (a) $[_{PP} [_P$ 'zaw] $[_N$ 'mo]]

             toward   horse

        'toward the horse'

    (b)   // 'zaw // 'mo //

    (c)   / 'zaw / 'mo /   (n=1)

    (d)   (　LH) (LH)

(29) (a) $[_{VP} [_V$ peq] $[_N$ 'mo] $[_N$ tshaw]]

              give   horses grass

        'give horses grass'

    (b)   // peq // 'mo // tshaw //

    (c)   / peq / 'mo / tshaw /   (n=1)

    (d)   (MH) (LH) (MH)

The phrase structures in (28a) and (29a) are interpreted as (28b) and (29b) by the mapping rule (6) and some of their boundaries are deleted as in (28c) and (29c) to make the prosodic domain shown in (28d) and (29d).

12.4.2 Phonological properties in Shanghai

A question arises here: why does Shanghai prefer small tonal domain? In our terms, why does Shanghai set the number of boundaries to be deleted (n) as 1 instead of 2? To answer this question, we need to consider phonological properties in Shanghai carefully. Selkirk and Shen (1990) show three rules applying in a Prosodic Word: Obligatory Tone Deletion, LR Association and Contour Tone Association:

(30) Obligatory Tone Deletion

     $(T_i\, T_j \ldots T_k \ldots)_{PW}$ → $(T_i\, T_j \ldots \ldots)_{PW}$

This rule deletes all the tones following the first pair of tones in a prosodic word domain. LR Association associates the second tone with the second syllable in a prosodic word, as shown in (31).

(31) LR Association

     $(\,T_i\, T_j \ldots)_{PW}$ → $(\,T_i\quad T_j \ldots)_{PW}$

      | | |

     $\sigma\ \sigma \ldots$ $\sigma\ \ \sigma \ldots$

Contour Tone Association associates the last pair of tones $T_i\ T_j$ with the last syllable in a prosodic word, as shown in (32).

(32) Contour Tone Association

     $(\ldots T_i\, T_j)_{PW}$ → $(\ldots T_i\, T_j)_{PW}$

      | V

     σ σ

Duanmu (2008) argues that Shanghai, which has CV syllables only, shows tone split, where contour tones break into level tones. Tone split is illustrated as in (33).

(33) Tone split in Shanghai

	Surface	H	L	L	H	L	H
	Citation	HL	0	L-H	0	L-H	0
		fii	lə$^{\,?}$	see	lə$^{\,?}$	zee	lə$^{\,?}$
		'flew'		'broke'		'earned'	

In contrast, other Chinese languages such as Standard Chinese, which have many CVX syllables (CVG and CVC), show stable tones.

(34) Lack of tone split in Standard Chinese

Surface	HL	(L)	LH	(L)	L	H
Citation	HL	0	LH	0	L-H	0
	mai	lə	lai	lə	mai	lə
	'sold'		'came'		'bought'	

Suppose that Shanghai set the number of boundaries to be deleted as 2 ($n = 2$) for Boundary Deletion. Then the examples in (28) and (29) would be (35) and (36).

(35) (a) $[_{PP} [_P$ 'zaw] $[_N$ 'mo]]
                    toward   horse
           'toward the horse'
      (b)   // 'zaw // 'mo //
      (c)   'zaw 'mo   ($n=2$)
      (d)   (L   H)   ← LH ~~LH~~

(36) (a) $[_{VP} [_V$ peq] $[_N$ 'mo] $[_N$ tshaw]]
                    give   horses   grass
           'give horses grass'
      (b)   // peq // 'mo // tshaw //
      (c)   peq 'mo tshaw   ($n=2$)
      (d)   (M   H)   ← MH ~~LH MH~~

Boundary Deletion would delete all the boundaries between words to give a tonal domain extending over all the words. However, this phrasing would make Tone Deletion delete the tone of nouns, which carry the most important information in the phrase. Thus, this phrasing must be avoided. Note that it is not possible to delete the tone of preposition or verb in order to keep the tone of nouns as shown in (37) and (38).

(37) 'zaw 'mo   ($n=2$)
        (LH)   ← ~~LH~~ LH

(38) peq 'mo tshaw ($n=2$)
        (LH MH) ← ~~MH~~ LH MH

This is impossible because Tone Deletion cannot delete the tone on the left in a tonal domain as formulated in (30). Moreover, even if the deletion of the tone of preposition or verb, no tone can be assigned to them by Tone Association, which applies only to the syllables on the right in a tonal domain as formulated in (32). Thus, Shanghai chooses small tonal domain in order to keep the tone of nouns.

Other dialect of Chinese have tone sandhi, which changes tones preceding the final tone in a tonal domain. For example, Beijing Chinese (Standard Chinese) has a tone sandhi rule which changes a sequence of third tones preceding the final third tone in a tonal domain. Chen (2000: 26) shows the following formulation of the tone sandhi:

(39) Beijing T3 Sandhi
     T3 → T2 / ___ T3
     T2 = MH
     T3 = L

Let us look at an example in (40).

(40) (a) *leng shui*
       cold water
       L   L   base
       MH L   sandhi

    (b) *mai ma*
       buy horse   'to buy a horse'
       L   L   base
       MH   L   sandhi

In (40), the complement of verb keeps its base tone while the verb changes its tone. No tone is deleted in a tonal domain in Standard Chinese. Thus, the deletion of prosodic boundaries between words can make a large tonal domain without deleting tone on the lexical item carrying important information. In other words, both Standard Chinese and Shanghai Chinese keep the tone of the object of verb or preposition. Thus, tone must be on the lexical items with important information in any language. Shanghai Chinese needs to divide sentences into small prosodic units in order to keep tone on the lexical items with important information.

12.4.3 Rhythm, function words and compounds

12.4.3.1 V-P/N

Let us consider three other types of phrasing in Shanghai: V-P/N, V-D/N and V-Q-CL/N. Yip (2002: 121) suggests that the prosodic domain in Shanghai is determined partly by rhythm. First, look at the following examples from Selkirk and Shen (1990: 321), which have the V-P/N phrasing pattern:

(41) (a) [$_{VP}$ [$_V$ 'z] [$_{PP}$ [$_P$ 'laq] [$_N$ 'zawNhe]]]
            live   at   Shanghai
        (L   H) (L   H)   <-   LH ~~LM~~ LH ~~MH~~
    'live in Shanghai'

    (b) [$_{VP}$ [$_V$ tsou] [$_{PP}$ [$_P$ taw] [$_N$ 'noetsiN]]]
            walk   to   Nanjing
        (M   H)(L   H)   <-   MH ~~MH~~ LH ~~HL~~
    'walk to Nanjing'

Selkirk and Shen (1990) explain this phrasing by the reference to the types of lexical categories in their formulation of Prosodic Word Rule (24), which is repeated here as (42).

(42)   Shanghai Chinese Prosodic Word Rule: (p. 320)
        Prosodic Word: {Left, Lex^0}
        where Lex^0 stands for word belonging to the lexical categories N, V, A.

In (42), the lexical categories are restricted to N, V and A, with P excluded. Thus, the left edge of preposition does not make a prosodic boundary.

This formulation of phrasing rule correctly explains the data in (41), which has the V P N sequence phrased as (V P) (N). However, they do not show why P is not included into the lexical categories. Selkirk and Shen (1990) show good observation of the phrasing facts, but we would like to know the reason behind their observation. Instead of postulating the edge parameter in (42), let us try to explain the phrasing in (41) with the bare mapping below.

For example, the verb phrase in (41a) has the phrase structure in (43a), which is mapped onto the phonological structure in (43b) by the mapping rule in (6).

(43) (a) [$_{VP}$ [$_V$ 'z] [$_{PP}$ [$_P$ 'laq] [$_N$ 'zawNhe]]]
               live   at   Shanghai
        'live in Shanghai'
     (b)   // 'z /// 'laq // 'zawNhe ///

Boundary Deletion (8) with $n = 2$ would derive a wrong phrasing pattern in (44).

(44)   (a)   'z / 'laq 'zawNhe /   ($n=2$)
       (b)   'z   'laq 'zawNhe
             (LH) (L   M)   ← LH LM ~~LH~~ ~~MH~~

This phrasing would delete the tone of N *'zawNhe*, violating the constraint on deletion of tone on important information. This phrasing is avoided in Shanghai. Then, how is the V P N sequence phrased into (V P) (N)?

I argue that two points are involved in the phrasing in (41). One is that the nouns in (41) in fact have two morphemes. The other is that prepositions are phonologically light and are likely to depend on the adjacent word. Let us look at each of them in turn.

First, note that each noun in (41) consists of two morphemes. *'zawNhe* and *'noetsiN* are a kind of compound noun as is evident from the fact that they consist of two Chinese characters (Shanghai 上海 is 'up-sea' and Nanjing 南京 is 'south-city'). I would like to argue that compound nouns N can be analyzed as [$_N$ [$_N$ …] [$_N$ …]] with its internal constituent structure. Then, the following structure is the input to the syntax-phonology mapping rule:

(45) (a)   [$_{VP}$ [$_V$ 'z] [$_{PP}$ [$_P$ 'laq] [$_N$ [$_N$ 'zawN] [$_N$ he]]]]
      (b)   [$_{VP}$ [$_V$ tsou] [$_{PP}$ [$_P$ taw] [$_N$ [$_N$ 'noe] [$_N$ tsiN]]]]

The mapped phonological representations are (46a) and (46b).

(46)   (a)   // 'z /// 'laq /// 'zawN // he ////
         (b)   // tsou /// taw /// 'noe // tsiN ////

It is not unnatural to put a prosodic boundary between the preposition and its object because there are three boundaries there (the maximum sequence in the example), as well as between the verb and the preposition. Eurhythmic considerations may well govern the actual phrasing.[4]

Second, prepositions in general are phonologically light and are likely to depend on the adjacent word. In this sense, prepositions may behave like enclitics. To review the discussion of clitics in Tokizaki (2008), consider the examples in (47).

(47) (a) Línda plays ténnis.
    (b) She pláys it.

I assume that (47b) has the syntactic representation (48a) which is interpreted as (48b).

(48) (a) [She [pláys] it]
    (b) / She / plays / it /

As shown in (48a), I assume that clitics and unstressed function words have a boundary on only one side of them. The side without consonants are likely to have no boundary. *She* has a boundary on its left and *it* has a boundary on its right.

    Let us go back to Shanghai examples in (41), which have a preposition prosodically grouped with the verb. This may suggest that the prepositions in these examples have no boundary on their left as shown in (49).

(49) (a) $[_{VP} [_V$ 'z] $[_{PP}$ 'laq] $[_N [_N$ 'zaw] $[_N$ Nhe]]]]
            live   at   Shang- hai
       'live in Shanghai'

    (b) $[_{VP} [_V$ tsou] $[_{PP}$ taw] $[_N [_N$ 'noe] $[_N$ tsiN]]]]
            walk   to   Nan- jing
       'walk to Nanjing'

Here it is assumed that prepositions *'laq* and *taw* have no boundary on their left. The syntactic structure in (49) are mapped onto the phonological structure in (50).

(50) (a) // 'z // 'laq /// 'zaw // Nhe ////
    (b) // tsou // taw /// 'noe // tsiN ////

The Boundary Deletion with $n = 2$ gives the right prosodic phrasing as shown in (51).

(51)   (a)   'z 'laq / 'zaw Nhe //   ('z 'laq) ('zaw Nhe)
      (b)   tsou taw / 'noe tsiN //   (tsou taw) ('noe tsiN)

The phrasing in (51) allows the verb and the first noun to keep its base tone within the prosodic domain, as shown in (41).

12.4.3.2 V-D/N

These points are also the case with a personal pronoun embedded as a possessive in a post-verbal noun phrase as in (52), which shows the V-D/N phrasing pattern.

(52) (a) [$_{VP}$ [$_V$ taN] [$_{DP}$ [$_D$ 'ngu] [$_N$ 'njitsz]]]
           hit   1SG   son
         (M   H) (L H) <- MH ~~LH~~ LH ~~MH~~
         'hit my son'
   (b) [$_{VP}$ [$_V$ taN] [$_{DP}$ 'ngu] [$_N$ [$_N$ 'nji] [$_N$ tsz]]]]
   (c) // taN // 'ngu /// 'nji // tsz ////
   (d) taN 'ngu / 'nji tsz //   (*n*=2)

The structure (52a) can be analyzed as (52b) where *'nji-tsz* 儿子 is a compound and a personal pronoun *'ngu* is like a clitic. The bare mapping applies to (52b) to give (52c), which is changed into (52d) by Boundary Deletion with $n = 2$. The phrasing in (52d) correctly predicts the prosodic units in (52a), where the verb and the noun keep their base tone.

12.4.3.3 V-Q-CL/N

However, there are some data which need careful examination. The following examples have four words, which are in a group of three words and a single word (V-Q-CL/N):

(53) (a)   [$_{VP}$ [$_V$ taw] [$_{NP}$[$_{QP}$ [$_Q$?iq] [$_{CL}$ pe]] [$_N$ 'zo]]]
             pour   one   cup   tea
           (M   H   L) (LH) ← MH ~~MH~~ ~~HL~~ LH
        'pour a cup of tea'

   (b)   [$_{VP}$ [$_V$ 'ma] [$_{NP}$[$_{QP}$ [$_Q$ tsi] [$_{CL}$ po]] [$_N$ taw]]]
         buy   how   many knife
         (L   H   L) (HL) ← LH ~~MH~~ ~~MH~~ HL
        'buy some knives'

These examples show that eurhythmic consideration is not always the crucial factor in phrasing in Shanghai. Selkirk and Shen (1990) argue that focus or semantic weight is involved in Shanghai. I speculate that this is the case in these examples as well. Duanmu (1992: 74) argues that *?iq* and *pe* in (53a) are 'function words' which do not carry stress. *Taw* and *'zo* are stress bearing units. This claim can be supported by the following examples, also from Selkirk and Shen (1990):

(54) (a) $[_{VP} [_V$ taw$] [_{NP}[_{QP} [_Q$?iq$] [_{CL}$ pe$]] [_N$ 'zo$]]]$

                pour   one   cup   tea

             (MH)   (M   H) (LH) ←   MH MH ~~HL~~ LH

        'pour one cup of tea'

(b) $[_{VP} [_V$ 'ma$] [_{NP}[_{QP} [_Q$ tsi$] [_{CL}$ po$]] [_N$ taw$]]]$

         buy   how   many knife

        (LH)   (M   H) (HL) ←   LH MH ~~MH~~ HL

        'how many knives ... buy?'

In (54a) and (54b), *?iq* and *tsi* are used as quantifiers. These words can start their own domains and keep their base tone if they have semantic content. This fact is not surprising if we assume bare mapping theory.

(55) (a) // taw //// ?iq // pe /// 'zo ///

      (b) // 'ma //// tsi // po /// taw ///

If we apply the boundary deletion rule with $n = 2$, we get the right phrasing:

(56) (a) taw // ?iq pe / 'zo /

      (b) 'ma // tsi po / taw /

Note that *pe* and *po* are used here as classifiers instead of nouns in these examples and need not keep their base tones.

To sum up the discussion in this section, I argued that the difference of phrasing between Shanghai Chinese and other Chinese dialects can be explained without the edge parameter. Shanghai Chinese has smaller prosodic units than other dialects of Chinese because Shanghai has CV syllables only while other Chinese dialects have many CVG or CVC syllables. Problematic data in Shanghai can be explained if we take into account the effects of rhythm, functional words and compounds on prosodic phrasing. Thus, we can explain the data in Shanghai which might have presented a problem in deriving the prosodic edge parameter from the syntactic head parameter. It is quite an advance, I believe, to be able to dispense with the edge parameter, which has been something of a problematic concept.

12.5 Conclusion

In this paper, I have argued that the edge parameter is not necessary for prosodic phrasing if we assume the bare mapping from syntactic structure onto phonology. The difference in syntactic structure can be determined by head parameter, i.e. head-initial or head-final. The phrasing in Shanghai Chinese, seemingly the problematic case for this analysis, is explained by its phonological properties such as syllable structure and Tone Deletion together with the constraint on deletion of important information expressed by nouns and verbs.

Thus we can dispense with the edge parameter. The remaining question is whether the head parameter can be derived by more basic elements. Kayne (1994) proposes the universal base hypothesis, which claims that all the languages have head-initial structure. The word order differences are due to the presence or absence of complement-movement. Tokizaki and Kuwana (2009) argue that complement-movement is possible if the language has leftward stress pattern. If this analysis is on the right track, what we need to explain the syntactic headedness and prosodic phrasing is the word stress canon in the language. I will leave this topic for a future study.

Notes

1   A part of this paper is based on Section 3.1 in Tokizaki (2008). I would like to thank Lisa Selkirk for her comments on the idea presented there. I also thank two anonymous reviewers for their valuable comments on an earlier version of this paper.

2   The mapping rule (6) can be considered as a generalized version of Chomsky and Halle's (1968: 366) #-Insertion:

  (i)   The boundary # is automatically inserted at the beginning and end of every string dominated by a major category, i.e., by one of the lexical categories 'noun,' 'verb,' 'adjective,' or by a category such as 'sentence,' 'noun phrase,' 'verb phrase,' which dominates a lexical category.

  Or as a generalized version of Selkirk's (1984: 314) Silent Demibeat Addition, which articulates the syntactic timing of a sentence:

(ii) Silent Demibeat Addition

Add a silent demibeat at the end of the metrical grid aligned with

(a) a word
(b) a word that is the head of a nonadjunct
(c) a phrase
(d) a daughter phrase of S.

The mapping rule (6) differs from Chomsky and Halle's #-Insertion (i) in that it counts all syntactic objects whether they are major categories N, V, A and their projections or not. The crucial difference between the mapping rule (6) and Selkirk's Silent Demibeat Addition (ii) is that only the former counts the beginning of a category as well as the end.

3   Shanghai Chinese Prosodic Word Rule (24) has a minor problem in explaining the phrasing of preposition phrases in citation form such as (26a). The left edge of the first prosodic word corresponds to the left edge of the preposition 'zaw. However, the rule in (24) cannot assign a prosodic word boundary to the left edge of P.

4   A reviewer points out that this claim also predicts that there will not be a prosodic boundary between a preposition and its complement if the complement is not a compound noun. In this case we would have the structure in (i), which is interpreted as (ii).

(i)   [$_{VP}$ [$_V$ 'z] [$_{PP}$ 'laq] [$_N$ ...]]]
                live   at   ...
         'live in ...'
(ii)   // 'z // 'laq // ... ///

In fact, we do not predict a prosodic boundary between P and N in (i) because there are only two boundaries there in (ii). However, we do not predict one between V and P either. Moreover, Chinese place names consist of two words as in (45), although there might be some exceptions that I do not know. Since I cannot test this case now, I will leave this matter for future research.

References

Chen, M. Y. (1987) The syntax of Xiamen tone sandhi. *Phonology Yearbook* 4: 109–149.

Chen, M. Y. (2000) *Tone Sandhi: Patterns across Chinese Dialects*. Cambridge: Cambridge University Press.

Cho, Y.-M. Y. (1990) Syntax and phrasing in Korean. In S. Inkelas and D. Zec (eds) *The Phonology-Syntax Connection* 47–62. Chicago, IL: The University of Chicago Press.

Chomsky, N. (1995) *The Minimalist Program*. Cambridge, MA: MIT Press.

Chomsky, N. and Halle, M. (1968) *The Sound Pattern of English*. New York: Harper & Row.

Clements, G. N. (1978) Tone and syntax in Ewe. In D. J. Napoli (ed.) *Elements of Tone, Stress, and Intonation* 21–99. Washington, DC: Georgetown University Press.

Duanmu, S. (1992) End-based theory, cyclic stress, and tonal domains. In J. M. Denton, G. P. Chan and C. P. Canakis (eds) *Papers from the 28th Regional Meeting of the Chicago Linguistic Society: Volume 2: The Parasession: The Cycle in Linguistic Theory* 65–76 Chicago, IL: Chicago Linguistic Society.

Duanmu, S. (2008) *Syllable Structure: The Limits of Variation*. Oxford: Oxford University Press.

Hale, K. and Selkirk, E. O. (1987) Government and tonal phrasing in Papago. *Phonology Yearbook* 4, 151–183.

Kayne, R. S. (1994) *The Antisymmetry in Syntax*. Cambridge, MA: MIT Press.

Kenstowicz, M. and Sohn, H-S. (1997) Phrasing and focus in Northern Kyungsang Korean. *PF: Papers at the Interface* (MIT Working Papers in Linguistics 30), 25–47.

Kisseberth, C. W. and Abasheikh, M. I. (1974) Vowel length in Chi-Mwi:ni – A case study of the role of grammar in phonology. In Bruck, A., Fox, R. A. and La Galy, M. W. (eds) *Papers from the Parasession on Natural Phonology* 193–209. Chicago, IL: Chicago Linguistic Society.

Liberman, M. and Prince, A. (1977) On stress and linguistic rhythm. *Linguistic Inquiry* 8: 249–336.

Odden, D. (1987) Kimatuumbi phrasal phonology. *Phonology Yearbook* 4: 13–36.

Selkirk, E. O. (1984) *Phonology and Syntax: The Relation between Sound and Structure*. Cambridge, MA: MIT Press.

Selkirk, E. O. (1986) On derived domains in sentence phonology. *Phonology Yearbook* 3: 371–405.

Selkirk, E. O. and Shen, T. (1990) Prosodic domains in Shanghai Chinese. In Inkelas, S. and Zec, D. (eds) *The Phonology-syntax Connection* 313–337. Chicago, IL: The University of Chicago Press.

Selkirk, E. O. and Tateishi, K. (1988) Constraints on minor phrase formation in

Japanese. In MacLeod, D., Larson, G. and Brentari, D. (eds) *Papers from the 24th Annual Regional Meeting of the Chicago Linguistic Society, Part One: The General Session* 316–336. Chicago, IL: Chicago Linguistic Society.

Selkirk, E. O. and Tateishi, K. (1991) Syntax and downstep in Japanese. In Georgopoulos, C. and Ishihara, R. (eds) *Interdisciplinary Approaches to Language: Essays in Honor of S.-Y. Kuroda* 519–544. Dordrecht: Kluwer.

Tokizaki, H. (1999) Prosodic phrasing and bare phrase structure. In Tamanji, P., Hirotani, M. and Hall N. (eds) *Proceedings of the North East Linguistic Society 29, Volume 1*, 381–395.

Tokizaki, H. (2008) *Syntactic Structure and Silence: A Minimalist Theory of Syntax-Phonology Interface*. Tokyo: Hitsuji Syobo.

Tokizaki, H. and Kuwana, Y. (2009) A stress-based theory of disharmonic word orders. Paper presented at Theoretical Approaches to Disharmonic Word Orders. Newcastle University, May 30–June 1, 2009.

Yip, M. (2002) *Tone*. Cambridge: Cambridge University Press.

Section 4
Prosodic hierarchy and
semantic interpretation (Focus)

13 Intonational phrase boundaries: A puzzle

Katy Carlson[a], Lyn Frazier[b] and Charles Clifton Jr[b]

13.1 Introduction

On all contemporary approaches to English intonation, a distinction is drawn between a high boundary tone at the end of an intonational phrase (H%) and a low boundary tone (L%). Although theories may differ in detail, the H% is associated with a continuation and the L% with closure (Pierrehumbert and Hirschberg, 1990; Bartels, 1997; Beckman and Elam, 1997; Zimmerman, 2000).[1] For example, with a low boundary (L%) tone, (1) is taken to be a declarative sentence; with a high boundary (H%) tone, it is interpreted as a question.

(1) (a) Josh left.
     (b) Josh left?

Similarly, in recent discussions of Alternative questions (Zimmerman, 2000; Pruitt, 2008), an example like (2) would be interpreted as a polar question with a rise on the final disjunct (2a), but interpreted as an alternative question with a fall on the final disjunct (2b). The two readings vary in what type of answer would be appropriate, as shown in the examples.

(2) (a) Would you like coffee or tea ...H%? Yes.
     (b) Would you like coffee or tea...L%? Coffee.

[a] Katy Carlson: Morehead State University, Morehead, KY, USA. Email: k.carlson@ morehead-st.edu.

[b] Lyn Frazier and Charles Clifton Jr: University of Massachusetts Amherst, Amherst, MA, USA.

In this paper, we report a series of experiments on the interpretation of ambiguous VP Ellipsis (VPE) sentences like (3) that are spoken with either a H% or L% boundary tone.

(3)   John said that Fred went to Europe (H%/L%) and Mary did too.

The elided VP at *did* may be interpreted with either the embedded VP *went to Europe* or the matrix VP *said that Fred went to Europe* as its antecedent. Our expectation was that the examples with a L% would behave more like the two sentence condition in a corresponding written study (described below), with more matrix interpretations, whereas examples with the H% would behave more like the one sentence condition in having fewer matrix interpretations. The expectation was not confirmed, with boundary tones being generally ineffective in biasing different interpretations of these VPE sentences. In what follows, we first present published and new experimental data and then discuss the results and their implications from the broader perspective of the various properties of prosodic constituents.

13.2 The experiments

13.2.1 Previous research

In written questionnaire studies, Frazier and Clifton (2005) investigated ambiguous ellipsis sentences like those in (4). They found that readers are more likely to take the matrix antecedent (*said that…*) across sentence boundaries, as in (4b), than within a sentence (4a).

(4)   (a) John said that Fred went to Europe and Mary did too.
      (b) John said that Fred went to Europe. Mary did too.

They proposed that salience relations in the discourse representation are determined by information structure notions like 'main assertion' rather than by locality (as in the syntactic representation). Across sentence boundaries, the syntactic representation decays and readers and listeners rely more heavily on the discourse representation than the syntactic representation. Thus readers were more likely to report the matrix VP antecedent in (4b) than in (4a). Specifically, in the one sentence condition (4a) there were 40% matrix interpretations, whereas in the two sentence condition there were significantly more (55% matrix interpretations).

Given this account of the results of the written study (which are backed up by other results supporting the Main Assertion hypothesis in Frazier and Clifton, 2005), one might expect that comparable results could be obtained with auditory input. If (4a) were spoken with an L% on *Europe,* this would indicate closure and favor matrix VP antecedents more than if (4a) were spoken with a H%. The H% might be taken to indicate continuation and favor making all three clauses part of a single sentence.

Frazier *et al.* (2007) tested this prediction in an auditory got-it study,[2] using sentences as in Table 13.1, where boundary tones are indicated in ToBI transcription and L+H* accents are indicated by uppercase letters.

Table 13.1: Response times in ms and % of matrix interpretations, Frazier *et al.,* 2007 experiment

	RT (ms)	*% matrix*
JOHN said Fred went to Europe L–H% and Mary did too.	2695	55
JOHN said Fred went to Europe L–L% and Mary did too.	2919	53
John said FRED went to Europe L–H% and Mary did too.	2854	42
John said FRED went to Europe L–L% and Mary did too.	2874	42

The prediction was not confirmed. The proportion of matrix VP antecedents did not differ at all between the two boundary tone conditions (though the position of a prominent L+H* accent did influence interpretations). In further studies, we pursue this puzzle.

13.2.2 Experiment 1

One possible reason why the boundary tones did not influence the interpretation of the sentences (and thus the presumed analysis as one versus two sentences) is the length of the pauses in the study above. The pauses before the conjunction *and* tended to be long (around 150–250 ms, on average). This raises the possibility that the second sentence might have sounded like an afterthought, essentially undermining the purpose behind the experimental manipulation. In effect, an afterthought might be a separate contribution to discourse, making it on a par with utterances involving two separate sentences or even two speakers (5), encouraging a high frequency of matrix antecedent interpretations.

(5)   A: John said that Fred went to Europe.
      B: (And) Mary did too.

To test for this possibility, the duration of the pauses was explicitly manipulated in Experiment 1. Experiment 1 tested the same sentences as Frazier *et al.* (2007), which are included here as Appendix 13.1. The sentences were spoken this time with H* accents on all of the noun phrases. But the sentences were altered by removing the pause after the first sentence conjunct to create two no-pause conditions, differing in boundary tones. It was expected that the no pause conditions might show fewer matrix antecedent responses than the pause conditions, due to the no pause conditions being easier to interpret as one sentence than the pause conditions. It was hoped that in the no pause conditions an effect of H% versus L% would now emerge.

The 16 sentences used by Frazier *et al.* (2007) were re-recorded by a trained phonologist, who attempted to put a mild H* accent on each proper name and place either a L% or H% boundary tone at the end of the first clause. One version of each sentence (all sentences appear in the Appendix) was recorded with little to no pause between the end of the first clause and the start of the second, and a second version was recorded with a pause of a moderate length. The no pause conditions had any existing silence removed, while the pause conditions were standardized to have pauses between 200 and 300 ms. The exact length of the pause was chosen so that the sentences sounded reasonably natural, depending on the speech rate and the lexical content. The best-sounding rendition of the second clause (containing the ellipsis) was chosen for each of the 16 items and spliced into all four versions of the item. The best-sounding rendition of each first clause with a certain boundary contour (L–H% vs. L–L%) was also chosen and spliced into the pause and no pause versions of each item. Sample pitchtracks of the no pause versions of one sentence appear in Figure 13.1. Average F0 and duration measurements were made using Praat (Boersma and Weenink, 2009) and appear in Table 13.2.

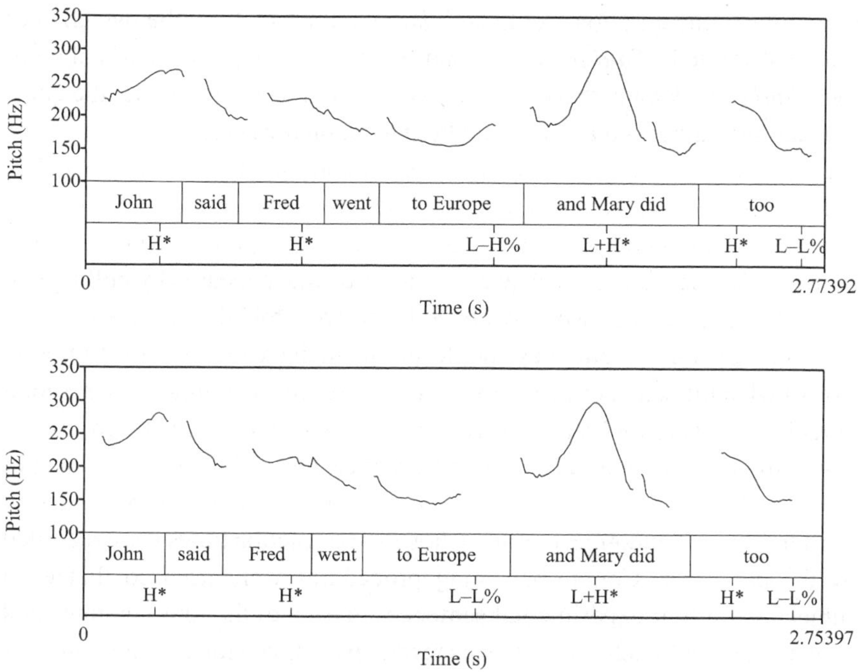

Figure 13.1: Sample pitchtracks, Experiment 1. Top panel: L–H% boundary tone; Bottom panel: L–L% boundary tone. No-pause conditions shown.

Table 13.2: Average F0 measurements in Hz and pause duration in ms (SDs in parentheses), Experiment 1

	Subject peak	*Object peak*	*L– or L–L%*	*H%*	*Remnant peak*	*Pause duration*
L–H% no pause	287 (21)	226 (11)	147 (5)	202 (18)	279 (14)	0
L–L% no pause	280 (19)	221 (11)	141 (5)		279 (14)[a]	0
L–H% pause	287 (21)	226 (11)	147 (5)	202 (18)	279 (14)	256 (24)
L–L% pause	280 (19)	221 (11)	141 (5)		279 (14)	249 (30)

[a] The same remnant was spliced into all four conditions of each sentence. A single L–H% rendition of each sentence was used to construct the pause and no pause conditions, and a single L–L% recording of each item was used for the pause and no pause conditions.

The 16 items were combined with 54 items from other experiments and 28 filler items (half ambiguous, half unambiguous) for presentation to the subjects. All sentences were stored as digital .wav files (16 bit, 22 kHz sample rate). A simple two-choice question was made up for each experimental item (e.g., for (5), the question would be *What did Mary do?* and the two choices provided would be *Said something* and *Went to Europe*). The matrix alternative, *Said something* in this case, always appeared on the left under the question and the embedded antecedent alternative, on the right.

Forty-eight University of Massachusetts undergraduates were tested in individual half-hour sessions, in a sound-attenuated chamber. The subjects were given instructions to listen to each sentence, pull a lever when the sentence finished, and then answer the question that appeared by pulling one of two levers under the two answers. Subjects were told that there was sometimes no right answer and they should simply indicate their intuitive impression of what the sentence probably meant. They were encouraged to respond quickly, and were told that their reaction times would be measured.

A computer presented a list of seven practice items while the experimenter monitored what the subject did. Then the list of 100 items was presented in an individually-randomized order. Choices and reaction times were recorded by the computer. Counterbalancing procedures were used so that each subject heard four experimental sentences in each of the four versions, and over all subjects, each sentence was tested in each version an equal number of times.

The results appear in Table 13.3, which presents the mean question-answering response time (RT) and the percentage of matrix choices, together with the 95% confidence intervals on the individual means.

Table 13.3: Response times in ms, % of matrix interpretations, and 95% CI on means, Experiment 1

	RT (ms)	*% matrix*	*95% CI*
L–H% no pause	2645	52	±9.9
L–L% no pause	2532	49	±9.3
L–H% pause	2593	50	±10.7
L–L% pause	2795	52	±9.9

The differences among the interpretation percentages were not significant. (The RT values were not of interest, apart from giving a general indication of how quickly subjects made their decision, and therefore were not analyzed.) The largest F value was for the interaction between the factors 'type of boundary' and 'presence of pause' ($F1(1,47) = 1.43$, $p = 0.233$, $F2(1,15) < 1.00$). This tendency reflects the observation that the percentage of matrix choices decreased numerically (but not significantly) from the H% to the L%

boundary conditions, but increased (again, nonsignificantly) when the pause was present. However, neither the main effect of type of boundary nor presence of pause approached significance (largest F in 2×2 ANOVAs = 1.04, all other Fs < 1.00).

13.2.3 Experiment 2

The expectation of fewer matrix antecedents was not confirmed in Experiment 1, nor was the hope that a difference between L% and H% would emergeonce the long pause of the original materials was eliminated. To further explore the possibility that duration and pause values were critical, Experiment 2 manipulated pause duration to a more extreme degree. Specifically, the no pause conditions used in Experiment 1 were retained, but very long pause versions of them were made by inserting a 500 ms silence between the end of the first conjunct and the start of the second using Praat. The original recordings which had undergone splicing to make the Experiment 1 materials were used in this experiment to create the no pause and long pause materials. Acoustic measurements are in Table 13.2. While there was no expectation of different results from Experiment 1 with the no pause items, we considered it possible that the extra-long pause would emphasize the 'afterthought' nature of the second conjunct, encouraging choice of matrix antecedents.

Table 13.4: F0 measurements in Hz (SDs in parentheses), Experiment 2

	Subject peak	*Object peak*	*L– or L–L%*	*H%*	*Remnant peak*
L–H% no pause	277 (22)	224 (11)	148 (3)	191 (10)	263 (11)[a]
L–L% no pause	273 (21)	220 (12)	145 (4)	[b]	264 (13)
L–H% long pause	277 (22)	224 (11)	148 (3)	191 (10)	263 (11)
L–L% long pause	273 (21)	220 (12)	145 (4)		264 (13)

[a] A single L–H% rendition of each sentence was used to construct the long pause and no pause conditions, and a single L–L% recording of each item was used for the long pause and no pause conditions.

[b] Two sentences in the L–L% conditions had a slight rise after the low target, averaging 165 Hz (10).

Forty-eight University of Massachusetts students were tested using the same procedures as in Experiment 1, except that the 16 experimental sentences were combined with 48 sentences from other, unrelated, experiments plus 24 filler sentences.

The results, in terms of RTs and percentage of matrix interpretations, appear in Table 13.5.

Table 13.5: Response times in ms, % of matrix interpretations, and 95% CI on means, Experiment 2

	RT (ms)	% matrix	95% CI
L–H% no pause	3141	53	±7.8
L–L% no pause	2913	54	±9.5
L–H% long pause	2944	54	±8.5
L–L% long pause	3053	58	±8.1

It is clear that the boundary and pause manipulations had no significant effects on choice percentages. All the F values in the analyses of variance that were conducted were < 1.0. The lack of an effect of pause duration is surprising. Most discussions of juncture cues would lead one to expect that longer pauses would indicate larger disjunctures, such as those that might exist between individual sentences or discourse segments, resulting in more choices of a matrix antecedent (as a full stop did in the written experiment discussed earlier). We delay further discussion of this matter until all experiments have been reported.

Given the surprising lack of effects in Experiments 1 and 2, the issue arises whether the effects of a full sentence boundary observed in the written study (which used the same sentences) are somehow specific to reading. To test whether comparable effects can be obtained in the auditory domain at all, Experiment 3 used both prosodic and syntactic means to disambiguate the input.

13.2.4 Experiment 3

In this study, the L–H% prosodic boundary co-occurred with the conjunction *and*, while the L–L% prosodic boundary appeared only in two-sentence discourses without the conjunction. Additionally, the position of a prominent (L+H*) pitch accent varied between the matrix subject (*John*) and the embedded subject (*Fred*), as shown by capitalized words in (6):

(6) (a) JOHN said Fred went to Europe (L–H%) and MARY did too.
    (b) John said FRED went to Europe (L–H%) and MARY did too.
    (c) JOHN said Fred went to Europe (L–L%). MARY did too.
    (d) John said FRED went to Europe (L–L%). MARY did too.

The same basic sentences used for Experiments 1 and 2 were re-recorded in four versions each by the same speaker as the previous experiments. Average acoustic measurements for critical points in the sentences appear in Table 13.6.

Table 13.6: F0 measurements in Hz and pause duration in ms (SDs in parentheses), Experiment 3

	Subject peak	*Object peak*	*L– or L–L%*	*H%*	*Remnant peak*	*Pause duration*
Matrix L–H% And	226 (16)	211 (13)	159 (8)	226 (16)	338 (17)	182 (84)
Embed L–H% And	233 (13)	352 (21)	157 (7)	228 (16)	322 (17)	129 (60)
Matrix L–L% No And	367 (14)	199 (11)	156 (5)	[a]	328 (12)	197 (88)
Embed L–L% No And	238 (5)	353 (13)	153 (7)	[b]	323 (11)	225 (79)

[a] Three sentences in this condition had a slight rise, averaging 166 Hz (6).
[b] Two sentences in this condition had a slight rise, averaging 160 Hz (2).

Twenty-eight students at Northwestern University participated in the study. They listened to the sentences over headphones in a sound attenuated room, pressing a button on the keyboard to hear the next sentence. The 16 experimental sentences were combined with various different filler sentences to make up a total list of 120 items. The question and answers corresponding to each sentence (as created for Experiment 1) appeared on a written questionnaire. Participants would mark on the questionnaire the interpretation they reached for each sentence. The items appeared in one of eight pseudo-randomized ordered lists, each list containing only one condition of each item. Equal numbers of subjects heard each condition of each item over the whole experiment.

The results are shown in Table 13.7.

Table 13.7: % of matrix interpretations, Experiment 3

	% matrix
Matrix L–H% And	61
Embed L–H% And	36
Matrix L–L% No And	70
Embed L–L% No And	54

The highest level of matrix responses was given in the condition with an accent on the matrix subject, no conjunction, and the L–L% boundary contour, the lowest in the condition with an embedded subject accent, a conjunction, and the L–H% boundary. In a 2×2 ANOVA, there was a significant main effect of the position of the pitch accent in the first clause ($F1(1,27) = 25.58$, $p < 0.001$; $F2(1,15) = 13.64$, $p < 0.005$) and a significant main effect of the conjunction plus boundary difference ($F1(1,27) = 7.25$, $p < 0.05$; $F2(1,15) = 7.23$, $p < 0.05$), but no interaction. When the L-L% appeared with no conjunction, participants did choose the matrix interpretation more often than with the conjunction plus the L-H% boundary.

The results of Experiment 3 show that comparable effects are observed in the visual and auditory modality when the sentences are clearly disambiguated to a one-sentence versus a two-sentence condition. Indeed, the results of the auditory study closely parallel those of the written study, not only in showing a significant effect in the predicted direction, with more matrix responses in the two sentence condition than in the one sentence condition, but even in the size of the effect (which is nearly constant across the two accent conditions). Experiment 3 thus eliminates any concern that 'sentence' might be, say, an artificial notion of conventional writing, and not of relevance to actual speech.

13.2.5   Experiment 4

Another attempt was made to intonationally induce a difference between a one-sentence and a two-sentence condition. In the earlier experiments, the heights of the pitch peak on the first clause subject and on the final clause subject (also known as the remnant, *Mary*) were closely comparable. The height of the pitch peak on the remnant may have been taken to indicate a pitch reset, which we will take to indicate the start of a new prosodic domain and thus may have masked any effect of the H% versus L% boundary tones or duration. Silverman (1987) provides some reason to believe that this could happen. His participants listened to connected discourses with the task of answering questions about sentences whose interpretation differed depending on whether they were heard as the end of the previous 'paragraph' or the beginning of the next. He found that, even when temporal factors were held constant and independent of the presence of a H* accent in the target sentence, listeners tended to associate the target sentence more with the following paragraph when the pitch range of the target sentence and the following material was expanded. That is, expansion of pitch range may signal the start of a new prosodic and interpretive domain. In our materials, the increased pitch range for the elliptical conjunct might have made listeners perceive it, in effect, as a separate sentence, masking any effect of the boundary tone. A similar suggestion comes from Cuendet *et al.* (2007), who reported that in broadcast news, where durational information becomes less informative because of the emphatic speech style, pitch range is more informative than duration in identifying sentence boundaries

Experiment 4 tested for this possibility by comparing the original materials with materials where the pitch peak of the final clause subject was in a range between the H% of the continuation rise (if present) and the peak on the object of the previous clause. If the resetting of pitch range effectively disambiguated the original sentences as two sentence discourses, then with a lower pitch range on the remnant, the L% and H% might have the originally expected effect, with more matrix antecedents in the lower L% condition than in the lower H% condition.

The no pause recordings used in Experiment 2 were used in Experiment 4. Their pitch contours were manipulated in Praat, using its 'stylize pitch' (at one semitone) and pitchdragging facilities (PSOLA method). Sentences that were to have a high pitch on the subject of the ellipsis clause were left intact. Sentences that were to have a lower pitch were manipulated by visually identifying the start and end of the pitch excursion on the subject and dragging its peak down to an imaginary line joining the start and end. A pair of sample pitch contours with a L–H% boundary appears in Figure 13.2. Acoustic measurements are in Table 13.8.

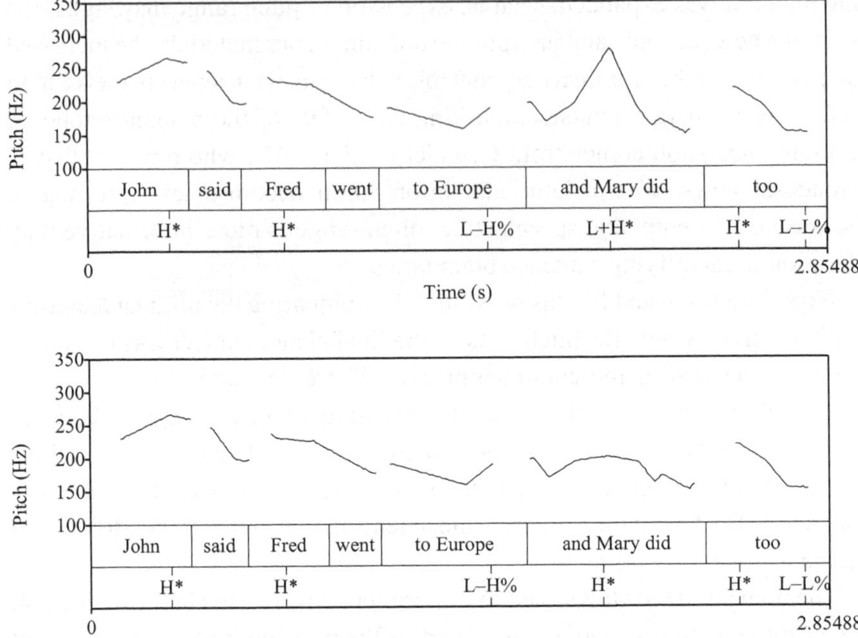

Figure 13.2: Sample pitchtracks, Experiment 4. Top panel: Original pitch accent on second clause subject NP; Bottom panel: Flattened pitch on second clause subject NP. L–H% boundary tone conditions shown.

Table 13.8: F0 measurements in Hz (SDs in parentheses), Experiment 4

	Subject peak	Object peak	L– or L–L%	H%	Remnant peak
L–H% high	273 (21)	221 (10)	151 (3)	188 (10)	259 (11)[a]
L–L% high	269 (21)	217 (13)	149 (5)		258 (12)
L–H% lower	273 (21)	221 (10)	151 (3)	188 (10)	200 (1)
L–L% lower	269 (21)	217 (13)	149 (5)		200 (1)

[a] A single L–H% rendition of each sentence was used to construct the high and lower conditions, and a single L–L% recording of each item was used for the high and lower conditions.

The resulting four versions of each of 16 sentences were combined with 58 other sentences from unrelated experiments plus the filler items used in Experiment 1. Forty-eight University of Massachusetts undergraduates were tested in individual half-hour sessions, following the same procedures used in Experiments 1 and 2.

The results appear in Table 13.9.

Table 13.9: Response times in ms, % of matrix interpretations, and 95% CI on means, Experiment 4

	RT (ms)	*% matrix*	*95% CI*
L–H% high	2941	57	±10.1
L–L% high	3091	57	±8.8
L–H% lower	3015	48	±9.7
L–L% lower	3168	56	±9.1

Numerically, it appears that the pitch level manipulation may have had the desired effect. An 8% reduction in choice of the matrix antecedent was associated with the change from a L% to a H% boundary tone when the second clause subject maintained a lower pitch range. However, statistical analyses do not encourage a secure belief in this difference. Overall 2×2 ANOVAs indicated that the two main effects were marginal at best (effect of boundary tone: $F1(1,47) = 1.81, p = 0.20; F2(1,15) < 1$; effect of pitch level: $F1(1,47) = 2.51, p = 0.12; F2(1,15) = 2.47, p = 0.14$; and the interaction $F1 < 1, F2(1,15) = 1.10, p > 0.30$). A simple t-test (by subjects) comparing the two lower tone conditions was no more encouraging: $t(47) = 1.41, p = 0.17$.

The differences among the conditions of Experiment 4 were not significant. However, there was a tantalizing hint in the predicted direction. This tendency for the lower H% condition to have fewer matrix antecedent responses than the lower L% condition encouraged us to conduct one more study.

13.2.6 Experiment 5

A set of 24 sentences, based on the 16 used in Experiments 1–4 with eight new sentences added, were recorded by a different female speaker, also trained in phonology and experimental phonetics. The sentences appear in Appendix 13.2. The speaker pronounced each sentence with H* accents on most nouns, but a L* and a L–H% boundary at the end of the first clause.[3] The subject of the second (elliptical) clause was on the same declination line as the remainder of the sentence – i.e., without the resetting of register common to the earlier experiments (apart from the lowered tone in Experiment 4). Praat was then used, as in Experiment 4, to lower the H% at the end of the first clause so that it was level in pitch with the previous L– tone for the L–L% condition. In addition, because some of the sentences were pronounced with an unnaturally long pause (500 ms) between clauses, the silence between the clauses was shortened to approximately 200 ms in both conditions. The resulting L–L% boundary was not as low as an utterance-final L–L%, but combined with the lengthy pause, should probably be analyzed as an IPh boundary rather than an ip. Sample pitchtracks are shown in Figure 13.3, and acoustic measurements in Table 13.10.

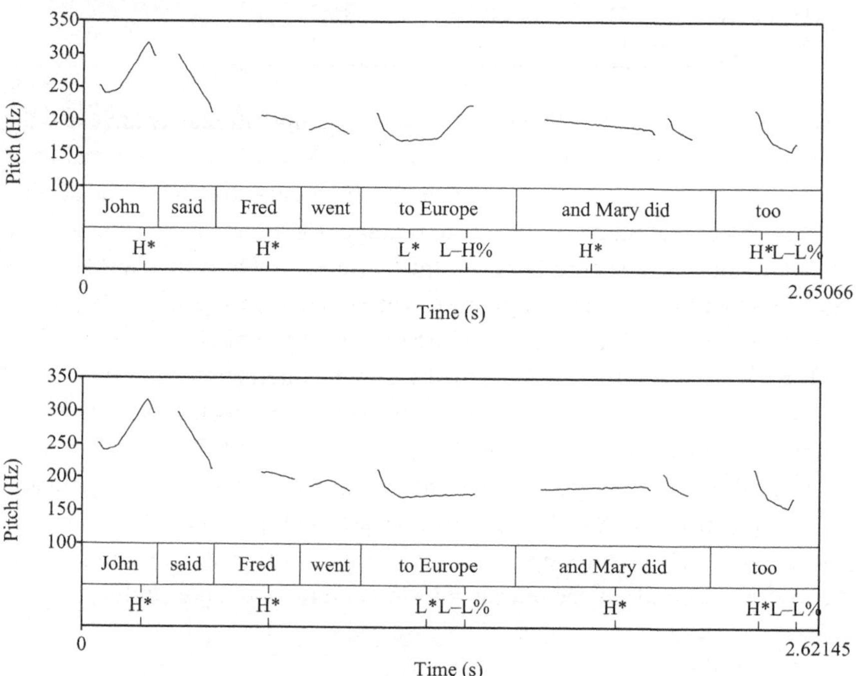

Figure 13.3: Sample pitchtracks, Experiment 5. Top panel: L–H% boundary tone; Bottom panel: L–L% boundary tone.

Table 13.10: F0 measurements in Hz (SDs in parentheses), Experiment 5

	Subject peak	*Object peak*	*L– or L–L%*	*H%*	*Remnant peak*
L–H%	266 (18)	204 (12)	163 (6)	206 (15)	200 (12)
L–L%	266 (18)	204 (12)	166 (6)		200 (12)

The 24 experimental sentences were divided into two counterbalanced lists, each with half the sentences in each of the two versions (L–L% and L–H%) and combined with 48 other sentences (fillers and unrelated experiments). Fifty-eight University of Massachusetts undergraduates were individually tested, using procedures like the previous experiments. Each experimental sentence was followed by a two-choice question asking whether the ellipsis had a matrix or embedded antecedent. Subjects answered the question by pulling a lever under one of the two answers.

The results showed that the L–H% conditions received 54.8% matrix interpretations, while the L–L% conditions received 51.8% matrix interpretations. The hypothesis that L–H% would result in fewer matrix attachments was clearly disconfirmed. The 3% difference between the two conditions (nonsignificant, $z = 1.16$, $p > 0.20$, when tested using a mixed logistic model (Jaeger, 2008)) is in the opposite of the predicted direction. The continuation rise resulted in numerically more, not fewer, matrix antecedent interpretations.

13.3 %-Boundary tones and spoken language interpretation

In the auditory domain, the expected one-sentence versus two-sentence effects appeared when signaled syntactically (by the absence of the conjunction between the two sentences, Experiment 3), just as they had been observed previously in the written domain (Frazier and Clifton, 2005). In both cases, the elliptical second clause was interpreted more often with a matrix antecedent as opposed to an embedded clause antecedent when a syntactic sentence boundary separated the clauses. The size of this sentence boundary effect remained essentially constant regardless of which potential antecedent contained a prominent pitch accent, even though an accent on the subject of a clause favored the choice of the corresponding VP (matrix or embedded) as the antecedent of the ellipsis.

The finding of comparable results of a sentence boundary for written sentences, with a period indicating a sentence boundary, and for spoken sentences with syntactic disambiguation is important. It suggests that the notion of sentence boundary really does apply in spoken language as well as in written language. One might have worried that the theoretical construct 'sentence' is really not applicable in spoken language. Often it is unclear how to break colloquial language into sentences and, with respect to capturing syntactic conditions, units other than individual sentences are clearly important, e.g., question-answer pairs. Thus it is of considerable interest to have empirical evidence suggesting the importance of the notion 'sentence' for spoken language.

It is also of interest that the biases of spoken and written ellipsis sentences are comparable when the two are equated with respect to ambiguity of the input. Certain structures or sentence-tokens may be ambiguous in one modality but not the other, of course. Kjelgaard and Speer (1999) showed that closure sentences have the same preferences in spoken and written language when an input is ambiguous in both modalities. The results of Experiment 3 show a similar pattern for ellipsis processing. Under circumstances where a two-sentence analysis is available in both written and spoken language, ellipsis interpretation preferences are similar in the two modalities. But under what circumstances an input is taken to be an instance of two separate sentences in the auditory modality remains an open issue.

When the division between clauses was signaled only by the nature of the boundary tone, our experiments found no difference in the frequency of matrix vs. embedded antecedents, unlike when the division into sentences was syntactically signaled. Very similar frequencies of choosing matrix vs. embedded antecedent were observed when the boundary tone was L–L% and when it was L–H% (a 'continuation rise'). This held true even when the duration of the pause before the final clause was manipulated (in Experiments 1 and 2). The lack of effect of pause duration indicated that the absence of an effect was not limited to conditions where the final clause could be interpreted as an 'afterthought,' i.e., it held even when no pause preceded the final clause.

In Experiment 4, when pitch range was manipulated by lowering the pitch peak on the final clause subject to discourage treating the two conjuncts as separate sentences, a hint of the expected effect of the boundary tone seemed to be seen (although the effect was not significant statistically). One could easily conjecture that the high pitch peak on the final clause subject in Experiments 1–3 may have suggested a pitch reset, indicating a new planning domain and thereby minimizing any effect of the boundary tone. However, Experiment 5 failed to provide any evidence at all for the suggestion that register was critical to the interpretation of %-boundary tones, despite having plenty of power to find such an effect if it existed. This in itself raises a new puzzle: why didn't register matter? Presumably answering this question must await precise models of how listeners track register and interpret boundaries and pitch peaks in the context of register changes.

In the present studies and many earlier ellipsis comprehension studies we have carried out (Frazier and Clifton, 1998; Carlson, 2002; Frazier *et al.*, 2007), pitch accents have a large influence on the preferred antecedent/correlate for an elided constituent. But the presence of extra prosodic boundaries intervening between an elided constituent/remnant and its antecedent/correlate does not (Carlson *et al.*, 2009). Carlson *et al.* (2009) argued that prosodic boundaries do not define the perceptual availability of linguistic material for all purposes. Rather, prosodic boundaries seem to constrain constituent structure and (possibly) movement dependencies (as in Price *et al.*, 1991; Kjelgaard and Speer, 1999; Schafer *et al.*, 2000 among many others), whereas prominence as conveyed by pitch accents influences selection of antecedents. With ellipsis, if the presence of prosodic boundaries does not influence the selection of antecedent, then perhaps the nature of the boundary also does not. But even if prosodic boundaries do not directly affect ellipsis processing, they could indirectly influence ellipsis by affecting discourse chunking. We assumed when we began this research that an L% boundary is interpreted as terminating an utterance or a sentence. So why didn't an L% on its own lead to more matrix VP antecedents in any of the studies?

We suggest that the L% in these sentences was interpreted as a marker of the end of a clause, which was the case in all conditions, and thus was not able to also indicate the end of a sentence. It is usually assumed that an H% is interpreted as a continuation rise, used when the speaker is not finished with her contribution. An L%, on the other hand, indicates that some significant unit has been closed, such as one of the alternatives in an alternative question 'CoffeeL%, or teaL%' (cf. example (2)). In the experimental sentences tested here, a syntactic clause always closed at the critical intonational phrase boundary position, whether the listener interpreted the input as one sentence or two. Perhaps an L% cannot do more than this. In short, the H% may have been taken to indicate that the speaker was holding the floor in all conditions, and the L% may have been interpreted as justified by the end of the current clause. Doing 'double duty' by also biasing toward a two-sentence analysis might be beyond the powers of the L% tone. This could explain the inability of our studies to prosodically favor a two-sentence analysis in any condition that was not also disambiguated syntactically. It would be interesting to also study distinct intermediate phrase boundary types, to see if this singleness of purpose holds for phrase accents (H– vs. L–, for example).

Acknowledgments

The research reported here was supported by Award Number R01HD18708 from the Eunice Kennedy Shriver National Institute of Child Health and Human Development. The content is solely the responsibility of the authors and does not necessarily represent the official views of the Eunice Kennedy Shriver National Institute of Child Health and Human Development or the National Institutes of Health. We are grateful to Caroline Féry and John Kingston for discussion of the issues addressed here, and to two anonymous reviewers for their suggestions on the paper.

Notes

1. We assume the prosodic theory behind the ToBI transcription system (Beckman and Elam, 1997; Pierrehumbert, 1980), in which there are two levels of prosodic phrasing in English. Intermediate phrases are the smaller units (corresponding to the Major Phrases of Selkirk, 2000), which must contain at least one pitch accent, and Intonational Phrases are larger units which must contain at least one intermediate phrase. This research is concerned only with Intonational Phrases.

2. In a got-it study, listeners press one button at the end of the sentence if they have understood the sentence (a got-it response), and they press another button if they did not understand the sentence. The response time (RT) for the got-it responses is recorded. Each sentence was followed by an interpretation question, providing a measure of how often matrix antecedents were chosen.

3. Because of the L* accent on the final noun of the clause (*Europe*), pitch movement to a low target for the L– of a L–H% boundary was not visible. Still, this condition had the same lengthy pause as the L–L% condition, and clearly ended with a rise, so a L–H% IPh boundary is a likely analysis.

References

Bartels, C. (1997) *Towards a Compositional Interpretation of English Statement and Question Intonation.* University of Massachusetts Amherst doctoral dissertation.
Beckman, M. and Elam, G. A. (1997) Guidelines for ToBI labelling, version 3. Columbus: Ohio State University. Retrieved on 9 April 2009 from http://anita.simmons.edu/~tobi/index.html
Boersma, P. and Weenink, D. (2009) Praat: doing phonetics by computer (version

5.1.11). [Computer program]. Retrieved on 19 July 2009, from http://www. praat.org/

Carlson, K. (2002) *Parallelism and Prosody in the Processing of Ellipsis Sentences*. New York: Routledge.

Carlson, K., Frazier, L. and Clifton, C., Jr. (2009) How prosody constrains comprehension: A limited effect of prosodic packaging. *Lingua* 119 (7): 1066–1082.

Cuendet, S., Hakkani-Tür, D., Shriberg, E., Fung, J. and Favre, B. (2007) Cross-genre feature comparisons for spoken sentence segmentation. *International Conference on Semantic Computing*: 265–274.

Frazier, L. and Clifton, C., Jr. (1998) Comprehension of sluiced sentences. *Language and Cognitive Processes* 13 (4): 499–520.

Frazier, L. and Clifton, C., Jr. (2005) The syntax-discourse divide: processing ellipses. *Syntax* 8 (2): 121–174.

Frazier, L., Clifton, C., Jr. and Carlson, K. (2007) Focus and VP ellipsis. *Language and Speech* 50 (1): 1–21.

Jaeger, T. F. (2008) Categorical data analysis: Away from ANOVAs (transformation or not) and towards logit mixed models. *Journal of Memory and Language* 59: 434–446.

Kjelgaard, M. M. and Speer, S. R. (1999) Prosodic facilitation and interference in the resolution of temporary syntactic closure ambiguity. *Journal of Memory and Language* 40: 153–194.

Pierrehumbert, J. (1980) *The Phonology and Phonetics of English Intonation*. MIT doctoral dissertation.

Pierrehumbert, J. B. and Hirschberg, J. (1990) The meaning of intonational contours in the interpretation of discourse. In P. R. Cohen, J. Morgan and M. E. Pollack (eds) *Intentions in Communication* 271–311. Cambridge, MA: MIT Press.

Price, P. J., Ostendorf, M., Shattuck-Hufnagel, S. and Fong, C. (1991). The use of prosody in syntactic disambiguation. *The Journal of the Acoustical Society of America* 90: 2956–2970.

Pruitt, K. (2008) Prosody and focus in alternative questions: accounting for interpretation. Poster presented at Experimental and Theoretical Advances in Prosody conference, Cornell University.

Schafer, A. J., Speer, S. R., Warren, P. and White, S. D. (2000) Intonational disambiguation in sentence production and comprehension. *Journal of Psycholinguistic Research* 29 (2): 169–182.

Selkirk, E. O. (2000) The interaction of constraints on prosodic phrasing. In M. Horne (ed.) *Prosody: Theory and Experiment* 231–261. Dordrecht: Kluwer Academic Publishers.

Silverman, K. (1987) *The Structure and Processing of Fundamental Frequency Contours*. University of Cambridge doctoral dissertation.

Zimmerman, T. E. (2000) Free choice disjunction and epistemic possibility. *Natural Language Semantics* 8 (4): 255–290.

Appendix 13.1
Materials used in Experiments 1–4.

Prosody for Experiment 1 is shown

Uppercase letters on remnants indicate H* or L+H* accents.

VPE sentences: mild accents, L–H% vs. L–L%, pause/no pause
1.   John (H*) said Fred (H*) went to Europe L–H% and MARY did too.
      John (H*) said Fred (H*) went to Europe L–L% and MARY did too.
2.   John (H*) claimed Tom (H*) left school L–H% and TINA did too.
      John (H*) claimed Tom (H*) left school L–L% and TINA did too.
3.   Michael (H*) wrote that Sam (H*) got married L–H% and EMILY did too.
      Michael (H*) wrote that Sam (H*) got married L–L% and EMILY did too.
4.   Fred (H*) thought Max (H*) opened a business L–H% and GLORIA did too.
      Fred (H*) thought Max (H*) opened a business L–L% and GLORIA did too.
5.   Kate (H*) announced that Anita (H*) passed the bar exam L–H% and ROGER did too.
      Kate (H*) announced that Anita (H*) passed the bar exam L–H% and ROGER did too.
6.   Lucy (H*) mentioned that Kathy (H*) got sick L–H% and JOE did too.
      Lucy (H*) mentioned that Kathy (H*) got sick L–L% and JOE did too.
7.   Melissa (H*) assumed Karen (H*) got a raise L–H% and ERNIE did too.
      Melissa (H*) assumed Karen (H*) got a raise L–L% and ERNIE did too.
8.   Julie (H*) said Maria (H*) went to the rally L–H% and GREG did too.
      Julie (H*) said Maria (H*) went to the rally L–L% and GREG did too.
9.   Henry (H*) claimed that Ian (H*) studied all yesterday evening L–H% and MARGO did too.
      Henry (H*) claimed that Ian (H*) studied all yesterday evening L–L% and MARGO did too.
10.   Roger (H*) thought Steve (H*) missed class L–H% and BARBARA did too.
      Roger (H*) thought Steve (H*) missed class L–L% and BARBARA did too.

11. Shawn (H*) remarked that Rob (H*) seemed preoccupied L–H% and
    TANYA did too.
    Shawn (H*) remarked that Rob (H*) seemed preoccupied L–L% and
    TANYA did too.
12. Luke (H*) noticed that Pete (H*) left work early L–H% and SUE did too.
    Luke (H*) noticed that Pete (H*) left work early L–L% and SUE did too.
13. Jessica (H*) assumed Sharon (H*) got an award L–H% and WILLIAM
    did too.
    Jessica (H*) assumed Sharon (H*) got an award L–L% and WILLIAM
    did too.
14. Jenny (H*) said Anne (H*) bought a Siberian husky L–H% and TOM did
    too.
    Jenny (H*) said Anne (H*) bought a Siberian husky L–L% and TOM did
    too.
15. Sonia (H*) observed that Mara (H*) took a second job L–H% and
    TIMOTHY did too.
    Sonia (H*) observed that Mara (H*) took a second job L–L% and
    TIMOTHY did too.
16. Lynne (H*) indicated Marcie (H*) signed up for a shop class L–H% and
    PETER did too.
    Lynne (H*) indicated Marcie (H*) signed up for a shop class L–L% and
    PETER did too.

Appendix 13.2
Materials used in Experiment 3, with sample question and answers for Item 1

1. John said that Fred went to Europe (L%/H%) and Mary did too.
          What did Mary do?
    Told someone about Fred   Went to Europe
2. John claimed Tom left school (L%/H%) and Tina did too.
3. Michael wrote that Sam got married (L%/H%) and Emily did too.
4. Fred thought Max opened a business (L%/H%) and Gloria did too.
5. Kate announced that Anita passed the bar exam (L%/H%) and Roger did too.
6. Lucy mentioned that Kathy got sick (L%/H%) and Joe did too.
7. Melissa assumed Karen got a raise (L%/H%) and Ernie did too.
8. Julie said Maria went to the rally (L%/H%) and Greg did too.
9. Henry claimed that Ian studied all yesterday evening (L%/H%) and Margo did too.
10. Roger thought Steve missed class (L%/H%) and Barbara did too.
11. Shawn remarked that Rob seemed preoccupied (L%/H%) and Tanya did too.
12. Luke noticed that Pete left work early (L%/H%) and Sue did too.
13. Jessica assumed Sharon got an award (L%/H%) and William did too.
14. Jenny said Anne bought a Siberian husky (L%/H%) and Tom did too.
15. Sonia observed that Mara took a second job (L%/H%) and Timothy did too.
16. Lynne indicated Marcie signed up for a shop class (L%/H%) and Peter did too.
17. Josh noticed that Mark went hiking every weekend (H%/L%) and Jocelyn did too.
18. Penny mentioned that Maria dropped out of statistics (H%/L%) and Emerson did too.
19. Liz observed that Sandra skipped classes a lot (H%/L%) and Paul did too.
20. Stan thought Sam got a job with Leisure Services (H%/L%) and Paula did too.
21. Mark assumed that Florian aced the exam (H%/L%) and Jessica did too.

22. Henry wrote that Matt got a post-doctoral fellowship (H%/L%) and Karen did too.
23. Susan knew that Kathy went to a garlic festival in Vermont (H%/L%) and Jackson did too.
24. Caitlin claimed Tanya acted childishly (H%/L%) and Richard did too.

14 Prosody and information structure of the German particles *selbst, wieder* and *auch*

Caroline Féry[a]

14.1 The phenomenon to be explained

Some German particles appear to change their meaning according to their accented or unaccented status. This is the case with *selbst* 'self/even', *wieder* 'again', *auch* 'too' and *schon* 'already'. Other particles, like *sogar* 'even' and *nur* 'only', do not show the same behaviour. However, in pure intonation languages such as English and German, a sentence-level pitch accent cannot have a contrastive function at the lexical level. Pitch accents are correlates of syntax and information structure, but are not able to distinguish two words, or even two interpretations of a word. This role is taken over by lexical stress, which is potentially distinctive. In a pair like *éxport* vs. *expórt* in English or *úmfahren* 'to run over' vs. *umfáhren* 'to drive around' in German, the distinction is made by the place of the lexical stress in the word rather than the actual realization of stress with pitch. In these languages, all words have a stressed syllable, a property called 'culminativity', and a monosyllabic word – like the particles studied here – obligatorily carries its lexical stress on the unique syllable.[1] Whether the lexical stress is realized by a pitch accent is not a property of the word itself, but of the sentence as a whole, especially of its information structure. As has been shown by Selkirk (1984, 1995), a pitch accent on a word signals that the word itself is the focus or that it is the focus exponent of a larger constituent. Because of this property, when a difference

[a] Caroline Féry: Goethe University, Frankfurt, Germany. Email: caroline.fery@gmail.com

in meaning due to pitch accent is observable, it can only be the reflex of a difference anchored in another part of the grammar.

In this paper, I propose that the difference in meaning and accent behaviour of *selbst*, *wieder* and *auch* is a function of their information structural roles. *Schon* 'already' is examined in a separate paper (see Féry 2010). When they are focus particles, they do not carry focus, but just associate with the focus constituent. In this case, they are not accented. But they can also carry a free focus themselves, and in this case, like all foci, they have a focus domain and they elicit a set of alternatives (see Rooth, 1985, 1992). In this function, they generally are accented at the level of the intonation phrase (Selkirk, 2008). The change of information structural role comes with a change of meaning, as illustrated in the examples (1) to (6). This change of meaning is only indirectly related to the change of accent status, and cannot be considered as definitional of two lexemes. German does not contrast words by the presence vs. absence of stress, and the particles under consideration are no exception.

When unaccented as in (1), *selbst* behaves like a focus particle with the same meaning as *sogar* 'even'. It associates with the accented constituent *Auto* 'car' and elicits the presupposition that Maria washed other things, which are 'less likely, less plausible, or more surprising' (Eckardt, 2001) than the car on the scale of the things Maria usually washes (see also Primus, 1991 for a scalar interpretation of *selbst*). The forward slash (/) stands for a proto-typical topic intonation, a rising contour, and the backslash (\) for a proto-typical focus intonation, a falling contour. *Selbst* in (2) is used in its inter-pretation as an 'intensifier' (see Jacobs, 1983; König, 1991; Siemund, 2000; Eckardt, 2001; Hole, 2008, among others). In this case it elicits the reading that it was Maria herself who washed the car, possibly in contrast to other persons who could have more plausibly washed the car.

(1) [MARIA/]_{TOP} hat selbst₁ [das AUTO\]_{FOC1} gewaschen.
     Maria   has even the car   washed
     'Maria has even washed the car.'

(2) [MARIA/]_{TOP} hat das Auto [SELBST\]_{FOC} gewaschen.
     Maria   has the car   herself   washed
     'Maria washed the car herself.'

Unstressed *wieder* in (3) is used in its restitutive interpretation. *Wieder* associates with the word *geschlossen* 'closed' in its domain of interpretation. The door is usually closed, or at least it had been closed before, but it has been opened, and Eva has restored it to its original closed state. In its restitutive use, the focus operator is sensitive for the element in its scope, which is often a predicate with a resultative component, expressing accomplishment or achievement. In (4), *wieder* is accented and has a repetitive meaning. Eva (or somebody else) has closed the door at least once in the past, and she repeats this act (see, among others, von Stechow, 1996; Klein, 2001; Beck, 2006).

(3) [EVA/]$_{TOP}$ hat die Tür wieder$_1$ [GESCHLOSSEN\]$_{FOC1}$
     Eva   has the door again   closed
     'Eva closed the door again.'

(4) [EVA/]$_{TOP}$ hat die Tür [WIEDER\]$_{FOC}$ geschlossen.
     Eva   has the door again   closed
     'Eva closed the door once more.'

The difference in meaning between the unaccented and the accented versions of *auch* 'also' is more subtle. A straightforward apprehension of the contrast between (5) and (6) is that unstressed and preposed *auch* in (5) associates with a following constituent, *Kuchen*, while accented *auch* in (6) seems to associate with the preceding element, *Maria* (see, among others, Reis and Rosengren, 1997; Krifka, 1999 for this explanation). However, there is also a difference in the interpretation of *auch* itself. In (5), it is just an association-with-focus particle with an additive meaning. Maria has eaten different things, and the sentence (5) adds cake to the list of the things she has eaten. In (6), *auch* is a focus and, as Krifka proposes, it emphasizes the affirmative part of the sentence. It contains a presupposition that at least one other person besides Maria has eaten cake, and affirms that Maria performed the same action. According to Krifka, *Maria* is a contrastive topic, and the remainder of the sentence says something about her. Reis and Rosengren (1997) propose that *auch* can sometimes mean 'likewise'.

(5) [MARIA/]$_{TOP}$ hat auch$_1$ [KUCHEN\]$_{FOC1}$ gegessen.
     Maria   has also   cake   eaten
     'Maria also ate cake.'
(6) [MARIA/]$_{TOP}$ hat [AUCH\]$_{FOC}$ Kuchen   gegessen.
     Maria   has also   cake   eaten
     'Maria ate cake, too.'

In this paper, it is proposed that, besides the well-studied semantic and syntactic features of these words, their prosodic and information structural properties are important for a proper analysis of the change of meaning. It is shown that they form a class of words with similar properties.

14.2 Two information structural roles: Association-with-focus and free focus

The main thesis defended in the present paper is that the three particles just introduced can have two main information structural roles, and that all other distinctions, in particular accent status and word order, are consequences of this primary distinction. The first role is association-with-focus and the second role is free focus.

14.2.1 Association-with-focus

In their first role, the particles associate with a focus, as illustrated in (1), (3) and (5) (see Jackendoff, 1972 for the expression association-with-focus). They are part of a larger class of focus-sensitive particles which typically evoke a set of alternatives on their associated constituent (Rooth, 1985). Additionally, they also express scalar (*sogar, selbst* 'even'), additive (*auch* 'also'), exclusive (*nur* 'only'), negative (*nicht* 'not') or restitutive (*wieder* 'again') functions. They usually associate with only part of the sentence, and are specialized for the kind of syntactic element with which they associate.

As already mentioned, the meaning of *selbst* as a focus particle is equivalent to that of *sogar* 'even'. The definition given by Eckardt (2001: 371) for *selbst* as a focus particle is: '(a) the proposition expressed is the least likely, least plausible, or most surprising proposition among the set of focus alternatives (scalar presupposition) and (b) all focus alternatives hold true as well (additivity)'.

Klein (2001) gives a unified meaning for both uses of *wieder* again: 'and this is not for the first time'. As a focus particle, *wieder* associates with teleological constructions, resultatives and the like, denoting a state which can be restored. This is often expressed by a predicate or an adjective, but see below for more uses.

As for *auch*, additivity is the meaning that most authors propose. *Auch* associates with different kinds of elements. Jacobs (1983) and Büring and Hartmann (2001) demonstrate a tendency for *auch* to adjoin to non-arguments, in other words to VPs, IPs, APs and root CPs. An adjunction to argument DPs or CPs is dispreferred, but not impossible (for example see Müller, 2002 and Reis, 2005). I will not contribute anything to this syntactic debate here.

When they associate with another element, the focus particles are functional elements with a scope. In this role, they keep their primary meaning. In the expression *selbst das Auto* in (1), the identity function identifies *Auto* as the element at stake, and presupposes that there are more plausible alternatives, yielding a true proposition when the background is applied to them. In (3), the complex *wieder geschlossen* has a resultative reading, due to the meaning of *geschlossen*, which is a state that can be restored, and the function of *wieder*, which says that it was already in this state before and that the initial or normal state has been restored. And finally, in the expression *auch Kuchen* in (5), *auch* is a functional element adding cake to whatever the action denotes.

14.2.2 Free foci

On the other hand, *selbst*, *wieder* and *auch* can also be foci themselves, without an associated element. In this case, they are not functional elements and do not associate with another constituent in the sentence. When they are free foci, they carry the focus role themselves. This is what distinguishes *selbst*, *wieder* and *auch* from other particles like *nur* 'only', *fast* 'almost' and *sogar* 'even', which cannot be free foci but only associate with another element in the sentence, and which, as a consequence, do not show the same twofold behaviour.[2]

I assume a tripartite division of the sentence into focused, given and topical parts (see Krifka, 2008). Every sentence has a focal part, but given and topical elements are optional. If *selbst*, *wieder* and *auch* are foci, the remainder of the sentence contains further information structural elements. The other constituents of the sentence may be given, or there may be another focus, or a topic. A topic may itself contain a focus and a given part. See below for examples of different constellations.

In (2), (4) and (6), the intended reading is one in which the subject is a topic, and the particle is the only focus of the sentence. The remainder of the sentence is undefined: it may be given or new information. The sentences can be paraphrased as in (9) to (11), respectively. These paraphrases express the fact that the particle has a meaning, tentatively rendered by the expression in brackets labelled FOC.

(9)   Selbst
       '[As for Maria]$_{TOP}$, [somebody washed her car], [and it
       was Maria who did it]$_{FOC}$'

(10) Wieder
       '[As for Eva]$_{TOP}$, [she has closed the door], [and this is not for the first time]$_{FOC}$'

(11) Auch
       '[As for Maria]$_{TOP}$, [she has eaten cake], [as did other persons]$_{FOC}$'

The narrowly focused part, indicated with square brackets and a subscripted FOC, is rendered in the examples above with pitch-accented particles. There is some loss in the interpretation of these words as compared to their function as association-with-focus particles. This loss may explain the drift in meaning observed when they do not associate.

As free foci always do, the particles elicit a set of alternatives, as shown in example (12). Since alternatives are of the same semantic type, modulo type-lifting, as the constituent of which they are alternatives (see Rooth, 1985, 1992), the words *selbst, wieder* and *auch*, which following Kleemann-Krämer (2008) I assume to be adverbs, should elicit propositional alternatives. As free foci, *selbst, wieder* and *auch* have a domain which, in the examples, includes the verb. We will see below that at least for *selbst*, the domain of the free focus does not necessarily include the verb. And of course, the particles also have a semantic meaning, which will be addressed in the following sections.

(12) (a) Alternatives for *selbst*: {and it was Anna herself
            who did it, and it was Anna's father who did it ...}

      (b) Alternatives for *wieder*: {and this is not for the
            first time, and this still happens, and this
            happens ...}[3]

      (c) Alternatives for *auch*: {and as did John, and as
            only Maria did, and as did other persons ...}

A primary focus may contain a secondary focus in its scope (Büring, 2008; Féry and Ishihara, 2009; Rooth, 2010). The adverbial particles addressed here may be primary foci, in which case they have wide scope over a secondary focus, or they are secondary foci, and are themselves subordinate to a focus with wider scope. Both cases are illustrated below. This happens in both the association-with-focus and free focus roles.

In the remainder of the paper, *selbst, wieder* and *auch* are discussed in turn, the proposal is elaborated with examples, and alternative accounts are discussed.

14.3 *Selbst*

Further examples of *selbst* as a focus particle are given in (13). *Selbst* preferably associates with a nominal constituent, argument or adjunct. In (13a), the constituent with which it associates, the subject, is the only focus of the sentence. There is no other focus, and also no topic. In (13b), *selbst* associates again with the unique focus of the sentence, but there is also a topic, as in (1), where the constituent associated with *selbst* was an object. (14) illustrates that a constituent introduced by *selbst* cannot play the role of a topic. This is due to the fact that *selbst* introduces a focus, and that the two roles are incompatible.

(13)   (a) Selbst$_1$ die   [REISE\]$_{Foc1}$ war ein Abenteuer.
           even   the   journey   was an   adventure
           'Even the journey was an adventure.'

        (b) [Den   NACHTISCH/]$_{Top}$ hat selbst$_1$ [ANNA\]$_{Foc1}$
           The.acc dessert   has even   Anna
           nicht mehr   geschafft.
           no   longer managed
           'As for the dessert, even Anna did not manage it.'

(14)   *Selbst1 [ANNA /]TOP1   hat [den   NACHTISCH \]FOC
           even   Anna   has the.acc dessert
           nicht mehr   geschafft.
           no   longer managed
           'Even Anna did not manage the dessert.'

In (15), *selbst* has a focal role. In discussing the role of *selbst* as a free focus, it is important to separate the strictly information structural issues from those related to pragmatic or contextual effects. It is, for instance, important to neutralize the effects that other particles of modality may bring into the same sentence. In (15a), *schon* 'already' contributes to the meaning of the sentence and adds a scalar nuance (see Féry 2010). (15a), where *selbst* is focused, and (13a), where it associates with *Reise* 'journey', convey equivalent meanings, but through different means. When *schon* is absent, as in (15b), the nuance is no longer there, because the scalar effect associated with *schon* in (15a) or with the focus particle in (13a) is absent.

(15) (a) Die Reise [SELBST\]Foc war <u>schon</u> ein Abenteuer.
the journey self   was already an   adventure
'The journey itself was already an adventure.'

(b) Die Reise [SELBST\]Foc war ein Abenteuer.
'The journey itself was an adventure.'

At this point, the function of *selbst* as an intensifier has to be clarified. In (15a) *selbst* intensifies *die Reise*, and resembles a focus particle. It seems to associate with this noun. And indeed, different authors have also analysed *selbst* as a focus particle in its role as intensifier (see König and Siemund, 1999; Siemund, 2000; but see Eckardt, 2001, who argues against this analysis). I agree with Eckardt and propose that even if *selbst* is the identity function for *die Reise* in (15a), its role in discourse is not that of a focus particle, but of a free focus. *Die Reise* is the topic of the sentence (or it may be given) and *selbst* is the focus. Neither has the other one in its association domain.

Selbst as 'intensifier' has been studied for its different interpretational uses (see especially König and Siemund, 1999 and Siemund, 2000), and has been shown to have several nuances, like scalar effects (or 'surprise effects') (16a), centrality effects[4] (16a–c), exclusivity (16a), and additivity (16d) (see Moravcsik, 1972; Edmondson and Plank, 1978; Siemund, 2000). However, these effects are not part of the meaning of the word *selbst* and, as a result, all nuances can be absent from the interpretation (see Eckardt, 2001 for a similar view). They arise because of world knowledge and/or context, if the construction in which *selbst* occurs suggests them. In fact, even though they are not part of the meaning of *selbst*, they often co-occur with this word, because of the strong identity function it denotes, shown in (17). We know that only one person is necessary to open a door, that parliamentary debates are supposed to be attended by all deputies, that the dessert is just a small part of a meal, and that many people are vegetarians. These pieces of information are not included in the literal meaning of the sentences in (16), but influence their meaning all the same.

(16) (a) Die CHEFIN hat die Tür [SELBST\]Foc aufgemacht.
      the boss has the door self opened
      'The boss opened the door herself.'

(b) Die KANZLERIN war bei der Parlamentsdebatte
    the chancellor was by the parliament-debates
    [SELBST\]Foc anwesend.
    self present
    'The chancellor herself was present at the parliamentary debates.'

(c) Der Nachtisch war [SELBST\]Foc eine ganze Mahlzeit.
    the dessert was self an entire meal
    'The dessert was a meal in itself.'

(d) BARBARA isst [SELBST\]Foc kein Fleisch.
    Barbara eats self no meat
    'Barbara herself doesn't eat any meat.'

For Moravcsik (1972), the core meaning contribution of *selbst* is the identity function ID on the domain of objects D_e, shown in (17) in Eckardt's (2001) formalization.[5] What is focused when *selbst* is a free focus is this identity function, causing the centrality effect evoked above and illustrated in (16a–c).

(17) ID: $D_e \rightarrow D_e$
    $ID(a)$ = a for all $a, a \in D_e$

An important distinction made in the work of König (1991), Siemund (2000), Eckardt (2001) and Hole (2008) is the adnominal vs. adverbial use of *selbst*. In the adnominal use, *selbst* is used as an intensifier of a noun and nothing else, whereas in its adverbial use, *selbst* is syntactically attached to a VP, even though it also intensifies a noun. (18) illustrates the adnominal use of *selbst*. In (18), the subject *Anna selbst* is divided into *Anna*, the topic, and *selbst*, the focus (of the topic). Together, they form the topic of the sentence. The primary focus of the whole sentence is the object *ein Kleid von Lagerfeld*.

(18) Adnominal
    [Anna [SELBST/]Foc]Top trug [ein Kleid von LAGERFELD\]Foc
    Anna self wore a dress by Lagerfeld
    'Anna herself wore a dress by Lagerfeld.'

Turning now to the adverbial use of *selbst*, a further distinction is made between its agentive (or exclusive) and its inclusive use, at least in the work of König (1991), Siemund (2000) and also Hole (2008), but not in the work of Eckardt (2001). König *et al.* (1999) propose the rough paraphrases 'alone', 'without help' for the exclusive use (19a) and 'too' for the inclusive one (19b), see also (16d).

(19) (a) Agentive/exclusive use of adverbial *selbst*
      Anna hat ihr Kleid [SELBST\]Foc geschneidert.
      Anna has her dress herself   sewn
      'Anna sewed her dress herself.'

   (b) Inclusive use of adverbial *selbst*
      Anna ist [SELBST\]Foc geflogen.
      Anna is   herself   flown
      (together with other people)
      'Anna has flown herself.'

Again I follow Eckardt (2001), who claims that the differences in interpretation between the different uses of adverbial *selbst* are a consequence of the context. Taking an example from Hole (2008) in (20) to illustrate this, but with a different analysis, glaciers cannot be deliberate agents, so that a sentence in which glaciers are portrayed as agents is not well formed; but this has purely pragmatic reasons. The agentivity effect is absent when *selbst* is adnominal (20b), because, in this case its domain is the DP. As illustrated with example (18), *der Gletscher selbst* is a topic, and *selbst* in (20b) is a focus inside the topic. There is no agentivity effect because *selbst* is not adverbial and does not modify the VP.

(20) (a) *[Der GLETSCHER]Top versperrt den Taleingang [SELBST]Foc
      The glacier blocks up the entrance of the valley itself
        *[…and it is the glacier that does it]

   (b [Der Gletscher SELBST Foc] versperrt den Taleingang
      The glacier itself blocks up the entrance of the valley

We are left with the distinction between the adnominal and adverbial uses of *selbst*. I propose that this distinction is a consequence of the information structure of the sentence as a whole. In the adnominal version of (18), the noun + *selbst* form a topic together. *Selbst* is a free focus, but its domain is reduced to the topic part of the sentence (see Truckenbrodt, 1995 for a definition of 'focus domain' as used here). In such a case, there is an independent and primary focus further in the sentence. The sentence (18) can be paraphrased as in (21). The paraphrase shows that the focus domain is now restricted to the DP. The difference is due to the different domains of the focus, and not to any intrinsic difference that the word itself can have.[6]

(21) [As for Anna [and it was Anna]$_{FOC2}$]$_{TOP}$ [she wore a dress by Lagerfeld]$_{FOC1}$

As for (19a), *selbst* is the primary focus, and the paraphrase shows that its focus domain is the whole sentence.

(22) [As for Anna]$_{TOP}$ she sewed her dress [and it was Anna who did it]$_{FOC}$

Beside the fact that *selbst* can have different focus domains, it may also be a primary or a secondary focus. If it is a secondary focus, it is subordinate or relative (Rooth, 2009) to a primary focus in the same sentence. In (15a) and (19a), *selbst* is the primary focus. In (18), it is a secondary focus, relative to the primary focus (the dress she wore).

Due to this property that focus may be a primary or a relative/secondary focus, *selbst* can combine with other particles in the same sentence. This is illustrated in (23), a sentence in which *Apfelstrudel* may be brand-new, as is the fact that Marie bakes this notoriously difficult cake by herself. *Sogar* is a focus particle taking *Apfelstrudel* in its scope. In one reading of this sentence, the baking of *Apfelstrudel* is primary focus, and that Marie is doing it herself is secondary focus (23a). In another reading, shown in (23b), *selbst* is a primary focus with larger scope than the one on *Apfelstrudel*. What is primarily focus is Marie's cooking talents. But even in the latter case, *selbst* does not carry the strongest accent of the sentence. It may even be completely unstressed. The reason is that it is too close to the accent on *Apfelstrudel*, and that this word is associated with a focus operator, a potent device for introducing pitch accents.[7] The information structural property of being a focus is marked by an accent when this is possible, but this is not obligatory. In this respect, this word behaves like other examples of the same sort (see Féry and Samek-Lodovici, 2006 for similar cases). In order for a word to carry a pitch accent, focus is not sufficient – the prosodic conditions for accent have to be fulfilled as well.

(23) (a) {Some cakes are very difficult to bake even for good cooks like her.}
Sie backt sogar₁ [APFELSTRUDEL\]$_{FOC1}$ [selbst]$_{FOC2}$
she bakes even   apple-strudel   herself
'She even bakes apple-strudel herself.'

(b) {Marie is a fantastic cook.}
Sie backt sogar₂ [APFELSTRUDEL\]$_{FOC2}$ [selbst]$_{FOC1}$

If *selbst* is a free focus, it should be able to elicit a set of alternatives which differs from the set of alternatives elicited by the element it intensifies. And indeed this is the case. A nice example of this sort, from Saebø (2007), appears in (25). The antecedent of *selbst* and *selbst* itself both carry a focus feature,[8] but the alternative sets that their information structural roles elicit are different: *My brother* is in an alternative set to which *I* belongs {my brother, me}, as members of the family about which the parents mind, and *himself* is in an alternative set to which *my fiancé* belongs {my brother, my fiancé}, the piano players.

> (25) A: Will your parents mind if you marry a piano player? (Saebø, 2007)
> B: Hardly. You see, [my BROTHER]$_{Foc}$ plays the piano [HIMSELF]$_{Foc}$

To conclude this section, *selbst* can be a focus-sensitive particle, or it can be a free focus. In the latter case, there is a distinction between the adnominal use, where its focus domain is limited to a DP, and the adverbial use, where its focus domain comprises a VP. As all foci it needs alternatives. An important factor is whether the focus is primary or secondary (or relative).

14.4 *Wieder*

In its restitutive use, when it is a focus particle, *wieder* takes an associated focused element. As illustrated in (3), the associated element is typically a state which is restored, often expressed by a predicate or an adjective. This has led researchers to concentrate on teleological constructions, resultatives and the like, which best illustrate the contrast between the two uses of *wieder*.

Some more examples of the restitutive use of *wieder* are given in (26) and (27). (26) presupposes that the normal situation is quietness,[9] and (27) presupposes that the refrigerator has been closed before.

> (26) Als   ich herein kam, gab es ein Riesenkrach,
> when I   in   came, was it a   huge-noise
> dann war es wieder$_1$ [RUHIG]$_{Foc1}$.
> then was it again   quiet
> 'When I came in, there was a loud noise, but then it
> was quiet again.'

> (27) Maria hat den Kühlschrank wieder$_1$ [ZUGEMACHT]$_{Foc1}$.
> Maria has the fridge   again   closed
> 'Maria closed the fridge.'

In its repetitive use, *wieder* is a free focus, and does not associate with another element. As observed for *selbst*, the difference in interpretation is a direct consequence of the information structural role of this word. In the example from von Stechow (1996) (his footnote 2) reproduced in (28), repetitive *wieder* is unstressed because it competes with an adjacent stronger contrastive accent. This shows that accent is not necessary for a repetitive interpretation of *wieder*, though focus is, see example (23). In the last part of (28), the focus is not on the fact that the bus is moving, but rather on the fact that it is doing it again. Actually, it is difficult to decide whether *wieder* is repetitive or restitutive in this sentence. Both seem to be possible. The speaker may assume that the normal situation for this bus is to be moving.

(28) Jetzt FÄHRT der Bus. Jetzt   bleibt er STEHEN.
      now   moves   the bus   now   stays   it stand
      Jetzt [FÄHRT]$_{Foc1}$ er [wieder]$_{Foc2}$.
      now   moves   it   again
      'Now the bus is moving. Now it is standing still. Now it is moving again.'

In von Stechow's (1996) structural account, the difference in interpretation of this word is due to an ambiguity in syntactic position and semantic scope. If *wieder* precedes an accusative object, as in (29a), only the repetitive reading is available. If *wieder* follows the accusative object, as in (29b), two readings are available, due to two possible positions of *wieder* (see (30)). This analysis goes together with lexical decomposition of the resultative predicate. *Geschlossen* 'closed' is decomposed into an adjective and an agentive verb.[10][11]

(29) (a) (weil)   Anna WIEDER das Tor   geschlossen
          (because) Anna again   the gate closed
          hat (repetitive)
          has
          '(because) Anna has closed the gate again.'

     (b) (weil) Anna das Tor wieder GESCHLOSSEN hat
          (restitutive/repetitive)
          'Anna closed the gate again.'

In von Stechow's proposal, (30a) corresponds to (29a) and *wieder* can only have a repetitive reading, whereas in (30b), which corresponds to (29b), it can have both readings.

(30) (a) [S <u>Again</u> [S [NP Anna] [VP CAUSE [S BECOME [S[NP the gate] be closed]]]]]

    (b) <u>Again</u> [S [NP Anna] [VP CAUSE [S BECOME [S <u>again</u> [S [NP the gate] be closed]]]]]

When *wieder* is a focus particle, it may associate with a word or expression which can have a restitutive meaning, such as a state (or a property, or an element in a pattern), and, in this role, it has to be prosodically adjacent to its associated element. There is, however, an alternative explanation for the word order facts, correlating with the newness of the object. The nuclear stress of the sentence is preferably preverbal in German, see Kratzer & Selkirk (2007) for an illuminating analysis of sentence accent in German. In (29a), it is unlikely that the object is unstressed, at least when the sentence is all-new, but the verb is preferably unstressed. The repetitive meaning is preferred in this sentence, and the object is new. In (29b) by contrast, *wieder* is preverbal. In this case, the object comes before *wieder*, making it old information and unstressed. But it is important to notice that word order and stress are only preferences. In a grammaticality judgement experiment, Meßmer (2007) demonstrated that the relationship between word order, accent and interpretation is far from being as clear as presented in the literature. Contextual information can override both word order and accent.

Stative verbs can also be related to a restitutive vs. resultative reading of *wieder*, as illustrated by the following examples from Klein (2001).

(31) (a) Im   Herbst 1980 waren sie in Riva
         in-the fall   1980 were they in Riva
         Faraldi. Im   folgenden Herbst waren sie
         Faraldi. In-the next   fall   were they
         wieder [auf der Axalp]$_{FOC}$. (restitutive/state)
         again   on the Axalp
         'In the fall of 1980 they were in Riva Faraldi.
         The next fall, they were again on the Axalp.'

    (b) Im   Herbst 1980 waren sie auf der
         in-the fall   1980 were   they on the
         Axalp. Im   folgenden Herbst waren sie
         Axalp. In-the next   fall   were they
         [WIEDER]$_{FOC}$ auf der Axalp. (repetitive/activity)
         again   on the Axalp
         'In the fall of 1980 they were on the Axalp.
         The next fall, they were again on the Axalp.'

According to Klein, the crucial aspect for the correct interpretation of *wieder* is the 'order of the situations that are stated in ongoing discourse', rather than the real temporal order, as shown in (32).

(32) (a) (Going back in time)

Es   gab   eine Eiszeit   vor   20,000 Jahren,
it   gave a   ice-age   before 20,000 years,
dann gab es wieder eine vor   60,000 Jahren.
then gave it again one before 60,000 years
'There was an ice age 12,000 years ago, and another one 60,000 years ago.'

(b) (Describing a pattern on the wall)
Es gibt   ein rotes Quadrat, dann ein blaues
it gives a   red   square   then a   blue
Dreieck, dann wieder ein rotes Quadrat.
triangle then again a   red   square
'There is a red square, then a blue triangle, then again a red square.'

Klein (2001) and Beck (2006) show that the restitutive/repetitive variants of *wieder* are a by-product not only of scope but also of information structure and discourse appropriateness. This is the analysis adopted here. However, there is a difference at least between Beck's analysis and the one I propose in the sense that Beck also claims that the predicate is given information in the repetitive reading, and new information in the restitutive one. In her view, there is a default complementarity between newness of the predicate and givenness of the adverb.[12]

In my view, the status of the predicate as focused is irrelevant for the repetitive interpretation. Focused *wieder* can be the only focus of the sentence (see (4)), or another focus may be present in the same sentence, either on the predicate or somewhere else. Examples of sentences in which *wieder* is not the only focus of the sentence are given in (33), with main stress on *vordere* 'front' or on the verb *zugemacht* 'closed', and secondary stress on *wieder*. As was illustrated for *selbst*, *wieder* can also be a primary or a secondary focus (33a-c). In (33c), it may even be a Second Occurrence Focus. In short, the accent behaviour is only a facultative but conspicuous reflex of this difference, and it cannot be considered as a necessary property of focus.

(33) (a) Eva hat [WIEDER/]~Foc2~ nur [die VORDERE\]~Foc1~
     Eva has again   only the front
     Tür zugemacht.
     door closed
     'Eva has again closed only the front door.'

(b) Eva hat [WIEDER/]~Foc2~ die Tür [ZUGEMACHT\]~Foc1~.
     Eva has again   the door closed
     'Eva has again closed the door.'

(c) [EVA\]~Foc1~ hat [wieder]~Foc2~ die Tür zugemacht.
     Eva   has again   the door closed
     'Eva has again closed the door.'

A case in which *wieder* is unambiguously repetitive comes from Fabricius-Hansen (2001). She shows that a repetitive reading is obligatory when *wieder* precedes the finite verb in V2 position, as in example (34a) (slightly changed from Fabricius-Hansen, 2001). In the analysis proposed here, *wieder* is a topic, and there is a focus later in the sentence. There is no reading in which *wieder* could be interpreted as restitutive. In my view, this impossibility illustrates the need for *wieder* as a focus particle to be prosodically adjacent to its associated element.[13]

(34) (a) [WIEDER/]~Foc~ musste Barbara [ihr altes
     again   had-to Barbara her old
     AUTO\ reparieren]~Foc~.
     car   repair
     'Barbara had to repair her old car again.'

(b) [Wieder REPARIERT/]~Top~ wurde Barbaras Auto
     again   repaired   was Barbara's car
     [am nächsten TAG\]~Foc~.
     on-the next   day
     'Barbara's old car was repaired the next day.'

When the verb is also topicalized, as in (34b), the resulting word order may trigger a restitutive reading, because *wieder* is adjacent to the predicate and can assign focus to it. If *wieder* is accented, the same sentence expresses that the action was repeated. In this case, *wieder* carries a free focus.

As for the difference in meaning between restitutive and repetitive interpretation, I refer the reader to Klein (2001) and especially Beck (2006), who elaborate accounts of the semantic contribution of the word in both readings.[14] In my view, the main difference lies in the fact that *wieder* as a focus particle needs an associated element which expresses that a state is re-established, whereas in its free focus reading, the main import of this word is that a certain state or action is true, 'and this not for the first time'.

In short, this section has shown that *wieder* resembles *selbst* in the sense that both particles can be focus-sensitive or free focus. The accent and word order behaviour are correlates of the crucial information structural distinction, and cannot be considered as the distinguishing property of the two uses.

14.5 *Auch*

As already mentioned, the data for *auch* are subtler than those for *selbst* and *wieder* because the difference in meaning between the focus particle and free focus uses of *auch* is not so obvious. The discussion in the literature is usually concerned with word order (preposed vs. postponed) and difference of accent (accented vs. unaccented), thus on correlates of information structure, rather than on a true difference in information structural role, Krifka (1999) being an exception. However, he only identifies a difference in information structure, and none in meaning. Reis and Rosengren (1997) find that *auch* (including preposed unstressed and postponed stressed *auch*) gives rise to two utterance meanings, 'in addition/furthermore' and 'likewise', which depend on whether or not the syntactic scope of *auch* contains stressed material, but they do not find a difference in information structure between postponed and preposed *auch*.

In the following, it is shown that *auch* has all the properties listed for *selbst* and *wieder*. In particular, word order and accent behaviour are only consequences of the two roles of this word, and cannot be considered as primary properties. *Auch* can associate or not; if it associates, it assigns focus and does not carry it. This relates to a strong tendency to be unaccented. If it does not associate, it is a free focus, without scope, but it then has a domain and triggers alternatives. In this role, it is often accented. I also propose to take the difference in meaning identified by Reis and Rosengren (1997) seriously, and to correlate 'in addition/furthermore' to the focus-sensitive particle and 'likewise' to the free focus use. However, as mentioned, the distinction between the two can be tenuous.

The two roles of *auch* can be illustrated with 'short replies', as in the contrast illustrated in (35) vs. (36) (see Vicente, 2006 and Konietzko, 2008 for different analyses). (35B) illustrates *auch* as a focus particle. In (35A), the list of the things that Maria ate is focused, and (B) just adds a new element which is also a focus. In this use as a focus particle, *auch* is truly additive. It is unmotivated to change the information structural content of the things she ate by making a topic out of it, as in (35B') , even though it is not impossible. However, (35C) is better as compared to (35B'). If *auch* is interpreted as 'likewise' in its free focus use, (35B') can be paraphrased as: 'Likewise, Mary ate different things', which is awkward in the context whereas in (35C) it is 'Likewise, she ate cake'. This could be the reason why (35C) fits the context better than (35B').

(35) A: Maria hat verschiedene Speisen gegessen: [LACHS, SUPPE, EIS, …]_FOC.
          'Maria ate different dishes: salmon, soup, ice-cream, …'
      B: [Auch KUCHEN\]_FOC.
          'Cake, too.'
      B': ?[KUCHEN/]_TOP [AUCH\]_FOC.
      C: [KUCHEN/]_TOP hat sie [AUCH\]_FOC gegessen.
          'She also ate cake.'

In (36) *Alain* is a topic, and the fact that this person has a cold is the focused part of the sentence. Speaker B changes the topic and focuses the fact that the same situation as expressed by A holds true for the new topic *ich* 'I'. In contrast, B' is not a good continuation because in this case, *ich* is a focus (and no longer a topic), and *auch* associates with this word. Notice that if the sentence is continued as *Auch ich bin erkältet*, it becomes better, probably because the VP is present and plays the role of *auch* in B, even if it is not stressed. In other words, it is a Second Occurrence Focus, and thus a focus.

(36) A: [ALAIN/]_TOP [ist ERKÄLTET\]_FOC.
          'Alain has a cold.'
      B: [ICH/]_TOP [AUCH\]_FOC.
          'Me too.'
      B': *[AUCH ICH\]_FOC.

Krifka (1999) claims that postponed *auch* is a focus, and that it needs a contrastive topic associated with it. One of his examples appears in (37). *Auch* 'too' gets its accent because it realizes an overt affirmative element, written as AFF, as illustrated in (37), an answer to the polarity question in curly brackets.

The set of alternatives of the second part of (37) is {Pia ate polenta, Pia did not eat polenta}. In the first part of (37), AFF is non-overt. In Krifka's account, *too* is an accented additive particle which receives its stress because it realizes an affirmative element explicitly, just like *did* and *certainly* in some other cases. Additive particles contrast with the non-overt affirmative element AFF and hence express a particular emphasis.

(37)   {Did Peter and Pia eat pasta?}
       [PETER]$_{Top}$ ate pasta AFF$_F$, and [PIA]$_{Top}$ ate pasta tòo$_{FOC/AFF}$..

But in fact, when *auch* is a focus, it does not need a contrastive topic over which it can take scope. A first example is shown in sentence (38). *Bohnen* is the contrastive topic, but it is *Peter* (*er* 'he') who is added to the list of persons who ate beans, and *er* is just given in the sentence. Contrastive topic and focus are thus independent of each other.

(38)   {Mary ate rice and beans. Did Peter eat the same?}
       [BOHNEN/]$_{Top}$ hat er   [AUCH\]$_{Foc}$ gegessen.
       beans   has he   also   eaten
       'He also ate beans.'

The following examples from Reis and Rosengren (1997) illustrate further that there is no need for a contrastive topic for *auch* to be a focus. A wh-word, as in (39), cannot be topical (it is not referential), and in (40), there is no element which could be a topic.

(39)   Ich stand vor   dem Eingang, und
       I   stood in-front-of the   entrance and
       <u>wer</u> stand da   plötzlich [AUCH/]$_{Foc}$?
       who stood there suddenly also
       'I stood in front of the entrance, and who suddenly appeared?'

(40)   Er bat   sie, ø [AUCH\]$_{Foc}$ zu kommen.
       he asked her   also   to come
       'He asked her to come, too.'

Auch does not always have an additive meaning, but, as shown by Krifka (1999), it sometimes has a meaning which is related to truth or affirmation. In these cases, it is affiliated to verum focus (Höhle, 1988). One of the crucial properties of verum focus in German, which is realized on the finite part of the sentence, is that all other constituents in the sentence must be deaccented in order for verum focus to emerge. Otherwise, the accent on the finite verb is overwritten, and the verum component is not perceived any more. Compare (41) with (42). In (41), verum focus is expressed by an accent on the finite verb *ist* 'is'. This is possible because all other constituents in the sentence are given, and as a result, can be deaccented.

(41) A. Maria ist nicht in Rom,   Tom hat sie
         Maria is not   in Rome, Tom has her
         gestern   gesehen.
         yesterday   seen
         'Maria is not in Rome. Tom saw her yesterday.'

     B. Doch, Maria IST in Rom.
         Sure, Maria is   in Rome
         'But Maria is in Rome.'

In (42), by contrast, only the fact that Maria went away is already given by the context, but not that she is Rome. If the speaker wants to highlight both the affirmative part of the sentence and Rome as the location, only the accent on Rome will be perceived, and the one on the finite verb will be lost. Because of the necessity of uniqueness of a verum accent, this focus is special.

(42) A. Maria ist nicht weggefahren, Tom hat sie
         Maria is not   away.driven, Tom has her
         gestern   gesehen.
         yesterday   seen
         'Maria did not drive away. Tom saw her yesterday.'

     B. Doch, Maria IST in ROM.
         Sure, Maria is in Rome
         'But Maria is in Rome.'

Accented *auch* sometimes plays the role of verum focus, in the sense that it provides a word which can be accented in order to affirm a sentence. When the whole sentence is given in the sense of Schwarzschild (1999), *auch* can be added to the sentence in the sense of likewise, and it then happens to be a good place for the necessary accent. An accent has to be there because of the focus (in this case the answer to the wh-question), but no other constituent can be accented. This is demonstrated in (43).

(43) (a) Marie thinks that Hannah is coming today, but what did Peter say?
      (b) He [ALSO]Foc said that Hannah is coming today.
      (c) *He SAID that Hannah is coming today.
      (d) *He said that HANNAH is coming today.
      (e) *He said that Hannah is coming TODAY.

Similarly, in the following sentence, it is not clear what should be added concretely (see Féry, 2009). Hans does not need to believe anything about Peter, and clearly Maria cannot be added to the set of persons who like this Christmas cake, since B mentions that Maria does not like it. But in the interpretation of 'likewise' *auch* is the only word to carry the necessary pitch accent of the sentence.

(44) A: Peter mag Christstollen.
          'Peter likes stollen.'
      B: Hans glaubt, dass Maria Christstollen [AUCH]Foc mag (aber Maria hasst Kuchen).
          'Hans believes that Maria likes stollen, too (but in fact Maria hates cakes).'

Another example in which additivity is not straightforward comes from Heim (1992). Imagine a situation in which John and Mary are competing for a job. John is chosen and informs Mary. She then answers (45). Again, Mary did not get the job, so she cannot be added as a successful candidate, and the parents do not need to know anything about John in order for the sentence to be well formed. There is thus no addition in the main clause either. If the meaning is changed to 'likewise', things improve a lot. Mary says to John that her parents think that she is, like John, the lucky candidate.

(45) Mary: My parents think that I also got the job.

To sum up this section, *auch* behaves in the same way as has been illustrated for *selbst* and *wieder*. It can be a focus particle or a free focus. It has been shown that the meaning difference between the two uses of this word is not as conspicuous as with *selbst* and *wieder*.

14.6 Summary

This paper has discussed three German particles, *selbst, wieder* and *auch*, which have the property of changing their meaning according to their accent status. It has been proposed that the difference cannot be lexical, because

German simply does not distinguish words by virtue of their pitch accent status. Only abstract lexical stress can do that, but since two of the words under study are monosyllabic, and the third one has an unstressable schwa syllable, this possibility is not available. Rather they vary their information structural properties. On the one hand, they can be focus particles, in which case they always associate with another element in the sentence. They then have a special scalar (*selbst* 'even'), additive (*auch* 'also'), or restitutive (*wieder* 'again') nuance. They are not accented because they assign focus, but do not carry it. On the other hand, they can be free foci, and in this role they have all the properties of focus: a domain and a set of alternatives. Moreover, they usually carry a pitch accent. Their meaning is different from the one they have when functioning as focus particles because they do not associate any more, but have to elicit alternatives all by themselves.

The other parts of the sentence in which they appear are crucial to fully understand the information structural properties of the particles. The remainder of the sentence also has an information structure, which interacts with the words under consideration, but which is largely independent of them. It is thus not possible to attribute a fixed information structural structure to the entire sentence. In other words, there is no complementarity between information structure of the particle and information structure of the remainder of the sentence.

The novelty of the proposal is, first, to account for these particles as a class. The analysis improves when they are treated as such. Second, to recognize that information structural behaviour is crucial, because it triggers conspicuous properties like word order and pitch accents in the whole sentence. Attempts to relate the particles' meanings to obligatory syntactic or phonological aspects are doomed to fail since these properties are just consequences of the information structure of the particles and of the whole sentence in which they appear. Word order and accents are contingent effects, which can be present or not.[15]

Acknowledgements

I am grateful to Gisbert Fanselow, Daniel Hole, Shin Ishihara, Ede Zimmermann and Malte Zimmermann for feedback on earlier versions of this paper. Thanks also to two reviewers, Stefan Sudhoff and an anonymous one, for constructive comments. Thanks also to the editors, Kirsten Brock and Joseph

De Veaugh-Geiss for technical help. All shortcomings are entirely my responsibility. This study is implemented in Lisa's tradition. Her work is a constant source of inspiration to me, and will remain so for the next 60 years.

Notes

1   *Wieder* is not monosyllabic, but it has only one stressable syllable.

2   I do not try to provide a list of focus particles here, and it may be the case that other particles may carry a free focus as well, like for instance the negative particle *nicht* 'not'. By contrast, the sentence *Ich bin nur MÜDE* 'I am only tired' in the sense of the only thing that I feel is tiredness, is not a counterexample to my claim. In this case, *nur* is a focus particle with an adjective as its associated constituent.

3   Beck (2006: 306) only admits *still* and the semantically empty adverb as alternatives for *again*. In doubt, I follow her proposal.

4   And the correlates of 'periphery' or 'entourage'.

5   *Selbst* establishes a relation between the referent and itself (x and x), in the same way as father of x, or sister of x is establishing a relationship between y and x.

6   *Selbst* can even be a topic alone if the context gives enough information about who we are talking about:

> (i) Edes Frau lebt in Berlin, sein Sohn in Wien, und [SELBST]$_{\text{Top}}$ [arbeitet er in FRANKFURT]$_{\text{Foc}}$
> 'Ede's wife lives in Berlin, his son in Vienna, and he himself works in Frankfurt.'

7   When enough material appears between the pitch accent on *Apfelstrudel* and *selbst*, the latter word may be accented. Thanks to Shin Ishihara for observing this.

8   *My brother* can be a topic, but as Büring (2003) proposes, a topic also elicits a set of alternatives.

9   In order for this sentence to be well-formed, the speaker does not need to have perceived the quietness at an anterior moment.

10   Fabricius-Hansen (2001) proposes two different lexical entries for *wieder*.

11   Von Stechow (1996) proposes the stress pattern shown in (29), but observes at the same time that the correlation between stress and interpretation is not watertight. In my view, the same holds even more so for word order.

12   Although she concedes that 'all tendencies can be overridden in suitable contexts'.

13   An alternative explanation (suggested to me by Ede Zimmermann) is that *wieder* is topicalized and is in a position where it is necessarily accented, and this is the

crucial point for its repetitive interpretation. The logic behind the explanation would be something like the following: While focus does not necessarily imply pitch accent, pitch accent necessarily implies focus.

14 From Beck (2006: 309): 'When *again* is not focused, the time interval t' that the presupposition of *again* makes reference to must be some salient time interval from the context. But when *again* is focused, it seems to have to be identified as the immediately preceding topic time – typically, the topic time of the immediately preceding sentence.

15 This paper has concentrated some of the German focus particles and has ignored the so-called 'modal' particles that can also be accented or not, like *ja* and *doch*.

References

Beck, S. (2006) Focus on again. *Linguistics and Philosophy* 29 (3): 277–314.

Büring, D. (2003) On d-trees, beans, and b-accents. *Linguistics and Philosophy* 26 (5): 511–545.

Büring, D. (2008) Been there, marked that: A theory of second occurrence focus. To appear in M. Kanazawa and C. Tancredi (eds) *Cross-Linguistic Focus Across the Grammar* (provisional). Amsterdam: John Benjamins.

Büring, D. and Hartmann, K. (2001) The syntax and semantics of focus-sensitive particles in German. *Natural Language and Linguistic Theory* 19 (2): 229–281.

Eckardt, R. (2001) Reanalysing *selbst. Natural Language Semantics* 9 (4): 371–412.

Edmondson, J. and Plank, F. (1978) Great expectations: An intensive self analysis. *Linguistics and Philosophy* 2 (3): 373–413.

Fabricius-Hansen, C. (2001) Wi(e)der and again(st). In C. Féry and W. Sternefeld (eds) *Audiatur Vox Sapientiae: A Festschrift for Arnim von Stechow* 101–130. Berlin: Akademie Verlag.

Féry, C. (2009) Postponed *auch*: Where does the accent come from?. *Snippets* 20. Special issue in honor of Manfred Krifka: 23–27. http://www.ledonline.it/snippets/

Féry, C. (2010) Information Structure of *schon*. In G. Fanselow & T. Hanneforth (eds) *Language and Logos: Festschrift für Peter Staudacher* 158–173. Berlin: Akademie Verlag.

Féry, C. and Ishihara, S. (2009) The phonology of second occurrence focus. *Journal of Linguistics* 45: 285–313.

Féry, C. and Samek-Lodovici, V. (2006) Focus projection and prosodic prominence in nested foci. *Language* 82 (1): 131–150.

Heim, I. (1992) Presupposition projection and the semantics of attitude verbs. *Journal of Semantics* 9 (3): 183–221.

Höhle, T. (1988) VERUM-Fokus. Vorwort and Nachwort in *Sprache und Pragmatik 5*. Lund, Germany: Arbeitsberichte, Germanistisches Institut der Universität Lund.

Hole, D. (2008) Agentive *selbst* and other instantiations of the identity function in German. Unpublished manuscript. Munich, Germany: Universität München.

Jackendoff, R. S. (1972) *Semantic Interpretation in Generative Grammar*. Cambridge, MA: MIT Press.

Jacobs, J. (1983) *Fokus und Skalen: Zur Syntax und Semantik der Gradpartikel im Deutschen*. Tübingen, Germany: Niemeyer.

Kleemann-Krämer, A. (2008) On apparent NP-internal focus particles in German. To appear in *Journal of Comparative Germanic Linguistics*.

Klein, W. (2001) Time and again. In C. Féry and W. Sternefeld (eds) *Audiatur Vox Sapientiae: A Festschrift for Arnim von Stechow* 267–286. Berlin: Akademie Verlag.

Konietzko, A. (2008) *The Syntax and Information Structure of bare Noun Ellipsis*. Talk presented at the CIL18, Seoul.

König, E. (1991) *The Meaning of Focus Particles: A Comparative Perspective*. London: Routledge.

König, E. and Siemund, P. (1999) Intensifiers as targets and sources of semantic changes. In R. Eckardt and K. von Heusinger (eds) *Meaning Change – Meaning Variation*. Workshop held at Konstanz, Germany, February 1999. Vol. I, 97–109.

Kratzer, A. and Selkirk. E. O. (2007) Phase theory and prosodic spellout: The case of verbs. *The Linguistic Review* 24: 93–135.

Krifka, M. (1999) Additive particles under stress. In *Proceedings of SALT 8* 111–128. Ithaca, NY: Cornell, CLC Publications.

Krifka, M. (2008) Basic notions of information structure. *Acta Linguistica Hungarica* 55 (3–4): 243–276.

Meßmer, E. (2007) *Die Lesarten von* wieder *– abhängig von Wortstellung und Betonung?* Bachelor Thesis. Germany: Universität Frankfurt.

Moravcsik, E. (1972) Some cross-linguistic generalizations about intensifier constructions. In *Papers from CLS 8* 271–277. Chicago, IL: Chicago Linguistic Society.

Müller, S. (2002) *Complex Predicates: Verbal Complexes, Resultative Constructions, and Particle Verbs in German*. Stanford University, CA: CSLI Publications.

Primus, B. (1991) *Selbst –* Variants of scalar adverb in German. *Linguistische Berichte, Sonderheft 4* (1991/1992), 54–88.

Reis, M. (2005) On the syntax of so-called focus particles in German: A reply to Büring and Hartmann 2001. *Natural Language and Linguistic Theory* 23 (2): 459–483.

Reis, M. and Rosengren, I. (1997) A modular approach to the grammar of additive particles: The case of German *auch*. *Journal of Semantics* 14 (3): 237–309.

Rooth, M. (1985) *Associations with Focus*. PhD Dissertation. Amherst, MA: University of Massachusetts.

Rooth, M. (1992) A theory of focus interpretation. *Natural Language Semantics* 1 (1): 75–116.

Rooth, M. (2010) Second Occurrence Focus and Relativized Stress F. In M. Zimmermann and C. Féry (eds) *Intonation Structure from Different Perspectives* 15–35. Oxford: Oxford University Press.

Saebø, K. J. (2007) *Autofocus, Custom Focus*. Talk presented at the Fairwell Workshop for Arnim von Stechow, March 2007. Tübingen, Germany.

Schwarzschild, R. (1999) GIVENness, AvoidF and other constraints on the placement of accent. *Natural Language Semantics* 7: 141–177.

Selkirk, E. O. (1984) *Phonology and Syntax: The Relation between Sound and Structure*. Cambridge, MA: MIT Press.

Selkirk, E. O. (1995) Sentence prosody: Intonation, stress and phrasing. In J. Goldsmith (ed.) *Handbook of Phonological Theory* 550–569. Oxford: Blackwell.

Selkirk, E. O. (2008) Contrastive focus, givenness and the unmarked status of 'discourse-new'. *Acta Linguistica Hungarica* 55 (3–4): 331–346.

Siemund, P. (2000) *Intensifiers in English and German: A Comparison*. London: Routledge.

Stechow, A. von (1996) The different readings of *wieder* 'again': A structural account. *Journal of Semantics* 13 (2): 87–138.

Truckenbrodt, H. (1995) *Phonological Phrases: Their Relation to Syntax, Focus and Prominence*. Unpublished Doctoral Dissertation. Cambridge, MA: MIT.

Vicente, L. (2006) Short negative replies in Spanish. In B. Los and J. van de Weijer (eds) *Linguistics in the Netherlands 23* 199–211. Amsterdam: John Benjamins.

15 Prosodic phrasing of wh-questions in Tokyo Japanese

Masako Hirotani[a]

15.1 Introduction

This paper investigates the prosodic phrasing of wh-questions in Tokyo Japanese. Specifically, it examines whether the scope of a wh-phrase in a sentence like (1) is disambiguated using prosody by speakers of Tokyo Japanese.[1]

(1) [CP [IP John-wa [CP [IP Mary-ga   **nani**-o   katta]-**ka**] kikimasita]-**ka**]?
     John-TOP   Mary-NOM what-ACC bought-Q   asked-Q

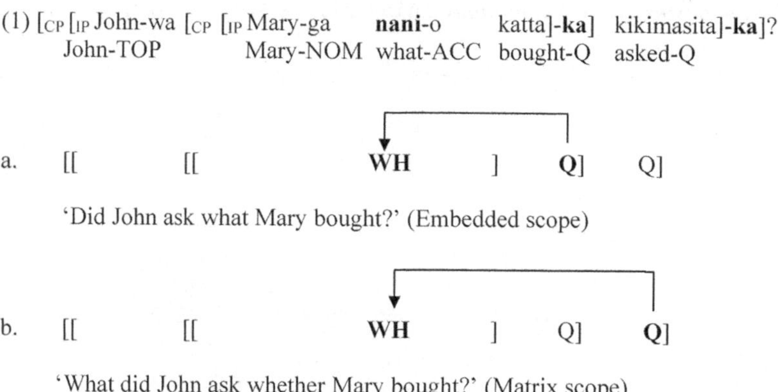

a. 'Did John ask what Mary bought?' (Embedded scope)

b. 'What did John ask whether Mary bought?' (Matrix scope)

As depicted in (1a, b), the scope of a wh-in situ phrase is ambiguous in Japanese (Tomioka, 1997; Lasnik and Saito, 1984; Takahashi, 1993; Deguchi and Kitagawa, 2002; Ishihara, 2002, 2003; Kitagawa and Deguchi, 2002; for empirical evidence, see Hirotani, 2003, 2004, 2005). Since the syntactic

[a] Masako Hirotani: Carleton University, Ottawa, ON, Canada and Max Planck Institute for Human Cognitive and Brain Sciences, Leipzig, Germany. Email: masako_hirotani@carleton.ca

location of a question marker (Q-marker) determines wh-scope (Nishigauchi, 1986, 1999), if a sentence has a Q-marker in both embedded and matrix clauses, the wh-phrase, which is embedded inside the embedded clause, can take either the embedded clause as its scope, as shown in (1a), or the matrix clause, as in (1b). In the recent literature on Japanese processing, studies using self-paced reading and Event Related Potentials (ERPs) report that matrix scope wh-questions are more costly and thus more difficult to process than embedded scope wh-questions (Miyamoto and Takahashi, 2002; Ueno and Kluender, 2003; Aoshima *et al.*, 2004). Hirotani (2003, 2004, 2005) showed that certain prosodic phrasing associated with a wh-question facilitates listeners' assignment of embedded scope to the wh-phrase but not the assignment of matrix scope. But do speakers use prosodic phrasing to disambiguate wh-scope in scopally ambiguous wh-questions?

When a scopal ambiguity exists, as in (1), it is an interesting question to ask whether a speaker uses prosodic phrasing to disambiguate wh-scope assigned to a sentence. According to the previous research in psycholinguistics, whether a speaker utilizes prosody for disambiguation seems to depend on the type of ambiguity associated with a sentence. The pioneering work by Lehiste (1973) showed that surface structure bracketing ambiguities are disambiguated by prosody, whereas thematic ambiguities are not. In a Japanese sentence with a wh-in situ phrase, it is commonly assumed that its structure is represented in LF (Lasnik and Saito, 1984; Hoji, 1985; Nishigauchi, 1986, 1999). Therefore, the question is whether the ambiguity represented in LF is disambiguated by prosody. If a speaker is only sensitive to syntactic ambiguities at surface structure, he or she may not necessarily disambiguate the assignment of wh-scope to a sentence by prosody. This is not a surprising speculation to make, given that a rather wide range of options is available in the prosodic phrasing of a sentence (e.g., Venditti *et al.* 1996). Linguistic analyses allow certain options in prosodic phrasing (Selkirk, 1984, 2000; Gussenhoven, 1999). Selkirk (2000), for instance, assumes that some syntactic elements are visible to the syntax-phonology interface component in the grammar but not all. In psycholinguistics, Schafer *et al.* (2000) noted a wide range of variation in speakers' production of prosodic phrasing.

Besides certain type of syntactic ambiguities, what are the factors that influence the prosodic phrasing of a sentence? The previous research shows that information structure of a sentence (i.e., focus and Given/New information) is a critical factor for the prosodic phrasing of a sentence. In many languages Given/old information tends to receive reduced pitch compared to new information (see Ladd (1996) for an overview). In Japanese, whenever a phrase is focused, it starts a new Major Phrase (MaP, a.k.a., intermediate phrase, corresponding to a phonological domain for pitch resetting) and dephrasing of a MaP boundary occurs subsequently (Nagahara, 1994; Truckenbrodt, 1995; Uechi, 1998). Another crucial factor in speakers' production of prosodic phrasing is the pragmatic context where a sentence is uttered. The study by Schafer *et al.* (2000) demonstrated the importance of a speaker's pragmatic goal being fulfilled when the natural production of a sentence is investigated. These previous studies point to the fact that various factors play a role in determining the prosodic phrasing of a sentence. It is reasonable to assume that Japanese wh-questions are also subject to multiple factors.

With only a few exceptions, the prosodic phrasing of Tokyo Japanese wh-questions has not been the subject of empirical investigation.[2] Maekawa (1994, 1997) tested short one-clause wh-questions like *Nani-ga mieru-no?* 'What can (pro) see?', contrasting with sentences containing (non-wh-)indefinites like *Nani-ka mieru-no?* 'Can (pro) see something?' He observed a lower $F0$ maximum on the verb of wh-questions, compared to sentences containing (non-wh)indefinites. Adopting Maekawa's paradigm, Ishihara (2003) conducted a production experiment to test prosodic structures of multiple wh-questions. In his experiment, two out of six speakers showed results similar to Maekawa's. Both Maekawa and Ishihara's studies are important precursors of the present study. However, since different structures were tested, the design of their studies may not be suitable to answer the questions addressed in the present paper.

The present research reports two production experiments which tested the prosodic phrasing of Japanese wh-questions. Experiment 1 investigated whether wh-scope is disambiguated by the prosodic phrasing when speakers of Tokyo Japanese utter the sentences. Experiment 1 additionally examined whether distinct experimental methodologies have an influence on speakers' production of the prosodic phrasing of sentences. Specifically, it investigated whether the speakers' awareness of a contrast between different scope assignments of wh-phrase forces or invites them to produce the distinct prosodic phrasing for the sentences. Experiment 2 tested whether contexts that influence the Given/New informational status of materials influence the production of prosodic phrasing of wh-questions.

Two linguistically different approaches will be contrasted when the prosodic phrasing of Japanese wh-questions is investigated. In the first approach the wh-scope and prosodic structure of a sentence are assumed to be mapped in a one-to-one relation in the syntax-phonology interface. We will refer to this approach as the *Obligatory Pairing Hypothesis*. The proposals made by Deguchi and Kitagawa (2002), Kitagawa and Deguchi (2002), and Ishihara (2002, 2003) fall under this approach. Descriptively their proposal is that wh-scope is disambiguated by the domain of pitch range compression, which follows a focused wh-phrase. Assume that the end of a pitch compression domain coincides with the end of a MaP boundary. With this assumption, the proposals of Deguchi and Kitagawa, Kitagawa and Deguchi, and Ishihara are understood in the following way: A MaP boundary appears immediately after the embedded Q-marker for an embedded scope interpretation of the wh-phrase, as in (2a), since pitch compression ends at the embedded Q-marker for an embedded scope interpretation. For a matrix interpretation of wh-scope, on the other hand, no MaP boundary occurs after the embedded Q-marker, as in (2b), as pitch compression continues until the matrix Q-marker for a matrix scope interpretation. Parentheses indicate MaP boundaries in (2) and hereafter.

(2) [$_{CP}$ [$_{IP}$ John-wa [$_{CP}$ [$_{IP}$ Mary-ga   nani-o   katta]-ka] kikimasita]-ka]?
    John-TOP   Mary-NOM what-ACC bought-Q   asked-Q
    'Did John ask what Mary bought?' (Embedded scope)
    or 'What did John ask whether Mary bought?' (Matrix scope)

a.   (John-wa)   (Mary-ga) (nani-o   katta-ka)   (kikimasita-ka)?

b.   (John-wa)   (Mary-ga) (nani-o   katta-ka   kikimasita-ka)?

A wh-phrase receives high pitch due to its focus status and starts a new MaP in both embedded and matrix interpretations of the wh-phrase, as shown in (2a, b). Under the Obligatory Pairing Hypothesis, it is unclear how a context effect (i.e., Given/New informational status of materials) interacts with the mapping of wh-scope and prosodic boundaries.

The second approach allows options in the prosodic phrasing of wh-questions regardless of the interpretation of wh-scope. This approach will be called the *Multiple Pairing Hypothesis*. In this approach, the prosodic phrasing of a wh-question is derived by an interaction of constraints in the syntax-phonology and semantics-phonology interfaces. This approach assumes that the prosodic phrasing of a sentence is determined by an inter-action of constraints in Optimality Theoretic terms (McCarthy and Prince, 1993; Prince and Smolensky, 1993), following Selkirk (1995, 2000), Sugahara (2003), and Truckenbrodt (1995).[3] A constraint relevant in our discussion is Align$_L$ (XP, MaP), proposed by Selkirk and Tateishi (1988, 1991). Selkirk and Tateishi observed that there is a tendency for the left edge of a syntactic maximal projection (i.e., XP) to coincide with the left edge of a MaP boundary in Japanese (see also Selkirk *et al.*, 2003, 2004). In (2), since no left edge of an XP appears immediately after the embedded Q-marker, a MaP boundary is not obligatory at that position. This results in the optional-ity of a MaP boundary after the embedded Q-marker. More importantly, this constraint makes no distinction between the two scopes, and therefore both prosodic options are available for both embedded and matrix scope inter-pretations of wh-phrases.

There are cases when such an option in prosodic phrasing is absent in the Multiple Pairing Hypothesis. The optionality disappears when constraints ranked higher than Align$_L$ (XP, MaP) are effective. First, when the matrix verb is focused, a MaP boundary is inserted immediately after the embedded Q-marker, as shown in (3). This is due to Align$_L$ (focus, MaP), which requires the left edge of a focus phrase to coincide with the left edge of a MaP boundary.

(3)   (John-wa)   (Mary-ga)   (nani-o   katta-ka)   ([$_F$ kikimasita]-ka)?
       John-TOP   Mary-NOM   what-ACC   bought-Q   [$_F$ asked]-Q

Second, when the Given/New status of constituents was controlled by a pre-ceding context, prosodic options as in (2) are no longer available. In the context where the matrix verb is interpreted as Given information, the prosodic phrasing without a MaP boundary between the verbs, as in (4b), is preferred over the prosodic phrasing with the boundary, as in (4a). (A tick mark used in an example indicates that the given prosodic phrasing is optimal while an asterisk indicates the ungrammatical prosodic phrasing.) This preference is expected given that Given information cannot bear MaP Promi-nence, hence it cannot constitute a MaP on its own (Selkirk, Class notes, Spring, 2004). In (4) underlines indicate Given information.

(4) [$_{CP}$ [$_{IP}$ John-wa [$_{CP}$ [$_{IP}$ Mary-ga   nani-o   katta]-ka]   kikimasita]-ka]?
    John-TOP   Mary-NOM what-ACC bought-Q   asked-Q

    'Did John ask what Mary bought?' (Embedded scope)
    or 'What did John ask whether Mary bought?' (Matrix scope)

a. * (John-wa)   (Mary-ga) (nani-o   katta-ka)   (_{GIVEN}<u>kikimasita-ka</u>)?

b. √ (John-wa)   (Mary-ga) (nani-o   katta-ka   _{GIVEN}<u>kikimasita-ka</u>)?

Note that Align$_L$ (focus, MaP) is responsible for the insertion of a MaP boundary immediately before the wh-phrase. This boundary is also harmonious with Align$_L$ (MaP, Max).

The two hypotheses described above diverge on the point whether the presence or absence of a MaP boundary after the embedded Q-marker correlates with wh-scope in a sentence like (2). In addition, they differ on the explanation for the insertion or absence of a MaP boundary after the embedded Q-marker. In the Obligatory Pairing Hypothesis, the boundary is present to indicate the embedded scope of the wh-phrase, whereas the Multiple Pairing Hypothesis requires the boundary to be there when the matrix verb is focused. Similarly, in the Obligatory Pairing Hypothesis the absence of a MaP boundary after the embedded Q-marker marks matrix wh-scope, whereas in the Multiple Pairing Hypothesis no boundary appears when the matrix verb is Given information. Since the prosodic phrasing at the embedded Q-marker is important to evaluate the two hypotheses, Experiments 1 and 2 focus on investigating whether a MaP boundary is inserted or not after the embedded Q-marker.

Some factors that are not mentioned above, such as the location of an accent within a word and the length of phrase, also play an important role in the assignment of prosodic phrasing to a sentence (for Japanese accent and prosodic phrasing, see e.g., Sugahara (2003); for length effect, see e.g., Ferreira, 1993; Watson and Gibson, 2004; Carlson *et al.*, 2006). However, since those factors are beyond the scope of this paper, they will not be discussed in what follows. For a systematic investigation of prosodic phrasing with longer wh-questions in Tokyo Japanese, refer to Hirotani (2005).

15.2 Experiment 1

Unambiguous wh-questions like (5) were tested in Experiment 1. The location of lexical accent is indicated by an apostrophe in (5) and hereafter:

(5)   a. Embedded wh-question

Mi'nako-san-wa	Ya'tabe-kun-ga	**na'ni**-o	moyasita'-**ka**
Minako-Ms.-TOP	Yatabe-Mr.-NOM	what-ACC	burned-Q

gumon-sita'-**nokai**?
stupid question-did-Q
'Did Minako ask stupidly what Mr. Yatabe burned?'

U'n,	sonna-situmon-o	sita-rasi'i-yo.
Yes,	such-question-ACC	did-seem-SFP

'Yes, it seems (she) asked such a question.'

b. Matrix wh-question

Mi'nako-san-wa	Ya'tabe-kun-ga	**na'ni**-o	moyasita'-**ka**
Minako-Ms.-TOP	Yatabe-Mr.-NOM	what-ACC	burned-Q

gumon-sita'-**ndai**?
stupid question-did-Q
'What did Minako ask stupidly whether Mr. Yatabe burned?'

Waka'reta	gaaru hure'ndo-kara	moratta	tegami-da-yo.
became separated	girlfriend-from	received	letters-COP-SFP

'The letters (he) received from (his) ex-girlfriend.'

In (5a) the matrix Q-marker *nokai* attached to the matrix verb carries a [-wh] feature and it forces the embedded Q-marker to license the wh-phrase in the embedded clause, as illustrated in (6a). As a result, the wh-phrase is interpreted in the embedded clause and the whole sentence becomes a yes/no question (embedded wh-question). On the other hand, the matrix Q-marker in (5b) *ndai* has a [+wh] feature and the wh-phrase is interpreted in the matrix clause, as diagrammed in (6b). Thus, the whole sentence is a wh-question (matrix wh-question). (See Yoshida (1998) for the discussion of the special matrix Q-markers adopted here.)

(6) a. Embedded wh-question

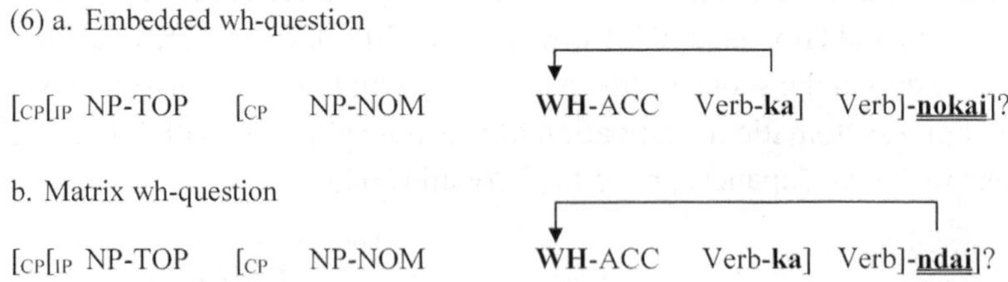

[CP[IP NP-TOP   [CP   NP-NOM   **WH-ACC**   Verb-**ka**]   Verb]-__nokai__]?

b. Matrix wh-question

[CP[IP NP-TOP   [CP   NP-NOM   **WH-ACC**   Verb-**ka**]   Verb]-__ndai__]?

To facilitate speakers' interpretation of the sentences, appropriate answers were presented following each question (e.g., the Japanese equivalent of *Yes, it seems (she) asked such a question./ The letters (he) received from (his) ex-girlfriend.*), as shown in (5). This created a short dialogue where speakers and an experimenter participate in a conversation.

There were several reasons why unambiguous short sentences, as in (5), were used in the present study. First, the purpose of this experiment was to investigate whether speakers produce distinct prosodic phrasing based on the reading assigned to a sentence. In this case, it was important to test unambiguous sentences, so that speakers were clear about the meaning of the sentences. Second, by using different matrix Q-markers (*nokai* vs. *ndai*), the string could be kept exactly the same for embedded and matrix wh-questions up to the matrix verb. This made acoustic measurements easier and more accurate for both types of questions. Third, Hirotani (2005) compared short sentences, as in (5), with sentences that were made longer by adding an adjunct phrase between the verbs. Hirotani (2005) demonstrated that regardless of the scope interpretation of a wh-phrase, a MaP boundary was inserted after the embedded Q-marker 100% of the time when an adjunct phrase appeared between the verbs in the longer sentences. Since this insertion of a MaP boundary is purely due to a syntactic factor (at surface level)[4] and not interacting with wh-scope, long sentences are not suited for the present purpose of the experiment.

Besides investigating whether speakers disambiguate prosodically two types of wh-questions (embedded vs. matrix scope wh-questions), the current experiment also addressed the question of whether the speakers' awareness of the contrast between the two wh-questions influences the prosodic phrasing of sentences. In order to answer this question, the experiment contained three blocks where the degree of speakers' awareness of the contrast between the two types of questions was systematically controlled.

15.2.1 Methods

15.2.1.1 Materials

Ten sentences were constructed for each type of wh-questions, described in (5). Each sentence was followed by an appropriate answer corresponding to the assigned wh-scope. No context preceded the wh-questions. To make the experimental task communicative, speakers asked the target wh-questions and an experimenter, playing the role of addressee, answered them. Test sentences appear in the Appendix.

In the experiment, the same sentence was read only once for one question type, i.e., the same sentence was not used for both types of wh-questions in the same block. (7) and (8) below are examples where embedded and matrix scope wh-questions are represented by a distinct sentence in the same block. Across different blocks, sentences were exactly the same except the disambiguating Q-markers, as shown in (5). (For the block manipulation, see below.)

(7)   Embedded question
      Ri'kako-san-wa   Ya'suko-san-ga   **da're**-o   norotteita'-**ka**
      Rikako-Ms.-TOP   Yasuko-Ms.-NOM   who-ACC   cursed-Q

      yogensiteita'-**nokai**?
      had predicted-Q
      'Had Rikako predicted who Yasuko would curse?'

      U'n,   so'o-mitai-da-yo.
      Yes   so-seem-COP-SFP
      'Yes, it seems so.'

(8)   Matrix question
      Ya'maki-isi-wa   Yo'neda-hutyoo-ga   **da're**-o   dokusatusita'-**ka**
      Yamaki-doctor-TOP   Yoneda-head nurse-NOM   who-ACC   killed by poison-Q

      mitometa'-**ndai**?
      admitted-Q
      'Who did Dr. Yamaki determine whether Yoneda, (the) head nurse, killed by poison?'

      Sango'ositu-no   gan-ka'nzya-rasii-yo.
      Three-No.-room-GEN   cancer-patient-seem-SFP
      'It seems (it was) (the) cancer patient in room No. 3.'

All words in the experimental sentences were accented. The location of lexical accents was strictly controlled. An accent fell in the following places: the first mora of each noun phrase (for both matrix and embedded subject NPs and wh-words) and the last mora of embedded and matrix verbs. The length of each prosodic word was also controlled. All the words except the wh-word were at least three mora, long enough to be a MaP (Shinya, 2000). Critical words (i.e., wh-words and embedded and matrix verbs) and their accent-carrying mora always started with sonorant consonants.

15.2.1.2 Block manipulation

One of the purposes of the present experiment was to investigate whether speakers' awareness of the contrast between embedded and matrix scope wh-questions invites any difference in the prosodic phrasing of sentences. In order to test this, the experiment was divided into three blocks, as illustrated in Table 15.1.

Table 15.1: Block manipulation in Experiment 1 (Numbers in parentheses indicate the number of items included in the experiment for each construction type)

Group	Block 1	Block 2	Block 3
Embedded Group	Embedded questions (6) Fillers (6)	Embedded questions (4) Matrix questions (4) Fillers (8)	Embedded questions (2) Matrix questions (2) Fillers (4)
Matrix Group	Matrix questions (6) Fillers (6)		

Speakers (see below for participants) were divided into two groups: Embedded Group and Matrix Group. Speakers in the Embedded Group read aloud only embedded scope wh-questions in the first block. In contrast, speakers in the Matrix Group saw only matrix scope wh-questions. In the second block, both groups received a list of sentences which contained both embedded and matrix scope wh-questions. In the final block, speakers from both groups were asked to read aloud both members of a pair of embedded and matrix scope wh-questions. That is, an embedded and matrix scope wh-question, which were exactly the same except for the disambiguating matrix Q-marker, appeared on the computer screen at the same time, just like the examples in (5). Then, speakers were instructed to compare the meaning of the two sentences carefully before uttering them one by one in a sequence. Therefore, the experiment was set up in the way that speakers became aware of the existence of different types of wh-questions as they moved on to the later blocks: It was likely that speakers were familiar with only one type of questions in the first block, whereas the existence of different types of question was made explicit to the speakers in the final block. The same number of filler sentences as target sentences was included in each block.

15.2.1.3 Participants

Eight Japanese speakers from the Tokyo area took part in the experiment as paid volunteer participants. Five of them were female speakers (Speakers 1, 3, 5, 6, and 8) and three were male speakers (Speakers 2, 4, and 7). Six speakers were undergraduate exchange students from Japan who took courses at the

University of Massachusetts Amherst, while two speakers (Speakers 2 and 4) were regular undergraduate students of the same university whose length of stay in the US was less than two years. All speakers were in their early twenties. Half of the participants were grouped into the Embedded Group (Speakers 1 to 4) and the other half into the Matrix Group (Speakers 5 to 8).

15.2.1.4. Procedures

Sentences were randomized in each block. Three experimental blocks described previously (see Table 15.1) were provided to each speaker with a short interval (ten minute break) between the blocks. Each sentence together with a short appropriate answer, as shown in (5), (7) and (8), was presented on the computer screen, using Japanese fonts on Microsoft PowerPoint. Speakers were instructed to read each sentence silently before reading it aloud. They were asked to read the sentence as naturally as possible and to convey the meaning of the sentence to the experimenter, who responded to them by giving an appropriate answer to each sentence. Each sentence was repeated three times. That is, after going through a list once, the sentences in the same block were randomized again and presented to the speakers to read out loud again. This procedure was taken once again, so that three repetitions of the same sentence were obtained before moving on to the following block. A short break (three minutes) was given before each repetition. The experiment took place in a sound deadened room and speakers' utterances were recorded by a SONY mini-disk recorder. Speakers' utterances were digitized into audio files (16 bit, 22 kHz) for acoustic analyses.

15.2.1.5 Data analysis

To carry out acoustic measurements on recorded materials, the acoustic software Praat (Boersma and Weenink, 2009) was used. For each prosodic word, i.e., each constituent in the present experiment, both $F0$ maxima and minima were identified manually.

15.2.2 Results

This section reports two kinds of data: (a) percentage insertion of a MaP boundary after the embedded Q-marker; and (b) $F0$ maxima of embedded and matrix verbs. To obtain data on boundary insertion, the number of occurrences of a MaP boundary following the embedded Q-marker was counted.

The judgment whether a MaP boundary was inserted or not was based on auditory impressions of the author and two other phonetically trained Japanese speakers. The task for these informants was to check whether pitch was reset between the embedded and matrix verbs, as the occurrence of pitch resetting is an index for an appearance of a MaP boundary in Japanese (Pierrehumbert and Beckman, 1988; Kubozono, 1993; Sugahara, 2003). These impressionistic judgments regarding a MaP boundary insertion were augmented by acoustic analyses of the verbs. The purpose for looking into the two kinds of data sets, as described above, was to determine whether embedded and matrix questions were disambiguated by the insertion of a MaP boundary following the embedded Q-marker. The data were also used to examine whether the prosodic phrasing of sentences was influenced by speakers' awareness of the contrast between embedded and matrix questions (i.e., the block manipulation described above).

Table 15.2 presents percentages of MaP boundary insertion after the embedded Q-marker for each type of wh-questions (embedded vs. matrix scope wh-questions) for each speaker in each group (Embedded vs. Matrix Group) in each block. The numbers in parentheses indicate the number of cases where a MaP boundary appeared after the embedded Q-marker, given a total number of cases measured. As described above, each block was repeated three times, so three scores were obtained for each sentence, resulting in a total of 18, 12, and 6 data points to be analyzed for each speaker in each block.

As shown in Table 15.2, in Block 1 where only one type of questions was presented to speakers, speakers of the Embedded Group, who were asked to produce only embedded questions, systematically inserted a MaP boundary after the embedded Q-marker (100% insertion). Most of the speakers of the Matrix Group, who uttered only matrix questions in the first block, varied their insertion of MaP boundaries (average % insertion for Speakers 6, 7, and 8: 42%). Interestingly Speaker 5 of the Matrix Group produced a MaP boundary in her production of matrix questions consistently (100%). These data show that when speakers were given one type of questions to produce, they systematically inserted a MaP boundary in embedded questions. In matrix questions, however, such a consistent insertion of a MaP boundary did not hold for most of the speakers.

Table 15.2: Percentage insertion of a MaP boundary after the embedded Q-marker in embedded and matrix scope wh-questions for Experiment 1 (the number of cases where a MaP boundary appeared after the embedded Q-marker, given a total number of cases measured).

Speaker	Embedded Questions			Matrix Questions		
Embedded Group	Block 1	Block 2	Block 3	Block 1	Block 2	Block 3
1	100 (18/18)	100 (12/12)	100 (6/6)		0 (0/12)	0 (0/6)
2	100 (18/18)	100 (12/12)	100 (6/6)		17 (2/12)	0 (0/6)
3	100 (18/18)	100 (12/12)	100 (6/6)		92 (11/12)	0 (0/6)
4	100 (18/18)	100 (12/12)	100 (6/6)		100 (12/12)	100 (6/6)
Matrix Group	Block 1	Block 2	Block 3	Block 1	Block 2	Block 3
5		100 (12/12)	100 (6/6)	100 (18/18)	67 (8/12)	0 (0/6)
6		100 (12/12)	100 (6/6)	33 (6/18)	42 (5/12)	0 (0/6)
7		75 (9/12)	100 (6/6)	50 (9/18)	25 (3/12)	0 (0/6)
8		42 (5/12)	100 (6/6)	44 (8/18)	50 (6/12)	17 (1/6)

Pitchtracks in Figures 15.1, 15.2, and 15.3 are examples of embedded and matrix questions that some of the speakers produced in Block 1. Figure 15.1 shows a pitchtrack for a typical utterance of an embedded question, which illustrates the insertion of a MaP boundary following the embedded Q-marker (Speaker 1). In the figure, the $F0$ maximum of the matrix verb is higher than the $F0$ maximum of the preceding embedded verb. The location of H* on the matrix verb was indicated by an arrow in the figure.

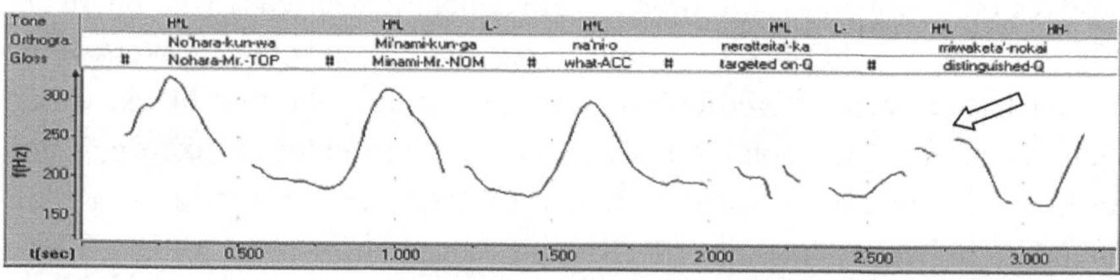

Figure 15.1: Pitchtrack for an embedded scope wh-question produced by Speaker 1 in Block 1, showing an insertion of a MaP boundary after the embedded Q-marker. The example sentence is *No'hara-kun-wa Mi'nami-kun-ga na'ni-o neratteita'-ka miwaketa'-nokai?* 'Did Mr. Nohara say what Mr. Minami was aimed for?'

Speaker 6's production of matrix questions was a typical case showing that the MaP boundary after the embedded Q-marker was optional. As shown in Figures 15.2 and 15.3, for the same sentence in the same block (i.e., different repetitions of the same sentence in Block 1), this speaker sometimes inserted a MaP boundary following the embedded Q-marker and sometimes did not. Again, an arrow indicates the position of H* on the matrix verb in the figures.

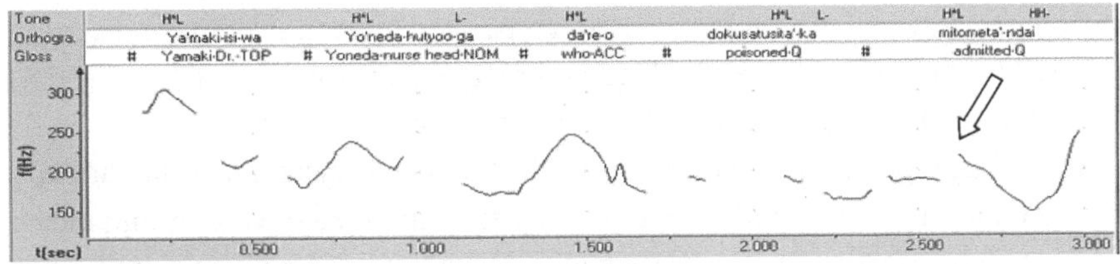

Figure 15.2: Pitchtrack for a matrix scope wh-question produced by Speaker 6 in Block 1, showing a MaP boundary after the embedded Q-marker. The example sentence is *Ya'maki-isi-wa Yo'neda-hutyoo-ga da're-o dokusatusita'-ka mitometa'-ndai?* 'Who did Dr. Yamaki determine whether Yoneda, (the) head nurse, killed by poison?'

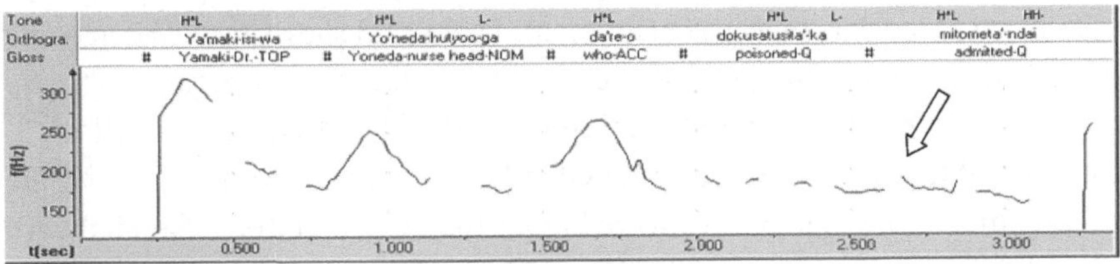

Figure 15.3: Pitchtrack for a matrix scope wh-question produced by Speaker 6 in Block 1, showing no MaP boundary after the embedded Q-marker. The example sentence is *Ya'maki-isi-wa Yo'neda-hutyoo-ga da're-o dokusatusita'-ka mitometa'-ndai?* 'Who did Dr. Yamaki determine whether Yoneda, (the) head nurse, killed by poison?'

Next, Block 2 had two types of questions mixed in the same block. This block allowed a systematic comparison between embedded and matrix questions within single speakers' production of the sentences. A one-way ANOVA, comparing the percentage of boundary insertion between the two types of questions, showed a significant effect of question type ($F(1, 7) = 8.47$, $p < 0.05$). Descriptively, for five speakers (Speakers 1, 2, 5, 6, and 7), the percentage of MaP boundary insertion after the embedded Q-marker was different between embedded and matrix questions, whereas such a discrimination was not found for the rest of the speakers (Speakers 3, 4, and 8). The speakers who differentiated the two types of questions inserted in embedded questions a MaP boundary systematically (Speakers 1, 2, 5, and 6) or more often, compared to matrix questions (Speaker 7), while their production of matrix questions had either no boundary (Speaker 1) or fewer boundaries when compared to embedded questions (Speakers 2, 5, 6, and 7). The speakers who showed no difference between the distinct question types had either a systematic insertion of MaP boundary in both embedded and matrix questions (Speakers 3 and 4) or an optional boundary in both types of questions (Speaker 8).

In the last block (Block 3), all the speakers except Speaker 4 systematically showed an insertion of the MaP boundary in embedded questions and a lack of boundary insertion in matrix questions. Recall in this block both embedded and matrix questions were constructed using the same lexical items (except the disambiguating matrix Q-markers) and were put side by side on a computer screen before speakers uttered them one by one, so that they could compare directly between the two types of questions. Under this situation, most of the speakers disambiguated the two types of questions by manipulating the insertion of a MaP boundary after the embedded Q-marker.

Turning to the data on $F0$ measurement, Table 15.3 shows mean $F0$ maxima of embedded and matrix verbs in embedded and matrix questions. The $F0$ maximum corresponds to an H* of embedded and matrix verbs. In Block 1, for most of the speakers of the Embedded Group (Speakers 1, 2, and 3), the $F0$ maxima of the matrix verb were higher than those of the embedded verb in embedded questions (mean difference 58 Hz), whereas such a relation between the two verbs was held only for one speaker (Speaker 5) in the Matrix Group who produced matrix questions. For the rest of the speakers in the Matrix Group, the $F0$ maxima of the embedded and matrix verbs did not differ (mean difference 1 Hz). These results support an analysis in which for the majority of the speakers, pitch was likely to reset following the embedded Q-marker in embedded questions but this pitch resetting was optional in matrix questions. This is consistent with the data on the MaP boundary insertion presented previously. Statistical tests were conducted to compare the two types of questions in terms of the $F0$ maxima of the verbs. However, the results showed no significance. This is probably due to the variability observed for matrix questions, reflecting the fact that those questions allowed an optional insertion of a MaP boundary following the embedded Q-marker.

Table 15.3: Average $F0$ maxima (Hz) of embedded and matrix verbs in embedded and matrix scope wh-questions for Experiment 1.

	Embedded Questions						Matrix Questions					
Speaker	Block 1		Block 2		Block 3		Block 1		Block 2		Block 3	
Embedded Group	Embedded Verb	Matrix Verb	Embedded Verb	Matrix Verb	Embedded Verb	Matrix Verb	Embedded Verb	Matrix Verb	Embedded Verb	Matrix Verb	Embedded Verb	Matrix Verb
1	215	273	201	243	202	356			200	193	207	194
2	108	134	103	144	109	146			112	103	111	103
3	210	279	215	281	216	290			218	236	220	214
4	96	102	93	110	97	112			96	113	95	113
Matrix Group	Embedded Verb	Matrix Verb	Embedded Verb	Matrix Verb	Embedded Verb	Matrix Verb	Embedded Verb	Matrix Verb	Embedded Verb	Matrix Verb	Embedded Verb	Matrix Verb
5			201	268	208	292	202	223	198	215	215	187
6			196	246	203	252	199	197	198	193	204	198
7			149	171	142	181	127	122	142	126	127	116
8			197	214	191	236	196	198	191	187	193	189

For the data in Block 2, when speakers from the two groups were all pooled, a 2 × 2 ANOVA showed both the main effect of question type and verb, and a significant interaction between the two factors (question type: $F(1, 7) = 29.63$, $p < 0.001$, verb: $F(1, 7) = 16.20$, $p < 0.05$, interaction: $F(1, 7) = 33.37$, $p < 0.001$). The statistical results indicate that the matrix verb of embedded questions had higher $F0$ maxima than that of matrix questions (mean difference on the matrix verb between embedded and matrix questions 39 Hz), while the two questions did not differ in terms of the $F0$ maxima of the preceding embedded verb (mean difference 0 Hz). In addition to the general pattern of the data described above, individual differences with respect to the $F0$ relation between the verbs should be noted. For all speakers, embedded questions had the matrix verb higher than the preceding embedded verb. For matrix questions, on the other hand, only Speakers 3, 4, and 5 produced the matrix verb higher than the embedded verb and other speakers showed either the opposite $F0$ relation, or a small or close to no difference between the verbs.

Results obtained for Block 3 are straightforward. For all the speakers except Speaker 4, embedded questions had the matrix verb higher than the embedded verb, whereas the $F0$ relation between the two verbs was reversed in matrix questions. These results were supported by the main effect of question type and verb, and a significant interaction of the two factors (question type: $F(1, 7) = 17.51$, $p < 0.001$, verb: $F(1, 7) = 17.22$, $p < 0.001$, interaction: $F(1, 7) = 14.74$, $p < 0.05$). Thus, for the majority of the speakers, when embedded and matrix questions were explicitly compared in the final block, the matrix verb of matrix questions was pronounced with a lower pitch than that of embedded questions while keeping the $F0$ maxima of the embedded verb constant, so that a distinction could be made between the two types of questions.

In sum, most of the speakers inserted a MaP boundary after the embedded Q-marker in embedded questions. This was true in all blocks. Accordingly, embedded questions had the $F0$ maxima higher on the matrix verb than the preceding embedded verb. As for matrix questions, the first two blocks showed an optional insertion of a MaP boundary. The acoustic data support this conclusion: The $F0$ relation between the embedded and matrix verbs was variable in matrix questions. In the final block, for all but one speaker, no MaP boundary appeared in matrix questions and the matrix verb was consistently lower than the embedded verb. Therefore, a systematic distinction was made between the two types of questions in the last block.

15.2.3 Discussion

The present experiment investigated the prosodic phrasing of embedded and matrix scope wh-questions. In the first two blocks, where embedded and matrix questions were not explicitly compared, there was an overlap in the choice of prosodic phrasing for embedded and matrix questions. This is because a MaP boundary was usually inserted after the embedded Q-marker in embedded questions while matrix questions allowed variability in their prosodic phrasing. This data pattern fits with the Multiple Pairing Hypothesis better than the Obligatory Pairing Hypothesis. Crucially, in the first two blocks, no one-to-one mapping of wh-scope and the prosodic phrasing of a sentence was obtained for most of the speakers.

Of course, the consistent appearance of a MaP boundary in embedded questions needs an explanation, as the strong version of the Multiple Pairing Hypothesis predicts an optional boundary for both types of questions. A speculative explanation follows. When speakers uttered embedded questions, they were likely to have an interpretation where the matrix verb was FOCUSed (i.e., contrastively focused). If the matrix verb was FOCUSed, it was likely to start a new MaP in virtue of Align_L (focus, MaP). Such a focus interpretation was available to speakers probably due to the answers provided by the experimenter as a reply to the speakers' utterance of embedded questions. Recall, as a reply to a sentence *John-wa Mary-ga nani-o katta-ka kiita-nokai?* 'Did John ask what Mary bought?', answers like *Un, kiita-mitai-da-yo.* 'Yes, (it) seems (he) asked' or *Uun, kiitenai-mitai-da-yo.* 'No, (it) seems (he) hasn't asked' were given to the speakers after they uttered the sentence. These answers may be ambiguous because of the elided embedded clause: In case a positive answer was provided, they could either mean that (a) the whole proposition 'John asked what Mary bought' is true, or they could mean that (b) it is unknown whether or not the denotation of the embedded clause is true but the denotation of the matrix clause (i.e., John's asking about something) is true. If the speaker had the second interpretation, he or she may have interpreted an embedded question as a questioning whether or not John ASKed about something is true, where the matrix verb was contrastively focused (i.e., asked vs. not asked). If the speaker had the first interpretation, then such a focus interpretation does not arise. The discussion above shows one advantage of the Multiple Pairing Hypothesis. Under this approach, no unique mapping between a specific scope interpretation of a wh-phrase and the prosodic phrasing of a sentence is proposed. Rather, the prosodic phrasing of a sentence is determined by an interaction of the relevant constraints. For the FOCUS interpretation discussed above, the constraint $Align_L$ (focus, MaP) was ranked higher than $Align_L$ (XP, MaP), which is responsible for the observed optional insertion of a MaP boundary after the embedded Q-marker.

It was clear in this experiment that the prosodic phrasing of sentences can be heavily influenced by whether speakers are aware of the contrast between embedded and matrix questions. In the final block, where the speakers were asked to compare the two types of questions before uttering them, all the speakers except one (Speaker 4) systematically inserted in embedded questions and removed in matrix questions a MaP boundary after the embedded Q-marker. In terms of $F0$ maxima, the matrix verb of matrix questions was consistently lower than the corresponding verb of embedded questions. The majority of the speakers thus completely disambiguated between embedded and matrix questions in the final block.

The block effect raises an important question about what counts as the grammatical prosodic phrasing of embedded and matrix questions. Does the prosodic phrasing obtained in the final block represent the grammar of Japanese? Given the nature of the task, this paper suggests that the prosodic phrasing speakers produced in the final block is not the representative phrasing for the grammar of Japanese. It was produced when the speakers deliberately contrasted the prosody of embedded vs. matrix questions. This is not an ordinary circumstance in speaking. Normally, speakers do not compare two construction types nor they are aware of the contrast in the meaning between similar constructions. In the final block, through a comparison, the existence of the two different types of wh-questions was made clear to the speakers. In this circumstance, when speakers were asked to convey the meaning of two sentences simultaneously that were similar but yet differed in wh-scope, they were likely to produce a distinct prosody for each question type, so that the different types of questions could be disambiguated. The results of this experiment suggest that if one wants to investigate the grammatically permissible prosodic phrasing of sentences, testing sentences in a context where speakers' attention is drawn to a contrast between similar yet different construction types is not an appropriate way to collect data. This probably includes the case where tested sentences are presented right next to each other, as it is more likely that speakers notice differences between the sentences before they read the second sentence.

In the present experiment, no context was provided for the tested sentences. If contexts which manipulate the information status of a matrix verb precede embedded and matrix scope wh-questions, do they influence the prosodic phrasing of the sentences? Under the Multiple Pairing Hypothesis, Given/New status of constituents is one of the factors that plays a role in the prosodic phrasing of sentences. The experiment in the following section tested a context effect (Given/New information) on the production of prosodic phrasing.

15.3 Experiment 2

As a follow-up to Experiment 1, the present experiment investigated whether the production of embedded and matrix scope wh-questions is influenced by the information status of constituents. The hypothesis tested in this experiment was the following: Given constituents undergo pitch compression and as a result, the frequency of MaP boundary insertions before those constituents is decreased, compared to the case of New constituents. Sugahara (2003) has shown that the Given/New status of constituents has an effect on the pitch range found after focused phrases in Japanese and induces dephrasing of a MaP. Thus, a similar effect in wh-questions arising from the information status of constituents after wh-phrases is predicted. The effect of dephrasing of a MaP can be understood by assuming Major Phrase Prominence (Selkirk, Class notes, Spring, 2004), which requires one and only one prominent element in a MaP. The material interpreted as Given information lacks prominence and does not constitute a MaP on its own.

In the experiment, target sentences in the same form as in Experiment 1 were supplemented with two different contexts. In a Given context, the verbs used in a target sentence were made into Given information by being already mentioned in the prior context. In a New context, those verbs were not mentioned before the speakers' utterance of the sentence. If both embedded and matrix questions are sensitive to these Given/New contexts, the verbs in those questions will be realized in lower pitch in Given contexts than in New contexts (i.e., context effect). If such an effect arises, it indicates that the Given/New status of constituents is a factor that influences the presence or absence of a MaP boundary after the embedded Q-marker.

15.3.1 Methods

15.3.1.1 Materials

Embedded and matrix scope wh-questions were tested in exactly the same form as those tested in Experiment 1. In addition to the materials constructed for the previous experiment, ten sentences were newly created to make a total set of eight sentences for embedded questions and a separate set of eight sentences for matrix questions. Each sentence was preceded by two different contexts (i.e., Given or New). In the Given context, both embedded and matrix verbs in the target sentence were mentioned and those verbs were made into Given information. This manipulation was adopted in order to reduce an insertion of a MaP boundary before the embedded verb. There is a chance that a MaP boundary might be inserted before the embedded verb if the embedded verb is New. If a MaP boundary appeared before the embedded verb, both embedded and matrix verbs may be grouped into the same MaP. Any prosodic bias such as this should be avoided in the course of investigation of prosodic phrasing for sentences. In the New context, the verbs were not mentioned and thus treated as New information. Example contexts (translated into English) are shown in (9). The target sentence, which participants of the experiment uttered, is boldfaced. The critical words in the context which were made into Given information are underlined:

(9)   A. Context for embedded question, Given

Yatabe's girlfriend left him. He had bunch of things he got from her. However, he decided to burn the most favorite present he received from her in order to forget about her. So he was <u>burning</u> a particular thing behind the school building. Minako came by and checked whether the <u>burnt</u> ashes came from that particular thing. Then she <u>asked</u> him <u>a stupid question</u>.

B. Context for embedded question, New

Yatabe's girlfriend left him. He had bunch of things he got from her. However, he has decided to get rid of the most favorite present he received from her in order to forget about her. So he threw a particular thing in a fireplace. Then, Minako, who is a chatter box, came by and checked whether that particular thing is in the fireplace.

Target embedded question

Mi'nako-san-wa   Ya'tabe-kun-ga   na'ni-o   moyasita'-ka
Minako-Ms.-TOP   Yatabe-Mr.-NOM   what-ACC   burned-Q

gumon-sita'-nokai?
stupid question-did-Q
'Did Minako ask stupidly what Mr. Yatabe had burned?'

Ha'i,   tazuneta-mi'tai-desu-yo.
Yes   asked-seem-COP-SFP
'Yes, it seems (she) asked (such a question)'.

C. Context for matrix question, Given

Three patients in the hospital, who were in room 1, 2, and 3, respectively, got <u>poisoned</u> by possibly different nurses. Three nurses were under suspicion. Although Dr. Yamaki knew whether Yoneda <u>poisoned</u> one particular patient, he did not <u>confirm</u> anything Yoneda did. However, last night he <u>finally confirmed </u>whether Yoneda <u>poisoned</u> that particular patient.

D. Context for matrix question, New

Three patients in the hospital, who were in rooms 1, 2, and 3, respectively, died because some nurses injected to the patients medicine that induces heart attack. Three nurses were under suspicion. Although Dr. Yamaki knew whether Yoneda injected the medicine to one particular patient, he did not say anything about what Yoneda did. However, last night he finally spoke about whether Yoneda injected the medicine to that particular patient.

Target matrix question

Ya'maki-isi-wa   Yo'neda-hutyoo-ga   da're-o   dokusatusita'-ka
Yamaki-doctor-TOP   Yoneda-head nurse-NOM   who-ACC   poisoned-Q

mitometa'-ndai?
admitted-Q
'Who did Dr. Yamaki confirm whether Yoneda, (the) head nurse, killed by poison?'

San-go'o-situ-no   gan-ka'nzya-mitai-desu-yo.
Three-No.-room-GEN   cancer-patient-seem-COP-SFP
'It seems (it was) (the) cancer patient in room No. 3.'

As shown in (9), different sets of target sentences were tested for embedded (A, B) and matrix questions (C, D). The same target sentence followed either a Given (A, C) or New context (B, D). In the Given context, the critical words which made the verbs of the target sentence Given information appeared immediately before the target sentence, in order to make clear to speakers the information status of the words (see the location of underlined words in the context.). In the New context, those words were not mentioned in the prior context before an utterance of the target sentence. Contexts which might induce a pragmatic inference about the denotation of the verbs in the target sentence were also avoided as much as possible. In both Given and New contexts, an alternative set for the wh-phrase was first introduced and then it was mentioned that a specific entity which fits the description of the alternative set exists. In these contexts, both embedded and matrix questions are felicitous. For example, in the contexts for the embedded questions in (A, B), Yatabe received many presents from his girlfriend and then he burned one of them. The contexts for the matrix questions in (C, D) mention that a set of people that were killed by poison is introduced and then it is described that Yoneda may have killed one of those people. The complexity and length of contexts were matched between Given and New contexts as much as possible. Two native speakers of Japanese checked whether the contexts (both Given and New) were natural for each target sentence. Experimental sentences were supplemented with four declarative sentences as fillers.

15.3.1.2 *Procedures*

Contexts were recorded by the experimenter before the experiment. This was to ensure that the contexts speakers heard sounded exactly the same to all speakers. A native speaker of Tokyo Japanese checked whether those recorded contexts sounded natural. In the experiment, speakers sat in front of a Dell laptop computer in a sound deadened chamber. A target sentence appeared briefly on the computer screen before the context was played. At this time, speakers were allowed to skim through the sentence but were instructed not to read aloud the sentence. Speakers were told that the purpose of flashing the target sentence once before the recording was to let them be ready for the experiment and not to give any bias for the target sentence. Therefore, speakers were instructed to listen to the context as soon as they became ready for the recording. When they were ready, the context was played. Speakers were asked to listen to the context for comprehension. When the context was over, speakers uttered the target sentence as a reply to the context they just heard. In order to make the task communicative, just like Experiment 1, the experimenter sat next to the speaker and played the role of addressee. The experimenter recorded speakers' utterances of target sentences by a SONY mini-disk recorder and digitized them into audio files (16 bit, 22 kHz) for later acoustic analysis. There were three blocks in the experiment. Thirty-two context-target sentence pairs appeared in one block. The context-sentence pairs were randomized before each block. A ten to fifteen minute break was given to the speakers between the blocks.

15.3.1.3 Participants

Four Japanese speakers from the Tokyo area, who participated in the previous experiment, also participated in the present experiment (i.e., Speakers 2, 3, 5, and 8 in Experiment 1). At least a one-month interval was given between the current experiment and the previous experiment, so that any influence from the previous experiment could be minimized.

15.3.2 Results

Table 15.4 presents percentages of MaP boundary insertion after the embedded Q-marker in embedded and matrix scope wh-questions when they were preceded by Given or New context.

Table 15.4: Percentage insertion of a MaP boundary after the embedded Q-marker in embedded and matrix scope wh-questions for Experiment 2 (the number of cases where a MaP boundary appeared after the embedded Q-marker, given a total number of cases measured).

Speaker	Embedded Question		Matrix Question	
	Given	New	Given	New
2	46 (11/24)	96 (23/24)	0 (0/24)	88 (21/24)
3	96 (23/24)	96 (23/24)	50 (12/24)	75 (18/24)
5	63 (15/24)	100 (24/24)	33 (8/24)	79 (19/24)
8	58 (14/24)	71 (17/24)	46 (11/24)	67 (16/24)

The overall pattern of the data is as follows. A context effect was found: the insertion of a MaP boundary after the embedded Q-marker increased about 35% in New contexts, compared to Given contexts. Moreover, the percentage increase of a boundary insertion was larger in matrix questions (45% increase) than embedded questions (25% increase). In addition, all speakers had a preference for inserting a MaP boundary after the embedded Q-marker in embedded questions (78%) and the insertion of a MaP boundary was optional in matrix questions (55%). The latter results are consistent with the findings in the previous experiment (Experiment 1). These patterns of the data are supported by the results of a 2×2 ANOVA: question type: $F(1, 3) = 18.59$, $p < 0.05$, context: $F(1, 3) = 7.25$, $p = 0.07$, and interaction: $F(1, 3) = 7.82$, $p = 0.07$.

Speakers 2, 5, and 8 followed the overall pattern of the data discussed above, though the context effect seemed to be smaller for Speaker 8 than Speakers 2 and 5. In Speaker 3's production of the sentences, matrix questions were sensitive to contexts but embedded questions were not. In other words, embedded questions did not differ in terms of a boundary insertion in Given and New contexts (96% in both Given and New contexts).

Interestingly, when the data of Speaker 3 were excluded, embedded questions numerically showed an optional boundary insertion in Given contexts (56%) while keeping the preference for the boundary in New contexts (89%). For matrix questions, the boundary was inserted infrequently in Given contexts (26%) and preferred in New contexts (78%). Considering the results of the present and previous experiments together, it is clear that the preference for the boundary insertion is obtained only in New contexts for embedded questions. Moreover, both embedded and matrix questions favor the boundary in New contexts, though the preference is slightly stronger in embedded questions over matrix questions.

Table 15.5 presents the $F0$ maxima of embedded and matrix verbs when embedded and matrix questions were uttered following Given or New contexts.

Table 15.5: Average *F0* maxima (Hz) of embedded and matrix verbs in embedded and matrix scope wh-questions for Experiment 2.

| Speaker | Embedded Question | | | | Matrix Question | | | |
| | Given | | New | | Given | | New | |
	Embedded Verb	Matrix Verb	Embedded Verb	Matrix Verb	Embedded Verb	Matrix Verb	Embedded Verb	Matrix Verb
2	116	137	127	171	115	109	133	191
3	218	279	220	279	222	218	224	226
5	212	233	205	263	209	203	206	235
8	205	217	203	236	191	190	198	200

The results are basically consistent with the data on the percentage of MaP boundary insertion presented in Table 15.4. A $2 \times 2 \times 2$ ANOVA showed the following results. Although the context effect was not significant ($F(1, 3) = 4.31, p = 0.13$), a marginally significant interaction between context and verb was found ($F(1, 3) = 5.70, p = 0.10$). This interaction indicates that Given contexts led speakers to produce sentences with lower pitch, compared to New contexts and that this context effect was larger on the matrix verb than the embedded verb (the mean difference between Given and New contexts: 4 Hz (embedded verb) and 27 Hz (matrix verb)). In addition, the statistical test showed a marginally significant interaction between question type and verb ($F(1, 3) = 6.55, p = 0.08$): Embedded questions had a larger $F0$ difference between the embedded and matrix verbs (39 Hz) than matrix questions (9 Hz). Overall, embedded questions had higher $F0$ maxima than matrix questions (208 vs. 192 Hz, $F(1, 3) = 8.12, p = 0.07$) and the matrix verb was pronounced with higher $F0$ maxima than the embedded verb (212 vs. 188 Hz, averaged across two question types, $F(1, 3) = 31.79, p = 0.01$).

Similarly to the data on the percent insertion of a MaP boundary, Speaker 3 showed a context effect only in matrix questions. The context effect appeared to be smaller for Speaker 8 than other speakers.

To sum up the results, the frequency of the occurrence of a MaP boundary after the embedded Q-marker was increased by whether the verbs were New in both embedded and matrix questions for three speakers (Speakers 2, 5, and 8) and only in matrix questions for Speaker 3. Accordingly, the $F0$ maxima of the matrix verbs were higher in New contexts than in Given contexts in both question types for three speakers (Speakers 2, 5, and 8) and only in matrix questions for Speaker 3.

15.3.3 Discussion

A context effect was found for most of the speakers who participated in the current experiment, though the effect was significant only in matrix scope wh-questions for Speaker 3. These results suggest that the prosodic phrasing of wh-questions is influenced by the Given/New status of material in the sentences, as in the non-interrogative sentences studied by Sugahara (2003). As discussed already, MaP Prominence (Selkirk, Class notes, Spring, 2004), requiring one and only one prominent element to occur in a MaP, accounts for the absence of a MaP boundary before the Given information.

Besides the sentence length effect demonstrated in Hirotani (2005), the information status of constituents is another factor that has an effect on the presence of a MaP boundary after the embedded Q-marker. This further suggests that the optionality in the prosodic phrasing of matrix questions observed in the preceding experiment conducted in an out-of-the blue context (Experiment 1) may come from the way speakers accommodated or made up some specific contexts in their minds.

It was consistent with the results of the previous experiment that embedded scope wh-questions had more frequent insertion of a MaP boundary after the embedded Q-marker and higher $F0$ maxima on the matrix verb than matrix questions. As suggested previously, this is probably because the contrastive FOCUS interpretation of the matrix verb was available to speakers in embedded questions, partly due to the answers provided after the target sentences were uttered by the speakers. In case of matrix questions, no FOCUS interpretation of the matrix verb was likely to exist; this may explain why the insertion of a MaP boundary was subject to the information status of the matrix verb.

It was interesting that the embedded verb was not affected by the context as much as the matrix verb. It could be because the embedded verb was positioned immediately after the focused element (i.e., wh-phrase) and underwent pitch reduction due to a post-focus effect (Nagahara, 1994; Sugahara; 2003). That is, the context effect was probably attenuated on the embedded verb; being adjacent to the wh-phrase, the embedded verb was more likely to be affected by the post-focus effect than the matrix verb was.

15.4 General discussion

In this paper, the prosodic phrasing of Japanese wh-questions was investigated. The results of the first experiment showed that matrix scope wh-questions had an optional MaP boundary after the embedded Q-marker. What is meant by 'optional boundary' here is that prosodic renditions with and without a MaP boundary after the embedded Q-marker were both observed. In embedded scope wh-questions, there was a preference for the insertion of a MaP boundary over the absence of such a boundary. It was clear from the second experiment that the insertion of a MaP boundary is highly sensitive to the information status of the matrix verb. In the second experiment, a context was provided prior to an utterance of the test sentences. The preceding contexts made the matrix verb of a sentence either Given or New information. In New contexts both embedded and matrix scope wh-questions favored the MaP boundary insertion while in Given contexts, the boundary was optional for embedded scope wh-questions and infrequent for matrix scope wh-questions.

Is the scope of wh-phrases disambiguated by prosody in Tokyo Japanese? Given the production results reported in the present paper, it is reasonable to conclude that wh-scope is not disambiguated by the prosodic phrasing of a sentence. This view is supported by wh-questions produced both in out-of-the-blue contexts (Experiment 1) and contexts where information status of the matrix verb was controlled (Experiment 2). Out-of-blue contexts showed an overlap in the choice of prosodic phrasing for two types of wh-questions. This was precisely due to the fact that matrix scope wh-questions allowed an optional insertion of a MaP boundary following the embedded Q-marker. The results were even more striking when contexts made the matrix verb New information. Under this context, both embedded and matrix scope wh-questions preferred a MaP boundary after the embedded Q-marker. The above conclusion about the relation between prosody and the scope of a wh-phrase is not a surprising one, even compared to the recent results of the empirical research conducted in other languages (e.g., Baltazani (2000) for quantifier scope in Greek; Johnson (2006) for English quantifier scope; Jun and Oh (1996) for Korean questions). In those studies, though a certain prosodic preference was shown to a certain scope interpretation of a sentence, prosody did not completely disambiguate scope ambiguities. This may contrast with some of the production results with surface syntactic ambiguities (e.g., Schafer *et al.*, 2000; Jun and Koike, 2008). The difference could be attributed to the different nature of the ambiguity inherent in the types of sentences examined (e.g., ambiguities at the level of LF for wh-questions in Tokyo Japanese).

The data presented in the current paper are in favor of an account in which multiple factors play a role in determining the prosodic phrasing of a sentence (the Multiple Pairing Hypothesis). As discussed earlier, the optional appearance of a MaP boundary after the embedded Q-marker is expected given the grammatical constraints of Japanese prosody (see Sugahara (2003) for an extensive discussion of the constraints proposed for Japanese prosody). As for the preference for a MaP boundary in embedded scope wh-questions, this paper suggests that it is probably because of the contrastive FOCUS interpretation of the matrix verb available to those questions. When the matrix verb was Given information (Experiment 2), the pitch of that phrase was compressed and as a result, the frequency of the appearance of a MaP boundary was decreased, compared to when the phrase was New information. The contrasting hypothesis (the Obligatory Pairing Hypothesis) is not fully compatible with the results of the present studies. As mentioned above, the prosodic phrasing of embedded and matrix scope wh-questions is not strictly determined by different wh-scope assignments. Crucially, the Obligatory Pairing Hypothesis does not account for the optional boundary observed in matrix scope wh-questions. Moreover, a context effect (Experiment 2) cannot be explained without an additional constraint being stipulated.

Some issues regarding the optional insertion of a MaP boundary for matrix scope wh-questions (in out-of-the-blue contexts) need further discussion. One might still hold the view of the Obligatory Pairing Hypothesis and argue that optional boundary insertion in matrix scope wh-questions comes from a conflict with the default prosody, i.e., the insertion of a boundary after the embedded Q-marker. That is, matrix scope wh-questions require no boundary after the embedded Q-marker. However, with the assumption that insertion of a MaP boundary after the embedded Q-marker constitutes the default prosodic phrasing for wh-questions, it must be stipulated how the boundary insertion is attenuated, or becomes optional, in matrix scope wh-questions. Embedded scope wh-questions do not run into this kind of problem because the prosodic phrasing associated with an embedded scope wh-question is matched with the default prosody. Two problems can be pointed out for this approach. First, it is very difficult to decide which prosodic phrasing is the default one. While Kitagawa and Fodor (2003) claim that short prosody (i.e., the one with a boundary in the current case) is the default, many researchers hold the view that optionality is one of the core features of prosody. Selkirk (1995), for example, shows that there are many different ways to pronounce a sentence 'Mary bought a book about [F bats].' with a logically equal meaning. Second, some of the results obtained in the current work and Hirotani (2005) cannot be explained under the hypothesis provided above. Recall that not only embedded but also matrix scope wh-questions favored a MaP boundary in New contexts (Experiment 2). In the study by Hirotani (2005), a MaP boundary was likely to appear even for matrix scope wh-questions when an adjunct phrase was inserted between the verbs. Instances of this sort cannot be explained without postulating an additional constraint which specifically encourages a boundary insertion for matrix scope wh-questions.

Another important finding of the present production studies is that experimental methodologies heavily influence speakers' production of prosodic phrasing. In Experiment 1, speakers' awareness of the contrast between embedded and matrix scope wh-questions demonstrated an effect on the prosodic phrasing of the sentences. When embedded and matrix scope wh-questions were presented right next to each other, speakers deliberately produced distinct prosodic phrasing for the two types of questions: A MaP boundary was systematically inserted after the embedded Q-marker in embedded scope wh-questions while such a boundary was systematically omitted in matrix scope wh-questions. Accordingly, the $F0$ maxima of the matrix verb were higher in embedded scope wh-questions than in matrix scope wh-questions. This paper suggests that the prosodic phrasing obtained in such an environment is not a typical utterance that mirrors directly the grammar of Japanese prosody. In other words, given the special task (i.e., comparison between sentences), an extra force was present to disambiguate between embedded and matrix scope wh-questions. What this implies is that comparing similar but different constructions may not be an appropriate way to study natural prosodic phrasing of sentences. It may eliminate the overlapping prosodic phrasing which is in fact completely grammaticized (see e.g., Venditti *et al.*, (1996) for the prosodic variation found in a language). Thus, experimental methodologies must be carefully chosen when the prosodic phrasing of sentences is tested. Regarding the 'extra force' just mentioned, the reason why speakers chose not to insert a MaP boundary after the embedded Q-marker in matrix scope wh-questions may be that the context which makes the matrix verb Given information fits better with matrix scope wh-questions than embedded scope wh-questions. This is because asking something about what the matrix verb denotes is less plausible with an embedded scope wh-question when the matrix verb is already established as Given information in the discourse. Therefore, if speakers are forced to choose between embedded and matrix scope wh-questions to assign such a context to the sentences, they are more likely to select matrix scope wh-questions than embedded scope wh-questions.

Another interesting and important question left to be addressed concerns the relation of the current work to the (auditory) comprehension of wh-questions. The results of the present studies imply the following. Assume that it is easier for listeners to comprehend sentences when they are accompanied by the appropriate (i.e., grammatical) prosodic phrasing and discourse contexts than when they are not. In case of embedded questions, they are expected to be easier when there is a MaP boundary following the embedded Q-marker than when no such boundary appears at the location. In addition, those questions should be comprehended more easily when they appear in the context in which the matrix verb is (contrastively) focused than when they do not. For matrix scope wh-questions, the presence or absence of a MaP boundary after the embedded Q-marker should not influence the interpretation of the sentences. If the context in which the matrix verb is made into Given information goes well with matrix scope wh-questions, as speculated above, the prosodic phrasing without a MaP boundary after the embedded Q-marker may facilitate the scope interpretation of matrix wh-questions. These predictions based on the present production studies are rather speculative. Thus, further research is needed to explore how listeners use prosodic boundaries to assign wh-scope to a sentence and to investigate whether the use of prosodic boundaries is the same between speakers and listeners.

Finally, besides those already mentioned above, one of the issues remaining to be solved is whether production results will be the same when wh-questions are recorded in a completely natural setting. In the present production experiments, the sentences were recorded in the form of a dialogue to make the task for speakers communicative. However, such a dialogue may not be sufficient to avoid all the effects coming from 'lab speech' (Beckman, 1997). It will probably be interesting to compare the present results with those collected in a completely natural environment.

Acknowledgments

This research was conducted as a part of the author's Ph.D. dissertation submitted to University of Massachusetts Amherst. The studies presented in this paper were supported by the research grants HD18708 from NIH and BCS 0090674 from NSF to the University of Massachusetts Amherst. The author would like to thank Lyn Frazier, Charles Clifton, Elisabeth Selkirk, and three anonymous reviewers for their valuable comments for the reported studies. Many thanks goes to Charles Clifton for his help preparing the present paper.

Notes

1. The following abbreviations are used for glosses in the present paper: ACC (accusative), COP (copula), GEN (genitive), NOM (nominative), Q (question marker), SFP (sentence final particle), and TOP (topic).

2. Ito (2002) investigated the prosodic structure of the sentences produced by Tokyo Japanese speakers as a reply to wh-questions. Her study found that the $F0$ peak of a narrowly focused word was consistently higher than that of a broadly focused word. In Kubo (1989) and Smith (2005), wh-scope and its prosodic structure in Fukuoka Japanese are discussed. According to their studies, the scope of a wh-phrase is completely disambiguated by the locus of H-tone in the Fukuoka dialect.

3. This paper does not discuss a constraint ranking for Japanese prosody because this is beyond the scope of the paper. For the previous proposals, see Truckenbrodt (1995) and Sugahara (2003).

4. The presence of a MaP boundary when an adjunct phrase was inserted after the embedded Q-marker can be captured by the grammatical constraint, Align$_L$ (XP, MaP). When an adjunct phrase is inserted after the embedded Q-marker, as in [NP-TOP [NP-NOM Wh-ACC V-Q]$_i$ [Adjunct t$_i$ V-Q]], the embedded clause undergoes scrambling (Saito, 1985) before the matrix adjunct, which creates an XP boundary at the left edge of the adjunct phrase to be aligned with a MaP boundary.

References

Albritton, D. W., McKoon, G. and Ratcliff, R. (1996) Reliability of prosodic cues for resolving syntactic ambiguity. *Journal of Experimental Psychology: Learning, Memory, and Cognition* 22 (3): 714–735.

Aoshima, S., Phillips, C. and Weinberg, A. (2004) Processing filler-gap dependencies in a head-final language. *Journal of Memory and Language* 51: 23–54.

Baltazani, M. (2000) *Prosody and Scope*. Ph.D. Dissertation, University of California, Los Angeles.

Beckman, M. E. (1996) The parsing of prosody. *Language and Cognitive Processes* 11: 17–67.

Beckman, M. E. (1997) A typology of spontaneous speech. In Y. Sagisaka, N. Campbell, and N. Higuchi (eds) *Computing Prosody: Computational Models for Processing Spontaneous Speech* 7–26. New York: Springer.

Beckman, M. E. and Pierrehumbert, J. (1986) Intonational structure in Japanese and English. *Phonology Yearbook* 3: 255–309.

Boersma, P. and Weenink, D. (2009) Praat: Doing phonetics by computer (Version 5.1.07) [Computer program]. Retrieved 12 May 2009, from http://www.praat.org/.

Carlson, K., Clifton, C. Jr. and Frazier, L. (2006) Effects of constituent length on boundary informativeness. Paper presented at the 19th Annual CUNY Conference on Human Sentence Processing, The City University of New York, New York.

Deguchi, M. and Kitagawa, Y. (2002) Prosody and wh-questions. In M. Hirotani (ed.) *Proceedings of the North East Linguistic Society, Vol. 32* 73–92. Amherst MA: Graduate Linguistic Student Association.

Ferreira, F. (1993) The creation of prosody during sentence production. *Psychological Review* 100 (2): 233–253.

Fodor, J. A. (1983) *Modularity of Mind.* Cambridge MA: MIT Press.

Fodor, J. D. (2002) Prosodic disambiguation in silent reading. In M. Hirotani (ed.) *Proceedings of the North East Linguistic Society, Vol. 32* 113–137. Amherst MA: Graduate Linguistic Student Association.

Gussenhoven, C. (1999) Discreteness and gradience in intonational contrasts. *Language and Speech* 42 (2–3): 281–305.

Hamblin, C. L. (1973) Questions in Montague English. *Foundations of Language* 10 (1): 41–53.

Hirotani, M. (2003) Prosodic effects on the interpretation of Japanese wh-questions. In L. Alonso-Ovalle (ed.) *University of Massachusetts Occasional Papers in Linguistics 27: On Semantic Processing* 117–137. Amherst, MA: Graduate Linguistic Student Association.

Hirotani, M. (2004) Prosodic boundaries in the comprehension and production of wh-questions in Tokyo Japanese. Paper presented at the 17th Annual CUNY Conference on Human Sentence Processing, University of Maryland, College Park.

Hirotani, M. (2005) *Prosody and LF Interpretation: Processing Japanese wh-questions.* Unpublished Ph.D. Dissertation, University of Massachusetts Amherst.

Hoji, H. (1985) *Logical Form Constraints and Configurational Structures in Japanese.* Unpublished Ph.D. Dissertation, University of Washington.

Ishihara, S. (2002) Invisible but audible wh-scope marking: Wh-constructions and deaccenting in Japanese. In L. Mikkelsen and C. Potts (eds) *Proceedings of the 21st West Coast Conference on Formal Linguistics* 180–193. Somerville MA: Cascadilla Press.

Ishihara, S. (2003) *Intonation and Interface Condition.* Unpublished Ph.D. Dissertation, Massachusetts Institute of Technology.

Ito, K. (2002) *The Interaction of Focus and Lexical Pitch Accent in Speech Production and Dialogue Comprehension: Evidence from Japanese and Basque.* Unpublished Ph.D. Dissertation, University of Illoisnois, Urbana-Champaign.

Johnson, S. (2006) Prosody and logical scope in English. Paper presented at the 19th Annual CUNY Conference on Human Sentence Processing, The City University of New York, New York.

Jun, S. and Koike, C. (2008) Default prosody and relative clause attachment in Japanese. *Japanese/Korean Linguistics, vol. 13* 41–53. Stanford CA: CSLI.

Jun, S. and Oh, M. (1996) A prosodic analysis of three types of wh-phrases in Korean, *Language and Speech* 39(1): 37–61.

Karttunen, L. (1977) Syntax and semantics of questions. *Linguistics and Philosophy* 1 (1): 3–44.

Kitagawa, Y. and Deguchi, M. (2002) *Prosody in Syntactic Analyses*. Ms, Indiana University.

Kitagawa, Y. and Fodor, J. D. (2003) Default prosody explains neglected syntactic analysis in Japanese. In W. McClure (ed.) *Japanese/Korean Linguistics, vol. 12* 267–279. Stanford CA: CSLI.

Kratzer, A. and Shimoyama, J. (2002) Indeterminate pronouns: The view from Japanese. In Y. Otsu (ed.) *The Proceedings of the 3rd Tokyo Conference on Psycholinguistics* 1–25. Tokyo Japan: Hitsuji Syobo Publishing.

Kubo, Tomoyuki. (1989) Fukuoka-si hougen no, dare · nani-tou-no gimonsi-o fukumu bun–no pitti-pataan [The pitch patterns of sentences containing WH-words in the Fukuoka City dialect]. *Kokugogaku* 156: 1–12.

Kubozono, H. (1993) *The Organization of Japanese Prosody*. Tokyo Japan: Kuroshio.

Ladd, D. R. (1996) *Intonational Phonology*. Cambridge UK: Cambridge University Press.

Lasnik, H. and Saito, M. (1984) On the nature of proper government. *Linguistic Inquiry* 15 (2): 238–289.

Lasnik, H. and Saito, M. (1992) *Move α: Conditions on its Application and Output*. Cambridge MA: MIT Press.

Lehiste, I. (1973) Phonetic disambiguation of syntactic ambiguity. *Glossa*: 7: 107–122.

Maekawa, K. (1994) Is there 'dephrasing' of the accentual phrase in Japanese? In J. J. Venditti (ed.) *Papers from the Linguistics Laboratory, Ohio State University Working Papers in Linguistics, vol. 44* 146–165. Columbus, OH: Ohio State University.

Maekawa, K. (1997) Nihongo gimonsi gimon-bun no intoneesyon [The intonation of the Japanese wh-question]. In Onsei Bunpoo Kenkyuukai (ed.) *Bunpoo to onsei [Grammar and Sound]* 45–53. Tokyo, Japan: Kuroshio.

McCarthy, J. and Prince, A. (1993) Generalized alignment. In G. Gooij and J. v. Maarle (eds) *The Yearbook of Morphology 1993* 89–164. Dordrecht Holland: Kluwer.

Miyamoto, E. T. and Takahashi, S. (2002) The processing of wh-phrases and interrogative complementizers in Japanese. In N. M. Akatsuka, and S. Strauss (eds) *Japanese/Korean Linguistics, vol. 10* 62–75. Stanford CA: CSLI.

Nagahara, H. (1994) *Phonological Phrasing in Japanese*. Unpublished Ph.D. Dissertation, University of California, Los Angeles.

Nespor, M. and Vogel, I. (1986) *Prosodic Phonology*. Dordrecht Holland: Foris.

Nishiguchi, T. (1986) *Quantification in Syntax*. Unpublished Ph.D. Dissertation, University of Massachusetts Amherst.

Nishigauchi, T. (1999) Quantification and wh-constructions. In N. Tsujimura (ed.) *The Handbook of Japanese Linguistics* 154–190. Malden MA: Blackwell.

Pierrehumbert, J. and Beckman, M. E. (1988) *Japanese Tone Structure*. Cambridge MA: MIT Press.

Prince, A. and Smolensky, P. (1993) *Optimality Theory: Constraint Interaction in Generative Grammar*. Technical report #2 of the Rutgers Center for Cognitive Science. New Brunswick NJ: Rutgers University.

Rooth, M. (1996) Focus. In S. Lappin (ed.) *The Handbook of Contemporary Semantic Theory* 271–297. Oxford: Blackwell.

Saito, M. (1985) *Some Asymmetries in Japanese and their Theoretical Implications*. Ph.D. Dissertation, Massachusetts Institute of Technology.

Schafer, A., Speer, S., Warren, P. and White, S. (2000) Intonational disambiguation in sentence production and comprehension. *Journal of Psycholinguistic Research* 29 (2): 169–182.

Schwarzschild, R. (1999) GIVENness, avoidF and other constraints on the placement of accent. *Natural Language Semantics* 7 (2): 141–177.

Selkirk, E. O. (1984) *Phonology and Syntax: The Relation Between Sound and Structure*. Cambridge MA: MIT Press.

Selkirk, E. O. (1995) The prosodic structure of function words. In J. Beckman, S. Urbanczyk and L. Walsh (eds) *Optimality Theory, University of Massachusetts Occasional Papers in Linguistics, vol. 18* 439–469. Amherst MA: Graduate Linguistic Student Association.

Selkirk, E. O. (1995) Sentence prosody: Intonation, stress, and phrasing. In J. Goldsmith (ed.) *The Handbook of Phonological Theory* 550–569. New York NY: Blackwell.

Selkirk, E. O. (2000) The interaction of constraints on prosodic phrasing. In M. Horne (ed.) *Prosody: Theory and Experiment* 231–261. Dordrecht Holland: Kluwer.

Selkirk, E. O. (2004) Class notes. Spring, 2004. Ms., University of Massachusetts Amherst.

Selkirk, E. O. and Tateishi, K. (1988) Constraints on minor phrase formation in Japanese. In M. G. Larson and D. Brentari (eds) *Proceedings of the 24th Annual Meeting of the Chicago Linguistics Society* 316–336. Chicago IL: Chicago Linguistic Society.

Selkirk, E. O. and Tateishi, K. (1991) Syntax and downstep in Japanese. In C. Georgopoulos and R. Ishihara (eds) *Interdisciplinary Approaches to Language: Essays in Honor of S.-Y. Kuroda* 519–543. Dordrecht Holland: Kluwer.

Selkirk, E. O., Shinya, T. and Kawahara, S. (2004) Phonological and phonetic effects of minor phrase length on F0 in Japanese. Paper presented at Speech Prosody 2004, Nara, Japan.

Selkirk, E. O., Sugahara, M. and Shinya, T. (2003) Degree of initial lowering in Japanese as a reflex of prosodic structure organization. In *Proceedings of the 15th International Congress of Phonetic Sciences* 491–494. Barcelona, Spain.

Shimoyama, J. (2002) *Wh-constructions in Japanese*. Unpublished Ph.D. Dissertation, University of Massachusetts Amherst.

Shinya, T. (2002) The intonational asymmetry between argument and adjunct in Japanese. Ms., University of Massachusetts Amherst.

Smith, J. (2005) On the WH-question intonational domain in Fukuoka Japanese: Some implications for the syntax-prosody interface. In S. Kawahara (ed.) *Papers on Prosody, University of Massachusetts Occasional Papers in Linguistics, vol. 30* 219–237. Amherst MA: Graduate Linguistic Student Association.

Snedeker, J. and Trueswell, J. (2003) Using prosody to avoid ambiguity: Effects of speaker awareness and referential context. *Journal of Memory and Language* 48: 103–130.

Sugahara, M. (2003) *Downtrends and Post-focus Intonation in Tokyo Japanese.* Unpublished Ph.D. Dissertation, University of Massachusetts Amherst.

Takahashi, D. (1993) Movement of *wh*-phrases in Japanese. *Natural Language and Linguistic Theory* 11: 655–678.

Tomioka, S. (1997) Wh-insitu, subjacency, and LF syntax. Course handout from Linguistic Society of America Summer Institute, Cornell University.

Truckenbrodt, H. (1995) *Phonological Phrases: Their Relation to Syntax, Focus, and Prominence.* Unpublished Ph.D. Dissertation, Massachusetts Institute of Technology.

Uechi, A. (1998) *An Interface Approach to Topic/focus Structure.* Unpublished Ph.D. Dissertation, University of British Columbia.

Ueno, M. and Kluender, R. (2003) On the processing of Japanese wh-questions: Relating grammar and brain. In G. Garding and M. Tsujimura (eds) *Proceedings of the 22nd West Coast Conference on Formal Linguistics* 491–504. Somerville MA: Cascadilla Press.

Venditti, J. J., Jun, S. and Beckman, M. E. (1996) Prosodic cues to syntactic and other linguistic structures in Japanese, Korean, and English. In J. L. Morgan and K. D. Demuth (eds) *Signal to Syntax: Bootstrapping from Speech to Grammar in Early Acquisition* 287–311. Hillsdale NJ: Lawrence Erlbaum Associates.

Watanabe, A. (1992) Subjacency and S-structure movement of wh-in-situ. *Journal of East Asian Linguistics* 1 (3): 225–291.

Watson. D. and Gibson E. (2004) The relationship between intonational phrasing and syntactic structure in language production. *Language and Cognitive Processes* 19 (6): 713–755.

Yoshida, T. (1998) Wh-operator vs. yes/no-operator. *International Christian University Language Research Bulletin* 13: 159–172.

Appendix. Materials for Experiment 1

Participants in the Embedded Group read unambiguous embedded wh-questions (1)–(6) in the first block, which was then followed by the second block containing both unambiguous embedded ((1), (2), (6), (7)) and matrix wh-questions ((10)–(12) and (14)). In the final block, a pair of unambiguous embedded ((1) and (5)) and matrix question ((8) and (11)), which were the same in form except for the disambiguating matrix Q-marker, were presented to speakers simultaneously. Likewise, the first block for the Matrix Group contained only unambiguous matrix wh-questions (8)–(13). The second and final blocks for this group were the same as those provided for the Embedded Group. In the sentences below, apostrophes indicate the location of accents in each word. Non-target sentences, which were uttered by an addressee in reply to speakers' utterances, are shown in parentheses.

1.

Mi'nako-san-wa	Ya'tabe-kun-ga	na'ni-o	moyasita'-ka
Minako-Ms.-TOP	Yatabe-Mr.-NOM	what-ACC	burned-Q

gumon-sita'-nokai?

stupid question-did-Q

'Did Minako ask stupidly what Mr. Yatabe burned?'

(Un,	sonna-situmon-o	sita-rasii-yo.)
Yes,	such-question-ACC	did-seem-SFP

'Yes, it seems (she) asked such a question.'

2.

No'riko-san-wa	Ma'sako-san-ga	na'ni-o	mokugekisita'-ka
Noriko-Ms.-TOP	Masako-Ms.-NOM	what-ACC	witnessed-Q

mokunin-sita'-nokai?

tacit consent-did-Q

'Was Noriko tolerant (about) what Masako witnessed?'

(Iie,	tyanto	keesatu-ni	itta-mitai-da-yo.)
No,	properly	police-DAT	said-seem-COP-SFP

'No, it seems (she) properly told (the) police (about it).'

3.

No'hara-kun-wa	Mi'nami-kun-ga	na'ni-o	neratteita'-ka
Nohara-Mr.-TOP	Minami-Mr.-NOM	what-ACC	was aiming for-Q

miwaketa'-nokai?

distinguished-Q?

'Did Mr. Nohara say what Mr. Minami was aiming for?'

(Iya,   miwakewadekinakatta-mitai-da-yo.)

No,   could not tell-seem-COP-SFP

'No, it seems (he) could not tell (it).'

4.

Ya'maki-isi-wa	Yo'neda-hutyoo-ga	da're-o
Yamaki-doctor-TOP	Yoneda-head nurse-NOM	who-ACC

dokusatusita'-ka	yokensita'-nokai?
killed by poison-Q	had foreseen-Q

'Had Dr. Yamaki foreseen who Yoneda, (the) head nurse, killed by poison?'

(Un,   sonna-yoken-o-siteita-yoo-da-ne.)

Yes,   such-foreseeing-ACC-did-seem-COP-SFP

'Yes, it seems (he) had such sight.'

5.

Go'roo-kun wa	Ni'sida-san-ga	da're-o	yusutteita'-ka
Goroo-Mr.-TOP	Nisida-Ms.-NOM	who-ACC	was extorting-Q

yosokusita'-nokai?

predicted-Q

'Did Goroo predict who Ms. Nisida was extorting?'

(Un,   yosokusiteita-mitai-da-ne.)

Yes,   predicted-seem-COP-SFP

'Yes, it seems (he) had (the) prediction.'

6.

| Na'gano-san-wa | Ya'gami-tizi-ga | | da're-o | yondeita'-ka |
| Nagano-Mr.-TOP | Yagami-governor-NOM | | who-ACC | invited-Q |

matagiki-sita'-nokai?
hearsay-did-Q
'Did Mr. Nagano learn by hearsay who (the) governor, Yagami, invited?'

| (Iya, | sonna-koto-wa | matagiki-sitenai-mitai-da-yo.) |
| No, | such-thing-TOP | hearsay-did not-seem-COP-SFP |

'No, it seems (he) has not learned about (it) by hearsay.'

7.

| Ri'kako-san-wa | Ya'suko-san-ga | da're-o | norotteita'-ka |
| Rikako-Ms.-TOP | Yasuko-Ms.-NOM | who-ACC | cursed-Q |

yogensiteita'-nokai?
had predicted-Q
'Had Rikako predicted who Yasuko would curse?'

| (Un, | soo-mita-da-ne.) |
| Yes | so-seem-COP-SFP |

'Yes, it seems so.'

8.

| Mi'nako-san-wa | Ya'tabe-kun-ga | na'ni-o | moyasita'-ka |
| Minako-Ms.-TOP | Yatabe-Mr.-NOM | what-ACC | burned-Q |

gumon-sita'-ndai?
stupid question-did-Q
'What did Minako ask stupidly whether Mr. Yatabe burned?'

| (Wakareta | gaaru hurendo-kara | moratta | tegami-da-yo.) |
| became separated | girlfriend-from | received | letter-COP-SFP |

'(The) letters (he) received from (his) ex-girlfriend.'

9.

No'riko-san-wa	Ma'sako-san-ga	na'ni-o	mokugekisita'-ka
Noriko-Ms.-TOP	Masako-Ms.-NOM	what-ACC	witnessed-Q

mokunin-sita'-ndai?

tacit consent-did-Q

'What was Noriko tolerant (about) whether Masako witnessed?'

(Hikinige-genba-rasii-yo.)

hit-and-run-spot-seem-SFP

'It seems (she saw) a hit-and-run accident.'

10.

No'hara-kun-wa	Mi'nami-kun-ga	na'ni-o	neratteita'-ka
Nohara-Mr.-TOP	Minami-Mr.-NOM	what-ACC	was aiming for-Q

miwaketa'-ndai?

distinguished-Q?

'What did Mr. Nohara say whether Mr. Minami was aiming for?'

(Naikaku-no   sutoreeto-da-yo.)

inside corner -GEN   straight-COP-SFP

'(The) inside fast ball.'

11.

Go'roo-kun-wa	Ni'sida-san-ga	da're-o	yusutteita'-ka
Goroo-Mr.-TOP	Nisida-Ms.-NOM	who-ACC	was extorting-Q

yosokusita'-ndai?

predicted-Q

'Who did Goroo predict whether Ms. Nisida was extorting?'

(Tonari-mati-no   daikigyoo-no   syatyoo-da-yo.)

neighboring-town-GEN   big enterprise-GEN   president-COP-SFP

'(The) president of (the) big company in (the) neighboring town.'

12.

Ya'maki-isi-wa	Yo'neda-hutyoo-ga	da're-o
Yamaki-doctor-TOP	Yoneda-head nurse-NOM	who-ACC

dokusatusita'-ka	mitometa'-ndai?
killed by poison-Q	admitted-Q

'Who did Dr. Yamaki determine whether Yoneda, (the) head nurse, killed by poison?'

(Sangoositu-no	gan-kanzya-rasii-yo.)
Three-No.-room-GEN	cancer-patient-seem-SFP

'It seems (it was) (the) cancer patient in room No. 3.'

13.

Na'gano-san-wa	Ya'gami-tizi-ga	da're-o	yondeita'-ka
Nagano-Mr.-TOP	Yagami-governor-NOM	who-ACC	invited-Q

matagiki-sita'-ndai?
hearsay-did-Q

'Who did Mr. Nagano learn by hearsay whether (the) governor, Yagami, invited?'

(Minzi-too-no	Sirai-kanzityoo-da-yo.)
Minzi-party-GEN	Sirai-chief secretary-COP-SFP

'Mr. Sirai, (the) chief secretary, of Minzi party.'

14.

Ha'mada-san-wa	Ma'miko-san-ga	na'ni-o
Hamada-Mr.-TOP	Mamiko-Ms.-NOM	what-ACC

manandeita'-ka	bakanisita'-ndai?
was learning-Q	made a fool of-Q

'What did Mr. Hamada laugh at whether Mamiko was learning?'

(Boki-no	kihon-da-yo.)
bookkeeping-GEN	basic-COP-SFP

'(The) basic bookkeeping.'

16 Effects of indefinite pronouns and traces on verb stress in German

Hubert Truckenbrodt[a]

16.1 Introduction

Kratzer and Selkirk (2007) develop an innovative account of phrasal stress in terms of phases (see Chomsky, 2008). In developing the account with German examples, they notice an interesting difference concerning the indirect effect of indefinite pronouns as opposed to traces on whether stress is assigned to a following verb. This effect is further explored in this paper, along with some related issues.

By way of background, notice first that in all-new-sentences, a non-pronominal subject and a non-pronominal object both receive phrasal stress as in (1). I indicate stress by underlining. The last stress is strengthened to the strongest of the clause, which I indicate by double underlining. The absence of stress on the final verb is in some sense tied to the presence of the preceding stressed direct object (see Gussenhoven, 1983: Krifka, 1984; Selkirk, 1984 and much later literature). If the verb is preceded by an adjunct as in (2) the final verb is stressed.

(1) [What happened while I was gone?]

  Ein <u>Mann</u> hat ein <u>Buch</u> gekauft.

  a man has a book bought

  'A man has bought a book.'

[a] Hubert Truckenbrodt: Zentrum für Allgemeine Sprachwissenschaft, Berlin and Humboldt-Universität zu Berlin, Germany. Email: truckenbrodt@zas.gwz-berlin.de

(2)   [What are you laughing about?]

Ein <u>Mann</u> hat während einer <u>Vorstellung</u> <u>geschlafen</u>.

a   man   has during   a   show   slept

'A man has slept during a show.'

There is a sense, then, in which a direct object exempts the following verb from being stressed. Can the subject of a transitive verb likewise exempt the final verb from being stressed, across a pronoun or across the trace of a direct object? Kratzer and Selkirk (2007) show that this is not possible across an intervening indefinite object pronoun as in (3). Interestingly, they also show that, when the direct object is given and scrambled as in (4), the subject does exempt the final verb from requiring stress. Their examples show the stress-patterns of all-new sentences, except where otherwise noticed (as with the given constituent in (4)).

(3)   Ich hab gehört, dass <u>Maria</u> *was*   <u>gekauft</u> hat.

I   have heard   that Maria something bought has

'I have heard that Maria has bought something.'

(4)   Ich weiss, dass dieses Haus$_G$ <u>Mafiosi</u> besitzen.

I   know that this   house Mafiosi own

'I know that Mafiosi own this house.'

In this paper, further cases of this contrast are introduced, the contrast is extended to configurations with an indirect and a direct object, and a related case from Kratzer and Selkirk (2007) involving PPs without phrasal stress is addressed. The data is introduced in Section 16.2. In Section 16.3 I review the account of Kratzer and Selkirk (2007) and offer an extension for the cases involving indirect and direct object. In Section 16.4 I discuss an account in the theory in terms of Stress-XP (Truckenbrodt, 2007), though the case of the stressless PPs will remain open. I will not seek a choice between the two accounts, and will conclude by addressing the relation of the two accounts in Section 16.5.

16.2 Stress patterns with indefinite and definite pronouns

16.2.1 Indirect object + direct object + verb

The perspective assumed here is that the syntax plays a role in the assignment of phrasal prosodic structure and phrasal stress that can be stated independently of the deaccenting role of givenness (Ladd, 1983; Féry and Samek-Lodovici, 2006; Selkirk, 2006) and independently of the stress-attracting role of focus (Jackendoff, 1972, refined in Truckenbrodt, 1995: Ch. 4; Rooth, 1996). Context questions are employed to ensure that a sentence, or the relevant part of it, consists of new elements inside of a larger focus.

Again some background first: A stressed new indefinite (i.e. unscrambled) direct object makes a following verb stressless obligatorily, as in (5).

(5) [What did she do?]

    a. # Sie hat ein <u>Buch</u> <u>gekauft</u>.

    b. Sie hat ein <u>Buch</u> gekauft.

       she has a   book bought

       'She has bought a book.'

Now, an indirect object and a direct object both carry phrasal stress. Here the stressed direct object has the effect that the verb need not carry phrasal stress:

(6) [What did she do?]

    Sie hat einem <u>Kind</u> ein <u>Buch</u> vorgelesen.

    she has a.DAT child a   book read

    'She has read a book to a child.'

In (7) the direct object is replaced with an indefinite pronoun. Can the indirect object exempt the final verb from carrying phrasal stress in this case? As shown, stress on the verb as in (7a) is obligatory in such a configuration. (7b) is not a possible stress pattern in this case, unless the verb 'vorgelesen' is contextually given.

(7)   [What did she do?]

    a.   Sie hat einem <u>Kind</u> *(et)was*   <u>vorgelesen</u>.

    b. # Sie hat einem <u>Kind</u> *(et)was*   vorgelesen.

        she has a.DAT child something read

        'She has read something to a child.'

In (8) the direct object is realized by a definite object pronoun. This is fronted within the middle field of the clause obligatorily. As shown in (8), the stress facts change in the case considered here. Both stress patterns are now possible. Importantly, the stressless verb in (8b) is allowed, while it is disallowed in (7b).

(8)   [What did she do next with the book?]

    a.   Sie hat *es* einem <u>Kind</u> <u>vorgelesen</u>.

    b.   Sie hat *es* einem <u>Kind</u> vorgelesen.

        she has it a.DAT child read

        'She has read it to a child.'

The same two stress-patterns are found when the direct object is not expressed, as in (9).

(9)   [What did she do?]

    a.   Sie hat einem <u>Kind</u> <u>vorgelesen</u>.

    b.   Sie hat einem <u>Kind</u> vorgelesen.

        she has a.DAT child read

        'She has read to a child.'

In sum, a direct object exempts the following verb from carrying stress. An indirect object cannot exempt the verb from carrying stress across an intervening direct object pronoun. Where the position of the direct object is phonetically empty, the verb is stressed optionally.

16.2.2 Subject + direct object + verb

As reviewed initially in this paper, a subject and a following unscrambled direct object both receive phrasal stress, and a following verb remains unstressed. Another example is shown in (10). I employ an initial adverbial for reasons explained later in this paper.

(10)   [What happened on Tuesday?]

    Am <u>Dienstag</u> hat ein <u>Kunde</u>   ein <u>Buch</u> geklaut.

    on   Tuesday has a   customer a   book stolen

    'On Tuesday a customer has stolen a book.'

The observation of Kratzer and Selkirk (2007) concerning a direct object pronoun is reproduced in (11). The verb cannot be stressless as in (11b) when the subject is followed by an indefinite direct object pronoun. (It could be stressless only it it were contextually given.)

(11)   [What happened on Tuesday?]

    a.   Am <u>Dienstag</u> hat ein <u>Kunde</u>   *etwas*   <u>geklaut</u>.

    b. #   Am <u>Dienstag</u> hat ein <u>Kunde</u>   *etwas*   geklaut.

        on   Tuesday has a   customer something stolen

        'On Tuesday a customer has stolen something.'

When the direct object is a personal pronoun that is moved to the left of the subject, as in (12), the stressless verb is possible, as in (12b). This is parallel to the example (4) of Kratzer and Selkirk (2007). Alternatively, stress on the verb is possible, as in (12a).

(12)   [What happened to the new hammer?]

    a.   Am <u>Dienstag</u> hat *ihn* ein <u>Kunde</u> <u>geklaut</u>.

    b.   Am <u>Dienstag</u> hat *ihn* ein <u>Kunde</u> geklaut.

        on   Tuesday has it   a   customer stolen

        'On Tuesday a customer has stolen it.'

Kratzer and Selkirk (2007:122) observe for their example (4) that it does not allow the alternative stress-pattern with the verb stressed. I believe this may be because of the following reason. It seems to me that in the domain of optionality where the syntax does not determine the stress, subtle preferences arise due to expectability of the predicates involved. These may be more intricate than the givenness that we normally take into account. Thus, in (4) it may be that 'Mafiosi' and 'house' together make the verb 'own' in some sense expected. I seek to avoid this by using 'customer' and 'steal' in (12). Further examples to document the optionality are shown in (13)–(16).

(13)   [What do you know about Peter's trip?]

    a.   <u>Überall</u>   haben *ihn* <u>Frauen</u> <u>verehrt</u>.

    b.   <u>Überall</u>   haben *ihn* <u>Frauen</u> verehrt.

        everywhere have   him women admired

        'Women admired him everywhere.'

(14)   [What did Peter see on his trip?]

    a.   <u>Überall</u>   haben <u>Frauen</u> *jemand*   <u>verehrt</u>.

    b. # <u>Überall</u>   haben <u>Frauen</u> *jemand*   verehrt.

        everywhere have   women someone admired

        'Women have admired someone everywhere.'

(15)   [What happened to the apparatus?]

    a.   In der <u>Werkstadt</u> haben *ihn* <u>Fachleute</u> <u>geölt</u>.

    b.   In der <u>Werkstadt</u> haben *ihn* <u>Fachleute</u> geölt.

        in the garage   have   it   specialists oiled

        'Specialists have oiled it in the garage.'

(16)   [What happened in the afternoon?]

    a.   In der <u>Werkstadt</u> haben <u>Fachleute</u> *etwas*   <u>geölt</u>.

    b. # In der <u>Werkstadt</u> haben <u>Fachleute</u> *etwas*   geölt.

        in the garage   have   specialists something oiled

        'Specialists have oiled something in the garage.'

As seen initially, then, a subject can exempt a following transitive verb from being stressed across the trace of the direct object, but not across an intervening indefinite pronoun. The patterns are parallel to those of indirect and direct object.

16.2.3 Directional and locative PPs

Kratzer and Selkirk (2007: 107f) discuss a pattern of stress from Uhmann (1991) and others that is unexpected for earlier accounts that assign phrasal stress to each verbal argument, including the account in terms of Stress-XP. When a direct object (or unaccusative subject) is followed by a directional or locative PP, the PP need not carry phrasal stress. (Agentive verbs seem to be excluded from this, as Kratzer and Selkirk 2007 show.) In (17), the PP 'an einen Freund' does not carry phrasal stress. Importantly, this pattern of stress is possible even if the PP is not contextually given.

(17)   ... dass ein <u>Junge</u> eine <u>Geige</u> an einen Freund schickte

         that a   boy   a   violin to a   friend sent

    '... that a boy sent a violin to a friend.'

Notice that this suggests that adjacency of the verb to the stressed object is not a general precondition for a stressless verb in German. Similar patterns of leftmost stress within the VP in Persian are reported in Kahnemuyipour (2004).

16.3 The account of the phase-based theory of phrasal stress by Kratzer and Selkirk (2007)

16.3.1 CP and vP phases

Kratzer and Selkirk (2007) formulate a new theory of phrasal stress that postulates a connection to the phases of Chomsky (2008). In doing so, they build on suggestions of Kahnemuyipour (2004). They also integrate suggestions about topics by Jäger (2001). German plays a central role in the illustration of the theory.

According to Chomsky, vP and CP are phases, i.e. cyclic nodes on a cycle where each cyclic node undergoes a derivation that includes interpretation at LF and PF. Phases are divided into edges (specifier and head of the highest projection in the phase) and spellout domains (the complement of this highest projection of the phase). Only the spellout domain of a phase is processed at PF. Processing at PF is taken to result in structures that no longer allow syntactic movement. Elements that undergo syntactic movement out of the phase must therefore stand at the edge of the phase, outside of the spellout domain, to escape being spelled out as part of the phase. The starting point for Kratzer and Selkirk is that the spellout domain of CP is TP and the spellout domain of vP is VP.

Kahnemuyipour (2004) suggested that the highest constituent in a spellout domain receives phrasal stress. Kratzer and Selkirk (2007) modify this to a formulation in which the highest syntactic *phrase*, i.e. XP, in the spellout domain receives phrasal stress (and first forms a prosodic major phrase, an aspect that I do not address here).

(18)   Kratzer and Selkirk (2007)

The highest phrase condition on prosodic spellout – stress-based version:

Assign phrase stress within the highest syntactic phrase within the spellout domain.

Consider the structure in (19) for a transitive German *dass*-clause. Kratzer and Selkirk analyze the subject as being in Spec,TP.

(19)   [CP-PHASE-1 dass [TP-SPELLOUT-1 Maria$_k$ [vP-PHASE-2 t$_k$ [VP-SPELLOUT-2 Gesetze studierte]]]]
         that   Maria   laws   studied

In the lower spellout domain VP, the direct object 'Gesetze' is the highest XP and receives phrasal stress by (18). In the higher spellout domain TP, the subject is the highest XP and receives phrasal stress by (18). Stress is thus correctly assigned to these two arguments.

An empirical strength of the proposal by Kratzer and Selkirk (2007) lies with its ability to generalize to the unexpected stress pattern involving the stressless PP discussed in the preceding section: The PP argument that follows the direct object need not receive phrasal stress. (20) illustrates how the account of Kratzer and Selkirk (2007) works. In the vP-phase, the direct object is the highest XP in the spellout domain VP, and thus receives phrasal stress. No other phrasal stress is assigned in this lower spellout domain, therefore the PP argument remains without phrasal stress.

(20)   [CP-PHASE-1 dass [TP-SPELLOUT-1 ein Junge$_k$

                [vP-PHASE-2 t$_k$ [VP-SPELLOUT-2 eine Geige an einen Freund schickte]]]]
         that   a   boy   a   violin to a   friend sent

16.3.2 A topic phase

Kratzer and Selkirk (2007) adopt the suggestion of Jäger (2001) that sentences have to have a syntactically represented topic. In assessing stress-patterns in clauses that only consist of subject and verb, this is important: If the sentence takes the subject as its topic, the subject cannot carry the sentence stress because it is the topic. Following Jäger, one can avoid this effect with the help of an initial overt sentence topic. This disengages the subject from the topic-requirement and allows us to study the remaining effects of the syntactic structure on phrasal stress. Jäger also argues that the effect of stage- vs. individual-level predicates on argument position and interpretation (Diesing, 1992; Kratzer, 1995) is real but indirect, mediated by this topic requirement.

Kratzer and Selkirk (2007: 113) show that when this is taken into account, it becomes apparent that unergative verbs in German show an all-new stress pattern in which the subject is stressed and the verb stressless. Two examples are shown in (21).

(21)   a.   Im   <u>Wohnzimmer</u> hat ein <u>Besucher</u> telefoniert.

in_the livingroom   has a   visitor   phoned

'A visitor has made a call in the livingroom.'

b.   In der <u>Küche</u> haben einige <u>Männer</u> gearbeitet.

in the kitchen have   some   men   worked

'Some men have worked in the kitchen.'

In the absence of reasons to contrast the verb or to take the subject as in some way given, a stress-pattern in which the verb is also stressed is dispreferred in such sentences.

Kratzer and Selkirk (2007) postulate a topic phrase TopP between CP and TP. They suggest that the TopP is itself a phase. In this way both the topic and the following subject in examples like (21) receive phrasal stress. This is shown in (22), the embedded clause equivalent of (21a). The topic 'im Wohnzimmer' in Spec,TopP receives phrasal stress as the highest XP of the TopP spellout domain of the CP phase. The subject 'ein Besucher' in Spec,TP receives phrasal stress as the highest XP of the TP spellout domain of the TopP phase.

(22)   dass   im   <u>Wohnhimmer</u> ein <u>Besucher</u> telefoniert hat

    [CP-PHASE-1[TopP-SPELLOUT-1   ]]

        [TopP-PHASE-2   [TP-SPELLOUT-2   ]]

    that   in_the livingroom   a   visitor   telephoned has

16.3.3 Verb stress and verb position

The definition (18) requires that the highest XP inside of the spellout domain receives stress. For the spellout domain VP in (19), this is the direct object. If there are no arguments inside the VP, there are no XPs in the spellout domain. A natural amendment for this case is the condition in (23) from Kratzer and Selkirk (2007: 110). It requires a prosodic major phrase, and thus ultimately phrasal stress, inside of a spellout domain. Thus, if there is no highest XP to be stressed by (18) inside of the spellout domain, stress is assigned to some element in the spellout domain, which is then the verb.

(23)   The Elsewhere Condition on prosodic spellout

    A spellout domain with eligible material must contain a major phrase.

Crucial for the issue of whether the verb is stressed by the Elsewhere Condition is then the position of the verb. If it remains within VP, it receives stress by (23) when VP is a spellout domain. Kratzer and Selkirk assume that the verb (or verb cluster) can also undergo head-movement and raise to v, the head of vP. There it is outside of the spellout domain VP and will end up without phrasal stress.

In the suggestion of Kratzer and Selkirk, the presence of the indefinite pronoun vs. trace intervening between the subject and the verb has a crucial effect on the position of the verb. As shown in (24), the verb does not raise to v in the presence of the the indefinite pronoun 'was'. The pronoun rejects stress for independent reasons. The verbs are therefore the target of the Elsewhere Condition (23) and receive phrasal stress in this manner.

(24)   [CP-PHASE-1 dass [TP-SPELLOUT-1 <u>Maria</u>k [vP-PHASE-2 tk [vP-SPELLOUT-2 *was* <u>gekauft</u> hat]]]]

        that   Maria   something

                                                            bought has

In the absence of an overt pronoun, on the other hand, the verbs are assumed to raise to v. There is no material left in the overt VP. Therefore, the Elsewhere Condition does not apply on the lowest cycle, as in (25). The verb will not be stressed in the head position of vP: The next larger spellout domain is TP, the spellout domain of TopP. The highest XP in the TP is the subject, so that the Elsewhere Condition does not end up stressing the raised verb.

(25)   dass   dieses Haus$_j$ <u>Mafiosi$_k$</u>   besitzen.

    $[_{\text{CP-PH-1}}[_{\text{TopP-SP-1}}$]]

        $[_{\text{TopP-PH-2}}$ $[_{\text{TP-SP-2}}$]]

                   $[_{v\text{P-PH-3}}$ t$_k$ $[_{\text{VP-SP-3}}$ t$_j$ t$_i$] besitzen$_i$]

    that   this   house   Mafiosi   own

Kratzer and Selkirk suggest that raising is motivated by prosodic spellout economy. Where the moving verb would leave behind a phonetically empty spellout domain, as in (25), this spellout domain can ultimately be 'skipped'. This economical advantage motivates and thus forces raising of the verb in their account. In (24), the presence of the indefinite pronoun prevents this advantage: even if the verb raised, the spellout domain would still contain the overt pronoun, and thus could not be 'skipped' in this manner. Therefore, raising of the verb would not be motivated and is not allowed.

As was seen, the position taken in the current paper is that the stress pattern in (25) alternates with an optional variant in which the verb is stressed. One way of looking at this optionality is that raising of the verb is possible but optional in this case. Where the verb does not move, the Elsewhere Condition assigns stress to it in the spellout domain VP. I leave open the details of integrating this with Kratzer and Selkirk's account.

16.3.4 Extension to ditransitive verbs

The extension to ditransitive verbs offered here assumes a verbal domain that is further structured into VP shells (Larson, 1988; see Ramchand, 2008 for recent suggestions). It further builds on the suggestion by Kratzer and Selkirk (2007: 123) that there are multiple topic projections in the German clause, including one between subject and object positions. If I understand correctly, the suggestion is that the targets of scrambling may more generally be identified with TopPs (scrambling applying only to elements with topic properties, such as given DPs or indefinites with presuppositional readings).

The extension requires a separate layer of the VP shell for the indirect object, as well as a topic projection on top of the VP of the direct object, the latter briefly introduced by Kratzer and Selkirk (2007: 123). The objects are taken to be in the specifiers of these VP projections, as in (26).

(26)   ... [$_{vP\text{-}PH\text{-}1}$ t   [$_{VP1\text{-}SP\text{-}1}$ einem <u>Kind</u> [$_{TopP\text{-}PH\text{-}2}$ [$_{VP2\text{-}SP\text{-}2}$ ein <u>Buch</u> vorgelesen]]]]
                    a.DAT child   a   book   read

In this fashion, the indirect object IO receives stress as the highest XP in the spellout domain VP_1 of the phase vP. The direct object receives phrasal stress as the highest XP in the spellout domain VP_2 of the lower TopP phase.

Consider then the case with the indirect object pronoun 'etwas' in (27). The pronoun prevents the verb from raising: It would not leave an empty VP spellout domain behind. The verb is consequently stressed by the Elsewhere Condition on the lower TopP phrase with the spellout domain VP_2.

(27)   ...[$_{vP\text{-}PH\text{-}1}$ t   [$_{VP1\text{-}SP\text{-}1}$ einem <u>Kind</u> [$_{TopP\text{-}PH\text{-}1}$ [$_{VP2\text{-}SP\text{-}2}$ *etwas*   <u>vorgelesen</u>]]]]
                    a.DAT child   something read

With the direct object moved as in (28), the verb may also raise, leaving an empty spellout domain VP behind. The verb remains unstressed (the spellout domain it is in, TP, normally assigns stress to its highest XP, the subject). The indirect object is stressed, as in the preceding examples, as the highest XP in the spellout domain VP_1.

(28)   ... es_k [$_{vP\text{-}PH\text{-}1}$ t   [$_{VP1\text{-}SP\text{-}1}$ einem <u>Kind</u> [$_{TopP\text{-}PH\text{-}2}$ [$_{VP2\text{-}SP\text{-}2}$ t_k t_i]]] vorgelesen$_i$]
          it   a.DAT child   read

The additional TopP above the direct object is suggested by Kratzer and Selkirk (2007). It can also be motivated as a target of scrambling (see Müller, 1999; Haider and Rosengren, 2003 on scrambling). The verb 'eintauschen', 'trade' in (29)–(31) takes a direct object and a prepositional object and allows an optional benefactive dative argument. Direct object and PP object are bare plurals in (29) and (30). The context in these cases does not motivate an information structure asymmetry between them. In these cases, scrambling into a topic position is not motivated. The deviance of (30) shows that (29) is the underlying word order. In (31) the PP object is made into a potential topic in two ways. It is definite and it is given. In this case, scrambling as in (31) is possible. Crucially, scrambling here targets a position below the indirect object and above the direct object. This is the position for which a topic projection is postulated in (26).

(29)   [What did he do?]

   Er hat einem Kunden   Nägel gegen Schrauben eingetauscht.

   he has a.DAT customer nails against screws   traded

   'He has traded nails against screws for a customer.'

(30)   [What did he do?]

   ?# Er hat einem Kunden   gegen   Schrauben Nägel eingetauscht.

   he has a.DAT customer against screws   nails traded

(31)   [What did he trade against these screws?]

   Er hat einem <u>Kunden</u>   gegen diese <u>Schrauben</u>G <u>Nägel</u> eingetauscht.

   he has a.DAT customer against these screws   nails traded

Summing up, the extension of the stress patterns involving indefinite pronouns and traces to ditransitive verbs can be accommodated in the theory of Kratzer and Selkirk (2007) with plausible additional means: an additional layer in a VP shell representation, and a second topic phrase above the direct object.

16.4 Account in terms of Stress-XP

16.4.1 Background on Stress-XP

Like so much in this area, Stress-XP builds on work by Lisa Selkirk. Stress-XP builds on the claim of the universal relevance of XPs to the syntax-phonology interface, elaborated in terms of Align-XP for Chi Mwi:ni in Selkirk (1986), for Shanghai Chinese in Selkirk and Shen (1990) (here the restriction on lexical XPs plays an important role) and for Japanese in Selkirk and Tateishi (1991). See also Selkirk (1995) for implementation of edge-alignment with XPs in Optimality Theory and for some consequences of it in English.

Stress-XP is from Truckenbrodt (1995). It was applied to German briefly in Samek-Lodovici (2005) and Truckenbrodt (2006, 2007) and in some more detail in Truckenbrodt and Darcy (2010). See Féry and Samek-Lodovici (2006) for application to English, Samek-Lodovici (2005) for application to Italian and a range of other languages.

The constraint is formulated as follows:

(32)   Stress-XP: Each lexical XP must contain a beat of phrasal stress.

The effects of Stress-XP are to be assessed on the assumption that phrasal stress is assigned only where forced by this constraint. The assumption that the last phrasal stress thus assigned is strengthened to the strongest of the intonation phrase is shared with the account of Kratzer and Selkirk (2007).

In the Stress-XP account, each argument and each adjunct correctly receives phrasal stress because, and so long as, it includes a lexical XP. The lexical XP requires phrasal stress by Stress-XP. I take DP, PP, vP, TP, and CP to be functional projections that do not invoke Stress-XP. Stress-XP is invoked by the lexical projections NP and VP (as well as AP, not discussed here). DP argument often contains a lexical NP, and it is this NP that requires phrasal stress by Stress-XP. These NPs in the arguments are bracketed in (33). If each of them attracts phrasal stress, the correct beats of phrasal stress are derived here. An adjunct such as [während einer [$_{NP}$ <u>Vorstellung</u>]] in (2) likewise contains such a lexical XP, typically an NP as in this case, which correctly attracts stress by Stress-XP.

(33)   [$_{NP}$ <u>Peter</u>] hat einem [$_{NP}$ <u>Kind</u>] ein [$_{NP}$ <u>Buch</u>] vorgelesen.

       Peter has a.DAT   child a   book read

       'Peter has read a book to a child.'

The theory in terms of Stress-XP claims in its favor a conceptual edge over earlier theories like that of Gussenhoven (1983, 1992): the argument-adjunct distinction in stress-assignment is not written into the account. Instead, it is derived from standard assumptions about the different syntactic structure of arguments and of adjuncts with the help of the simple formulation in (32). This relates to the application of Stress-XP to the lexical projection VP. An argument, as in (34a), is genuinely inside of the projection of the verb, the VP. The NP in the argument needs to carry phrasal stress to satisfy Stress-XP. Given this phrasal stress on the argument, Stress-XP is also satisfied for the

VP, since the stress on the argument is also stress inside of the VP. No additional stress is required on the verb following the argument. Matters are different for the adjunct, as shown in (34b). The adjunct to VP is not genuinely inside of VP. Instead, there is one segment of the VP, the lower one, which is a sister to the adjunct. For some purposes, including the assignment of thematic roles, this lower segment is decisive, i.e. the adjunct counts as being outside of VP. Truckenbrodt (1999) argued that the lower segment is also decisive for the syntax-prosody mapping. This is assumed here as well. With this, Stress-XP, applied to the VP in (34b), requires phrasal stress in this VP. Stress in this circled VP can only fall on the verb. Put differently, phrasal stress on the argument satisfies Stress-XP in (34a), where the following verb is only a head; in (34b), the verb following the adjunct is really a VP, and therefore requires phrasal stress by Stress-XP.

(34)

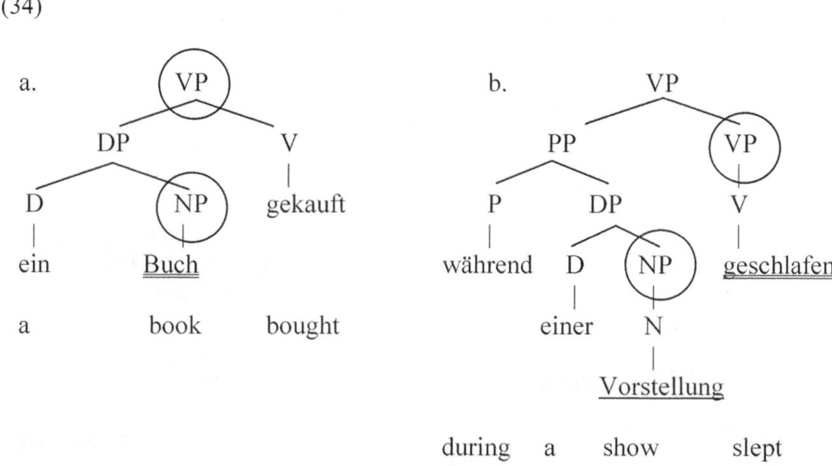

More generally, if a lexical XP is inside of another one (cf. the two circled lexical XPs in (34a)), no additional phrasal stress is required for the higher XP: A single instance of phrasal stress will satisfy Stress-XP for both projections. On the other hand, where two lexical XPs are disjoined and next to each other (cf. the two circles in (34b)), Stress-XP will of course require phrasal stress in each of them.

16.4.2 Pronouns and traces

The stress-pattern [… <u>IO</u> pron$_{DO}$ <u>V</u>] in (7) suggests the presence of an internal VP as follows: [… <u>IO</u> [$_{VP}$ pron$_{DO}$ <u>V</u>]]. This VP will correctly attract stress by Stress-XP, which cannot fall on the pronoun for independent reasons (nor on the IO, which is crucially outside of this VP) and thus falls on the verb. (35a) is a structure of this kind that is suggested for verbal arguments by Haider and Rosengren (2003): the lowest argument joins with the verb to form a VP, higher arguments occur in VP-adjoined positions. In this structure, the circled VP that comprises the direct object and the verb invokes Stress-XP and thus correctly derives stress on the verb. In this paper I mainly employ VP shell structures as in the discussion of Kratzer and Selkirk (2007) above. The VP shell structure in (35b), crucially with a separate VP for direct object and verb, derives the correct stress pattern. The lower VP$_2$ of the shell-structure (circled) here invokes Stress-XP and derives the stress on the verb.

(35)

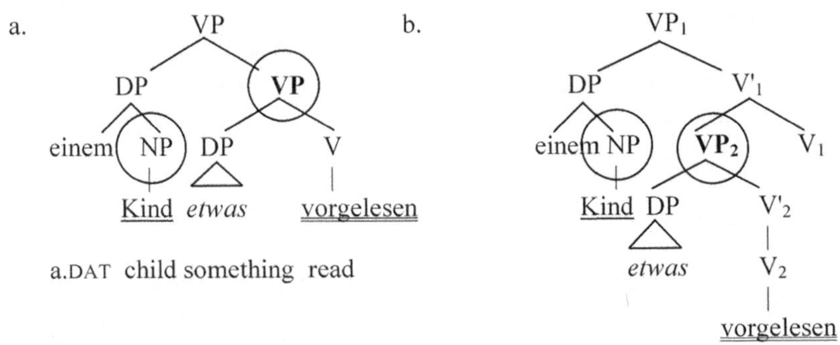

The VP-shell structure employed here also correctly derives the stressless verb in (33) as shown in (36). The lexical XPs are bracketed here. Stress in the direct object noun 'Buch' is also stress in VP$_2$ so that Stress-XP provides no reason to stress the final verb.

(36)   [Peter] hat [$_{VP1}$ einem [Kind] [$_{VP2}$ ein [Buch] vorgelesen]]
        Peter has   a.DAT child   a   book read

Let us turn to the case involving the direct object trace in (8), where both stress-patterns [… IO t V] and [… IO t V] are allowed. The choice of the account turns on correctness of the Uniformity of Theta-assignment Hypothesis by Baker (1988: 46):

(37)   *Uniformity of Theta-assignment Hypothesis* (UTAH)

Identical thematic relationships between items are represented by identical structural relationships between those items at the level of D-structure.

If the UTAH is correct, it entails a fixed underlying order of the arguments for a given German verb. For example, the verb 'vorlesen' has an agent, a beneficient/experiencer and a theme argument. The UTAH requires that the underlying order of these is constant regardless of their surface order. German word-order in the Mittelfeld is fairly flexible. A standard analysis for this flexibility is to assume an underlying order (either the unmarked word order or an order inferred by other syntactic arguments) and to hold scrambling responsible for the flexibility. See, for example, Frey (1993) and Haider and Rosengren (2003). However, it has also been suggested by Bayer and Kornfilt (1994), Fanselow (2001, 2003), and others, that the assumption of a fixed underlying order be given up and that word order in the Mittelfeld is base-generated. This amounts to giving up the UTAH.

An account that allows different underlying orders to be base-generated can derive the two stress-patterns as shown in (38). 'Kind' is stressed as an NP in both a. and b. Where it is followed by the trace of the direct object in a lower VP, this lower VP attracts stress as in (38a), in parallel to (35a). The assumption of flexible underlying order also allows (38b), where the indirect object is base-generated in the lowest VP, thus exempting the following verb from being stressed.

(38)   *Structures in an account that allows different underlying orders*

   a.   *es*ᵢ   [vp einem Kind [vp tᵢ vorgelesen]].

   b.   *es*ᵢ [vp tᵢ [vp einem Kind   vorgelesen]].

         it   a.DAT child   read

In that account, the difference between the indefinite pronoun in situ in (7) and the dislocated definite pronoun in (22) is due to the fact that the dislocated pronoun need not originate in the lowest VP, while a pronoun in situ must be in the lowest VP due to its overt position.

Here I pursue an account that retains the spirit of the UTAH, as does Ramchand (2008). Following Kratzer and Selkirk (2007), I relate the difference between pronoun and trace to the position of the verb in its shell. As in Kratzer and Selkirk's account, a higher position of the verb is to be prohibited in the presence of the indefinite direct object pronoun, as shown in (39). Here the verb is to receive the phrasal stress assigned due to Stress-XP in VP$_2$. If it were to stand in a higher position, there would be no incentive for stressing it. We are led to assume that raising is not an option in this case.

(39)

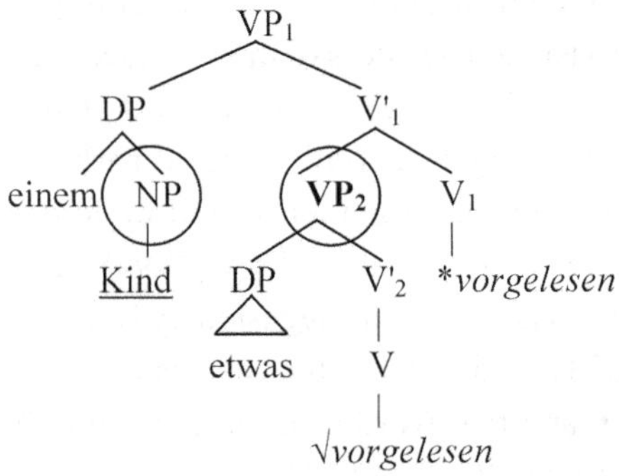

a.DAT child   something read

I assume for concreteness that the verb always raises in its shell for theta-role assignment, and that its traces are copies of the verb. The question at issue is then which of these copies is spelled out. I will return to (39).

In the case of the direct object trace in (8), one would ideally want to allow the structure (40a) with a low verb position as well as the structure (40b) with a higher verb position. In (40a), Stress-XP, applied to VP$_2$, will lead to stress on the verb. In (40b), VP$_2$ is empty-headed and phonetically empty. By the Lexical Category Condition (LCC), a general provision formulated in Truckenbrodt (1999), lexical XPs invoke the phrasal mapping constraints but neither functionally headed XPs nor empty-headed XPs do. (The distinction between lexical and functional elements goes back to Selkirk and Shen (1990) and Selkirk (1995).) VP$_2$ in (40b) is empty-headed (and phonetically empty), and so does not invoke Stress-XP by this general provision. VP$_1$ is now overtly headed and so invokes Stress-XP. This is satisfied without stress on the verb, since VP$_1$ contains stress on the word 'Kind', which is independently required by the application of Stress-XP to this NP. This derives the stress-pattern with the stressless verb.

(40)

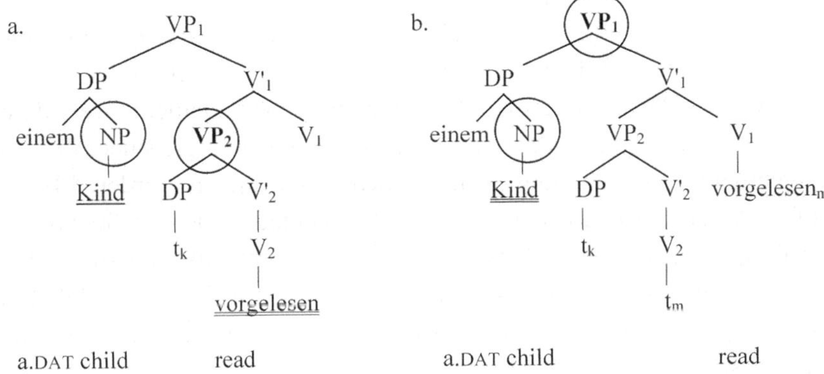

a.DAT child   read   a.DAT child   read

Why would low spellout be the only option in (39) and high spellout be allowed in (40)? The present account cannot invoke the economy considerations suggested by Kratzer and Selkirk (2007) for their account. A different possibility outlined here is a combination of the traditional headedness parameter in (41) with a weakened version of the Linear Correspondence Axiom (LCA) of Kayne (1994). The weakened LCA, here wLCA, orders only overt elements. Furthermore, adjuncts are ignored here. For the purposes at hand, the much-simplified version in (42) is sufficient.

(41)   The VP is head-final in German.

(42)   wLCA

        For overt specifiers, overt heads and overt complements:

        A specifier of XP precedes X and any complement of X.

        A head precedes its complement.

(39) is in accord with the wLCA so long as the verb does not raise in its shell: The indirect object, a specifier of VP$_1$, precedes the complement VP$_2$ of V$_1$. The direct object, in specifier position of VP$_2$, precedes the head V$_2$.

The wLCA prohibits a higher spellout of the verb in this structure. If the verb were to be spelled out in the position of V_1, it would be an overt head that follows its complement VP_2, in violation of the wLCA. (It would have to follow the pronoun because of the headedness parameter (41).) Notice that only overt elements matter to the wLCA in (42). A phonetically empty verb V_1 is therefore not relevant to the wLCA.

Where the direct object position is occupied by a phonetically empty trace as in (40), spellout of the verb in the higher position in (40b) is not blocked by the wLCA. This is because only phonetically overt elements are ordered by the wLCA in (42). (40b) does not violate the wLCA, since VP_2, the complement of V_1 is empty in this structure and thus not ordered by the wLCA. Among the overt elements, the indirect object in the specifier position of VP_1 precedes the head V_1, as required. We may tentatively assume, then, that the spellout positions in (40a) and (40b) are both allowed, and that the optionality of stress-assignment in (8) is optionality between these two structures.

Let us then briefly turn to the syntactic cases involving a subject, a direct object and the verb. It was seen above that the stress-facts of this case (Section 16.2.2.) are parallel to the cases involving an indirect object, a direct object and a verb (Section 16.2.1.). The account employs the structure used throughout in which the direct object stands in the specifier of a separate VP as in (43). The account is parallel to the account of the objects in a ditransitive structure above (here with the subject in place of the indirect object above). Raising of the verb needs to be constrained by the wLCA, in parallel to (39) and (40).

(43)

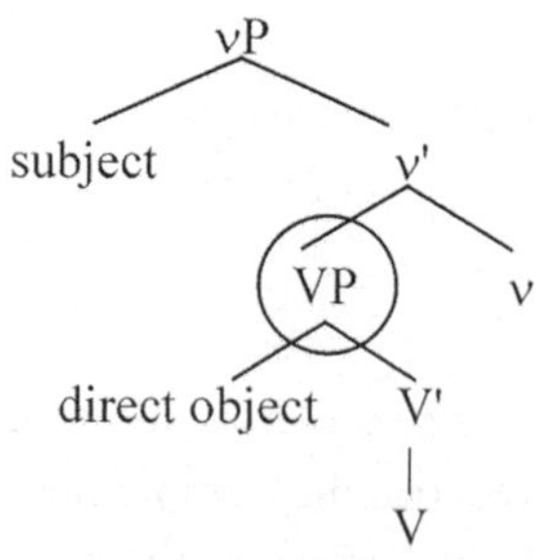

The projection hosting the subject is the functional vP. Notice that in the examples discussed here, the verb receives stress only in the application of Stress-XP to the lower (and always lexical) VP.

16.4.3 Stressless PPs

The stress-pattern with stressless locative and directional PPs presents what seems to be a serious problem for the account in terms of Stress-XP. As shown in (44), there is a lexical NP in the PP, and Stress-XP would predict phrasal stress on this NP. The surprise here is with the fact that the stressless PP is allowed even if the PP is new. (I concur with the assessment of Kratzer and Selkirk (2007) that stress on the PP is also a possibility.)

(44)   ... dass ein [Junge] eine [Geige] an einen [Freund] schickte

        that a   boy   a   violin to a   friend   sent

    '... that a boy sent a violin to a friend.'

I agree with Kahnemuyipour (2004) and Kratzer and Selkirk (2007) that such stress-patterns motivate exploring new paths in this domain. Still, for me personally it is too early to give up Stress-XP as a contender in the discussion. I plan to explore in future work the possibility that we are facing a case of untypical syntax.

Hale and Keyser (2002: Ch.3) discuss similar constructions in English, shown in (45) on the left. They are interested in the verb formation process shown on the right.

(45)   a.   John put the wine in (a) bottle(s)   John bottled the wine.

       b.   John put the apples in (a) bag(s)   John bagged the apples.

       c.   John put the calves in the corral   John corralled the calves.

These verbs can include the concepts of the directional PP as shown. Hale and Keyser argue that more is involved than syntactic head movement (incorporation). First, they argue that head movement can proceed from the specifier of a complement to a higher head. In the cases in (45), this would result in inclusion of the theme in the verb: A construction like 'John put the apples in bags' would result in verb formation like *'John appled in bags'. This does not occur. Second, this word formation process will sometimes allow the kind of complement originally incorporated into the verb:

(46)   John shelved the books on the windowsill.

John bagged the potatoes in a gunnysack.

Hale and Keyser define a novel process of conflation with these properties. For them, the input to conflation is the structure [$_{VP}$ V [$_{PP}$ [the apples] (in) bag]], with conflation of '(in) bag' with the higher verb.

For the sake of exploration, let us tentatively redefine conflation in terms of the VP-shells employed in this paper. In these terms, conflation may be thought of along the lines of V' reanalysis in Larson (1988), namely as a process in which a V' is turned into a verbal head. (47) shows the derivation of 'bag the apples'. In step b. the original V' is turned into V by conflation. In step c., this newly formed head undergoes head movement in the shell.

(47)

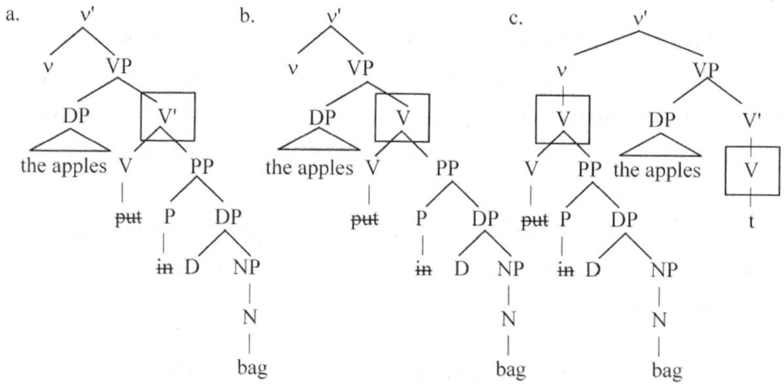

The understanding of conflation as V' reanalysis would have the desired properties. First, the theme ('the apples' in (45)) does not participate in this word formation process, since it is in a specifier position outside of V'. Second, the observation in (46) finds a place. Assume that after the joining of V and PP to [$_{V'}$ V PP] conflation applies to give [$_V$ V PP]. This newly formed head can now take a directional PP complement into its (to-be-created) V' projection. To be sure, conflation violates traditional assumptions about structure preservations: Phrases do not normally become parts of heads.

The parallel of interest for the German stress-facts is that in those cases in which English allows verb formation, i.e. somehow joining what is otherwise a phrase into a verbal head, German allows absence of stress. Assume that conflation applied to the relevant structure (48a) in German, deriving (48b).

(48)

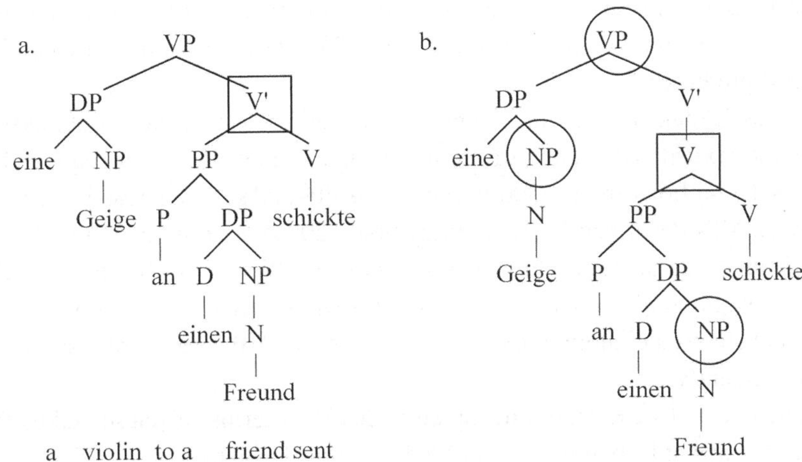

In (48b), there would be a plausible reason for not stressing the PP. The demands of Stress-XP in the PP may be in conflict with demands on the boxed constituent V to be mapped to, or wrapped in, a prosodic word. Where this latter requirement would win out, the PP would end up stressless.

Some syntactic arguments for a particular closeness of this class of PPs to the verb in German can be found in Steinitz (1989) and Frey (1993). For the syntax of Persian, Kahnemuyipour (2004: 95f) cites references for the syntactic analysis he adopts, and cites Karimi (2003), who presents arguments that point in the direction outlined here.

I leave all this to future work, merely noting here that a defense of Stress-XP may not be entirely hopeless in the face of the German stressless PPs and related facts in Persian.

16.5 Phases vs. phrases: Concluding remarks on the relation of the two accounts

Here I wish to highlight some elements in which the two accounts discussed differ, and some elements that they share.

Let us take a generalization from the SAAR of Gussenhoven (1992) as a starting point: Inside of a focus, non-given arguments and adjuncts receive accent (here: phrasal stress; Gussenhoven, 1992: 98ff treats stressless locative PPs as predicates).

Stress-XP takes this surface-generalization at face value, and maintains that it is the lexical XPs inside of the arguments and adjuncts that require this stress. Exceptions are the German stressless PPs and similar stress-patterns in Persian VPs described by Kahnemuyipour (2004), assuming standard syntactic analyses of these. Stress-XP extends to VPs without further ado: the verb is stressed if it constitutes a VP on its own (or together with a pronoun). It is not stressed if another lexical XP inside of the VP requires phrasal stress independently.

The account of Kratzer and Selkirk (2007) in terms of phases takes the observations of Kahnemuyipour (2004) and the German stressless PPs as one of their starting points. In some sense, matters are here shifted up in the tree, relative to earlier accounts including the Stress-XP account. For the typical argument and adjunct, stress-assignment is triggered with the constituent dominating them, a spellout domain of a phase, of which the argument or adjunct is the highest XP. This requires, in the end, a phase for each beat of phrasal stress in the sentence. This was shown for DP arguments in the text above. Adjuncts will similarly require additional phases. A plausible conception for additional phases of this kind lies with the suggestion of Kratzer and Selkirk (2007) that topic phrases introduce additional phases, where these topic phrases are identified with landing sites of scrambling.

The 'shift up in the tree' leads to the need for a separate statement concerning stress on the verbs, the Elsewhere Condition, which mirrors the effect of Stress-XP: The VP spellout domain requires phrasal stress. Seen from the point of view of Stress-XP, the resulting dichotomy in principles of stress-assignment may be seen as a price to pay for 'shifting up in the tree' of the stress-trigger of constituents other than the verb. However, if the phasal account is on the right track, the Elsewhere Condition seems to be natural.

I have mainly explored how the effects of indefinite pronouns and traces of the direct object generalize from transitive sentences to ditransitive sentences. Kratzer and Selkirk (2007) suggested that the option of raising of the verb or verbs in the VP-shell correlates with the absence of an overt direct object pronoun. This proves to be fruitful in the extension of their account to ditransitive sentences. It also proves to be fruitful in an account of these patterns in terms of Stress-XP. I pointed out that a weakened version of Kayne's LCA may also be at play in restricting possible verb positions.

Lisa, I hope that there is something in this discussion that you enjoy thinking about. Much pleasure in the years ahead, with time for research!

References

Baker, M. C. (1988) *Incorporation: A Theory of Grammatical Function Changing.* Chicago, IL: University of Chicago Press.

Bayer, J. and Kornfilt, J. (1994) Against scrambling as an instance of Move-alpha. In H. v. Riemsdijk and N. Corver (eds) *Studies on Scrambling: Movement and Non-movement Approaches to Free Word-order Phenomena* 17–60. Berlin: Mouton de Gruyter.

Chomsky, N. (2008) On phases. In R. Freidin, C. P. Otero and M. L. Zubizarreta (eds) *Foundational Issues in Linguistic Theory. Essays in Honor of Jean-Roger Vergnaud* 133–166. Cambridge, MA: MIT Press.

Diesing, M. (1992) *Indefinites*. Cambridge, MA: MIT Press.

Fanselow, G. (2001) Features, theta-roles, and free constituent order. *Linguistic Inquiry* 32 (3): 405–437.

Fanselow, G. (2003) Free constituent order: a minimalist interface account. *Folia Linguistica* 37 (1–2): 191–231.

Féry, C. and Samek-Lodovici, V. (2006) Focus projection and prosodic prominence in nested foci. *Language* 82 (1): 131–150.

Frey, W. (1993) *Syntaktische Bedingungen für die semantische Interpretation. Über Bindung, implizite Argumente und Skopus*. Berlin: Akademie Verlag.

Gussenhoven, C. (1983) Focus, mode and the nucleus. *Journal of Linguistics* 19: 377–417.

Gussenhoven, C. (1992) Sentence accents and argument structure. In I. Roca (ed.) *Thematic Structure, its Role in Grammar* 79–106. Berlin, New York: Foris.

Haider, H. and Rosengren, I. (2003) Scrambling: nontriggered chain formation in OV languages. *Journal of Germanic Linguistics* 15 (3): 203–267.

Hale, K. and Keyser, S. J. (2002) *Prolegomenon to a Theory of Argument Structure*. Cambridge, MA: MIT Press.

Jackendoff, R. S. (1972) *Semantic Interpretation in Generative Grammar*. Cambridge, MA: MIT Press.

Jäger, G. (2001) Topic-comment structure and the contrast between stage level and individual level predicates. *Journal of Semantics* 18 (2): 83–126.

Kahnemuyipour, A. (2004) *The Syntax of Sentential Stress*. Doctoral thesis, University of Toronto.

Karimi, S. (2003) On object positions, specificit and scrambling in Persian. In S. Karimi (ed.) *Word Order and Scrambling* 91–125. London: Blackwell.

Kayne, R. (1994) *The Antisymmetry of Syntax*. Cambridge, MA: MIT Press.

Kratzer, A. (1995) Stage-level and individual-level predicates. In G. N. Carlson and J. F. Pelletier (eds) *The Generic Book* 125–175. Chicago, IL: Chicago University Press.

Kratzer, A. and Selkirk, E. (2007) Phase theory and prosodic spellout: the case of verbs. *The Linguistic Review* 24 (2–3): 93–135.

Krifka, M. (1984) Focus, Topic, syntaktische Struktur und semantische Interpretation. Ms. Universität München.

Ladd, D. R. (1983) Even, focus, and normal stress. *Journal of Semantics* 2 (2): 257–270.

Larson, R. (1988) On the double object construction. *Linguistic Inquiry* 19 (3): 335–391.

Müller, G. (1999) Optimality, markedness and word order in German. *Linguistics* 37 (5): 777–818.

Ramchand, G. (2008) *Verb Meaning and the Lexicon. A First-phase Syntax*. Cambridge: Cambridge University Press.

Rooth, M. (1996) Focus. In S. Lappin (ed.) *The Handbook of Contemporary Semantic Theory* 271–297. Oxford and Cambridge, MA: Blackwell.

Samek-Lodovici, V. (2005) Prosody-syntax interaction in the expression of focus. *Natural Language and Linguistic Theory* 23: 687–755.

Selkirk, E. and Shen, T. (1990) Prosodic domains in Shanghai Chinese. In S. Inkelas and D. Zec (eds) *The Phonology-Syntax Connection* 313–337. Chicago, IL: The University of Chicago Press.

Selkirk, E. and Tateishi, K. (1991) Syntax and downstep in Japanese. In C. Georgopolous and R. Ishihara (eds) *Interdisciplinary Approaches to Language: Essays in Honor of S.-Y. Kuroda* 519–543. Dordrecht: Kluwer.

Selkirk, E. (2006) Contrastive focus, givenness and phrase stress. Ms., University of Massachusetts, Amherst.

Selkirk, E. O. (1984) *Phonology and Syntax: The Relationship between Sound and Structure*. Cambridge, MA and London: MIT Press.

Selkirk, E. O. (1986) On derived domains in sentence phonology. *Phonology Yearbook* 3: 371–405.

Selkirk, E. O. (1995) The prosodic structure of function words. In J. Beckman, L. W.

Dickey and S. Urbanczyk (eds) *Papers in Optimality Theory. University of Massachusetts Occasional Papers 18* 439–469. Amherst, MA: GLSA.

Steinitz, R. (1989) V^u, I^y und I^z: Überlegungen zum Prädikativ. In W. Motsch (ed.) *Wortstruktur und Satzstruktur* 210–234: Akademie der Wissenschaften der DDR, Zentralinstitut für Sprachwissenschaft.

Truckenbrodt, H. (1995) *Phonological Phrases: Their Relation to Syntax, Focus, and Prominence.* Doctoral thesis, MIT.

Truckenbrodt, H. (1999) On the relation between syntactic phrases and phonological phrases. *Linguistic Inquiry* 30 (2): 219–255.

Truckenbrodt, H. (2006) Phrasal stress. In K. Brown (ed.) *The Encyclopedia of Languages and Linguistics, 2nd Edition, Vol. 9* 572–579. Oxford: Elsevier.

Truckenbrodt, H. (2007) The syntax-phonology interface. In P. de Lacy (ed.) *The Cambridge Handbook of Phonology* 435–456. Cambridge: Cambridge University Press.

Truckenbrodt, H. and Darcy, I. (2010) Object clauses, movement, and phrasal stress. In N. Shir and L. Rochman (eds) *The Sound Patterns of Syntax* 189–216. Oxford: Oxford University Press.

Uhmann, S. (1991) *Fokusphonologie. Eine Analyse deutscher Intonationskonturen im Rahmen der nicht-linearen Phonologie.* Tübingen: Niemeyer.

Author Index

Keyword Index